Contents at a Glance

SAMS Teach Yourself

Adobe® Premiere® Pro in 24 Hours

Jeff Sengstack

 SAMS 800 East 96th St., Indianapolis, Indiana, 46240 USA

Sams Teach Yourself Adobe® Premiere® Pro in 24 Hours

International Standard Book Number: 0-672-32607-8

Library of Congress Catalog Card Number: 2003094092

Printed in the United States of America

First Printing: February 2004

07   06   05   04   4   3   2   1

Trademarks

All terms mentioned in this book that are known to be trademarks or service marks have been appropriately capitalized. Sams Publishing cannot attest to the accuracy of this information. Use of a term in this book should not be regarded as affecting the validity of any trademark or service mark.

Warning and Disclaimer

Bulk Sales

Sams Publishing offers excellent discounts on this book when ordered in quantity for bulk purchases or special sales. For more information, please contact

U.S. Corporate and Government Sales
1-800-382-3419
corpsales@pearsontechgroup.com

For sales outside of the U.S., please contact

International Sales
1-317-428-3341
international@pearsontechgroup.com

Acquisitions Editor
Betsy Brown

Development Editor
Jonathan Steever

Managing Editor
Charlotte Clapp

Senior Project Editor
Matt Purcell

Copy Editor
Mike Henry

Indexer
Chris Barrick

Proofreader
Wendy Ott

Technical Editor
Doug Dixon

Publishing Coordinator
Vanessa Evans

Designer
Gary Adair

Production
Michelle Mitchell

Table of Contents

Part IV: Higher-End Visual Effects and Editing Techniques

Part V: Working with Other Adobe Products and Exporting Your Videos

About the Author

Jeff Sengstack has worn many hats: TV news reporter/anchor, video producer, writer focusing on PC technology, high school math/science teacher, radio station disk jockey, music publisher marketing director and (presently) school board trustee. As a news reporter he won a regional Emmy and two Society of Professional Journalists first-place awards. He's an Adobe Certified Expert and Trainer on Premiere and wrote Adobe's *Higher Education Digital Video Curriculum Guide*. He's written 300 articles and five books, including *Sams Teach Yourself DVD Authoring in 24 Hours*. His focus these days is creating family tree DVDs and video tutorials to supplement this book. Visit his Web site at www.sengstack.com.

Acknowledgments

My hat's off to Adobe and the Premiere Pro development team. They have created a terrific product. One reason Premiere Pro is so much better than the competition is that Adobe listened to and addressed user and beta tester comments and concerns. Adobe is the only company I know of that gives so much weight to its customers' views.

Several members of that development team fielded many questions from me during the beta testing and book writing process. I appreciate their help.

This book's technical editor, Douglas Dixon, and the editorial staff at Sams worked hard to make this book better. I appreciate that.

Tell Us What You Think!

As the reader of this book, *you* are our most important critic and commentator. We value your opinion and want to know what we're doing right, what we could do better, what areas you'd like to see us publish in, and any other words of wisdom you're willing to pass our way.

You can email or write me directly to let me know what you did or didn't like about this book—as well as what we can do to make our books stronger.

Please note that I cannot help you with technical problems related to the topic of this book, and that due to the high volume of mail I receive, I might not be able to reply to every message.

When you write, please be sure to include this book's title and author as well as your name and phone number or e-mail address. I will carefully review your comments and share them with the author and editors who worked on the book.

Email: graphics@samspublishing.com

Mail: Mark Taber
            Associate Publisher
            Sams Publishing
            800 East 96th Street
            Indianapolis, IN 46240 USA

Introduction

Sams Teach Yourself Adobe Premiere Pro in 24 Hours is different from the rest of the dozen or so other Premiere how-to books. Those books tend to be highly detailed or greatly simplified reference manuals using impenetrable vernacular, or collections of step-by-step instructions focusing solely on Premiere functions. Both types fail to create lasting impressions, and they don't teach you how to make videos.

What's missing is context. I think of those books as sort of like instructing budding artists how to use a paintbrush by telling them to swab the brush in paint and slather it on a canvas. Where's the art?

My goal with *Sams Teach Yourself Adobe Premiere Pro in 24 Hours* is to help you create high-quality, professional-looking videos. Rather than simply presenting a collection of disconnected tutorials, I'll frequently remind you of the big picture and what you're trying to accomplish. That said, I haven't skimped on useful nuts-and-bolts instructions. I've tried simply to present them in a logical, easy-to-follow manner that reflects the way most Premiere users approach editing.

A Collaborative Effort

In a departure from traditional Premiere Pro how-to books, I turned this into a collaborative project. I contacted several of my friends and former colleagues in the TV and video production business who provided dozens of expert tips to supplement this book's coverage of Premiere Pro functionality. For instance, they provided advice about shooting high-quality video, writing effectively, and creating professional voice-overs.

The timing is right for this book, both on a personal level and in the marketplace. It fits my career path to a T. I'm an Adobe Certified Expert (ACE) in Premiere and have extensive television production credentials—TV anchor, reporter, photographer, and editor—plus I'm a recipient of a regional Emmy award and two Society of Professional Journalists first-place awards. I've written hundreds of articles, written or worked on eight books, and have been a high school science and math teacher. I tapped all that experience to create what I think is a logical, instructional flow using readily digestible chunks of information placed in a real-world context. *Sams Teach*

Yourself Adobe Premiere Pro in 24 Hours will ensure that you can track how each new task fits into your project goals.

The market is primed for Premiere Pro. *Convergence* might be an overused word (third only to *paradigm* and *epiphany*), but it applies. Adobe continues to bring a reasonably priced, increasingly powerful video production tool to Windows users. High-quality digital video (DV) camcorders have dropped in price. Anyone with a laptop and a DV camcorder can operate as an independent video producer or TV news reporter.

Premiere Pro: Built from Scratch

With Premiere Pro, Adobe has raised the bar, thrown down the gauntlet, and upped the ante (yep, three clichés, but they all apply). Premiere Pro clearly is the PC video editor of choice for budding video producers and professionals alike. Two-and-a-half years in the making, Adobe created Premiere Pro with entirely new code. The development team's goals were ease-of-use, fast editing, and compatibility across Adobe's entire DV product line. While testing early beta versions and reading comments from other beta testers, I enjoyed seeing how some experienced users first felt that Premiere Pro's workflow changes were a bit awkward. But light bulbs soon began switching on as the online testing community started to discover the logic behind the changes and the improved functionality they fostered.

Premiere Pro signals a tidal shift in Adobe's approach to the digital video market. It now offers a tightly integrated, five-product DV suite: Premiere Pro, After Effects 6, Photoshop CS, Encore DVD, and Audition. The latter two products you might not have heard about.

While working on Premiere Pro, Adobe teamed up with the DVD authoring industry-leader, Sonic Solutions, to create a professional DVD authoring product: Adobe Encore DVD. Anything you create in Premiere Pro, you can use within Encore DVD as part of a full-featured DVD project. I'll cover DVD creation with Encore DVD in Hour 24 of this book.

In addition, in mid-2003, Adobe bought Syntrillium Software, producers of the professional-level audio editing tool named Cool Edit Pro. Adobe added 5,000 music loops to Cool Edit Pro and released it in the fall of 2003 as Adobe Audition. I give you a brief overview of Audition in Hour 15, "Professional Audio Tools: SmartSound Sonicfire and Adobe Audition."

Adobe After Effects is the industry-leading text animation and 3D graphics product. The latest revision works smoothly with Premiere Pro. And Photoshop continues to dominate the graphic creation landscape. I show you how to use both products in Hour 22, "Using Photoshop and After Effects to Enhance Your DV Project."

Book Organization

Sams Teach Yourself Adobe Premiere Pro in 24 Hours consists of 24 "lessons." Each should take about an hour—more or less—to complete. That's not to say that at the end of each lesson you'll have mastered its particular topic. To really become proficient in Premiere Pro you'll need to reinforce what you've learned with practice. I'd suggest moving through a lesson, doing some additional work, and then taking a breather before tackling the next lesson.

I've tried to follow my own video production advice and keep it simple—and short—but I do know that some of you want higher-level Premiere and video production tips. So, I've scattered such advice throughout all the chapters in the form of notes ("By the Way"), tips ("Did You Know?"), and cautions ("Watch Out!").

By buying Premiere Pro, you've joined the ranks of more than 750,000 video editors who recognize a high-quality video production product when they see one. Now, with the help of this book, you soon will be able to fully exploit all the powerful tools Premiere Pro brings to bear. The ultimate goal is that you'll create videos that shine.

Conventions Used in This Book

This book uses the following conventions:

Text that you type and text that you see onscreen appears in `monospace` type.

By the Way presents interesting information related to the discussion.

By the Way

Did You Know? offers advice or shows you an easier way to do something.

Did you Know?

Watch Out! alerts you to a possible problem and gives you advice on how to avoid it.

Watch Out!

PART I

Getting Started

HOUR 1

Touring Premiere Pro and Presenting the DV Workflow

What You'll Learn in This Hour:

- ▶ Premiere Pro—a nonlinear editor
- ▶ Touring Premiere Pro's workspace
- ▶ Premiere Pro's special features and technologies
- ▶ Diagramming the digital video workflow

You probably want to dive right into Premiere Pro. I don't blame you. If you've had any experience editing videos with Premiere or other PC video editors you may be able to do a lot with Premiere Pro right off the bat. However, formal, hands-on work with Premiere Pro in this book doesn't begin until Hour 4, "Premiere Pro Setup."

That said, in this first hour, I take you on a tour of Premiere's workspace and, if you're so inclined, you can fire up Premiere and follow along. I explain how video editing on your PC with Premiere Pro is a tidal change from editing on videotape machines. I show you that Premiere Pro's workspace organization helps you edit quickly, efficiently, and creatively. Its developers gave it numerous, clever features and incorporated new technologies that place it head and shoulders above all other PC-based video editors.

Premiere Pro is the hub of a digital video workflow involving four other Adobe products. I outline how you can work with all of them to enhance your video projects.

Premiere—A Nonlinear Editor

Premiere is a *nonlinear editor* (NLE). It looks and feels a whole lot different from standard, nondigital (or analog) linear videotape-editing systems. This might be patently obvious to you, but bear with me a bit.

On tape systems, you need to lay down edits consecutively and contiguously. If you decide to expand a story already edited on tape by inserting a sound bite in the middle, you simply cannot slip that bite into the piece and slide everything after it farther into the story. You need to edit in that sound bite *over* your existing edits and *reedit* everything after it. Alternatively, you first can make a dub (or copy) of the story segment after the new edit point and lay that down after adding the sound bite (causing generation quality loss in the process).

Mid-Story Changes—The Horror

Makes me shudder to think of the news stories I produced, back in the days of videotape-only editing, that screamed for some minor mid-story fixes. But I knew those fixes would have taken too much time and caused too much reporter/editor grumbling. Such is life in deadline-driven TV news.

As newsrooms have moved to NLEs, reporter/editor tension (at least over silly little things such as adding a sound bite in the middle of a piece…ah-hem) has dissipated.

Premiere Pro and other NLEs like it have come to the rescue. Now you can make changes with a few mouse clicks. If you want to edit the all-important production closing shots before editing anything else, that's fine. It's nonlinear. Feel free to do things nonsequentially.

The other overwhelming improvement over videotape-editing systems is immediate access to your video clips. No longer do you need to endlessly fast forward or rewind through miles of tape to find that one snippet of natural sound. With Premiere Pro and other NLEs, it's all a mouse click away.

Touring Premiere Pro's Workspace

Before diving into nonlinear editing (in Hour 6, "Creating a Cuts-Only Video"), I want to give you a brief tour of the video-editing workspace.

Checking Out Premiere Pro's Interface

Try it Yourself

This is the first of many tasks I present in this book. In most cases, they're detailed, step-by-step instructions. The best way to get some value out of this book is to complete those tasks. In this particular case, this is kind of a task-lite. You don't have to open Premiere Pro at this point, but if you want to, feel free. In either event, here's a look at Premiere Pro's workspace:

1. Install Premiere Pro. It's fairly straightforward, but you'll need to restart your PC.

2. Double-click the Premiere Pro icon on your desktop to open it. After the splash screen disappears, the opening interface displays, as shown in Figure 1.1.

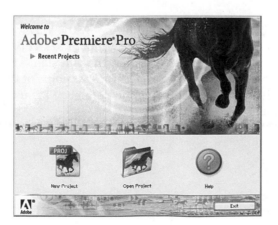

FIGURE 1.1
Premiere Pro's opening dialog box enables you to quickly access projects-in-progress or start a new project.

▼

3. Click New Project to open the New Project dialog box shown in Figure 1.2.

By the Way

Out with the Old

I can't say it enough (and I do say it several more times throughout this book): Adobe built Premiere Pro from the ground up to streamline the video creation process. The New Project dialog box is a case in point. Previous Premiere iterations presented about two dozen choices. Premiere Pro offers up eight: four each for NTSC and PAL (you can create your own customized project settings). Why so few? Briefly stated, it's because of new internal video and audio processing. I explain more in a later section, "Premiere Pro's Special Features and Technologies."

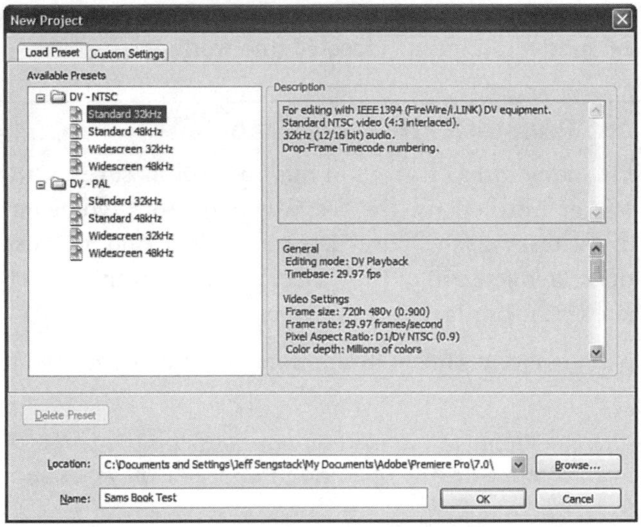

FIGURE 1.2
This simple interface exemplifies the streamlined workflow in Premiere Pro.

4. If you're working with NTSC (see following By the Way for more information on TV standards) select DV-NTSC, Standard 32kHz (kHz is the audio sampling rate). If you're a PAL user click the plus sign (+) next to DV-PAL and select Standard 32kHz. Give your project a name at the bottom of the screen and then click OK. That opens the Premiere Pro user interface (UI) shown in Figure 1.3.

▲

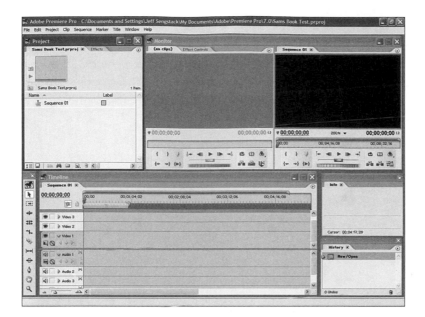

FIGURE 1.3
Premiere Pro's workspace might seem daunting to first-time NLE users, but you'll soon see the logic behind its layout.

TV Standards

NTSC, PAL, and SECAM (although it's not an option in Premiere Pro)—what's with all the different (and incompatible) standards?

▶ National Television Standard Committee (NTSC) is the TV standard for most of North America and South America as well as Japan. It's clearly the worst of these three TV standards. It has only 525 lines of resolution and displays at a nearly incomprehensible 29.97 frames per second (film displays at 24 frames per second [FPS]).

▶ Phase Alternate Line (PAL) at 625 lines has better resolution and displays at 25 frames per second. It's available in Western Europe and Australia.

▶ Sequential Couleur A'memorie (SECAM) has the highest resolution—819 lines—as well as a separate channel for color information. Like PAL, it runs at 25 FPS. It's used in France and in scattered locations around the Middle East and Africa.

Because of NTSC's tendency toward color variability, engineers jokingly refer to it as "Never The Same Color." There is a glimmer of hope: North America is grudgingly elbowing the higher-resolution PAL and SECAM folks aside with High-Definition TV (HDTV), which is set for full adoption in the United States by 2006.

Premiere Pro's Workspace Layout

If you've never seen a nonlinear editor, this workspace might throw you for a loop. Not to worry. The layout reflects many years of experience on the part of Premiere Pro's development team. It understands the NLE workflow and has put innumerable fixes into Premiere Pro to further refine it. I've identified its principal elements in Figure 1.4.

FIGURE 1.4
Premiere Pro's workspace windows and palettes.

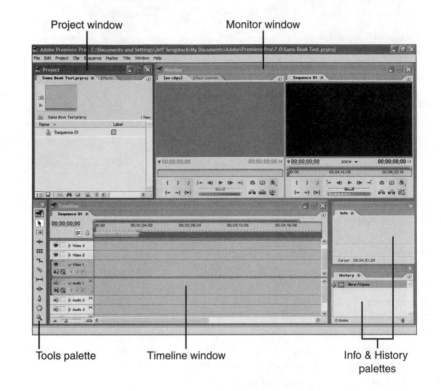

Project window   Monitor window

Tools palette   Timeline window   Info & History palettes

 By the Way

Windows, Palettes, and Dialog Boxes

Premiere Pro's developers use a potentially confusing nomenclature for elements of this NLE. They sometimes exacerbate that by using different terms for the same thing. I'll try to clarify those items as they arise. In this case, *windows* are resizable work areas in which you take some action, *palettes* present essentially unchangeable items like effects and editing tools, and *dialog boxes* request user input such as preferences.

In the following sections, I briefly explain the salient elements of the Premiere Pro user interface (UI). I go into greater detail in later hours.

Project Window

Start by taking a look at the Project window in the upper-left corner of the UI in Figure 1.4. This is where you store and access your original video clips—your raw footage—as well as audio files, graphics, and *sequences* (Adobe's new name for timelines). It uses *bins* (Adobe's name for file folders) to organize your assets.

Figure 1.5 shows how it looks after I add a few files to it and expand the view to display the characteristics of the those video, audio, and image files.

Adding Files to the Project Window

I explain this process in detail in Hour 5, "Scene Selection and Video Capture." If you want to add some files now, select File→Import, navigate to some media files, select them, and click Open. You can also use a shortcut: In the Project window, double-click in the blank area below the word Sequence to open the Import window. After you've added a few files and expanded the width of your Project window, it should look something like Figure 1.5.

In Figure 1.5, the Project window displays characteristics such as media type, length, video resolution, and audio information. You can sort on characteristics by clicking their column names and click-drag columns to new locations. Note that the Project window uses icons and label colors to further differentiate media types.

Effects

Clicking the Effects tab in the Project window opens the Effects palette. As Figure 1.6 shows, effects include scene transitions, such as dissolves and wipes; video effects to alter the appearance of your clips; two audio crossfade transitions; and numerous audio effects to spice up your sound. I'll begin covering these powerful (but frequently overused) tools in Hour 6.

Dockable Palettes

Palettes, such as the Effects palette, are *dockable*. That is, you can drag their tabs to other windows or palettes if those new locations suit your workflow. This is a good thing. The reason I'm pointing this out now is that your version of Premiere Pro (as opposed to the beta version I used to write this book) might have the Effects tab in a location other than the Project window. If so, it's probably in the Monitor window.

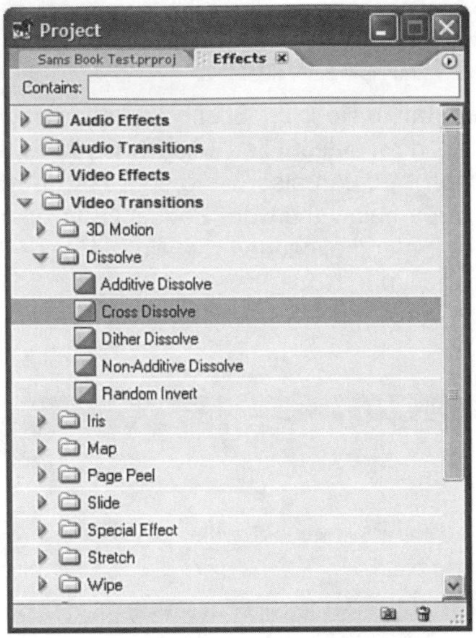

FIGURE 1.6
The Effects palette gives you immediate access to dozens of transitions and effects.

You apply an effect by dragging it to a clip and you place transitions between clips and—new to Premiere Pro—*on* clips. That nifty new trick, combined with another very cool new feature—the ability to apply transitions on any track instead of only on clips on track one—means that you can create all sorts of animated effects. That's particularly true with geometric shapes created in Premiere Pro's Title Designer. I cover that in Hour 8, "Tackling Text: Using the Title Designer."

Monitor Window

You use the Monitor window to view and trim raw clips (your original footage) and view your project-in-progress. You can open the Monitor window with only one screen—the Program screen—or, as shown in Figure 1.7, with two screens—Program and Source.

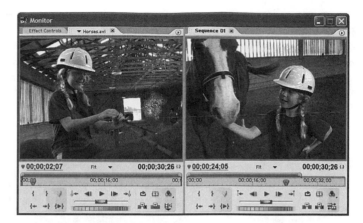

FIGURE 1.7
You view your raw clips in the Monitor window's Source screen (left) and your finished product in the Program screen (right).

The controls at the bottom middle of each screen work much like your VCR with the addition of a very nice shuttle (the wide button in the middle of that group). The other controls are principally for editing. I start covering them in Hour 6.

Timeline Window

This is where you'll do *most* of your actual editing (because this is Premiere Pro, there are always multiple means to perform any one task). Figure 1.8 shows the Premiere Pro timeline window.

Timeline or Sequence?

In my view, this is Premiere Pro 1.0, not Premiere 7.0. It's a new product with new code and new terminology. This is an opportune time to establish crystal clear naming conventions.

In the case of *sequences,* I think Adobe slipped up. *Sequences* are *timelines.* All NLE video editors work with timelines. The window where you work with sequences in Premiere Pro is called the *Timeline window.* So, I think those things in the Timeline window should be called *timelines,* not *sequences.* I asked the Premiere Pro team leader why they chose to use sequences. Here's his reply:

"The name sequences *is designed to reflect the new functionality. Since timelines/sequences are now nestable, they can be used to segment a video edit and enable a production to be broken up into manageable 'sequences.'*

The word timeline *seemed very self-contained, so we changed it to sequence to reflect this extra capability.*

The variation in terminology (in the manual and marketing literature) is largely due to the fact existing Premiere users will be familiar with timeline *and so...we use both terminologies as we felt this was easier for our existing customer base."*

By the Way

The Real Version Number

When I wrote this in the fall of 2003, Adobe hadn't decided what version number to give to Premiere Pro (even though it had already shipped). I clearly see Premiere Pro as a new product; therefore, calling it version 1.0 makes sense to me. But some in the Adobe community think calling it version 7.0 shows that it's a revision of a well-respected and strongly established franchise.

FIGURE 1.8
The sequences (timelines) in Premiere Pro's Timeline window will look familiar to anyone who has worked with other nonlinear editors.

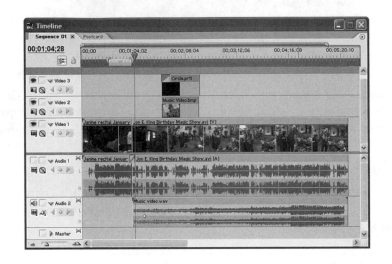

The Timeline window can have multiple sequences, each accessible via a tab at the top of the window. In this case, in Figure 1.8, there are two sequences: one for my project and the other for the Photoshop PSD file I added to the Project window. Basically each sequence is a collection of video and audio tracks.

Anyone who has edited with an NLE will feel comfortable working with Premiere Pro's sequences (although there is a bit of a learning curve that I cover in Hour 6). Anyone coming from the linear, videotape-editing world might find sequences a bit daunting at first but soon will come to love them.

You can layer—*composite*—video clips, images, graphics, and titles in up to 99 tracks. Clips in higher-numbered tracks cover whatever is directly below them on a sequence. Therefore, you need to give clips in higher-numbered tracks some kind of transparency or reduce their size if you want to let clips in lower tracks show through. I start covering those topics in Hour 17, "Compositing Part I—Layering Images and Clips."

Tools Palette

This thin, vertical palette, shown in Figure 1.9, is a refinement of a similar tools collection found in previous versions of Premiere.

FIGURE 1.9
The Tools palette is another example of Premiere Pro's streamlined editing methodology.

Each icon represents a tool that performs a specific function, typically different kinds of edits. What makes this updated Tools palette better than its predecessors is that there are no hidden submenus within this palette. What you see is what you get. The reason for the change? A new context-sensitive cursor. Depending on the situation, the cursor in Premiere Pro changes to indicate a new function that matches the circumstances. If you choose, you can press keyboard shortcuts to change the cursor.

History and Info Palettes

Here are two useful tools:

▶ The History palette (shown in Figure 1.10) tracks every step you take in your video production and lets you back up if you don't like your latest efforts. If the History palette isn't showing up in your workspace, select Window→History from the main menu. Note that when you back up to a previous condition, all steps that came after that point remain in the History palette but are grayed out. That means you can move around without obliterating all your work. The one caveat: You cannot extract a single misstep buried within the current list.

▶ The Info palette has a limited purpose. It offers only a brief data snapshot of whatever element—clip, transition, or effect—you've currently selected in a sequence or the Project window. In the case of Figure 1.11, it notes that the selected clip is an AVI (audio/video interleaved) file with stereo audio. One neat little feature: The Info Palette notes the location of your cursor (as opposed to the Current Time Indicator—edit line). As you move the cursor around a sequence, the Cursor readout notes your location within the sequence.

FIGURE 1.10
The History palette tracks every step— large or small—you make as you edit your project.

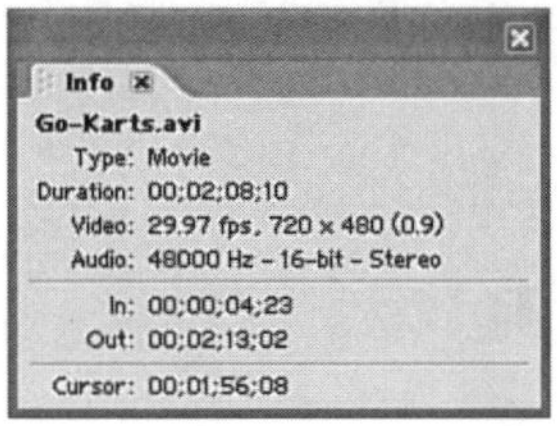

Figure 1.11
The Info palette displays facts about whatever clip you've selected.

By the Way

The Navigator Has Lost Its Way

If you worked with a previous version of Premiere, you might note the passing of the Navigator palette. It was a small, graphical representation of the entire timeline that enabled you to jump around in a project without having to scroll through the timeline. One Premiere Pro keyboard shortcut, the \ backslash, puts your entire project within the width of the displayed portion of the sequence and is a good work-around.

Premiere Pro's Special Features and Technologies

Previous versions of Premiere had a kind of cobbled together, hodgepodge feel. Some things worked elegantly, others did not.

For me, what sets Premiere Pro apart from its predecessors and the competition is how carefully the development team worked to create a consistent look and functionality, to incorporate industry-standard technologies, and to aim high.

Premiere Pro Developer Comments

During beta testing, Premiere Pro's development team frequently commented on the product's new features and functionality. I asked Adobe if I could use some of those quotes in my book. Adobe declined, citing legal issues, but said paraphrasing developer comments without attributing them to specific individuals would be fine.

By the Way

It's exciting to work with such carefully crafted software. That so much effort went into getting the fundamentals right and that the development team took the high road in terms of technology demonstrate that Adobe is making a long-term commitment to creating a powerful, compelling, market-leading product.

The following developer comment, which came the day Adobe informed the beta team that Columbo (Premiere Pro's code name) had gone gold master, reinforces that.

Developer Comment—Technology

Premiere Pro is set to go forward. By modernizing the code we laid the groundwork for rapid future development. I think we will surprise the video editing community by how quickly we will incorporate new features into future versions. Premiere Pro is not the end. It is the beginning.

By the Way

Here are a few examples of Premiere Pro's special features and technologies.

Native YUV Video Processing

Previous versions of Premiere converted video to the computer-friendly RGB (red, green, blue) color scheme. Then, when exported, Premiere converted it back to a TV standard called YUV (Y is luminance and UV is color). These multiple conversions caused some visual quality degradation. Now all video is stored on your hard drive in its native YUV scheme. Only when displaying video on your PC monitor does Premiere Pro convert YUV to RGB.

Color Correction

Premiere lacked a true color correction tool. Premiere Pro rectifies that. Its new color corrector, coupled with the vector scopes shown in Figure 1.12, help you maintain a consistent look for your project (despite changing lighting conditions during a video shoot) or give it a hue that helps set a mood. I cover the color corrector in Hour 16, "Using Higher-Level Effects—Part 2."

FIGURE 1.12
Use these vector scopes plus a color corrector to ensure the highest visual quality for your projects.

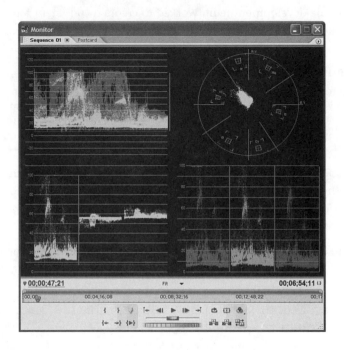

New Audio Technologies and Tools

Audio quality and editing in Premiere Pro nearly matches that found in high-end audio-only production suites. There are two reasons: audio *conforming* and sample-level editing.

As you add—*import*—an audio clip or a video clip with audio to your Project window, Premiere Pro conforms it (you might note the little *conforming* progress bar in the lower-right corner, shown in Figure 1.13).

FIGURE 1.13
As you add audio, Premiere Pro conforms it to match the audio project settings.

Conforming Sams Test Video.avi

Conforming converts your audio into a separate file instead of keeping it inter-leaved with video. It also converts it to 32-bit, floating-point quality (see the fol-lowing By the Way) and up-converts all audio to match the kHz rate set for your project.

Floating-Point Versus Integer

Converting audio to 32-bit floating-point ensures that it remains at its absolutely highest quality possible—even after applying effects and volume changes. For instance, CD audio is in a 16-bit integer format, which limits it to 65,536 incre-ments. 32-bit floating point represents sound using a full-range of numbers using a variable number of decimal places, thereby giving the audio reproduction more accu-racy.

What this all means is that no matter what changes you make to audio within Premiere Pro, all your audio will remain at its original quality. Instead of editing audio only at video frame junctions (one every 1/30 of a second), you can edit audio at the sample rate (at every 1/32,000 or 1/48,000 of a second depending on your selected kHz setting). This leads to absolute audio editing precision. These changes lead to better real-time performance. No longer does Premiere need to process video as it plays audio since audio is now kept in separate files.

The small downside is the conversion time (during which you can still edit and listen to whatever portion of the clip that has been conformed) and the use of additional hard drive space—typically about 1.4GB per hour of DV.

Premiere Pro enables you to work in mono, stereo, and 5.1 Dolby Digital. One other major improvement is the audio mixer, shown in Figure 1.14 and accessed by selecting Window→Audio Mixer.

Maximize the Audio Mixer

By the Way

Sometimes when opening the audio mixer using Window→Audio Mixer, only a little Master Meter displays. If that's the case, click its wing-out triangle and select Audio Mixer (your only choice)—doing so opens the full audio mixer.

The Audio Mixer makes it possible for you to combine audio tracks into separate *sub-mixes*, to apply audio effects to entire tracks to improve consistency, and to add a real-time voice over narration. I cover audio topics in Part III: "Acquiring, Editing, and Sweetening Audio."

FIGURE 1.14
The revamped
Audio Mixer gives
you greater control.

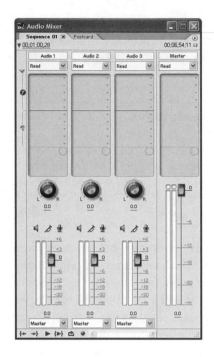

If you want to take your audio editing to even higher levels or to create custom music using loops or your own compositions, you might consider working with Adobe Audition. I give you some hands-on instructions on that product in Hour 15, "Professional Audio Tools: SmartSound Sonicfire and Adobe Audition."

Tight Integration with Photoshop CS and After Effects 6

Back in Figure 1.5, you might have noticed a file folder called Postcard. That file folder holds a Photoshop *PSD* file. Figure 1.15 shows an expanded view.

If you've worked with Photoshop, you know you can create graphics in layers—typically one graphic element or effect per layer. If you import a layered PSD graphic into Premiere Pro, it gives you the option of breaking it down into those separate layers so that you can manipulate them individually on sequences. This is a very powerful tool and is new to Premiere Pro.

Likewise, when you import a Premiere Pro project into After Effects 6, Adobe's industry-standard graphic animation tool, it displays it in its separate tracks. I demonstrate how to use Photoshop and After Effects for Premiere Pro projects in Hour 22, "Using Photoshop and After Effects to Enhance Your DV Project."

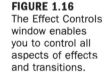

FIGURE 1.15
When you import layered Photoshop PSD files into Premiere Pro, you have the option of splitting that file into its constituent layers.

Effect Controls Window

Another workflow improvement is how Premiere Pro displays and enables you to customize effects, transitions, transparencies, and motion control. Its revamped Effect Controls window gives you absolute control including changing clips over time. Figure 1.16 shows one example of a transition applied between two clips (in this case, the Doors transition).

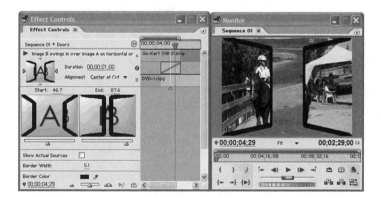

FIGURE 1.16
The Effect Controls window enables you to control all aspects of effects and transitions.

Instead of opening separate windows or dialog boxes for different effect, transition, transparency, and motion control elements, Premiere Pro puts all controls in the Effect Controls window (ECW).

For instance, in its upper-right corner, the ECW displays transition placement. Elsewhere in the ECW, you control the color and width of the transition edge border and its duration. You can watch all these changes in real-time in the monitor or use the Play button in the upper left corner of the ECW. The Effect Controls window is a very powerful tool. It's the hub of Premiere Pro's workflow.

Customizable Keyboard Shortcuts

This nice feature (shown in Figure 1.17), accessed by selecting Edit→Keyboard Customization from the main bar, enables editors to create their own comfortable workflow. As topics come up throughout this book, I'll fill you in on the applicable keyboard shortcuts.

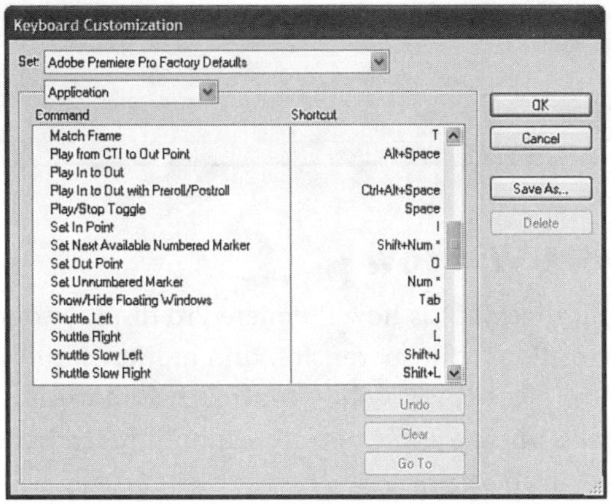

FIGURE 1.17
The Keyboard Customization dialog box enables you to set a workflow that matches your style.

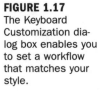

Diagramming the Digital Video Workflow

Premiere Pro is the hub of a newly expanded, five-product Adobe suite of tools geared to digital video production. All five tools feature tight integration and complement and enhance each other. Here's a brief rundown of Premiere Pro's four teammates:

▶ Photoshop CS (Creative Suite)—The latest update to this industry-standard graphic creation and editing product.

▶ After Effects 6—The tool-of-choice for video editors looking to animate graphics and text.

▶ Encore DVD—A new DVD-authoring product built from the ground up to work closely with Premiere Pro, After Effects, and Photoshop CS.

▶ Audition—A professional-level audio editing and sweetening product. Adobe purchased it (Cool Edit Pro) from Syntrillium Software in the summer of 2003 and supplemented it with 5,000 *loops*—music snippets that editors can use to create entire musical selections.

This book is about Premiere Pro, but I would be remiss if I didn't demonstrate how you can use these other Adobe products to improve the quality of your video projects.

It might sound like I think Adobe is the only company that makes video, audio, and graphics-editing products and DVD-authoring tools. I recognize there is plenty of competition. But taken individually and collectively, nothing can come close to the power, productivity, creativity, and integration these Adobe products will bring to your video projects.

That became apparent as I was working on the Premiere Pro beta. Adobe let beta participants take a look at these upcoming products. As we got our hands on them, they blew us away. One tester noted that "as the sun came up," he figured he better stop playing with Audition and get some sleep.

In particular, as the author of *Sams Teach Yourself DVD Authoring in 24 Hours*, I've tested more than a dozen DVD authoring products. Adobe Encore DVD is the best of breed for its price point. Built with a team augmented by engineers from DVD authoring industry leader, Sonic Solutions, Encore DVD is an excellent, carefully engineered, and powerful product with a solid pedigree.

I cover each of these products in separate hours later in this book. For now, take a look at Figure 1.18 to get an idea of how they all work together.

Digital Video Workflow

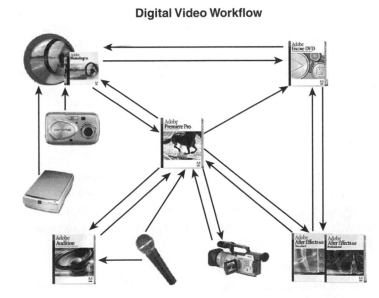

FIGURE 1.18
The digital video workflow using Adobe's Video Collection.

Your workflow might vary depending on your production needs. Basically, Premiere Pro assembles raw and finished parts into a completed whole. Here are a few mini-workflow scenarios:

▶ Photoshop CS captures and touches up photos from a digital camera or a scanner and then exports them to Premiere Pro.

▶ Photoshop CS creates images from scratch or edits still images created in Premiere Pro and then sends them on to Premiere Pro.

▶ Audition enables you to create custom music and edit existing music and sounds either to an existing video clip or production or as a separate audio file. That audio might come from digital video captured by Premiere Pro. Do fine-tuning in Audition and send it back to Premiere Pro.

▶ Premiere Pro captures raw video from a camcorder or VCR. You then edit it and can record it to tape using a camcorder or VCR.

▶ Send sequences created in Premiere Pro to After Effects 6 to apply complex motion and animation, then send those updated motion sequences back to Premiere Pro.

▶ Use After Effects 6 to create and animate text in ways far beyond the capabilities in Premiere Pro.

▶ Send Premiere Pro–created video projects to Encore DVD to use in DVD projects. You can use those videos as the foundation of a project or as motion menus.

▶ Create menus and menu buttons for Encore DVD in Photoshop CS or use Photoshop CS to edit menus created using Encore DVD templates.

▶ Use After Effects 6 to build motion menus for Encore DVD using Photoshop CS or Encore DVD-created static menus.

Summary

Premiere Pro is a nonlinear editor. That means you can place audio, video, and graphics anywhere on a sequence (timeline), organize sub-tasks in separate sequences to focus on them, rearrange media clips within a sequence, add transitions, apply effects, and do any number of other video editing steps in basically any order that suits you.

Premiere Pro has a logically laid-out workspace that facilitates a smooth and efficient workflow. At its center are the Effect Controls and Timeline windows.

Premiere Pro now puts many of its editing tools in the ECW, giving you immediate access to many features that heretofore required a lot of rummaging around in various windows and dialog boxes.

Premiere Pro's developers clearly focused their attention on planning and looking long term. Premiere Pro uses industry-standard technologies and always aims for the highest common denominator. That means there is no degradation in quality at any stage of the production and that Adobe will be able to upgrade Premiere Pro quickly and effectively.

Finally, Premiere Pro is the central processing unit for a five-product digital video–editing suite from Adobe. That company pulled out all the stops in the second half of 2003 to put together a complete package of the industry's best tools that give you limitless possibilities.

At this point in each hour, I normally present a Q&A, a quiz on the hour's tasks, and some suggested exercises as a means to reinforce what you learned and to give you opportunities for extra credit work. Because this hour had no in-depth, step-by-step tasks, I'm leaving out the quiz.

Q&A

Q *I don't see any reason to display two monitor screens. One that shows your finished product seems to be enough.*

A Many editors work with only one monitor screen. When working on an effect, I'll frequently switch to a single-monitor view to save screen real estate. But the second monitor—the Source Monitor—comes in real handy. You'll end up doing a lot of editing with the Source Monitor. One standard workflow is to place raw video clips in the Source Monitor, trim those clips using the Source Monitor editing controls, and then place those trimmed clips on a sequence.

Q *That comment from the Premiere Pro team leader mentioned that the sequences are nestable. What did he mean by that?*

A I cover this concept in Hour 19, "Tips, Tricks, and Techniques—Part 1." Basically, nested sequences replace an awkward editing process called *virtual clips*. It was fraught with gotchas and was a difficult concept to grasp. Nested sequences give you that same ability, but function much more elegantly. In essence, you can create a segment on one sequence and place that sequence in another sequence. There are several reasons for that, including using the same sequence several times but applying a different effect to it. I'll go over the other reasons to use nested sequences in Hour 19.

Workshop

Exercises

1. I'm a real believer in learning from experts. You'd be surprised how willing most experts are to give you some tips. Contact local video production companies, ask whether they use nonlinear editors (even if they're not Premiere Pro), and make an appointment to watch an editor at work. You'll learn a lot.

2. Take your own tour of Premiere Pro's workspace. Open menus, check out preferences (Edit→Preferences—and—Project→Project Settings), take a look at the keyboard shortcuts, and examine the various pre-set workspaces (Windows→Workspace→Effects—and—Audio—or—Color Correction.

3. Go to the Adobe Web site and visit the Video Suite section—http://www.adobe.com/motion/main.html. There you can download trial versions of the four other Video Suite products. Later in this book, I'll suggest you do that individually for each product covered, but now is as good a time as any.

HOUR 2

Camcorder and Shooting Tips

What You'll Learn in This Hour:

▶ Going digital

▶ Choosing a camcorder

▶ Moving up (way up) to high-definition video

▶ Eighteen tips on shooting great video

▶ Expert advice from Karl Petersen

To make an excellent video production, you need to start with high-quality raw material—the original footage. Most books on Premiere Pro gloss over this subject, but no amount of clever, whiz-bang editing can turn mediocre raw video or audio into a dazzling final product. The old computer-programming adage applies: garbage in, garbage out. In the TV world, that adage has a slightly different twist: You *can't* fix it in post. That is, postproduction techniques will not resurrect reels of video junk.

I have 15 years experience in broadcast TV and video production. I've done my own shooting and have worked with some of the best photographers in the business. In this hour, I pass along some of their video-shooting tips to start you on the right track to a finished product you can be proud of.

Going Digital

Great video quality aside, the true *coup de grace* to the high-end video production world is that today's top consumer and **prosumer** (a step up from consumer, but still not broadcast quality) camcorders are digital. This might be yesterday's news to some of you, but for those of you just getting your feet wet in the video production world, listen up. Digital video (DV) changes everything.

In the old days (a couple years ago), analog was it. DV was ridiculously expensive and definitely not a budget video production option.

An analog video signal is a continuous waveform. Small disruptions to that otherwise smooth, continuous signal lead to degradation in image and color quality. Simply dubbing (recording) an analog tape to another tape results in some quality loss. With each additional dub—each added generation—images look less defined, colors become increasingly washed out, and the pictures get grainy. Audio quality also suffers with each generation.

In tape-only editing systems, to make simple scene transitions such as dissolves or to add special effects such as showing videos in moving boxes means doing multiple edits or recording passes. Each pass adds more video noise to the tape. Editors using analog tape machines have to plan carefully to avoid creating projects with obvious shifts in video quality from one section to another.

DV makes generation quality loss a thing of the past. DV is a binary signal—a stream of ones and zeros. Unlike an analog signal, which has a wide range of data possibilities and many ways for electronic equipment to misinterpret it, a digital signal rarely loses quality during transmission and doesn't suffer from generation loss.

By the Way

Long-Distance Digital Video

Home satellite systems that use those pizza-sized dishes are digital. To reach your home, those digital TV signals travel from an earth-based transmitter to a satellite in geosynchronous orbit (22,000 miles into space) back to your parabolic pizza pie receiver—44,000 miles and the picture is crystal clear.

Although some noise might creep into the signal, electronic equipment easily can filter this out because all it's looking for are zeros and ones (see Figure 2.1). Little ragged edges on the signal are rarely large enough to lead to obvious signal quality loss.

More importantly for our purposes, multiple DV edits or dubs do not lead to generational loss. The signal simply remains zeros and ones. You're no longer constrained to limiting your creative considerations to ensure low-noise video. No matter how many edits you perform, no matter how many layers of elements you pile up in a clip, there should be no discernible noise or degradation to fidelity.

Therefore, your first order of business is to buy, borrow, or rent a DV camcorder. A purchase will run you between $500 and $4,000 (see the upcoming sidebar for a rundown of several prosumer camcorders). Three things drive camcorder prices:

lens quality, features, and whether they have one or three image gathering and processing integrated circuits or chips. As you move up the price range, you'll see an increasing number of competitive features—longer focal length lenses, larger LCD screen viewfinders, programmable settings, and fast shutter speeds. But the biggest differentiator is that top-end camcorders have three chips versus a single chip for lower-priced products.

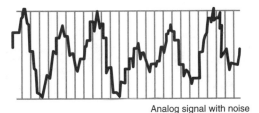

Analog signal with noise

Digital (binary) signal with noise

FIGURE 2.1
Signal noise can dramatically affect analog signals but has virtually no affect on binary signals.

Choosing a Camcorder

First up is your gear—and topping the list is your camcorder. This is an exciting time. For years, video pros have lugged around shoulder-numbing Sony Beta SP and Ikegami broadcast-quality cameras. Their rich colors and low-light capabilities used to put prosumer and consumer **prosumer** camcorders to shame.

Not any longer. Some might quibble and say today's top prosumer camcorders are not true broadcast quality, but only the most highly trained eye can discern an appreciable difference between the $3,300 Canon XL1S or the $2,300 Sony DCR-VX2000 and anything a $15,000+ broadcast camera can crank out. See Figure 2.2 for some high-quality prosumer camcorder models. In the meantime, even lower-priced prosumer and consumer models are more than acceptable and work fine with Premiere Pro.

Camcorder Selection Tips

Camcorders use a charged coupled device (CCD) chip to convert brightness and color to a digital signal. Single-chip camcorder CCDs have to crunch a lot of data. Three-chip camcorders use a prism to divide incoming light into separate red, green, and blue (RGB) hues, thus letting each respective CCD gather more information within its designated segment of the color spectrum. Even though single-chip camcorders use special RGB filters to help their one CCD interpret color data, three-chip cameras have distinctly better color and low-light capabilities.

FIGURE 2.2
Top-of-the-line pro-sumer DV cam-corders: the Canon XL1S (estimated street price $3,300), the Sony DCR-VX2000 ($2,300), and the Panasonic PV-DV953 ($1,300). You can't go wrong with any of these models.

Canon XL1S

Panasonic PV-Dv953

Sony DCR-VX2000

Your choice in camcorders comes down to your audience. If your videos are only for home or Web page viewing, a single-chip camcorder will work fine. If you'll be projecting your videos on large screens for sales presentations or shareholder meetings, you should give strong consideration to a three-chip camcorder. And if you want to move into the professional video-production business, a three-CCD camcorder is a must. Showing up at a client's office with a palm-sized, single-chip camcorder is a sure way to jinx a deal.

Prosumer Camcorder Rundown

Camcorder buying is one of those things that might simply come down to feel. You pick up a camcorder and it fits well in your hands, the controls are logical and accessible, the menus make sense, and the images look right. Or not. When you start digging into the details—all those features—it becomes brain numbing.

So, here are the basics: Top-of-the-line gets you three CCDs and plenty of manual override options: focus, iris, shutter speed, and white balance. If you're serious about shooting high-quality videos, you'll want to have that level of control. For example, setting a higher shutter speed—the Panasonic PV DV952 I tested for this book has a super-fast 1/8000th of a second shutter speed—means that you can capture very crisp images of a very fast subject. Race cars and sprinters all look sharp at such shutter speeds. You do need plenty of light to make this work, though.

Other features of importance include the following:

▶ Substantial optical zoom—at least 10×, but 25× is better.

▶ Input and output capabilities. IEEE 1394 (the industry-standard means to transfer digital video) is a given, as is a means to record from and to a VCR or other camcorder (S-Video connectors are better than composite). Analog-in enables you to record analog video to DV and/or pass it through directly to your PC via the IEEE 1394 cable.

▶ An external mic plug is a necessity as well as a headphone plug.

▶ Optical image stabilizing using prisms or some other means (versus the less desirable electronic stabilization).

Superfluous features—and there are many—include the following:

▶ Digital zoom. All you get are chunky pixels. Use Premiere Pro's Motion or Transforms effects to handle this.

▶ Titler; fade-in, fade-out; digital effects (picture in picture, wipes, multipicture mode, sepia, and so on). Premiere Pro handles all these without forcing you to fumble with awkward on-camera controls and menus.

▶ Widescreen view (unless it's a true 16:9—few offer this). *Faux widescreen* simply adds black bars to the top and bottom of the screen covering parts of the image. Again, you can create this look in Premiere Pro.

▶ Built-in lighting compensation modes, including back-lit, low light, portrait, sports, and extremely bright settings (surf and snow). You should use the manual features to more accurately handle these situations.

The prosumer industry de facto standard camcorder is the Canon XL1S, followed closely by the Sony DCR-VX2000, the Canon GL2, and the Panasonic PV-DV953.

Stepping down a notch, but still a prosumer-quality 3CCD camcorder, is the Sony DCR-TRV950.

Panasonic PV-DV953

The Panasonic PV-DV953 is a high-end prosumer camcorder. Although Sony and Canon grab plenty of prosumer mind share, the DV953 might just muscle its way into that vaunted group.

Panasonic loaned me the PV-DV952—the predecessor to the PV-DV953—to review. The PV-DV953 is nearly identical. The two significant improvements are 50% more pixels on its CCDs (leading to better image quality) and a lower price. The PV-DV953 is the first three-CCD prosumer camcorder with a list price less than $1,500.

Outstanding standard features include three CCDs with 2.4 mega pixels (the Sony TRV950 is 1 mega pixel, or one million pixels), 30× optical zoom, 3.5'' color LCD monitor, color viewfinder, easy-to-access manual controls, easy-to-use VCR controls, and a comfortable feel.

Other good features: The provided battery charges quickly and runs the camcorder for about two hours, the thumbwheel/pushbutton menu control is effective, audio quality is very good and minimizes sound from behind the camera, and the USB connection allows easy downloading of still images and audio to your PC.

Some minor nitpicking: The DV953 tries to be the be-all, end-all prosumer/consumer camcorder. There are just too many superfluous features that probably jack up the price without giving much added benefit. The digital photo quality cannot match standard digital still cameras, the memory card audio recording feature is unnecessary (just use the DV tape and an IEEE 1394 connector), the zoom mic appears only to increase the recorded audio volume without narrowing the focus of the sound, image stabilization had no obvious effect, and the low-light video quality is noisy.

The PV-DV953 represents a significant leap forward for Panasonic. Its predecessor—the DV51D—was bulky and had a small monitor, a cheap feel, and some awkward controls. The PV-DV953 has resolved all those flaws.

Legacy Analog Camcorders

You might own a legacy analog camcorder—VHS (dread the thought), S-VHS, or Hi-8—and aren't ready to shell out the cash for a DV camcorder. Your old clunker might get the job done, but the results will be several cuts below pure DV video. Image quality from most legacy camcorders falls below today's DV camcorders (Hi-8 still looks pretty good, and professional Beta SP is better than prosumer DV). But no matter how good the original video looks, the final edited product will not look that great. That's largely because when loading the analog video into your PC (video capture), Premiere Pro converts it to a digital video file (losing some quality in the process). When recording it back to analog tape for viewing, it will lose even more quality. Because Premiere Pro stores video digitally, there will be no generation loss for converted analog video (or DV) during editing.

One other minor fly in the ointment: You'll need to buy a video capture card (see Hour 4, "Premiere Pro Setup") with analog input connectors. A straightforward DV-only capture card will not work.

Moving Up (Way Up) to High-Definition Video

High-definition TV (HDTV) is imminent. Sort of. It's been imminent for nearly two decades. Back in 1987, I did a news story about how KSL-TV (my employer at the time) in Salt Lake City was going high-def. The consumer response since then has been decidedly underwhelming.

That's about to change. Top-down pressure from the Federal Communications Commission on TV networks, their affiliates, and independent stations, to switch to digital TV (including high-def) by 2006 is one reason.

But I think bottom-up pressure will be the main reason we move to HDTV. Video producers, advertisers, independent filmmakers, and consumers will lead the charge to HDTV.

HD image quality nearly matches 35mm film, comparable quality cameras and editing equipment are less expensive (about $200,000 for top-end HDTV versus $400,000 for a high-quality film camera), and high-def videotapes cost much less. With processing included, film costs about $5,000 an hour. A one-hour HD tape costs $60.

Premiere Pro can handle HDTV, but it takes some specialized hardware and software to do it. As of this book's release, only one company had announced an HDTV-style product for Premiere Pro: CineForm's $1,200 Aspect HD software plug-in (a separate piece of software that works within Premiere Pro) coupled with the $4,000 JVC JY-HD10U prosumer HD camcorder (see Figure 2.3). I present an overview of these products in Hour 21, "Third-Party Products."

FIGURE 2.3
The JVC JY-HD10U is the first pro-sumer-priced HD camcorder.

HD is a small part of Premiere Pro's current feature set. So, I'll limit my overview. But that feature set won't stay limited for long. Adobe says it's working with several camcorder manufacturers and high-definition video card companies and expects to announce several partnerships in the near future.

Eighteen Tips on Shooting Great Video

With your camcorder of choice in hand, it's time to venture off and shoot videos.

Here are my video-shooting axioms:

- ▶ Stripe your DV tapes
- ▶ Adhere to the "rule of thirds"
- ▶ Get a closing shot
- ▶ Get an establishing shot
- ▶ Keep your shots steady—use a tripod
- ▶ Let your camera follow the action
- ▶ Use trucking shots to move with the action
- ▶ Try out unusual angles
- ▶ Lean into or away from subjects
- ▶ Get wide and tight shots to add interest
- ▶ Try to match action in multiple shots
- ▶ Shoot sequences to help tell the story
- ▶ Avoid fast pans and snap zooms—they're for MTV only
- ▶ Remember to shoot cutaways to avoid jump cuts
- ▶ Make sure you don't break the "plane"
- ▶ Get plenty of natural sound
- ▶ Use lights to make your project brilliant
- ▶ Plan your shoot

I've jammed a lot into these 18 items. All will help make your video shine with a professional glow. I've discussed each in detail in the following sections.

Stripe Your DV Tapes

This is a tedious but ultimately timesaving step. Your DV camcorder lays down timecode as it records. Later, as you transfer DV to your computer, you'll likely use that timecode to create a video clip log. After you've completed logging your tape or tapes, you'll tell Premiere Pro to automatically retrieve the logged clips by automatically shuttling the tape to the timecodes noted in the log and then record them to your hard drive.

Most camcorders, when powered up, reset their timecode to zero seconds. If you do that more than once using the same videotape, you'll end up with several instances of the same timecode on one tape. As a result, Premiere Pro probably will retrieve the wrong clip. Striping your tapes before doing any shooting resolves that. You stripe tapes by simply placing a fresh tape in your camcorder, capping your lens, pressing Record, and waiting for your camcorder to stripe the entire tape. Rewind the tape and you're ready to go. Now, as you use your camcorder, it'll record new video over the black video you taped but won't change the timecode.

Adhere to the Rule of Thirds

Composition is the most fundamental element of camerawork, and the rule of thirds is the textbook. When composing your shot, think of your viewfinder as being crisscrossed by two horizontal and two vertical lines. The center of interest should fall on one of the four intersections. See Figure 2.4 for a simple diagram. The standard amateur photographer mistake is to put the center of attention at the center of the image. The most common is portraits in which the eyes of the subject are dead center in the photo. One rule of thumb is to look around the viewfinder as you shoot, not just stare at its center. Check the edges to see whether you're filling the frame with interesting images. Avoid large areas of blank space.

FIGURE 2.4
The rule of thirds: Putting your image's most important element at one of these intersections will make it more pleasing to the eye.

Get a Closing Shot

This might seem like I'm taking things way out of order, but the one shot that should be uppermost in your mind is the closing shot (the opening shot or shots are important but have a much less lasting impact). Your closing images are what stick in people's minds. They're what your audience takes away from your video production. If you start a shoot without knowing what your closing shot will be, you should be constantly on the lookout for that one shot or sequence that best wraps up your story.

Dotson's Rule

The importance of the closing shot came through loud and clear at a seminar I attended given by NBC-TV feature reporter Bob Dotson (see Hour 3, "Story Creation, Writing, and Video Production Tips"). He and his photographer never fail to find a closing shot. It could be as simple as someone closing a door, capping a pen, petting a dog, turning out the lights, or releasing a butterfly from their cupped hands. If you happen to see a Dotson feature story, consider its close. It's sure to be memorable.

Get an Establishing Shot

An establishing shot sets a scene. It doesn't have to be the opening shot. One of the greatest establishing shots of all time is in Robert Redford's *The Natural*. Those who have seen this marvelous film know what I'm talking about: The shot from the top row of the baseball stadium during a night game that takes in the entire field with blazing lights ringing the park. Anyone who has been to a major league ballpark gets goose bumps when that image appears onscreen. It tells a dramatic story in one image.

That should be your goal for your project's establishing shot or shots (you might need several if you're covering several topics in one video).

Did you Know?

Think Different

Although super-wide works sometimes—aerials make great establishing shots—it pays to think "outside the box." Don't fall back on the old standbys, such as the scoreboard, the corporate sign, or the medium shot of a hospital operating room. Try something different: a tight shot of a soccer ball with natural sound of children's voices, a low-angle image through a glass table of someone using your client's product, or a close-up of a scalpel with light glinting off its surface.

Each grabs the viewer's attention and helps tell your story.

Keep Your Shots Steady—Use a Tripod

We all know that photographers take the images we view on TV, and that they uses a camera to create them. But, as video producers, we don't want to remind viewers of that. We want to give them the sense that they're looking through a window or, better yet, are there on location.

A shaky camera shatters that illusion.

Despite a recent trend away from the use of tripods—MTV started it and shows such as *48 Hours* have run with it—there's plenty to be said for smooth-looking video. If you're doing a sit-down interview or grabbing close-ups, put your camcorder on "sticks." When possible, use a tripod with a fluid head. That'll enable you to make smooth pans or tilts. Good tripods aren't cheap. Reasonably high-quality sticks start at about $150. See Figure 2.5 for a top-of-the-line example.

FIGURE 2.5
The Sachtler DA 75 L aluminum tripod (right) weighs only 2kg. Its DV 2 fluid head works well with lightweight camcorders.

Makeshift Tripods

If a tripod is too expensive, cumbersome, or inconvenient; if the action is too fast paced; or if you need to move the camera during the shot, try to find some way to stabilize the shot. For still shots, lean against a wall, put your elbows on a table, or place the camcorder on a solid object. For moving shots, get the camcorder off your shoulder, hold it about waist high, and let your arms work as shock absorbers.

Another alternative is to buy or make a Steadicam. A Steadicam Jr—complete with a built-in monitor—that works with prosumer camcorders costs $900. See http://www.steadicam.com/prohh_jr.htm.

Here's a Web site for a home-built steady cam: http://www.student. virginia.edu/~fms-uva/steadycam/. It's a heck of a lot cheaper.

Did you
Know?

Let Your Camera Follow the Action

This might seem obvious, but keep your viewfinder on the ball (or puck, face, conveyor belt, and so on). Your viewers' eyes will want to follow the action, so give them what they want.

One nifty trick is to use directed movement as a pan motivator. That is, follow a leaf's progress as it moves down a stream and then continue your camera motion past the leaf—panning—and widen out to show something unexpected: a waterfall, a huge industrial complex, or a fisherman.

Use Trucking Shots to Move with the Action

This is an excellent way to follow action (so named because using a camera on a moving vehicle is one way to get this shot). Truck right along with some action. If you're shooting a golf ball rolling toward the cup, tag along right behind, in front of, or beside it. When walking through tall grass, dangle your camcorder at knee level and walk right through it, letting the grass blades smack into the lens. Ever wonder how they get those cool downhill snow-skiing shots? The cameraperson skis backwards with a heavy electronic news-gathering (ENG) camera on his shoulder or dangling from his hand at snow level (see the next section). I've watched my good friend Karl Peterson (see the upcoming section, "Expert Advice from Karl Petersen") do that amazing maneuver several times.

Try Out Unusual Angles

Move your camcorder away from eye level. Shoulder shots have their place—they represent probably as much as 80% of all video—but getting the camcorder off your shoulder leads to more interesting and enjoyable shots. Ground-level "ferret-cam" shots are great for cavorting puppies or crawling babies. Climb a ladder or use a tall building to get a crane shot. Shoot through other objects or people while keeping the focus on your subject.

Stop Action Tips

You'll need a tripod to create stop-action or time-lapse photography. Both methods require that the camera remain steady. The other requirement is that the focal length and aperture cannot change. So, when you set up your camcorder to shoot the same scene for a long time, planning to compress time during editing, make sure that your auto-focus, auto-white balance, and auto-iris are turned off.

Lean Into or Away from Subjects

Too many shooters rely too heavily on the zoom lens. A better way to move in close or away from a subject is simply to lean in or out. Lean way in and start your shot tight on someone's hands as he works on a wood carving; then lean way back (perhaps widening your zoom lens as well) to reveal that he is working in a sweatshop full of folks hunched over their handiwork. It's much more effective than a standard lens zoom and a lot easier to pull off.

Get Wide and Tight Shots to Add Interest

Most novice videographers create one boring medium shot after another. The reason: It fits our experience. Our eyes tend to take in things the same way. Instead, think wide and tight. Grab a wide shot and a tight shot of your subject. It's much more interesting.

Did you Know?

Get Close to the Subject

When you grab your tight shots, try to avoid relying on your zoom lens. Instead, get as close as practical to your subject and then grab that tight shot. Unless you want your shot to look like you took it from a distance, it's much more interesting to change positions rather than simply toggle that zoom button. Also, audio is much better when you're closer to the subject.

Try to Match Action in Multiple Shots

Repetitive action—running assembly-line machinery, demonstrating a golf swing, or working in a barbershop—lends itself to matched action shots. A barber clips someone's hair and it falls to the floor. Get a shot of the scissors, the hair hitting the floor, a wide shot of the entire shop, and a close-up reflection of the scissors in the mirror or the barber's glasses. You'll later edit those separate shots into one smooth collection of matched action.

Shoot Sequences to Help Tell the Story

Shooting repetitive action in sequence is another way to build interest and even suspense. A bowler wipes his hands on a rosin bag, dries them over a blower, wipes the ball with a towel, picks the ball up, fixes his gaze on the pins, steps forward, swings the ball back, releases it, slides to the foul line, watches the ball's trajectory, and then reacts to the shot. Instead of simply capturing all this in one long shot, piecing these actions together in a sequence of edits is much more compelling. You can easily combine wide and tight shots, trucking moves, and matched action to turn repetitive action into attention-grabbing sequences.

Avoid Fast Pans and Snap Zooms

These moves fall into MTV and amateur video territory. Few circumstances call for such stomach-churning camerawork. In general, it's best to minimize all pans and zooms. As with a shaky camera, they remind viewers that they're watching TV.

If you do zoom or pan, do it for a purpose: to reveal something, to follow someone's gaze from his or her eyes to the subject of interest, or to continue the flow of action (as in the floating leaf example earlier). A slow zoom in, with only a minimal change to the focal length, can add drama to a sound bite. Again, do it sparingly.

Keep on Rolling Along

Don't let this no-fast-moves admonition force you to stop rolling while you zoom or pan. If you see something that warrants a quick close-up shot or you need to suddenly pan to grab some possibly fleeting footage, keep rolling. You can always edit around that sudden movement later.

If you stop recording to make the pan or zoom and adjust the focus, you might lose some or all of whatever it was you were trying so desperately to shoot. Plus you'll lose any accompanying natural sound.

Remember to Shoot Cutaways to Avoid Jump Cuts

Cutaways literally let you cut away from the action or interview subject. One important use is to avoid **jump cuts**—two clips that, when edited one after the other, create a disconnect in the viewer's mind.

Consider the standard news or corporate interview. You might want to edit together two 10-second sound bites from the same person. Doing so would mean the interviewee would look like he suddenly moved. To avoid that jump cut—that sudden disconcerting shift—you make a cutaway of the interview. That could be a wide shot, a hand shot, or a reverse-angle shot of the interviewer over the interviewee's shoulder. You then edit in the cutaway over the juncture of the two sound bites to cover the jump cut.

The same holds true for a soccer game. It can be disconcerting simply to cut from one wide shot of players on the field to another. If you shoot some crowd reactions or the scoreboard, you can use those shots to cover up what would have been a jump cut.

Make Sure That You Don't Break the Plane

This is another of those viewer disconnects you want to avoid. If you're shooting in one direction, you don't want your next shot to be looking back at your previous camera location. For instance, if you're shooting an interview with the camera peering over the left shoulder of the interviewer, you want to shoot your reverse cutaways behind the interviewee and over his right shoulder. That keeps the camera on the same side of the plane—an imaginary vertical flat surface running through the interviewer and interviewee. To shoot over your subject's left shoulder would break that plane, meaning the viewer would think the camera that took the previous shot should somehow be in view. Figure 2.6 shows an interview with correct and incorrect (broken plane) camera placements. This also applies to larger settings, such as shooting from both sides of a basketball court or football field.

In general, you want to keep all your camera positions on one side of that plane. This isn't true for all situations. Consider a TV show of a rock group performance. Camera crew members typically scramble all over the stage, grabbing shots from multiple angles, and frequently appear on camera themselves. That's much different from breaking the plane in a formal sit-down interview.

Switch Sides

If you conduct formal, sit-down interviews with more than one person for the same piece, consider shooting each subject from a different side of the interviewer. That is, if you shoot one subject with the camera positioned over the left shoulder of the reporter, position the camera over the right shoulder of the reporter for the next interview. That avoids a subtle jump cut that happens when you edit two bites from two individuals who are both facing the same way.

Did you Know?

Get Plenty of Natural Sound

This is absolutely critical. We tend to take sound for granted. However, relying on your camcorder's built-in mic and taking extra steps to improve the audio quality will dramatically improve the production value of your projects. I'll cover audio issues in depth in Part III, *"Acquiring, Editing, and Sweetening Audio."* For now, think in terms of using additional mics: *shotgun* mics to narrow the focus of your sound and avoid extraneous noise, *lavalieres* tucked out of sight for interviews, and *wireless* mics to get sound when your camera can't be close enough to get just what you need.

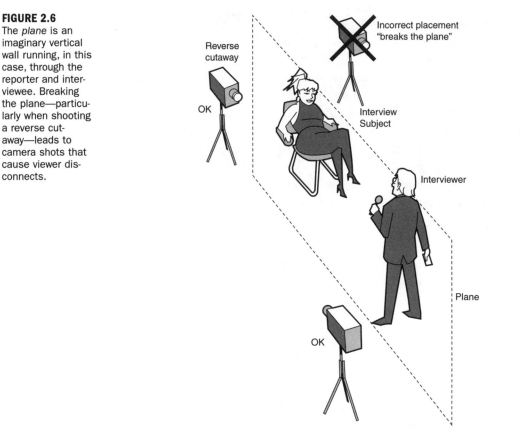

Reverse cutaway

OK

Incorrect placement "breaks the plane"

Interview Subject

Interviewer

Plane

OK

Use Lights to Make Your Project Brilliant

Lights add dazzle and depth to otherwise bland and flat scenes. An onboard cam-corder fill light is a convenient way to brighten dull shots. And a full (but admit-tedly cumbersome) lighting kit with a few colored gels can liven up an otherwise dull research laboratory. If you don't have the time, money, patience, or person-nel to deal with adding lights, do whatever you can to increase the available light. Open curtains, turn on all the lights, or bring a couple desk lamps into the room. One caveat: Low-light situations can be dramatic and flipping on a few desk lamps can destroy that mood in a moment.

Watch Your White Balance

Did you Know?

No matter what kind of lighting situation you're in, you always need to watch your **white balance**. Different lights operate with different color temperatures. Your eyes automatically compensate for those color differences, but your camcorder is not that proficient. These days, most camcorders have auto–white balance, and many have manual–white balance as well. Auto–white balance works in most situations. As you move from room to room or from inside to outside, the camera "assumes" that everything in its field of view is gray and adjusts its color balance accordingly.

Tricky Lighting Situations

Watch Out!

Problems arise when you shoot indoors and have a window in the scene. In that circumstance, whatever you see through the window probably will have a blue tint. The other tricky white balance situation is when you shoot a scene with a predominant color, such as doing product shots using a solid-color background. The auto–white balance will think that solid color is gray, and the image will look horrible. That's when you need to place a gray or white card in the scene, fill the viewfinder with that card under whatever lighting you plan to use for the product shots, and click the manual–white balance button. For a fun practical lesson in the value of a manual–white balance, roll tape throughout this procedure or when you walk from indoors to outdoors to watch the colors change.

Plan Your Shoot

When you consider a video project, plan what you need to shoot to tell the story. Videotaping your kid's soccer championship match, a corporate backgrounder, or a medical procedure each require planning to ensure success. Know what you want your final video project to say and think of what you need to videotape to tell that story.

Even the best-laid plans and most carefully scripted projects might need some adjusting once you start rolling and recording in the field. No matter how you envision the finished project, be willing to make changes as the situation warrants.

Expert Advice from Karl Petersen

Karl Petersen is my favorite TV news photographer. We met in Boise, Idaho, where we worked at competing stations. We later worked together at KSL-TV in Salt Lake City. We formed a video production company in Oregon called Glint Video (we always tried to get a "glint" shot in all our news pieces). Then Karl moved on to KGW-TV in Portland, where he is now chief photographer.

Karl Petersen—
Chief Photographer,
KGW-TV, Portland,
OR

Karl has seen and done it all. Absolutely nothing fazes him. He'll venture into the tensest situation and shoot with aplomb. When we went out on stories, we had an unspoken understanding: I never had to tell Karl what kind of images and sound I needed. I knew he would always get exactly what would make the story work. Karl's regular beat these days is chopper photog. "Sky 8," KGW's Bell 407 helicopter, has two Flir cameras. One is infrared and can operate in *total* darkness. Karl's advice is worth much more than the price of this book. Take it to heart:

▶ My first shooting advice is, don't do it. Pursue a career of doctor, lawyer, teamster, stevedore, bordello piano player, whatever.

▶ Having failed that, my first tip is always to shoot as an editor. Always think about how to get from one shot to the next. Try to get some kind of transition shot with either an entry or exit. Close-ups are especially helpful in editing to get from point A to point B.

▶ Get a good shot mix—wide, medium, close-up (extreme close-ups work well), and unusual angles. Get lots of shots. Variety is an editor's friend.

▶ Get an establishing shot that tells viewers where you are.

▶ Fundamentals: Make sure that you have freshly charged batteries, always monitor audio by wearing an earpiece (if you don't you're guaranteed to get burned), and watch your color balance.

▶ For all indoor interviews, I recommend using at least two lights, three if you have time (I usually don't—TV news is hectic). If I'm to the reporter's right, I place a light with an umbrella reflector slightly to his left. That means the interviewee is looking toward the light. I place a Lowel Omni with "barn doors" (to keep it from shining into the lens) behind and over the left shoulder of the interview subject (that is, to my right). This adds nice highlights.

If I have time, I place a third umbrella well behind the camera to add fill (see Figure 2.7).

FIGURE 2.7
A Lowel Tota with an umbrella (left) and a Lowel Omni with barn doors. Images courtesy of Lowel-Light.

- ▶ If I'm shooting in a room with sunlight coming in a window, I use blue gels—especially balanced for daylight—and then color balance for sunlight.

- ▶ For underwater photography, I recommend using an Ewa-Marine plastic bag video camcorder housing (see `http://www.ewa-marine.de/English/e-start.htm`). They're good to a depth of about 30 feet, easy to use, and relatively inexpensive (about $350).

When shooting from "Sky 8," I sit in the warmth and comfort of the back seat and operate the cameras with a laptop and a joystick. Not many video producers have this luxury. For those who must shoot from a side window, here are some tips:

- ▶ Think safety first. Make sure that nothing can fall off the camera—such as a lens shade—or out of the back seat and possibly hit the rotor. That makes the chopper spin like crazy, so you get real dizzy before you die.

- ▶ Shooting with the door off is ideal (remove it *before* you take off).

- ▶ Try to keep the camera slightly inside the door frame to keep it out of the wind.

▶ Have the pilot "crab" (fly sort of sideways) so that you can shoot straight ahead. That's much more dramatic. It's a great way to fly along a river for instance.

▶ Have the pilot fly low. This allows cool reveal shots, such as flying over a ridge to reveal an expansive vista.

Finally, don't forget to grab that "glint" shot.

Summary

A high-quality video production must start with excellent video. Your gear is paramount—high-end camcorder (preferably DV or broadcast-quality analog), lights, mics, and sticks. When shooting your raw video, think outside the box. Don't settle for standard, boring shoulder shots. Get in close, get down low, look for that unusual angle. Natural sound is essential, and lighting adds sizzle.

Q&A

Q *When I do quick interviews in the field using my handheld camera, people always stare in the camera and act. Is there a way to fix that?*

A You bet! *You* need to stop staring—at the viewfinder, that is. Try to frame up your man on the street (*MOS* in TV news parlance) in the viewfinder as casually as possible and then move your head away from the camera. Look your subjects in their eyes and instead of interviewing them—talk to them. They'll return the favor.

Q *How am I supposed to keep my camera steady if I'm doing a trucking shot? What about videotaping something such as whitewater rafting? There's no way to keep it steady then.*

A Correct! One powerful element of video is that it can transport viewers to someplace besides their living room or office. You keep your shots steady to avoid shattering that illusion. But if that place is full of action, any camera movement simply mirrors what it would be like for the viewer to be there and to experience that excitement. Camera movement in moments of action, especially from a first-person perspective, is tremendously effective.

Workshop

Quiz

1. If you're shooting a formal sit-down interview and the camera is positioned over the left shoulder of the interviewer, where should you place the camera for reverse cutaways?

2. What's the principal advantage of digital video over analog video?

3. Why should you stripe your tapes?

Quiz Answers

1. Place the camera behind the interview subject and shoot over his right shoulder. You can shoot a wide two-shot of the reporter and interviewee and a tight shot of the reporter to use as cutaways. If the reporter isn't going to be part of the story (typically the case in corporate productions), keep the camera in its original location and shoot tight hand shots and wider establishing shots.

2. Digital video is simply a collection of zeros and ones. There is no signal quality degradation during transmission or generation loss after multiple edits. Analog video suffers from both maladies.

3. Striping your tapes—that is, laying down continuous timecode from beginning to end before doing any videotaping—ensures that there will be no duplicate timecodes on the same tape. That means when Premiere Pro later does an automated video transfer of selected clips, there will be no confusion about selecting between clips with the same timecode.

Exercises

1. Grab your camcorder and shoot some video. Keep my tips in mind. Remember the rule of thirds. Get wide, tight, and trucking shots. Follow the action, use unusual angles, and record plenty of natural sound.

2. Critically view your videos, looking for poorly framed shots, shaky camera work, and lousy lighting. Learn from your mistakes.

HOUR 3

Story Creation, Writing, and Video Production Tips

What You'll Learn in This Hour:

- ▶ Getting the story right: story creation tips from NBC-TV correspondent Bob Dotson
- ▶ Writing in the active voice: Mackie Morris' writing tips—"The Good Writer's Dazzlin' Dozen"
- ▶ Storytelling with video: scriptwriting tips from Hollywood screenwriters Stephen Black and Henry Stern
- ▶ Stepping up to film: expert advice from cinematographer Charly Steinberger
- ▶ The business of video production: Sam Prigg's tips on starting a video production company
- ▶ Doing the video production thing: Joe Walsh's event shooting tips

Premiere Pro is a powerful video production tool. By choosing Premiere Pro, you've made a commitment to take your video production quality up several notches. To do that requires more than learning new editing techniques. You also need to hone your story-creation skills, writing style, and even business acumen. By moving to Premiere Pro, you're showing the kind of interest in video production that frequently leads to a profession within that industry.

This hour addresses those issues. I've turned to some colleagues and friends in the TV news, film, and video production industry and asked them to offer expert tips within their specialty.

Getting the Story Right

I worked in the TV news business as a reporter and anchorman as well as shooter and editor. In my 11 years working on-camera and off, I constantly critiqued my work and asked others to do the same. Some offered their advice in writing and I hung on to those words of wisdom:

- ▶ An NBC producer who ran the affiliate **feed**—a daily collection of stories made available to local network stations for their use—once wrote about a prison counseling piece that I submitted to him. He said that my "story *talked* about" the subject "but *showed* nothing" about it. My tape "cried out for some natural sound of a session in progress."

- ▶ A Seattle TV news director wrote that my stories had a sameness—a voice track, a sound bite, more voiceover, another sound bite, and a standup close. "Mix 'em up," he suggested.

- ▶ And a consultant took me aside to tell me to "break up my on-camera pacing with pauses."

I took all those tips to the bank. The NBC producer ended up buying about a story a week from me. The news director helped me get a job in a much larger market. And the consultant's advice helped me land an anchor job at that station.

I'm a believer in heeding expert advice.

In putting together this book, I've had the enjoyable opportunity to contact many of the people who have given me advice or from whom I have gained a lot of practical knowledge. Each agreed to provide expert tips focusing on their specialty. You've already met photographer Karl Petersen in Hour 2, "Camcorder and Shooting Tips." In Hour 7, "Applying Professional Edits and Adding Transitions," you'll hear from editor John Crossman. And in Hour 12, "Acquiring Audio," Chris Lyons, an audio engineer from the world's leading microphone manufacturer, Shure, Inc., offers up his expert advice.

For this hour, I compiled six expert columns. I think they all speak to enhancing your skills beyond the fundamentals of camerawork, editing, and simply learning how to use Premiere Pro's toolset. Further, you might want to take what you do with Premiere Pro and move into a career in video production. These experts speak to that.

Up first, Bob Dotson.

Story-Creation Tips from Bob Dotson

Bob Dotson,
NBC-TV
reporter.

NBC-TV *Today Show* correspondent Bob Dotson is, I think, the best human-interest feature-story TV reporter. Dotson has received more than 50 awards. The National Press Photographers Association award committee wrote, "Bob Dotson's reports help us understand ourselves a bit better. They show that all our lives are important and really matter. After all, this country was built not by great heroes or great politicians, but by ordinary people—by thousands whose names we don't know, may never know, but without whose influence America wouldn't exist."

Although you probably aren't a TV newsperson, you'll probably create human-interest stories—Dotson's forte. If there's a storyteller out there you should emulate, I think he's the one. During my TV reporting days I tried to watch all his stories, and when a station I worked for offered me the chance to attend one of his seminars, I jumped at it.

I've reproduced my notes, with his approval, here. I took many things away from his class. Three points stand out:

▶ **Give viewers a reason to remember the story.**

▶ **When interviewing people, try not to ask questions.** Merely make observations. That loosens people up, letting them reveal their emotional, human side to you.

▶ **Make sure that you get a closing shot.** Most video producers look for dramatic opening shots or sequences (and that's still a good thing), but your viewers are more likely to remember the closing shot.

Bob Dotson's Storyteller's Checklist

Dotson's Storyteller's Checklist inspired his book *Make It Memorable* (Bonus Books) and a companion videotape of all the stories in the book. He prepared his list (and book) with TV news reporters in mind, but his tips apply to professional, corporate, and home video producers as well:

▶ **Always remember that the reporter is not the story.**

▶ **Make sure the *commitment* is present.** Commitment is your description of the story, stated in one sentence. That is, what you want the audience to take away from the report. You should be able to state the commitment as a complete sentence with subject, verb, and object. "Outside money is altering the city's architecture," "This cow has never taken an order in her life," "You can't murder a pumpkin," and so on. You formulate this commitment to yourself to help guide the story creation. Then you use your images to prove the commitment visually. Very seldom will you state the commitment verbally in any story.

▶ **Write your pictures first.** Give them a strong lead, preferably visual, that instantly telegraphs the story to come.

▶ **The main body of the story should usually be no more than three to five main points**, which you prove visually after you've identified them.

▶ **Create a strong close that you can't top**, something you build toward throughout the story. Ideally, the ending is also visual.

▶ **Write loose.** Be hard on yourself as a writer. Say nothing in the script that your viewers would already know or that the visuals say more eloquently.

▶ **Throughout the story, build your report around sequences**—two or three shots of a guy buying basketball tickets, two or three shots of a husband and wife drinking coffee at a kitchen table, and so on. Sequences demand matched action.

▶ **Allow for moments of silence.** Stop writing occasionally and let two or three seconds or more of compelling action occur without voiceover. For a writer, nothing is more difficult to write than silence. For viewers, sometimes nothing is more eloquent.

▶ **Use strong natural sound** to heighten realism, authenticity, believability, and to heighten the viewer's sense of vicarious participation in the events you're showing. Some reports merely enable you to watch what happened. The best reports make it possible for you to experience what happened.

▶ **Tell your story through people.** People sell your story. Try to find strong central characters engaged in compelling action that is visual or picturesque.

▶ **Build in surprises to sustain viewer involvement.** Surprises help viewers feel something about the story; surprises lure uninterested viewers to the screen. Surprises can be visual, wild sounds, short bites, or poetic script. Always, surprises are little moments of drama.

▶ **Short sound bites prove the story you are showing.** Don't use sound bites as substitutes for more effective storytelling.

▶ **Address the larger issue.** "A trailer home burned down." Such a story fails to meet the "so what?" test. "The trailer home burned down because the walls are full of flammable insulation" describes the larger issue and meets the "so what?" test.

▶ **Finally, make your story memorable.** Can your viewers feel something about the story and its subjects? If feeling is present, the story will be memorable. It will stick in the viewers' minds.

Keep It Simple...and Short

As a coda to Dotson's advice, I'll add that you need to remember, this is only TV. You need some mighty compelling or entertaining material to keep viewers glued to the tube for more than a few minutes. Think about whatever message you're trying to get across in your video project and consider what images, sound, and graphics will convey that message in the briefest, most effective manner. Then shoot with brevity in mind.

That's not to say that you don't grab unplanned video that looks great. Or that you cut interviews short even if you haven't heard some compelling sound bites. Videotape is expendable. Feel free to shoot plenty. Although it's true that you might have to wade through a lot to find the best shots, the advantage of DV is that after these shots have been located, you can simply capture them to your hard drive and they become immediately accessible.

Writing in the Active Voice

It's a rare classroom experience that can cause a tidal change. One of those for me was a seminar with Mackie Morris (see the upcoming section). Morris makes his message clear: "Write in the active voice." For example, instead of writing

A bill was passed by the Senate.

write this instead:

The Senate passed a bill.

Put the receiver of the verb's action after the verb. Instead of the passively voiced "John Doe was arrested by police" (Doe is the receiver of the action and is ahead of the verb), change that to "Police arrested John Doe."

Morris emphasizes that passive voice deadens, complicates, and lengthens writing. It's not ungrammatical, but it's more suitable for print than television copy. You use passive voice sparingly in everyday conversation, and you should use it sparingly in video productions. You're asking people to listen to your words, not read them. Make it easy. Make it active.

It takes some effort to make the shift from passive voice to active. Simply recognizing passive voice takes extra attentiveness. The biggest giveaway is some form of the *to be* verb in a verb phrase. The following sentences are all in the passive voice:

> The students were praised by the teacher.
>
> The unruly customer was told to leave by the maitre d'.
>
> The forest was destroyed by fire.

Make them active by moving the receiver of the action to after the verb:

> The teacher praised the students.
>
> The maitre d' told the unruly customer to leave.
>
> Fire destroyed the forest.

That one fundamental technique makes your sentences simpler and shorter.

Morris calls it *straight-line meaning*. The listener understands the copy better because it flows in a straight line. You know that when you read a newspaper you frequently go back and reread some sentences because something didn't add up. Video viewers don't have that luxury.

Besides simply switching the sentence around (*relocating the actor*, as Morris puts it), you can fix passive sentences in three other ways:

▶ **Identify the missing actor and insert it into the sentence.** Change "The airplane was landed during the storm" to "A passenger landed the airplane during the storm."

▶ **Change the verb.** Instead of writing "The bell was sounded at noon" write "The bell rang at noon." (Or tolled, pealed, chimed—using active voice fosters the use of more descriptive words.)

▶ **Drop the *to be* verb.** Change "The spotlight was focused on downtown" to "The spotlight focused on downtown."

Not all *to be* verb phrases are passive. "The man was driving south" contains a verb phrase and a *to be* helper. But the man was performing the action, not receiving it. Therefore, the sentence is active. A sentence is passive only if the receiver of the verb's action precedes the verb.

Writing in the active voice forces you to get out of your writing rut. Instead of saying the same old things in the same old *to be* passive way, select new active verbs and constructions. You'll write more conversationally and with a fresher and more interesting style.

That's not to say that you'll write exclusively in the active voice. You should write, "He was born in 1984," or "She was injured in the accident" because that's what people say.

Focusing on active voice makes your copy more interesting and easier to understand.

Mackie Morris' Writing Tips

Few if any media consultants match Mackie Morris' 25-year record as a journalism and communications seminar leader, teacher, coach, and practitioner. Founder and president of Mackie Morris Communications, he works with a wide range of corporate and public service clients to enhance their communication skills.

Mackie Morris.

Morris previously served as chairman of the Broadcast News Department at the University of Missouri School of Journalism. He later worked as a vice president and lead consultant for Frank N. Magid Associates, a major media consulting firm, where he implemented a series of instructional workshops for broadcast professionals. It was at one of those seminars that I became a devotee of Morris's "active voice." Morris continues to be one of the most sought-after broadcast writing seminarians ever.

The Good Writer's Dazzlin' Dozen

At his seminars, Morris relentlessly hammers home his active voice message. But peppered throughout his presentation he interjects other useful writing tips. He calls them "The Good Writer's Dazzlin' Dozen":

▶ **Write factually and accurately.** The best technique and the finest form mean nothing if your copy's wrong.

▶ **Write in the active voice.** This technique makes your copy tighter, complete, easier to listen to, and more interesting. Do whatever you must to avoid the passive voice.

▶ **Write in the present or present perfect tenses.** They make your copy more immediate, and immediacy is more interesting. Avoid the word *today*. If you use past tense, make sure that you give a time reference to avoid confusion.

▶ **Keep your writing simple.** Choose positive forms over negative forms. Write one thought to a sentence. Don't search for synonyms; repetition is not a sin. Don't search for complicated, intellectual language. Give the audience the best possible chance to understand the story.

▶ **Be complete and clear.** In your quest for brevity and conciseness, don't omit necessary information.

▶ **Be creative.** Stick to the rules, but develop your own style. Try to say the same old thing in a different, new way. Make use of writing devices that make copy easier to listen to and more interesting, such as using the "rule of threes" (that is, grouping items by threes, such as red, white, and blue; left, right, and center; over, under, and through). Saying things in groups of three always sounds better. Pausing before saying the third item is even more effective.

▶ **Write to be heard.** Maintain a sense of rhythm in your writing. All life has rhythm, and rhythmic writing is easier to hear. Avoid potentially confusing homonyms. Always, always test your copy by reading it aloud.

▶ **Avoid interruptives.** Don't force the listener to make difficult mental connections. Put modifiers next to what they modify. Don't split verb phrases (split infinitives).

Incorrect: Will eventually decide.

Correct: Eventually will decide.

Incorrect: Doctors only gave him six months to live.

Correct: Doctors gave him only six months to live.

▶ **Avoid commas.** A comma demands a hitch in reading and the resulting jerkiness frustrates the listener. Avoiding commas also eliminates subordinate clauses. Such clauses kill the impact of copy, especially if they come at the top of a story or sentence.

▶ **Avoid numbers.** The listener has trouble remembering them.

▶ **Avoid pronouns.** If you must use a pronoun, make sure that the pronoun agrees with its antecedent and appears close to the antecedent. For example, "John Doe hit Bob Smith on the head and paramedics took him to the hospital." In this case, instead of *him* use *Smith*.

▶ **Write to the pictures but not too closely to the pictures.** Remember that more specific video requires more general writing, and vice versa. Utilize the touch-and-go method, wherein you write directly to the video at the beginning of a sequence, and then allow the writing to become more general with background information and other facts as the video continues.

Storytelling with Video

That's what you do. You're a storyteller. In most cases, you might go out on a shoot with only a basic idea of what you're going to tape and how you're going to piece it together. That kind of approach will get you only so far.

As you up the ante in your work, there will be times when you'll want to work from a script. It may be as straightforward as a corporate safety production with employees doing the acting, or you may have aspirations to create a dramatic feature.

In either case, some fundamental scriptwriting skills will help you raise the bar of your production. I've tapped two of Hollywood's top writers to do the honors.

Stephen Black and Henry Stern's Scriptwriting Tips

Stephen Black (left) and Henry Stern (right), TV scriptwriters and producers.

I count myself fortunate to have Stephen Black and Henry Stern as neighbors and friends. Their TV scriptwriting and producing credits would fill this page. They forged new directions in episodic dramas with their work on *Dynasty*, *Falcon Crest*, *Flamingo Road*, *Matlock*, and *Knot's Landing*. Their work as head writers on *As the World Turns* and consultants for *One Life to Live* stirred things up and added sizzle to both of these long-running daytime staples. They've had a hand in a half-dozen TV movies, including the only TV film starring Audrey Hepburn, *Love Among Thieves*.

They got their start as a writing team doing comedies in the mid-1970s. Stern had been one of Broadway's youngest producers, and Black had written a couple plays. Despite failing to sell their first comedy script to *The Mary Tyler Moore Show*, they were given free access to the set where they watched rehearsals and show tapings, all the while taking copious notes. That led to a brief stint writing for a new show called *The Love Boat* ("It paid the bills and got us in the Writers Guild") and finally landed them a job with Norman Lear Productions, the company behind *All in the Family*.

These days they're working on their second novel and a movie script. Here's their advice to aspiring scriptwriters:

- ▶ **The most important thing is that we like to tell stories.**

- ▶ **And the most important thing in stories is the characters.** The best kind of character is one with the ability to surprise you. The audience is not dumb. You've got to come up with something unpredictable. You don't want a white hat or black hat. You want people wearing gray hats. People you can't read. You want to be interested in what happens to them.

- ▶ **It's *not* a good idea to start your script writing with a plot.** It's better to start with a theme. Know what you want to say, how you want to say it, and where you want to be at the end. The theme of our current film script is, How does the death of someone affect his three closest friends?

- ▶ **With the theme in hand, we next create the characters.** What is their arc and how will that change throughout the story? We invent detailed character bios. Where did they go to school? What were their parents like? What was their childhood like? We don't have to use all that in the script, but it's good for us to know to help craft the story.

- ▶ **Next we sit down with a yellow legal pad and make 30 to 40 story points**, such as guy robs bank, hides in mother's house, falls in love with neighbor, and so on.

- ▶ **Then we write an extensive narrative outline**—30 pages or more. We include texture—the tone and detail. We take time to describe settings and characters. Instead of merely using physical descriptions of characters, such as Bob is 6'2" with the torso of a long distance runner, we're more likely to write, "As John was driving up Canyon Avenue, he looked out his rain spattered window and caught sight of Bob, one more time, running in the rain." That says a lot. We love doing that. It makes it easier to do the script.

- ▶ **It's really crucial that you learn how to structure a piece so that your story makes sense.** Know where your story is going and how plot elements and character elements will build on each other so they peak at certain points. An excellent film example of structure is *Two for the Road*, with Audrey Hepburn and Albert Finney. Even though they use multiple flashbacks, you know that from beginning to end this is a story of a marriage on the skids.

- ▶ **Tell as much of the story as you can without dialogue.** Tell it cinematically. Don't give camera directions such as wide, tight medium. That's the director's job and disrupts the story flow. But it's okay to script camera *angles*. We wrote a scene where a woman was about to tell her husband their son was killed in combat. The husband ran a steak house and happened to be in the walk-in freezer when his wife arrived. We directed the camera to look through the window and, without any dialogue, watch the woman tell the husband and see the reaction.

▶ **You can't write if you're not an observer.** We're constantly eavesdropping in restaurants. We're acutely aware of dialogue going on around us. Our characters have to speak in the vernacular of the time.

▶ **Dialogue is more than just writing down what two people say to each other.** Good dialogue is succinct, crisp, entertaining, and rich. It's a level above conversation.

▶ **Bury the "pipe."** The *pipe* is the exposition, the conduit of information, the stuff that the audience needs to know to make sense of the story. Say the character's been divorced three times, has six kids with six different women, and runs a grocery. You don't come out and say that. You impart it to the audience in an interesting way.

▶ **Scriptwriting is collaborative.** Everyone has a hand in it. A screenplay will go through 10 to 15 drafts before shooting begins.

▶ **Writing is hard work.** To sit there in front of a blank, empty computer screen knowing that you have to come up with compelling characters and stimulating plots, week after week after week can be daunting. Back in 1970, we were working with Leon Uris on a musical production of his novel *Exodus*. After several tiring meetings with potential backers, Stephen asked him if he had any advice for aspiring playwrights. He said, "Put your ass in a chair in front of a typewriter." This was the most succinct, valuable information we were ever given.

Unblocking Creativity

Writer's block strikes us all. As Black and Stern noted, it's darned hard to sit down in front of a blank computer screen and start putting words in the computer.

Here are some ways to get the creative juices flowing:

▶ **Bounce ideas off others.** Simply talking about your project typically will give you a whole new perspective. Listening to questions posed to you about your work will help you focus your writing.

▶ **Change your work environment.** I have the luxury of going outside and sitting on a rocking chair overlooking a lovely valley. That moment in the fresh air helps bust loose a few cobwebs.

▶ **Scribble down some ideas.** Turn away from your computer and grab a yellow legal pad and a felt-tip pen. Connect the thoughts on paper.

▶ **Take a break.** Listen to a great tune. Take a jog. Then get back to work—you're on deadline!

Stepping Up to Film

Charly Steinberger, cinematographer.

I count myself fortunate to have one of Germany's top cinematographers, Charly Steinberger, as a friend. He's served as director of photography on scores of movies and TV shows. His films have won numerous prestigious awards, including German Film Award – Best Cinematographer, Venice Film Festival – Best Film, and the New York Critics Award – Best Film.

Steinberger has worked with some of Europe's most famous actors: David Niven, Roger Moore, Kim Novak, Gina Lollobrigida, Sophia Loren and, topping his personal list, Marlene Dietrich. Few readers of this book will have the opportunity to work at this top end of the film production scale, but I think everyone can take Steinberger's advice to the bank.

Charly Steinberger's Tips for Prospective Filmmakers

Steinberger's guidance comes from the perspective of a filmmaker who has seen absolutely everything. He has a pragmatic view. Here are his filmmaking tips:

▶ **The most important component of a film is a good script.** Unfortunately that happens only rarely.

▶ **Next in importance is a solid budget.**

▶ **A good production team can make or break a film.** Topping the list is the director and the cinematographer, followed by the set designer, costume designer, makeup artist, lighting specialist, grip, and editor. Overseeing it all should be a producer with a reputation for spending money wisely. Too many producers try to cut corners and save money by hiring less experienced (that is, *cheaper*) crew members.

▶ **The photographer's primary responsibility is to use the camera to tell the story well.** Too many cinematographers get lost attempting to create brilliant and grand images.

▶ **A point that often gets neglected is the critical search for and selection of locations**—be they cafes, apartments, or offices—to help give characters their correct motivation. The right settings bring life and depth to your characters.

▶ **In the post-production world, there is no longer any difference between film and video.** Both now use nonlinear digital editors.

▶ **I still work with film instead of video** because film has higher resolution, truer colors, more accurate reproduction, more brilliance, and solid contrasts. That said, it won't be long before video will equal film in quality.

The Business of Video Production

I've been here. In the early 1990s, photographer Karl Petersen and I started Glint Video in Portland, Oregon. We had two good-sized clients and occasionally picked up smaller gigs along the way.

We sought advice from our mutual friend, news photographer Sam Prigg, who had turned some weekend freelance assignments into a growing video production business—with an office and his own gear and even employees! When we saw all that he had done to get where he was, it gave both Karl and me the jitters.

We stuck to what amounted to a freelance, on-call arrangement. Soon there were dry spells and too many wannabe competitors with NewTek Video Toasters and low-ball bids. Karl got an offer to be chief photographer at the local NBC-TV affiliate, and one of our clients asked me to write a book. So, we parted ways.

It's tough to get into any business, especially into a high-tech, creative field such as video production, where client expectations shift as quickly as the technology.

Despite that, Sam Prigg is still at it. While other production firms in Utah have folded their tents, Prigg has adjusted to the shifting landscape and grabbed greater market share. Here's his advice.

Sam Prigg's Tips on Starting a Video Production Company

Sam Prigg, the "Head Wabbit" at White Rabbit Productions in Salt Lake City (http://www.whiterabbitproductions.com) has never taken himself too seriously. That hasn't stopped him from creating one of Utah's most successful video production houses. His client list and "statues," as he puts it, make that clear. He's

Sam Prigg, "Head Wabbit," White Rabbit Productions.

worked for all the major networks, plus Disney, Apple, Intel, and many other big-name clients. During the 2002 Winter Olympics, he had eight crews working full-time for folks such as Jay Leno, David Letterman, and MTV. His "statues" include Emmys, ADDYs, Tellys, DuPonts, and "Most Improved" in bowling.

Sam Prigg is one of the good guys. I thoroughly enjoyed working with him in the mid-1980s during my 4-year stint at KSL-TV in Salt Lake City. He has a degree in broadcast journalism and a minor in cinematography. For the first half of his 27-year TV and film career, he thought he was going to live and die working for a TV station. But then the business changed and so did he.

Local news operations cut staff while adding news shows (news is relatively inexpensive programming), and TV networks found it was cheaper to make layoffs and hire local freelance crews instead. Sam began shooting on the side and soon started making more money working on weekends and vacations than he was in his day job.

Since he also was becoming disenchanted with that TV news job, he knew it was time to leave. How hard could it be, he thought, to do freelance full time and make a killing? He soon found out, and along the way, acquired a few tips that others might use to *not* make the same mistakes. Here's what he has to say:

- ▶ **Learning about business is essential to survival.** I have a degree in communications and lots of worldly experiences, but the business world is a whole different animal. You'll need to learn about insurance, taxes, bonding, business plans, advertising, equipment purchases or leases, office space, phones, faxes, furniture, marketing, pricing, invoicing, bad debts, good demo reels, production schedules, contracts, the IRS, accounting, hiring freelance workers, firing freelance workers, security, and credit. It's no surprise that most small startups fail after a few years.

- ▶ **Working with a partner...or not.** I started our company with a partner, thinking our skills complemented each other. Turns out we had conflicting ideas about how to run a business, and I ended up buying him out. Dissolving a partnership can be like getting a divorce. Partner up if you must, but be aware of the ramifications. Put your expectations in writing. Spell out the roles each partner will take, where the money will go, and be prepared to review the contract frequently.

► **Don't put all your eggs in one basket.** When I started my business, I had one client that accounted for most of my work. It was great. I traveled around the United States, shot all kinds of neat stuff, edited to my heart's content, and enjoyed life in the freelance world. Two years later, the client's company got sold and everything stopped. I forgot to broaden my base and to do that marketing thing. I had to scramble to find some new clients. It took a couple of years until I felt comfortable again, but I learned a few things. One is that eggs-in-one-basket rule, and the other is that the time to do your marketing is when you're busy with the project that you're currently working on.

► **Figure out what kind of video production company you are.** When I started out, I was going to offer to do anything at the highest possible level. I planned to shoot, write, and edit commercials, news, documentaries, corporate videos, sports, accident re-creations, school plays, weddings...well, no weddings, but just about anything else. My market was the world. And I could do it on film or video—I thought. It took a long time to discover who I was, but now I can say our mission statement in one sentence: We shoot high-end video for television networks, news magazine shows, and corporations, and we specialize in making people look good. After we figured that out, it was easier to focus our marketing and purchase the right equipment.

► **Create a demo reel.** Your demo reel represents who and what you are. It is your most valuable marketing tool. There are plenty of views about what makes a good reel. My take is that you may have only 30 seconds to make a favorable impression. Why? I know of TV news directors who view aspiring reporters' demo reels—chock full of stories, on-camera stand-ups, and clever on-set repartee—for all of 30 seconds. That's all the time they need to make such important decisions. Make sure that you gear your reel for your target audience and have it quickly demonstrate your core values. Our reel has a fast-paced introduction with several shots of well-lit people, well-composed shots of a variety of subjects, and lively music. It includes a few graphics-laden segments and ends with contact information. It runs about seven and a half minutes. I like to watch it. And it has helped us get lots of jobs.

► **Educate your clients.** When I meet a new client for the first time, I usually have to educate them about the steps involved with producing an effective video. It starts with identifying the audience members—their ages, educations, and preconceived attitudes about the subject. I then outline the dozen or so steps involved with most productions—concept, writing, storyboarding, casting, location scouting, crew, equipment, production shoot, narration, editing, graphics, and music.

▶ **Don't burn a client.** If you make a mistake with some clients—bad lighting, poor composition, arriving late, faulty equipment, dead batteries—they might forgive you once. TV networks are less forgiving. One mistake and they won't come back.

▶ **Adapt to change because things will change.** I try to stay up on the newest trends in equipment and technology, such as new recording formats and delivery systems. It's important to understand why they have been developed and how they change the way we do business. Many clients now ask about having their video streamed or converted to DVDs or CD-ROMs. High-definition formats are now being offered at the high-end and low-end. New recording formats include hard drives, memory sticks, and re-recordable DVDs. As a means to stay current, subscribe to technology magazines and join an industry organization such as the International Television Association for its conferences and seminars. View the work of others to see what kind of competition you might be facing and what kind of markets you might be missing.

▶ **Deciding what to charge.** For the high end of the video production market, it's easier to determine what to charge because TV networks, union contracts, and a universal fee schedule set the parameters for what the market will pay. In the television news, news magazine, and corporate worlds, using broadcast Betacam SP cameras, professional audio equipment, extensive lighting, and grip equipment and being backed by 15 to 20 years of experience, a two-person crew, consisting of a camera person and audio tech, can get between $1,200 to $1,500 for a 10-hour day. You can charge additional fees for the use of a wide-angle lens, matte box with filters, HMI or daylight-balanced lighting, and other production tools. Beginning photographers can usually charge $200 to $350 a day plus $150 to $200 for a mini-DV camera, a small lighting package, and a selection of microphones.

▶ **Consider working for someone else.** It's easier and much less expensive to work for the kind of company you would like to become. Get your experience with another production company that has its own equipment and clients. Perfect your techniques and broaden your knowledge by working for someone else. Then, as you understand the market and maybe find your niche, you can branch off on your own with a better understanding of the business and where your market might be. Our company is always looking for a photographer with a good eye as well as audio techs, gaffers, grips, teleprompter operators, writers, producers, and just about anyone else who can help make us look good.

Doing the Video Production Thing

White Rabbit's specialty is making interviewees look great. Painting them with the right lights, placing them in visually appealing settings, and creating a film-like look using videotape—normally a harsh and all-too-realistic-looking medium.

Other production houses have other specialties. One focus for Cinemagic Studios in Portland is on-location, multicamera videotaping. Corporate roundtable discussions, live musical performances, and sporting events all fall into this realm. It takes a team of pros who have worked together for years to pull off something this fraught with complexities and possible snafus.

Joe Walsh's Event Shooting Tips

Joe Walsh,
Cinemagic
Studios, CEO.

Joe Walsh and his team at Cinemagic Studios were my go-to guys when I worked as an independent video producer in Portland. I knew I could count on Cinemagic Studios to tackle whatever I threw at them. Walsh founded Cinemagic in 1980. His truly dedicated team, several of whom have worked for him for many years, has gained the confidence of a broad range of clients by meeting their unique needs and solving their communication problems.

Cinemagic offers a full range of film, video, animation, and multimedia services for commercials, documentation, promotion, training, instruction, seminars, business meetings, and corporate backgrounders. Their work has garnered 30 Telly Awards (www.cinemagicstudios.com).

One of Cinemagic's fortes is shooting events using multiple cameras and switching them live. Here's Walsh's checklist:

▶ **Make sure you have a clear understanding of your client's expectations and budget.** Crew prices vary depending on the market. In Cinemagic's case, we charge $1,500 per day for a standard DVCAM or Beta SP camera package with a cameraman and an audio person.

▶ **Do a site check and rehearsal to determine the best camera locations.** For two-camera remotes, it's best to have a back and front position. Place the cameras on risers so that you can shoot over people's heads. Position the cameras so that you don't "cross the plane" and shoot toward each other. Use the rehearsal to iron out details with the people in charge of the location.

▶ **Use multiple cameras and switch the event live to minimize editing afterward.** Later, if the budget allows it, you can improve the product by tossing in some post-production editing and graphics. Cinemagic's remote multicamera setup includes a digital switcher, intercom system, audio mixer, studio recorder, and monitors for each camera crew, plus preview and program feed monitors. Budding producers take note: To buy the equivalent gear that we use for your own two-camera remote setup would cost about $75,000.

▶ **Always have the cameras record separate tapes.** Even though we switch events live, if the technical director makes a bad switch or a cameraman makes an awkward move, we *can* fix it in post.

▶ **"Jam sync" all recorders before starting to record.** Setting the timecode to match all recorders makes it much easier to find footage that you need if you have to fix something in editing (see Hour 21, "Real-World Applications and Third-Party Products," for a review of Multicam, a product that enables you to "live edit" multiple-camera shoots).

▶ **Have a pre-production meeting with your crew to discuss the project and assign their responsibilities.** Onsite setup usually takes one hour for a single camera and two hours for multiple cameras. Make sure that all the cables are tucked away or taped down. After the setup, do a test record and playback check. During the event, we always monitor the audio and video signals.

▶ **Ensure that your location is well lit.** For a lot of our events, the house handles the lighting, which makes our job a lot easier. If not, we typically turn to our basic light kit: a Lowel light system with two broad throw Tota lights and one wide-focus-range Omni to use as a key- or backlight (see Figure 3.1).

FIGURE 3.1
Lowel Tota light (left) and Lowel Omni light. (Images courtesy Lowel-Light Manufacturing, Inc.)

Lowel Tota   Lowel Omni

► **Audio is crucial.** When events handle their own audio, we take a line feed from their soundboard and use shotgun mics for backup and ambient audio. Otherwise, we rely on our standard mic kit: camera mic, shotgun, lavaliere, handheld, and PZM (pressure zone microphone, useful for a conference table with several speakers).

► **When using wireless mics, select UHF instead of VHF to avoid frequency conflicts.** All sorts of fun stuff can go wrong with wireless mics. Your receiver can pick up other sources on your channel, such as radio stations (I always get country music), pizza delivery guys, or other wireless mics from local commercial TV stations. The UHF wireless mics have multiple channels at the higher MHz frequency range, so there is less chance of interference. Always keep fresh batteries on hand. As the batteries grow weak, reception problems occur.

Our favorite wireless mic story happened when we were taking an audio line feed from the house. The house audio man placed a wireless mic on the presenter. Just moments before he was to go on, the presenter went to the bathroom. Not only did *we* pick up the very graphic audio, so did the 500 people in the auditorium.

Summary

Premiere Pro is not like a word processor. You didn't buy it just to do some writing and not worry about all those other hard-to-decipher bells and whistles. You bought it because it offers so much more power than, well, those lower-priced also-rans.

The likelihood then is that you want to do something other than create vacation movies to show your (ungrateful) relatives. To up that production ante means improving your story creation, writing, and video production business acumen. The advice given here comes from folks who've been in the trenches for years. They know from where they're speaking.

Workshop

We'll dispense with the usual Q&A and Quiz for this hour. However, some exercises are in order.

Exercises

1. Scriptwriter Stephen Black's dad fostered his writing from very early on. One exercise he asked his son to do while they were working on a novel together was to sit down during a large family gathering and invent characters for the novel using the characteristics of the gathered guests as his inspiration. It worked for Black. It's also a great way for you to avoid the usual idle family chitchat.

2. Take a local newspaper story about an event or breaking news. Read it aloud with an ear for passive-voice phrases, such as "She was hit by a speeding car," "The house was destroyed by the blaze," and "The budget was presented by the governor." Rewrite the story in active voice.

3. Contact a local TV station or production company and get permission to tag along during a remote, multicamera taping. They might let you help set up (it's called *gaffer's tape*, not *duct tape*) and sit in the control room. That will be an eye-opening and educational experience.

HOUR 4

Premiere Pro Setup

What You'll Learn in This Hour:

- ▶ Configuring a powerful DV workstation
- ▶ Video capture cards—adding editing magic
- ▶ Reviewing the Alienware DV workstation
- ▶ Starting Premiere Pro for the first time
- ▶ Organizing the workspace

Adobe created Premiere Pro with high-performance PCs—or, more aptly, *DV worksta-tions*—in mind. To get the best out of Premiere Pro, you need a PC DV workstation with plenty of horsepower. In this hour, I give you some tips on what to consider when buying a DV workstation or upgrading your PC.

While testing the Premiere Pro beta and writing this book, I used a PC loaned to me for those purposes by Alienware (that's its logo on the cover). I give you a rundown of what that Alienware DV workstation has to offer later this hour.

That workstation has a specialized video capture card that enhances the Premiere Pro editing experience. I cover that card and its competitors later in this hour. And I conclude this hour by showing you how to start up Premiere and make a few user interface tweaks to get you ready for editing.

Configuring a Powerful DV Workstation

Premiere Pro's developers aimed high. If you have anything less than a truly top-end PC, you will not see Premiere Pro operate at its best.

As I wrote this book, I used two PCs: the Alienware DV workstation powerhouse and a PC that slightly exceeded Premiere Pro's minimum specs. The differences were dramatic.

Premiere Pro's Minimum Specs

If you've looked at your Premiere Pro retail box, you might already know the minimum specs. Here's a quick rundown:

- ▶ Intel Pentium III 800MHz processor
- ▶ 256MB of RAM
- ▶ 800MB of hard-disk space for installation
- ▶ Dedicated, large-capacity 7200RPM hard drive for media assets
- ▶ 1024×768 32-bit color video display adapter
- ▶ Microsoft Windows XP

If your PC barely meets these minimum specs, you'll end up working with a very sluggish machine. Here's what you can expect with such a PC:

- ▶ You'll have to scale Premiere Pro back to a lower-resolution display to achieve real-time playback.
- ▶ Rendering—converting any files with special effects applied or that don't match the project audio and video data rates—will take a long time and will consume 100% of your processor's cycles.
- ▶ Audio conforming will take a long time and will bog down performance.
- ▶ As you move around on a sequence or work with effects, there will be noticeable lags between mouse clicks and on-screen actions.

My System Recommendations

Premiere Pro takes advantage of certain technologies. Here's a few to keep in mind, starting with the top three, most effective performance enhancers:

- ▶ **RAM.** The more RAM you have the better. Premiere Pro uses 90-120MB of RAM simply to function. As you scrub through a video project, Premiere Pro consumes even more RAM for media caching, thereby creating smoother playback. By design, Premiere Pro will use up to about one-third of your total RAM for caching. On a 1GB RAM PC, total RAM usage will peak at about 400MB, or several video frames. If you have 2GB, that'll more than double the number of cached frames, meaning even better playback performance.

▶ **Hyperthreading.** Premiere Pro takes advantage of Intel Pentium 4's hyperthreading technology. That is, if Premiere Pro detects that you have a hyperthreading CPU, it divides its processing into multiple streams to work faster and more efficiently. The corollary to this is that it also takes advantage of PCs with multiple processors (both nonhyperthreading and hyperthreading—such as the Alienware DV workstation described later in this hour in "Reviewing the Alienware DV Workstation"). Theoretically (at least until someone makes such a PC), Premiere Pro can use up to 16 threads!

Dual CPUs and Hyperthreading in Action

To see graphic evidence that dual CPUs with hyperthreading really are doing their job, take a look at Windows Task Manager (shown in Figure 4.1). Access the Task Manager by right-clicking the task bar (or pressing Ctrl+Alt+Delete) and then clicking the Performance tab. In the case of the Alienware DV workstation, two Intel P4s with hyperthreading means the PC functions as if it has four CPUs.

By the Way

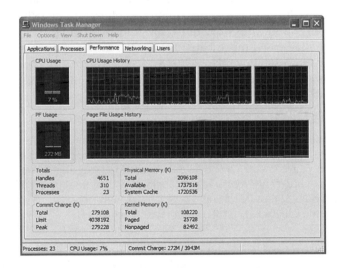

FIGURE 4.1
Windows Task Manager displays a CPU utilization graph for each CPU—two hyperthreading CPUs equals four graphs.

▶ **RAID.** Using a RAID (Redundant Array of Inexpensive—or Independent—Disks) array opens the tightest bottleneck on your PC, your hard drive's throughput. Premiere Pro frequently asks your hard drive to max out. With a RAID, that max is significantly higher than with a single hard drive. A typical two-drive RAID makes a huge difference in video performance.

> ### Developer Note—Hard Drives
>
> If you don't go with a RAID, you still will get better performance with two hard drives (two 60GB or two 120GB drives, for example) instead of one. To get that performance boost, break up your file storage so that Premiere Pro pulls from both drives. For instance, you could put the conformed audio and video preview directories on one drive, and keep your captured media on the other. Doing so balances which drives you're seeking from to get media. You set those file locations by selecting Edit→Preferences→Scratch Disks.

▶ **Dual monitors**. Premiere Pro demands screen real estate. To create screen shots for this book, I worked with only one monitor running at 1024×768 (a higher resolution would have led to images with typeface and icons too small to reproduce in this book). That meant repeatedly opening and closing windows and palettes to avoid clutter, to make room for edits, and to find clips. Two monitors is the standard, professional editing setup and will make your life a whole lot easier. To do that, you'll need a dual-monitor video card. My Alienware system uses an NVIDIA Quadro FX 1000 with dual DVI (digital video interface) plugs.

▶ **ASIO audio hardware**. Audio Stream In/Out (ASIO) technology, developed by Steinberg (the Germany-based audio subsidiary of Pinnacle Systems), ensures that sound cards have much lower latency and are more responsive. Such cards give you a much better feel for the final product when mixing audio, especially when working with 5.1 Dolby Digital. The SoundBlaster Audigy in my Alienware system is ASIO compliant and works like a charm.

> ### ASIO and VST
>
> Premiere Pro uses another Steinberg technology: VST (Virtual Studio Technology). This nearly ubiquitous software technology ensures that third-party created, VST-compliant audio plug-ins work smoothly in Premiere Pro. Plug-ins are mini programs that, in this case, augment Premiere Pro's audio effects suite. The Premiere plug-in industry is surprisingly robust. I cover the VST plug-ins in Hour 14, "Sweetening Your Sound," and some others in Hour 21, "Third-Party Products."

▶ **Video capture card**. Full-featured video capture cards serve three primary functions: analog (as well as DV) video capture, hardware-based MPEG encoding (converting video into the compressed MPEG format used on DVDs and digital satellites),and real-time video effects and transitions. The three main contenders on the PC side are Canopus, Matrox, and Pinnacle. I present an overview of those cards in the next section, "Video Capture Cards—Adding Video Editing Magic."

These components are not inexpensive. A fully tricked-out DV workstation will cost about $6,000. If you're a PC hobbyist, you can take the build-it-yourself route but the price difference between buying the components separately and purchasing a *turnkey* system is much less than it was a couple years ago.

You can take a middle road. That is, upgrade your existing PC. The biggest performance boosts will come from additional RAM, RAID, and a hyperthreading CPU (Pentium 4 Xeons).

If you choose the turnkey approach, I recommend looking first at Alienware (http://www.alienware.com). I take the system Alienware loaned me for a test drive later this hour in "Reviewing the Alienware DV Workstation." There aren't many other PC makers that focus on this high-end market. Here are two companies with product lines that approach the full-featured Alienware DV workstation: Dell's Dimension XPS series (http://www.dell.com) and Falcon Northwest's Mach V high-end gaming PCs (http://www.voodoocomputers.com).

Video Capture Cards—Adding Video Editing Magic

Video cards are a specialized part of a DV workstation. You *can* spend several thousand dollars for a high-end, broadcast-quality card. But the more likely scenario is to buy a mid-priced but still very powerful and feature-rich card for $500 to $1,100. Keep in mind that most of these cards come bundled with full versions of Premiere Pro, which has a retail price of $700.

There are only two principal competitors: Canopus (http://www.canopus.us) and Matrox (http://www.matrox.com) each offer two excellent cards (Pinnacle's Pro-One card works with Premiere 6.5, but Pinnacle is not supporting Premiere Pro):

- ▶ Canopus DVRaptor RT2, $600 (list price)
- ▶ Canopus DVStorm2—$1,088 without Premiere, DVStorm2 Plus—$1,200 with Premiere
- ▶ Matrox RT.X10 Xtra, $500
- ▶ Matrox RT.X100 Xtreme, $1,100

I won't attempt to dissect all the strengths and weaknesses of these cards. They all offer amazing functionality for the price.

I tested the Canopus DVStorm2 that came installed on my Alienware DV workstation (see Figure 4.2). I'll use it to introduce you to the kind of capabilities you can expect from a full-featured capture card.

FIGURE 4.2
The Canopus DVStorm2 features smooth multitrack video playback and dozens of special effects and transitions.

The DVStorm2 has both a hardware card and a faceplate for the front of your PC. That faceplate has in/out connectors for DV (digital video) and analog video (consumer-*ish* composite and higher-quality S-video). The hardware card has an MPEG encoder that enables you to convert incoming DV and analog video to MPEG on the fly. That card also has video processors that relieve your PC's CPU of some work and allow for smoother multitrack video and special effect real-time playback within Premiere Pro.

DVStorm2's video capture software helps busy production houses or newsrooms. With it you can capture up to three separate DV streams concurrently (you'll need two additional DV ports—also known as *IEEE 1394* or *FireWire* ports).

Where DVStorm2 really shines is with its package of video and audio special effects and transitions. These include some eye-popping, exciting 2D and 3D visual effects as well as some innovative transitions and audio sweetening tools. Adding the DVStorm2 suite of effects nearly doubles the number shipped with Premiere Pro.

Here's a quick rundown:

- ▶ **2D effects.** Take a look at Figure 4.3. Those three 2D effects are representative of what DVStorm2 has to offer. You can instantly change a scene into a pencil sketch, blur the action, or give your video the look of an old film.

- ▶ **3D effects.** DVStorm2 facilitates putting pictures in pictures. You can apply motion, change shapes, and add a 3D feel to those moving video clips. Premiere Pro offers similar features, but some video producers might find the DVStorm2 controls, shown in Figure 4.4, to be more intuitive.

Canopus DVStorm2 2D Effects

Pencil Sketch   Motion Blur   Old Movie

FIGURE 4.3
Three DVStorm2 video effects: Pencil Sketch, Motion Blur, and Old Movie.

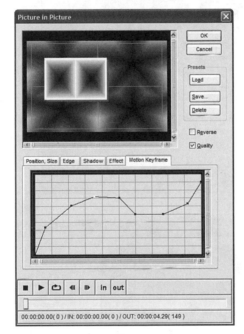

FIGURE 4.4
DVStorm2's PIP (picture-in-picture) offers some intuitive controls and other elements, such as shadows and borders.

► **2D transitions**. Most of these are a bit gimmicky. But gimmicky can be good—fun even—when used in a video project. The Jet Wipe, shown in Figure 4.5, is one of many such object-style transitions that move you from one video clip (usually called the *A-clip*) to the next clip in a sequence (the *B-clip*). Its control panel gives you numerous options to control its behavior.

► **3D transitions**. This is where a video capture card like the DVStorm2 really shines. Its Cube Spin, shown in Figure 4.6, is one of a dozen or so super-slick 3D transitions. Both the A-clip and the B-clip play in real-time on the cube's sides. You can adjust all the parameters of how and where the cube spins and use a custom background (or select a solid color). Other DVStorm 3D transitions include page peels in which the back of the page reflects the next video clip—very cool. And you can combine all of these effects. For instance, apply page peels to a bunch of pictures-in-pictures.

FIGURE 4.5
Fun, creative, and sometimes gimmicky DVStorm2 wipe transitions add zest to a video production.

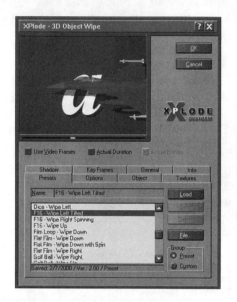

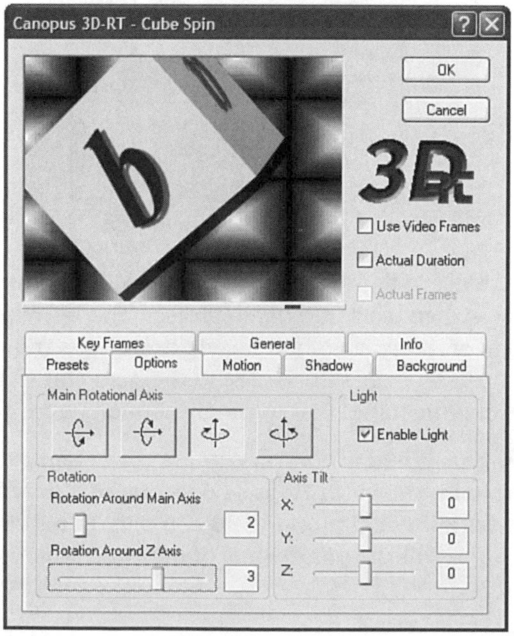

FIGURE 4.6
DVStorm2's 3D effects, like this cube spin, are its biggest selling point.

Reviewing the Alienware DV Workstation

I'm a long-time fan of Alienware, from its early days in the late 1990s as a maker of PCs geared to hardcore PC gamers to its position today as a market leader in high-performance PCs. I purchased Alienware to use while writing my previous book on Premiere, *Sams Teach Yourself Adobe Premiere 6.5 in 24 Hours*. (See Figure 4.7.)

FIGURE 4.7
Alienware—the leading PC maker for hardcore gamers and DV enthusiasts.

This time around, with Premiere Pro's new tack as a technology-driven NLE, I knew I'd need even more PC power. So, I turned once again to Alienware. I proposed that the company provide a loaner DV workstation with the understanding only that Sams would include an Alienware logo on the book's cover.

Alienware obliged. And I'm darned glad it did because the DV workstation those folks provided—the MJ-12 model shown in Figure 4.8—has every technological component available to enhance the Premiere Pro experience. Running side-by-side with a reasonably powerful PC dramatically demonstrates the performance enhancements it provides.

FIGURE 4.8
The Alienware MJ-12 DV workstation powerhouse.

It has every element I enumerated earlier this hour:

- Dual Pentium 4 Xeon 2.8GHz CPUs
- Two GB Corsair DDR SDRAM

- ▶ A two-disk RAID array (plus a third system drive) using Seagate Barracuda 120 GB hard drives
- ▶ An NVIDIA Quadro 1000 dual-monitor video card with dual DVI (digital video interface) connectors that support the latest digital flat panels and also work with standard analog PC monitors
- ▶ An ASIO-compliant SoundBlaster Audigy 2, 6.1 digital surround sound card with six speakers and a subwoofer
- ▶ A Canopus DVStorm2 video capture card
- ▶ A Plextor PX-504A DVD recorder

These are more than vanilla components; they all are the best of breed at the moment Alienware built my MJ-12. And Alienware doesn't just cobble these components together. What sets Alienware apart from other system builders is its attention to detail. The company cuts no corners. From the high-quality case and extra strength power supply down to the multi-fan cooling system and neat and tidy "cable management," Alienware consistently delivers the best DV systems.

Starting Premiere Pro for the First Time

If you performed the task in the first hour, "Touring Premiere Pro and Presenting the DV Workflow," you've already installed and opened Premiere. In this section, we take a closer look at Premiere Pro's opening screens.

Premiere Pro's developers greatly simplified its project settings, limiting the default choices to various flavors of DV—digital video. The only other choice—Video for Windows (VFW)—is for projects that use a variety of PC or analog video.

Adobe gives this VFW option short shrift. The printed manual merely refers readers to the online help file. And the online help file has only one line about VFW:

> "The Video For Windows editing mode can be useful for projects based on analog video or a square-pixel aspect ratio."

In my *Sams Teach Yourself* book on Premiere 6.5, I explained all the various VFW and other non-DV settings in great detail. In hindsight—way too much detail. This time I'll take the hint from Adobe and focus on DV while giving you only a glimpse into the VFW options.

Checking Project Preferences

The basic rule of thumb when selecting project settings is this: match settings to your source material and not to the final output. Even if your goal is to create a low-resolution video to run on the Internet, wait until you *finish* editing and then reduce the *output* quality settings. One other advantage to matching your source material settings is that you have more output options later. Here's how this works:

1. Open Premiere Pro by double-clicking its icon on the desktop. That pops up the Welcome screen I showed you in the first hour. If you started a project then, your welcome screen will look something like Figure 4.9. It lists recent projects. Clicking on one takes you to the workspace as you left it when you previously worked on Premiere Pro. For this task, start anew by clicking New Project to open the New Project dialog box.

FIGURE 4.9
How the Welcome screen looks after you've worked on a couple projects.

2. Your only obvious options are NTSC or PAL, 32 or 48kHz, and Standard (4:3 aspect ratio) or Widescreen (16:9). Most of you will simply choose the setting that matches your original DV and move on. In this case, though, click the Custom Settings tab circled in Figure 4.10.

What kHz Setting to Choose

By the Way

Many DV camcorders give you two audio quality options: 16-bit audio recorded at 48kHz or lower quality 12-bit audio recorded at 32kHz. The latter lays down two

▼

stereo tracks: one with audio recorded by the on-camera mic and the other giving you an option to insert a narration or some other audio. **Kilohertz** refers to the number of samples recorded per second. More is better. CD audio is 44.1kHz. MPEG audio for DVD playback is 48kHz. Bottom line, select 32kHz or 48kHz depending on how you set up your camcorder. If you recorded at 32kHz and set your project to 48kHz, that is not a problem. Premiere Pro will simply take a little longer to *up-convert* your audio during the conforming process.

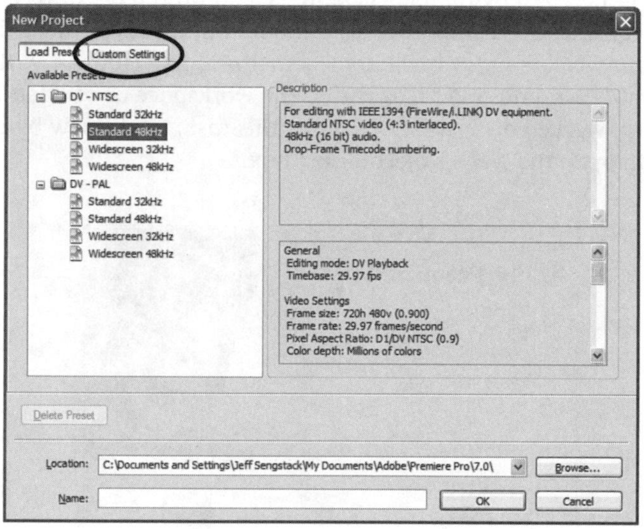

FIGURE 4.10
The New Project screen offers up only three basic choices. Clicking the Custom Settings tab presents many more options.

3. The Custom Settings dialog box has dozens of options, most of which you might never access. So, I'll simply gloss over them. Select Video for Windows from the drop-down list shown in Figure 4.11.

4. After you've selected VFW, many options become available (DV has very few options because it's a standardized video format). Click through the various drop-down lists, basically just to see what's available. Your choices fall into frame rate and size plus extra audio quality options.

Watch Out!

VFW: Not Fully Functional in Premiere Pro

Premiere Pro's developers failed to fully implement VFW editing. What's missing is *edge view*. That feature makes it possible for you to see exactly what frame you've selected to cut or move or edit in some other fashion. This is one of about a

▼

half-dozen features found in Premiere 6.5 that did not make it into Premiere Pro, largely due to time constraints (I'm guessing it'll show up soon in a *point* release). Although the lack of edge view is an inconvenience, it's not what developers (or users) would call a show stopper.

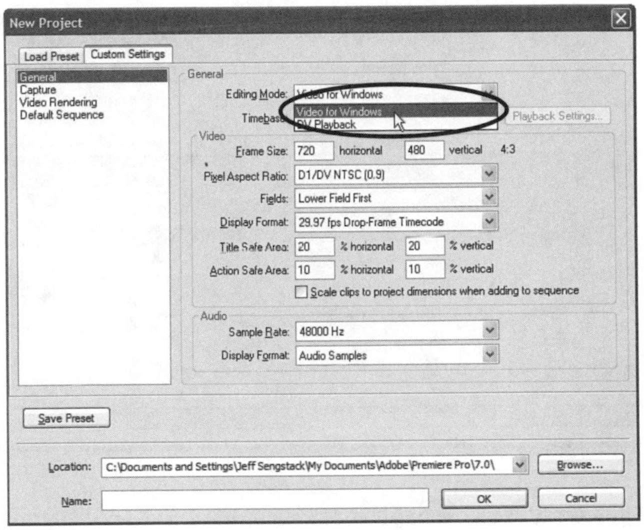

FIGURE 4.11
The Custom Settings dialog box enables you to fine-tune your project settings.

5. Click through the three other dialog boxes by selecting in turn: Capture, Video Rendering, and Default Sequence. Under Capture, unless you have an analog video capture card like the Canopus DVStorm2, your only "choice" will be DV/IEEE 1394 Capture. Video Rendering offers up several **codecs** (COmpression/DECompression algorithms) to convert analog video or other video files to DV for use in Premiere Pro. Default Sequence has nothing to do with DV or VFW; it's how a newly opened sequence (timeline) will look.

6. Click the Load Preset tab to return to the default dialog box, select a DV preset that matches your source material, give your new project a name (change that file's disk storage location if that suits you), and then click OK. That opens the main Premiere Pro user interface—UI—shown in Figure 4.12.

FIGURE 4.12
Premiere Pro's default, new project user interface.

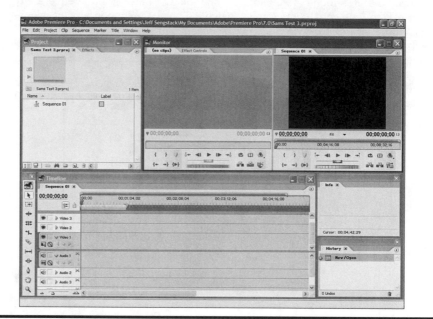

Organizing the Workspace

After you've worked with Premiere Pro for a while, you'll want to organize the workspace to suit your needs. Here's an approach I use.

Because I'm working in 1024×768 for this book, I need as much editing screen real estate as I can get. For starters, I combine the History and Info palettes by dragging and dropping the Info tab next to the History tab. It ends up looking like the palette in Figure 4.13. Then I close it by clicking the little x in its upper-right corner. If I need to open either History or Info, I select Window→History—or—Info.

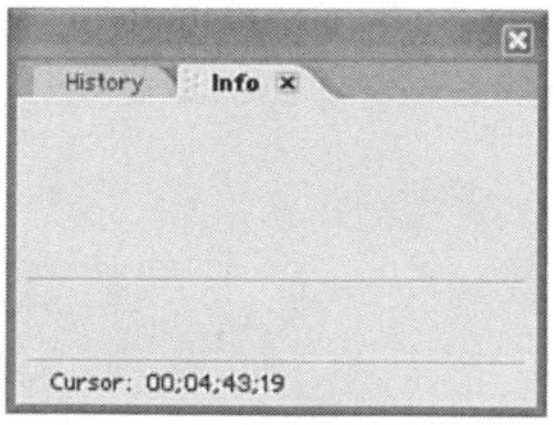

FIGURE 4.13
Combine History and Info by dragging and dropping the Info tab next to the History tab.

Then I get rid of the Tools palette by using an Adobe keyboard shortcut that works on all Adobe digital imaging products: Tab. Pressing Tab removes the Tools palette and pressing Tab again brings it back. That way, when I need a tool, I simply press Tab, select the tool, use it, change back to the default Pointer tool, and press Tab again to lose the Tools palette.

Tab Shortcut Key Behavior

If I had not clicked the little x to close the combined History/Info palette, pressing Tab would have closed it along with the Tools palette. Pressing Tab again would then pop open both palettes. That's not the behavior I want. So, by manually closing the History/Info palette, Tab then opens/closes only the Tools palette. Premiere Pro is nothing if not insanely configurable.

Did you Know?

With the History, Info, and Tools palettes gone, I drag the edges of the Timeline window all the way to the right and left sides of the screen as shown in Figure 4.14.

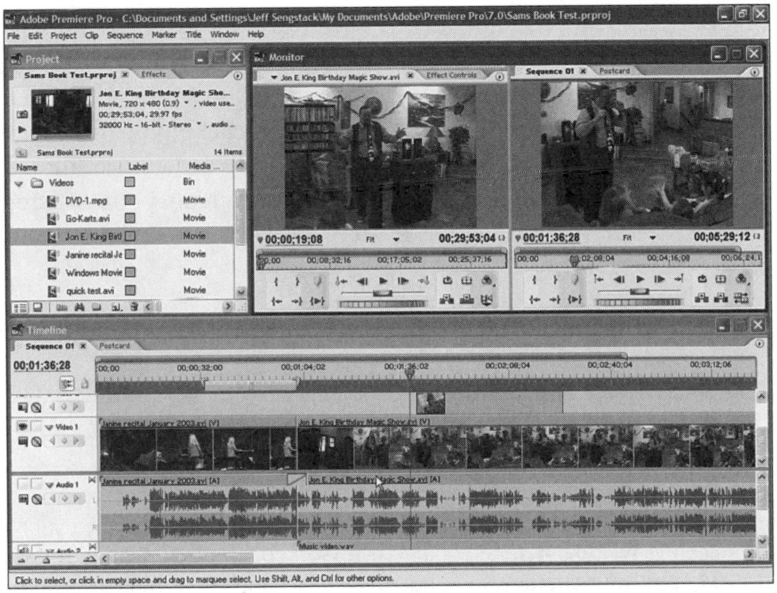

FIGURE 4.14
My personal work-space features a wider timeline and closed History, Info, and Tools palettes.

There are other means to adjust the look of your workspace. As shown in Figure 4.15, you can change from a dual-monitor view to a single-monitor view by click-ing the wing menu (sometimes called the *fly-out menu*) triangle in the upper-right corner and selecting Single View. (Figure 4.15 shows how the Monitor window looks *after* making that selection.)

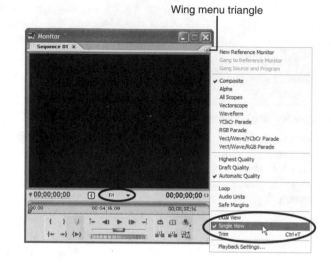

Wing menu triangle

FIGURE 4.15
Switch between
dual- and single-
monitor views.

I prefer a dual-monitor view, but some editors do not. In any event, when I'm
working on a complex effect, sometimes it's good to work in single-monitor view
and expand the Monitor window. In particular, when working with Motion
Control settings, sometimes you need to drag motion paths outside the monitor
screen. For example, expanding the Monitor window, clicking the little *Fit* wing
menu triangle at the bottom of the screen, and selecting 50% places the screen in
the middle of a lot of empty space, giving you room to create your off-screen
motion path. I explain motion settings in Hour 11, "Putting Video and Still Clips
in Motion."

Use Workspace Pre-sets

Did you Know?

Save Your Customized Workspace

Because I'm the only one who uses my PC, I don't need to worry about some other
editor messing with my customized Premiere Pro workspace changes. If you share
your computer with other editors who don't like your layout, you can save your workspace by selecting Window→Workspace→Save Workspace. Then type in a name and
click Save. To open your custom workspace, select Window→Workspace and then
select your named workspace.

Different editing modes demand different workspaces. As shown in Figure 4.16,
Premiere Pro accommodates those needs with four workspace pre-sets. Access
them by selecting Window→Workspace and then choosing from the four pre-sets.

Click through all four (Editing is the default opening screen) to see how they differ. Effects brings the Effects Palette and Effect Controls window front and center. Audio opens the Audio Mixer. And Color Corrector opens a second reference monitor.

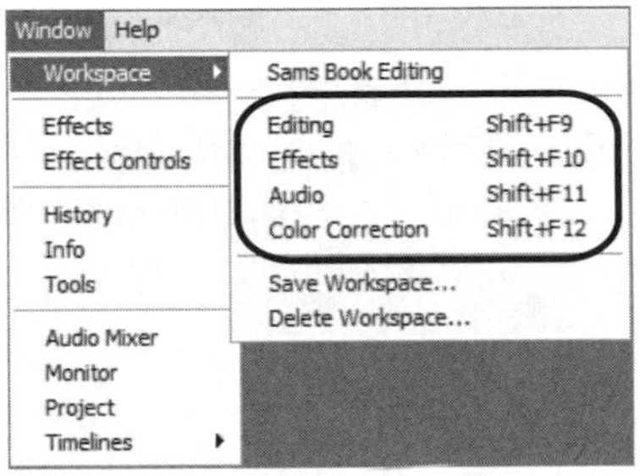

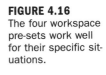

FIGURE 4.16
The four workspace pre-sets work well for their specific situations.

Finally, take a look at the General Preferences dialog box. It has a nice feature that enables you to set the brightness level for Premiere Pro's overall look. Access it by selecting Edit→Preferences→General from the main menu bar. That opens the screen shown in Figure 4.17.

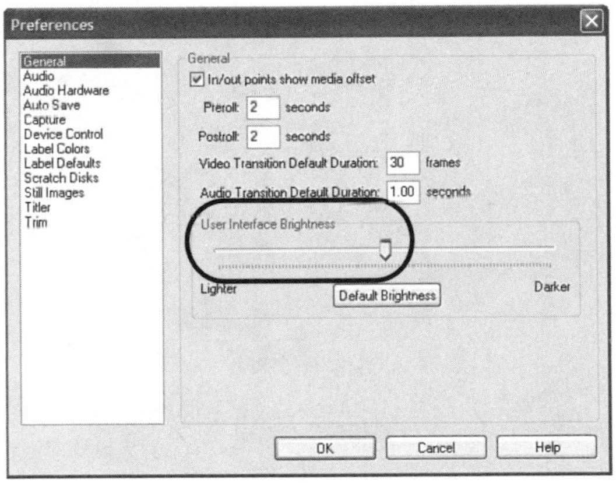

FIGURE 4.17
Use the Preferences dialog box to set screen brightness and to access a plethora of other options.

Move the User Interface Brightness slider to adjust brightness. This comes in real handy for those production studios that keep their NLEs in a dark room to emphasize the quality displayed on the monitor(s).

While in the Preferences dialog box, click Scratch Disks to set the locations for where you'll store captured audio and video as well as conformed audio and audio and video previews. If you have two hard drives but no RAID, it's a good idea to put captured audio and video on one drive and the conformed audio and previews on the other.

Summary

By design, Premiere Pro exploits the latest PC technologies. More RAM, RAID arrays, and hyperthreading dual CPUs top the list. Dual monitors, ASIO-compliant audio cards, and high-end video capture cards (with all their exciting special effects) also enhance Premiere Pro's performance.

Of all the PC DV workstation system makers, Alienware tops my list. It understands what the DV enthusiast needs, builds workstations with only the best components, and uses extra care in how it assembles those high-performance machines.

When you fire up Premiere Pro for the first time, you need only choose a project setting that matches the source material. If you venture from DV, you'll need to adjust some VFW settings.

Premiere Pro is eminently configurable. Tweak to your heart's content and work style. The more you edit, the more likely you'll create a collection of personal workspaces.

Q&A

Q *As PCs get more powerful, why do I need to buy a video capture card as a way to boost performance?*

A My message is not that you must buy a high-end video capture card. That said, consider that a card's performance boost is only one benefit. Most cards also offer analog video in/out capability, hardware MPEG encoding, and a boatload of special effects that you'd pay hundreds of dollars for if purchased separately from third party plug-in providers.

Q *ASIO, VST, RAID, and MPEG. Help! I'm getting acronymed out. Do I need to know all these terms?*

A My teaching (and book writing) philosophy is that I want students (and readers) to at least have a feel for why developers make certain decisions. And what sets Premiere Pro apart from its competition and predecessors is the care its developers put into building its foundation. A large part of that decision-making process was choosing to support current (and likely coming) industry standards. You don't have to know how ASIO reduces latency (thus improving audio responsiveness), just that writing code that supports it makes Premiere Pro a faster racehorse.

Workshop

Quiz

1. How do you make palettes disappear?

2. What three changes will give your PC the greatest performance boost when working with Premiere Pro?

3. If you're using DV and building your video project to run in low resolution on the Internet, should you select VFW for your project settings?

Quiz Answers

1. Either click their little x's to close them (then use Windows→[Palette Name] to reopen them), or use Adobe's ubiquitous keyboard shortcut: Tab.

2. Ranked from biggest boost down (depending on your system): RAM, Hyperthreading and/or Dual Processors, and RAID.

3. No. Match your project settings to your original video. In this case, DV set to whatever audio level you used in your camcorder. If you don't know the audio kHz level (32kHz or 48kHz), choose DV 48kHz to ensure maximum quality. When you complete your project, select output settings to suit the output medium. I cover outputting projects in Hour 23, "Exporting Premiere Frames, Clips, and Projects."

Exercises

1. Experiment with the Premiere Pro workspace. Click every main menu drop-down list. Check all the preferences by selecting Edit→Preferences and Project→Project Settings (the latter are the same items as in the opening New Project dialog box).

2. Visit Canopus.com and Matrox.com to check on their video capture cards. Prices and features change rapidly in this exciting DV editing environment. Both companies frequently offer special bundles that throw many additional special effects into the mix.

HOUR 5

Scene Selection and Video Capture

What You'll Learn in This Hour:

▶ Selecting video clips

▶ Capturing digital video

▶ Tackling manual analog movie capture

▶ Using Scenalyzer to automate video capture

▶ Managing your assets

The editing process begins as you plan and shoot your video. But even the best photographers get more material than they need. And there are always those shots that just don't turn out right. So, the next step in editing is when you review your original videotapes. Before you transfer, *capture* your video in NLE parlance format to your PC.

Premiere Pro offers some tools to take some of the manual labor out of that process. You can set up Premiere Pro to simply record your entire videotape as one long clip, mark individual clips for automated capturing later, or have Premiere Pro use its *scene detection* feature to analyze your tape and automatically create separate clips whenever you press the Pause/Record button on your camcorder.

What Premiere Pro's scene detection process does not do is detect visual scene differences when you did *not* press the Pause/Record button. A typical example is a wedding when the photographer keeps the camera rolling while panning quickly to get a different angle. A third-party program—Scenalyzer—does just that. I demonstrate that program in this hour.

Finally, after you've captured your video to your PC, it's best to organize it. That is, give the different clips descriptive names and place them in applicable folders to make them easier to find as deadlines loom.

Selecting Video Clips

Before you use Premiere Pro to capture—or transfer—video to your PC's hard drive, critically view your raw footage. You want to look for "keeper" clips and sequences, the best interview sound bites, and any natural sound that will enhance your production.

The purpose is twofold: to better manage your media assets and to speed up the video capture process. The latter is an example of how DV really shines—the capability to automatically transfer selected video clips to your computer. You simply create a list of video clips, tell Premiere Pro to transfer them, and then take the dog for a walk while Premiere Pro handles the chores. Nice.

Before you grab the leash, I want to run through some scene-selection tips.

Shoot Plenty of Video

The basic tenet in the video or film production world is that you'll shoot a whole lot more raw footage than you'll put in your final production (probably at least five times what you'll need). You've heard of film scenes *hitting the cutting room floor*. Next time you watch a DVD movie, check to see whether it has deleted scenes. You'll be amazed at how many difficult-to-shoot, well-acted, and expensive scenes did not make it into the final cut.

Your task now is to critically review your tape(s) and weed out the chaff while retaining the grain. True, you can transfer entire tapes to your hard drive and do weeding later. But an hour of DV and Premiere Pro's associated conforming audio consume about 14GB of hard drive space. Having a collection of named clips makes finding those special shots much easier than scanning through a one-hour video file.

You want to transfer only the best sound bites, the coolest scenes, and the highest-quality natural sound. If you did more than one take of a scene, find the one that works best. If you videotaped that soccer championship game, select all the goals, great plays, and enthusiastic crowd reactions, skipping most of the up-and-down-the-field ball handling.

Getting Good Bites

My view is that the video producer or writer can do a much better job telling the story than the folks you interview for the story. It's your job to distill factual information and create a coherent, cohesive story.

So, it's best to use interview sound bites *not* to state facts but to present emotions, feelings, and opinions. You should be the one to say, "At the bottom of the ninth, the bases were loaded, with two outs." Let the batter, who is recalling this dramatic moment say, "My legs felt like jello."

Even in a corporate backgrounder, employees should be the ones stating how enthusiastic they are about a new product. Your job is to say what that product does.

In general, keep sound bites short. Let them be punctuation marks, not paragraphs.

Exceptions for Idiosyncratic Characters

A caveat: None of these admonitions are carved in stone. Some characters you'll videotape are so compelling, quirky, or humorous that your best bet is to let them be the primary narrator. Then you'll want to consider what scenes you can use to illustrate their commentary. You don't want to fill your entire video with a "talking head."

By the Way

Listening for Effective Natural Sound

As you review your raw footage, you should keep your ears tuned for brief instances of dramatic sound: a wire cutter clipping a piano wire (one of the most memorable for me—see "Editing Tips from an Expert—John Crossman" in Hour 9, "Advanced Editing Techniques and Workspace Tools"), the crack of a baseball bat, a gurgling brook, a hawk screeching.

You'll want to transfer these as separate clips even though you might also transfer a long clip of the soaring hawk with that sound somewhere in it. Why? Later, when you edit in that soaring hawk, you easily can find and edit in the screech *nat-sound* (which means *natural sound* in TV news parlance) to give the image more punch.

Capturing Digital Video

Capturing or transferring video from your camcorder to your PC can be mindlessly easy or maddeningly difficult. Digital video—DV—transfer falls on the easy end of the scale.

On the other hand, analog video capture is fraught with potential snafus. You need a video capture card with analog video inputs and you cannot automate the capture process. It's completely manual. If your only camera is analog—Hi-8, SVHS, or VHS—read the following section, "Preparing for Video Capture," and then move on to the "Tackling Manual Analog Movie Capture" section later in this hour.

Preparing for Video Capture

Before you transfer your first frame of raw video to your PC, you need to decide where to store your clips. It all depends on your computer's hard drive configuration. Ideally, you have more than one hard drive: one for your Windows XP operating system (OS) and program files (including Premiere Pro), and another for video, images, graphics, and sound—your A/V (audio/visual) drive. The OS frequently accesses its hard drive even in the middle of an edit or video capture. Having separate OS and A/V drives ensures a smoother operation. Regularly defragmenting your hard drives as well as closing background applications will also improve performance.

Watch Out!

Sufficient Throughput

Your A/V drive should be able to sustain a throughput of 4MBps (more if you're working with analog video). Most recent hard drive models can handle that easily, typically operating at more than 10Mbps.

If you have only one drive and it's reasonably fast, you should have no noticeable problems during video capture.

Now it's time to tell Premiere Pro where to store your video clips and to make sure that Premiere Pro and your DV camcorder can communicate with each other. After that has been resolved, you can view, log, and transfer video to your computer.

Try it Yourself

Tell Premiere Pro Where to Store Your Clips

First you'll tell Premiere Pro where you want to store captured clips. In a bit of confounding legacy nomenclature, Premiere Pro calls these hard disk locations *scratch disks*. That's a holdover to the days of massive, removable storage devices. Now, 120GB internal hard drives are common, and removable storage is not that critical to computerized video editing. Here are the steps to follow for this task:

1. Open Premiere Pro. In the Welcome dialog box, select one of your projects.

2. From the Main Menu bar, select Edit→Preferences→Scratch Disks to open the Preferences dialog box with the Scratch Disks entry already selected (see Figure 5.1).

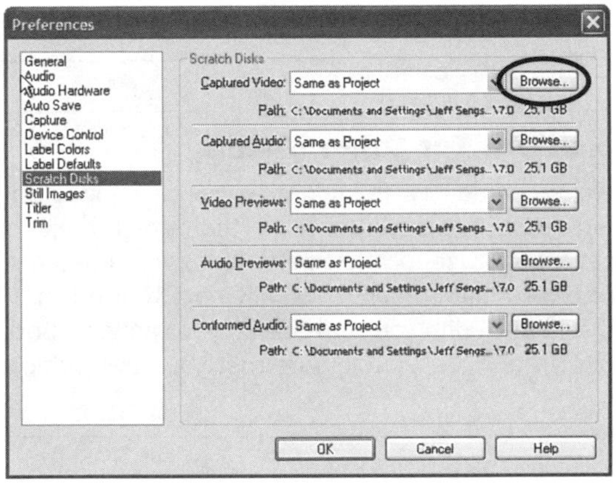

FIGURE 5.1
Use this dialog box to tell Premiere Pro where your scratch disks are.

3. Click the Browse button next to Captured Video. Navigate to the directory you want to use to store your captured A/V files, click Make New Folder, type in a name (I suggest *Captured Video*), and click OK.

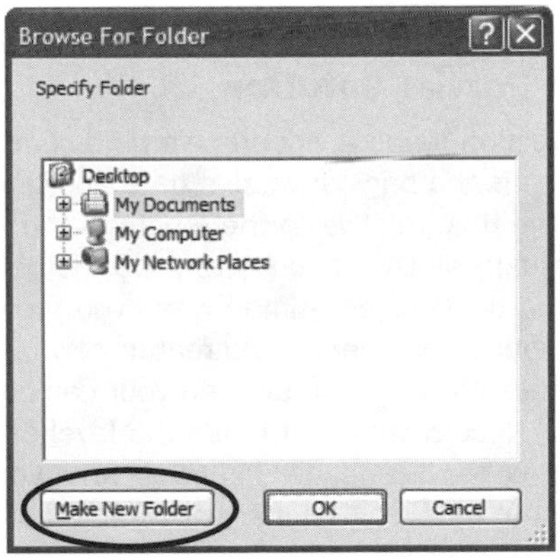

FIGURE 5.2
Use the Make New Folder feature to set a location for your captured A/V files.

4. Do the same thing for Captured Audio (in the same Scratch Disks dialog box). You'll use that file folder to store music ripped from CDs, narrations recorded directly to your PC, and other audio created in programs like Adobe Audition.

Confirm Your Folder Location

When you select Make New Folder to create the Captured Audio file folder, Premiere Pro will automatically want to create a subfolder in the Captured Video folder. So, before you click Make New Folder, select the main directory where you want that file folder to reside.

Use Default Locations for Other Media

You might go through the same new file folder process for Video and Audio Previews as well as Conformed Audio, but leaving them in the default project file location will work fine. The project file storage location defaults to your Premiere Pro directory in My Documents. Your project file does not actually hold your original clips—only data noting their location and any edits you've made to your project. Because My Documents is on your system disk, make sure that you have sufficient space to handle these files.

Using Premiere Pro to Control Your Camcorder

Transferring digital video to your hard drive is a two-step process: logging and capturing. You can log clips manually or have Premiere Pro do it using its Scene Detection feature (see the following By the Way). We'll take the manual approach and you'll start the process by using Premiere Pro to control your camcorder.

Scene Detection: A Partial Solution

Premiere Pro's Scene Detection reads a videotape's *time stamp*—as opposed to its *timecode.* The **time stamp** is the original video's date and time of day, recorded in a data track (**timecode** is the time relative to the length of the video you've shot—that is, elapsed time). Virtually all DV camcorders have the data time stamp feature. Premiere Pro detects any *discontinuities*—times when you pressed the Pause/Record button on your camcorder—and creates new clips at each juncture. It does not notice those instances when you pointed your camcorder at a new scene without clicking the Pause/Record button. If that's the level of scene detection you need, a third-party product called Scenalyzer might be what you're looking for. I demonstrate it later this hour in "Using Scenalyzer to Automate Video Capture."

For Premiere Pro's time stamp scene selection to work well, it's best if you follow the advice I gave in Hour 2, "Camcorder and Shooting Tips": stripe your tapes. Failing that, do not eject a tape and then put it back in your camcorder to shoot more video. Doing so will create a time stamp discontinuity.

Remotely Controlling Your Camcorder

The fun is about to begin. If you haven't used a computer to control a DV device, this task is guaranteed to elevate your heart rate:

1. Turn your camcorder to VCR/VTR (playback) mode (as opposed to Camera [record] mode).

Use AC, Not a Battery

When firing up your camcorder, use its AC adapter, not its battery. Here's why: When using a battery, camcorders go into sleep mode after a while. And the battery will invariably run out in the middle of an automated transfer.

2. Using an IEEE 1394 (FireWire) cable, connect your camcorder to your PC's video card, IEEE 1394 card, or other DV outlet. That probably will cause Windows to display the dialog box shown in Figure 5.3. If it does, keep things simple and click Cancel.

Avoid Nagging Windows Queries

Did you Know?

You can get Windows to stop bugging you whenever you plug in a DV device (or any other piece of hardware like that). When that dialog box pops up, select the Take No Action icon and click the Always Perform the Selected Action check box.

FIGURE 5.3
The Digital Video Device AutoPlay dialog box opens when you connect your camcorder to your PC.

3. Open Premiere Pro, select an existing project (or start a new one).

▼ **4.** Open the Capture window by selecting File→Capture. Figure 5.4 represents what you should have in front of you: a TV screen with standard video-editing-style VCR controls.

What to Do if You Don't See Your Video

DV camcorders have become standardized such that just about any DV camcorder or other DV device will connect flawlessly with your PC. You'll know yours is not making the connection if the word Stopped does not appear at the top of the capture screen or if the VCR controls have no effect. If that's the case, click the Settings tab and then click Device Control / Options (I've circled it in the lower-right corner of the Capture window). That opens a drop-down list of camera manufacturers (Device Brand) and camcorder models (Device Type). Select yours and see whether that clears things up.

FIGURE 5.4
The Capture window. Using standard VCR and videotape-editing controls, you easily can scan through your tape to find "keeper" video clips to transfer to your hard drive.

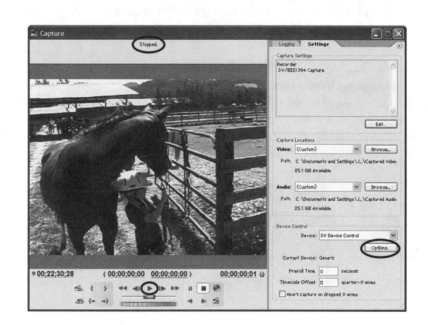

5. Click the Play button (circled in Figure 5.4). Is this not cool? There is your raw video playing on your computer.

▼ **6.** Try out some of the other buttons: Fast-forward, Rewind, and Stop.

Use Pop-up Tooltips

If you're not sure what just about any button or icon in Premiere Pro does, simply place your cursor on it. As shown in Figure 5.5, after a moment, that object's tooltip—and keyboard shortcut (if any)—will appear.

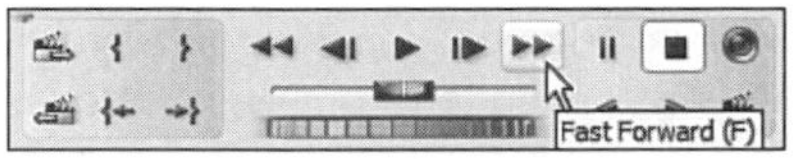

By the Way ▼

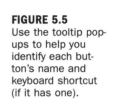

FIGURE 5.5
Use the tooltip pop-ups to help you identify each button's name and keyboard shortcut (if it has one).

7. Now try some of the special buttons: Shuttle (the wide button in the middle) enables you to move slowly or zip quickly—depending on how far you move the slider off center—forward or backward through your tape. You also have frame-at-a-time Step Forward and Backward buttons, Forward and Reverse Slow Play, and a single-frame Jog control (the ruled line beneath all the other controls).

▲

Using Video Clip Naming Conventions

As you log your clips, you'll give each clip a name (you can let Premiere Pro do that automatically, such as Clip01, Clip02, and so on, but doing so is ineffective). Think through how you're going to name your clips. You might end up with dozens of clips, and if you don't give them descriptive names, it'll slow down editing.

You might use a naming convention for sound bites such as Bite-1, Bite-2, and so forth. Adding a brief descriptive comment, such as Bite 1 Laugh, will help. With natural sound, you could say Nat 1 Hawk screech.

Automatic Naming Not So Helpful

If your video clip naming convention uses numbers at the end of each clip name, Premiere Pro will automatically add one to that number when you return to the Logging page (I cover that process in the next Try it Yourself task, "Log and Capture Your Clips." So, if you name a clip Home Run-1, when you click Log In/Out, Premiere Pro stores that clip information in the Project Window and then returns to the Logging page and automatically places Home Run-2 in the File Name window.

Nice? Sort of. Turns out that you don't necessarily have all the home runs back-to-back on your tape, so the next clip you log might be Crowd Reacts-3 and you'll have to type that over Home Run-2.

Did you Know?

With all other scenes (that is, besides natural sound and sound bites), you can drop the prefixes and just give them consistent yet descriptive names: Goal-3, Crowd React-2 Applause, Hawk Soaring-4, and Interview cutaway-1 reverse.

Did you Know?

Using a Naming Convention Eases Project Window Organization

Later, just before you make your first edit, you'll organize your clips in file folders (Adobe calls them *bins*). My suggestion is to put each category of clip into a separate folder—for example: natural sound, sound bites, and scenes. Depending on your project's size, you might want to use subcategories for scenes. Using a consistent naming convention will help in other areas. Because you can sort clips alphabetically, you can find all the nat-sound clips, select them all, and easily place them in the Nat-Sound file folder (bin).

Try it Yourself
▼

Log and Capture Your Clips

The standard operating procedure is to log a number of clips and then have Premiere Pro automatically transfer them to your PC. Or you can simply mark the in-point and out-point for a single clip and capture it.

As you log your tapes, you give each clip a name (or Premiere Pro does that automatically) and then Premiere Pro stores each clip's in-point and out-point data in your Project Window under each clip's name. You specify in which folder you want to store that data (you can change the folder for each clip if you choose) so that when you do the actual capture, Premiere Pro places that clip's reference information in that Project Window bin.

Here are the steps to follow:

1. In the Capture window Setup area, click the Logging tab.

2. As shown in Figure 5.6, select where you want to store each clip's in- and out-data. By default, the Capture window displays whatever bins you have in your Project Window. Because you probably haven't created any bins, your only choice will be your project's main bin. In my case, it's Sams Book Test.prproj (prproj is the file extension for Premiere Pro projects).

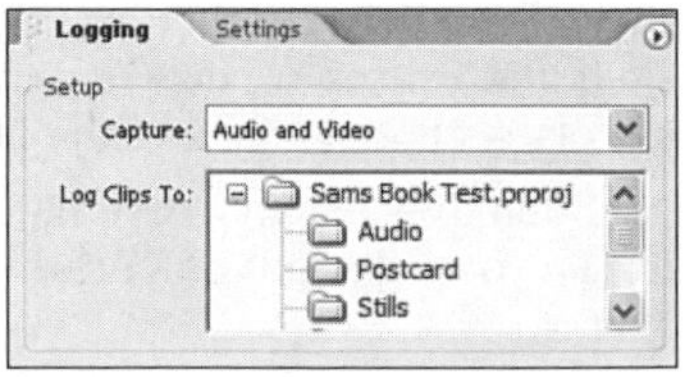

FIGURE 5.6
Select a bin from the Project window list to store clip information.

▼

3. Change the *Handles* setting (found in lower right of Logging tab in Capture window—see Figure 5.7). This adds a user-specified number of frames (using 30 FPS) to the start and finish of a clip. By adding handles to each clip, you're guaranteed to have enough extra video to add transitions without covering up important elements of the clip.

Using the Mouse Drag Method to Change Numeric Values

You can type in a figure—I recommend at least 30 frames or 1 second—or just place your cursor over the handles number and drag it left or right to change the value. This method to change a numeric value is used throughout Premiere Pro, especially in the Effect Controls window, so give it a try here to get a feel for it.

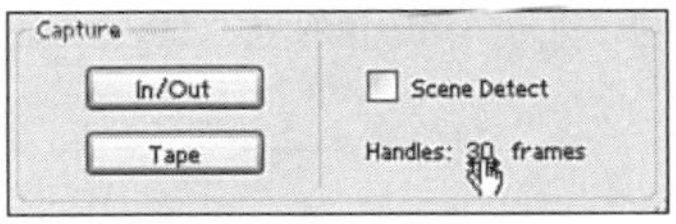

FIGURE 5.7
Add handles to ensure that you have enough slop at the start and end of your clip for a transition (if needed).

4. In the Clip Data section, as shown in Figure 5.8, give your tape a unique name (Premiere Pro remembers clip in/out data based on tape names). And, if you know what your first clip will be, add its name.

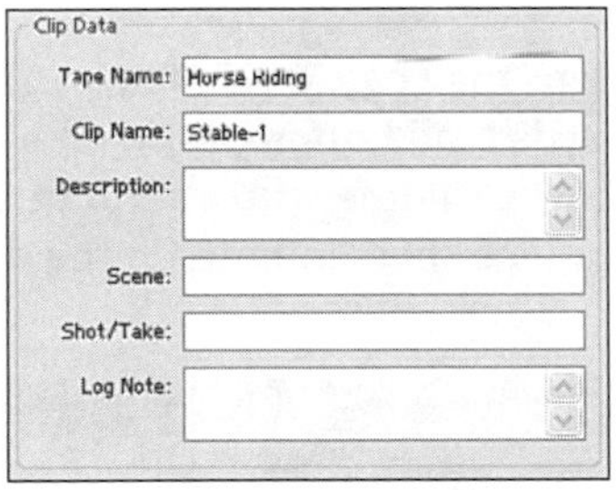

FIGURE 5.8
Give your videotape a name (write it on the tape as a reminder) to begin logging.

5. Start logging your tape. To do that, rewind it and then play it. When you see the start of a clip you want to transfer to your PC, stop the tape, rewind to that spot, and click the Set In button, as shown in Figure 5.9, at the beginning of that clip. When you get to the end of that clip (you can use Fast-forward or simply Play to get there), click Set Out. The in/out times will display as well as the clip length.

FIGURE 5.9
Use the Timecode
section of the
Capture window to
log in/out times for
each clip that you
want to capture.

Timecode		
ꜛ 00;23;07;01	Set In	
ꜜ 00;23;12;20	Set Out	
↔ 00;00;05;20	Log Clip	

Did you
Know?

Three Other Ways to Set In/Out Points

As is the case with just about anything you do with Premiere Pro, there are other means to set in-points and out-points for selected clips. You can click the brackets shown in Figure 5.10 on the play controls, use the keyboard shortcuts—I for in and O for Out—or you can change the in/out time directly in the Timecode area by clicking on the timecode and dragging your cursor left or right.

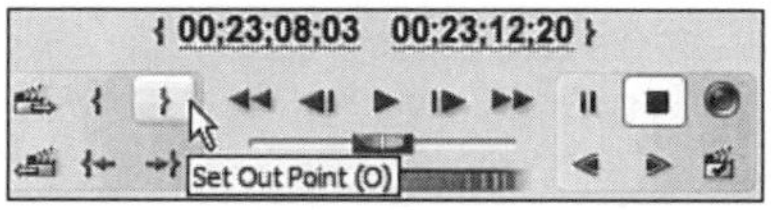

FIGURE 5.10
You can set in-
points and out-
points using the
brackets next to
the VCR controls.
Note the keyboard
shortcut shown in
the tooltip: O.

ꜛ 00;23;08;03 00;23;12;20 ꜜ

Set Out Point (O)

6. Click Log Clip. That opens the Log Clip dialog box shown in Figure 5.11. Change the name, if needed, add appropriate notes if you want, and then click OK. That adds this clip's name with its in/out and tape name info to the Project Window. You'll go there later to do the actual capture.

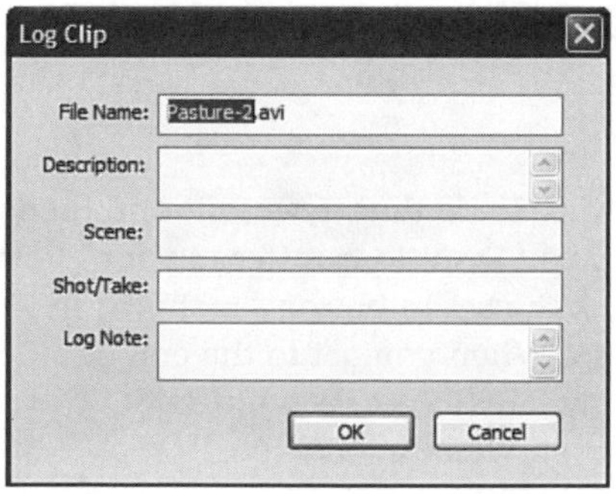

FIGURE 5.11
Use the Log Clip
dialog box to add
any additional infor-
mation about your
clip before adding
its name to the
Project window.

Log Clip	✕
File Name:	Pasture-2.avi
Description:	
Scene:	
Shot/Take:	
Log Note:	
	OK Cancel

7. Log clips for the rest of your tape using the same method.

Capture? Not Really. More Like Transfer.

Before you capture your first clip, I want to clarify one point. *Capture* is a somewhat misleading term used throughout the NLE world. On the digital video (DV) side of things, *transfer* would be a more descriptive term. Because DV already is digital, all Premiere Pro does is tell your camcorder to transfer the selected digital clip data through the IEEE 1394 interface and onto your hard drive. Done. No capturing necessary. It does use a codec to place the clip into a file wrapper that Premiere Pro can recognize, but that codec does not change the original DV data.

In the analog world, *transfer, conversion, compression,* and *wrapping* would more accurately describe the capture process. In that case, your camcorder transfers the video and audio as analog data to a video capture card. Then that card's built-in hardware converts the waveform signal to a digital form, compresses it using a codec, wraps it in the AVI file format, and then stores it to your hard drive. It's a much less user-friendly process made even more tedious by the inability to remotely control your camcorder (in most cases). I'll explain that process in the next section, "Tackling Manual Analog Movie Capture."

8. To perform the actual capture, open the Project Window (see Figure 5.12) and select all the clips that you want to capture (see following Did You Know? for three methods to do that). As shown in Figure 5.12, Premiere Pro calls already captured video clips **movies** and gives them a film/speaker icon (they have both audio and video). Uncaptured clips are called **offline** and have a different icon. You can sort them by media type to group all offline clips.

Three Ways to Select More Than One Item

Windows and Premiere Pro offer three ways to select more than one object. If they are contiguous, mouse-click on the top one and Shift+click on the last one in the group, or click to the left and above the top click and drag to the last one to highlight a group. If the objects are scattered about, click first one and then Ctrl+click on each additional one in turn.

Pasture-1.avi	☐	Movie
Pasture-2.avi	☐	Movie
Pasture-3.avi	☐	Movie
Pasture-4.avi	☐	Offline
Pasture-5.avi	☐	Offline

FIGURE 5.12
In the Project window, Premiere Pro identifies captured *(movie)* versus ready-to be-captured *(offline)* clips.

9. Select File→Batch Capture. That opens a very simple Batch Capture dialog box that asks whether you want to override the camcorder settings. Leave that box unchecked and click OK.

10. The Capture window opens, as does another little dialog box telling you to insert the proper tape (in your case, it's probably still in the camcorder). Click OK.

11. Premiere Pro now takes control of your camcorder, cues up the tape to the first clip (or to whatever number of frames ahead of it if you set using handles), and transfers that clip and all other clips to your hard drive. You can monitor the capture process by watching the PC screen or your camcorder's display. When completed, take a look at your Project window to see the results. Offline files have become movies.

> **Discontinuities Lead to Capture Breakdowns**
>
> If your tape does not have continuous timecode and you logged clips from different areas of the tape, Premiere Pro might not be able to automatically capture your clips. Your tape will not have continuous timecode, for instance, if you eject the tape then reinsert it. To avoid this inconvenience stripe your tapes.

Tackling Manual Analog Movie Capture

If you need to transfer analog video—consumer-level VHS, SVHS, Hi-8, or professional-grade video such as Beta-SP—you need a video capture card with analog inputs. Most such cards, like the Canopus DVStorm2 covered in Hour 4, "Premiere Pro Setup," have consumer-quality composite connectors as well as S-video and sometimes top-of-the-line component plugs.

> **Convert Analog to DV to Automate That Capture Process**
>
> If you have access to a DV camcorder, there is one way to avoid the manual analog capture process: dub your analog tapes to that DV camcorder. That's a fairly straightforward procedure. Most DV camcorders have analog inputs (composite or S-video outlets). After your tapes have been dubbed over, you can use the DV camcorder to automate the capture process. One side benefit: you have a digital backup of your analog tape.

You'll need to use your card's documentation to set up the capture criteria. Typically you do that when you first open Premiere Pro and refine the criteria later when you open the Project Settings, Capture dialog box. The drop-down menus will display options with your card's manufacturer listed.

You'll then go through the movie-capture process in a much more hands-on fashion. For starters, the only way that you can log clips for later automated capture is if your camcorder records industry-standard timecode on the tape and has device control. Most consumer analog camcorders do not do that. If you do have such a camcorder—it's probably a broadcast-quality Beta-SP device—follow the capture process used for DV. If not, you'll manually transfer each clip, one by one.

A Typical Video Capture Card Scenario

If you do step up to a specialized video capture card, each has its own set steps to capture video. But they typically match those listed here:

1. Make sure that your camcorder is turned on and set to VCR/VTR.

2. Open the Capture window, click the Settings tab, and change the Device Control setting to your capture card.

3. Press Play on your camcorder (again, unless yours is a professional grade camcorder, there will be no means for Premiere Pro to control it).

4. If your video card installation and setup went smoothly, you should see the video in the Movie Capture window.

5. Using the controls on your camcorder, search for a scene you like, back up the tape a few seconds, press Play, and then click the Record button on the Movie Capture window.

Analog Capture Processing

By the Way

Your capture card converts that analog video signal into a digital format, compresses it, and sends it to the designated file folder on your hard drive. Some capture cards will split the signal into video-only and audio-only files (you easily can sync them up during editing).

---

6. When you reach the end of that particular scene, press Esc or click the Record button to stop the recording.

7. Premiere Pro will ask you to name the clip, just as it did during DV movie capture.

8. Click OK to return to the Movie Capture window and continue selecting and transferring clips, one at a time.

Using Scenalyzer to Automate Video Capture

Premiere Pro's scene detection algorithm works only by noting discontinuities in the time stamp. It cannot detect visual scene changes. Scenalyzer can. This easy-to-use $39 program is available for download from the Vienna, Austria-based Web site: http://scenalyzer.com/.

Its interface, shown in Figure 5.13, offers intuitive controls and tips.

FIGURE 5.13
Scenalyzer takes scene detection to its most helpful level.

You can simply accept the default conditions and click the Capture Video to Your Harddisk button or, as shown in Figure 5.14, tweak the heck out of it.

The caveat is that scene analysis is tricky. It's often better than nothing, but it can miss many scene breaks or create too many clips. That said, if you want greater control and more automation during video capture, Scenalyzer is the right choice.

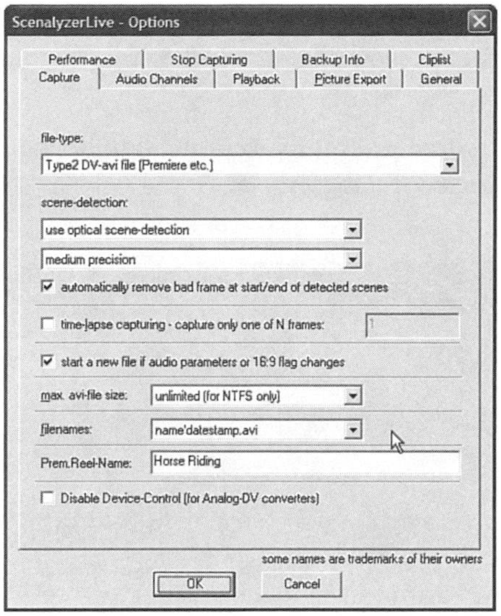

FIGURE 5.14
Scenalyzer's many options make it possible for you to fine-tune your video capture to the *n*th degree.

Managing Your Assets

You used naming conventions to make accessing your video and other media assets easier. One additional step will enhance that ease-of-access: organizing your Project window.

The Project window is simply a means to access your **assets**—video clips, audio cuts, and graphics. Each listed media asset is basically just a link. The files themselves—the video clips and so on—remain in their scratch disk file folder(s).

Project Windows Holds Only Small Bits of Data

It's a good thing that the Project window contains only links and not actual asset files. It saves disk space by not copying assets to a new location. This means that you can have multiple projects access the same assets without duplicating them. It also means that you can delete a project file without mistakenly deleting your precious video clips.

Even when you trim a clip, the original clip remains untouched. Premiere Pro doesn't lop off the unwanted sections, it merely records the data that *describes* how you trimmed the clip. Premiere Pro is nondestructive.

By the Way

Organize Your Assets

Try it Yourself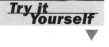

Logically arranging your assets in the Project window is simple. It's not much more than adding a few bins then doing some dragging and dropping. Here's how it works:

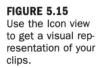

1. Take a look at the Project window. You should see all your newly captured video clips. Expand the view of that window by dragging its lower-right corner.

2. Change the display to Icon (more accurately, *thumbnail*) view by clicking the Monitor button, circled in Figure 5.15.

FIGURE 5.15
Use the Icon view to get a visual representation of your clips.

3. Test the Project window media viewer by selecting one of your clips and clicking on the Play triangle next to the screen in the upper-left corner of the Project window.

4. Create new file folders (*bins*) by clicking the folder button to the right of the Icon view button (also circled in Figure 5.15). That displays a bin in the Project window. Give it a name that matches your planned video clip organization. Do that for all the bins you planned for your clips.

5. Select and drag video clips to their respective bins. You can select more than one clip using the methods described earlier: Shift+click or click+drag to select contiguous clips or Ctrl+click to select scattered clips. After the clips have been selected, click on the image portion of a clip (as opposed to a beige border) and drag the clip collection to its respective bin. Repeat that for all your clips. As with folders in Windows Explorer, you also can drag folders into other folders to create *nested* folder collections.

Summary

Before you can edit your video, you need to *capture* it—transfer it to your PC. That process can be as simple as copying an entire tape to your hard drive and storing it as one long clip or it can take a more selective route. That latter approach gives you the chance to review your raw footage to choose keepers and to give your chosen clips descriptive names that will make it easier to track down elusive clips later.

Premiere Pro has a scene selection feature that relies on breaks in a DV tape's time stamp. If you want to split your tape automatically into clips based on visual scene changes, Scenalyzer handles that well.

Finally, after you've captured your clips, organize your clips into bins in the Project window.

Q&A

Q *I get a report that there were dropped frames during the batch capture. What's going on?*

A If you experience dropped frames, you might have too many programs running in the background that are interfering with video capture. In Windows, press Ctrl+Alt+Del to open the Task Manager, and take a look at the Applications tab and the Processes tab to see what programs and processes are running in the background. If it's more than three or four programs, you might disable some of them. Also check what programs load automatically during startup by selecting Start→Run, typing in `msconfig`, and clicking OK. That opens the System Configuration Utility. Click its Startup tab. I'm a firm believer in not having anything running in the background (except virus checking software). You can probably unclick everything else there to free up some resources. One other point: If you're capturing analog video, you might be using an outdated codec or one with too high a data rate.

Q *When I open the Capture window, I don't see an image in the video monitor and I can't control my DV camcorder. Why not?*

A This could be one of several things: Your camcorder is not turned on (if you're using a battery, it might be in sleep mode); you have it in Camera mode instead of VCR/VTR; or you haven't inserted your tape.

Workshop

Quiz

1. During the capture process, it's a good idea to add some extra frames to the start and end of each clip to ensure that you have enough footage to do transitions. How do you do that?

2. You want to capture a clip for its video plus a portion of that clip for a snippet of natural sound. How do you do that?

3. Why should you store your captured video and audio files on a hard drive other than the one your operating system is on?

Quiz Answers

1. Put some number of frames in the Handles option in the Capture section of the Capture window. A reminder: One second of video equals approximately 30 frames for NTSC or 25 frames for PAL.

2. Simply log that entire clip and then go back and log the natural sound portion. It's not a problem to capture a video from the same location on your original tape more than once. Premiere Pro simply treats each instance as a separate clip and shuttles the tape to the proper in- and out-points, whether or not it's been there before.

3. Your operating system regularly accesses its hard drive, even when your computer is otherwise idle. If that happens while you're viewing or transferring a clip, it might interrupt the flow. You also should install Premiere on a drive other than the one you're using for your video clips.

Exercise

If you have any analog tapes, now is as good a time as any to convert them to DV. Obtain a DV camcorder with analog video inputs (S-video is better than composite) and dub your tapes to DV. DV lasts longer than analog and is much easier to work with.

HOUR 6

Creating a Cuts-Only Video

What You'll Learn in This Hour:

▶ Video editing: from engineers to artists
▶ Using a storyboard approach
▶ Taking a Timeline window tour
▶ Editing clips in a sequence

Video editing has come a long way from massive tape machines operated only by engineers to desktop PCs offering anyone an opportunity to enjoy the art of video editing. A good introduction to nonlinear editing is via the storyboard. I explain that in this hour. After you've organized your clips on the storyboard and then moved them to a timeline—or **sequence** in Premiere Pro parlance—you have count less options to trim, move, add, and delete clips. Those topics conclude this hour.

Video Editing: From Engineers to Artists

Premiere Pro and other nonlinear editors like it have opened new opportunities. Anyone with a PC, even a laptop, now can do broadcast-quality video editing. What was once reserved for high-end video production studios and well-equipped TV stations, has now reached the mass market (at least those willing to spend $2,000 for software and a digital video (DV) camcorder).

Old-Fashioned Editing

To gain some perspective on the video editing process, a little history is in order. In the early days of TV, engineers did the editing. They had to. They were trained to deal with unruly, bulky, and complex tape machines. They had to monitor things such as color framing, sync timing, and blanking.

Here's how John Crossman, a long-time editor friend of mine, puts it (see "Editing Tips from an Expert—John Crossman" in Hour 9, "Advanced Editing Techniques and Workspace Tools"):

> *The logic was that the same people who pushed the "record" and "playback" buttons in the tape room should be the ones to run the editing machines. Videotape editing then was considered a very technical job, not an artistic job.*

Microprocessors eventually resolved and automated many of those technical issues, and nonengineering people—folks with an eye for editing—started populating the editing bays. However, prohibitive costs limited access to those machines.

As recently as a few years ago, whenever I created a video that called for some special transitions, I worked offline (that is, I used copies of my original master tapes on a lower-priced editing system to create an edit decision list [EDL]). Figure 6.1 shows an example created in Premiere 6.5.

By the Way

EDLs—On Their Way Out

Premiere Pro no longer creates EDLs. Adobe chose to migrate to an emerging cross-platform technology called AAF—Advanced Authoring Format. It resolves two drawbacks to EDLs: They're text only and they have limited transition and effect options. According to the AAF Association (`http://www.aafassociation.org`), "AAF is a multimedia file format that enables content creators to easily exchange digital media and metadata across platforms, and between systems and applications. The AAF simplifies project management, saves time, and preserves valuable metadata that was often lost when transferring media between applications in the past."

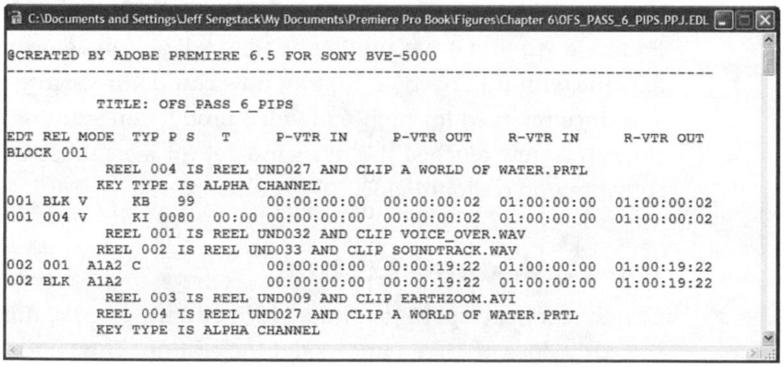

```
C:\Documents and Settings\Jeff Sengstack\My Documents\Premiere Pro Book\Figures\Chapter 6\OFS_PASS_6_PIPS.PPJ.EDL

@CREATED BY ADOBE PREMIERE 6.5 FOR SONY BVE-5000
--------------------------------------------------------------------------------

         TITLE: OFS_PASS_6_PIPS

EDT REL MODE  TYP P S   T      P-VTR IN     P-VTR OUT    R-VTR IN     R-VTR OUT
BLOCK 001
          REEL 004 IS REEL UND027 AND CLIP A WORLD OF WATER.PRTL
         KEY TYPE IS ALPHA CHANNEL
001 BLK V     KB   99         00:00:00:00  00:00:00:02  01:00:00:00  01:00:00:02
001 004 V     KI 0080  00:00 00:00:00:00  00:00:00:02  01:00:00:00  01:00:00:02
          REEL 001 IS REEL UND032 AND CLIP VOICE_OVER.WAV
         REEL 002 IS REEL UND033 AND CLIP SOUNDTRACK.WAV
002 001  A1A2 C               00:00:00:00  00:00:19:22  01:00:00:00  01:00:19:22
002 BLK  A1A2                 00:00:00:00  00:00:19:22  01:00:00:00  01:00:19:22
          REEL 003 IS REEL UND009 AND CLIP EARTHZOOM.AVI
         REEL 004 IS REEL UND027 AND CLIP A WORLD OF WATER.PRTL
         KEY TYPE IS ALPHA CHANNEL
```

FIGURE 6.1
An EDL created by Premiere 6.5.

Then I took my original raw footage and that EDL data file, with all the transition commands built in, to an expensive online facility that automatically (with some manual labor) cranked out a polished product. That process, although more time-consuming than working online from start to finish, saved a ton of money.

Today the pendulum has swung to the opposite extreme, and you're riding that pendulum. Anyone can work solely online (that is, use the original video footage from start to finish). No longer do video producers need to rely on high-priced production houses. Heck, now you can do it at home. The purpose is to do it well, and that starts with getting your assets arranged.

Using a Storyboard Approach

I think the easiest way to take your first steps into nonlinear video editing is by using a storyboard. You've probably seen how feature film directors sometimes use photos or call on artists to sketch out scenes to help visualize story flow and camera angles. I've seen animated feature film storyboards that filled several conference room walls.

Few video editors rely on the storyboard. It's more a bridge to editing than a true productivity tool. In previous versions of Premiere, it was a separate feature. Premiere Pro's developers chose to drop the storyboard, but changed the Project window to replace most of the storyboard's functionality.

Missing Storyboard Features

By the Way

What's missing in Premiere Pro's implementation of the storyboard versus previous versions are little arrows showing the storyboard flow (it's still left-to-right and top-to-bottom), a total running time for the selected clips, and the capability to remove clips without deleting them from the Project window. (I offer up a workaround for that latter issue in the coming Try It Yourself tasks.) It also has some confounding usability issues that I explain in a moment.

You can display video clip thumbnails in the Project window—in storyboard fashion—to help structure the flow of your production. This approach can come in handy by revealing gaps in your story—places that need fleshing out with more video or graphics. It's also a way to note redundancy. It's also an easy way to quickly place a whole bunch of ordered clips on a sequence. But for most folks, it serves solely as a one-time introduction to nonlinear editing. Use it once and move on.

Creating a Storyboard

▼

The methodology is fairly simple, but there are some limitations. The first limitation is that switching to Icon view in the Project window displays thumbnails of clips only from a single bin (folder). Because you have multiple bins, this makes creating a storyboard darned inconvenient. Here's a workaround for that as well as an explanation of the rest of the storyboard creation process:

1. In the Project window, create a Storyboard bin by clicking the new Bin button and naming it Storyboard.

2. The goal is to place copies of all the clips you intend to use in your storyboard in this newly created bin. Open a bin with clips that you intend to use and select all the needed clips from that bin.

3. As shown in Figure 6.2, right-click (*context-click* in Premiere Pro parlance) on one of the selected clips to bring up the context menu. Select Copy (that will copy the entire collection of clips).

By the Way

Context-Clicking

Premiere Pro is rife with context-sensitive menus that are accessible by right-clicking on objects or within windows. Feel free to right-click on scattered items in the Premiere Pro workspace. You'll find that clicking in the Monitor, Timeline, and Effect Controls windows presents you with numerous options.

FIGURE 6.2
Open bins one at a time, select clips you want to place in your storyboard, and use the right-click context menu to copy them.

▼

4. As shown in Figure 6.3, right-click on the Storyboard bin and select Paste. Repeat this for all the clips you want to place in your storyboard.

Audio Re-conforming

The unfortunate side effect of all this copying is that Premiere Pro will re-conform all the audio for these clips, which consumes extra hard drive space and ties up your processor for a while. This behavior was one of the regular gripes among beta testers. We'll watch to see whether Adobe fixes this in future versions of Premiere Pro.

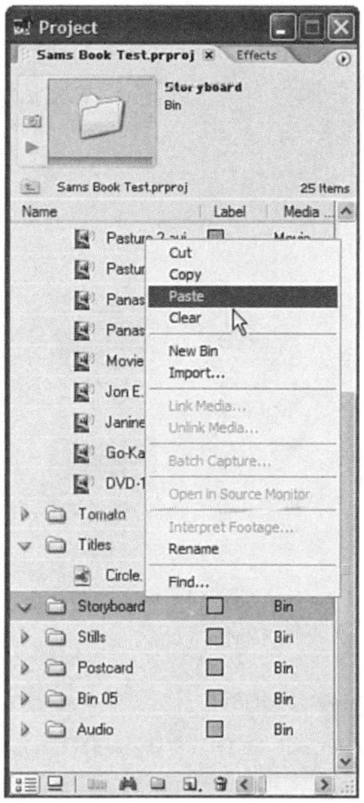

By the Way

FIGURE 6.3
Highlight the Storyboard bin with a right mouse click and then paste your clip copies there.

5. With your Storyboard bin loaded to the brim, expand your Project window view as wide and tall as you can and change the view to display clip thumbnails by clicking the Icon button (circled in Figure 6.4) at the bottom-left corner of the Project window.

6. For reasons unknown, this causes Premiere Pro to close any opened bins and display bin icons only. Remedy that by double-clicking the Storyboard bin to display all its clips. Your Project window should look like Figure 6.4. If the thumbnails don't display, click the wing menu triangle (in the upper-right corner in Figure 6.4), and select Thumbnails→Large, Medium or Small.

By the
Way

No Word Wrap

Here's another limitation to Premiere Pro's storyboard implementation. The old Premiere storyboard used something like word wrap. If there were too many thumbnails for the Project window screen size, they'd fill the screen width and then scroll down the window (standard behavior for most windows). You could at least see a group of consecutively placed thumbnails in the window.

With Premiere Pro, the thumbnails generally run past the right side of the window, meaning that you have to use the slider on the bottom of the window to see consecutively placed thumbnails. To gather them within the width of your expanded Project window, open the wing menu (the little triangle in the upper right corner) and select Clean Up.

FIGURE 6.4
Expand your Project window and convert it to Icon (thumbnail) view by clicking the circled Icon button. Use the wing menu and select Clean Up to remove any empty storyboard frames.

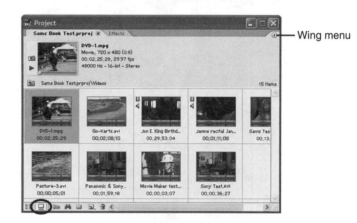

Wing menu

7. A clip's thumbnail image—or *poster frame*—defaults to the first frame of video for that clip. You can set a new thumbnail image by selecting the clip and then playing it in the little Project window video monitor. When you see a more representative image, click the camera button highlighted in Figure 6.5.

FIGURE 6.5
If you choose to do so, you can change the thumbnail poster frame image by using the small video screen and camera button.

Arrange Your Storyboard

Now you can look over the storyboard and do two things: rearrange and delete clips. Remember, you're just deleting clips from the Storyboard bin. The original clip references remain in their respective Project window bins.

To move a clip, simply drag it to a new location. A black vertical line indicates placement.

To use the same clip or portions of the same clip in more than one location, right-click on that clip and select Duplicate. That instantly adds a copy of that clip (adding the word *Copy* at the end of its filename) someplace in the storyboard. Track it down and place it where it suits you. I tell you how to trim it in the next task.

To remove a clip from the Storyboard, select it and press Delete (or right-click and select Cut). That leaves an empty placeholder. You can remove such gaps later by opening the Project window wing menu (the triangle in the upper-right corner) and selecting Clean Up.

Trim Clips in the Source Monitor

Try it Yourself

▼

It's helpful to trim clips before moving them from the Storyboard to the sequence. Do that by double-clicking a thumbnail to display it to the Source Monitor window and trim it there. Here's how it's done:

1. With your Storyboard still open, double-click a clip you'd like to slim down. The Monitor window pops up (depending on your screen resolution, it might pop up on top of the storyboard) with your clip's first frame on display on the Source screen (another way to open a clip like this is to simply drag it from the storyboard to the Source Monitor window).

2. As shown in Figure 6.6, play the clip to where you'd like it to start. Use the Play button or scrub through the clip using the Current Time Indicator (CTI). Mark that in-point by clicking the Set In-Point "{" bracket (or pressing the I shortcut key). Do the same for the out-point. No need to be too exact. You can make more precise edits when you work in the Timeline window.

3. Refer back to the Storyboard bin (see Figure 6.5) and you'll see that the clip duration displayed below the clip thumbnail has changed to reflect the new in-points and out-points.

▼

▼

FIGURE 6.6
You can trim your
storyboard clips in
the Source Monitor
window using the
in- and out-
markers.

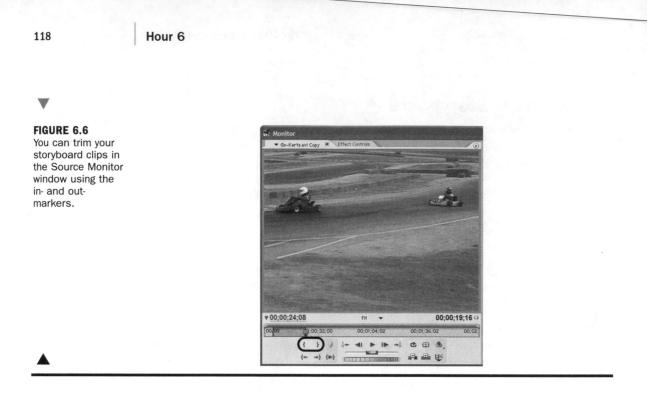

▲

Feel free to trim down as many of your clips as you like (you always can adjust those in-points and out-points later in the timeline).

When you're satisfied that your clips are in the right sequence and that you've weeded out the redundancies and trimmed the fat, it's time to send your project to the timeline window for additional editing.

Try it Yourself   **Automate Your Storyboard to a Sequence**

▼

Now you're going to move your storyboard clips to the timeline window—placing them contiguously, in sequential order. Premiere Pro calls this **automate to sequence**. Here's how you do it:

1. Select the clips to place on a sequence. You probably want to select all clips. To do that, select Edit→Select All. You can Ctrl+click to select scattered clips or drag a marquee over a group of contiguous clips.

2. Click the Automate to Sequence button in the lower-left corner of the Project Window. I highlighted it in Figure 6.7.

FIGURE 6.7
The Automate to
Sequence button
will place your sto-
ryboard clips on
the timeline.

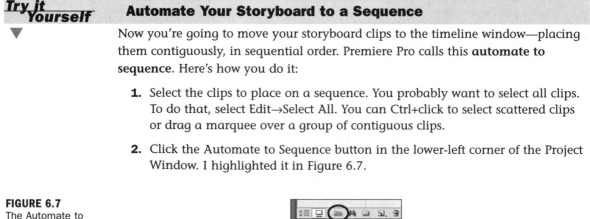

▼

3. In the newly opened Automate to Sequence dialog box, shown in Figure 6.8, you face several options:

Ordering—Sort Order puts clips on a sequence in the order you established in the Storyboard. Selection Order places them in the order you selected them by Ctrl+clicking on individual clips.

Placement—Places your clips sequentially on the timeline as opposed to at unnumbered markers (something we haven't covered anyway).

Method—The choices are Insert or Overlay. I discuss both concepts later this hour in the "Editing Clips in a Sequence" section. Because you probably are placing the clips on an empty sequence, both methods do the same thing.

Clip Overlap—Here's where I suggest that you deviate from the defaults. Overlap presumes that you'll put a transition such as a cross-dissolve between all clips. The goal this hour is to create a **cuts-only** video; that is, a video with no transitions or special effects. Set Clip Overlap to zero.

Keep Transitions in Check

I will mention more than once in this book that transitions (and special effects) are overused and distracting. Fewer is better.

By the Way

Apply Default Audio/Video Transition—Because you'll opt for no transitions, uncheck these boxes.

Ignore Audio/Video—Because you want to put both the audio and video portions of your DV clips on a sequence, keep these boxes unchecked.

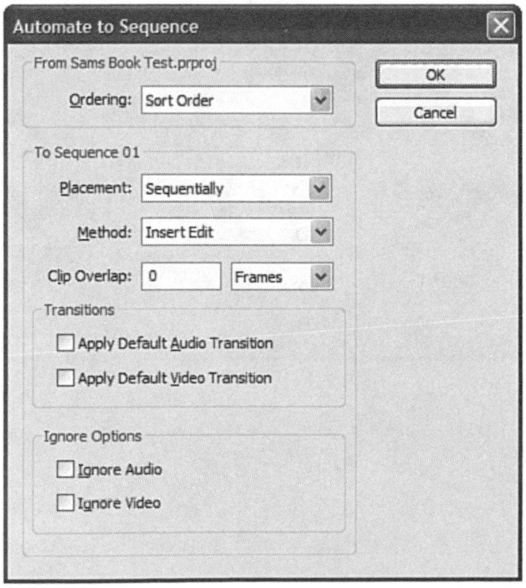

FIGURE 6.8
Adjust settings in the Automate to Sequence dialog box to complete the process.

Checking the Destination Sequence

Before you click OK, check your Timeline window. Premiere Pro will place your clips on whatever sequence is open, starting wherever you have placed the CTI in that sequence. If you've followed this book to a T, there should be one empty sequence in the Timeline window. If not, cancel out of the Automate to Sequence dialog box, select File→New→Sequence, and click OK in the New Sequence dialog box. Now return to the Automate to Sequence dialog box, make the appropriate adjustments, and go to step 4.

4. Click OK. This places your clips in order on the Sequence in the Timeline window.

Taking a Timeline Window Tour

The Timeline window and its sequences are the heart and soul of Premiere Pro. Everything you do in Premiere Pro relies on the timeline sequences. You do further editing of your clips here, add special effects, and place transitions between clips—and your output emanates from it.

The first thing you'll notice is that your ordered clips residing on Video Track 1 and their audio (in this case, natural sound) is on Audio Track 1. It should look a lot like Figure 6.9. The name of each clip appears right after each edit point.

Current Time Indicator – CTI

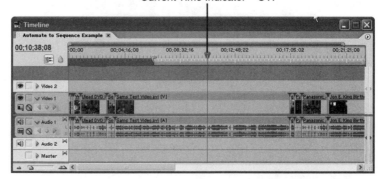

FIGURE 6.9
The timeline immediately after completing the Automate to Timeline process.

Timeline Window Keyboard Shortcuts

Depending on the length of your project, you probably see only a few of the clips you automatically added to the sequence. You can change the scale of the sequence to show more clips (or fewer—your choice). Here are three keyboard shortcuts:

▶ / (backslash) will display your entire project within the width of the Timeline window.

▶ - (hyphen key—*not* the numeric keypad minus sign) incrementally increases the time displayed in the timeline, thereby showing more of your project assets. This is the same as the Zoom Out—small mountain—button in the lower-left corner of the Timeline window.

▶ = (equal key) incrementally reduces the time displayed. The + is an uppercase =, but you don't need to use the Shift key for this shortcut. It's the same as the Zoom In—double mountain—button.

To take a look at your masterpiece in action, drag the CTI (noted in Figure 6.9) to the beginning and press the spacebar (the keyboard shortcut for Play/Pause). Your cuts-only video will display in the Monitor window's program screen. You can stop it by pressing the spacebar again. You also can use the VCR button controls in the program screen.

Scrubbing

You quickly can scrub through your project by clicking and dragging the CTI (or the edit line below it and outside any clips).

Editing Clips in a Sequence

In a departure from standard Premiere Pro how-to books, I think the best way to learn about using the sequence is to experiment with it a bit. When I first learned to use earlier versions of Premiere by reading how-to books, their narrow, specific, step-by-step explanations kept me from seeing the big picture. I think the way around that is for you to take Premiere Pro's sequence for a test drive by doing a few straightforward edits.

And don't worry. There's really no way you can mess up your storyboard handiwork. Premiere Pro is fairly forgiving. If you do something that looks wrong, you always can click Edit, Undo to fix it (or the standard Windows shortcut: Ctrl+Z). Do several things wrong and you can use the History palette to move back as many steps as you like, even as far back as to the original Automate to Sequence (see Figure 6.10).

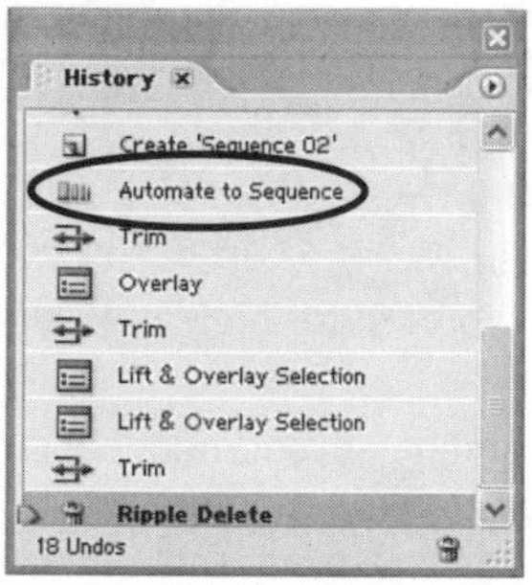

FIGURE 6.10
If things get out of hand, use the History palette to back up any number of steps, even all the way back to Automate to Sequence.

One of the beauties of Premiere Pro is how easy it is to add clips anywhere in the project, move them around, remove them altogether, and change their lengths. Here's how you do all that.

Changing a Clip's Length

Note that as you move your Selection tool (the default arrow cursor) across a clip, it changes shape to a left or right red square bracket—either [or]. This little tool, shown in Figure 6.11, enables you to change the length of a clip.

FIGURE 6.11
The Selection tool's Trim mode makes it possible for you to change the length of a clip by moving the beginning or end of a clip.

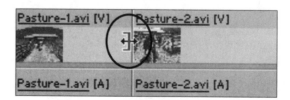

Move the bracket to the end of a clip directly before the edit point with the next clip. Notice that the bracket faces left. If you click and drag it to the left, you'll trim the end of that clip. You can look for an appropriate trim edit point by watching the Program Monitor screen. Release the mouse and your clip shrinks, leaving a gap where the trimmed footage used to be. I explain how to get rid of that gap in a few minutes.

By the Way

Trimming Changes Audio, Too

As you trim your video, its associated audio gets trimmed as well. You can trim only the video or only the audio portion of such a linked clip. I show you how in the next hour, "Applying Professional Edits and Adding Transitions."

To trim the beginning of a clip, do the same thing except make sure that the bracket faces right—into the clip. Then drag it to the right and release when you reach an appropriate edit point.

Snap to Edges

Premiere Pro has a tremendously useful attribute called Snap to Edges. It's a default setting, and in only a few instances will you want to deselect it. Snap to Edges means that as you drag a clip toward another clip, it'll jump to the edge of the clip to make a clean, unbroken edit. With Snap to Edges turned off, you'd have to slide the new clip very carefully next to the other clip to ensure there is no gap.

Snap to Edges is also useful when making precise edits. Using the Selection tool (in its trim mode) to trim a clip is a bit inexact. You *can* make it frame specific. Locate the frame you want to edit to by dragging the CTI through your sequence to that frame's approximate location and then using the Step Forward/Back buttons (keyboard shortcuts: right-arrow key and left-arrow key) in the Program Monitor window to move to the specific frame. That places the CTI right at that frame on the clip in the timeline. Use the Selection tool and drag the edge of the clip toward the CTI line. When it gets near it, it will snap to the CTI, and you'll have made a frame-specific edit.

You can use this technique in all sorts of circumstances.

Removing a Clip

Select a clip by clicking it and pressing Delete. Gone. There's that gray gap again. We'll fix that later. If you want your clip back, select Edit→Undo (Ctrl+Z).

Closing the Gaps—Ripple Delete

By now, you might have left a few gaps in your production. Removing them and closing the gaps is a snap. As shown in Figure 6.12, right-click a gap and click Ripple Delete (so named because its effect ripples through the entire sequence). Ripple Delete removes the gap by sliding all the material after the gap to the left. Do this for all the gaps, and your production will play back smoothly.

Pasture-2.avi [V]

Ripple Delete

FIGURE 6.12
Ripple Delete slides everything in a sequence, on all video and audio tracks, to the left (earlier in the production) to fill a gap.

Save yourself a step by applying Ripple Delete to a clip. Right-click on a clip; that opens the lengthy context-sensitive menu shown in Figure 6.13. I cover some of that menu's commands later in this book. In this case, select Ripple Delete. Doing so removes the selected clip and slides everything else on the sequence (video and audio clips) over to the left to fill the gap.

FIGURE 6.13
Right-click on a clip to open this extensive context-sensitive menu. In this case, use it to Ripple Delete the clip.

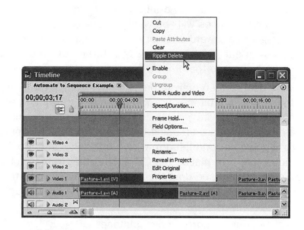

Using the Ripple Edit Tool

Another way to avoid creating those gaps is to use the Ripple Edit tool. It's one of the 11 tools in the Tools palette. I've highlighted the Ripple Edit tool in Figure 6.14 (keyboard shortcut: B).

FIGURE 6.14
The Ripple Edit tool. Using it saves you the extra step of doing ripple deletes on gaps in your timeline.

You use the Ripple Edit tool to change the length of a clip. It works much like the Selection tool (its icon is a thicker Selection tool bracket). The basic difference between the Selection and Ripple Edit tools is how the rest of the clips on a track behave once you change the length of a clip.

You know that when you use the Selection tool to shorten a clip by dragging in one end of that clip, doing so leaves a gap between two clips. To close that gap, you right-click it and select Ripple Delete.

If you use the Ripple Edit tool instead, there's no need to do that final step. When you use the Ripple Edit tool to lengthen or shorten a clip, your action ripples through the sequence. That is, all clips after that edit slide to the left to fill the gap or slide to the right accommodate a longer clip.

Position it at the beginning or end of a clip you want to shorten and then click and drag it accordingly. If the edit point abuts another clip, Premiere Pro shows adjacent frames in the Monitor window as you are dragging. After you've found the point where you want to make your edit, release the mouse button. The Ripple Edit tool shortens the clip and slides everything on every track (audio and video) of the sequence over to the left to close the gap. I introduce the other Tools palette items later in this hour, in the "Using Other Editing Tools" section.

Lifting and Moving a Clip

There are two kinds of moves: lift and extract. Lift leaves a gap. Extract is the equivalent of what is usually referred to as a *ripple delete* in that other clips move over to fill the gap. Extract uses a keyboard modifier (see next section). To lift and move a clip (both the video and its linked audio), click and drag the clip from one point on the Video 1 track and drop it at the end of your clip collection. The behavior should match that shown in Figure 6.15.

Overlaying a Clip

If you lift a clip and then place it on top of another clip or clips, the moved clip will cover those clips and its audio will replace what was on the sequence before. That's called an *overlay edit* and I discuss that a bit more later this hour in "Adding a Clip Inside a Sequence—Overlay or Insert."

By the Way

Using a Keyboard Modifier to *Extract* and Move

Extract introduces something new to Premiere Pro: keyboard modifiers. By holding down Ctrl or Alt+Ctrl when adding, removing, or moving a clip, you change how the rest of the clips on the sequence behave. At first it might seem confusing, but the behavior is logical and predictable. You use the Alt key only for sequences with clips on more than one set of tracks. I cover it in Hour 17, "Compositing Part 1—Layering Images and Clips." We'll stick with using the Ctrl keyboard modifier in this hour.

FIGURE 6.15
The lift and move behavior.

Third-Biggest Beta Group Gripe

The Premiere Pro development team dropped a number of tools in lieu of adding keyboard modifiers. For some members of the beta testing group, these new behaviors caused a fair amount of confusion and consternation. All that came to a screeching halt when one member posted a brief video on his Web site, giving a practical demonstration of this new functionality. Light bulbs began clicking on and it didn't take long before the beta folks began singing the praises of keyboard modifiers.

Extract is the same as ripple delete. You remove a clip and all other clips slide to the left to fill the gap. In this case, because you're doing an extract and move, those sliding clips include the extracted clip.

Take a look at Figure 6.16 to see how this behavior plays out. You click on a clip and hold down the Ctrl key as you extract it from its place on the sequence. You now can release the Ctrl key and move it to the end of your sequence. When you drop it there (release the mouse button), the moved clip and the clips ahead of it slide to fill its former position—an extract and move.

Modifier Key Feedback

Note that as you drag a clip to or from the Project window to a sequence or from one place on a sequence track to another, Premiere Pro displays a little text message at the bottom of the user interface. If you aren't using the Ctrl key, it'll say, Drop in Track to Overwrite. Use Ctrl to enable insert. Press the Ctrl key and Premiere Pro will let you know that you can use the Alt key to limit the tracks that shift.

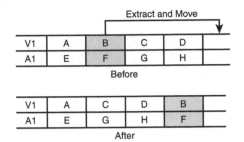

FIGURE 6.16
The extract and move behavior.

Adding a Clip Inside a Sequence—Overlay or Insert

No matter how carefully you selected clips for your storyboard, you can add clips to your sequence later (see Figure 6.17).

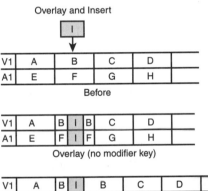

FIGURE 6.17
Overlay (no keyboard modifier) and insert (using Ctrl modifier) behaviors.

An overlay (or *overwrite*) does just what it says. Here's how it works. Drag a clip from the Project window to the sequence. As shown in Figure 6.18, the Monitor window Program screen changes into two images. The left side is the new out-point of the clip that precedes your newly positioned clip. The right side is the in-point of the clip that follows your newly placed clip (you don't see an image of the clip you're positioning). As you slide the clip left and right, those side-by-side images change accordingly.

If you want to position your new clip at an edit point or at the CTI edit line, Snap to Edges will take care of that and give you a visual reference by popping up a thin, black, vertical line at those points as you move close to them. When you're satisfied with the new position, release the mouse button.

FIGURE 6.18
Use the Monitor window Program split-screen to locate the new in-points and out-points for the overlaid clip.

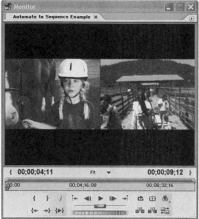

FIGURE 6.18
Use the Monitor window Program split-screen to locate the new in-points and out-points for the overlaid clip.

By the Way

> ### Razoring Behavior
>
> This overlay (as well as insert) behavior—positioning a clip anywhere within an existing clip or set of clips—is called **razoring**. In one step, you're making two razor slices, removing the stuff between the cuts, and dropping a new clip in that gap. This is a new, very powerful, time-saving feature in Premiere Pro.

Take a look back at Figure 6.17 to see how an insert edit behaves. In this case, it does not overwrite a clip or set of clips; it razors a clip at the left edge of the new clip, slides everything to the right of that razor cut to the right, and drops the new clip on the sequence in that newly created gap. Nothing is covered up. All previously placed video and audio remain on the sequence.

To perform an insert edit, follow the same process as you did with an overlay. But this time, hold down the Ctrl key as you position the clip in the sequence. In this case, the Monitor window Program split-screen will show the same image on both sides (unless you position the left edge of the new clip at an edit point). When you find an edit point that suits you, release the mouse button. Voilá—an Insert edit.

Using Other Editing Tools

The Tools palette has lost weight in Premiere Pro. Previous versions of Premiere packed 18 tools in an even smaller space than the current Tools palette. Premiere Pro places only 11 on that vertical bar. Table 6.1 shows a quick rundown.

TABLE 6.1   Tools Palette Tools

Icon	Tool Name	Function	Keyboard Shortcut
	Selection	Multipurpose, all-around aide	v
	Track Select	Discussed later this hour	m
	Ripple Edit	Already discussed	b
	Rolling Edit	See Hour 9	n
	Rate Stretch	See Hour 9	x
	Razor	Discussed later	c
	Slide	See Hour 9	u
	Slip	See Hour 9	y
	Pen	Discussed later this hour	p
	Hand	Discussed later this hour	h
	Zoom	Discussed later this hour	z

Track Select

Not to be confused with the Selection tool, the Track Select tool enables you to select all clips to the right of wherever you click it on a video or audio track. You can Shift-click to select other tracks. After they've been selected, you can slide them, delete them, cut/paste them, or copy/paste them.

Edit Tools

I've already explained the Ripple Edit tool. I'll cover Rolling, Rate Stretch, Slide, and Slip in Hour 9. The one you might experiment with now is the Rate Stretch tool. Select it and then click and drag it on a clip to stretch or compress that clip and in the process slow it down or speed it up.

Razor

Razor slices a clip or clips in two. It has multiple uses, and I'll cover them in several different hours.

Pen

A very limited use tool used to add, select, move, or delete keyframes on a sequence. I briefly explain it in Hour 14, "Sweetening Your Sound."

Hand

A limited-use tool. Use the Hand tool to move an entire sequence by grabbing a clip and sliding it to one side. It works the same as moving the scrollbar at the bottom of the Timeline window.

Zoom

This works like the Zoom In and Zoom Out buttons in the lower-left corner of the Timeline window and the Zoom bar at the top of the sequence above the time ruler. Default is Zoom In (the + cursor). Hold down Alt to change that to Zoom Out (the - cursor). When you want to see a set of clips in greater detail, click and drag the Zoom tool around those clips.

Summary

Video editing has moved from an engineering function to art. Nonlinear editors (NLEs) have opened this art form to anyone with a PC and a camcorder. An easy introduction to nonlinear editing is a storyboard. It enables you to visualize the flow of your production as it moves from one video clip to the next.

Premiere Pro's Project window storyboard implementation is not as elegant as the dedicated storyboards in its predecessors, but it achieves the same results. You can use the Project window's icon view to arrange clips and then trim them in the Monitor window Source screen.

After you've automated the clips to a sequence, it's easy to trim, delete, add, extract, and insert clips. Premiere Pro's new keyboard modifier—Ctrl, in the instances covered this hour—gives you more control without the need to change tools or perform extra steps.

Q&A

Q *The storyboard is fine as an introduction to nonlinear editing, but I want to skip it and work directly on the timeline. How can I do this?*

A This is the approach you'll probably end up taking as you gain experience working with Premiere Pro. Instead of opening a new storyboard each time you start a new production, just drag clips from your Project window and drop them on the timeline. Drop them all on the Video 1 track. You can select a number of clips at once in the Project window and drag them all to the timeline. In that case, they'll appear in the same order they appeared in the Project bin or in the order you selected them.

Q *Because Premiere Pro can have up to 99 video and audio tracks, why can't I place video in some other track besides Video 1?*

A You can place your clips on any track you want. And as you gain experience, you will do that for every project. It's just that placing clips on multiple tracks introduces a level of complexity that might be more than you want to tackle at this stage. Feel free to experiment. The basic rule is that video clips on higher-numbered tracks cover whatever is below them on a sequence, whereas audio tracks all play at once. Later in the book, I show you how to composite—or layer video—and how to mix multiple audio tracks.

Workshop

Quiz

1. You set up the Project window to display thumbnails. But one thumbnail is black. Why? What can you do about it?

2. You've created a storyboard, but several clips are obviously too long. How do you trim that excess baggage?

3. How do you trim a clip in a sequence without creating a gray gap?

Quiz Answers

1. It's black because the first frame of that clip is black. The thumbnail defaults to the first frame. To change the thumbnail image, select the clip, play it in the little Project Monitor window, and when you see an image

that represents the clip, click the little box in the lower-right corner. That sets a new thumbnail image. It should show up right away in the Project Bin window.

2. Double-click each extra-long clip to open it in the Source Monitor. Play it or drag the CTI to where you want the edited clip to start. Click the left in-point bracket ({). Then do the same for the out-point. Notice that your clip's new time shows up in its storyboard thumbnail caption.

3. Use the Ripple Edit tool. You'll find it in the Tools palette. It's the third one down—a fat vertical line with arrows sticking out both sides. Move it to the end of the clip you want to shorten. Drag it to the new edit point and release. The clip will shrink and the rest of the project automatically will fill the gap.

Exercises

1. Take the right-click menu for a test drive (you've already used this technique to use Ripple Delete). Right-click a clip in the timeline and check out the various options. Speed/Duration and Frame Hold are both excellent editing tools that I'll cover later. Try them out on some clips.

2. Grab your camcorder and head out looking not for a subject but rather for a sequence. For example, go to a public place such as a park and tape some-one tossing a ball to his dog. Get wide and tight shots and various angles (oh, and get permission). Then transfer that video and build a sequence. This is a real test of editing skill because it involves editing techniques such as wide/tight and matching shots.

3. Practice, practice, and practice all the various editing moves described in this hour. Trim, delete, overlay, insert, lift, and extract. Use the Ctrl modifier key. Note that that Insert/Overlay icon changes as you press and release the Ctrl key. The more you work with this new functionality, the more it will become second nature.

PART II

Enhancing Your Video

HOUR 7

Adding Transitions Between Clips

What You'll Learn in This Hour:

▶ Using transitions with restraint
▶ Trying some transitions
▶ Manipulating transitions in the A/B window

Applying transitions between clips—dissolves, page wipes, spinning screens, and many more—is a nice way to ease viewers from one scene to the next or to grab their attention.

Adding transitions is a simple drag-and-drop process. Most transitions offer additional options and all let you fine-tune their exact placement between clips and duration. Editors new to Premiere Pro's wealth of transition possibilities might opt to overuse them. I strongly suggest restraint.

Using Transitions with Restraint

Watch some TV news stories. Most use cuts-only edits. I'd be surprised if you see any transitions. Why? Time *is* a factor. But more and more stations these days have ready access to nonlinear editors such as Premiere Pro, and it takes almost no time to add a transition using an NLE.

The principal reason for the dearth of transitions is that they can be distracting. If a TV news editor uses one, it's for a purpose. Transitions typically take what would have been a jarring edit—such as a major jump cut—and make it more palatable. An oft-heard newsroom phrase applies: "If you can't solve it, dissolve it."

On the other hand, consider the *Star Wars* movies. Remember all the highly stylized transitions? Obvious, slow wipes for example. George Lucas knows what he's doing. Each of those transitions has a purpose. In general, they are reminiscent of old serialized movie and TV shows. Specifically, they send a clear message to the audience: "Pay attention. We're transitioning across space and time..."

Transitions can add whimsy. Here are a few examples:

▶ Start on a tight hand shot of someone cutting a deck of cards and make a Swap transition—one image slides to one side and another slides over it—to another card-related shot.

▶ Start with a tight shot of a clock (analog, not digital) and use the aptly named Clock Wipe—a line centered on the screen sweeps around to reveal another image—to move to another setting and time.

▶ Get that James Bond, through-the-bloody-eye effect using the Iris Round transition.

▶ Take a medium shot of a garage door and use a Push—one image moves off the top while another replaces it from below—to transition to the next shot of the garage interior.

▶ With some planning and experimentation, you can videotape someone pushing against a wall while walking in place and use that same Push transition (after applying a horizontal direction to it) to have that person "slide" the old scene off screen.

Transitions can work with your video to add visual interest:

▶ Take a shot of a car driving through the frame and use a wipe, synchronized with the speed of the car, to move to the next scene.

▶ Transition from a shot of driving rain or a waterfall using the Slash Slide transition, in which streaks, like driving rain, slice through an image revealing another image behind it.

▶ Use the aptly named Venetian Blinds transition as a great way to move from an interior to an exterior.

▶ A Page Peel transition works well with a piece of parchment.

The possibilities are truly endless. During this hour, I'll encourage you to experiment with all that Premiere Pro has to offer.

Trying Some Transitions

Premiere Pro ships with more than 70 transitions. Some are subtle, and some are "in your face." The more you experiment with them, the more likely you are to use them well.

Applying a transition between two clips starts with a simple drag-and-drop. That might be enough for many transitions, but Premiere Pro gives you a wide variety of options to fine-tune transitions. Most of that work takes place in the Effect Controls window. Some transitions have a Custom button that opens a separate dialog box with sets of options unique to each.

In the following Try It Yourself tasks, I'll start you off on simple transitions and gradually introduce you to the extra options available.

Prepare Your Workspace to Test Transitions

Try it Yourself

I want to keep things simple. In this task, you'll work on a very basic sequence with only two video clips. After you've complete that setup I'll introduce you to the Effects palette. Here's how:

1. Open Premiere to your current project.

2. Select Windows→Workspace→Effects to change the workspace to Effects. That makes it easier to work with transitions.

3. Open a new sequence by selecting File→New Sequence. That opens the New Sequence dialog box shown in Figure 7.1.

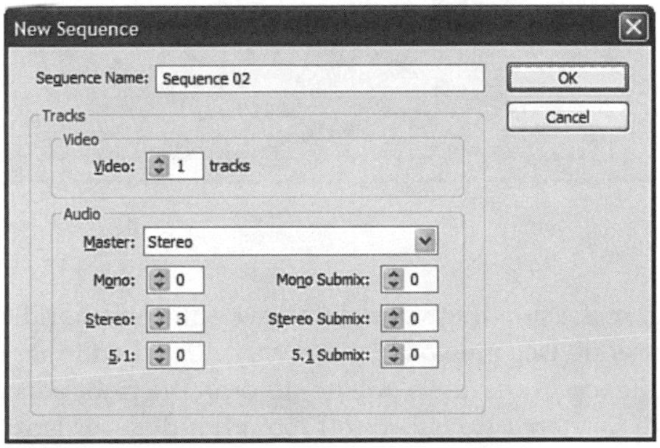

FIGURE 7.1
Use the New Sequence dialog box to open a very basic, one-track sequence.

4. Change the number of video tracks to 1 and click OK. That opens a second sequence in your Timeline window.

By the Way

Transitions on Any Track

New to Premiere Pro is the ability to add transitions between two clips on any track in a sequence. This is a very useful improvement that saves several awkward steps that were needed to accomplish the same thing in previous versions of Premiere. I limit you to a single track here to simplify things and because transition behavior on track one is the same as on any other track.

5. Open your Project window (if it's closed or you can't find it, select Window→ Project). Select two short clips and, by clicking on their icons, drag them to the newly created sequence. Press the \ (backslash) key to display both clips within the Timeline window. Your Timeline window should look like Figure 7.2.

By the Way

Head and Tail Handles Make for Smoother Transitions

Take a look at the junction of your two clips. Because you probably haven't trimmed them, the clips are their original full length. If that's the case, small triangles, like those circled in Figure 7.2, will be in the top right or left corners of any untrimmed edges of a clip. For transitions to work smoothly, you need handles—some *head* and *tail* overlap between the clips. That is, trimmed video that will be used in the transition (see step 6 for a how-to). Head and tail room are not absolutely necessary. Premiere Pro gives you several options to deal with in the event you have no *slop*. I discuss this whole issue in the upcoming section, "Manipulating Transitions in the A/B Window."

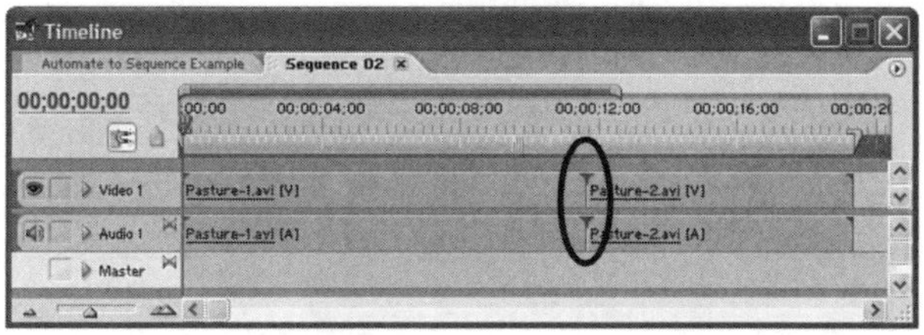

FIGURE 7.2
A basic sequence with only one video, one audio, and one master audio track plus two clips. Note that the little triangles mean there are no handles available to do a smooth transition.

6. You need to make sure that your clips have sufficient handles—or head and tail room overlap (see previous By the Way). Use the Ripple Edit tool (third icon from the top in the Tools palette) to drag the right edge of the first clip to the left to shorten it (to give it tail room handles—at least a second) and drag the left edge of the second clip to the right to give it some head room handles. By using the Ripple Edit tool, these two trims should leave no gap. If there is a gap, right-click on it and select Ripple Delete.

7. In the Effects palette (if you changed to the Effects workspace, it should already be open), click the Video Transitions tab. Note that the transitions are organized into 10 folders or bins. Click the triangle next to the Dissolve folder to open it, and, as shown in Figure 7.3, note that Cross Dissolve has a red box around it. That means it's the default transition. Drag Cross Dissolve to the edit between your two clips on the sequence.

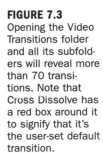

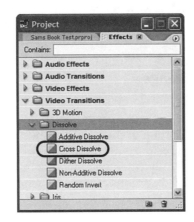

FIGURE 7.3
Opening the Video Transitions folder and all its subfolders will reveal more than 70 transitions. Note that Cross Dissolve has a red box around it to signify that it's the user-set default transition.

Changing the Default Transition

There are two primary uses for the default transition: when automating a storyboard to a sequence or as a quick means to add a transition using the keyboard shortcut—Ctrl+D. As you gain experience with transitions, you might want to set a different default transition. To do that, select the transition you want to use, click the Effects palette's wing-menu triangle, and select Set Default Transition. A red box will appear around that transition. If you select Default Transition Duration, you open the General Preferences dialog box where you can change that setting.

Did you Know?

A Plethora of Transitions

Where to begin? The many choices can be a bit mind-boggling. To bring some order to this chaos, I'll take you through several transitions, each of which offers some additional options.

Testing Transitions

Try it Yourself

You'll start with the Cross Dissolve transition, and then move on to Page Peel, Wipe, Iris Round, and Pinwheel. Here's how you add transitions and adjust their characteristics:

▼

1. Click on the Cross Dissolve icon and drag it to the junction between your two clips. That junction should look like Figure 7.4.

By the Way

Transition Placement Counts

If you drag the transition slightly to the right or left of that junction, Premiere Pro will display little icons showing that your transition either ends or begins at the junction. You can make that placement later in the Effect Controls window, so it's not critical at this point. For now, center the transition on the cut point between the two clips.

By the Way

Sequence Display Changes

Two things about how your sequence should look:

▶ A short red horizontal line will appear above any new transition. That red line means that this portion of the sequence must be rendered before you can record it back to tape or create a file of your finished project. Rendering happens automatically when you *export* your project, but you can choose to render selected portions of your sequence to make those sections display more smoothly on slower PCs.

▶ If your video or audio tracks are taller than those in Figure 7.4, the little purple transition marker might be too small to select with your Selection tool. Switch your video track to its shortest setting by clicking the little triangle to the left of Video 1. Doing so should flip the triangle so that it points to the right, reduce the height of the track display, and more prominently display the transition in the video track. You also might have to zoom in on your sequence to expand the width of the transition to enable you to select it.

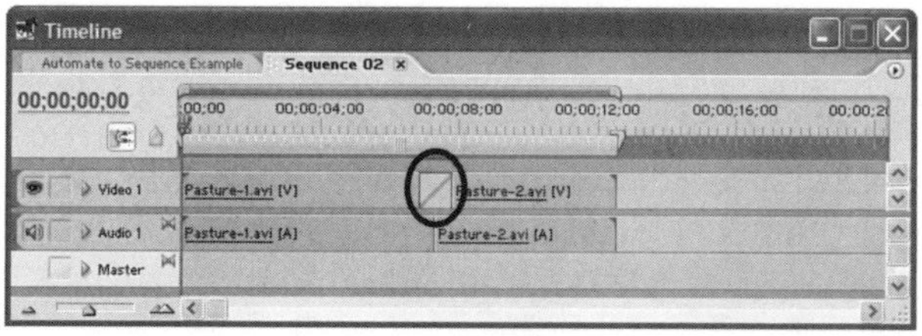

FIGURE 7.4
Dragging a transition to your sequence adds a little purple box with a diagonal line running through it.

2. Click on the transition marker in the sequence to select it. That displays the transition settings in the Effect Controls window (ECW). Your ECW should look like Figure 7.5. I've expanded the Monitor window to make adjusting transitions settings go more smoothly. You should do the same.

▼

Open the ECW's Timeline Display

If the Timeline section of the ECW is hidden, click the Show/Hide button annotated in Figure 7.5.

Show/Hide button

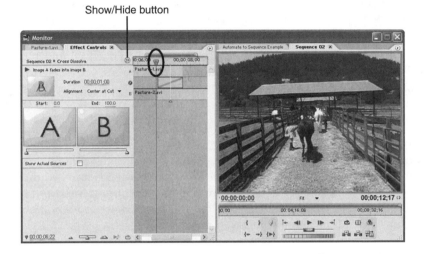

FIGURE 7.5
Make adjustments to the transitions settings in the Effect Controls window.

3. There are several ways to preview your transition. The most effective is to view it in real-time in the Program Monitor screen. In the ECW, click on the timeline ruler just ahead of the transition (I've circled that spot in Figure 7.5) to move the Current Time Indicator (CTI) to that point. Then press the space-bar to do a real-time preview. You'll see the first clip dissolve—or fade—into the second clip. Neat.

Other Preview Methods

Try two other preview methods: First, click the small triangle in the upper-left corner of the ECW. That plays a representation of transition using the A & B color boxes. Second, drag the slider below the large A rectangle. To view those transitions using your actual video clips, click the Show Actual Sources box.

Note: Leaving the slider in that new position will cause your dissolve to start at that point in the dissolve process. So, for now, slide it back.

Did you Know?

Dissolve Up from—or Down to—Black

To ease in or out of a video, most producers dissolve—or fade—up from or down to black. You can do both with simple transition drag and drops. Just drag Cross Dissolve (or any other transition, if you want a different look) to the beginning of your first clip and/or the end of your last clip. Done. I show you how to adjust the length of that fade up or down—making it more dramatic or more abrupt—in the next task, "Manipulating Transitions in the A/B Window."

4. Change the transition to Page Peel by opening the Page Peel folder, clicking on the Page Peel transition icon, and dragging it to the Cross Dissolve transition in the sequence. Doing so automatically replaces the Cross Dissolve with the Page Peel. Click on the transition (the purple marker with the diagonal line) to open the Page Peel transition in the ECW.

5. Page Peel offers additional options. In this case, as shown in Figure 7.6, you can change the direction of the Page Peel by clicking the triangles around the preview screen. Click the little Play button to see the changed transition behavior. Click Reverse to change from a Page Peel that reveals the second clip to a Page Peel that covers the first clip. You'll see both motion direction triangles and the Reverse option in many transitions.

FIGURE 7.6
Clicking the triangles around the preview screen changes the Page Peel direction. Clicking Reverse changes the transition from a peel away to a peel onto.

6. Change to the Wipe transition by locating it in the Effects palette's Video Transition Wipe folder and dragging it to the Page Peel transition in the sequence. Click on the purple marker to select it and display it in the ECW.

7. As shown in Figure 7.7, Wipe offers four more directions (eight in all) for the transition movement, plus a new feature: a border and anti-aliasing (see the sidebar titled "Clean Up the Jaggies with Anti-Aliasing"). Experiment with the border width and give it a color by either clicking the rectangular Border Color swatch and selecting a color from the standard Windows Color Picker shown in Figure 7.8 or clicking and dragging the Eyedropper tool to the Monitor window Program screen. As you roll the Eyedropper tool over the images, it picks up a color from the scene and displays it in the color swatch. Releasing the mouse button grabs the current color. Selecting a color this way keeps the border color from clashing with the images.

Easy Search Tool

If you know the name of a transition but have forgotten its folder, simply start typing its name in the Effects palette's Contains window. As you type, all transitions and effects with those starting letters will display in the Effects palette. The more letters you type, the more your search will be narrowed. That the transitions and effects appear in real-time as you type (as opposed to after you press Enter) is a laborsaving feature.

Did you Know?

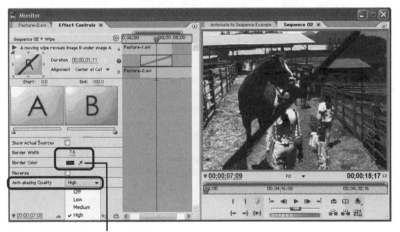

Eyedropper tool

FIGURE 7.7
Wipe offers more movement directions plus a border.

▼

FIGURE 7.8
Use the Color Picker (shown here) to select a color for the border or use the eyedropper tool to select a color from the Monitor window Program screen. Make sure that they're NTSC safe by avoiding oversaturated colors (those that cause the caution sign to pop onscreen).

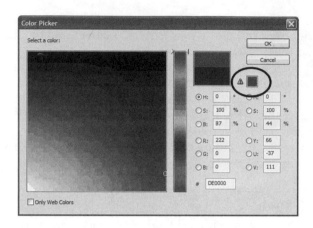

Clean Up the Jaggies with Anti-Aliasing

Every transition that offers a border option also has an anti-aliasing option. **Aliasing** is the jagged edge common along sharply defined diagonal lines in computer graphics and TV sets. If you look closely enough at a diagonal line, even in your PC monitor (which has a higher resolution than your TV set), you'll see stair steps—that's aliasing.

To get rid of aliasing, you select, ahem, *Anti*-Aliasing. Premiere's default setting is to disable anti-aliasing. I don't get this. Aliasing looks bad, so the default should be *anti*-aliasing. Nevertheless, on an effect such as a vertical or horizontal wipe, there should be no noticeable aliasing, whether or not you've opted for anti-aliasing. But if you click one of those little white triangles in the corners of the little ECW preview monitor and switch to a diagonal wipe, you'll probably want to turn on anti-aliasing.

You do that by clicking the little Anti-aliasing Quality triangle and, as shown in Figure 7.7, selecting Low, Medium, or High. You get immediate feedback in the Monitor window Program monitor. The diagonal border edges become increasingly softer as you ratchet up anti-aliasing.

Stay Safe

If you click around the Color Picker long enough, you'll eventually select a color that prompts Premiere to pop up a little yield/exclamation mark sign (see Figure 7.8). That's because you've selected a non-NTSC-safe color that will not display well on a standard TV set (it'll work fine on your PC monitor, though). For instance, selecting a highly saturated color value of 250 or more for the red, green, or blue (the R, G, or B number) color components, with a very low number for one of the other two colors

▼

will create an oversaturated color that will smear on an NTSC monitor. You can fix that by clicking on the yield sign a few times until Premiere Pro finds a similar but NTSC-safe color. You can click around the Color Picker to find a safe color or type in a lower number (249 or less should work) in the offending color's box.

8. Change to the Iris Round transition. You'll find it in the Iris folder. You know the drill by now; just remember to click on the transition in the sequence for it to show up in the ECW.

9. What sets Iris Round and several other similar transitions apart (see the next By the Way) is the option to set a start or ending location—or both— within the video image. As shown in Figure 7.9, simply drag the tiny start location icon in the Start windows (circled in Figure 7.9) to a place that suits the scene. You might start the Iris Round transition on a circular object in the scene, for instance.

Similar Transitions

By the Way

Other transitions that allow a custom starting or ending point are 3D Motion Tumble Away, Iris Cross, Iris Diamond, Iris Square, Zoom, Zoom Cross, and Zoom Trails.

Go in Reverse

Did you Know?

Try Reverse on Iris Round (and on any other transitions, if you like). Instead of starting as a small dot and growing to reveal the next clip, selecting Reverse means that the circle starts large and shrinks to that spot. So, by using Reverse, Iris Round actually has a startpoint or an endpoint—it's your choice.

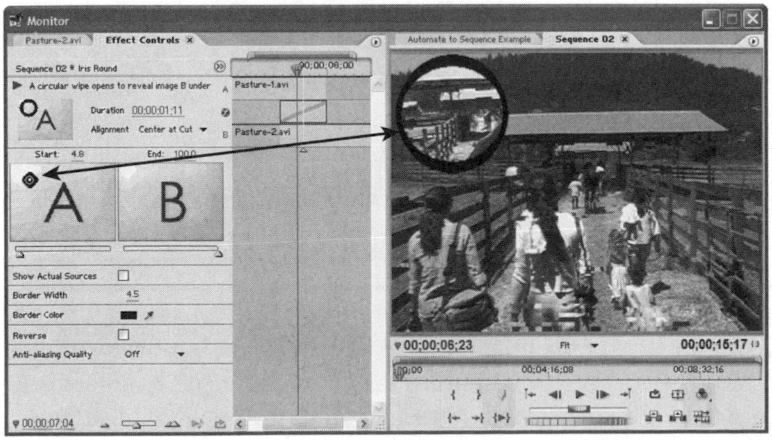

FIGURE 7.9
Some transitions enable you to set the specific start point or endpoint for extra dramatic effect.

▼

10. Change to the Pinwheel transition (it's in the Wipe folder) and check it out in the ECW.

11. Pinwheel, as well as about a dozen other Premiere Pro transitions, has a Custom button. Click it. In this case, your only option is the Number of Wedges. Type in a number (32 is the maximum allowed in this case) and, as shown in Figure 7.10, if the CTI is somewhere within the transition, you'll get real-time feedback on how your number selection looks.

12. Save your project; I want to keep this setup available for use in the next section, "Manipulating Transitions in the A/B Window."

13. Try out some other transitions with custom settings: Venetian Blinds, Random Blocks, Slash Slide, Iris Shapes, Band Slide, and Swirl.

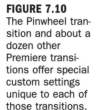

Fiddle with Flip Over

Give the Flip Over transition a test drive. It's in the 3D Motion folder—a collection of transitions that use perspective to give your transitions greater depth. The Flip Over transition takes the A clip and spins it like a flat board horizontally or vertically and then reveals the B clip on the board's other side. That flipping motion briefly leaves an empty space behind the board. You can change the color of that space and split the board into as many as eight slats by opening the Custom dialog box.

FIGURE 7.10
The Pinwheel transition and about a dozen other Premiere transitions offer special custom settings unique to each of those transitions.

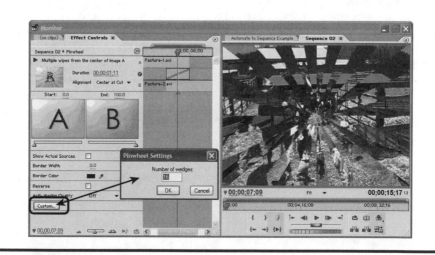

▲

I've touched on most of the primary types of transitions, but have purposely skipped two. They are specialized transitions that require a little more editing experience to tackle, so I'm saving them for Hour 9, "Advanced Editing

Techniques and Workspace Tools," which is a catchall for other editing techniques. There, I'll go over the Image Mask and Gradient Mask transitions.

Manipulating Transitions in the A/B Window

Because Premiere Pro's developers created this product from the ground up, they had the opportunity to make some fundamental decisions. One was to no longer include A/B editing in the Timeline window.

A/B editing is old-school, film-style editing. Film editors frequently use two reels of film: an A-roll and a B-roll, usually duplicates made from the same original. The two-reel approach permits nice, easy-on-the-eyes cross-dissolves, gradually fading down the images from one reel while fading up the other (see sidebar: "Still 'Grabbing B-Roll' After All These Years").

There was one advantage to having A/B editing in older versions of Premiere. You could more easily modify certain transition characteristics—the exact locations where the transition began on one clip and ended on the other, the length of the transition, and its midpoint—more intuitively in an A/B mode interface layout.

Well, here's the good news for both A/B and single-track editing camps: Premiere Pro includes all of that functionality in its Effect Controls window. I take you through its paces after the following three notes in "Using the A/B Mode to Fine-tune a Transition."

To A/B or Not to A/B

In my book on the previous version of Premiere, *Sams Teach Yourself Premiere 6.5 in 24 Hours*, I recommended that readers simply ignore the A/B mode. In my view, in this NLE era, it's counterintuitive.

But there are some editors who swear by it, including some Premiere Pro beta testers. Removing A/B editing was the single most discussed (to the point of derisive name-calling) decision in the beta group.

To Adobe's credit, it stayed the course. Not only because A/B editing is archaic but, more importantly, because removing A/B editing meant Adobe could design Premiere Pro to allow transitions on any track (see next By the Way).

This is such an improvement over previous versions of Premiere that even the naysayers should recognize that its benefits far outweigh any lost functionality.

By the Way

Developer Comment—Dropping A/B

The development team had to field a lot of questions about dropping A/B editing. Here is a compilation of their responses:

"We knew when we made this decision that it would be controversial. Editors are passionate about the way they work."

"When we made the change it was for very legitimate reasons. It avoids a great deal of complication when allowing the application of effects to clips on tracks other than just Video 1."

"To ease in this method of operation we elected to represent the A/B method of display in the Effect Controls window. We believed that the controls in this window provide the same level of adjustment that A/B mode offered in previous versions."

"When we made this decision, our goal was to have a net gain in terms of features, functionality, and flexibility as well as solve a problem."

"We are bringing Premiere into the 21st century. This is not just about the product that we are building today, but the construction of a solid foundation, which we can continue to build on."

Still "Grabbing B-Roll" After All These Years

In the TV news business—back when everyone used film and didn't have time to make duplicate reels—the A-roll typically was the interview and the B-roll was everything else. They relied on two reels because the audio and images were not synchronized in the same place on the film. Older film projectors use a sound track that is 20–26 frames (about a second) ahead of the associated images because the sound pickup in the projector is not in the lens. If you've ever threaded a film projector, you know how important it is to get just the right size loops to ensure the sound synchronizes to the images.

So, in the old TV news film era, to get a sound bite to play audio at the right time, that clip had to play behind the B-roll for about a second to allow enough time for the sound to reach the audio pickup device. Only then would a director cut to the A-roll image to play the interview segment and then would cut back to the B-roll once the sound bite ended. Despite this now-outmoded means of editing or playing back news stories, news photographers still say they're going to go "grab some B-roll."

When stations began switching to ENG (electronic news gathering) video gear, there was no longer a need to use A/B-rolls. Audio and video were on the same place on videotape, but the only way to do those smooth cross-dissolves was to make a copy of the original videotape (leading to some quality loss), run it on a second VCR, and make the cross-dissolve with an electronic switcher. That was a time-consuming and cumbersome process fraught with timing problems. Older VCRs frequently were not frame-accurate and you ended up with spasmodic-looking dissolves.

DV changes that. No more dubbing, no more generation loss, no more timing problems, and no more need to edit using ancient A/B-roll methods.

Using the A/B Mode to Fine-tune a Transition

Basically, A/B editing splits a single video track into two sub-tracks. What would normally be two consecutive and contiguous clips on a single track now display as individual clips on separate sub-tracks, giving you the option to apply a transition between them and to manipulate their head and tail frames—or handles—and other transition elements.

Working with the ECW's A/B Feature

Try it Yourself ▼

This is yet another very clever, useful, and powerful new feature in Premiere Pro. After you've gotten a sense for its functionality, I think you will see what an excellent little tool it is. Here's how it works:

1. If Premiere Pro is open to where you left off (with the Pinwheel transition loaded), that will work fine. If not, select File→Open Recent Project and select the project you saved in the previous task. You can use any transition for this task.

2. Take a look at Figure 7.11. Take note of a few things:

   ▶ The light green color on each clip is the portion of that clip that will display during playback.

   ▶ The darker green portion is the extra head or tail handles or frames you have available if you want to lengthen the transition duration. Clip A (the first clip in the two-clip sequence) has tail handles. Clip B has head handles.

Miscue in Color Scheme?

By the Way

A minor gripe here: The dark green sections of the clips don't delineate the full extent of the head or tail handles. They are truncated. I think the display would be more intuitive if those dark green sections extended all the way to the edit point (the thin white line), the spot where you made the original cut edit before adding the transition.

The other side of coin is that the light areas *do* show that tail and head frames from both clips contribute to the transition.

   ▶ The thin white line is the Edit Point where you butted the two clips together. Its default position is centered in the transition. You can move that edit (keeping the transition centered over it) and you can move the transition off-center without adjusting the Edit Point.

▼

▼

- The purple rectangle is the transition. The box width shows its relative duration. A display to the left of the Timeline Display notes the actual duration
time.

- You can move the CTI within the purple transition box to display how the
transition will look at any point.

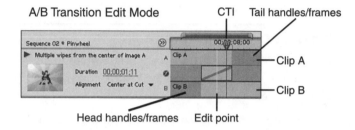

3. There are two ways to lengthen the transition: First, position your cursor
over either end of that purple box and it will change to a Trim tool. Just as
you would with a clip, drag the end to lengthen or shorten it. Second,
change the duration time by typing in a new time or clicking on the time
display and dragging your mouse left or right to change the duration.

4. To change the position of the transition relative to the edit point, simply
move the cursor over the transition box until it changes into the Slide
Transition icon shown in Figure 7.12 and then drag left or right. You might
notice that if you move the transition, the Alignment display (to the left of
the Timeline display window) changes from the default Center at Cut to
Custom Start.

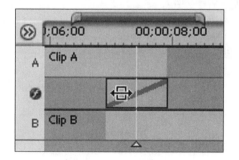

▼

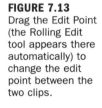

Placing the Beginning or the End of the Transition at the Cut Junction of the Two Clips

Instead of dragging the transition to position it at the exact beginning or end of the original cut edit (aligning it with the edit point), use the Alignment drop-down list. Click the triangle and select Start at Cut or End at Cut. If you've moved the transition at all, the alignment will be called Custom Start.

5. You can change the Edit Point by positioning the cursor over that thin white line (as shown in Figure 7.13, the cursor turns into a Rolling Edit tool) and dragging it right or left. In essence, you're changing the out- and in-points of the adjacent clips without changing the overall length of the two clips taken together. A split-screen display in the Program monitor (see Figure 7.14) shows you the new out- and in-points as you drag the Rolling Edit tool.

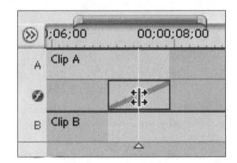

FIGURE 7.13
Drag the Edit Point (the Rolling Edit tool appears there automatically) to change the edit point between the two clips.

FIGURE 7.14
A split-screen view pops on automatically to show you the new in- and out-points as you move the centerline.

Dealing with Inadequate (or No) Head or Tail Handles

Eventually, you will want to place transitions at edit points where you don't have adequate head or tail handles. This might be because you paused the camcorder too soon or didn't get it started fast enough. You might want to add a transition to ease what would be an abrupt cut edit. Premiere Pro deals with that elegantly.

Try it Yourself

▼

Working Without Handles

What you'll do here is un-trim a clip. Drag its in- or out-point as far as it will go, butt a trimmed clip up to that point, and then apply a transition. Then you'll see how Premiere Pro deals with that differently than two clips with adequate head and tail room. Here's how it works:

1. On your sequence, grab the B-clip (the second clip) and drag it to the right—far enough to let you un-trim the A-clip.

2. Drag the A-clip's out point as far as it will go. If you deselect it by clicking outside that clip, you'll see it has those little triangles I discussed earlier this hour, showing that there are no frames left to use as handles. Now slide clip B back to the right edge of clip A. Your sequence should look like Figure 7.15.

FIGURE 7.15
The little triangles indicate clip A has no tail handles. Clip B has no triangles; therefore, it does have head handles.

3. Drag a transition to that edit point (I recommend Wipe because it's easy to see the freeze frames Premiere Pro is about to make to ensure this transition works). You'll notice that you cannot center the transition on the edit point. Premiere Pro forces you to locate it completely to the left of the edit point because the A-clip has no extra tail handles to make the transition. Premiere Pro also displays a transition icon that represents a transition that ends at the clip junction. Select the transition so that it shows up in the ECW (refer to Figure 7.16). You'll see that the ECW already has identified this as an End at Cut transition.

By the Way

▼

No Head Handles—Start at Cut Placement

If, instead, your B-clip had no head handles and the A-clip had enough handles, Premiere Pro would have forced placement of the transition starting at the edit point—a Start at Cut transition.

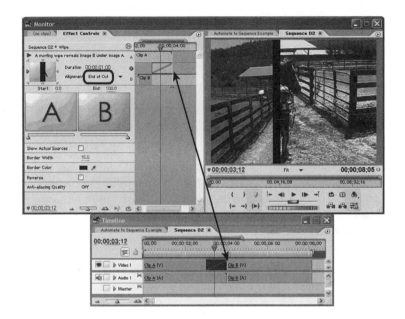

FIGURE 7.16 ▼
Premiere Pro automatically creates an End at Cut transition for a clip that has no tail handles (I added a border to better display the transition).

4. Drag the CTI to see that the transition works smoothly. It starts sooner than it would have if you had two clips with enough tail and head handles, but viewers probably will not notice the subtle shift.

5. You can extend the transition farther into the B-clip. Drag the transition's right edge or the entire transition to the right. As shown in Figure 7.17, parallel diagonal lines appear. These signify that Premiere Pro has created freeze frames of the last frame of the A-clip, to make the transition.

Freeze Frame Marker in Wrong Place?

I think the diagonal line display indicating the use of freeze frames to create the transition makes sense. But in my mind, those diagonal lines are in the wrong place. To be more informative, those lines should display on the portion of the specific clip to which they are being applied. This is my second minor gripe about this new ECW, A/B display. Perhaps Adobe might make these small fixes in the next revision.

By the Way

---

6. Drag the CTI and note that once it passes the edit point, Clip A becomes a still image. Because most transitions happen quickly and most viewers' attention will be on clip B, they might not even notice that clip A has become a still image. It works similarly if clip A has tail handles and clip B does not.

FIGURE 7.17
If you extend a transition from clip A (with no tail handles) into clip B, Premiere Pro adds freeze frames to the transition.

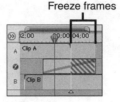

7. Finally, extend both of your clips to their original untrimmed state and butt them together. Now, neither has any tail or head handles. Apply a transition to them and, as shown in Figure 7.18, you get an *information* message that there is insufficient media and parallel diagonal lines appear in the purple transition rectangle.

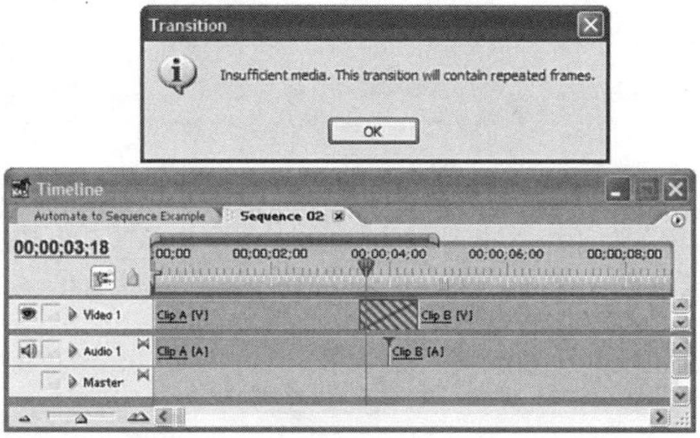

FIGURE 7.18
Applying a transition to two clips with no tail or head room leads to this informational message.

8. Take a look at this transition in the ECW. Slowly drag the CTI to see how it works. Clip A plays fine until the edit point (halfway through the transition) and then changes to a still image. Meanwhile, clip B starts as a freeze frame, but goes into motion at the moment Clip A becomes a freeze frame.

Using Transitions on Your Clips

Now is the time to experiment. Look for clips that lend themselves to specific transitions. Try out a variety. After you've had some fun, be sure to use transitions judiciously. Restraint is a good thing when it comes to transitions.

To give you an overview of virtually all the transitions Premiere has to offer, take a look at the next few pages of transitions. I have grouped them in Figure 7.19 by their respective file folders (bins).

3D

Cub Spin

Curtain

Doors

Flip Over

Fold Up

Spin Away

Swing In

Swing Out

Tumble Away

FIGURE 7.19
Virtually every tran-
sition available in
Premiere Pro.

Dissolve

Additive

Cross

Dither

Non-Additive

Random Invert

Special

Displace

Image Mask

Texturize

Three-D

Iris

Iris Cross

Iris Diamond

Iris Points

Iris Round

Iris Shapes

Iris Square

Iris Star

Page Peel

Center

Page

Page Turn

Peel Back

Roll Away

Zoom

Boxes

Cross Zoom

Zoom

Zoom Trails

Slide

Band Slide

Multi-Spin

Push

Slash Slide

Slide

Split

Swap

Swirl

Center Media

Center Split

Sliding Bands

Sliding Boxes

Stretch

Cross

Funnel

Stretch

Stretch In

Stretch Over

Wipe

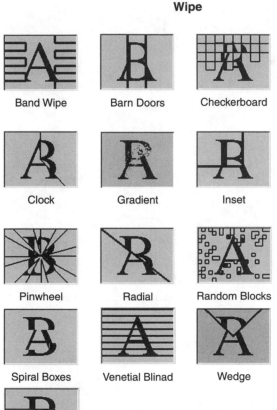

Band Wipe	Barn Doors	Checkerboard	Checker
Clock	Gradient	Inset	Paint Splatter
Pinwheel	Radial	Random Blocks	Random Wipe
Spiral Boxes	Venetial Blinad	Wedge	Wipe
Zig-Zag Blocks			

Summary

Transitions can make a video move more smoothly or snap the audience to attention. Some can be whimsical, others draw attention to a portion of the scene, and still others create a frantic mood. Fun stuff but use restraint.

Applying transitions takes not much more than a simple drag and drop. You can add things such as colored borders, change directions, and start and end locations. Plus some have custom options unique to those individual transitions. The Effect Controls window's A/B timeline display makes it easy to move transitions relative to the edit point, change the transition duration, and apply transitions to clips that don't have sufficient head or tail handles.

Q&A

Q *All the transitions I add last for only one second. I want all of them to last longer. I know I can change them one at a time, but is there an easier way to do this?*

A Two ways to do that: One, select Edit→Preferences→General and change the Video Transition Duration from the default 30 frames (one second) to whatever length you want. Two, with the Effects palette tab open, click the wing menu, select Default Transition Duration. That too opens the General Preferences dialog box.

Q *Finding transitions by name is cumbersome. I remember seeing some with descriptive names but searching through all of the Video Transition folders is tedious. Is there a better way?*

A You bet. Simply start typing in the Contains field. As you type, Premiere Pro displays all effects and transitions (audio and video) that contain that letter combination. The more you type, the shorter the list becomes.

Workshop

Quiz

1. You apply a transition to a clip but it's not what you're looking for. So, you want to replace that transition. How do you do that?

2. You have a clip with no tail handles and you want to use every frame. However, the next clip looks very similar so to avoid a jump cut you need a transition. How do you do that?

3. The Iris Square transition starts as a square somewhere on clip A with clip B inside the square. It then expands to fill the screen to reveal the next clip. You want it to start as a full screen square and shrink, revealing the clip B behind it. How do you do that?

Quiz Answers

1. Drag and drop the replacement transition on top of the rejected transition. The new one automatically replaces the old one.

2. Just apply the transition as you would normally. Premiere Pro will automatically end the transition at the edit point. You can slide that transition to

the right, ensuring that special video snippet gets its full due. If you move the out-point of the transition, Premiere Pro will add freeze frames of clip A's last frame to use as tail handles.

3. Simple. Check the Reverse box. That switches the movement from starting small and ending full screen to starting full screen and ending small.

Exercises

1. Scan your video collection for clips that lend themselves to transitions. Those could be cars or other things moving horizontally or vertically through the screen, rain splattering in a puddle, curtains, playing cards, clock faces (analog clocks, that is), or kids' alphabet blocks. Try some transitions on them and see what works and what does not work.

2. The Effects Palette enables you to create a personalized collection of favorites. Do that by clicking the Effect palette's wing menu and selecting New Custom Bin. That creates a folder called Favorites 1. You can change its name by clicking on it twice and typing in a new name. Then you can drag and drop individual transitions or entire folders. All the original transitions remain in their original folders but your Favorites folder makes the ones you use more accessible.

HOUR 8

Tackling Text: Using the Title Designer

What You'll Learn in This Hour:

- ▶ Using supers to tell your story
- ▶ Using a template to examine properties
- ▶ Creating text
- ▶ Adding motion and putting your text on a path
- ▶ Creating geometric objects

Onscreen text helps tell your story. Using a location **super** (superimposed text) sets the scene and saves the narration for other relevant points. Displaying an interviewee's name and title at the bottom of the screen reminds viewers who this person is. Using onscreen bulleted points reinforces the message you're trying to get across. Or you can give your production an opening title screen or rolling credits at the end.

Premiere Pro's Title Designer is such a full-featured product that you might never fully tap its potential. With the Title Designer, you can create simple text, rolling credits, and colorful shapes. You can use any font stored on your PC, your text can be any color (or multiple colors), any degree of transparency, and darned near any shape. Using the Path tool, you can place your text on the most convoluted curved line you can imagine. The Title Designer is an engaging and powerful tool. Anything you create in the Title Designer, you can save as a clip and use in any project.

Using Supers to Help Tell Your Story

Consider this opening sequence: A telephoto shot of scorched desert sand with rippling heat distorting the scene. Dry, desiccated, lifeless sagebrush. A lizard slowly seeking shade beneath a small stone. And a small plume of dust in the distance. Attention-getting stuff.

Now a narrator intones, "The summer heat beats down on the Bonneville Salt Flats." Effective. But what might work better is a *super* (onscreen text)—something such as Bonneville Salt Flats. Then, as the plume of dust moves toward the camera, add another super: Speed Trials—Summer 2003. Then a rocket-shaped vehicle screams through the scene.

Rather than interrupt the building suspense with a dulcet-toned narrator, save him for later. Instead, simply slap on a couple supers to set up your story.

Here are a couple other sample instances in which text can be an effective alternative to voice-overs:

▶ Instead of using a voice-over to say, "John Jones, president of the XYZ Association for the Preservation of Salient Sayings," put that information in a super at the bottom of the screen.

▶ Instead of simply saying a collection of statistics, such as 12 drummers drumming, 11 pipers piping, 10 lords a-leaping, and so on, use a collection of bulleted points that you pop onscreen with each new numbered item. If you have small graphic images of each element, you can add them along with the text.

Text strengthens your project.

Using a Template to Examine Properties

Open Premiere Pro to your workspace and locate the Title Designer. It's not where you might expect—under the Windows drop-down menu along with Audio Mixer, Navigator, History, and the like. Instead, it's in the File menu.

Select File→New→Title (or use the keyboard shortcut: the F9 key). Doing so pops up the Title Designer. The default opening view displays whatever video frame is under the CTI. For now, turn that display off by unchecking Show Video at the top of the Title Designer window (see Figure 8.1).

The background now consists of a grayscale checkerboard. That signifies a transparency. That is, if you place text created in this window on a sequence video track above other video, that video will display wherever you see that checkerboard. As you create text or geometric objects, you can give them some transparency. In that case, you'll see the checkerboard through an object, which means the video will show through but it'll appear that it's covered with smoked or tinted glass.

FIGURE 8.1
Premiere Pro's new Title Designer with the Templates button and the Show Video checkbox highlighted.

I'm going to take a different and, I think, more intuitive approach to explaining this Premiere Pro functionality. Instead of having your first tasks be to build text from scratch, you'll start by dissecting a finished product. In that way, you'll get a practical view of a number of title creation methods.

You'll work with some of Premiere Pro's built-in title templates. These are tremendously useful. Simply open one in the Title Designer and replace the placeholder text with your own copy, change a color to suit your project, or change a shape to suit your style. You can select Lower- or Upper-Third templates and use them to identify an interviewee or a location. Select a matte to frame part of a scene. Or you can use a bulleted list template to add such a list to your project.

Try it Yourself — Dissecting a Template's Text

In this task, my expectation is that you'll do lots of experimenting. I'm going to ask you to click on just about every title option and change just about every title characteristic. The purpose is to give you an idea of the breadth and power of the Adobe Title Designer. Here we go:

1. Open the Templates dialog box by clicking the Templates button highlighted in Figure 8.1.

2. As shown in Figure 8.2, open as many template folders and click through as many templates as you like. When you've seen enough, open the Lower Thirds folder, select lower third 1024_7, and click Apply.

By the Way — Why This Template?

I chose this particular template because it has a number of features, including four-color gradient, transparency, sheen, and outer strokes. I explain these in the upcoming steps.

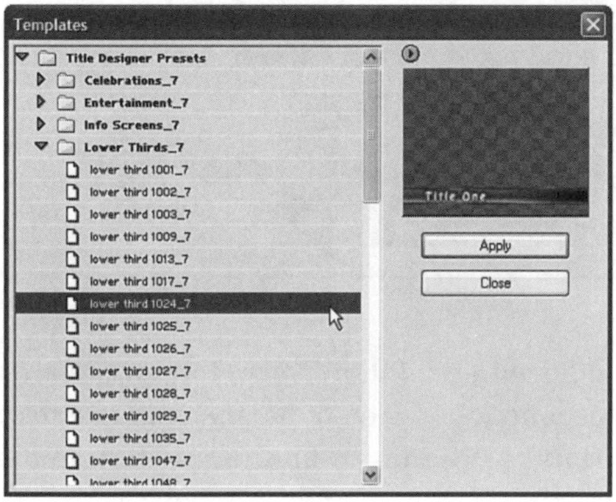

FIGURE 8.2
Use a template to see how to create titles.

3. Back in the Title Designer, click the Selection tool (the keyboard shortcut is V) and then hover it over the template. As you move it around, bounding boxes will appear, delineating the three elements of this title. Grab each box in turn and drag each element up the screen so you can see the template's components. Your screen should look like Figure 8.3.

FIGURE 8.3 ▼
Breaking a template into its constituent parts clarifies the title creation process.

4. Select Title One to display its bounding box with its eight sizing handles. That opens up its Properties listing in the Object Style window on the right side of the Title Designer window (see Figure 8.4). Note the various Properties' elements, including Font, Font Size, Slant, and Underline.

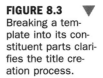

FIGURE 8.4
Selecting the template's Title One text opens its Properties listing.

5. Click on the Font drop-down list. Overwhelming, isn't it? To give you some clarity, select Browse from the top of that long list to open the dialog box shown in Figure 8.5. You can drag its top and bottom to see more fonts at once and select a new one if you want.

▼

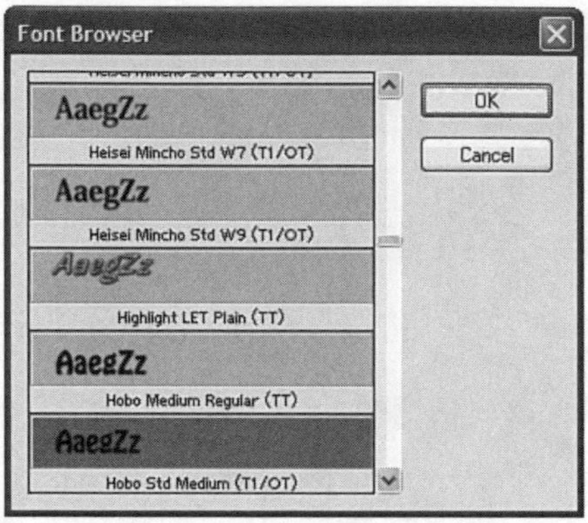

▼

FIGURE 8.5
Use the Font
Browser to get a
clearer picture of
what will work well
with your project.

6. Check the Small Caps and Underline check boxes to see how they work. Then select the numeric properties in turn and drag your cursor left and right to change their values noting the effect on the Title One text. Here is a brief rundown of what those items do:

   ▶ **Aspect** changes the width of the individual characters.

   ▶ **Leading** is the amount of space between lines of type. In the case of this template, there is only one line of type, so changing the Leading value has no apparent effect.

   ▶ **Kerning** changes spacing between characters' pairs.

   ▶ **Tracking** changes spacing between groups of characters.

   ▶ **Baseline Shift** moves selected characters vertically. It's useful when you want to use superscripts or subscripts.

   ▶ **Slant** adjust and angle of an object.

   ▶ **Small Caps, Small Caps Size, and Underline** are all self-explanatory.

   ▶ **Distort** stretches or shrinks text along either the X-axis, Y-axis, or both (to see it, click the disclosure triangle).

7. Click the Fill disclosure triangle to open that collection of Properties (see Figure 8.6). Click the Fill Type drop-down list and scroll through its options. I'll cover gradients in the next task. For now, select Bevel and experiment with the various options (Bevel gives each text character a 3D feel). You'll quickly see that the possibilities are endless. Clicking one of the color boxes opens the standard Premiere Pro color picker.

▼

FIGURE 8.6 ▼
Use the Fill properties to change the text's interior characteristics.

8. Click the Strokes disclosure triangle. This template's text has no inner strokes, but does have three outer strokes. Click the second Outer Stroke disclosure triangle (it has more features applied than the other two).

What Are Strokes?

Strokes is Adobe's term for inner or outer text or graphic borders. These strokes or borders have the same collection of properties available as are available for text and other Title Designer objects.

By the Way

9. To get a better feel for how strokes work, drag the corner handles of the Title One bounding box to expand it. To see additional stroke features, select Depth from the Type drop-down list and click the Sheen disclosure triangle. Your window should look something like Figure 8.7.

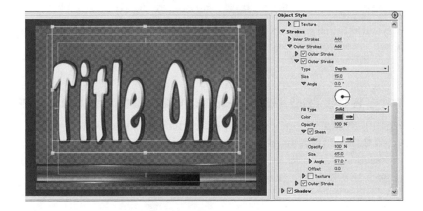

FIGURE 8.7
Strokes give outer or inner borders to text or graphic objects. Selecting Depth adds unique shading to those strokes.

▼

▼

10. Experiment with the size and angle of the outer stroke. By using Depth and a larger size, plus adjusting the angle, you can create true 3D text.

11. Sheen is a soft-edged color that typically runs horizontally through text or, in this case, through only the outer stroke. You can change that angle plus its size and where it's located in the stroke text by altering the size, angle, and offset. Check out Figure 8.8 for an example of how you can use all these stroke options.

FIGURE 8.8
How your text can look after giving it some depth and apply a sheen to its outer stroke.

12. Finally, as far as this Title One text goes, click the Shadow disclosure triangle to reveal its properties and click the Shadow Angle disclosure triangle to open that feature, too. You might note that Title One doesn't have an obvious shadow. That's because the shadow opacity is 100% and its size is only 2 points. Change all the characteristics to see how the Shadow feature works. Take a look at my example in Figure 8.9.

Everything is self-explanatory, with the exception of Spread. Increasing the Spread value softens the shadow.

▲

Working with the Template's Geometric Shapes

The lower-third template has two other elements: rectangles. The graphics artist who created this template used the Title Designer to make these as well. As with the text dissection, taking a look at why these shapes look the way they do will go a long way to showing you how to do it on your own.

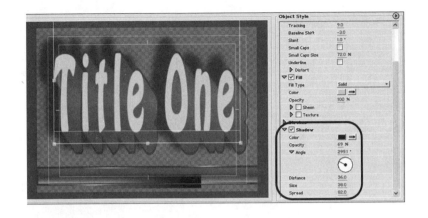

Dissecting a Template's Shapes

Shapes can have the same set of features that you can apply to text. In this task, I take a look at those features that were not used in the template's text line or were not used in an interesting fashion. Here's how these objects were put together:

1. Continue where you left off in the previous task. Either grab a handle of the Title One bounding box and drag it to shrink it and get it out of the way, or simply select it and press Delete. You can always start fresh by reopening the Templates dialog box and reselecting this or any other template.

2. Select the black rectangle. As shown in Figure 8.10, doing so opens its Properties display. It has very few properties, so I close the disclosure triangles for all the unused properties to clean up the workspace.

> **Why Use Only Black in a Four-Color Gradient?**
>
> The black rectangle gradually becomes transparent on its left side. This is a nice way to give text a slightly more dramatic look. To create that effect, use the four-color gradient's four **color stops**—the colors you set for each corner. In this case they are all black. Then apply transparency to the stop(s) of your choice (see step 3).

By the Way

3. To achieve that graduated transparency look, the Adobe graphics artist selected the upper and lower left color stops and then set their Color Stop Opacity values to 0%. Click on all the color stops and adjust their opacities to see how that works.

FIGURE 8.10
The black rectangle
has only a couple
properties of inter-
est: 4 Color
Gradient and Stop
Color Opacity.

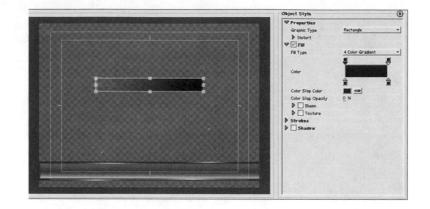

4. Drag the black rectangle out of the way (or delete it) and slide the
   yellow/brown rectangle into the workspace. Drag the bounding box corners
   to dramatically expand it. Take a look at its properties and you'll see it has
   a lot going on with it: 4 Color Gradient, Sheen, and two Outer Strokes. I
   expanded those outer strokes to better display the sheens applied to them.

FIGURE 8.11
This rectangle
(expanded to better
display its charac-
teristics) has two
outer strokes, each
with a sheen.

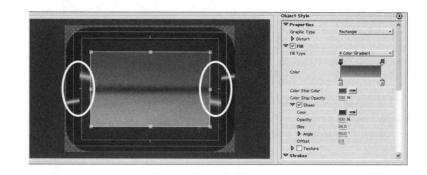

5. Double-click on each of the four color stop boxes around the 4 Color
   Gradient display. Note that each color is just slightly different than the
   other four and that the colors at the top are slightly darker than the bottom
   colors. This gives this rectangle some extra depth. Feel free to change the
   colors and reduce the opacities a bit.

Lift a Color from Your Video

Instead of using the Color Picker to change the color stop color (or any other colored item), use the Eyedropper tool to select a color from your video. To see the video, click the Show Video check box at the top of the Title Designer window. Move to a clip you want to use by clicking on the timecode and dragging left or right. Click the Eyedropper tool next to the color swatch and drag it into your video scene. Note that the eyedropper acts in real-time. The color in the 4 Color Gradient window (in this case) changes as you move around the video clip in the window.

6. Note the sheen running horizontally through the rectangle is a dark brown to complement the other colors. Change its color and angle to see what else works well.

7. Uncheck and recheck the two Outer Stroke check boxes to see how those two strokes look. Note that both are only 3-points wide and fall on top of one another. The artist used two as a means to apply two sheens to the box border.

Nothing Is Cut in Stone

As is the case in anything you do with Premiere Pro, you can always undo an editing step. In the case of the Title Designer, step back any number of steps by using the History palette (select Window→History), selecting Edit→Undo, or using the keyboard shortcut Ctrl+Z.

Did you Know?

8. Take a look at the Outer Strokes Sheens' properties. Note that the angle is 281 degrees for the first and 81 degrees for the second. That is, the sheen appears just a bit above the center line on one side and a bit below the center line on the other. If the sheens ran through the box, they'd form a flat X. This is a clever bit of visual artistry. When you're done experimenting, delete all the objects and text to create a clean slate for the next task.

Creating Text

Up to this point, you've worked with a template. In upcoming tasks, you'll create text from scratch. One admonition: As with video transitions, it's mighty tempting to go overboard and create text using some wild styles. The purpose is to make your text interesting but readable. Splashy, 3D-style text with sheens, strokes, and drop shadows can distract viewers from whatever message you're trying to get across. And if you're applying text over video or still images, you need to take care that the text stands out from the video without clashing with it.

The Adobe Title Designer offers three text creation approaches: anywhere within the title window, within a text box, or along a path. In each of those instances, as shown in Figure 8.12, you can orient your text horizontally or vertically.

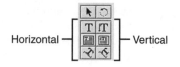

Here's an explanation of each type:

▶ **Point Text**—This style builds a text bounding box *as you type*. If you change the shape and size of the box after you stop typing, that action correspondingly changes the shape and size of the text. Stretching the box stretches the text.

▶ **Area Text**—In this case, you set the size and shape of your text box before entering text. After selecting this tool, you need to define your text boundary by dragging and dropping a box in the text window. Changing the box size later displays more or less text. It does *not* change the shape or size of the text.

▶ **Path Text**—You can build a path for your text to follow by clicking and moving your cursor around the text window. This is not an animation tool. It merely creates a line—albeit as contorted as you want—for the text to set on. You can use Path Text style to create something simple, such as a rainbow-shape curve of text. After it has been built, you can grab a path's handles to reshape it. And after adding text to a path, you can change its font size.

Try it Yourself

Create Point Text

If you've worked with just about any graphics program, you'll get the hang of manipulating text in the Adobe Title Designer. Here's how to get started:

1. Select the horizontal Text Tool (the capital letter T) or use the keyboard shortcut: T. Click anywhere in the Title Designer window on top of the grayscale checkerboard.

2. Clicking in the Title Designer window switches on the text property display. Click the Font drop-down list, select Browse, and select a wild font, such as Wingdings.

3. In the Premiere Pro main menu bar, select Title to open its drop-down menu (see Figure 8.13). Open the various wing menus to see what's offered. In this case, see to it that Word Wrap is checked. Also, note menu items that are not available in the Title Designer window:

   ▶ **Type Alignment** enables you to choose left, center, or right.

   ▶ **Word Wrap** means that as you type and reach the title-safe margin (the inner box defined by the thin white lines), the text automatically continues on the next line instead of running off screen to the right.

   ▶ **Tab Stops** opens a little window that enables you to state how far the cursor will move each time you click Tab.

   ▶ **Logo** enables you to add images or graphics to the Title Designer, either within a text box or as a separate object.

   ▶ **Select** is useful if there are several objects on top of one another and it's difficult to select a specific one.

   ▶ **Arrange** takes a selected object and moves it front or back one layer or all the way depending on the command you choose.

   ▶ **View** lets you choose whether to display the title-safe and action-safe boxes (both are on by default), the text baselines (the line that shows where the bottom of the text will run), and tab markers.

Title and Action Safe Zones

NTSC TV sets cut off the edges of the TV signal. How much they cut varies from set to set. To ensure that your text is completely within the edges of everyone's TV screens, keep your text within the title-safe zone (the inner box) and any action you want viewers to see within the action-safe zone. Despite this admonition, it's still okay to extend the background graphics, like the rectangular boxes used in the template earlier in this hour, to the edges of the screen to fill the frame for viewing on TV monitors and computer screens.

By the Way

---

4. Start typing. Because you selected Wingdings (or a nutty looking equivalent) and word wrap, you should get some crazy-looking text filling your screen within the confines of the title-safe area—something like what's shown in Figure 8.14.

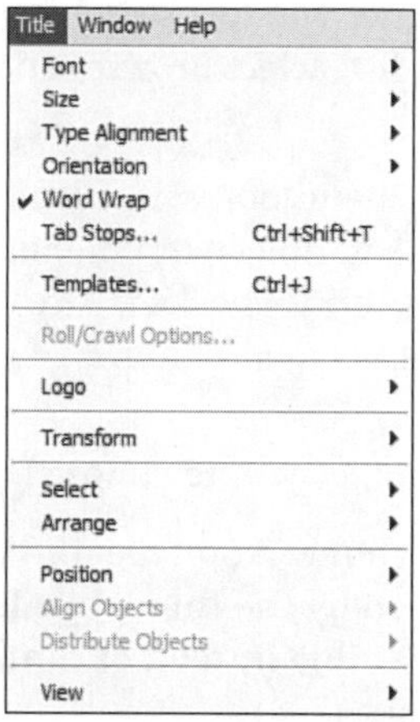

FIGURE 8.13
The Title menu offers additional Title Designer features.

FIGURE 8.14
Taking the Title Designer for a test drive with Wingdings.

5. Click the Selection tool (keyboard shortcut V) and click inside the text bounding box to switch on its handles. Move your cursor to the corners of the bounding box. As you approach each corner, the cursor turns into a double-arrow to indicate that you can stretch the box. But if you move the cursor a bit farther out of the box, it changes into a curved double-arrow like the one in Figure 8.15. Use that to spin the box to any angle you choose.

6. As you spin the box, look at the Transform section in the lower-right corner of the Title Designer window. I've highlighted it in Figure 8.16. Note how the Rotation values change.

More Than One Way to Move a Box

Instead of dragging bounding box handles, you can change values in the Transform window. Either type in new values or place your cursor on a value and drag left or right to set a new value. You will get immediate feedback as whatever object you selected adjusts its position as you change values.

By the Way

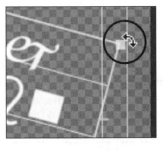

FIGURE 8.15
Move the cursor just outside the bounding box handles to turn it into a rotation tool.

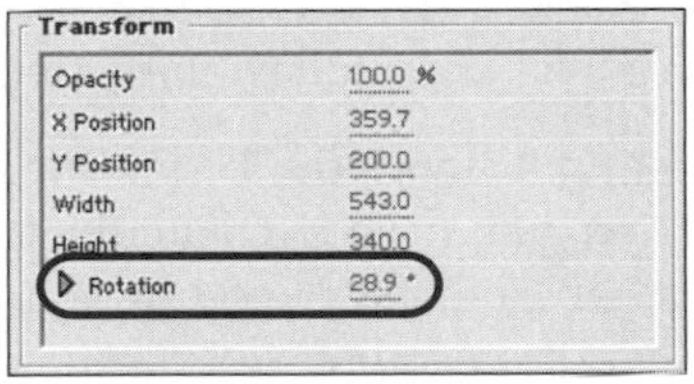

Transform	
Opacity	100.0 %
X Position	359.7
Y Position	200.0
Width	543.0
Height	340.0
▷ Rotation	28.9 °

FIGURE 8.16
As you rotate or move the box, note how the values change in the Transform widow.

7. Move the box around the text window and watch the X-position and Y-position change.

8. Finally, change the box shape and watch Width and Height values change.

Saving Text

At any point in your text creation process, you can save your work by selecting File→Save from the main menu bar. Doing that would normally save your project, but with the Title Designer window open, Premiere Pro saves your text.

Doing so places that new title in your Project window. Once there, you can drag it to a sequence either on a track above a clip or clips or on Video 1 to display as a standalone object.

Did you Know?

Reediting Text—Retaining a Style

After your text has been saved, you can always reedit it. If you create a unique text and graphic style that you think will help viewers recognize your productions or give them some consistency, you can simply change the wording in saved text files while retaining the style. This comes in very handy if you've created a standard way to superimpose locations or interviewees' names. Or you can save that text format as a style by selecting the text's bounding box, clicking the Styles wing menu triangle, and selecting New Style. Give your style a name, click OK, and it will appear as a two-letter icon in the Styles thumbnail collection.

In this case, there's no need to save this work, so delete all your text by clicking the Selection tool, clicking inside the bounding box, and pressing Delete. Alternatively, you can use the Text tool, drag it over the text to highlight it, and then press Delete or Backspace to remove all the selected text.

Try it Yourself   **Test the Area Text Style**

To experiment with the Area Text style, follow these steps:

1. Try Area Text by selecting its tool—the T in a lined box. In this case, *before* you can start typing text, you need to create the text bounding box. Position your cursor in the text window, click to set an upper-left corner to your bounding box, and then drag your cursor down and to the right to create the bottom-right corner.

2. Fill the box with text. You'll notice the first difference between Area Text and Point Text. Instead of expanding to accommodate more text, as the Point Text box did, the Area Type box has your type disappear off the bottom of the screen. Figure 8.17 demonstrates that.

3. If you expand the box, the text doesn't change shape or size, but the altered box reveals the text that ran outside the box's original confines.

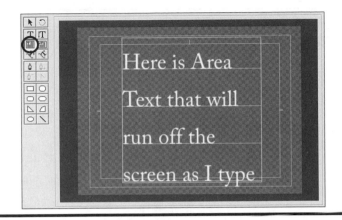

FIGURE 8.17 ▼
The Area Text
bounding box does
not expand laterally
to accommodate
more text. Rather,
your text runs down
and off the screen.

▲

Vertical Text

While you're doing your text testing, try the two vertically oriented text types. They're the two large T's with arrows pointing down. There really is hardly any difference between these two and their horizontal partners. True, as you type, the letters run from the top of the bounding box to the bottom, but they still display side by side, not standing on top of each other. The only difference is in the rotation. Instead of rotating on an axis at the center of the box, as do the horizontally oriented text tools, the vertical text boxes rotate on a point outside and above the boxes. Give that little feature a try.

Did you
Know?

Adding Motion and Putting Text on a Path

You've seen opening and closing movie and TV show credits hundreds of times. In Premiere Pro, that's **rolling text**—words that scroll vertically up or down the screen.

Also, you've seen news bulletins that slide horizontally along the bottom or top edges of the page. In the TV news business, we used to call them *Chyron crawls* after the once de facto industry-standard, text-creation tool (Chyron Corp. is still a major player in the graphics and TV production world). In Premiere Pro, they're **crawling text**.

In either case, they take only a couple additional text-creation steps to make.

Try it Yourself

Set Up Rolling Text

To set up rolling text, follow these steps:

1. In the upper-left corner of Title Designer interface, click the Title Type drop-down list and select Roll. I've highlighted this in Figure 8.18.

By the Way

> **A Scrollbar Appears**
>
> When you select Roll, the Title Designer adds a scrollbar on the right side of its window that enables you to view your text as it runs off the bottom of the screen. If you select the Crawl option, that scrollbar will appear at the bottom to enable you to view text running off the right edge of the window.

FIGURE 8.18
Title Type with Roll selected.

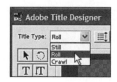

2. Click the Type tool (the capital T) instead of the Area Type tool. Type in your rolling text. If you don't press Enter and word wrap is on, you'll continue typing down the page. At the end of each line of text, you can press Enter to start a new line or let the word wrap take care of that for you.

3. When this is done, click the Roll/Crawl Options (next to the Title Type drop-down list) to open the dialog box shown in Figure 8.19 (alternatively, you can select Title→Roll/Crawl Options from the workspace's main menu bar). You have the following options (note that rolling text always moves *up* the screen):

   - **Start Off Screen**—Specifies whether the credits start completely off the screen and roll on
   - **End Off Screen**—Indicates whether the credits roll completely off the screen
   - **Pre-Roll**—Specifies the number of frames before the first words appear onscreen
   - **Ease-In**—Indicates the number of frames to get up to full speed when the first words appear
   - **Ease-Out**—Slows the credits down at the end

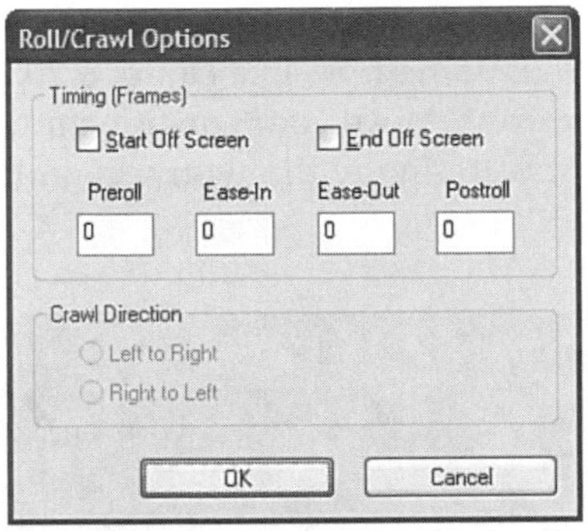

Roll/Crawl Options ☒

Timing (Frames)
☐ Start Off Screen   ☐ End Off Screen

Preroll   Ease-In   Ease-Out   Postroll
[0]   [0]   [0]   [0]

Crawl Direction
○ Left to Right
○ Right to Left

[OK]   [Cancel]

FIGURE 8.19
The Roll/Crawl Options dialog box enables you to control the timing of moving text and, in the case of crawling text, whether it moves from right to left or from left to right.

Creating Crawling Text

You create crawling text the same way as rolling text, only you start by selecting Crawl in the Title Type window. As you type, your text rolls off the right side of the text window. In this case, the scrollbar appears at the bottom of the text window, enabling you to see all your text.

Using the Path Tool

The Path Text tool is both elegant and tricky. It enables you to build simple or complex, straight and/or curved paths for your text to follow.

Text on a Path

Try it Yourself

If you've worked with the Pen tool in Adobe Photoshop, you know how to use the Path Text tool. Basically, you define a path by clicking a number of locations in the Title Designer window and dragging handles at each point to use to define the curves. Here's how it works:

1. Delete any text in the Title Designer window and select the Path tool (the T on a slope).

2. Click *and hold down the mouse button* anywhere in the text creation window. Drag the mouse to create long handles. You'll use these to define the curve's characteristics.

3. Click, hold, and drag somewhere else to create another anchor point and handles. The Title Designer automatically connects the two anchor points. Move the cursor to the handles. Your cursor will change to a black arrow—use it to drag the handles. Make them longer, shorter, or move them around to see how this works.

▼

4. Adjust the curve by clicking on the handle endpoints and dragging. Your text window should look something like Figure 8.20. You can add as many anchor points as you want. Move your cursor near the curve and it will change to a black arrow to signify that you can grab the curve and drag it to reshape it.

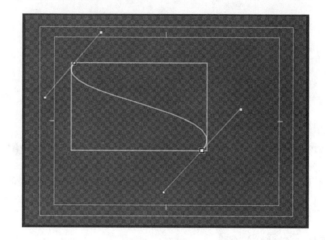

5. When you've finished your path creation work, change the cursor to the Selection tool (click the Arrow or press V), place your cursor somewhere inside the newly created bounding box, and click. Doing so places a text cursor at the beginning of the curved line. Type some text. That text will position itself on your line. I created a simple three-anchor point curve for Figure 8.21. It takes practice to perfect this technique, but if you give it a few tries, you'll get a basic idea how it works.

Did you Know?

Grabbing a Path Can Be Tricky

To change the shape of the curve means clicking on the path line—the little handles on the path or at the end of each handle's extension lines. It can be tricky to make those connections. Try one of these methods:

After setting all the path points, you can roll the cursor on that path, note when it turns into a black arrow, and grab the line or a handle to move it.

Or you can click the Selection tool, double-click in the path bounding box to redisplay the path line, and know that if you inadvertently click off the path, you will not create a new path point.

Did you
Know?

Other Pen Tools

When you use the Pen tool and click anywhere in the Title Designer window, you activate the three other Pen tool icons for the Add, Delete, and Convert Anchor Point tools. Select one and then click on any path point to make the respective changes.

FIGURE 8.21
The Path Text tool can create a twisting text display.

Creating Geometric Objects

If you've created shapes in graphics-editing software such as Photoshop or Illustrator, you know how to create geometric objects in Premiere Pro. Select from the various shapes to the left of the text window, drag and draw the outline, and release the mouse. The Line tool creates line segments and curves by using the same procedure you used with the Path Tool. Click to set a starting point and then drag and click to set the endpoint. Each segment has its own bounding box.

As you learned when working with templates, you can use the numerous properties to give your shapes special characteristics. In Figure 8.22, I drew a few shapes and added some gradients, various opacity levels, strokes, and shadows to demonstrate what you can do.

FIGURE 8.22
Some graphic objects created with gradients and various opacity levels.

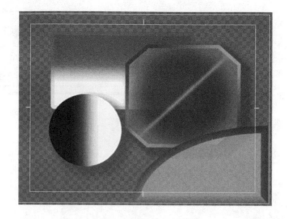

When you draw objects, they appear as solid white with no borders. Add a border with an inner or outer stroke.

Special Drawing Keyboard Shortcuts

If you want to create a square, circle, right triangle, or a square clipped rectangle (as opposed to a rectangle, oval, non-right triangle, or stretched clipped rectangle), hold down the Shift key when dragging the shape's border. If you want to maintain the aspect ratio for a shape you've already made, hold the Shift key before resizing that shape.

It's fairly easy to build layers of graphic objects and add text as well. You can send an object backward or forward by highlighting it, selecting Title→Arrange and then choosing from Bring to Front (that is, on top of all other objects), Bring Forward (on top of the next highest object), Send to Back (that is, make it the bottom/deepest object), or Send Backward (behind the next lower object).

Using transparent layers as backgrounds for supers is an excellent way to create a production studio or product line identity. When you have a look you like, save it as a style or save an entire text design, including graphics, and reuse it like a template.

Summary

Adding text or supers to your video project gives it another element and adds depth. Text sometimes can send a message much more succinctly and clearly than a narration. It can reinforce narrated information or remind viewers about the people in your piece and the message you're trying to convey.

The text tools in Premiere Pro are similar to those in standard graphics/text programs, with several extra features tossed in. The infinite customizability of your text's appearance means that you can create a look unique to your productions.

Q&A

Q *When I resize my text bounding box, the text changes shape and size. How do I change the box without changing the contents?*

A You're using Point Text, Premiere Pro's default text style. Instead, select the T in the lined box (Area Text), drag and drop a text bounding box, and start typing. If you need to increase the size of the box, the text will remain the same shape and size.

Q *I want to make a circle in a square, but all I get are ovals in rectangles.*

A You need to hold down the Shift key before you define the size of the quadri-lateral or round figure. Doing that keeps all sides equal and forces your oval to be a circle.

Workshop

Quiz

1. How do you keep text from running outside the viewable area on a typical NTSC TV set?

2. There are too many typefaces! How can you wade through all that and quickly find one that works for you?

3. How do you create a rectangle with a gradient inside it and a two-color border?

Quiz Answers

1. Use the Title Safe Zone option, which is accessible in the Title menu or in the Monitor menu for viewing in the Source and Program Monitors. If you select the Word Wrap option, the Title Designer automatically keeps all text within the title safe zone as you type.

2. Browse. Go to Title→Font→Browse and scroll all the font samples. Or click the Font drop-down list and select Browse.

3. Open the Title Designer. Create a rectangle by selecting the Rectangle tool and clicking and dragging within the text window to define a rectangle. In the Properties window, click the Fill disclosure triangle, select Linear

Gradient from the Fill Type drop-down list, and select two colors in turn. Select Strokes, Inner and Outer Stroke, in turn, and give each inner and outer border a color and other characteristics to suit you.

Exercises

1. Create rolling credits with different font sizes and text alignments. Main headings could be aligned left and individuals' names centered.

2. Make a rainbow using the Line tool. Click one side of the text window and then click the other, making a straight line. Then drag the center handle to make a curve. Repeat this three or four more times and color each line to create a rainbow look. Now add text along another arc over the rainbow. Do you feel a song coming on?

3. Create a three-layer collection of rectangles with varying transparencies and drop shadow values. Create the three rectangles by dragging and dropping them in separate locations. Make the large one opaque (100% opacity) with a drop shadow of 50% opacity, the middle one 40% opacity with a drop shadow of 20% opacity, and the small one 25% opacity with a drop shadow of 30% opacity. Then select colors and gradients that give a contrast so that you can see one through the other. One other suggestion: Give one or two of the rectangles a Repeat value to create parallel lines to make them stand out even more. Also, pick a drop shadow that is similar in color to the object on which the shadow falls.

4. Watch TV news stories and note how their interview supers look. Attempt to emulate those styles by creating a standard interviewee super with one font, two text sizes (larger for the name, smaller for the title), a colored line running between the two text lines, and three overlapping and transparent boxes on the left, acting as a unique production studio identifier. Make sure that you save this—you actually might want to use it.

HOUR 9

Advanced Editing Techniques and Workspace Tools

What You'll Learn in This Hour:

- ▶ Adding a professional touch to your project
- ▶ Playing clips backward, changing speed, and freezing frames
- ▶ Adding cutaways
- ▶ Rolling, slip, and slide edits
- ▶ Special transitions: masks and gradient wipes
- ▶ Editing tips from an expert—John Crossman

I believe that you should start specializing only after you learn the fundamentals. If all a basketball player practices is a spinning, reverse, wrong-handed flip shot, he'll make no more than a bucket a game. Not many opportunities for that shot arise.

By now, given enough practice, you might have mastered straightforward Premiere Pro cuts-only editing techniques. You've worked with transitions and all their options, and have created text and geometric shapes.

That being the case, this hour ramps up those fundamental techniques a bit. I explain some standard professional editing concepts, show you some other ways to manipulate clips, go over some time-saving editing tools, and explain two higher-end transitions. Finally, I believe in learning from experts. The best video editor I've worked with offers up his advice at the conclusion of this hour.

Adding a Professional Touch to Your Project

One reason to use the video shooting tips in Hour 2, "Camcorder and Shooting Tips," is to open up more creative opportunities during editing. Right now you're doing fundamental, simplified editing, but trying out some standard professional editing techniques will help as we move to more complex editing later.

Using Establishing Shots

Do you have establishing shots? As I mentioned in Hour 2 you need them to let viewers know where they are. Try to place establishing shots near the beginning of any new setting or location.

Using Matching Shots

If you shot any repetitive action, look for matching shots. You might have a wide shot of someone typing at her computer and a tight shot of that person's hands on the keyboard. Edit them together and make sure you avoid jump cuts. The person in the wide shot might take her hands off the keyboard for a moment. If the tight shot is of her hands *on* the keyboard, make sure that you trim the wide shot to the point where the person still has her hands on the keyboard.

Using Wide and Tight Shots

These shots add interest. You might have a wide shot of a football game with the quarterback barking out signals. The next edit could be a tight shot of his face. You could have shot these two clips during two different plays, but by editing them back-to-back, they appear to be one play.

Sequences

This is a great way to build interest. The fish shops at Seattle's Pike Place Market provide a nonstop sideshow full of repetitive action. Most videographers would opt for a medium shot or two. Instead, put together a sequence of a tight shot of hands grabbing a fish from the display case, a medium shot from behind the shopkeeper as he tosses the fish to an employee, that employee catching the fish and placing it on a scale, and so on. Look for sequences like that in your raw video. Build your sequences well by using tight and wide shots and matching shots.

Cutaways

Avoid putting two very similar shots together. Two wide shots of the same soccer game, for instance. Instead, between the two wide shots edit in a cutaway—a crowd shot, a parent shouting encouragement, or the scoreboard—to avoid creating a viewer disconnect. The same holds true for interviews. If you "butt together" two bites from the same interviewee, put a cutaway between them—a hand shot or a reverse cutaway of the interviewer.

Resolving Cutaway Audio Conflicts

When using cutaways, you usually lay only video over the edited video and audio clips. For instance, if you use a reverse cutaway of an interviewer during a sound bite, you don't want to hear whatever sound is on that cutaway clip. But in the case of the soccer parent shouting encouragement, you do want to mix both the shout and the original game natural sound. The techniques in this hour's "Adding News-Style Cutaways" section covers the first method. I leave the audio cutaway to Hour 13, "Editing Audio."

Playing Clips Backward, Changing Speed, and Freezing Frames

By the time you finish this section, you'll know how to create a video sequence that incorporates all three of these concepts.

Going in Reverse and Altering Speed

First, two fun and simple techniques: playing a clip backward and changing its speed. Consider the possibilities. Kids diving *out* of a pond, a pitcher *retrieving* his fastball, and a reverse replay of an explosive building demolition. Combine that with slow-motion or speed things up and you can add drama or humor.

Play a Clip Backward and Change Clip Speed

Try it Yourself

You can apply both effects within the same dialog box. This small interface updates a less user-friendly process in previous versions of Premiere. It now packs a lot of fun into a small package. Here's how it works:

1. Select any clip, either on a sequence or in the Project window.

2. Right-click on that clip to open the context menu and select Speed/Duration. As shown in Figure 9.1, that opens the Clip Speed/Duration dialog box. Here are its features:

▼

> ▶ **Speed**—set a percentage of the original clip speed here. 200% doubles the speed, whereas 50% slows things down by half. As you change the percentage, the duration changes as well. 200% cuts the duration in half.
>
> ▶ **Link/Unlink**—If you want to retain the length of the clip on the sequence, but want to change its speed, click this icon to unlink the percentage with the duration.

Unlink Doesn't Always Work

Premiere Pro can override your unlink command. That happens when you increase the clip speed and there aren't enough unused head or tail frames to accomplish the change without changing the duration.

Doubling the speed normally shortens the clip by half. To keep the clip the same length, Premiere Pro uses those head or tail frames to fill in the clip length. If there aren't enough head or tail room frames, Premiere Pro behaves as if the Link icon were unbroken and changes the clip length accordingly.

> ▶ **Reverse Speed**—Does what it says: plays the clip backward at whatever speed you set. It also plays the audio backward. You can disassociate that audio by *unlinking* it from the video (not to be confused with the Link/Unlink feature in the Clip Speed/Duration dialog box). In this case, you're unlinking the audio and video elements of an A/V clip. I explain that in the next task.
>
> ▶ **Maintain Audio Pitch**—This is a very clever feature. When audio speeds up, it normally sounds like Alvin and the Chipmunks. When it slows down, it's a slow drawl. Maintaining the audio's pitch means that the audio changes speed, but keeps the original pitch.

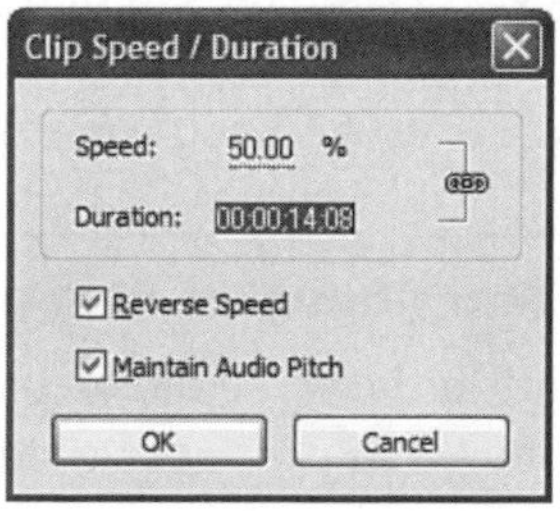

FIGURE 9.1
You can dramatically change the nature of your video using this simple Clip Speed/Duration dialog box.

▼

Rapid-Fire Narrations

The Maintain Audio Pitch feature is great if you want to speed up an announcer's voice to fit his copy into that end-of-commercial disclaimer common to car financing commercials.

3. Take a look at how Premiere Pro displays your altered clips on the sequence. Previous versions of Premiere changed the clip name by adding a reference to the new clip speed. Premiere Pro doesn't do that. But as shown in Figure 9.2, if you hover your cursor over the clip, a pop-up message indicates the new speed percentage.

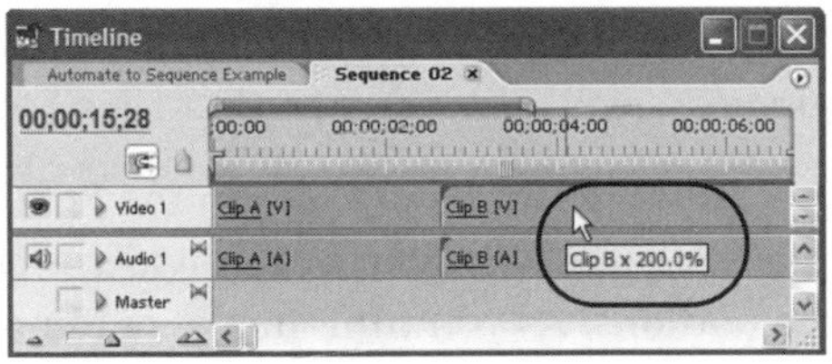

FIGURE 9.2
When you hover your cursor over a speed-altered clip, Premiere Pro displays its new rate.

Rate Stretch Tool

You can forgo the dialog box approach to changing a clip's speed. Use the Rate Stretch tool (the fifth tool down on the Tools palette). You can use it only on clips that have no clips adjacent to them on the right. And the audio automatically adjusts accordingly with the associated pitch change. It is an imprecise tool, but it's an easy way to stretch a clip to exactly fill a gap.

4. Check your work by playing the clip either by dragging it from the Project window to the Source Monitor screen or by playing it from the sequence. Use the keyboard shortcut—the spacebar—to see it play in real-time.

Getting That Slow-Mo Music Video Look

You've seen those MTV videos of vocalists lip-synching their tunes while loping in slow-motion on a beach. How, you ask, can they apply slow-motion and still have the lip-synch work right?

The video director makes a speeded-up version of the song and plays it while shooting the video. So, the singer lip-synchs at a faster rhythm. Then the video editor slows down that video to match the beat of the original tune.

For example, if you use Premiere Pro to speed up the original tune to 150% of its original speed, you'll need to play back the video at 66.67% to get it to synchronize to the original tune. Cool.

If the math isn't clear, here's a different take:

Use the Clip Speed dialog to change the duration and don't worry about the speed percentage. Just shorten it so that the percentage is about 150% (fast enough to create a slow-mo look without making your singer go into a frenzy to keep up). When you drop the video you made using the speeded-up song into the sequence, use the Duration setting to lengthen it to match the original clip length. The speed should read about 68% in this case.

Unlinking Clips

If you have audio associated with the clip, any speed or reverse direction applied to the video portion of the clip changes the audio accordingly. You can override that by *unlinking* that audio.

All video clips that have audio appear as one clip in the Project window, but when you place them on a sequence, Premiere Pro divides them into their constituent video and audio portions. As you trim, move, or remove them, the video and audio act in concert. If you want to deal with them independently, unlink them.

Did you Know?

Unlink for Cutaways

Unlinking audio also comes in handy when you add cutaways to your piece. I discuss that general editing style in Hour 17, "Compositing Part 1—Layering Images and Clips." In this hour's "Adding News-Style Cutaways," I show you a different way to add a cutaway without adding its associated audio.

Try it Yourself

Unlinking Audio and Video

▼

Unlinking and relinking video and audio is a bit nonintuitive. Especially if, after unlinking the audio, you move it to some other place, and then want to link it back up to the original video and have the audio and video get back into synch. Here's how you do all of that:

1. Take a look at Figure 9.3. Clip A is linked and clip B is *unlinked*. You can tell because clip A is underlined, and clip B is not. The unlinked clip B also loses its video (V) and audio (A) designators.

▼

2. To unlink a linked A/V clip, right-click on that clip to open the context menu shown in Figure 9.4 and choose Unlink Audio and Video.

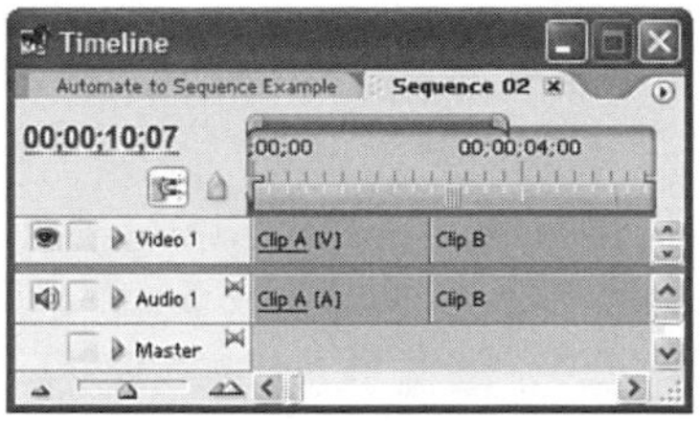

FIGURE 9.3 ▼
Clip B is unlinked (meaning that you can edit its audio and video portions independent of each other). Unlinking a clip changes the appearance of its name in a sequence, removing the underline and (V) and (A) notations.

FIGURE 9.4
To unlink a clip, right-click on it and select Unlink Audio and Video.

3. That simple right-click and select action doesn't quite finish the job. As long as both clips are highlighted, they'll continue to act as if they were linked. To finish the task, click anywhere in the sequence besides on the video or audio portion of the formerly linked clips. That deselects them so that you can change the video speed without affecting the audio.

Unlink Keyboard Shortcut

There is a handy keyboard shortcut that enables you to briefly unlink audio and video so that you can trim either one while keeping both in synch. Hold down Alt as you make that trim. This greatly simplifies what used to be a kind of complex process to make what are called *J and L cuts*. I explain both in Hour 13.

▼

4. Drag an unlinked audio or video segment away from its formerly linked sibling. The two are now out of synch, but Premiere Pro does not note that in any way.

5. To relink and re-synch those two unlinked clips, select both clips by clicking on either the audio or video clip and then Shift+clicking on the other clip. Right-click on either one to open the clip's context menu, and then select Link Audio and Video.

6. As shown in Figure 9.5, relinking the clips causes Premiere Pro to display a time box that notes how out of synch they are. It's easy to re-synch them—that is to slide either the audio or video segment so that it realigns with its partner and makes the audio synch up properly with its associated video. Choose which clip you want to move, right-click the time code display, and choose Move into Synch. That moves that clip so that it lines up with the other clip.

▲

Watch Out!

Re-Synch Caveats

Two things: If you trimmed either the video or audio portion of this relinked clip, the clips will line up to synch the audio so that the ends are not flush. In addition, the portion of the clip that moves does an overlay edit by default, so it'll cover up whatever is on its track at its new location.

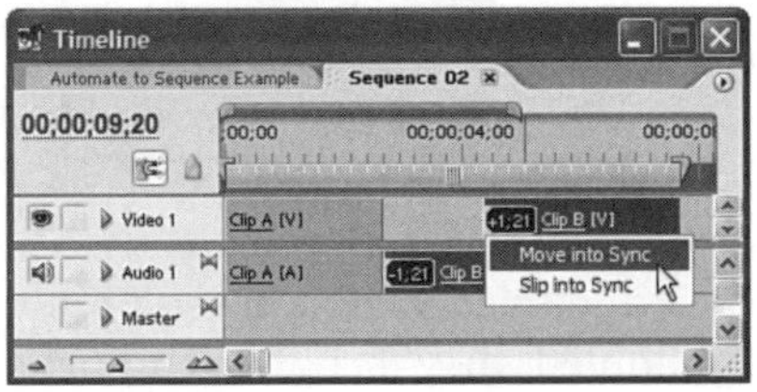

FIGURE 9.5
After relinking a clip (and before re-synching it) Premiere Pro displays how much the video and audio portions are out of synch.

Using Freeze Frames

If you want to create a sequence of clips that starts with a regular-speed clip, slows down, stops, shifts to a slow reverse, and finishes at full-speed reverse, you need to create a freeze frame (along with two razor edits).

You also can use a freeze frame as an effective way to close a segment or an entire production. Freeze the final frame and then fade to black. To do either, you first need to create a freeze—or *hold*—frame.

Working with Freeze Frames

To end a piece with a freeze frame and then a fade to black takes a few steps: clip trimming, copying, pasting, freezing, and adding a transition. The process to place a freeze frame in the middle of a series of clips takes a few more steps. Here's how to do both:

1. Place a clip on a sequence and trim its end to the frame you want to hold and then fade to black.

2. Right-click on that clip and select Copy.

3. Move the CTI to the end of your clip or just past the end.

4. Select Edit→Paste from the main menu. That places a copy of the original clip on the sequence, right after its twin clip.

No Right-Click Paste Option

I'm a big fan of right-click, context-sensitive menus. So, I fully expected to be able to right-click on an empty space on a video or audio track and see a context menu to enable me to paste the clip to the sequence. No such luck. Thus, the need to use the Main menu bar to do the Edit→Paste or the keyboard shortcut: Ctrl-V.

5. Right-click on that duplicate clip, select Rename and, as shown in Figure 9.6, give that clip a descriptive name. In my case: Freeze-Clip A.

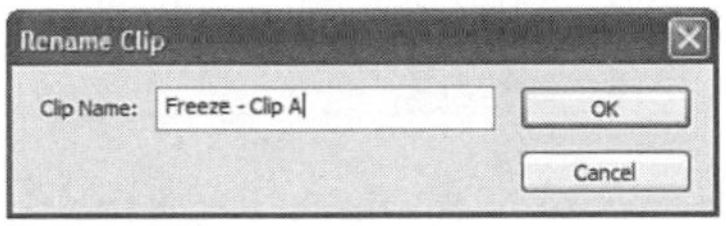

FIGURE 9.6
When creating a duplicate clip that you'll use as a freeze frame, give it a descriptive name.

6. Right-click on the duplicate clip and select Frame Hold. In the dialog box shown in Figure 9.7, check the Hold On box, select Out Point from the drop-down list, and click OK.

7. Now if you place the CTI over the first clip and press the spacebar to play the sequence, the video will get to the end of that clip and then play the next clip, which is a still image of the first clip's last frame. In other words, the video will freeze on the last frame of the first clip.

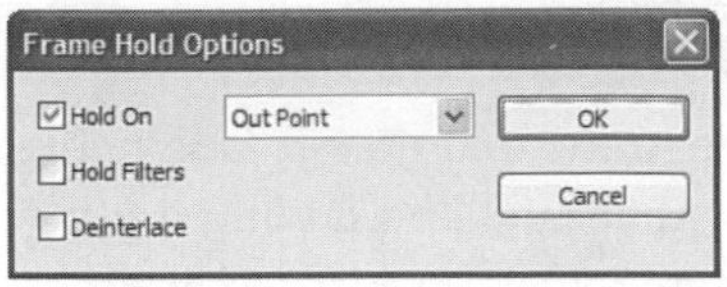

▼

FIGURE 9.7
Use the Frame
Hold dialog box to
create a freeze
frame; in this case,
using a clip's out-
point.

Watch
Out!

Trim After the Fact

If you want to trim the length of the duplicate clip, don't trim from the endpoint. If
you do, the freeze frame will change to match the new out-point. Here are two ways
to shorten a clip with a frame hold set to the out-point:

- ▶ Use the Ripple Edit tool (keyboard shortcut: B) to trim it from its in-point.
- ▶ Use the Selection tool to trim the still frame clip's *left* edge (creating a gap in
  the process), right-click on the gap, and select Ripple Delete to close that gap.

Did you
Know?

Fix the Audio

The audio for your duplicated clip will be the same as the original clip, even with a
Hold Frame applied. So, if you do nothing with the audio on the second clip, you'll
have an awkward moment as the audio from the first clip jumps back to its start
and plays again. I explain how to fix that in Hour 13. It involves unlinking the
audio/video of both clips, deleting the audio portion of the freeze-frame clip, dragging the right-edge of the audio from the original clip under the freeze frame, and
gradually fading it out.

8. To have that freeze frame fade to black, drag the Cross Dissolve transition to
   the end of the freeze frame. You can adjust the length of the Cross Dissolve
   in the Effect Controls window.

9. Here's a quick explanation of how to add a freeze frame in the middle of a
   clip (it uses many of the same steps you just completed). Find the frame to
   duplicate, use the Razor tool to cut the clip at that point, and right-click.
   Copy the portion of the clip to the right of the slice.

10. Slide the right-side clip out of the way, paste the duplicate in front of it, and
    rename that duplicate to something like Freeze A-2. Right-click the dupli-
    cate, select Frame Hold, check Hold On and In Point, and click OK. Your
    sequence should look something like Figure 9.8—a freeze frame in the mid-
    dle of a clip. You can adjust the length of that freeze frame by using the
    Ripple Edit tool on its out-point.

▼

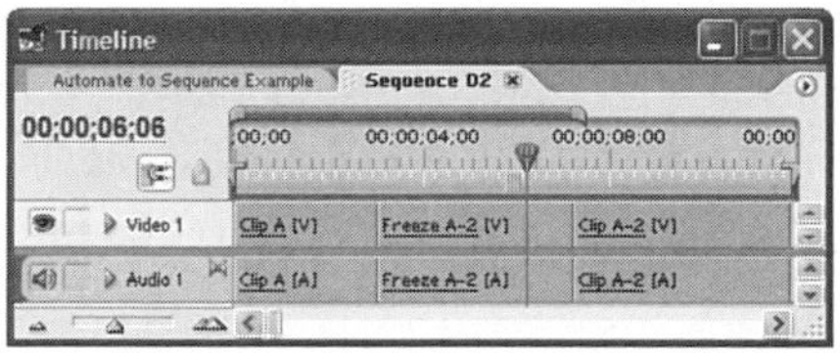

FIGURE 9.8
To add a freeze frame in the middle of a clip, slice that clip, duplicate the second half, place that duplicate between the two halves, and apply a Frame Hold to its in-point.

11. For a final bit of legerdemain, split the two outside clips and apply slow motion and reverse slow motion to them, respectively. I've labeled clips in Figure 9.9 to show you how this works. Delete the right-side clip (you'll replace it with the split opening clip). Move the freeze frame to the right to give the left clip enough room to expand when you apply slow motion to it. Use the razor to slice the first clip and apply slow motion to the right slice to ease into the freeze frame. Copy that right clip and paste it after the freeze frame. Apply reverse motion to it (it already has slow motion applied). Copy the first clip and paste it at the end. Apply reverse motion to it.

Mid-Clip Speed Change Can Be Abrupt

Slicing a clip to change its speed mid-clip is not all that elegant. What Premiere Pro does not let you do is to gradually change clip speed over time. This takes some real programming time and energy and did not make it into version one of Premiere Pro, but it might show up in the first upgrade.

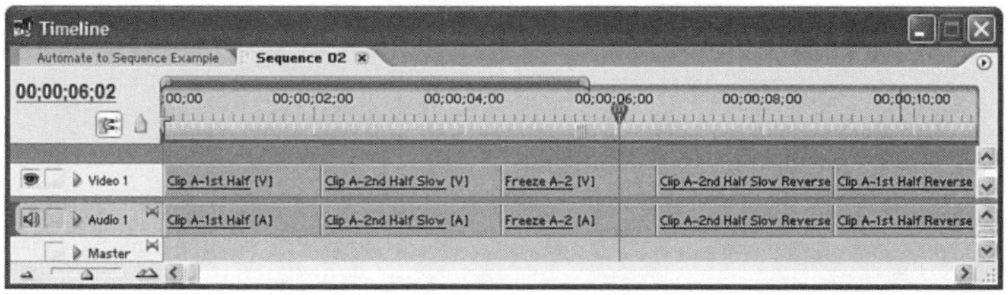

By the Way

FIGURE 9.9
Going from regular to slow-motion, to a freeze frame, and then reverse slow-motion and regular speed reverse motion takes several razor slices, speed changes, and clip copies.

Adding News-Style Cutaways

To see cutaways in action, simply watch some TV news stories. During some interviews, the view typically shifts to the interviewer listening intently. This is primarily used when the news reporter chose to butt-together two brief sound bites to make one longer one. The editor adds a cutaway there to avoid a jump cut. Or, if the story is about a football game, for example, the view might switch in the middle of a play to a tight shot of screaming fans and then switch back to the play itself.

Both of these edits are cutaways. The first would have no audio added, the second might mix the crowd audio with the audio from the play. The upcoming task deals only with the former: nonaudio cutaway. I leave adding cutaways with audio to Hour 13.

Try it Yourself   **Editing Cutaways**

This task uses the Source Monitor screen as a means to define the in-points and out-points for a cutaway and then to remove audio before you add the cutaway to your sequence. Here's how to do it:

1. Clear your sequence of clips or create a new one. Then add a clip to Video 1.

By the Way

> **My Cutaway Task**
>
> Because this task is simply for practice, you don't need to find the perfect cutaway nor the perfect place to edit it in. In this case, I'll show you how I did it with my magic show video. I shot a kids' magic show and want to insert a tight shot of one of the trick set-ups. I don't want to disrupt the audio flow, only insert a brief cutaway (three seconds typically works well).

2. Drag the video clip with the cutaway you want to use to the Source Monitor screen.

3. Locate that cutaway and mark its in-point and out-point using the brackets below the Source Monitor screen.

4. To edit in a video-only cutaway, click the Toggle Take Audio and Video button highlighted in Figure 9.10 and select the filmstrip icon. The other choices are video with audio—a filmstrip with a speaker—and audio-only—a speaker.

5. Move the CTI on the sequence to the frame where you want to place the cutaway.

6. Click in the Source Monitor screen and drag that to the clip on the sequence, using Snap to Edges to line up its in-point with the CTI edit line. Release the mouse. As a reminder, this is an *overlay* edit. It replaces whatever was on the sequence at that point and, in this case, does not add audio.

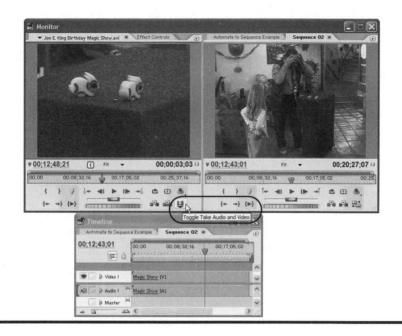

FIGURE 9.10 ▼
Set the in-points and out-points for your cutaway in the Source Monitor window and then tell Premiere Pro to edit in only video by selecting the highlighted filmstrip icon in the Toggle Take Audio and Video button.

What Happens If You Add Audio Too

If you had selected the audio/video option and dragged the clip from the Source Monitor screen to the clip on the sequence, it would have overlaid the audio portion of the selected clip as well. As I explain in Hour 17, the workaround for that is to add another audio track, target that track, and then use the Overlay button in the Source Monitor window instead of dragging the clip to the sequence.

Alternative Method to Find Edit Location

You don't have to mark the cutaway location with the CTI edit line. You simply can drag the cutaway to the clip and then drag it left or right, watching the split-screen in the Program Monitor to find a good location.

Rolling, Slip, and Slide Edits

You'll tap this set of editing tools when you want to preserve the overall length of your program. They come in handy for precisely timed projects such as 30-second advertisements.

In many cases, it might be easier to make individual edits and forgo these special tools, but it's good for any professional editor to know how to do rolling, slide, and slip edits. It can be a challenge to remember what each tool does (during one demo I attended, a Premiere Pro team member struggled in vain to remember which tool did what). So, here's a quick run-through. Table 9.1 provides a slightly different overview of these three specialized edits:

▶ Rolling edit—Rolls the cut point between two adjacent clips

▶ Slide edit—Slides the clip along its track in the sequence.

▶ Slip edit—Slips the in—and outpoints of a clip *without* moving it along its track.

TABLE 9.1   Rolling, Slide, and Slip Edits

Edit	Effect	Clip Length(s)	Clip(s) In/Out
Rolling edit	Changes the duration and in-points and out-points of two adjacent clips.	Changes	Changes
Slide edit	The selected clip remains unchanged, but out-points, in-points, and lengths of both adjacent clips are changed.	Unchanged	Unchanged
Slip edit	Changes only the selected clip's in-points and out-points.	Unchanged	Changes

Make Rolling, Slide, and Slip Edits

We'll start with the Rolling edit (the easiest of the three) and then move on to Slide and Slip edits. Here are the steps to follow:

1. Place three clips side by side on a sequence's Video 1 track. Make sure that all of them have plenty of head and tail frames to allow for the edits. The easiest way is to shorten each clip by dragging in the beginning and end (the in-points and out-points) with the Selection tool.

2. Select the Rolling Edit tool from the Tools palette (keyboard shortcut N). Move its cursor between the two clips that you want to edit. I've highlighted the Rolling Edit Tool palette icon and its edit-point cursor in Figure 9.11.

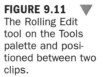

FIGURE 9.11 ▼
The Rolling Edit tool on the Tools palette and positioned between two clips.

3. What makes this Rolling Edit different from any you've done to this point is that you'll use the Program Monitor screen to make the edit. Click the Rolling Edit tool at the cut between the two clips and drag it in either direction. If you drag it left, you're shortening the first clip (clip A, in my example) and lengthening clip B. As shown in Figure 9.12, as you move the Rolling Edit tool, the monitor shows the new out-point and in-point of the adjacent clips.

Rolling Edits Change Adjacent Clip Lengths

Simply to confirm what you just experienced: The Rolling Edit tool preserves the overall project length, but *rolls* the out-points and in-points of two adjacent clips—shortening one clip while lengthening the other.

FIGURE 9.12
As you drag the Rolling Edit tool, use the Program Monitor to view the changing out-point and in-point of the two adjacent clips.

4. Switch to the Slide Edit tool and place it over the middle clip (not at an edit point) as shown in Figure 9.13.

5. Click on the middle clip and drag it left or right. Take a look at the Program Monitor screen shown in Figure 9.14. The two top images are the in-point and out-point of the selected clip. They will not change. The two larger images are the out-point and in-point of the adjacent (left and right, respectively) clips. As in a Rolling Edit, these edit points do change as you move the selected clip.

▼

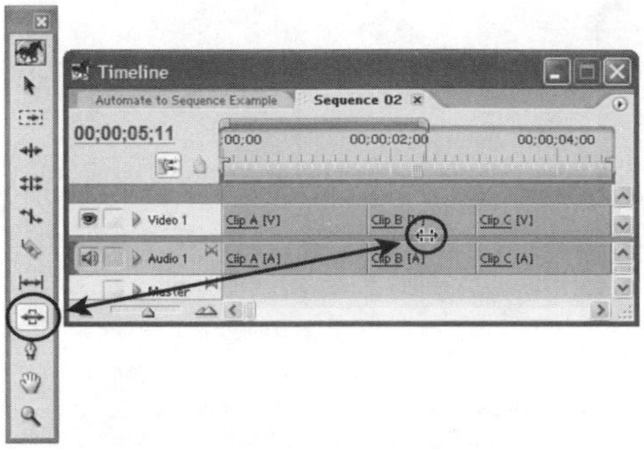

▼

FIGURE 9.13
The Slide Edit tool on the Tools palette and positioned on a clip.

FIGURE 9.14
As you drag the Slide Edit tool, the Program Monitor displays the changing out-point and in-point of the two adjacent clips and the unchanged selected clip's in-point and out-point.

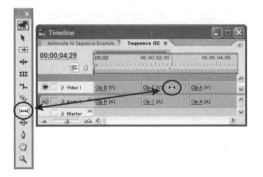

6. Switch to the Slip Edit tool and place it over the center clip (you can place it over any clip because it affects only the selected clip, but the center clip presents a more descriptive example). Use Figure 9.15 for reference.

FIGURE 9.15
The Slip Edit tool on the Tools palette and positioned on a clip.

7. Click on the middle clip and drag it left or right. Take a look at the Program Monitor screen shown in Figure 9.16. The two top images are the out-points and in-points of the two adjacent clips. They will not change. The two larger images are the in-point and out-point of the selected clip. These edit points change as you move the selected clip left or right.

▲

Using the Slip Tool at the Beginning or End

Although the Slip Edit tool is intended to adjust the in-point and out-point of a clip between two other clips, you can use it on the first or last clip of your piece. Give that a try to see how it works.

Did you Know?

FIGURE 9.16
As you drag the Slip Edit tool, the Program Monitor displays its shifting in-point and out-point, and the unchanged out- and in-points of the adjacent clips.

The Rolling, Slip, and Slide Edit tools work with both cuts-only edits and transitions. However, I recommend you remove any transitions before using these tools and then reapply those transitions to make sure that they work the way you expected. One example: You might have created a transition with a move that starts at a specific point in clip A and moves to a point in clip B. Those start points and endpoints will likely shift as you make adjustments using a rolling, slip, or slide edit.

Creating Special Transitions

Back in Hour 7, "Adding Transition Between Clips," I skipped two of the more-involved transitions: Image Mask and Gradient Wipe. I'll run them by you here.

Using the Image Mask Transition

This is more like a special effect than a transition. Basically, you use any image—black-and-white, grayscale, or full color—as a means to display part(s) of clip A and part(s) of clip B at the same time.

For instance, you might want to display part of an image in the sky of another image or have a clip play in a frame on a wall or through a window. In each case, you'd create a black mask to match the area where you want the video to show through the first video.

Clip A shows through the black area of your image (or any part of it that is 50% or more gray), and clip B shows through the white area (or any part that is less than 50% gray). To reiterate, when using the Image Mask transition, Premiere Pro sees the mask only as black or white. Even if you use a mask with color, Premiere Pro makes the transition by converting the color image to grayscale and then calculating which portions are more or less than 50% gray.

To do this, you'll need a mask. To get some hands-on experience, I'd suggest you make a rudimentary mask using a tool such as Microsoft Paint or Premiere Pro's Title Designer. Create your mask and save it on your Premiere Pro scratch disk.

Figure 9.17 shows how a mask might look. It's basically a stark black-and-white graphic. Remember that the black area lets that part of clip A show through, and the white area displays that section of clip B.

FIGURE 9.17
A rudimentary mask created in Microsoft Paint for use with the Image Mask transition.

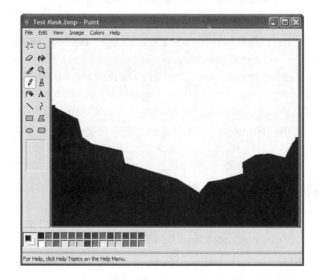

 Create an Image Mask Transition

To create an Image Mask transition, follow these steps:

1. Delete the three video clips from your sequence or create a new sequence.

2. To make it clear how the Image Mask transition works, I'd like you to make two color mattes—solid color graphics that you can use as clips in your project. As shown in Figure 9.18, click on the New Item icon in the Project window and select Color Matte (or right-click on any blank space in the Project

window to open the context menu and select New Item→Color Matte). Select a color from the Color Picker and give your matte a descriptive name. Do that again for a distinctly different color.

Color Mattes Are Useful Objects

Now that you know about how to make color mattes, consider using them in your projects. For instance, use them if you want a simple color background for text or for pictures-in-pictures.

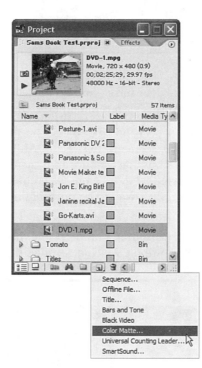

FIGURE 9.18
Create color mattes by clicking the New Item button.

3. Drag each matte to the Video 1 track of your sequence. Your sequence should look like Figure 9.19.

4. Locate the Image Mask transition in the Special Effect folder in the Effect palette's Video Transitions folder and drag it to the edit point between the two mattes. This pops up a small Image Mask Settings dialog box, as illustrated in Figure 9.20. This is a tad confusing because you'd expect to see a standard Transitions Settings dialog box with a Custom button instead (we'll get to that dialog box in a moment).

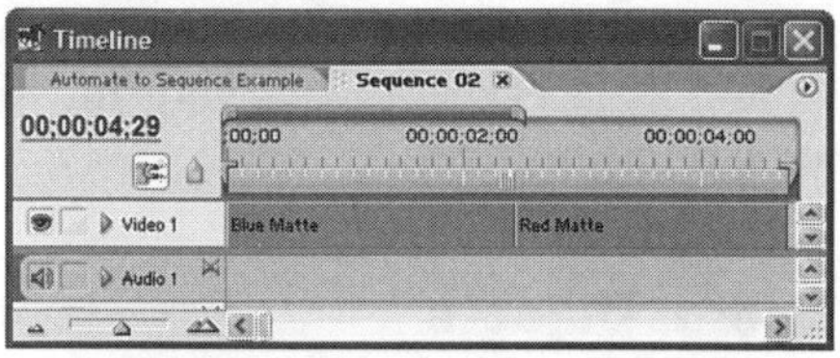

▼

FIGURE 9.19
The Image Mask transitions sequence setup.

FIGURE 9.20
The preliminary Image Mask Settings dialog box.

5. Click Select Image, locate your mask, and double-click it. When this brings you back to the Image Mask Settings dialog box, click OK.

6. Now open the Effect Controls window and click on the purple Image Mask transition rectangle on the sequence to select it. Ah-ha. This looks more familiar (see Figure 9.21), but you'll notice that there is no A and B preview window, there's only a window that combines both clips. Although this is called a transition, it's really a way to let parts of one clip show through on another.

7. You can give your mask transition a border. Note that whatever portion of the original Image Mask graphic was black shows the A clip and whatever was white shows the B clip.

▲

FIGURE 9.21
The actual Image Mask Effect Controls window settings.

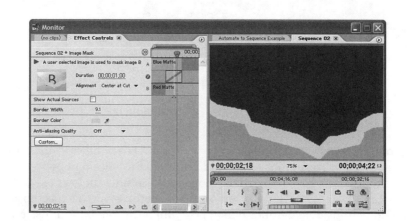

As with most transitions, if you click the down arrow, you'll switch how Premiere Pro performs this transition. Instead of letting clip A show through the black portion of your mask, clip A now shows through the white and clip B shows through the black.

Creating a Gradient Wipe Transition

This is more like what you'd expect to see in a transition. It works like the Image Mask transition in that it lets parts of clip A and clip B display together using a custom mask, but the Gradient Wipe transition actually moves from one scene to the next using a smooth animation. It's like other Wipe transitions, but in this case you control the shape of the edge.

In a reversal of the Image Mask transition, clip B shows through the black area, whereas clip A shows through the white area. Also, in this case, Premiere Pro does see things as gray—gradually. As the transition progresses, the gray areas darken and more of clip B shows through until at the end of the transition only clip B is onscreen.

As in the previous task (the Image Mask transition), I suggest that you create a grayscale gradient mask. Figure 9.22 shows a very rudimentary example using black, two grayscale areas, and white.

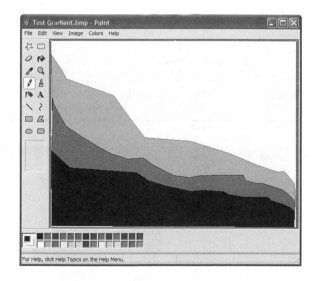

FIGURE 9.22
A rudimentary grayscale mask created in Microsoft Paint for use with the Gradient Wipe transition.

Try it Yourself   Create a Gradient Wipe Transition

To create a Gradient Wipe transition, follow these steps:

1. Return to your timeline and replace the Image Mask transition with the Gradient Wipe transition (it's in the `Wipe` folder).

2. This, too, pops up a little preliminary Gradient Wipe Settings dialog box, as shown in Figure 9.23. Click Select Image, locate your gradient graphic, and double-click it.

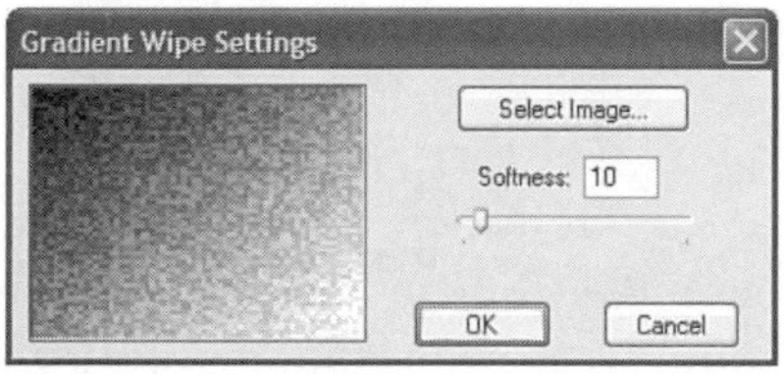

FIGURE 9.23
The preliminary Gradient Wipe Settings dialog box.

3. This returns you to the preliminary Gradient Wipe Transition dialog box. Select a Softness setting (this smoothes sharp edges in your gradient graphic). Click OK.

4. As with the Image Mask transition, click the transition on the sequence to display its settings in the Effect Controls window. As shown in Figure 9.24, this display has all the trappings of a real transition, including separate A and B clip windows.

5. Click Show Actual Sources and drag the slider under clip A to see how this transition works. As you move the slider, Premiere Pro is in effect making the Image Mask graphic darker and letting more of clip B appear in the increasingly black areas of the graphic you created for this transition.

FIGURE 9.24
The Gradient Wipe transition works like other transitions with the extra feature of a user-created gradient graphic.

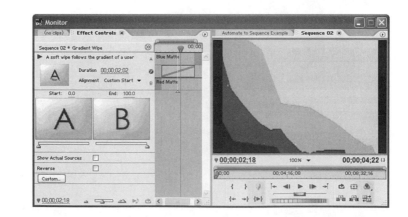

Similar to the Image Mask transition, you can change how this transition works by clicking, in this case, the R button. This starts the transition from the top instead of the bottom.

Sequence and Project Window Label Colors

As you've worked with the Project and Timeline windows, you might have noticed that objects in both windows follow a certain color scheme (Adobe favors pastels). Those colors are customizable. Here's a rundown of the default color scheme:

▶ Video-only clips are blue.

▶ Audio-only clips are green.

▶ Linked or formerly linked video/audio clips are cyan.

▶ Graphics or mattes are violet.

▶ Sequences are gray.

▶ Red bar(s) near the top of a sequence indicate segments that need rendering before the project is completed.

▶ Project window bins are orange.

The one small flaw is that there is no distinctive color for the unlinked portions of a formerly linked A/V clip.

In any event, if the pastels don't resonate with you, you can change the color scheme by selecting Edit→Preferences→Label Colors. Then select new colors using the Color Picker. Associate those new colors with their labels by selecting Label Defaults from the same Preferences dialog box.

Editing Tips from an Expert—John Crossman

Forever seared in my brain is one edit. It was in my first "magazine" piece for KSL-TV in Salt Lake City. This was back in the mid-1980s. The national Radio and Television News Directors Association had just named KSL the TV news station of the year—an honor that KSL would win an unprecedented two years in a row. KSL had the highest-rated (by percentage of viewers) news shows in the country. It was a TV news powerhouse. I had just moved there from a medium-sized market and was in awe of the professionalism, the scope of the news operation, and the array of high-tech goodies.

Buried deep in the editing bays was something akin to the command center of the Starship Enterprise. At its helm was John Crossman, KSL's chief editor. For me, having come from a station with *no* editors (the photographers did all the editing), this was a tad overwhelming. One of my first assignments was a long feature story on a local piano manufacturer. I'd never done a magazine-style piece and handed John a straightforward news-style voice-over. He barely batted an eye.

A couple hours later he called me into his realm wanting to show me how the piece was coming together. It sang. It danced. It had rhythm. I was confounded. The segment ended with a Billy Joel piano crescendo followed by a loud "clip" of a wire cutter snipping a piano string. I looked at John and at all his whiz-bang electronics and said one of the dumbest comments I've ever muttered in my TV career: "This equipment is amazing!" Fortunately, he forgave me my egregious error and we got on famously after that.

John spent eight years at KSL and now runs Crossman Post Production (www.xman-post.com) just outside of Salt Lake City. He provides video editing, graphics, and computer-generated animation for a lengthy list of corporate, educational, and broadcast clients. He's won five regional Emmys, 26 national Tellys, and a slew of other awards.

John is a wonderfully talented guy who has a true passion for the art of editing. Here are his editing tips.

To begin, good editors need certain basic talents:

- ▶ **Rhythm**—Life has a rhythm, so does editing. If you can't feel it, it's very hard to learn.

▶ **Visualization**—Good editors can see the completed project before they start. The actual editing is just the detail work. The images are already completely edited in their minds.

▶ **Patience**—Even when you can see it in your mind's eye, you'll have to make compromises on every project. The true test of an editor is whether he can make compromises work well. The best editors make it look like every single choice was the best choice.

▶ **Positive attitude**—Your attitude will go a long, long way toward determining your success. You'll spend numberless hours editing in a small dark space, usually on a deadline, and always with budget pressure, client pressure, spouse pressure...you name it. And the better the attitude, the better the job will go.

▶ **Team player**—You're part of a team. Try not to criticize the other members. Remember, you didn't have your eye in the viewfinder when the bomb went off. Thinking you could have had that shot when you're looking at the tape hours and miles away is easy, but not productive. Let the producer say, "I wish he had gotten closer." You say, "Well, let's do it this way and it will still work." That's where the editor earns his money, his reputation, and his loyalty.

To edit well, you need to do the following:

▶ **Use motivation and logic.** This is the most important concept in editing. Your editing should be motivated. You should have a reason for the shots you select and the order in which you select them. There should be a purpose to why you dissolve, why you use a wipe, as well as why you cut. Your goal is to communicate clearly what has happened. Your shot selection and the time spent on each shot should reinforce the narration while conveying information.

▶ **Plan as you digitize.** As you digitize the video, you should see in your mind's eye how the pictures are going to line up to get you to where you want to be at the end. Is the shot a great scene-setter (beginning)? Is it incredibly beautiful (possible ending shot)? Is it self-explanatory or incomprehensible (possible cutting-room floor material)?

▶ **Build new skills.** If you're in the professional ranks, or want to be, you must budget a considerable amount of time and money toward keeping current. At the very least, you're going to need to learn about how to incorporate graphics, animation, compositing, and special effects into your editing to serve the demands of your clients.

▶ In the world of broadcast television, you are surrounded by people who know how to create good stories. In corporate production, you might be working with someone who has no clue. At this point, you become 90% teacher and 10% editor. Your attitude will win you a loyal client or lose you a lifetime customer.

▶ Like music in a movie, good editing helps communicate your message and shouldn't really stand out to the viewer. The editing is not the message, but the editing can make the message work, not work, or work better than it should.

Summary

Professional video editors have a handful of editing tricks up their sleeves: establishing shots, wide and tight, sequences, and cutaways. Editors are so accustomed to adding these nifty touches to their projects, they are almost second nature. Keep them in mind as you shoot your raw video and do your initial edits.

As you use those techniques, you'll come to rely on several Premiere Pro editing tools. Adjusting clip speed and direction plus adding freeze frames expands your editing possibilities. Rolling, slip, and slide edits take that cuts-only style even further. The two mask transitions enable you to use custom images to display two clips at once. Adding cutaways makes it possible for you to add some visual interest to an interview or other video clip.

Q&A

Q *When I use the Rolling, Slip, and Slide Edit tools, the clip frames shift in the monitor screens, showing the new edit points, but after a while they stop and won't let me move the edit point any farther. What's up?*

A You've reached the end of the line—the beginning or end of the original clip. There are no additional head or tail frames to enable you to move the edit any farther.

Q *I create a freeze frame by selecting Frame Hold and checking Hold On the Out Point. That freeze holds for a bit too long, so I trimmed it and now the freeze frame image is different than the one I wanted. What's going on?*

A You trimmed your clip by dragging its out-point. Because that's the image you told Premiere Pro to hold, it updates that freeze frame as you change the out-point. To avoid this issue, use the Ripple Edit tool and trim the clip from its in-point.

Workshop

Quiz

1. You've completed a project that is exactly one minute long and needs to stay that length. You like one clip, but you want to shift its position slightly between two other clips. What edit tool do you use? Why?

2. What are the principal differences between the Image Mask and Gradient Mask transitions?

3. You want to make sure that when you drag a cutaway from the Source Monitor screen, it doesn't alter the audio of the original clip. How do you do that?

Quiz Answers

1. The Slide Edit tool. It enables you to slide a clip between two others, changing their in-points and out-points while keeping the selected clip intact.

2. The Image Mask transition sees everything in black or white—no gray area for that guy. And it's not a true transition. It's merely a means to sandwich two clips together. The Gradient Mask transition has a built-in transition

motion, revealing the next clip from either the bottom of the screen going up or from the top and going down, and sees things in shades of gray.

3. Click the little Toggle Take Audio and Video button until it turns into a film-strip icon without a speaker (that button is below the lower-right corner of the monitor screen). Now drag the image in the Source Monitor screen to the Video 1 track of your sequence. The original clip's audio should remain untouched. Take care not to click it one time too many—that turns it into an audio-only edit.

Exercises

1. I demonstrated the process to create a sequence using regular forward motion, slow motion, stop action, reverse slow motion, and reverse full-speed motion. Now, find a clip of your own that would work well with those edits and apply them.

2. To really get a feel for the four edit tools presented in this hour—Rolling, Slide, Slip, and Rate Stretch—plus the Ripple Edit tool, you need to use them. I guarantee that if you use them a half-dozen times each, they'll become second nature. And you'll see the beauty of how well Premiere Pro's developers implemented all this functionality. It's a marked improvement over previous versions of Premiere.

3. Combine two concepts presented in this hour: professional editing techniques and the Ripple, Rolling, Slide, and Slip Edit tools. Use these tools to make matching edits and build sequences. What makes these tools so powerful is that you can view just how the edits will work in the Program Monitor screen.

Adding Video Effects

What You'll Learn in This Hour:

▶ Introducing Premiere Pro's video effects
▶ Working with simple video effects
▶ Changing effects over time—keyframing
▶ Using keyframe interpolation controls

Premiere Pro's video effects give you more ways than you can imagine to jazz up your video and dazzle viewers. You can put clips in motion, distort them, shrink them, fly them across other clips, and change their color, style, and overall appearance.

You can apply these effects—video *and* audio—gradually over time or immediately. You can combine effects. For instance, you can posterize a clip, flip it around, and fly it off screen. It's a cliché, but it applies: The only limit is your imagination.

Introducing Premiere Pro's Video Effects

This hour marks the first of several during which I cover Premiere Pro's many video effects. I introduce the Effects palette here and go over some of the simpler effects; those that have few, if any, options. I present most of the remaining video effects in Hours 15 and 16, "Using Higher-Level Video Effects—Parts 1 and 2" (see following By the Way: "Keying—Newly Categorized As an Effect," for an explanation about the remaining effects).

Premiere Pro ships with 93 effects and dozens more are available from third-party providers. If you have Premiere Pro open, click in the Effects tab in the Project window and open the Video Effects palette. I've illustrated part of that palette in Figure 10.1.

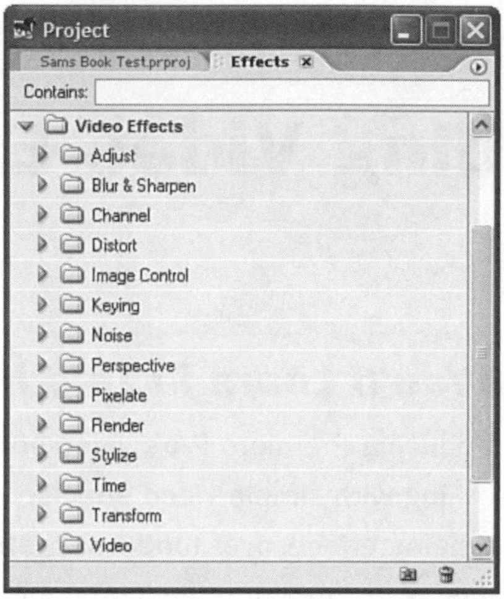

FIGURE 10.1
The Video Effects palette.

As a convenience, Adobe created 14 categories to organize these video effects, but you'll find that one category can sometimes seem a lot like another, and video effects in different palettes can be very similar.

Keying—Newly Categorized As an Effect

Until this release of Premiere Pro, keying was not considered an effect. Keying falls more into what most editors would call a *compositing* tool. That is, it's a means to give a video clip some transparency to enable layering—or compositing—it with other clips. Keying is a concept that takes some explanation as well as a shift from single-track editing to multiple tracks. I introduce keying in Hour 17, "Compositing Part 1—Layering Images and Clips."

There are three basic types of video effects: Standard, Photoshop, and After Effects. Adobe used to differentiate the After Effects group by giving it effects a special icon. No longer. The only obvious way you can discover which effect falls into which group is by looking in Premiere Pro's main file directory.

Digging into the Effects

If you're so inclined, navigate to wherever you installed Premiere Pro. If you opted for the default installation, you'll find it at `C:/Program Files/Adobe/Premiere Pro/`. Open the Plug-ins folder. In it, among other things, you'll see a collection of files that all start with the word *Filter* and have PRM file extensions. Those are the old Premiere stand-by video effects (they called them *filters* in previous Premiere iterations).

You also might notice a collection of AEFilter files with AEX file extensions. Most of these are the keying filters discussed in the previous By the Way. New to this group and to Premiere Pro are the Color Corrector and ColorMatch After Effects filters, (for some programming reason, they're stored in the Plug-ins folder, not the After Effects folder) and Motion and Opacity After Effects filters. The latter two are called *fixed effects* because they are always available for your use in the newly revamped, all-in-one, Effect Controls window (ECW). I cover opacity in Hour 17, and I explain motion in the next hour, "Putting Video and Still Clips in Motion."

Dig a little deeper into separate AEFilters and PSFilters folders, and you'll find the After Effects and Photoshop effects used in earlier versions of Premiere. The Photoshop effects (all have 8BF file extensions) tend to have few options, so I'll cover some of them in this hour. Basically, they're lifted straight from Photoshop where they are used on static graphics or photos. Premiere Pro gives you the opportunity to use them on moving pictures and change their characteristics over time. This *keyframing* capability, even with only a few parameters, can be very powerful.

The After Effects' effects tend to be a little wilder and more involved. Many have built-in animations and multiple features. I take you through that group in Hour 16.

You apply video effects by simply dragging and dropping them to a clip on a sequence or in the Effect Controls window. You can add multiple video effects to a single clip. Doing so can produce surprising and unpredictable results.

I concentrate on the simplest video effects in this hour to give you a taste of their variety and value. Then I show you one of the real strengths of Premiere Pro: the capability to change effects over time. Even static effects like those lifted from Photoshop can be animated.

Convert a Clip to Grayscale

Try it Yourself

I'll begin with Premiere Pro's simplest video effect: Black & White. It converts any clip to grayscale (shades of gray). Follow these steps:

1. You can open Premiere Pro to your own workspace, but make sure that we're on the same plate, switch to the Effects workspace by selecting Window→Workspace→Effects.

2. Add a brief video or linked video/audio clip to your timeline by dragging it from the Project window.

3. Select the video portion of that clip by clicking it with the Selection tool.

4. Note that the name of the clip shows up in the Effect Controls window (it should be open in the Source side of the Monitor window by virtue of your having switched to the Effects workspace).

▼

5. In the Video Effects folder (under the Effects tab in the Project window), open the Image Control file folder and drag and drop Black & White on the clip on the timeline or to the left side of the Effect Controls window. This action adds the video effect name to the Effect Controls window, below Motion and Opacity and above Volume (if you're using a linked audio/video clip). I've illustrated this in Figure 10.2. Note that there's a little f icon on the left side. Clicking this turns off the effect while keeping it in the ECW.

Did you
Know?

Finding Effects (and Transitions)

With the many video effects file folders, it's sometimes tricky to locate an effect. If you know an effect's name (or part of its name), type it in the Contains: line at the top of the Effects palette. Premiere Pro immediately displays all effects that match those letters, narrowing the search as you type.

**By the
Way**

New Horizontal Lines in the Sequence

You might note that when you add an effect to a clip, two thin horizontal lines show up in the sequence. A red line below the Time Ruler indicates that this clip will need rendering before final output. And a line at the bottom of the clip in the sequence serves simply as a reminder that you've added an effect to this clip. That line is green when the clip is selected and purple when it's not selected.

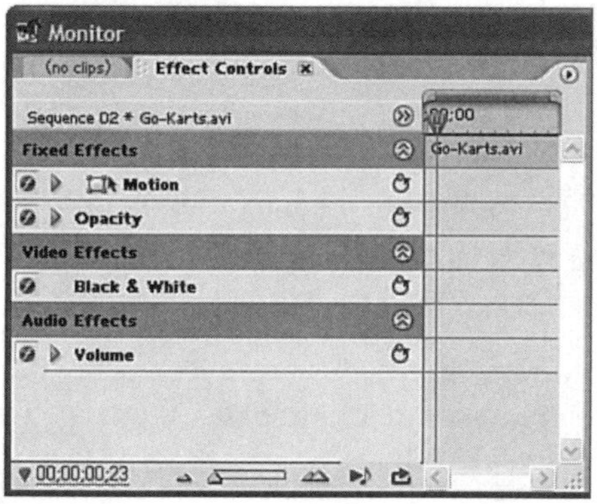

FIGURE 10.2
After the Black & White video effect is applied to a clip, it appears in the Effect Controls window.

6. The Black & White video effect happens immediately. Place the CTI edit line on the clip and note that its image in the Program Monitor screen shifts instantly to a grayscale image. Preview your clip (press the spacebar) to see the Black & White effect in action.

▼

7. Using the Black & White video effect can be abrupt. To make this clip gradually shift to black-and-white, use the Razor tool to slice it, put the Black & White video effect on the second section, and add a cross-dissolve on the sliced edit between the two clips.

Try the Camera Blur Video Effect

Black & White is as basic as Premiere Pro's video effects get. To move things up a notch, try the Camera Blur video effect:

1. Remove Black & White from the Effect Controls palette by clicking on its name and pressing Delete (or right-click on the effect name and select Cut).

2. Open the Blur & Sharpen file folder and drag and drop Camera Blur onto the timeline or the Effect Controls window.

3. Note that as I've illustrated in Figure 10.3, there are three extra items in expanded view of the Camera Blur section in the ECW: a little window icon, two disclosure triangles, and a stopwatch (the latter is to set keyframes, which I cover in the next section, "Changing Effects Over Time— Keyframing"). The window icon and the disclosure triangles both access this effect's one control: Percent Blur.

Accessing Parameters

Virtually all effects have a disclosure triangle. Clicking it typically displays a list of nested parameters, most of which have disclosure triangles of their own.

However, only some clips have the little window icon that accesses a separate settings dialog box.

Settings Dialog Box Opening by Itself

When you add this effect, and others that use a settings dialog box (see step 4), the dialog box should not open until you click its little window icon in the ECW. But, as a result of what might be a minor glitch in Premiere Pro's code, sometimes when you add such an effect to the ECW, its settings dialog box opens on its own. It's a nonissue really, but this is just a heads-up in case it throws you the first time it happens.

4. Click the window icon to view the Camera Blur Settings dialog box.

5. Move the percentage slider to see its effect in the Settings dialog box preview window (see Figure 10.4). Click OK.

▼

FIGURE 10.3
Camera Blur has three additional features in its Effect Controls window display: a window icon to access a setup dialog box, a disclosure triangle to access that setup info within the ECW, and a stopwatch to switch on keyframes.

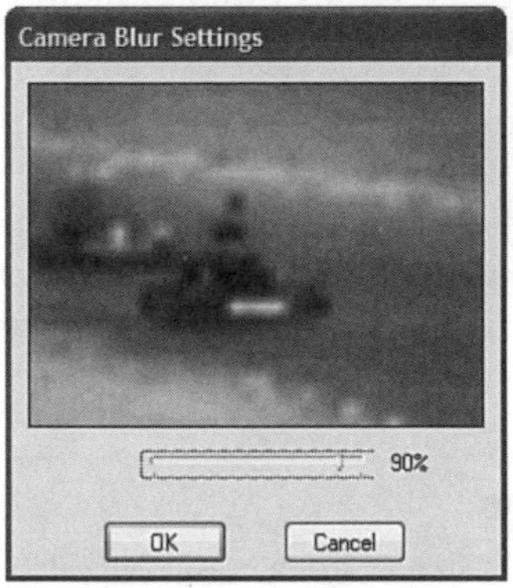

FIGURE 10.4
Camera Blur has only one option: Percent Blur.

Did you Know?

Preview Frame Behaviors

When you preview an effect in its Settings dialog box, the image displayed might not be what you expect to see. If you have the CTI (current time indicator) on the clip (clicking on the clip to select it does *not* move the CTI to it), the Settings dialog box displays the frame under the CTI. If the CTI isn't on the clip, the Settings dialog box displays a frame from the clip, but there does not appear to be any rhyme or reason as to which frame. If you instead preview your work in the Monitor window's Program screen (see steps 6 and 7), you'll need to move the CTI edit line to the clip to see the effect in action.

6. To see how the controls in the ECW work, click the disclosure triangle next to *Camera Blur* and click the disclosure triangle below and to the left of the first one. Your screen will look like Figure 10.3 shown earlier.

▼

By the Way ▼

ECW Controls—Eminently Keyframable

That these settings dialog box controls are also available in the ECW means that you can apply keyframes to any or all of them. This is a major improvement in Premiere Pro over its predecessors.

7. Move the CTI to your clip to see it in the Monitor window Program screen, and then move the slider to change the percent blur. Note the immediate change in the Monitor.

▲

Did you Know?

Photoshop Video Effects

Camera Blur is the first of several Photoshop video effects you'll work with. Most have similar, simple settings dialog box interfaces and offer most of those dialog box controls in the Effect Controls window. This demonstrates the elegance of Premiere Pro. Previous versions of Premiere presented effects in myriad ways; now all are accessible within the ECW as well as in their former interfaces.

For your information, here's a list of the Photoshop video effects: Crystalize, Lens Flare, Pinch, Pointillize, Polar Coordinates, Radial Blur, Shear, Spherize, Tiles, Twirl, Wave, Wind, and ZigZag. All but one use a Settings dialog box and most are simple and fun.

Experiment with the following simple video effects. Although you can apply multiple effects to a clip (sometimes with unpredictable and exciting results), in this case it's best to delete each effect before moving on to the next one:

Crystallize—Found in the Pixelate file folder, this effect creates a distorted mosaic by placing adjacent pixels into solid-colored polygons. Choose a value from 3 to 300 pixels per polygon. A setting of 5 works nicely.

Facet—Found in the Pixelate file folder, this effect is reminiscent of Gauguin paintings. It creates a smooth oil painting–like effect by clumping together pixels of similar color values. As with Black & White, there are no options.

Pointillize—Found in the Pixelate file folder, this effect is reminiscent of a Seurat painting. But even at the lowest setting (3), the chunky points don't match his fine style. Pointillize does work well with landscapes.

Replicate—Found in the Stylize file folder, this effect divides the screen into tiles and displays the whole clip in each tile—from a 2×2 grid to 16×16.

Solarize—This effect is found in the Stylize file folder. By blending between a negative and a positive image, Solarize makes your clip look like film briefly exposed to light during developing. A setting of 0% leaves your clip unchanged, whereas 100% turns it into a negative image.

Before moving to keyframes, I want to fill you in on a few more basic, but useful effects.

Apply the Spherize Video Effect

The Spherize effect distorts your image, making it look as if someone's pushing a basketball against it. Here are the steps:

1. Remove Camera Blur (and all other effects) from the Effect Controls window by selecting it and deleting it.

2. Open the Distort file folder and drag and drop Spherize into the Effect Controls window or on to the clip in the sequence.

3. Click on the settings dialog box icon to open it (if it hasn't opened automatically). As shown in Figure 10.5, this video effect has a numeric value, an adjustable screen size, and an additional control: *Mode*. Adjust these as desired. Here are some points to keep in mind:

   ▶ **Amount**—A setting from –100 to +100 either pushes or pulls the clip into a spherical shape.

   ▶ **Mode**—You have three options: Normal, Horizontal Only, and Vertical Only. Normal looks like a ball, whereas Horizontal Only and Vertical Only expand out and squeeze in along their respective axes.

   ▶ **Preview Window**—The little buttons (+ and –) beneath the preview window let you zoom in on or away from your subject to more clearly see the change in shape, but this does not affect the final effect.

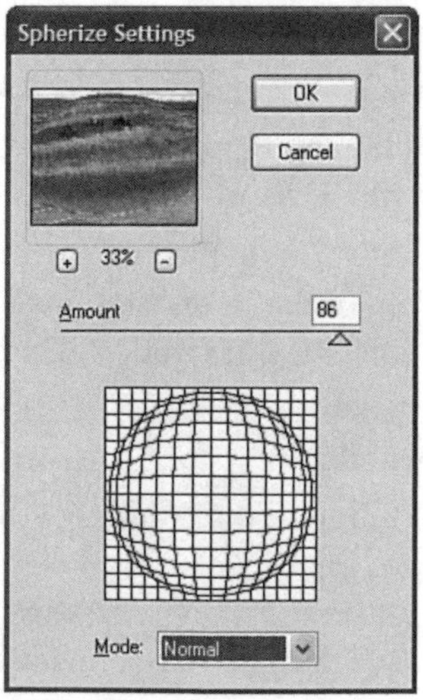

FIGURE 10.5
Spherize offers two options to create the appearance of a basketball pressed against your clip.

ECW Missing Controls

In the case of Spherize (and several other video effects), not all its dialog box controls or options show up when you twirl down its disclosure triangles in the Effect Controls window. What's missing in this case is the Mode option. It pays to check both sets of controls. Whichever dialog box controls are not listed in the ECW are therefore not available for keyframing. I cover that topic in a moment.

Watch
Out!

Take a look at three other effects from the `Distort` file folder:

Pinch—The pull move squeezes/pinches the center of the image. The push move bulges out the image like Spherize.

Shear—This is the fun-house mirror effect. It distorts your clip along a line that works much like the Path Text tool. Drag the line's two endpoints around the perimeter of the box, create handles anywhere on the line, and drag and contort that line. The effect of your handiwork shows up immediately in the preview window.

ZigZag—You can create pond ripples and other radial effects with ZigZag. The Amount setting (–100 to 100, with 0 being no distortion) represents the magnitude of distortion and the reflection angle. Ridges is the number of ripples (direction reversals), and Style sets the general appearance (Pond, Out from Center, or Around Center).

Changing Effects Over Time—Keyframing

Keyframing has changed dramatically for the better in Premiere Pro versus previous versions. Virtually all options for all effects are keyframable. That is, you can change the effect's behavior over time in myriad ways.

For instance, you can have Camera Blur gradually "rack" the scene out of focus or start out of focus and gradually sharpen the image. Or you can use the Spherize effect to bulge out a scene a little at the start and gradually make the entire scene blow up like a balloon.

This new functionality has the same look and feel as Adobe's very powerful motion graphics and text animation product: After Effects. This duplication of functionality is purposeful. Adobe has gone whole hog to create a tightly integrated suite of DV tools—Premiere Pro, After Effects 6, Photoshop CS, Audition and Encore DVD—that look and behave similarly (Audition has not yet received an Adobe face-lift, but the other four do feature similar user interfaces).

Try it
Yourself
▼

Try Out Video Effect Keyframing

To see keyframing in action, you'll apply it to the Crystallize effect, gradually increasing and decreasing the cell size over time. To see how keyframing works, follow these steps:

1. Remove Spherize and any other effects from the ECW.

2. Drag the Crystallize video effect (from the Stylize file folder) to the Effect Controls window. Twirl down the disclosure triangle.

*By the
Way*

> ### Skip the Effect Settings Dialog Box
>
> If the Crystallize Settings dialog box opens, simply click OK (you'll select actual settings in a moment).

3. Move the CTI to somewhere near the middle of your clip (either drag the CTI within the ECW or in the Timeline window).

4. As shown in Figure 10.6, click the Keyframe stopwatch to turn on keyframes. When you do you'll note several changes:

   ▶ The stopwatch displays a sweep hand to let you know that you have activated keyframes.

   ▶ A set of icons appears on the right side of the display. You use them to move from one keyframe to the previous or next one in a collection. The diamond in the middle enables you to set a keyframe wherever the CTI edit line is at that moment.

   ▶ A little diamond appears in the ECW timeline area. That marks this new keyframe. At the moment, it's solid gray. That will change when you add the next keyframe.

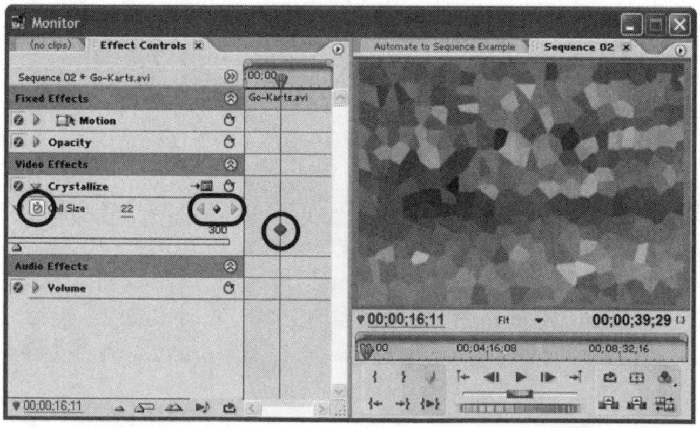

FIGURE 10.6
Switching on the keyframe stopwatch adds a keyframe at the current CTI location plus turns on the keyframe navigation controls.

▼

5. Change the Crystallize Cell Size setting to a large number. Something greater than 150 pixels will do.

6. Move the CTI edit line to the beginning of the clip either by using the Home keyboard shortcut or dragging the CTI to the beginning in the ECW or the sequence.

ECW's Mini-Timeline

One other very cool feature of the ECW is its mini-timeline—that section on its right side. If you don't see it in your ECW, click the little chevron button in the upper-right corner to open it. You can drag its left edge to widen its view and use the zoom icons at the bottom of the ECW to change its view. It's a very handy tool.

7. Decrease the Cell Size setting to something very small (the smallest value is 3 pixels).

What Just Happened?

When you move the CTI *and* change the effect's value, Premiere Pro automatically adds another keyframe icon in the ECW. Simply moving it *without* changing an effect value does *not* set a new keyframe. In this case, the keyframe icon is a triangle pointing to the right, indicating that it's marking the keyframe for the first frame in the clip. (When you apply a keyframe to the last clip, it'll be a triangle pointing to the left.) All other keyframes are diamond-shaped unless you apply interpolation controls to them (see "Using Keyframe Interpolation Controls" later in this hour).

8. Move to the last frame of your clip either by using the keyboard shortcut End or by dragging the CTI in the ECW mini-timeline or in the sequence.

When *End* Means *Beginning*

Using the End shortcut key can be disconcerting. When you use it on a clip, it doesn't take you to the *last* frame of *that* clip, it takes you to the *first* frame of the *next* clip (if there is no clip at the end of the selected clip, it'll display black).

Premiere Pro's development team queried the beta group about this behavior and I voiced my opposition to it. As it turns out, there apparently was a programming reason that forced their hand and they had to stick with this counterintuitive approach.

The team members admit it's not ideal and they're working on fixing it for the next release. In the meantime, if you want to go to a clip's last frame, press End and then press the Left Arrow key once to move back one frame so that you can see your work.

Watch Those Keyframe Icons

With two keyframes in your clip, notice how their appearance changes. The one on the left is a white (actually, a very light gray) triangle. The one in the middle is white on the left and dark gray on the right. The dark gray indicates it's the last keyframe—chronologically—in this clip. If you now put a keyframe after it (and you will in step 9), it'll turn completely white to indicate there are keyframes on both sides of it.

9. Add another keyframe by changing the cell size back to something small like three. Your ECW should look something like Figure 10.7.

FIGURE 10.7
After adding keyframes at the beginning, middle, and end of a clip, your ECW should look something like this.

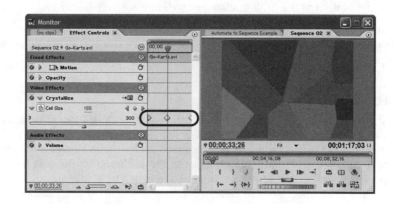

10. Play your clip. Your video clip transitions from a lovely postimpressionist painting to a screen full of animated solid-color polygons and then back to that lovely painting again.

Keyframe Manipulation

After you add keyframes, they're not immutable. You can move them, delete them, add more, and change their attributes. Here's a rundown of those methods:

▶ **Add a Keyframe**—You already know that you can add a keyframe by moving the CTI to a new location and changing an effect value there. Another way is by moving the CTI to a frame where you want to add a keyframe and clicking the little diamond between the two triangles. You can change the value now or come back to it later.

▶ **Move a Keyframe**—First, move the CTI to the new location so that you can see that spot. (If the effect is so drastic that you can't see the video well enough, turn off the little f icon until you find the right spot, and then click the effect f icon back to its on state.) Click and drag the keyframe to position it directly under the CTI edit line. Unfortunately, Snap to Edges does not work when moving keyframes, so you might not get absolutely frame-accurate placement.

▶ **Delete a Keyframe**—Click on the keyframe and press Delete or right-click on it and select Cut.

▶ **Delete All Keyframes**—Click the stopwatch. Premiere Pro will prompt you before removing all keyframes from the ECW.

▶ **Move to a Keyframe**—Move to a keyframe by using the two little keyframe navigation triangles or moving the CTI to a keyframe and noting when the little diamond between those two triangles changes its appearance, which indicates that you've landed on a keyframe.

▶ **Change a Keyframe's Attributes**—Move to a keyframe and then adjust whatever setting(s) you've already applied.

Multiple Keyframable Attributes

Most video effects offer more than one adjustable attribute. Lightning, for instance, has 25! The ECW makes it easy to set keyframes for each attribute at any number of points within a clip. This is a huge improvement in Premiere Pro over its predecessors. I present many of those multiple-feature video effects in Hours 15 and 16.

For now, feel free to experiment. I suggest using ZigZag. It's in the Distort folder. It has two attributes that create a very cool, pebble-dropped-in-a-pool effect. When animated with keyframes, you can start with a few ridges, increase that number, and then decrease it. Follow the same procedure for the size of the ridges.

Using Keyframe Interpolation Controls

Another very slick additional tool new to Premiere Pro is keyframe interpolation. You use this to adjust the way an effect attribute behaves as it moves away from a keyframe and approaches the next keyframe. Adobe likes to say you use interpolation controls to change the way an effect behaves both *spatially* and *temporally*—in space and time.

Effects normally change linearly over time. That is, if you were to graph an effect's values on the Y axis and time on the X axis, it would define a straight line.

Try it Yourself   Using Keyframe Interpolation

Using keyframe interpolation, you can turn the start points and endpoints of that line into curves; that is, ease out of a keyframe and quickly accelerate into the next one. Here's how it works:

1. If you still have the Crystallize effect applied to a clip, use that for this exercise. Otherwise, add some other simple effect covered in this hour (other than Black & White—it's not keyframable) and give it at least three keyframes.

2. Right-click on the first keyframe and take a look at the context menu (refer to Figure 10.8). You have five options:

   ▶ Normal Out—Straight line interpolation

   ▶ Fast Out—Accelerate then slow down to a linear rate

   ▶ Slow Out—Gradual acceleration to a linear rate

   ▶ Easy Curve Out—A more logarithmic and slower Slow Out

   ▶ Hold Out—Holds the current keyframe attribute until the next keyframe or the end of the clip

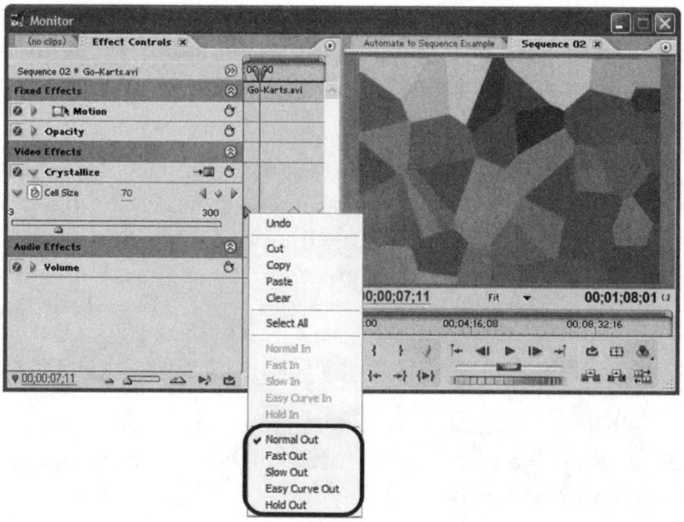

FIGURE 10.8
Keyframe interpolation tools enable you to give attribute changes a bit more of a realistic feel.

3. Select Fast Out. That does two things: It changes the keyframe's icon to indicate that it's a Fast Out and changes the *next* keyframe into a Slow In. This

dual-keyframe behavior happens whenever you use keyframe interpolation. (See the following Watch Out! and sidebar for additional information on this.)

4. Check your handiwork by previewing this clip. Note that if you have more than two keyframes, you can change the interpolation behavior between them as well.

Rippling Interpolations

Watch Out!

I'm not a fan of this automatic, adjacent keyframe interpolation changing behavior.

I think that when you change the interpolation behavior of one keyframe, the next keyframe should *not* change. However, this behavior happens for every changed interpolation value. The adjacent keyframe always shifts to the complement or opposite of its neighbor.

To see that, right-click on the *center* keyframe and change it to Fast In. That changes the first keyframe from Fast Out to Slow Out.

This side-by-side keyframe interpolation is by design. What you're seeing is a compromise that Premiere Pro's design engineers made to avoid changing the user interface. See the following Developer's Comment sidebar for an explanation.

Developer's Comment—Between Keyframe Interpolation

Premiere Pro's method of interpolation works in the area *between* two keyframes, not for individual keyframe (as our user interface tends to make you believe—each keyframe seems to have its own settings in the UI).

For instance, if you change a keyframe to Easy Curve In, this actually applies to the whole interval between this keyframe and the *previous* one, and that is why you see the previous keyframe settings change to Easy Curve Out. The same applies in the other direction: If you change a keyframe to Hold Out, the next keyframe automatically changes to Hold In.

Here's an implementation detail that might help clarify this: We never store the *In* value for a keyframe anywhere in memory during an editing session (for example, Ease In, Normal In, Hold In, and so on). It's always derived from the Out value of the previous keyframe.

Table 10.1 shows how we find the In value for a specific keyframe, by looking at the previous keyframe.

To be fair, the interpolation mode should not have been set on the keyframes themselves but rather as a property of the interval between the two keyframes. But that would have required a new user interface. Our UI design team is very aware of these issues in the interface, and we'll be looking into them in the future.

TABLE 10.1   Keyframe Interpolation Pairings

Left Keyframe Setting	Right Keyframe Setting
Normal Out	Normal In
Fast Out	Slow In
Slow Out	Fast In
Easy Curve Out	Easy Curve In
Hold Out	Hold In

Try it Yourself   **Keyframe Parameter Values in Action**

Here's a nifty way to help you get a grasp on what's really happening to the keyframe parameter values over time:

1. Expand the video track by twirling down the disclosure triangle next to the track's eyeball icon.

2. Drag the top of the track to expand it even more.

3. Simplify the clip view by clicking the Clip Display icon below the track eyeball and selecting Show Name Only.

4. Click the next icon to the right and select Show Keyframes.

5. Click the Effect Keyframe drop-down list at the top of the clip by clicking the word *Opacity* and selecting Crystallize→Cells.

6. Change the first Crystallize keyframe in the ECW to Easy Curve Out.

7. Your clip display in the Timeline window should now look like Figure 10.9. By adding interpolation, the Cell values now change along a curve both moving from the left keyframe and moving into the right keyframe.

8. To check this out even more, change the interpolation controls. In particular, choose Hold Out and note that a straight line appears in the clip display, meaning that the Crystallize cell count remains unchanged until it reaches the next keyframe.

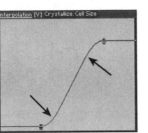

FIGURE 10.9
Use a clip's keyframe display to see how interpolation controls change an effect's parameters over time. The arrows point out the curved lines associated with Easy Curve Out and In.

Non-Keyframable Effects

Not all video effects are keyframable—they simply do something with no parameters. Here's a list:

Anti-Alias—This effect is found in the Blur file folder. Just as anti-aliasing in transitions blurs sharply defined diagonal lines, this effect softens the edges between highly contrasting colors.

Black & White—Found in the Image Control file folder, this effect converts color clips into grayscale.

Facet—Found in the Pixelate file folder, this effect creates the oil-painting look.

Field Interpolate—Found in the Video file folder. This is a technical fix, not a creative tool. It re-creates missing scan lines dropped during capture.

Gaussian Sharpen—Found in the Sharpen file folder, this effect is supposed to dramatically sharpen a clip, but it looks more like the Crystallize effect.

Ghosting—Found in the Blur file folder, this very nifty effect creates a "comet tail" on any moving object (including camera moves). It's great for showing the flight of a thrown/hit/kicked ball. A steady camera is a must.

Horizontal Flip—Found in the Transform file folder, this effect reverses a clip left to right but still plays the clip forward. Use it if you broke the plane while shooting a cutaway.

Sharpen Edges—Found in the Sharpen file folder, this effect looks just as odd as Gaussian Sharpen. Apparently, it's only effective for very soft focus clips.

Vertical Flip—Found in the Transform file folder, this effect flips clips upside down.

Vertical Hold—Found in the Transform file folder, this effect makes your clip look like the vertical hold is out of whack.

Summary

Premiere's video effects run the gamut from mundane and technical to dazzling and exciting. Adding video effects is a simple drag-and-drop process. It's easy to combine a variety of effects on one clip.

By putting virtually all the effects' features in the Effect Controls window, Premiere Pro makes it easy to set the behaviors of those effects. In addition, you can change those behaviors over time by using keyframes. And you can apply keyframes individually and independently to every attribute listed in the ECW. Using keyframes to control those effects make them that much more entertaining and effective.

Q&A

Q *When I apply a video effect to a clip it doesn't show up in the Monitor window's Program screen. How am I supposed to see any changes I apply to this clip?*

A Even though you've selected that clip by clicking on it or dragging an effect to it, you still need to move the CTI's edit line to that clip for it to display in the Monitor window Program screen.

Q *I've selected a clip and am working on it in the ECW. I clicked End to move to that clip's last frame, but all I see is a black screen in the Monitor window Program screen. What's going on?*

A This is a Premiere Pro anomaly. Pressing End takes you to the *first* frame of the *next* clip. To see the *last* frame of the selected clip, press the Left Arrow key once.

Workshop

Quiz

1. You want to make a clip gradually shift to black-and-white for the duration of that clip. How do you do that?

2. How do you make an effect start within a clip rather than at the beginning?

3. You want your effect to jump out of the gate but slide gradually into the next clip. How do you do that?

Quiz Answers

1. Razor the clip somewhere near the middle. Apply Black & White to the second half. Apply a Cross Dissolve transition to the edit. In the ECW, drag the ends of the Cross Dissolve transition all the way to the beginning and end of the razored clips. If you can't see the entire clip in the ECW, expand your view by clicking the little hill icon at the bottom of the window.

2. Use a keyframe. Move the CTI to the frame where you want to start the effect and click the keyframe stopwatch. That sets the first keyframe. You can add other keyframes after that point if you want.

3. Use keyframe interpolation controls. Right-click on the first keyframe and select Fast Out. That automatically sets the next keyframe (the last keyframe in this case) to Slow In.

Exercises

1. Layer multiple video effects on the same clip. You might try Crystallize, Solarize, and Replicate. Alternatively, apply Horizontal Hold and Vertical Hold to the same clip. Change the order to see whether that makes any difference.

2. With those or some other multiple effects, apply keyframes to turn them on and off at different times. You might set Pointillize to start changing off the top, and then bring in ZigZag later to give that animation a "ripply" feel. The more you experiment, the better the chance that you'll discover some very cool effect combos that work well for you.

3. Use video effects to make apparent video transitions. To do that, apply the same effect to adjacent clips. Use keyframes to gradually change the effect in the first clip until, in the case of Crystallize, for example, it's a jumbled mess by the end of the clip. Then start the next clip at that same jumbled mess setting and gradually minimize the mess to reveal the true clip appearance.

HOUR 11

Putting Video and Still Clips in Motion

What You'll Learn in This Hour:

▶ Applying motion

▶ Enhancing motion—changing size and adding rotation

▶ Giving clips a 3D look

▶ Working with still images—special issues

Applying Motion and Changing a Clip's Size

You've seen videos with clips flying over other images or that spin video clips onscreen—having them start as small dots and expanding to full-screen size. You can create those effects using Premiere Pro's motion settings.

Premiere Pro's Motion effect is a significant improvement over the Motion Settings window used in its predecessors. That previous, separate interface presented editors with some arcane and nonintuitive controls. For me, its two redeeming features were its looping preview mode that gave immediate feedback for any changed motion settings and its Skew feature.

With Premiere Pro's capability to play every effect in real-time in the Monitor window Program screen, the loss of the looping preview is inconsequential. And you can use the Transform effect to apply Skew to a clip.

What you gain is three things:

▶ All your motion control work takes place within the Effect Controls and Monitor windows

▶ Direct motion settings using either onscreen drag-and-drop methods or numerical values in the Effect Controls window

▶ Precise keyframe control over several motion aspects

To see motion controls in their best light means displaying them over a background. To do that in Premiere Pro means placing the clips in a track other than Video 1 and using some other clip on Video 1 to serve as a background. This is an example of *compositing* or *layering*. I'll cover that subject in detail starting in Hour 17, "Compositing Part 1—Layering Images and Clips." For this coming exercise, you'll keep things simple and use a solid color matte as that background.

Setting Up Premiere Pro to Apply Its Motion Effect

As you become more comfortable with Premiere Pro, working with the Motion effect will become second nature. But I believe in starting with the basics and that means, for now, I want to present the Motion effect in its simplest form. To do that, you first need to set up your sequence, Effect Controls window, and Monitor window to get a clear picture of how this effect works. Here's how to do that:

1. Switch to the Effects workspace by selecting Window→Workspace→Effects. Then clear your sequence by deleting all clips on it.

2. Create a color matte by clicking the New Item button in the Project window, selecting Color Matte, choosing a color, clicking OK, giving it a name, and clicking OK.

3. Drag that color matte to Video 1.

Did you Know?

Why a Color Matte for a Background?

You could place a video clip or still image on Video 1 to serve as a backdrop for the clips you'll put in motion over that backdrop. I prefer using a matte at this point because it's less distracting and makes it easier to see how the Motion effect works.

4. Drag a video or linked video/audio clip to the Video 2 track (if your sequence does not have a Video 2 track, drag the clip to the gray area

above Video 1 to automatically create a new video track). This will be the clip you'll put in motion. Trim it to about 20 seconds.

5. Extend the color matte to equal the length of the video clip. Your sequence should look like Figure 11.1.

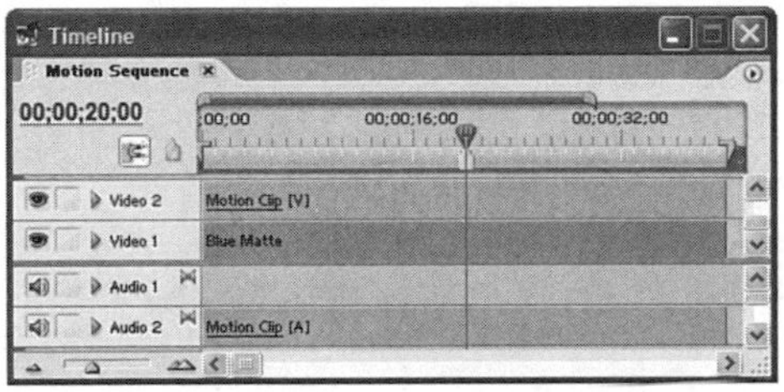

FIGURE 11.1
How your sequence should look to carry out this exercise.

6. Click on your clip in Video 2 to select it.

7. Open the Effect Controls window. Click Motion to switch on that effect and twirl down all the disclosure triangles. As shown in Figure 11.2 that opens up five, "keyframable" options:

- ▶ **Position**—The screen location of the clip's *anchor* point (its center unless you change the anchor point). Because the NTSC screen size is 720×480, the default starting values of 360 and 240 place the center of the clip at the center of the screen. 0,0 puts the center in the upper-left corner and 720, 480 puts it in the lower right. You can drag the clip completely off-screen, meaning that the values can be less than 0 and greater than 720 and 480.

- ▶ **Scale**—The relative size of the clip. The slider has a range from 0% to 100%, but you can use the numerical representation to increase the clip size to 600% of its original size.

- ▶ **Scale Width**—You need to uncheck Uniform Scale to make that active. Doing so changes Scale to Scale Height and enables you to change the width and height independently.

- ▶ **Rotation**—The first figure represents the number of full 360-degree spins. A positive number is clockwise and a negative number is counterclockwise. The maximum value for each direction is 90, meaning that you can apply up to 180(!) full rotations to a clip. The second figure represents a partial rotation and goes from –360 to 360 degrees.

- ▶ **Anchor Point**—The center of the rotation, as opposed to the center of the clip. You can set the clip to rotate around one of its corners or around a point outside the clip, if you so choose.

8. To work more effectively with the Motion effect, change the zoom level of the Monitor window Program screen by clicking the drop-down list highlighted in Figure 11.2 and selecting 50% or less. This will give you more screen real estate when dragging a clip completely off-screen.

By the Way

Effects with Motion Controls

Several video effects have a Motion Control component. I cover them in Hour 16, "Using Higher-Level Video Effects." For now, if you want to see what I'm talking about, take a look at Transform, Twirl, or Crop. Each sports that little bounding box icon that indicates it offers motion controls.

Each of those effects has its own unique application of motion controls. Of particular interest is Transform. It's the video effect used by Premiere Pro's design team to serve as the foundation for the fixed Motion effect. The team included it as a separate video effect, in part, because it offers additional features such as the capability to skew the clip and enables you to add a drop shadow that works properly with a rotating clip.

FIGURE 11.2
Select Motion and twirl down the disclosure triangles to view the five, keyframable motion settings' options. Reduce the Monitor zoom level to better display how Motion parameters work.

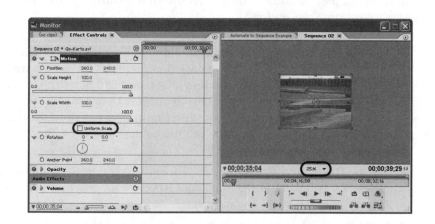

Try it Yourself   **Applying Motion to a Clip**

Working with the Motion effect is a lot like working with a text bounding box. Switching on the Motion effect places a bounding box around the perimeter of the video clip or still image. Not only can you adjust it using numeric values in the ECW (Effect Controls Window), but you also can manipulate it directly in the Monitor Program screen. You can drag it to a new location, change its shape and size, and rotate it. Here's how it works:

1. Press Home to put the CTI (current time indicator) edit line at the beginning of your clip.

2. Turn on keyframes for position by clicking on its stopwatch.

3. Click on the word *Motion* to switch on that effect. That places a bounding box around the clip in the Monitor window Program screen. Click on its center crosshairs and drag the bounding box (and the clip inside it) completely off the left side of the screen. Use Figure 11.3 as a reference.

Checking Position Numeric Values

In my example (shown in Figure 11.3), the Position numeric values in the ECW are –360 and 240. That means the clip's center is 360 pixels to the left of the left edge of the screen, which puts the full-screen clip just off screen. The 240 means the center of the clip is on the extended horizontal centerline of the screen. Because you've slid the entire clip off screen, the Monitor window Program screen should display a full-screen view of the color matte on Video 1.

By the Way

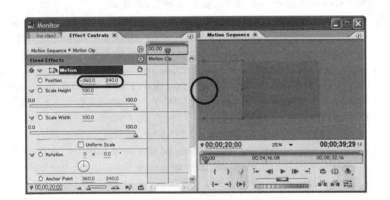

FIGURE 11.3
Click on the clip bounding box crosshairs and then drag the clip off screen. Note the Position numeric values that correspond to moving the clip off the left side of the screen.

4. By moving the CTI, turning on keyframes, and dragging the clip to a new location, you automatically added a keyframe at the start of the clip. You'll do the same for the clip's last frame. Move the CTI edit line to the end of the clip by clicking End and clicking the left arrow once.

5. Instead of dragging the clip to a new location, change the numeric values to 1080 and 240. That will put it completely off the right side of the screen—720+360=1080—and keep it on the screen's horizontal center line.

6. Press Home and the spacebar to play the clip. It should start completely off screen to the left then gradually work its way horizontally until it slides off screen to the right.

7. Now you'll add two more positions toward the middle of the clip to make the clip move from the left to above the center of the screen, straight down

to the bottom and angle off beyond the right side of the screen. Start that process by moving the CTI edit line about a third of the way into the clip and then dragging the clip bounding box or inputting numeric values to move the clip off the top center of the screen (numeric values: 360, –240).

When Up Is Negative

The vertical Motion effect numeric value is a disconnect for me. Premiere Pro's design engineers chose to set 0,0 as the upper-left corner of the screen (for those into Cartesian coordinates, that's the junction of the X and Y axes) and then determined that any point *above* the screen would be a *negative* number. To keep things intuitive, they should have set 0,0 at the lower-left corner of the screen and had anything above be a positive number and anything below that be negative—just as you'd expect.

Developer Comment—Why Upper Left Is 0,0

There's no official answer, but the likely reason has to do with the standard way coordinate systems work on Windows, which has the (0,0) coordinates point to the upper-left corner of the screen. This has been the case since Windows 1.0.

There are more evolved (some might say *resolution-independent*) coordinate systems available on Windows that have the lower-left corner defined as (0,0), but most app developers never use these, since it makes it harder to design good-looking interfaces with that system.

8. Move the CTI edit line about two thirds of the way into the clip and then drag the clip or input numeric values to move the clip off the bottom center of the screen (numeric values: 360, 720).

9. Take a look at the motion tracking lines in the Monitor window's Program screen. Figure 11.4 shows how yours should look with the CTI set to slightly past the mid-point of your clip. Move the CTI and note how the tracking line display moves with the CTI, always showing the motion path before and after the current location of the CTI. Also note that the dotted line indicates the relative speed of the clip along the path. The wider the spacing between dots, the faster the motion.

What Happened to the Motion Tracking Lines?

If you click somewhere outside the Motion effect portion of the ECW, the motion tracking lines disappear (as will the clip bounding box).

The reason? By clicking elsewhere, you deselect the Motion effect. To switch those lines and the clip bounding box back on (along with other motion features), simply reselect Motion by clicking its name in the ECW.

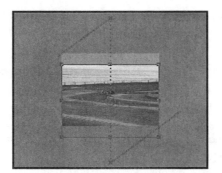

FIGURE 11.4
The motion tracking dotted lines show the Position path starting a bit before the current location of the CTI and continuing to a few seconds after it.

10. Press Home and the spacebar to see the animation. You should see the lower-right corner of the clip slide diagonally from the left side to above the screen, move vertically straight down the screen (filling the view edge to edge at its midpoint), and then move diagonally off and up to the middle-right side.

Enhancing Motion—Changing Size and Adding Rotation

Simply sliding a clip around only begins to exploit Motion effect's possibilities. What makes the Motion effect really cool is the capability to shrink or expand the clip and to spin it.

In particular, you can start a clip full-screen (or zoom in even farther) and then shrink it to reveal another clip. You can spin a clip onto the screen starting as a small dot and then spin it off the screen, having it grow as it moves away. And you can layer multiple clips, creating several pictures-in-a-picture. I cover that latter technique in Hour 17.

Changing the Clip Size

Try it Yourself

The steps you follow to add these features are not much different than setting the position values. But there are some keyframe timing issues that you can use to enhance these motion features. Here's a basic rundown of how to enhance motion:

1. Clear the Motion Position settings you created in the previous task by clicking the Position Keyframe stopwatch icon. Premiere Pro will prompt you to make sure that this is what you want to do. Click OK.

▼

2. To remove any changed Motion setting vestiges, click the Reset button (located to the right of the word Motion in the ECW).

Why Not Use Reset to Clear *All* Motion Settings?

The Reset button can be a handy tool or an aggravating nuisance. Clicking Reset leads to one of three results:

▶ If you haven't set any keyframes (or have cleared keyframe settings by switching off all the keyframe stopwatches), clicking Reset returns all changed motion settings to their default values.

▶ If you've set keyframes for only one motion setting (such as Position, for example), moving the CTI to a keyframe and clicking Reset returns the values at that keyframe to their default setting.

▶ Things can get aggravating if you have set keyframes for more than one Motion feature (or multiple features for any other video effect). If you move the CTI to a keyframe and click Reset, Premiere Pro returns *that* keyframe to its default settings—*and*—*creates* keyframes at that point for all other motion settings that have keyframes turned on and sets all those new keyframes to their default settings. This can be a royal pain, so be careful when using Reset.

3. This part of this coming complex Motion effect will be to have the clip start as a tiny dot in the upper-left corner, grow to full-screen, and then shrink down to the lower-right corner. Start by pressing Home to place the CTI at the beginning of the clip, switch on keyframes for Position, and move the center of the clip to the upper-left corner (position 0,0).

4. Switch on the keyframe stopwatch for Scale and drag the slider to zero (or change the numeric value to zero). That sets the size to zero for the beginning of the clip.

By the Way

Uniform Scale—As It Pleases You

Feel free to uncheck the Uniform Scale box. Doing so means that you can set Width and Height independently and keyframe them separately.

5. Move the CTI about a third of the way into the clip and press Reset (yes, the Reset button can come in handy) to create two keyframes with default settings (clip at full size and centered in the screen).

6. Move the CTI about two thirds of the way into the clip and press Reset again. Doing that causes the clip to remain centered and at full screen for the time between the two keyframes.

▼

7. Move the clip to the lower right (720,480) and change the Scale back to zero. At this point, your ECW should look like Figure 11.5.

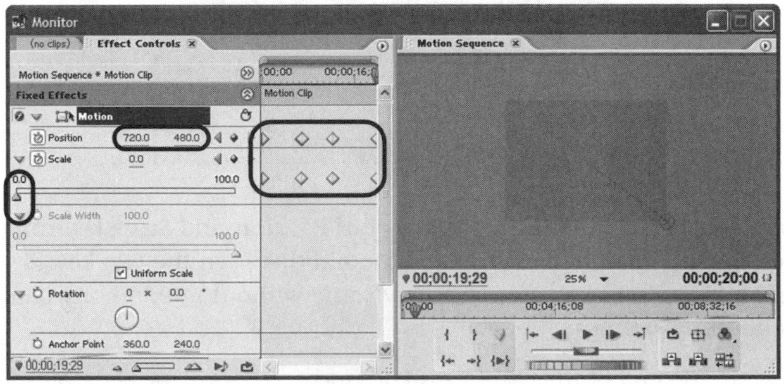

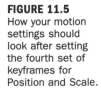

FIGURE 11.5
How your motion settings should look after setting the fourth set of keyframes for Position and Scale.

8. Preview this Position/Scale combo Motion effect by pressing the Home key and the spacebar. The clip should grow from a tiny dot in the upper left and move to full-screen in the center, hold there for a while, and then shrink to a dot while moving to the lower-right corner.

Adding Rotation

Try it Yourself

Finally, you'll add rotation using some new keyframes as well as change the rotation center—or anchor point. In the end, you'll impart your clip with some complex characteristics. This is the most detailed of all the tasks in this hour. Its purpose is to give you a complete look at rotation characteristics. Here's how to wrap up this effect:

1. Add Rotation to this clip by pressing Home to position the CTI edit line at the beginning of the clip. Switch on the Keyframe stopwatch for Rotation. That sets a starting keyframe for Rotation without applying any rotation to the clip.

2. To have the rotation stop just before the clip reaches full-screen size, move the CTI to just before the second set of keyframes.

3. You can manually rotate the clip a few times by moving the cursor to just outside the bounding box to switch on the rotation icon (as shown in Figure 11.6) and dragging it around the clip a few times (for this exercise, do it clockwise). The easier and more exacting method is to change the first Rotation value to something like 4 (for four full clockwise rotations). The second number is degrees and represents a partial rotation.

FIGURE 11.6
You can manually
rotate the clip by
moving the cursor
until this icon
appears and then
dragging it around
the clip bounding
box.

4. Move the CTI to just past the third set of Position and Scale keyframes and click the little Rotation keyframe diamond (between the two keyframe navigation triangles) to create a new keyframe without making any changes to the rotation settings.

5. Move to the end of the clip (press End and the left-arrow key—or—click either the Position or Scale keyframe right navigation triangle). Rewind your clip rotation by manually spinning it counterclockwise four times or changing the first Rotation setting back to 0 (four counterclockwise rotations to return it to its default position). If you set it to –4, it would rotate counterclockwise eight times.

6. Return the CTI to the clip's first frame by pressing Home.

7. Turn on the anchor point's keyframe stopwatch and set the numeric values to 0,0 (the clip will spin around its upper-left vertex).

8. Move to the Rotation's second keyframe by clicking its keyframe navigation triangle and then change the anchor point's numeric values to 720,480 (setting the clip's rotation vertex to its lower-right corner).

Watch Out!

Changing the Anchor Point Changes the Position

If you preview at this point, the results might surprise you. The clip will not settle in the center of the screen. Rather, it will end up in the upper-left corner. The reason? Changing the Rotation's anchor point sets that location as the point the Position "thinks" is the center of the clip. In this case, to get the clip centered in the screen, you'll need to change the Position values. Do that in step 9.

9. Move to the Position's second and third keyframes and change those values from 360,240 to 720,480. Because the anchor point is the clip's lower-right corner, using these values places that corner at the bottom-right corner of the screen, thereby placing the entire clip squarely in the center of the screen.

10. Use Rotation's keyframe navigation controls to move to that feature's third keyframe and then click the anchor point's keyframe diamond to set a new keyframe there without changing its current value (using Rotation's keyframes to set an anchor point keyframe means that they'll fall at the same place in the sequence).

11. Move to the clip's last keyframe by pressing End and the left-arrow key.

12. Change the anchor point to the clip's upper-right corner by changing its value to 720,0. Your ECW timeline should look something like Figure 11.7. (I moved the CTI edit line to a position near the beginning of the clip to better display its motion path in the Monitor window.)

13. Preview your motion settings by pressing Home and the spacebar. If all goes well, the clip will spin on screen from the upper-left corner, its vertex will shift as it spins, the clip will grow to full-screen size, and will then spin down to the right with the vertex shifting once again.

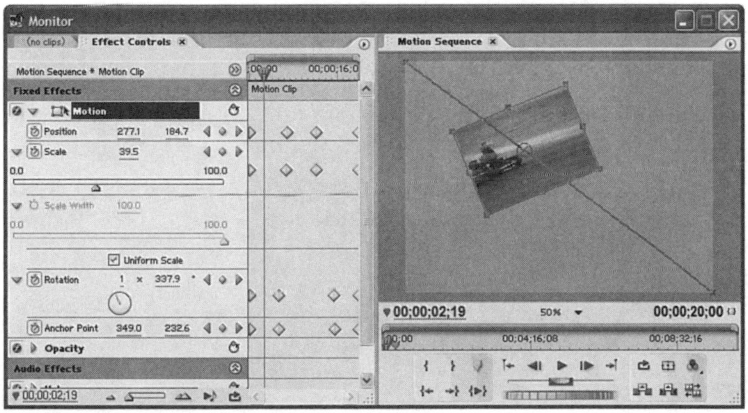

FIGURE 11.7
How your ECW timeline should look after adding keyframes for all Motion elements. Note that the position of the CTI sets the portion of the motion path you see in the Monitor window Program screen.

Giving Clips a 3D Look

Pictures-in-pictures have a much more realistic feel when those pictures have drop shadows. And adding borders or frames further enhances that look. You'll do both in this coming task.

Adding Shadows and Frames

Try it Yourself

Adding these two characteristics to moving clips is surprisingly easy. You simply use two video effects: Drop Shadow and Bevel Edges. Here's how you do this:

▼

1. Clear all motion characteristics by clicking each keyframe stopwatch and clicking the Reset button.

2. Shrink your clip by changing its scale to 50% (you can't see the drop shadow if your clip is full screen).

3. Apply the Drop Shadow video effect to your shrunken clip by dragging it from the Perspective folder to the ECW.

4. Twirl down all of Drop Shadow's disclosure triangles to reveal its six options:

   ▶ **Shadow Color**—Set it to any color you want. You might want to have it be a darker version of your matte color.

   ▶ **Opacity**—Most shadows aren't opaque. You can vary to match the lighting of the original clips.

   ▶ **Direction**—The point indicates in which direction the shadow will fall. Using keyframes, you can vary that direction such that the shadow spins around the clip.

   ▶ **Distance**—How far the shadow falls from edge of the clip.

   ▶ **Softness**—Give your shadow hard edges or let them disappear gradually.

   ▶ **Shadow Only**—Switch off your clip and display only its shadow.

5. Give your shadow some distance and some softness (values of 30 for both features work well). Your settings and Monitor window display should look something like Figure 11.8.

FIGURE 11.8
Use Drop Shadow's keyframable options to create a more realistic look for your motion effects.

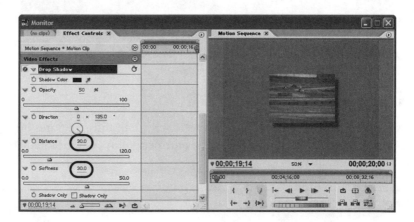

▼

6. Use Position keyframes to give your clip some motion. Preview your work and note that the shadow follows the clip perfectly.

Watch
Out!

Motion Effect's Rotation Does Not Work with Shadows

If you use the Motion effect to apply rotation to your shadow and clip, the shadow will rotate *with* the clip as a single unit. That's unrealistic. It should always fall away from the rotating clip in the same direction. To get a realistic drop shadow with rotation applied, you need to use the Transform video effect. I cover that in Hour 19, "Tips, Tricks, and Techniques—Part 1."

7. Add a very nice frame to your clip by dragging Bevel Edges from the Video Effects, Perspective folder to the ECW *above* Drop Shadow and *below* the Video Effects section label. Twirl down its disclosure triangles. Your setup should look like Figure 11.9.

Watch
Out!

Video Effects—Order Counts

You need to place the Bevel Edges effect above Drop Shadow because Premiere Pro applies effects in order from the top of the Video Effects group and down. Therefore, if Drop Shadow were at the top, Bevel Edges would apply its frame effect to the clip *and* the shadow. Not a desirable result.

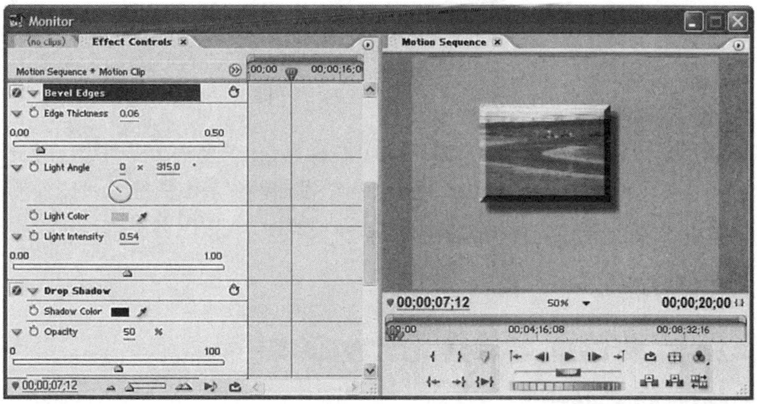

FIGURE 11.9
Use Bevel Edges to give your moving clip a nice framed look.

8. Change the Light Angle value to the complement of the Drop Shadow Direction (add or subtract 180 degrees from the Drop Shadow Direction value) so that the bevel and shadow look realistic.

▼

9. Adjust the Edge Thickness setting to suit your tastes and change the Light Intensity value so that it works well with your drop shadow's Opacity and Softness qualities.

▲

10. Preview your work.

Did you Know?

Making an Opaque Frame

It can be a bit disconcerting to have animated beveled edges. If you want to turn those edges into solid color (or at least darker) frames, simply select a dark light color (yes, the nomenclature can be confusing) and increase the Light Intensity value to bring out the 3D beveled look.

Did you Know?

Another Framing Option

Premiere Pro is chock-a-block with multiple means to an end. Along those lines, try the Clip video effect to make a frame. It adds a border using a color or colors (this feature is keyframable) you select to a solid rectangular border. That border steals pixels from the edge of your clip, so this is not a perfect solution, but it's easy and effective. I cover it in more detail in Hour 16.

Layering Clips in Motion

Placing one clip in motion—with a drop shadow and a frame—is a reasonably cool effect. It becomes much more interesting if you fly a collection of clips around the screen. I cover that technique in Hour 17.

In one of the upcoming end-of-hour exercises, I suggest you experiment with that. The basic procedure is to place several clips, one above the other, on separate video tracks. Then give motion settings, drop shadows, and beveled edges to each in turn.

Working with Still Images—
Special Issues

Unlike its predecessors, Premiere Pro does *not* automatically change the size and aspect ratio of imported still images and graphics to match the project settings (in most cases 720×480 pixels). Rather, Premiere Pro preserves those clips' original sizes and aspect ratios.

That means if you import a large image (greater than 720 pixels wide or 480 pixels tall in most cases), Premiere Pro centers it in the Monitor window screens and truncates it. Unless you take some steps to shrink that image to fit, only the center portion that fits the project resolution will end up in your final project.

On the other hand, if you import a small image, Premiere Pro does not blow it up to fit. Premiere Pro centers the image and displays it in its original resolution.

Blowing Up Small Resolution Images Can Be Messy

When possible, always use still images that are at least as large as your project resolution. If you use smaller resolution images and then zoom in on them, they lose visual quality. Sort of like a digital zoom on a camcorder. You end up with blocky chunks.

This resolution retention is an excellent development. It's predicable and, more importantly, it enables you to put large clips in motion while maintaining a relatively high screen resolution. You've seen those Ken Burns public TV specials with all their stills-in-motion. Premiere Pro lets you do the same thing easily.

Rather than take you through a Try It Yourself task, I'll briefly explain how to do it and illustrate that process with a few figures.

Zooming in on a High-Resolution Image

I like to make family tree videos and DVDs, so I frequently work with old family photos and documents. Figure 11.10 shows a portrait that I captured at 1150×1650 resolution. When placed on a sequence and displayed in the Monitor window Program screen, only the center 720×480 pixels display.

FIGURE 11.10
When working with a large format image, Premiere Pro displays only the center 720×480 pixel portion.

Here's how I turn that large format image into an attention-holding zoom:

1. I place the still image on Video 2 and drag its right edge to lengthen it from the default 5-second duration for still images.

2. I create a new color matte using a color that complements the photo's sepia tone and place it on Video 1 beneath my image clip.

3. I want to start wide on this image and zoom in on the faces of the two young men. To do that, I use the Motion effect and reduce the Scale setting (in this case to 30%).

4. As shown in Figure 11.11, I also switch on the Safe Margins display to ensure that I don't put important parts of the image outside the viewing area of most NTSC TV sets.

Turning on the Safe Margins Display

As a reminder, to turn on the Safe Margins display, click the Monitor window Wing Menu disclosure triangle and select Safe Margins.

FIGURE 11.11
Use the Motion effect Scale feature to zoom out from a high-resolution image. Turn on Safe Margins to avoid clipping important photo elements.

5. I place the CTI edit line on the photo's first frame and switch on the Position and Scale keyframe stopwatches to set the zoomed-out view as the starting point.

6. I move to the end of the clip. There I change the Position and Scale settings (thereby setting new keyframes) to zoom in on the portrait to the point shown in Figure 11.12.

FIGURE 11.12
Use the Motion effect to zoom in to add a little drama to a still image.

You can use the Motion effect in myriad ways to add interest to still images. Pan across wide shots, zoom out to reveal an interesting detail, or zoom in on an individual in a family portrait and then add an oval highlight (I show you how to do that effect in Hour 19).

Summary

Premiere Pro's new Motion effect is a wonderful tool. It can add drama to static images and it allows you to change image sizes, fly them anywhere on and off the screen, as well as rotate them. You can further enhance those motion characteristics by adding drop shadows and frames to your animated clips.

The Premiere Pro implementation of the Motion effect is a significant improvement over its predecessors. Now all the motion work takes place within the Effect Controls and Monitor windows, you can apply motion settings using a simple drag-and-drop method or the more precise numeric value approach, and all of its features are keyframable, giving you a full range of control.

Q&A

Q *I rotate a clip two times when bringing it on screen, and then set the rotation value to –2 to spin it back off. But it spins four times, not twice as I'd expect. What's going on?*

A The number of spins equals the difference between two keyframe rotation values. So, you rotated the clip twice to bring it on, using a Rotation numeric value of 2. But when you set the numeric value to –2 to spin it off, the difference between the two settings is 4—four counterclockwise spins. Set the Rotation value back to 0 (zero) to have it spin counterclockwise twice.

Q *I import a photo but when I view it in the Monitor window, I see only part of it. I changed the View Zoom Level value and the screen size changes, but I still see only that same portion. What's up?*

A Previous versions of Premiere used to shrink or expand still images to fit the project resolution and aspect ratio (usually standard TV—4:3). Fortunately, that behavior is now a thing of the past. Now you can import images as large as 4000×4000 pixels. But Premiere Pro will display only the center 720×480 pixel portion of such large format images. To see your entire image, use the Motion effect Scale setting to shrink it to fit the screen display.

Workshop

Quiz

1. You want a clip to appear full screen for a few seconds and then spin away. How do you make the Motion effect Rotation feature start within a clip rather than at the beginning?

2. You use Motion's Scale feature to shrink a clip and then add a frame using Bevel Edges. How do you give those edges a solid (or nearly solid) color while retaining the beveled look?

3. Using a high-resolution photo, how do you start tight on an individual, hold that position for a while, and then pull back to reveal the entire image.

Quiz Answers

1. Use keyframes. Move the CTI edit line to the point at which you want to start spinning the clip off screen and click the Rotation keyframe stopwatch to set its starting keyframe at that position. Then move the CTI edit line to the end of the clip and change the rotation setting to suit your purposes (update the clip Position and Scale settings if needed). That will automatically add an ending Rotation keyframe with its new values applied.

2. Although the nomenclature makes this sound counterintuitive, choose a dark light color and then increase the Light Intensity value to emphasize the beveled frame corners. You might also play with the Light Angle setting to find the direction that gives the greatest 3D look. Settings at the compass's cardinal points—0, 90, 180 and 270 degrees—work well for me.

3. Use the Motion effect Scale and Position settings for the initial tight view and proper framing, and then move the CTI edit line to the point at which you want to begin pulling back and switch on the keyframe stopwatches for those two motion elements (that will set keyframes using the Scale and Position values you set for the first frame). Move the CTI to the location in the clip where you want the move to end and change the Scale and Position values. That automatically sets new keyframes and concludes the move. You can use interpolation controls to have a Slow In or Easy Curve In effect to add even more drama.

Exercises

1. Do some extensive work with the Motion effect and its keyframes. Try moving keyframes around by clicking and dragging them. Change values for the five Motion effect features. Experiment with Rotation, Anchor Point, and Position to see how they interact. The more you work with this very powerful and important part of Premiere Pro, the more likely you are to use it effectively.

2. Try creating multiple pictures-in-a-picture. The basic way to do that is to start with a background matte, image or video on Video 1 and then place multiple clips, one above the other, on ascending video tracks. To create those additional tracks, simply drag each clip to the gray area in the sequence above the existing uppermost video track and Premiere Pro will

automatically create a new track. Switch off all the video track eyeballs except Video 1 and Video 2. Shrink the clip on Video 2 and put it in motion. Then switch on the eyeball of Video 3, shrink that clip, and give it motion (you'll see how it works with the clip on Video 2), and continue working up through the video tracks.

3. Scan in some photos in relatively high resolution—1,500×1,000 works well because it's about double DV resolution—and apply some pans and zooms to them, aiming to create a dramatic effect. Either reveal something or zoom in to draw attention to a subject.

PART III

Acquiring, Editing, and Sweetening Audio

HOUR 12

Acquiring Audio

What You'll Learn in This Hour:

▶ Selecting the right microphones for the job

▶ Connecting microphones to your camcorder or PC

▶ Expert audio tips from a Shure, Inc. engineer

▶ Building a voice recording area

▶ Voicing professional narrations

▶ Ripping music CDs

▶ Creating custom tunes with SmartSound's Movie Maestro

Audio is crucial. The best images will lose their impact if their audio is mediocre. Premiere offers plenty of ways to give your project a sonic boost.

You'll need to acquire some of that audio during on-location taping. Relying solely on your onboard camcorder microphone (or *mic*, for short) might lead to disappointing results. Choosing and using additional mics will sweeten your sound. After you're back in your studio—be it at home or work—you'll likely add a narration. There's no need to rent an expensive audio studio—your camcorder or soundcard and a simple makeshift audio recording area will do the trick. Some professional narration techniques will help as well. Finally, there's no need to hire a composer and musicians for noncommercial-use music: Rip CDs or use the fun music creation product that I introduce at the end of this hour.

Selecting the Right Mic for the Job

The first order of business: Get a good headset—one that covers your ears to block out extraneous sound. Plug it into your camcorder. As you record, listen. Is that how you want your video production to sound?

Onboard microphones take the middle ground. They pick up sound from every-where, including camera noise and wind. If you zoom in on a subject, onboard mics don't zoom with you. They still pick up noise from all around you. Crowd noise, sound reflecting off walls, the hum from the air conditioner, the zoom lens motor—as well as noise you create while handling the camcorder.

What you need are some external mics; specialized mics that serve narrow but useful functions. I've illustrated them in Figure 12.1. Here are the five basic types:

- ▶ Handheld
- ▶ Shotgun
- ▶ Wireless
- ▶ Surface mount
- ▶ Lavaliere

FIGURE 12.1
Five standard-issue mics: handheld, shotgun, wireless handheld, bound-ary, and lavaliere. (Products provided by Shure, Inc.)

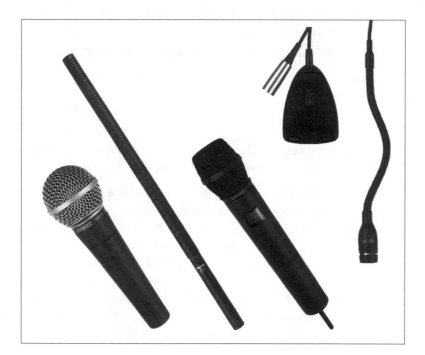

Handheld Mic

If you own only one external mic, make it a handheld. They're the rugged work-horses of the audio industry. Built with internal shock mounts to reduce handling noise, you'll use these mics for interviews, place them on podiums to record speeches, and use them to create narrations.

Many handheld mics are **omnidirectional**, meaning that they pick up sound from all directions. So, they'll pick up ambient room noise as well as close-up audio. To minimize that unwanted noise, keep the mic as close to your subject as practical—about a foot from the speaker's mouth works well.

A top-of-the-line, rugged, durable handheld costs from $150 to $250. Shure, Inc. (www.shure.com), the world's leading mic manufacturer, loaned me a handheld— as well as a lavaliere and a shotgun mic—to test while writing this book. (A senior engineer with Shure provided the expert sidebar later in this hour.) The Shure handheld SM63LB performed flawlessly within a wide frequency range, accurately capturing low and high voices. It retails for $225.

Most handheld mics use what's called a *dynamic transducer*. As Figure 12.2 illustrates, the transducer is a thin diaphragm attached to a tiny coil. As sound waves vibrate the diaphragm, the wire moves over a magnet, which converts that physical energy into an electrical signal. Dynamic transducer mics do not require any electrical power to operate.

Shure Inc., notes that "Dynamic mics are rugged and can handle high sound pressure levels, like those delivered by kick drums, snare drums, and high volume guitar amps. They're also good for loud, aggressive vocals. Most people start out recording with dynamic mics because of their lower cost and high durability."

The other type of mic—the *condenser transducer*, also shown in Figure 12.2—needs "phantom" power to be provided by a mixer or batteries. It uses a thin, flat plastic or metal diaphragm layered over another piece of metal or metal-coated ceramic. This type of mic is typically very small and has an extremely weak signal that requires preamplification before sending it to your camcorder or a mixer.

Shure adds that "Condenser mics are more sensitive than dynamic mics and are very responsive to high frequencies produced by an acoustic guitar or cymbals on a drum-kit." Condenser mics are excellent for interviews, narrations, and performance or studio music vocal recordings.

Lavaliere Mic

Most lavalieres use condenser transducer technology. They're perfect for formal, sit-down interviews. Their tiny size means that you can conceal them to minimize that "Oh, we're watching TV" disconnect. The downside is that most require batteries. As you know, batteries invariably fail at critical moments, so always use fresh, high-quality mic batteries. It *is* possible to power lavalieres directly from some mixers, but few budding video producers will use mixers.

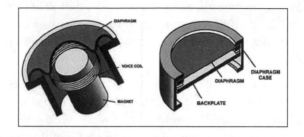

FIGURE 12.2
Cutaway views of a dynamic transducer mic (left) and a condenser transducer mic. (Illustration courtesy of Shure Inc., 2003.)

I tested Shure's WL50B. The clear and crisp sound was a cut above the handheld and is reflected in its higher price: $316.

Shotgun Mic

So-named because it resembles a shotgun barrel, the shotgun mic's unidirectional barrel (called an *interference tube*) narrows the focus of the audio field to about 30 degrees.

A shotgun mic can handle a number of tasks. I picked up one idea from top freelance photojournalist John Alpert. He's a one-man band who ventures into uncomfortable and frequently dangerous situations and uses his affable demeanor to get some amazingly revealing sound bites. Instead of shoving a handheld mic into his subjects' faces—which frequently leads to "mic-stare" and other nervous reactions—he uses a shotgun mic tucked under his armpit. He leans his head away from the camera viewfinder and simply chats with his subjects in his unique, gee-whiz kind of way. It works like magic.

One thing shotgun mics don't do is zoom. As Chris Lyons, the Shure engineer who wrote the audio expert sidebar says, "They're more like looking through a long tube at someone." They narrow your "view" of the sound.

By the Way

A Telephoto Mic

The telephoto lens equivalent in the microphone world is a parabolic dish. You've seen networks use them along the sidelines of NFL games to get those great crunching hits.

Good shotgun mics will set you back about $1,000. I tried out Shure's superb SM89 ($1,180). This is a condenser mic and needs phantom power that a standard prosumer camcorder cannot provide. A $100 (list price) PB224 portable phantom power adapter from the Rolls Corporation (www.rolls.com) will take care of that.

Boundary or Surface Mount Mics

You'll use these very specialized mics to pick up several speakers at a conference table or on a theater stage. They're built to be placed on a flat surface and pick up sound waves in both the air and from the hard surface. A good omnidirectional boundary mic costs about $160.

Wireless Systems

A wireless system is a major purchase that might set you back about as much as a medium-quality DV camcorder. And it can be a battery hog. But it can make your life a whole lot simpler and give you some incredible audio.

Wireless mics open a whole new spectrum of possibilities—a presenter at a trade show, the priest at a wedding, or a football coach working the sidelines. Wireless mics enable you to grab sound from a distance. After you've used one, you'll wonder how you got along without it. Wireless mics are a luxury, and good ones are priced to match. My Shure UP4 test unit, including receiver and an M58 mic with a built-in U2 transmitter, retails for $2,086 (see Figure 12.3).

FIGURE 12.3
The Shure UP4 wireless receiver with a combo mic and wireless transmitter.

Connecting Mics to Your Camcorder or PC

Surprisingly, this is the place where most mic problems arise. Most consumer and prosumer camcorders do not have decent mic input connections. They typically do not have enough amplification to "hear" standard handheld mics. What's more, they use mini-plugs, whereas most professional mics use rugged, reliable, three-pronged XLR jacks.

What you might need is a transformer with an XLR-to-mini–plug cable to increase the impedance and enable you to connect your mic to your camcorder. Such transformers are passive, meaning that they don't require electricity. Shure has just such a transformer—the A96F—for $54. If you use a powered mic such as a lavaliere, you might need only the XLR-to-mini–plug converter cable.

Making the PC Connection

Premiere Pro makes it possible for you to add a narration track to your project, live, as you watch your video play. To do that, you need to connect a mic to your soundcard. (I cover that recording process in the next hour, "Editing Audio.")

Voice-overs created with soundcards generally can't sound as good as those recorded with professional equipment in a recording studio or even as good as those made using a mic plugged into your camcorder. But they still can sound good enough for basic production work. You can take two routes: simple or not-so-simple.

Simple Approach

The simple approach is to visit your local Radio Shack and spend $20 to $30 on a mic. You'll have two basic choices:

- **Dynamic mics** come in two models. One is combined with a headset. Gamers and those who use their PCs to make phone calls like this hands-free approach. The other is a long-neck version that sets on your desk, which minimizes extraneous noise.

- **Condenser mics** offer slightly better voice-over quality and require a battery. They typically are lavaliere-style.

Buy a mic with a 1/8" (3.5mm) stereo mini-jack connection so that it can plug directly into your soundcard. Figure 12.4 shows a typical soundcard rear panel. Plug the mic into the correct jack (usually marked Mic or with a mic icon) and not the Line-in jack used with amplified devices such as CD players and sound mixers.

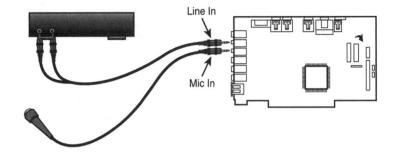

FIGURE 12.4
Plug your mic into the Mic jack on your soundcard's back panel. Use the Line-in jack only if you're using an amplified mixer with your mic.

Whichever mic you choose, make sure that you also get a headset. As I mention later this hour in "Voicing Solid Narrations," it's important to hear how the mic hears you.

Smooth Voice-over Recording

Recording a voice-over while editing video is a system-intensive process. To ensure glitch-free recording, free up resources: Close antivirus software, system-monitoring products, and other programs that might be running in the background with the exception of those required for the video, audio, and system components to function properly.

Did you Know?

Not-So-Simple Approach

Here's how you can up the soundcard voice-over ante. Buy two professional omni-directional mics. Most come with 1/4" or the much larger XLR connectors. Connect them to a pre-amplifier and a mixer. The pre-amp will improve the "color" of the sound. The mixer enables you to increase the stereo effect or sweet spot. To achieve that sweet spot, place the mics a few inches apart and then voice your narration into both of them. Doing so will better approximate the human ear spacing for stereo recording. You'll need an adapter to connect the mixer to the soundcard's 1/8" plug.

Getting the Most from Your Mics— Expert Audio Tips

When I considered whom I'd tap for audio expertise, only one name came to mind: Shure, Inc. Throughout my TV news and video production career, Shure mics have been the staple in our audio kits.

This 78-year old company is a world leader in microphone technology, playing a role in audio history from the Japanese surrender ending World War II and President John F. Kennedy's inaugural address to Woodstock and the 2002 Winter Olympics, where Shure's wireless systems captured all the opening ceremonies' audio moments. You heard Shure mics at the 2003 Montreux Jazz Festival, the 2003 Country Music Awards, and at the Rock and Roll Hall of Fame Museum.

Shure's "Elvis mic," the Unidyne, kicked things off when the company first introduced it in 1939. Frank Sinatra and the Rolling Stones field-tested the SM58—the world's best-selling, all-purpose vocal mic, which was introduced in 1966. And now groups such as N*SYNC and D'Angelo rely on Shure's Beta Series.

Shure put me in touch with Chris Lyons, a senior engineer in Shure's Applications Group. In his 12 years with Shure, he has served as technical liaison for Shure's broadcast customers and as product line manager for Wired Microphones. Chris has presented hundreds of audio training seminars to broadcasters, educators, government agencies, and audio/visual production specialists. He has written and edited numerous articles and technical papers, including the booklet *Guide to Better Audio for Video Production*, available for free download at www.shure.com/booklets/techpubs.html.

Chris offers this expert advice:

> ▶ **Advice on the position of the microphone:** Always place the microphone as close as is practical to the sound source. Every time the source-to-mic distance increases by a factor of two, the sound pressure level (SPL) reaching the mic decreases by a factor of four, making clear sound pickup progressively more difficult. This is called the *inverse-square rule*, and it applies

whether the distance increases from 6 inches to 12 inches or from 6 feet to 12 feet. This means that the talker-to-mic distance must be cut in half to cause a significant improvement in sound quality.

▶ **Advice on the number of microphones used:** Use the fewest number of microphones necessary for the situation. People sometimes have a tendency to over-mic a shot, using three or four microphones when one or two would be sufficient. Using excess mics means more background noise pickup, a greater chance of feedback or "tin can" sound, and more levels for the operator to keep track of. If additional mics don't make things sound better, they'll probably make things sound worse.

▶ **Advice for using a handheld mic:** Whether held in the hand or mounted on a stand, place this mic about 6–12 inches from the talker's mouth, pointing up at about a 45-degree angle (see Figure 12.5). With some types of microphones, holding the microphone very close (3–6 inches) will cause additional emphasis of the lower frequencies (known as *proximity effect*), resulting in a warmer, bass-heavy sound.

FIGURE 12.5
Proper placement for a handheld mic. (Illustration courtesy Shure, Inc. 2002.)

▶ **Advice for using a lavaliere mic:** For best results, clip a lavaliere mic on the outside of clothing, about 6 to 8 inches below the chin. You can clip the mic to the collar of a shirt or blouse, but sound quality in this position tends to be somewhat muffled because some high frequencies (which contain consonants) do not fully wrap around to the area under the chin.

▶ **Advice for concealing a lavaliere mic:** Concealing the mic gives your production an extra level of quality. Make sure that you keep both the microphone and the first few inches of cable from rubbing against either the body or clothing, which will cause noise. Try taping the "lav" under the shirt collar near the opening in front. The cable can be routed around to the back of the neck, over the collar, and under the shirt. Alternatively, tape it to the interviewee's eyeglasses on the inside by the temple. Route the wire over the ear and down the back.

▶ **Advice for using a surface mount mic:** These are great for panel discussions and work best when positioned on a smooth, flat surface, such as a table or desk. A thin piece of soft foam rubber or a computer mouse pad underneath the mic helps minimize problems created by surface vibrations. Small surfaces—less than 3-feet square—reduce the pickup of low frequencies and might improve the clarity of deep voices by reducing "boominess."

▶ **Advice for using a shotgun mic:** Avoid aiming shotgun mics at hard surfaces such as tile floors, brick walls, and flat ceilings. These surfaces reflect background noise into the microphone or cause the sound to be slightly hollow. Place a heavy blanket on a reflective surface to provide some sound absorption. Shotgun mics are more sensitive to wind noise than standard microphones, so use a foam windscreen and don't move them too rapidly. A rubber-isolated shock mount will help control handling noise.

▶ **Use only low-impedance microphones.** Low-impedance or "low-Z" mics (less than 600 ohms) enable you to use very long runs of cable (more than 1,000 feet) with negligible loss of sound quality. "High-Z" mics (greater than 10,000 ohms) lose high frequencies and begin to sound muffled with 20-foot cables. The impedance of a microphone should *not* match the impedance of the input to which it is connected. Matching the impedance causes significant signal level loss. Always connect low-impedance microphones to higher-impedance inputs—preferably 5 to 10 times greater. Inputs on professional mixers typically have an impedance of 1,000 ohms or more.

▶ **Tips on using wireless systems:** Try to keep the distance from the transmitter to the receiver as short as possible. Always do a walk-around with the mic before the event. If dropouts occur, try moving the receiver a few feet and repeat the walk-around. Dual-antenna diversity receivers minimize dropout because it is unlikely that the signal to both antennas will be interrupted at the same instant. If possible, do your sound check at the same time of day as the event to discover whether there are any nearby users of your wireless frequencies. When using belt-pack-type transmitters, make sure that the antenna cable is hanging straight. Coiling it up in the wearer's pocket significantly reduces transmission distance. With handheld transmitters that have an external antenna, discourage users from holding their hands over the antenna to avoid reducing transmission range and increasing dropout.

▶ **Use balanced cables and connectors.** Their metal shielding keeps the audio signal free of interference from things such as fluorescent lights, dimmer switches, and other audio or electrical cables. Use cables with braided or mesh shielding. They are more resistant than metal foil shielding to cracks or tears, which cause electrical shorts.

▶ **Plan ahead.** This is the most important thing you can do to improve the audio quality of your productions. When you set up your equipment, look for things that might cause a problem with your audio—air conditioning ducts, noisy doors, fluorescent lights, and so on. Check for things that you can use to your advantage—sound-absorbent carpeting or a built-in PA system. Experiment with different mic placements, but don't gamble an important project on a method you've never tried. Monitor your audio and listen carefully for anything that sounds unnatural. As the saying goes, "If you notice the sound, there's something wrong with it."

Building a Simple and Inexpensive Voice-Recording Area

To create your voice-over narration, you'll need a quiet, sound-absorbing location. I touched base with the industry leader in sound absorption material: Auralex Acoustics.

Auralex suggests that the easiest solution is to build a temporary recording area simply by hanging some thick blankets or fiberglass insulation on two joining corner walls. It is an old audio myth that egg cartons, carpeting, and foam rubber work well. Avoid them. If you can create something like a four-sided, blanketed cubicle, so much the better.

If you drape the blankets only in one corner, point the mic toward that corner, place yourself between the mic and the corner, and speak *away* from the blankets. It seems counterintuitive, but the mic is sort of like a camera. It "sees" what's in front of it (even if it is omnidirectional). In this case it "sees" your face and the hanging, sound-absorbing blankets.

If you want to take your voice-recording area quality up several notches, consider purchasing Auralex's studio foam sheets or a portable recording area kit. These kits range in price from $159 to $999. Figure 12.6 illustrates two of these *acoustic environments*, as Auralex calls them. The company emphasizes that these kits are not true isolation booths. Those are intended to keep sound out and require some serious construction. Visit www.auralex.com/ for product and dealer info, plus a contact phone number. Auralex is very customer-service oriented and will help you find a solution.

Voicing Solid Narrations

Creating narrations is as easy as turning on your camcorder. If you have a hand-held mic (or some other external mic), plug it into your camcorder. Otherwise, you can use the built-in, onboard camcorder mic.

Before you record your voice-over, go over this checklist to make sure that you're ready:

▶ **Read your copy out loud.** Listen to your words. They should sound comfortable, conversational, even informal.

▶ **Avoid technical jargon.** That demands extra effort from your listeners, and you might lose them.

▶ **Short sentences work best.** If you find yourself stumbling over certain long phrases, rewrite them.

▶ **Stress important words and phrases.** As you review your copy, underline important words. When you record your voice-over, you'll want to give those words extra emphasis—more volume and punch.

▶ **Mark pauses.** Go through your copy and mark logical breaks with short parallel lines. They'll remind you to pause at those points. Avoid overly smooth and constant pacing. That's characteristic of a scripted delivery and, once again, you don't want to remind viewers that this is TV. It's real life. It's conversational.

▶ **Break up your copy into shorter sentences.** Always be on the lookout for convoluted, wandering sentences. Too many modifiers can be unwieldy. Break long sentences into several shorter ones. Shorter sentences tend to have only one key point. It's easier to emphasize one key point in one sentence versus multiple points in a rambling speech.

▶ **Punch up your voice.** When reading copy, it's too easy to slip into a dull, monotone voice. Instead, add some zest and enthusiasm to your narration. As one consultant told me, "Pump up your projection." You want people to pay attention. You do that by speaking as if the subject truly interests you. On the other hand, you aren't trying to be a professional announcer. No need to put on airs or use a *basso profundo* voice.

▶ **Practice.** Record a couple narrations and listen. Have others listen. Most first-time narrators mumble or swallow words. Have you made yourself clear?

▶ **Use a wind screen.** Although you need to record close to the mic for best effect—12 inches away or so—getting too close can lead to "popping P's." As you say P-words, you project a small blast of wind at the mic. Using a wind screen minimizes that, as does not speaking directly into the mic.

▶ **Wear earphones.** In this case, the purpose is not to make sure that you're actually getting audio; rather, it's to hear yourself. That might seem a bit odd. You can hear yourself just fine without a headset. But you need the headset to see how the mic "hears" you. You'll also discover whether you're popping any P's or speaking with too much *sibilance*—an overemphasis on the S sound.

Ripping Music CDs

The easiest source for video production music is next to your stereo: your personal music CD collection. All CD cuts are digital and easily ripped to your hard drive. Once **ripped**—converted from CD audio a digital file on your hard drive—it's a simple matter to import CD music into Premiere Pro.

Beware the Copyright Police

Those tunes on your CDs are all copyrighted. I'm not an attorney and don't pretend to understand copyright law. That said, I'd suggest treading carefully when using someone else's music. Generally, if it's for personal use, it's considered *fair use* and there are no copyright issues. But just about any other use can step outside fair use.

Watch
Out!

To be on the safe side, compose your own music (see "Creating Custom Music with SmartSound Movie Maestro" later in this hour for one means to that end) or license or buy royalty-free music. To find out more about the latter, search on www.Google.com for *music licensing* or *royalty-free music*. I've worked with three such firms: www.LicenseMusic.com, www.dittybase.com, and www.Stock-Music.com.

Use Windows Media Player to Rip CD Cuts

No, the book is not taking a violent twist. *Ripping* is just how some describe the process of transferring music from a CD to a PC.

Several products are available to do that. The one most likely to be at your fingertips is Windows Media Player. Here's how it works:

1. Open Windows Media Player. It's probably in the Start menu under Accessories. If not, its default location is C:\Program Files\Windows Media Player\wmplayer.exe. You can open My Computer, go to this location, and double-click wmplayer.exe. Doing so opens the interface shown in Figure 12.7.

Automatically Opening Windows Media Player

You can open Windows Media Player another way. Simply insert a music CD into your DVD or CD drive and, depending on your version of Windows, either Windows Media Player automatically starts playing that CD or you're given an option of playing the CD with one of several programs that you have installed on your PC.

2. Click Copy from CD, as highlighted in Figure 12.7. That pops up a message asking you to insert an audio CD.

3. Insert a music CD. Either Windows will ask you which CD player you want to use (select Media Player) or Windows Media Player will automatically start playing the CD. Click the Stop button, at the bottom of the interface.

Online Album Details

All music CDs have unique identification numbers. Those numbers are generated by examining track times. If you're connected to the Internet, Media Player will send your music CD's number to www.allmusic.com (going through www.windowsmedia.com along the way). That site (owned by All Media Guide) is a repository of a huge database on music CDs. It uses that identifier number to retrieve your CD's information—title, artist, and track names—and then Windows Media Player displays them. As shown in Figure 12.8, click View Album Info for a full listing plus a review.

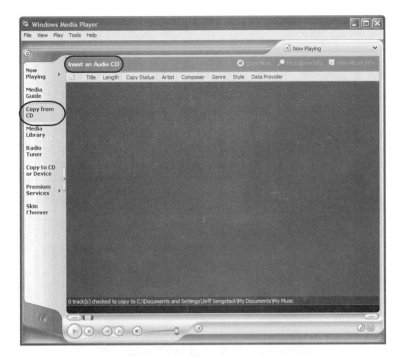

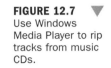

FIGURE 12.7 ▼
Use Windows
Media Player to rip
tracks from music
CDs.

FIGURE 12.8
Windows Media
Player's Copy CD
interface displays
information about
your CD retrieved
from the Internet
(to avoid any possi-
ble copyright con-
flicts, I created a
dummy screenshot
using my choir's
material).

▼

▼

4. By default, all tracks are check marked for copying to your hard drive. You can uncheck any that you don't want to copy.

Preview a Tune

If you want to preview a track, click it to select it and then click the Play button.

5. The default copy location is `C:\Documents and Settings\current user\My Documents\My Music`. Windows Media Player creates a folder for the artists and a subfolder for the selected album. If you want to change that location, select Tools, Options from the menu bar. Doing so opens the Options menu, shown in Figure 12.9. Select the Copy Music tab and change the directory.

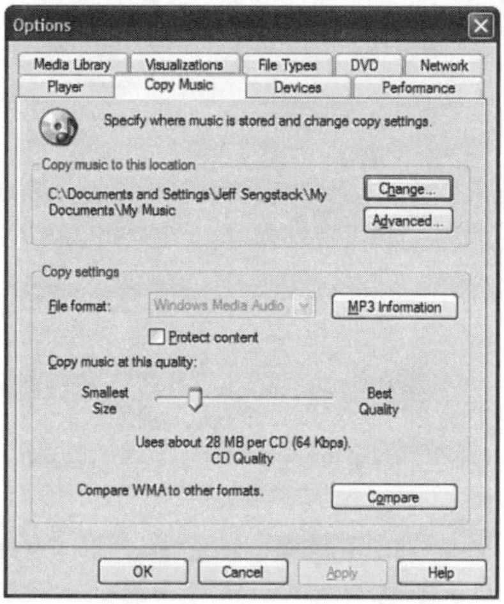

FIGURE 12.9
Use the Options interface to change the file folder storage location for your selected music tracks.

Avoid Vocals for Background Music

When selecting music for use in video or DVD productions, instrumentals generally work best. Vocals can step on your narration, natural sound, or voices in your videos.

6. When you're ready to copy the tracks, click the Copy Music button at the top of the interface. That opens two dialog boxes: The first reminds you to not make illegal copies and the second asks you about setting the recording quality level. It's best to use the highest quality setting for tunes you'll use in a Premiere Pro project. When you're past the dialog boxes, Windows Media Player displays progress bars to let you know how things are proceeding.

▲

Now that you've ripped a few tunes, you can use Media Player to burn a music CD. As shown in Figure 12.10, access that feature by clicking Copy to CD or Device, select the tracks you want to burn, place a recordable CD in your drive, and click the Copy button. This is a great way to create personalized CDs of your favorite tunes.

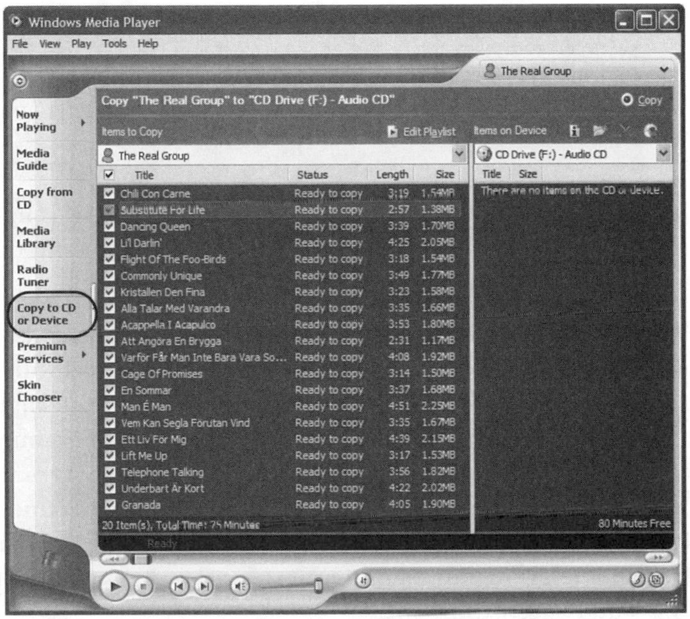

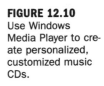

FIGURE 12.10
Use Windows Media Player to create personalized, customized music CDs.

Creating Custom Music with SmartSound Movie Maestro

Even if you can't carry a tune, you can create professional quality music. SmartSound Movie Maestro helps you compose custom music that fits not only the style of your video production, but also its exact length. The $50 retail version comes with 26 customizable songs (additional music collections, with themes such as Sentimental, Sports, and Vacation, retail for $30).

Here's what sets Movie Maestro created songs apart from any you'd receive from a licensing agency or royalty-free firm:

▶ SmartSound Movie Maestro can change the character of each tune to fit your needs by rearranging song segments in several distinct ways. Effectively, you get about eight songs for every one in the package.

▶ Using those same song segments and some smart software, Movie Maestro gives each song a clear, decisive ending right when you want it. There's no need to fade it out at your video's close.

Movie Maestro Music Usage Restrictions

Songs you create with the demo and retail versions of Movie Maestro are for non-commercial use only—meaning for home or school. If you want to use Movie Maestro for other purposes, such as business promotions, DVDs for retail sale, or in-house training DVDs, you must purchase music from SmartSound's Audio Palette or Edge series.

There are two ways to acquire the software needed to complete this up-coming task. You can download the demo version of Movie Maestro from www.smartsound.com/moviemaestro/index.html.

Or, if you upgraded to Premiere Pro from version 6 or 6.5, you can use the slightly different version of SmartSound, called Quicktracks, that shipped with those earlier versions of Premiere. Quicktracks comes on a separate CD that shipped with your retail version of Premiere. When installed, it resides in the Premiere 6 or 6.5 plug-ins folder (the default location is: C:\Program Files\Adobe\Premiere 6\Plug-ins). To use it with Premiere Pro, simply copy the SmartSound folder (right-click on it and select Copy) and paste it in your Premiere Pro plug-ins folder (right-click on that folder—default location: C:\Program Files\Adobe\Premiere Pro\Plug-ins—and select Paste).

To access the SmartSound Quicktracks plug-in, start Premiere Pro and then select File→New→SmartSound from the menu bar. The interface shown in Figure 12.11 looks different from the Movie Maestro demo, but the process to create music is very similar. Two significant advantages to using the Premiere plug-in are that it comes with 28 songs and the product does not expire. The downloaded demo has only 3 songs and times out 30 days after you first use it.

As we went to press, SmartSound was testing a beta version of a $99 retail Quicktracks plug-in for Premiere Pro.

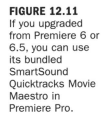

FIGURE 12.11
If you upgraded from Premiere 6 or 6.5, you can use its bundled SmartSound Quicktracks Movie Maestro in Premiere Pro.

Use Movie Maestro to Add Music to a Video

Try it Yourself

The downloaded version works the same way as its retail big brother. Here's how to use it:

1. Install the Movie Maestro demo by double-clicking the following file: MovieMaestroDemo.exe.

2. Open the program by double-clicking the SmartSound Movie Maestro icon on the desktop. That starts a brief musical introduction (as shown in Figure 12.12; you can click Skip to bypass it) and then the main user interface opens. A small dialog box, shown in Figure 12.13, pops up.

FIGURE 12.12
Create custom instrumental music in minutes with SmartSound Movie Maestro.

▼
FIGURE 12.13
You can create music to fit a particular video or as a standalone tune.

3. Click Create Music for a Movie, as shown in Figure 12.13. Doing so opens a file selection window with a default location of My Videos. If you have a video there, feel free to use it; otherwise, navigate to Movie Maestro's file folder (the default location is `C:\Program Files\Movie Maestro\Documentation`) and select `Sample Movie.mov`.

By the Way

Try the Tutorial

Feel free to use Movie Maestro's built-in tutorial by clicking the Tutorial button on the left side of the screen. It, too, uses the `Sample Movie.mov` file to demonstrate the software's functionality.

4. Click the Add Music button in the lower-left corner of the main interface to open the dialog box shown in Figure 12.14. This screen offers several musical styles as well as other means to make a musical selection.

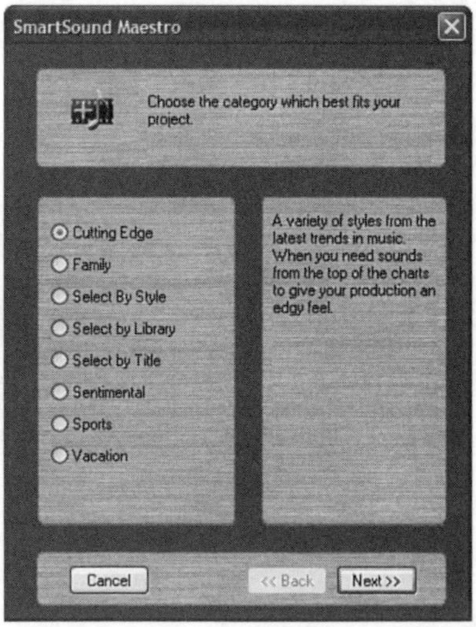

FIGURE 12.14
You can narrow your Movie Maestro music search using this interface. However, the demo version has only three songs, so don't expect too many choices.

▼

Demo Music Selection Limitations

It might appear that you have several choices in music, but this demo version has only three songs, so the various options don't have much meaning. If you click through the categories, you'll find little choice is available. If this were the retail product or the Premiere plug-in, there would be several tunes for each category, more than 25 in all.

5. Select a category and then select one of the three songs. Preview it by clicking the Play button at the bottom of the screen (see Figure 12.15). If it suits your needs, click Finish to automatically add it to the movie timeline and set its length to match the video.

Small Variation Between Products

At this point, the Premiere plug-in asks you to select a particular arrangement of this song. The downloaded demo version offers that option later.

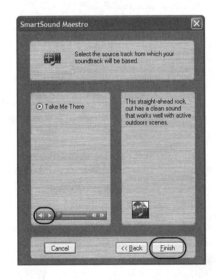

FIGURE 12.15
Listen to your selected tune by clicking the Play button.

6. Try your newly edited video (you might need to drag the Play Indicator to the start of the video—see Figure 12.16), by clicking the Play button.

FIGURE 12.16
Use this timeline interface to listen to how well your composition fits the video style.

Change the Length to Suit Your Needs

You can adjust the song's length by simply dragging and dropping its start and end-points. As you move the cursor, the video moves as well, so you can fine-tune the music to start or finish with a specific shot in your video. As you change the song's length, Movie Maestro automatically makes internal changes to the tune to ensure that it plays and ends smoothly and on time.

7. As the music is playing, try the variations by clicking the drop-down menu shown in Figure 12.16. Select any variation you want, and the video clip jumps back to the beginning. Each variation has a distinctly different start.

8. After you've chosen a variation, save your musical selection by clicking the Stop button and then click the Save Sound button in the upper-left corner of the screen. You have several save options: the sound file itself, as separate musical segments, or combined with the video. You also have three levels of audio: less than music CD quality (22KHz), music CD (44KHz), and digital video (48KHz).

Take Care When Saving with a Video

If you choose to save the combined movie and soundtrack, the Save window uses the original filename as the default saved filename. *Be careful*: You don't want to overwrite your original video file. Give this file a new descriptive name, such as *old-filename* with soundtrack.avi.

Other Save Options

The Advanced Save button enables you to convert the original video file into several other video formats. Some selections give you more options than you might have believed possible. For instance, select Export Movie to QuickTime Movie and then open the Use drop-down menu. None of these options is particularly suited to Premiere Pro video production, but feel free to experiment.

Boost Your Music Creation Level

You can take your music creation to a higher, more customized level with SmartSound's Sonicfire Pro and Adobe Audition. I'll take you through both product's paces in Hour 15, "Professional Audio Tools: SmartSound Sonicfire and Adobe Audition."

Summary

Audio is critical to a high-quality video production. Most important is the original footage. Take some extra measures to ensure high-quality audio. Select the right mics for the job, turn to wireless audio if your budget allows, and use professional voice-over techniques.

Strapped for cash and you need music for a video for personal use? Not to worry: Rip music from CDs or create custom music using SmartSound.

Q&A

Q **When I videotape indoors, my audio has a "tin-can" quality. What's going on?**

A This happens for one of two reasons. The simplest reason is that the mic is too far from your subject and you're in a room with reflective surfaces such as flat walls and an uncarpeted floor. Move the mic closer and, if possible, hang blankets where they won't show up in your video. The other is more complicated and involves what audio engineers call the *3-to-1 Rule*. If you use more than one mic for several speakers, as in a panel discussion, you need to place the mics three times as far apart as they are to the speakers. That is, if a mic is 2 feet from a panelist, the next mic should be at least 6 feet away from the first mic. Otherwise, the mics pick up audio at about the same time, cancel each other out, and create that tin-can sound.

Q **I bought professional-quality mics, but I can barely hear them in my headset and later when I listen to my tape. Why?**

A Unlike with professional camcorders, there are no mic standards for consumer and prosumer camcorders. If you read your camcorder's spec sheet, you probably won't see anything about the mic input, whether it's stereo or mono, and whether it needs external amplification. If you're using a low-impedance mic, such as a professional handheld mic with a cable longer than 20 feet, you'll probably need a transformer for most camcorders. That should resolve your low-volume problem. If you're using an unpowered condenser mic, such as a shotgun, you'll need phantom power, from a battery, a mixer, or a portable phantom power adapter.

Workshop

Quiz

1. Why should you use external mics?

2. If you had a budget for only one professional mic, what would it be?

3. When you set up a voice recording space in the corner of a room, which way do you face to voice the narration and why?

Quiz Answers

1. Your camcorder's onboard mic is a jack-of-all-trades and a master of none. It picks up sound all around you, including noise you make when handling the camcorder. External mics capture sound at the source. Using external mics is invariably better and greatly improves the quality of your production.

2. This is kind of a trick question. I think the best bet is a wireless shotgun mic. On news stories, a wireless shotgun gives reporters much greater mobility and puts interviewees at ease. Working with a shotgun mic means there's no need to stick a mic in someone's face. And going wireless obviates that awkward pause to plug a cable into the camera.

3. As counterintuitive as it seems, face *away* from the sound absorbing material. The mic picks up sound from the direction it's facing. The absorbing material minimizes the reflections it would pick up if the mic faced away from that material.

Exercises

1. Build a simple two-wall voice recording area using the methods described in this hour. Experiment with mic placement, distance from your mouth, and whether the mic points toward or away from the sound-absorbing material. Listen critically to the audio quality; tinny, noisy, muffled, too much echo or just right. Find what works best for you.

2. Work on your narration style. Do several voice-overs using the same script. Listen to your inflection, cadence, and pauses. Do you sound interested in the subject matter? Do you enunciate clearly without sounding pedantic? Try to find a comfort level between overly enthusiastic and bored. And feel free to combine narration segments from different takes. No one take has to be perfect.

3. Check the Yellow Pages for *Recording Service* or *Recording Studio* and pay one or two a visit. I took some high-school students to a studio in Portland, Oregon and we had a blast. The sound engineer demonstrated some amazing voice sweetening tricks.

HOUR 13

Editing Audio

What You'll Learn in This Hour:

▶ Premiere Pro—a new aural experience

▶ Basic Premiere Pro audio editing

▶ Higher-level audio editing

▶ Making an automated music video using markers

Premiere Pro—A New Aural Experience

As I mentioned in Hour 1, "Touring Premiere Pro and Presenting the DV Workflow," Premiere Pro features many new technologies. Heading the list is audio.

Adobe hired an audio software engineering expert to completely revamp Premiere Pro's take on audio. You can see (and hear) his work throughout Premiere Pro.

Here's a rundown of the changes he implemented (I go into more detail in upcoming sections and in the next hour):

▶ Two audio track types: clip and submix.

▶ Three audio track flavors: mono, stereo, and 5.1 surround sound

▶ A separate master audio track

▶ Conforming audio

▶ Sample-specific edits

▶ A new audio mixer

▶ Live voice-over recording

In addition, Premiere Pro's compliance with two audio industry standards: ASIO (Audio Stream In/Out) and VST (Virtual Studio Technology) ensures that it works smoothly with a wide range of audio cards and accepts dozens of audio effect plug-ins. I give you a taste of those plug-ins in Hour 14, "Sweetening Your Sound."

Audio Track Layout

There are now two distinct kinds of audio tracks in Premiere Pro: regular *clip* tracks and *submix* tracks.

Audio *clip* tracks are very similar to audio tracks in previous versions of Premiere. They are where you put your audio clips or audio portions of A/V clips. The new wrinkle is that you need to match the channel type of your clip to the track on which you are placing it—stereo to stereo, mono to mono, and 5.1 to 5.1. To simplify that, Premiere Pro automatically creates the proper track flavor, if necessary, when you drag a new clip to a sequence.

Submix tracks are completely new. They don't take clips at all. You use them to route or combine the output of multiple clip tracks and other submix tracks into a separate submix track so that you can apply effects, volume changes, and other characteristics to the group as a whole. I explain more about why you'll want to use submix tracks, how to create them, and how you route other tracks to them in the next hour, "Sweetening Your Sound."

Premiere Pro now enables you to place effects on entire tracks and submixes as well as on clips. You can edit keyframes on tracks in a sequence. In this way, you can create a consistent sound quality for an entire track rather than a clip at a time. For instance, you might lay down several narration segments on a track. Instead of applying the Reverb audio effect to each clip, you can apply it to the entire track.

Conforming Audio

Premiere Pro converts all audio to 32-bit floating-point data and matches audio to the project audio sample rate settings. (48kHz is the standard DV sample rate and 44.1kHz is CD audio.) If the original audio clip is at a lower quality setting than your project, Premiere Pro "up-converts" it. That audio conforming ensures that there is no loss in quality during any subsequent edits or when you apply audio effects to your clips.

To conform audio takes some time and consumes some disk space. Here is the basic hard disk space calculation:

Time in seconds×4×sample rate×number of channels = bytes

So, one hour of DV footage in a 48kHz project consumes

3,600 seconds×4×48,000×2 = 1,382,400,000 = 1.38GB

Taking that to its logical extreme, if you have a one-hour, 5.1 audio segment at 96kHz (the highest available setting), your conforming audio (CFA) file will be 8.28GB.

On a PC with a 2.8GHz hyperthreaded CPU, here's approximately how long it takes to conform a one-hour DV clip with 32k audio:

► Conforming into a 32k project—44 seconds

► Conforming into a 48k project—2 minutes

In the first case, Premiere Pro simply reads the audio from the DV clip and writes it as a 32-bit floating-point file to your hard drive. In the second case, Premiere Pro resamples the audio to 48kHz, which takes longer.

Conforming is a background process, which should not interfere with your work. It automatically pauses while you're playing or scrubbing through video. And you can place clips that are still conforming in a sequence.

As soon as Premiere Pro finishes conforming, you can switch on that clip's waveform in the sequence (I show you how to do that in "Basic Premiere Pro Audio Editing," later this hour).

Developer Comment—Conforming Audio File Management

By the Way

The biggest conforming audio development issue came down to the management of these files. There's no easy way for the user to know which files are associated with which projects. If you clean one project, will you regret it because you lost your CFAs for several other projects? Do we clean only those files that have not been used for some time?

Anyway, we know that Premiere Pro has some media management issues that need a comprehensive solution. This is on all of our lists of needed additions to subsequent revisions.

As for deleting the CFA files, simply find the folder (specified in the scratch disk preferences) and delete it. Of course, when you reopen the project, you'll have to regenerate them, which will take place in the background as it did originally.

I cover the other new developments—sample-specific editing, the audio mixer, and live voice-over recording—in the following sections and the next hour.

Basic Premiere Pro Audio Editing

Before you add scintillating sound to your project, I want to show you a few audio fundamentals.

Experiment with an Audio File Waveform

To experiment with an audio file waveform, follow these steps:

1. Open Premiere Pro, clear your sequence of clips, and select Window→Workspace→Audio.

2. If the Effects tab does not display in the Project window, you've run into a small bug. Take care of that by selecting Window→Effects to add the Effects palette to your workspace and then drag its tab to the Project window. Your workspace should look like Figure 13.1.

3. For future use, save this workspace as a slightly improved default audio workspace by selecting Window→Workspace→Save Workspace, giving it a name such as My Audio Workspace, and clicking Save. Next time, you can select that workspace from the Window→Workspace list.

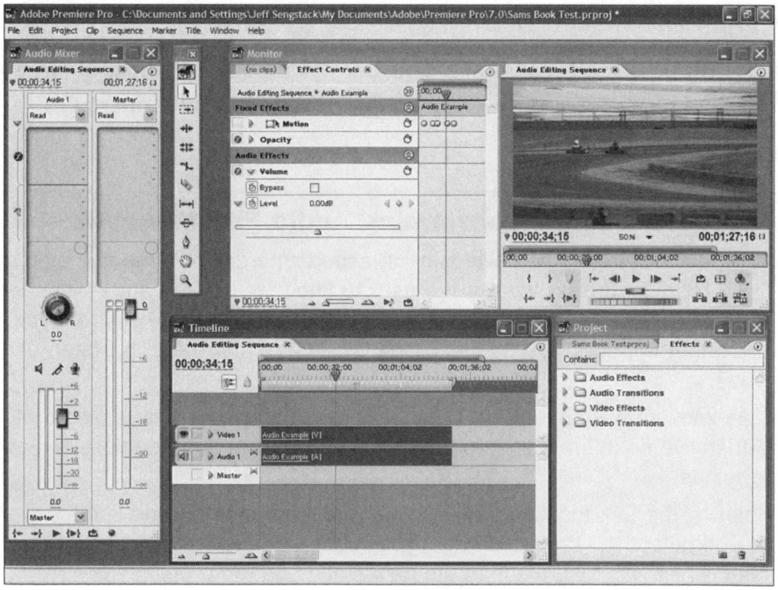

FIGURE 13.1
One way that your personalized audio workspace could look before you complete the following steps.

4. Drag any audio clip or linked A/V clip to your empty sequence. Premiere Pro handles most standard audio types, including AIF, AVI, MP3, M2V, MPEG, QuickTime (MOV), WAV, and Windows Media Audio (WMA).

5. Expand the audio track on which your new clip resides by clicking its Collapse/Expand Track triangle (to the left of Audio # and circled in Figure 13.2). Then greatly expand the height of the Timeline window by dragging its top and/or bottom edges. Finally, as shown in Figure 13.2, drag the bottom of the audio track to fill the screen.

6. By default, the clip's waveform should be visible. If not, click the little Set Display Style button circled in Figure 13.2 (below the speaker icon) and select Show Waveform.

FIGURE 13.2
Expand the audio track to see the clip's waveform. Note that in this stereo track, the top row is the left channel and the bottom is the right. I explain the various highlighted items in steps 5, 6, and 8.

7. Experiment with this waveform for a while. Drag the CTI edit line to the beginning and press the spacebar to play the waveform. The amplitude of the waveform reflects the volume of the original clip: The fatter/taller the line, the louder the sound.

Waveforms Are Immutable

Nothing that you do in Premiere Pro will affect the visible waveform of a media clip. Even if you change a clip's volume or apply audio effects to it, the waveform will always display the clip's original volume levels.

By the Way

▼

8. Press the =/+ key a couple times to expand—or zoom in—the view of the audio clip on the sequence. This will give you a clearer take on your audio levels. In my case (refer to Figure 13.2), the sudden drops in volume are when I pressed pause/record on my camcorder.

9. As shown in Figure 13.3, you change the audio time ruler markers to sample-level units by clicking the Timeline window wing menu and selecting Audio Units.

Sample Unit Time Ruler Markings

Take a look at Figure 13.3. With Audio Units selected, the time ruler markings change to hours:minutes:seconds:samples. In my example, the project setting is 32kHz, or 32,000 audio samples per second. Note that I have placed the CTI at 1 second and 31,999 samples—one sample shy of 2 seconds. This sample-specific editing enables you to precisely cut audio. Previous versions of Premiere let you cut audio only at each video frame, or every 1/30 of a second.

FIGURE 13.3
Change the time ruler to sample-specific editing by selecting Audio Units from the Timeline window wing menu.

10. Zoom in on the sequence view to its highest magnification: individual samples. The sequence width displayed in Figure 13.4 is 20 samples or 3/5,000 of a second. In my case, this spot is where the audio drops off dramatically. Premiere Pro makes it easy to cut one sample before that drop, if I so choose.

FIGURE 13.4
At its highest zoom level, you can make sample-specific edits and only a few-thousandths of a second fill a sequence width.

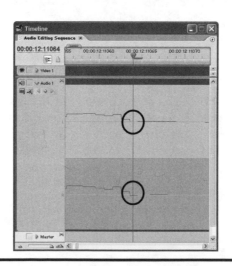

▲

Adjusting Volume

You might want to decrease or increase the volume of an entire clip or parts of a clip. For example, you might want to bring the natural sound down by half while you narrate, gradually fade up the audio at the start or end, or fade up an interview just as the narrator completes a segment. The latter is known as a *J-cut*. I explain that in the next section, "Higher-Level Audio Editing."

Adjusting the Volume

Try it Yourself ▼

To do any of those audio edits, you use the Volume audio effect in the Effect Controls window. Here's how it works:

1. To give yourself a little more screen real estate, reduce the size of the audio track and the Timeline window so that you can see the Effect Controls window.

2. Click the Show Keyframes button circled in Figure 13.5 and select Show Clip Volume.

3. Select your clip by clicking either the video or audio portion to display it in the ECW.

Watch Out!

Can't Select the Audio Clip? Uncheck Track Audio Options

When you open the Show Keyframes menu, you could select two *track* options: Show Track Keyframes and Show Track Volume. If you select either of these and you have an audio-only clip (no linked video associated with it), Premiere Pro will not allow you to select the audio clip to apply any volume changes or effects to it. If you have a linked A/V clip, the only way to select the audio portion is to click on its video partner. With either of these track options checked, you can apply volume changes and effects only on an entire track basis using the mixer. I explain that process in the next hour.

4. Raise or lower the overall volume of this clip by moving the level slider to the right or left. As shown in Figure 13.6, as you make those changes, the volume level indicator line moves to a higher or lower position.

5. Return the volume to 0.00dB.

▼

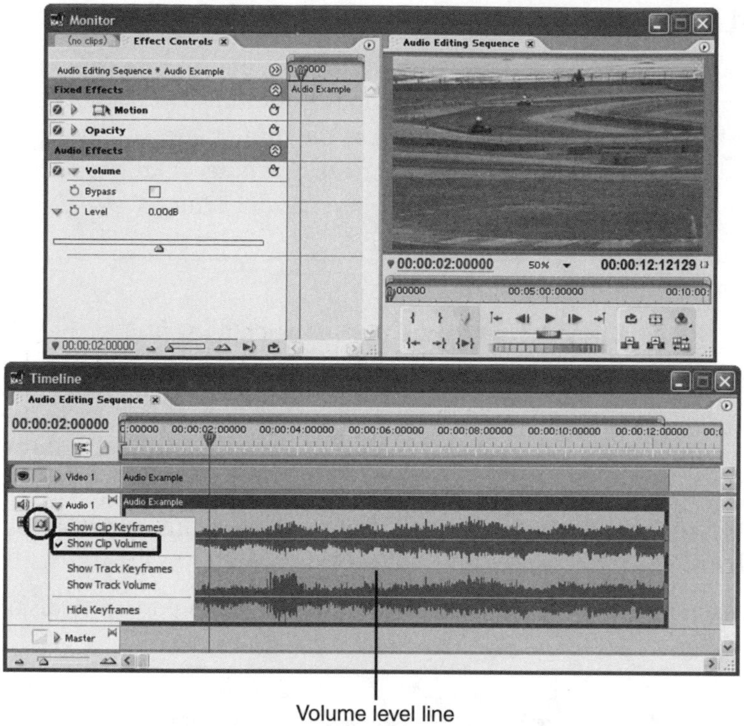

▼

FIGURE 13.5
Select Show Clip
Volume both to see
your work in the
clip's waveform and
to ensure that you
can apply a volume
change to the clip,
as opposed to only
the entire track.

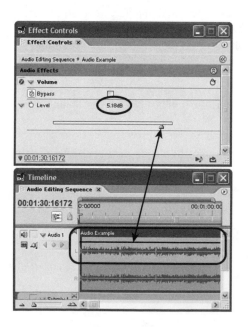

Volume level line

FIGURE 13.6
As you change the
clip volume by mov-
ing the level slider
in the ECW, the thin
yellow volume line
in the clip moves
up or down accord-
ingly (I darkened
and thickened the
line in this figure to
demonstrate that).

▼

Changing Volume Does Not Change Original Clip

Whatever changes you make to the clip volume in a sequence won't change the original clip's volume. They change only how the clip plays back in your project. The default volume setting is zero decibels. That is, Premiere Pro plays source audio clips at their original volume unless you tell it to do otherwise.

6. Take the first step to manually add a fade-in and a fade-out to your clip (in the next section, "Higher-Level Audio Editing," you use an audio transition to automate this) by pressing the Home keyboard shortcut, turning on keyframes by clicking the level stopwatch, and moving the level slider to the far left (-∞).

7. Move the CTI into your clip (about 2 seconds works well) and increase the Level to 0dB.

Consistent Workflow—But Missing Two Features

Changing clip audio volume in the ECW is new to Premiere Pro and a giant leap forward for this application. Previously, you had to use what Adobe called *audio volume rubberbands* in the timeline. Doing your volume (and audio effect) work in the ECW means that you have a consistent workflow.

There is one fly in the ointment: You cannot change the dB numeric value by selecting it and typing in a new number. The slider is your only choice.

8. Finish this process by moving the CTI to about 2 seconds from the end of your clip, clicking the keyframe diamond (between the two keyframe navigation triangles) to set a new keyframe without changing the volume level, and then moving to the end of the clip, and dropping the volume level back to the far left (-∞).

An Updated Waveform Display

Take a look at the clip's waveform display. Note two things: The yellow line (I darkened it in Figure 13.7 to make it easier to see) now has keyframe *handles* about 2 seconds from the start point and endpoint, and that line moves from the bottom (-∞) to the center of the clip (0dB) and back to the bottom.

Figure 13.7 also shows what happens if you drag a volume keyframe to a new location, as described in step 9.

9. After you've added keyframes, you can use the volume handles in the clip's waveform display (annotated in Figure 13.7) to change those keyframe settings. Simply grab one and drag it to increase or decrease volume and to

change the keyframe location. Note the real-time readout of your changes in the box at the bottom of the clip display.

FIGURE 13.7
As you make changes to the clip volume in the ECW, it changes the volume line in the clip waveform display (the lower line in this figure). You can grab and move the volume handles (keyframes) to change their location and dB level (the top line).

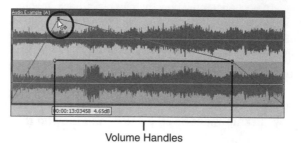

Volume Handles

10. Add some interpolation values to your audio to make the volume changes more appealing. As a reminder to do that, right-click on a keyframe in the ECW and select from the five choices. Applying Fast Out to the starting keyframe gets to the action more quickly and works well for my go-cart video. A Fast Out on the ending keyframe also works well.

11. Listen to your fade-in and fade-out by pressing Home and the spacebar.

Higher-Level Audio Editing

Just as you created transitions between video clips, you can make smooth transitions between audio clips. Premiere Pro offers only two; both are *crossfades* and they work just like a video cross-dissolve in that the audio in the first clip fades down as the audio in the next clip increases in volume. They add a real nice touch to your project. I recommend using them virtually every time you make some kind of smooth video transition.

On the other hand, you might want to have greater control over your transitions than the two crossfades offer. In that case, you need to place audio clips on separate audio tracks and use their individual volume controls to create the transition. You'll do both in this section.

Try it Yourself   **Crossfade Between Two Audio Clips**

New to Premiere Pro is the audio crossfade. You used to have to follow an elaborate manual crossfade process. Now you apply the Crossfade transitions to two audio clips just as you applied a cross-dissolve to two video clips. Here are the steps to follow:

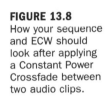

1. Add another audio-only or linked A/V clip to your sequence and butt it up against the first clip. Make sure that you've trimmed both clips to allow for some overlap.

2. Clear out the volume changes that you applied to the first clip by clicking the keyframe stopwatch to turn off keyframes, and then dragging the level slider to 0dB or press the Reset button.

3. Drag the Constant Power audio transition from the Crossfade folder in the Effects palette to the edit point between the two clips. To display it in the ECW, click on it in the sequence. Your sequence and ECW should look like Figure 13.8.

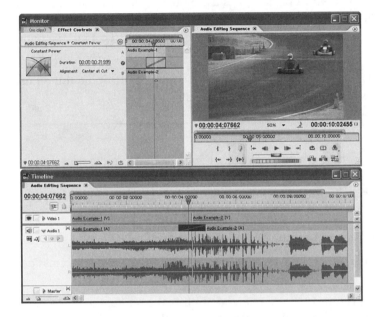

FIGURE 13.8
How your sequence and ECW should look after applying a Constant Power Crossfade between two audio clips.

4. As with video transitions, you can change the center point of the transition or change when it starts and ends by dragging it in its entirety or dragging its edges.

5. Lengthen it a bit to get a better feel for the transition and then listen to it and note how the volume levels change.

Use Crossfade to Start or End a Piece

Just as you can use the video Dissolve transition to ease into or out of the start or end of a video (fade from/to black), you can use the audio Crossfade to achieve the same results. Simply apply either Crossfade audio transition to the beginning or end of a clip.

By the Way

6. Replace the Constant Power transition with the only other audio transition by dragging Constant Gain to the transition on the sequence.

7. Lengthen and listen to it as well. You'll note that it does not have quite the same high level of sustained volume level as Constant Gain. Save your project so that you can use it in the next task.

News-Style Audio Editing: Using J-Cuts and L-Cuts

Frequently, you'll want to start a clip by having its sound play under the previous video clip and then transition to its associated video. This is a great way to let your audience know that someone is about to say something or that a transition is coming. It's kind of like foreshadowing. This is called a **J-cut**, so named because it looks like a J on the sequence.

Conversely, another slick editing technique is to let the audio tail off under the next video clip. This is an **L-cut** (it looks like an L).

Try it Yourself ▾   Making J-Cuts and L-Cuts

To do either of these cuts requires that you *unlink* the audio and video portions of a linked A/V clip. After they've been unlinked, you can move that audio segment to another audio track and then extend or shorten the audio portion to make the J- or L-cut.

Here's the basic approach you need to follow:

1. Use the project you saved in the previous task. Delete the crossfade by selecting it on the sequence and pressing Delete.

2. Using Figure 13.9 as a reference, unlink the audio and video portions of the second clip by right-clicking on it and selecting Unlink Audio and Video (see the next Did You Know? for a keyboard shortcut unlinking method).

3. Deselect that clip (this confirms the unlink) by clicking somewhere in the sequence besides on that clip.

4. Drag the audio portion of the second clip down to the gray area below the audio master track. Premiere Pro will indicate it's about to automatically add a new audio track to accommodate this clip; you can then release the mouse. Your sequence should look like Figure 13.11.

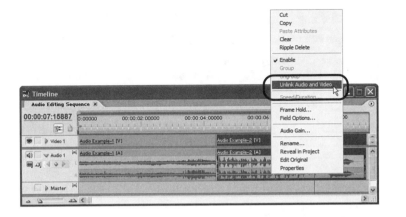

Figure 13.9 ▼
Right-click on a clip and select Unlink Audio and Video to enable you to separately edit the audio and video portions of an A/V clip.

Stay in Synch

As you move the audio portion of a clip in the sequence, take care that you don't slide it left or right when you drag it. Otherwise, the audio and video will get out of synch. Premiere Pro gives you a visual cue to help you line up your clips: As shown in Figure 13.10, if you see a black line with a triangle, your clips are properly lined up. If that black line disappears, you've moved out of synch.

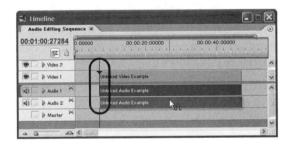

FIGURE 13.10
When dragging an unlinked audio clip to a new audio track, keep it in synch with the original video segment by noting when the highlighted black line pops on screen.

An Easy Way to Unlink and Move a Clip to a New Track

Here's a nifty keyboard shortcut that you can use to unlink and move a clip. Hold down the Alt key while you click on the portion of a clip that you want to move (that unlinks it), drag it to the new track (or, in this case, below the master audio track to make a new audio track), and drop it (see Figure 13.11).

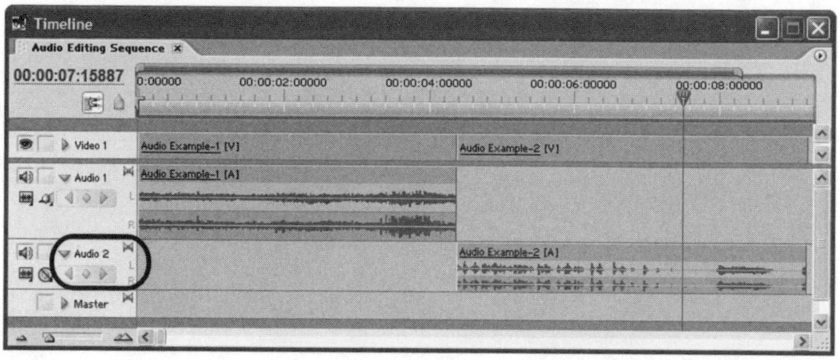

FIGURE 13.11
Drag the audio portion of the unlinked clip below the audio master track to add it to an automatically created new audio track.

5. Drag the end of that second audio clip under the end of the previous clip (refer to Figure 13.12).

Watch Out!

Drag the End—Don't Slide the Clip

Don't *slide* the audio clip. Doing so will un-synch it with its original video portion. Rather, drag the clip's starting point to the left to extend its duration.

6. Open the volume effect for that clip, switch on keyframes for level, move the cursor to the starting point, and decrease the volume to about –8dB (you can adjust this volume later to make it fit your purposes).

7. Move the CTI edit line to just before the end of the first clip and set a keyframe there by clicking the keyframe diamond between the two keyframe navigation triangles. This sets a keyframe with the same –8dB value.

8. Drag the CTI to the end of the first clip and increase the level to 0dB (automatically setting a new keyframe in the process). That is a J-cut. The audio in the second clip plays *under* the first clip and then increases in volume just as the second clip appears. Your sequence should look like Figure 13.12.

Did you Know?

Use a Video Dissolve to Further Ease the Transition

The purpose of a J- or L-cut is to ease viewers into or out of a clip. To enhance that transition, add a video Dissolve or some other smooth video transition between the two clips.

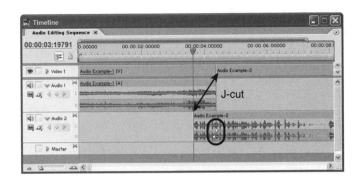

FIGURE 13.12
A J-cut is used to lay audio under a preceding video clip and then increase its volume at the point where its associated video pops onscreen.

Play your edited selection to see how that sound-under style works. The volume might increase too quickly or too slowly. It's a simple matter to adjust volume levels. Open the audio waveform portion of the audio track, switch on Show Clip Volume, and drag the volume keyframe handles around. You can also add an audio crossfade to the end of the first clip (or use the Volume effect) to fade it out or you might cut it completely just before the edit, depending on your needs.

You can make an L-cut using the same basic technique. In this case, you'll want to unlink the audio and video of the *first* clip, extend its audio segment *under* the second clip, and reduce its volume accordingly. Figure 13.13 is an example of an L-cut.

Use the Alt Shortcut to Extend an Audio Segment

You can use the Alt unlink keyboard shortcut for yet another unlinking use. Because you've already moved the second clip's audio to a new track and need only extend the first clip's audio segment to the right a bit, hold down the Alt key, click on the end of that first clip's audio segment, and then drag to the right. By holding down the Alt key, you'll extend only the audio segment of the clip.

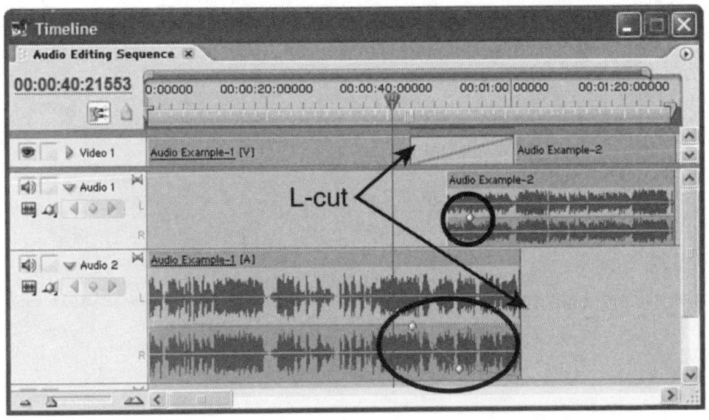

Did you Know?

FIGURE 13.13
Use an L-cut to ease viewers out of a clip. Note that I added a video Dissolve, eased out the audio in the first clip, and eased in the audio of the second clip.

Try it Yourself   Freeze Frame and Dissolve to Black

▼

One other L-cut-type edit is to end a piece with a freeze frame, and then dissolve to black while continuing the audio beneath both video elements. Here's a brief rundown of the steps:

1. As you did in Hour 9, "Advanced Editing Techniques and Workspace Tools," drag the CTI edit line to the ending point of the project's final clip—the frame you want to freeze.

2. Right-click on the clip and select Copy.

3. Click End to move the CTI to the end of that clip.

4. From the Main Menu, select Edit→Paste to add that duplicate clip to the end of your video.

5. Right-click on that duplicate clip and select Frame Hold→Hold On→OutPoint. Click OK.

6. Unlink the audio portion of that freeze-frame clip and delete that audio.

7. Add black video to your sequence by clicking the New Item button, selecting Black Video, and dragging that object to the end of your sequence.

8. Hold down Alt while dragging the audio segment of the final motion video clip all the way to the end of the piece. (You need enough extra, unused audio on the original clip to do this.)

9. Add a Cross Dissolve video transition between the freeze-frame and the black video.

10. Use the Volume effect and keyframes to drop the audio, starting at the beginning of the freeze frame and decreasing it to -∞ by the end of the black video. Your project should look like Figure 13.14.

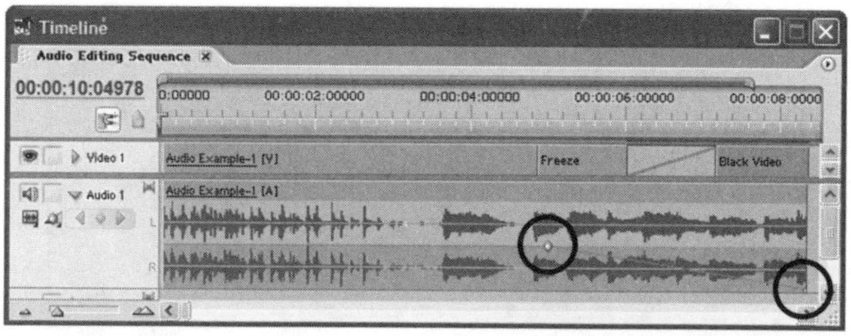

FIGURE 13.14
Using a freeze frame, black video, and an L-cut to create a gradual fade to black.

▲

Making an Automated Music Video Using Timeline Markers

I saved the fun task for last. Here, you're going to place a music clip on your timeline, add *markers* to match the beat (or wherever you want to place them), and then automatically add video clips, one for each marker. Voilá. A music video. Well, it's not exactly MTV, but at the very least it's a great way to make a slideshow.

Setting Timeline Markers and Automatically Adding Clips

Follow these steps to set the timeline markers:

1. Clear your timeline by deleting everything on it.

2. Drag a music track to the audio 2 track. (If you don't have a music track, return to Hour 12, "Acquiring Audio," and follow the instructions in the "Ripping Music CDs" section to use a track from an audio CD.)

Why Audio 2 Track?

You need to keep the audio 1 track free for any natural sound associated with the clips that you'll add to the video. When you use the Project window's Automate to Sequence feature, it places that nat-sound on Audio 1.

3. Move the CTI to that clip's first frame (use the Home key) and press the asterisk (*) key on the numeric keypad (*not* Shift+8). That adds a marker on that first frame. A little pointed icon appears right below the time ruler.

4. Play that audio clip and when you hear a place where you'd like to edit in a new clip, press the asterisk (*) key again to add another marker. Do that for each edit point. If you're using a laptop and don't have a numeric keypad, you can use Alt+Shift+=.

Use Markers with a Narration

You can use markers with other audio, notably narrations. As you listen to a narration, press the asterisk key when you hear a logical break in the narration copy or when the script calls for a specific shot. Even if you don't use the Automate to Sequence option, those markers will help you locate edit points.

5. At the end of the song, or when you think you've made enough markers, stop the music. As shown in Figure 13.15, a whole slew of little gray tab stops will populate your sequence.

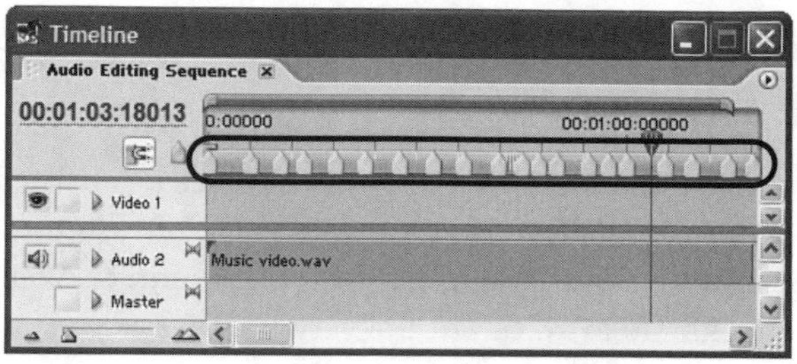

FIGURE 13.15
The timeline loaded
with markers, ready
and waiting to
make a music
video.

6. Use the Project window to select clips. You can change it to the Icon view and rearrange clips as you did in Hour 6, "Creating a Cuts-Only Video," or you can simply Ctrl+click on several to set the order in which they'll end up on the sequence.

7. After you have your clips arranged, click the Automate to Sequence icon (third icon in from the left at the bottom of the Project window).

8. That pops up the Automate to Sequence dialog box. Figure 13.16 shows the interface properly filled in for this music video. In this case, you want to change Placement to At Unnumbered Markers, set Method to Insert Edit, and leave the Ignore Audio and Ignore Video boxes unchecked. This means natural sound will end up on audio track 1, where you can change its volume or delete it to suit the video.

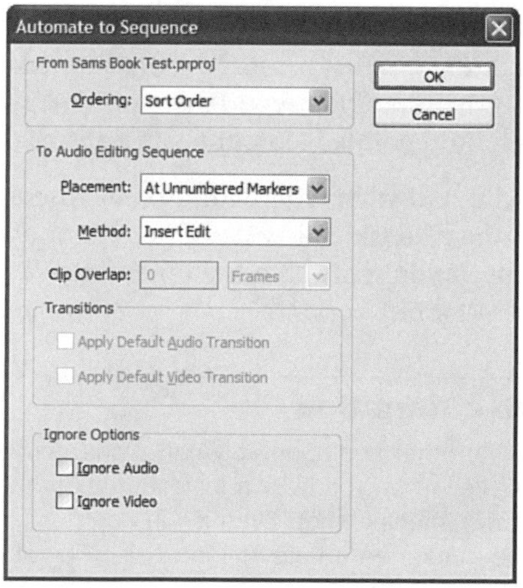

FIGURE 13.16
The Automate to
Sequence dialog
box, filled out to
make a music
video.

9. When you've made all the selections, click OK. Your timeline should fill up with clips. Move the edit line to the beginning and play. Slick.

Summary

Premiere Pro has taken audio editing to a new, much higher plane than in previous versions. By incorporating new technologies, industry-standard plug-ins, and high-end features such as audio conforming, sample-specific editing, and multiple track types, Premiere Pro gives audiophiles all they need to add a top-notch aural quality to their productions.

Basic audio editing—typically volume changes and crossfades—is now greatly simplified and takes place primarily in the Effect Controls window.

Some standard news-style audio-editing L- and J-cuts will take your audio one step higher. You can also create slideshows with a musical bed or timed to a narration by using markers and the Automate to Sequence option.

Q&A

Q *I adjusted the volume settings. Now my clip sounds different, but the waveform hasn't changed. What's going on?*

A This is Premiere Pro's default behavior. The waveform always represents the clip's original audio volume shape. And no matter how loud or quiet the original clip, the default starting Volume effect level for all clips is always 0dB.

Q *Right after I added a music clip to my Project window, I dragged it to the sequence and tried to view the waveform and play it. But no waveform displayed. Only after I clicked Stop did the waveform pop onscreen. What's going on?*

A Audio conforming is going on. When you add audio or an audio/video clip, Premiere Pro creates a new audio file using the project setting audio sample rate (usually 32kHz or 48kHz) and using 32-bit floating point data. That can take a little while. During the beta testing, you could not listen to the audio during conforming. Beta testers complained loudly and Adobe made some clever fixes allowing the audio to play at a reduced quality. But, it will not display the waveform until it's done conforming (you can't get everything you want). And if you play the clip while conforming is going on, it won't display the waveform until you stop playing it.

Workshop

Quiz

1. You want to start your piece by fading up your audio. Explain two ways to do that.

2. Why use an L-cut or a J-cut? What are the basic editing steps?

3. You have a quiet video clip, but in the middle someone honks a car horn. How could you remove that sound and replace it with the original quiet background of the original clip?

Quiz Answers

1. Add an Audio Crossfade transition (Constant Power or Constant Gain) to the beginning of the clip. Or use the Volume audio effect and keyframes to set the level to -∞ at the start and increase volume to 0dB within a second or two. Use interpolation controls to smooth what would otherwise be a straight-line fade-in.

2. In both instances, you're creating smooth transitions to either ease a cut with specific sound into your project or let it fade out. A *J-cut* starts audio under the preceding video cut (which also has associated audio) and then fades up as you transition or cut to the video portion of that clip. An *L-cut* fades audio under the next clip as a way to ease out of that audio/video clip. You create both edits by unlinking the audio from the clip you're going to extend, moving that audio to a different audio track, extending the audio in the appropriate direction, and then using the Volume effect to create a crossfade. It sounds best if you make those volume changes on both clips.

3. This one's kind of tough. First, remove the horn by using the Volume effect and keyframes to isolate it and reduce the volume to -∞ for that small segment. Then add that same clip somewhere out of the way on the sequence, unlink its audio, delete the video, drag in the ends of the audio clip to create a chunk of quiet audio that matches the rest of the original clip, and place it on the audio track right below the removed car horn. Listen to this passage. You might need to fade up and later fade out the quiet segment to ease in and out of it. If that sounds like a lot of work, it's only a small taste of what audio engineers do to enhance sound.

Exercises

1. J- and L-cuts should be a part of every production. The only way that's going to happen is if you get comfortable doing them. Make a few of each.

2. When using a narration, typically you'll lay down some of that voice-over, put in a clip with some nice natural sound, and then add more narration and more natural sound throughout your story. Give that process a try by cutting your narration with the Razor tool and inserting nat-sound clips at those breaks (hold down the Ctrl key when dragging clips to the razored point to perform an insert edit, thereby sliding clips to the right). Use J- and L-cuts liberally.

3. I'll cover audio special effects in Hour 14, but you can preview that process by adding effects to an audio clip. The best clip to use is a narration because you know what it should sound like and any changes you add will be more obvious. Open the Audio Effects tab in the Effects palette, open the folder that matches your clip (Mono, Stereo, or 5.1), and drag and drop Reverb on your audio clip. Select the clip and check out all the Reverb features in the Effect Controls window.

HOUR 14

Sweetening Your Sound

What You'll Learn in This Hour:

▶ Sweetening sound—Premiere Pro's audio effects
▶ Revealing the power of VST plug-ins
▶ Following Premiere Pro's new audio tracks
▶ Working with the new audio mixer

Premiere Pro's audio effects "sweeten" your sound. They can dramatically change the feel of your project. As with video effects, you set the parameters of audio effects from within the Effect Controls window. Some are specialized effects from a family of audio plug-ins using **VST—Virtual Studio Technology**—a new feature of Premiere Pro.

Premiere Pro's audio mixer is a leap forward in controlling audio for your projects. Combined with Premiere Pro's new submix track option, track-level audio effects, and live narration recording, it brings a lot of flexibility to your audio management.

Sweetening Sound—Premiere Pro's Audio Effects

Adobe has updated Premiere Pro's suite of audio effects. Most of the new effects arrive courtesy of VST software that fosters the integration of audio effect processors with PCs. In the case of Premiere Pro, it opens the door to a world of third-party audio effect plug-ins; little mini-programs that show up in the Audio Effects palette. You can add dozens of VST audio effects to that collection. I cover VST in the next section, "Revealing the Power of VST Plug-ins."

Previous versions of Premiere placed the audio effects into seven categories. Now you access them alphabetically. Unless you're an audio engineer, some of their names—*Bandpass*, *MultibandCompressor*, and *Parametric EQ*, for instance—might be a bit obtuse.

I take you through some of them to give you a taste of what to expect. For more information on what each effect does, take a look at the Premiere Pro online help section. Under Contents, select Applying Effects, and then select Audio Effects Included With Adobe Premiere Pro.

Ultimately, the best way to learn more about these effects is to try them out. They are nondestructive. That is, you can use them on any clip without changing the original clip's audio quality.

Try it Yourself   Working with Audio Effects

▼

Before I explain the audio effects function, I want to give you a brief overview of how to work with them. You'll start with a couple straightforward effects and then take a look at some of the higher-level tools. Here's how to add audio effects to clips:

1. Open Premiere Pro to either your customized audio workspace or the default workspace by selecting Window→Workspace→Audio—or—Your Audio Workspace.

2. Clear everything off your sequence and place a short (no more than 30 seconds) audio or linked audio/video clip on the Audio 1 track. The reason for the short clip duration is your audio playback convenience.

3. Open the Effects tab (its default location is in the Project window). Twirl down the Audio Effects disclosure triangle to reveal three subfolders: 5.1, Stereo, and Mono (with only a couple exceptions, such as Balance, all three have the same set of audio effects). Twirl down the Stereo disclosure triangle to reveal its 22 effects. Figure 14.1 shows how that should look.

4. Drag and drop the Balance effect on your audio clip. Select that clip to display it in the Effects Control window (ECW). Twirl down the two disclosure triangles to reveal the two keyframable parameters shown in Figure 14.2: Bypass and Balance.

▼

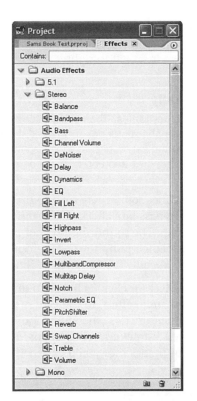

What's Bypass?

All audio effects (including the fixed Volume effect) have a Bypass parameter. Basically, checking Bypass means Premiere Pro will ignore any setting for this effect and play it at its default settings. What makes this an important feature of each audio effect is that Bypass is keyframable—you can set the exact moments when it switches off an effect and switches it back on.

Did you Know?

5. Using keyframes, set the balance completely to the left (-100%) at the start of your clip and then move it to the right (+100%) at the end. Play the clip. The audio should move from left to right.

Use Keyframes Liberally

Consider how you could use keyframes. The obvious usage is to change an effect over time. But consider those obnoxious ads in which the narrator suddenly has a booming, echoing voice. You too can duplicate those spots. Simply select Reverb and set keyframes for the beginning and end of that booming delivery.

6. Add two Bypass keyframes somewhere toward the middle of your clip. The first should have the Bypass box checked, but the second should be unchecked. Play the clip. The sound should begin to move from the left to the right, jump to the center, jump toward the right, and finish its move to the right channel. Bypass tells Premiere Pro to ignore any effect settings.

7. Remove the Balance effect (or click its little f to turn it off) and drag Delay, a slightly more complex audio effect, to the ECW. Twirl down its disclosure triangles to reveal three parameters (shown in Figure 14.3): Delay, Feedback, and Mix. Delay creates distinct echoes as opposed to Reverb, which creates more of a collection of echoes that you'd experience in a closed room.

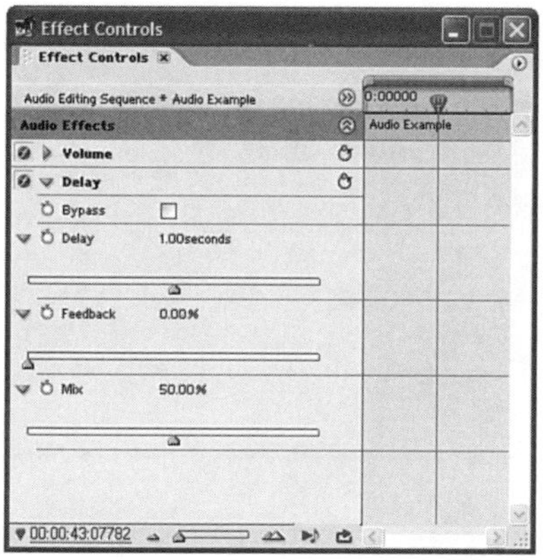

FIGURE 14.3
Delay—or echo—
has slightly more
complexity than
Balance.

Delay Equals Echo

The Delay parameter specifies the amount of time before the echo plays. Increasing the Feedback setting means you get echoes of echoes. And the Mix setting determines the prominence or subtlety of the echo.

Take a look at the Multitap Delay. This creates up to four distinct sets of delays or echoes using the same parameters as the Delay effect.

8. Remove the Delay effect, drag Parametric EQ to the ECW, and twirl down its disclosure triangles. As shown in Figure 14.4, this effect boosts or decreases the gain of a selected frequency region. If you want to boost the bass, move the Center slider to the left (lower frequencies), and increase the Boost. Cut the bass by moving the Boost slider to the left. Increase the width of the selected frequencies using the Q slider.

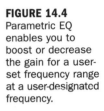

FIGURE 14.4
Parametric EQ enables you to boost or decrease the gain for a user-set frequency range at a user-designated frequency.

Multiple Uses of the Same Effect

You've probably seen an equalizer. Many car and home stereos have them. They enable you to punch up multiple, preset frequency ranges. Many enthusiasts use them to boost the heck out of the bass and rattle windshields and nerves of passing motorists.

Parametric EQ lets you select only one frequency range. But you can use Parametric EQ multiple times and select multiple frequencies. In effect, you can build a full graphic equalizer within the ECW. Or you can use Premiere Pro's EQ effect and its built-in five frequency ranges.

Did you Know?

Revealing the Power of VST Plug-ins

Take a look at one more audio effect. This one is guaranteed to make your head spin. Delete Parametric EQ and drag MultibandCompressor to the ECW. As Figure 14.5 shows, you'll need to dramatically expand the ECW to see only some of the parameters.

It works best if you drag the Effect Controls tab out of the Monitor window to create a separate Effect Controls window. Then drag the right edge of the parameter view by placing the cursor over the thin line until it turns into the double-arrow cursor circled in Figure 14.5.

Close the ECW Timeline to Free Up Space

To add a little screen real estate to the ECW, close its mini-timeline display. Do that by clicking the chevron indicated by an arrow in Figure 14.5. Reopen it using the same chevron button.

FIGURE 14.5
The Multiband-Compressor audio effect is one of several VST plug-ins. Its primary use is to reduce a clip's dynamic range. That is, decrease the gain for loud sounds and increase it for soft sounds.

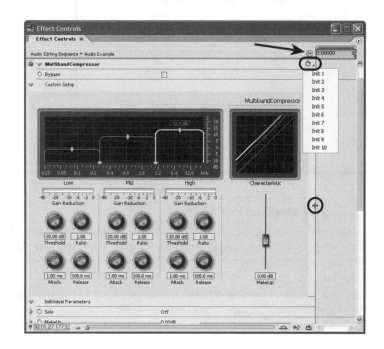

This sudden appearance of a rack of control knobs signals your first look at a VST plug-in. These are custom-designed audio effects that adhere to a standard set by Steinberg audio. Invariably, those who create VST audio effect plug-ins want them to have a unique look and offer some very specialized audio effects.

By the Way

Charlie Steinberg—Audio Visionary

To learn more about VST, I suggest you read an interview with Charlie Steinberg, the man behind VST and other audio innovations. You can start at http://www. steinberg.net or go directly to the interview at http://www.steinberg.net/ en/community/world_of_vst/vst_story/index.php?sid=0.

The MultibandCompressor's purpose is to narrow the dynamic range for up to three sets of frequency ranges. It works like the Dynamics effect but can create a softer sound.

Explaining its parameters could take a full hour. Instead, note that it offers a collection of presets. Premiere Pro alerts you to the presence of that collection by adding a tiny triangle below the reset button. I've put a box around it in Figure 14.5.

While the audio is playing, experiment with the MultibandCompressor by grabbing the diamond-shaped handles in the display screen and dragging the three boxes up or down or their vertices left or right. Finally, take a look at the mind-boggling array of additional individual parameters below the knobs. One real important reason to break them out individually is to let you set keyframes for any of them.

Other VST Effects

Take the Premiere Pro's other VST audio effects for brief spins:

- ▶ **DeNoiser**—Automatically detects and removes tape noise
- ▶ **Dynamics**—Compresses dynamic range
- ▶ **EQ**—A multiple-band parametric EQ
- ▶ **Pitch Shifter**—Raises or lowers pitch
- ▶ **Reverb**—Simulates various room sounds

Did you Know?

Some EQ Uses

You can use EQ to give oomph to a thin vocal by rolling off the high frequencies and boosting the bass.

If you have isolated recordings of instruments in a band, you can add presence to each one by boosting portions of their frequency range. Giving them a little more treble increases their "attack." If you have trouble with audio hum or "popped P's," reducing the low frequencies might help. You can use EQ to "carve out" a vocalist's range within an instrumental, giving that singer more "visibility."

There is a treasure trove of VST plug-ins available on the Internet. I suggest you start your quest at http://www.kvr-vst.com/. Check out Quick Effect Links for a lengthy listing of VST audio effects, all of which should work with Premiere Pro.

There's no need to check out K-V-R's Quick Instrument Links because Premiere Pro does not support instruments.

Most of these VST audio effect plug-ins cost something, but there are a few freebies. In particular, check out Little Duck. Figure 14.6 shows how it appears in Premiere Pro. It emulates a classic analog filter bank.

Little Duck's developer, Land of Cockaigne, offers several other free VST plug-ins featuring an older analog look at its Web site: http://www.funkelectric.com/~cockaigne/.

FIGURE 14.6
The Little Duck VST plug-in audio effect offers five analog-like filters as well as other controls.

Adding Multiple Audio Effects to a Clip

You can add multiple audio (and video) effects to the same clip. For instance, you might have a video with a bass player on the left and a guitar on the right. You could use Balance to start on the left and use Bass to emphasize that instrument. Then as you move the balance to the right using keyframes, you could reduce Bass and bring in Treble.

Combine Effects for Surprising Results

For a little fun, add both a Highpass and Lowpass filter to a clip. These effects pass through high or low frequencies and cut off the rest. Set each high and low cutoff frequency to the same value. The result should be near or complete silence.

Following Premiere Pro's New Audio Tracks

Premiere Pro's new audio tracks open up extra editing opportunities. There are now three track types: clip, submix, and master. As you work with Premiere Pro, you'll begin to see the value of these additional tracks.

Basically, your original clips go into clip tracks. You then can send them directly to the final master track (that's the default action) or send some or all of them to submix track(s). You can set volume levels and apply effects to the clips individually, to entire clip tracks, to entire submix tracks, and to the master track itself. Anything you do to a clip or clip track changes how it sounds in the submix and master tracks. Anything you do to a submix track changes how the master track sounds. To give you an idea of how this might work in real-world productions, here are two scenarios as suggested by the Premiere Pro development team:

▶ A two-camera shoot with additional narration and background music. You have two tracks of audio (one from each camera) and a narration, and then you have two tracks of music. You would like to be able to control the overall balance of voice and music. To do that, add two submix tracks. Assign all the voice tracks to one track and all the music tracks to the other. Now you can use the Volume effect in the voice submix track to control all the voice levels together and the Volume effect in the music submix track to control all the music together. This is called **stemming**. You still can adjust the relative levels of the clips within their own voice and music clip tracks.

▶ You want to add reverb to two tracks of vocals. To make this sound right, you want to use the same reverb parameters for both tracks. Add a submix track and add the reverb filter to that track. Assign each of the voice tracks to the submix track. Now you have what is known as a **dry** (original) signal in each clip track and a **wet** (edited) signal on the submix. You can control the amount of voice going to the reverb by changing the volume on the original clip track(s).

Adding and Sending Audio Tracks

You've noted that if you drag a clip to an empty space in a sequence, Premiere Pro automatically creates a new audio track that matches the type of audio: mono, stereo, or 5.1.

Try it Yourself   **Creating a Submix Track**

▼

If you want to add a submix track, you need to take a less automated route. You can use the same process to add any other type of track. Here's how you create a submix and **send**—or assign—an audio track to it:

1. As shown in Figure 14.7, right-click on an empty area on the left side (where the track names are) of a sequence and select Add Tracks.

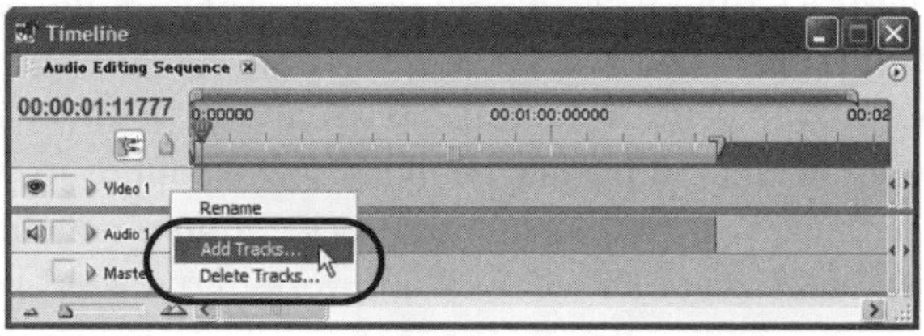

FIGURE 14.7
Use the sequence's context (right-click) menu to select Add Tracks.

2. In the Add Tracks dialog box shown in Figure 14.8, set Add Video Track(s) and Add Audio Track(s) to 0, set Audio Submix Tracks to 1, select a placement and track type, and click OK.

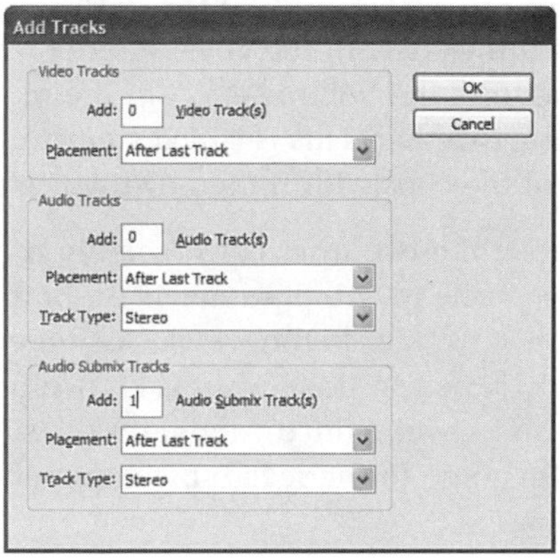

FIGURE 14.8
Use the Add Tracks dialog box to add an audio submix (or other video and audio tracks).

3. Take a look at the bottom of the audio mixer. As highlighted in Figure 14.9, Audio 1 (and any other clip tracks you have in your sequence) now has the option to send its signal to Submix 1. If you select Submix 1, whatever audio is on Audio 1 will also go to Submix 1. If you send several clip tracks to Submix 1, Premiere Pro combines them using whatever audio gain levels and effects you set in their original clip tracks.

▼

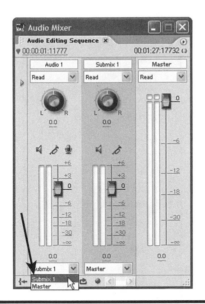

FIGURE 14.9 ▼
The drop-down list at the bottom of the audio mixer now enables you to send an audio clip track to a submix track.

▲

Working with the New Audio Mixer

Premiere Pro's new audio mixer is a giant step up from previous versions. It's the focal point of your audio production. In previous versions of Premiere, the audio mixer's primary task was to enable you to manually control audio levels (recording your actions as you applied them). This updated version improves on that functionality as well as offering two big improvements: the capability to apply effects to entire tracks and a means to record a narration directly to a sequence.

Recording a Narration and Adding Track Effects

Try it Yourself
▼

I won't go into too many details because the Adobe manual explains things well. However, I do suggest experimenting with the audio mixer:

1. If you haven't already done so, expand the Audio Mixer view by clicking the disclosure triangle circled in Figure 14.10.

2. To record a narration, make sure that your PC mic is plugged in to the Mic input on your sound card and turned on. To do that, open the Control Panel, and double-click Sounds and Audio. In the Volume tab, click Advanced and check to see that Microphone is not muted.

▼

▼
FIGURE 14.10
Open the audio mixer to display all its features by clicking the circled disclosure triangle.

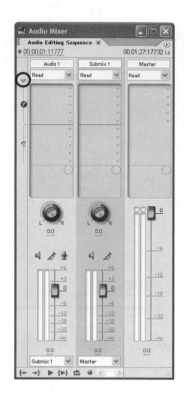

3. Activate the Premiere Pro narration record mode by clicking the Microphone button in one of the audio clip tracks (you can't record a narration to the master or submix tracks).

4. Click the red Record button at the bottom of the audio mixer. It'll start blinking. You can move the CTI edit line to where you want this narration to begin (it'll cover up any audio at that location) and then click the Play button to start recording. When you finish recording, click the Stop button and note that an audio clip appears on the selected audio track.

Watch Your Levels

Watch your voice levels in the mixer's audio track VU meter—the two parallel vertical bars next to the volume slider. You want to avoid too much volume (indicated by a red display in the VU meters) or too little. Occasionally jumping into the yellow zone toward the top is fine.

▼

What to Do About Feedback

If you record audio and you have taken no steps to mute the output, you might get **feedback**—that lovely screeching noise that happens when a mic gets too close to a loud speaker. There are several remedies:

▶ Use the Mute button on the track in the sequence.

▶ Drop the master fader bar to -∞.

▶ Change the assign for the track to a submix track and drop that submix track fader bar to -∞.

▶ Turn down your speakers (you can use headphones to hear yourself).

By the
Way

5. You use the audio mixer to add audio effects to the entire track by clicking the drop-down list triangle highlighted in Figure 14.11 and selecting from that list (it has all but a few of the clip-based effects).

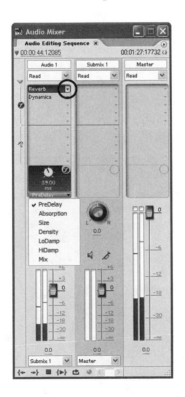

FIGURE 14.11
Add a track effect by clicking the triangle to reveal a drop-down list. Make adjustments using controls that display in the Mixer mini-window.

▼

▲

6. Each effect offers some level of control at the bottom of the audio mixer's mini-window. Some effects, such as Reverb shown in Figure 14.11, have drop-down lists of presets.

By the
Way

Effects Apply to Entire Track

These effects do not have the detailed control that you find when applying them to clips. Nor can you use keyframes. These effects apply to *entire* tracks. That's the beauty of track-based effects: their uniformity over an entire track.

Changing Track Gain and Balance or Pan

Premiere Pro's online help file has a thorough explanation of the audio mixer. Select Help→Contents→Mixing Audio to open that lengthy and detailed section.

Essentially, the audio mixer makes it possible for you to adjust audio gain and balance (or pan for mono tracks) on the fly, recording your changes as you make them. If you don't like the mix, you can make adjustments using the mixer or, as shown in Figure 14.12, by dragging the Track Volume handles in the audio track waveform display. To display those keyframes, click the Show Keyframes button and select Show Track Volume.

FIGURE 14.12
After using the audio mixer to set volume or gain levels for an entire track, you can move the volume handles in that track's waveform in the Timeline window to adjust those levels.

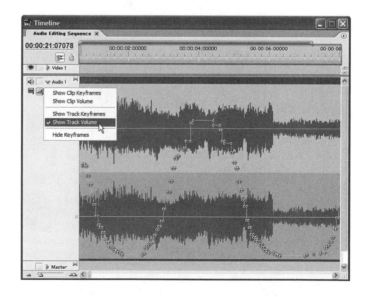

You make your audio gain and left/right balance changes after selecting an automation setting from the drop-down list (shown in Figure 14.13) at the top of the selected track. You have five automation setting choices:

▶ Off—Ignores any existing playback settings so that you can preview any changes as you make them without reverting to previous settings and without recording those changes.

▶ Read—Plays back any automation changes you've made.

▶ Write—Records adjustments as you make them and creates keyframe handles that display in the sequence's track waveform.

▶ Latch—Same as the Write setting except that nothing changes until you adjust a value; that value then holds until you change it.

▶ Touch—Same as the Latch setting except if you release the gain fader, the value returns to its previous setting.

FIGURE 14.13
Premiere Pro offers five **automation** controls in the audio mixer. Latch, Touch, and Write each give you slightly different levels of control over how you change a track's volume.

Surround Sound Panning

As far as automation is concerned, the surround panner works just like the stereo panner. As shown in Figure 14.14, if you create a 5.1 project, the audio mixer master track will have six VU meters and each clip track (mono, stereo, or 5.1) will have a panner setting display window.

To manually set panning for a track, set Automation to one of the Write modes, play your audio track, and grab and drag the little dot (highlighted with an arrow in Figure 14.14) to move the audio around the 5.1 surround location.

As you set these new locations, they show up as keyframe handles in your sequence. To view them and manually change them, click the Show Keyframes button and select Show Track Keyframes.

FIGURE 14.14
When working with 5.1 clips or projects, Premiere Pro enables you to manually adjust surround sound panner settings by dragging the little dot around inside this little window.

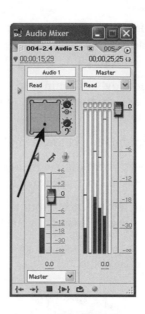

FIGURE 14.15
5.1 panner adjustments done in the audio mixer show up as keyframe handles in the audio track.

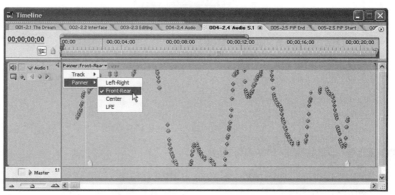

It would be impractical to show all keyframes for all six surround sound locations. Premiere Pro makes it possible for you to narrow down your view in the clip's waveform display. As shown in Figure 14.15, use the clip's drop-down list and select Panner→Left-Right, Front-Rear, Center or **LFE** (low-frequency effects that are routed to the subwoofer) to display the keyframe handles you created in the mixer.

You can use the Pen tool (it offers more precise control than the Selection arrow and enables you to add keyframes) from the Tools palette to add, delete, or adjust these handles:

▶ Add a keyframe by holding Ctrl and clicking on the yellow panning line.

▶ Move keyframes by grabbing and dragging them.

▶ Use the Pen tool (select it from the Tools palette or use its keyboard shortcut: P) to drag bounding boxes around groups of keyframes, and then hold down Shift, grab one of the highlighted keyframes, and drag the collection *en masse* to a new location.

▶ Delete a keyframe by selecting it with the Pen tool and pressing Delete. Delete a group by dragging a bounding box around them and pressing Delete.

Panner Seems Jerky—Not to Worry

The surround panner definitely tracks smoothly between points. If your PC is slower than most, you might see some jumpiness on the display updates in the mixer window but the internals will track smoothly.

By the Way

Summary

Adding audio effects to clips on a Premiere Pro sequence can bring a project to life. The Effect Controls window tracks each clip's effects, gives you detailed control over their individual features, and offers keyframes for those attributes. The addition of VST plug-in support means Adobe was able to include some very powerful and detailed effects.

The new audio mixer and audio tracks open up all sorts of extra control possibilities for Premiere Pro. It's a simple matter to apply effects to entire tracks and adjust volume and balance/panning changes on the fly.

Q&A

Q *I worked in the audio mixer for a while then returned to the Timeline window. When I play my video, I don't hear anything but I didn't mute the audio track. What's going on?*

A You probably muted the track in the audio mixer. Unfortunately, that action does not make itself apparent in the sequence display. Go back to the audio mixer and unselect the Mute button for your track. The button is right above the volume fader bar.

Q *I want to get a nice distinct echo effect, but Reverb sounds like a lot of echoes instead of only one. Is there a way to get only one echo, or at least some limited number of echoes?*

A Yes. Use Delay. It creates an exact duplication of whatever is on your audio clip. That can be very disconcerting if it's music—you'll hear every guitar strum twice, for instance. But if you have a voice shouting out a word or phrase, you can adjust the settings to have that echo come back quickly or with a delay of up to two seconds and have it blend with the original clip or not.

Workshop

Quiz

1. You need to boost treble and bass. You have several possibilities. What are they?

2. There are at least three ways to make audio move from the right channel to the left and back. What are they?

3. You recorded a speech but the presenter is too quiet and the waiter's clattering trays are too jarring. How can you fix those problems?

Quiz Answers

1. Take your pick. The easiest but least precise method is to add treble and bass to the clip. Using the Parametric EQ effect twice to boost each end of the audio frequency spectrum gives you a fine level of control. Or try EQ, turn off the midrange frequency bands, and adjust the low and high ends.

2. Use one of two effects: Balance adjusts the overall balance, left or right and Channel Volume enables you to adjust the volume of each channel individually. If you drop the left to -∞ and the right to full 6dB, you've accomplished virtually the same effect, but the clip will sound louder. To get audio to switch back and forth, use keyframes. Or use the audio mixer's Left/Right Balance control knob.

3. You want to minimize the clattering trays by reducing the high end of the volume when the clattering happens and remove it when the speaker pauses. Also, you want to increase the low-volume portions to better hear the speaker. Use Dynamics to do both. Use its Gate feature to cut off the signal when the speaker pauses, use Compressor to bring up the soft speaker levels, and use Limiter to cut off any loud sounds.

Exercises

1. Experiment with the Multitap Delay audio effect. Use it on a solo instrument, a solo voice (record your own, perhaps), and music with a hard beat. This is a slick and exciting toy that can give some real presence to audio.

2. Create a chorus using a voice. Use your camcorder or PC mic to record yourself (or a volunteer) singing a song. Add it to a sequence. Then use the PitchShifter audio effect on it. Add several audio tracks. Place the CTI edit line at the beginning of the original clip, copy the clip (right-click→Copy), select an empty track by clicking the track name, and then select Edit→Paste (or Ctrl+V) to place that copy on the sequence. Do that several times. Select each clip in turn and slightly adjust the PitchShifter's Fine setting. It takes some trial and error to avoid a warbling sound, but if all goes well, you'll turn a soloist into an ensemble.

3. Create a full-featured graphics equalizer by layering several Parametric EQ effects on the same clip. You can use EQ's five frequency presets, but using multiple instances of Parametric EQ is a good way to precisely control some very specific frequencies ranges. Preview your work as you make changes. After you've created a collection in the ECW, turn one or more of the effects off (click the f check box) and then listen to the difference.

HOUR 15

Professional Audio Tools: SmartSound Sonicfire and Adobe Audition

What You'll Learn in This Hour:

▶ Making music with SmartSound Sonicfire Pro
▶ Introducing Adobe Audition
▶ Audition's audio effects
▶ Using Audition to craft a tune

Music can make or break a production. If you aren't a dedicated musician with some fairly sophisticated PC music hardware and software, you probably can't create that music yourself. As I mentioned in Hour 12, "Acquiring Audio," you can rip music from a CD, but that raises the copyright infringement red flag. Or you can use the SmartSound QuickTracks plug-in that shipped with Premiere 6.5 or its new version for Premiere Pro that was in beta while I was writing this book.

None of these solutions is ideal. Two options that *are* ideal are SmartSound Sonicfire Pro 3 and Adobe Audition. SmartSound Sonicfire Pro 3 can create professional music that matches your project style and length. Adobe Audition enables you to take custom music creation further by offering 4,500 music loops that you can tap to create compositions. Plus it's loaded with professional audio editing tools and high-end effects that go beyond those available in Premiere Pro.

Making Music with SmartSound Sonicfire Pro

This full-featured big brother of QuickTracks from SmartSound (http://www.smartsound.com/), shown in Figure 15.1, makes it possible for you to create customized soundtracks that exactly fit the style and length of your work. You can use multiple tunes within a project, edit them to fit certain segments, and build transitions between them if that suits your production.

FIGURE 15.1
Sonicfire Pro 3 enables you to build customized original soundtracks that exactly fit the length and style of your production—and you pay no additional licensing fees.

Sonicfire Pro 3 works much like QuickTracks in that all its music is recorded from real instruments (as opposed to using MIDI files). QuickTracks transparently moves, adds, or removes little snippets of the song to make it fit a project length or user-selected style. Sonicfire Pro 3 offers those same features and enables you to select different phrases for dramatic effect and build your own arrangements by mixing and matching those snippets in whatever order and quantity suits you.

The *blocking* feature, shown in Figure 15.2, is a simple drag-and-drop process. Blocks that work well at the start, middle, or end of a song are easily identifiable.

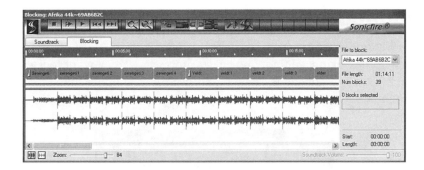

FIGURE 15.2
Sonicfire Pro 3 uses original tunes recorded by studio musicians in such a way that you can edit in, remove, move, and alter the length of snippets of music to fit your video production needs.

Sonicfire Pro 3 ($299) ships with 42 tunes at 44.1kHz (CD audio quality) and the Bundle Edition ($499) comes with 98 songs. Because you can edit them in uncountable ways, these songs open up a wealth of possibilities. You access those tunes directly or, as shown in Figure 15.3, narrow your search using criteria such as genre, instrumentation, and intensity.

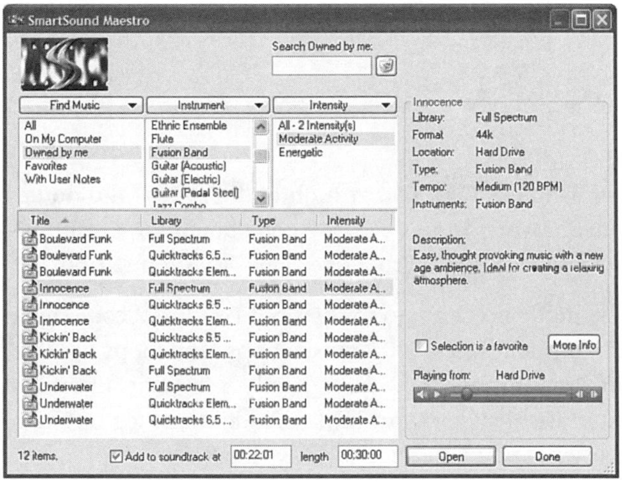

FIGURE 15.3
Access the SmartSound music library using the Maestro search tool.

You can limit your search to your existing collection or dramatically expand it by scouring the SmartSound collection on the company Web site. There you can preview and purchase tunes individually or select from several dozen themed CDs. CDs typically have 18 songs and retail for $100 (22kHz versions cost $50). Individual tunes sell for $20. Sonicfire Pro 3 is a great way to add a professional touch to your projects.

Introducing Adobe Audition

Adobe Audition is a complete, professional, 128-track recording studio that offers advanced audio mixing, editing, and effects processing. You'll want to use Adobe Audition for music productions, radio broadcasts, or to enhance audio for your Premiere Pro videos.

Audition started its life as Cool Edit, a high-end, professional audio editing tool from Syntrillium Software. In mid-2003, Adobe bought Syntrillium's technology assets and re-released Cool Edit Pro 2 as Adobe Audition ($299).

Although Adobe made no changes to the Cool Edit Pro 2 code, the company did add one tremendous feature: 4,500+ music loops. The loops are like the song snippets in Sonicfire Pro 3 in that they are typically a few bars of an instrument playing in a certain musical style. What makes Audition much different from Sonicfire Pro 3 is what you can do with those loops.

Here are some of Audition's features:

- **Change pitch and tempo without losing sonic fidelity**—Audition's beat-marking technology and superior stretch engine enable you to make pitch and tempo changes while retaining all the characteristics of the original instrument or voice.

- **Audio repair**—Noise reduction selectively removes room noise, hiss, hum, and even camera motors(!) while retaining full audio quality. Automated and user-defined click and pop removal cleans up vinyl recordings.

▶ **Sound your best**—Adobe Audition supports files with sample rates up to 10MHz (that's 10 MEGAHertz! as opposed to the standard CD-audio sampling rate of 44 KILOHertz), so whether your destination is tape, CD, DVD, or DVD-Audio, Audition can handle the files. All processing is done at the maximum 32-bit resolution for the highest quality sound. All edits are sample-accurate and short crossfades can be added for smooth, pop-free cuts every time.

▶ **Additional features**—It also offers real-time effects, loop creation, audio analysis tools, and video support.

Auditioning Audition

In the following tasks I'm going to put Audition through a few of its paces. I urge you to follow along by downloading the trial version of Audition from the Adobe Web site: www.adobe.com/products/audition. There you'll find links to the tryout download (30MB) and to the "loopology" content. The content is divided into musical genres. Knowing that 30MB might be a hefty download for you, I chose a genre with a relatively small file size: rockabilly (9MB).

Introducing Audition—Basic Editing

Try it Yourself
▼

Audition is really three products in one: a single waveform editor (meaning that you can narrow your audio processing down to a single audio element), a multitrack audio recorder and mixer, and a music creation tool. I give you a taste of all these elements in this and other upcoming tasks. We begin with a multitrack project:

1. Open Adobe Audition. If it opens to its default project, you'll see it populate its screen with a few music clips and then play the Audition theme. Your workspace should look like Figure 15.4.

What to Do If the Theme Does Not Appear

By the Way

The Audition theme might not appear (typically because you've opened Audition before). To load that project, do the following:

1. Make sure that you're in multitrack mode. There should be a little waveform icon in the upper-left corner of the user interface (I highlighted it in Figure 15.4). If the icon has three parallel waveforms instead, click that to open multitrack.

▼

2. Select File→Open Session. Clicking the highlighted Waveform button, switches to that workspace.

3. Go to the Audition directory (default location: C:\Program Files\Adobe\ Audition 1.0\Audition Theme).

4. Double-click on Audition-Theme.ses. Doing so will open the file in the main Audition multitrack user interface.

FIGURE 15.4
The Audition multi-track workspace with the Audition Theme open.

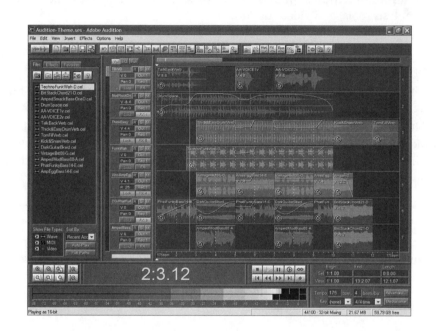

2. To play this 12-second spot, click the Play button at the bottom of the screen (or use the spacebar keyboard shortcut). With the exception of the narration, this theme was created using loops from the Audition library.

3. Slow down its tempo from 175 BPM to 125 BPM (or whatever new beat suits you) by highlighting 175 in the Tempo window in the lower-right corner of the screen, typing in the new BPM, and pressing Enter. After Audition finishes taking a few seconds to reprocess the audio, listen to the changes by pressing the Esc key to return the edit line to the beginning of the tracks and clicking Play.

By the Way ▼

Changed Tempo—Unchanged Pitch

I hope that what you're hearing amazes you. Everything slows down, but the instruments' characteristics remain unchanged. The narrator's voice still has the same pitch and he isn't dragging his words. The drums have the same presence and the instruments sustain their tonal qualities. This powerful feature opens up myriad possibilities. To whet your appetite, think of doing a 30-second spot with a 35-second narration. Use Audition to compress that narration without turning it into Alvin and the Chipmunks.

4. Take the tempo up to 200 BPM. Amazing, isn't it?

5. Now we'll change a clip's volume. We'll work with a clip in Track 5. To make it easier to hear your changes, solo that track by clicking the little S, which is indicated by an arrow in Figure 15.5. Also make sure that the track is not locked (the word *lock* should not be grayed out). If the track is locked, click the word *lock* to unlock the track.

FIGURE 15.5
Click the Solo button to listen to only that track. Change a clip's audio gain by clicking and dragging its volume handles.

6. Move the edit line to the beginning of that clip by dragging its small triangle at the top of the multitrack window.

7. To be sure that you can make volume changes within a clip display, select View and see to it that both Show Volume Envelopes and Enable Envelope Editing have check marks next to them.

8. Select the AmpEgg Bass clip to switch on its volume envelope handles (highlighted earlier in Figure 15.5). Grab them and move them around a bit. Press the spacebar to play the clip and check out the changes. Do this as much as you want with this or any other track. When done, switch off the Solo button.

9. Change the Pan settings for a clip by first clicking the Show Pan Envelopes button at the top of the interface (see Figure 15.6).

▼

FIGURE 15.6
Turn on the pan
envelope display by
clicking this button
at the top of the
user interface.

10. Audition color codes pan and volume lines: Pan lines are blue and volume lines are green. If you choose, you can make it easier to see the pan envelope handles by turning off the Volume Envelopes display by clicking its button (to the left of the Pan Envelopes).

11. Solo Track 6 and select the first clip: PhatFunkyBass14-E. Note that it pans left-to-right (top of the clip to the bottom). Grab and move those pan handles and listen to those changes. You can add handles by clicking on the Pan line and dragging it to a new location.

Audition's Audio Effects

As you've heard during the previous hour, Premiere Pro has a wealth of high-end audio effects. Not surprisingly, Audition does as well. What you'll note when working with them is all the extra features they offer.

 Test Audition's Audio Effects

Applying audio effects is a relatively simple task. But deciding what works well and when to do it takes a lot of trial and error. A good way to get to know what Audition can do for you is by sampling its effects. You can add them to entire tracks or to individual clips. Here's how:

1. Solo Track 6 by clicking its little S. Note that the track is unlocked (the Lock button is dark blue), so you can make edits to it.

2. Open its Effects dialog box, shown in Figure 15.7, by clicking the FX 8 button.

3. Play the clip by pressing the Play button and try out a few presets by selecting them from the drop-down list. Classical Cathedral gives your music a dramatic, rich sound. Move some of the sliders—especially Reverb (wet)—to see how that changes the sound.

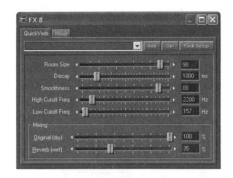

FIGURE 15.7 ▼
The track FX dialog
box gives you
access to all
effects added to a
track. Most effects
have a several slid-
er controls and
multiple presets.

What to Do When the Music Ends

If you want to play a clip over and over, you have two choices: When the song ends, click Stop and then click Play to start it over or use the Loop Play button (it's shaped like the ∞ infinity symbol).

Did you Know?

---

4. Add an effect to this track by clicking the Rack Setup button (in the upper-right corner) to open the Track 6 Effects Rack dialog box shown in Figure 15.8. Open the Special folder, select Distortion, click Add, and click OK to return to the FX 8 dialog box.

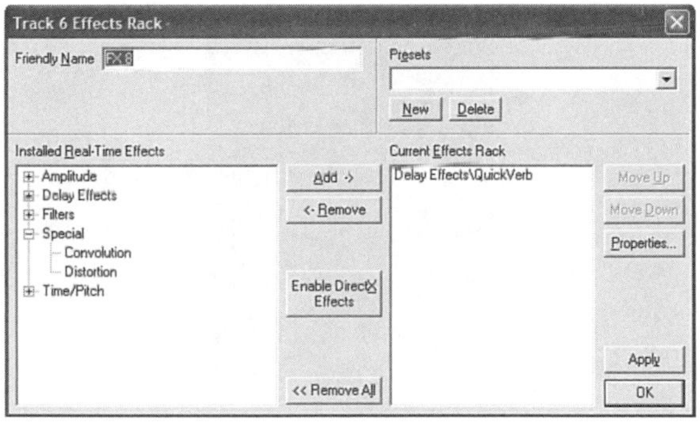

FIGURE 15.8
The Track Effects
Rack dialog box
enables you to add
effects to a track
or remove them.

5. Click the Distortion tab to open its control display, shown in Figure 15.9. Play the clip and try out some presets. Move the handles on the display. This effect can give your audio a grungy, garage band sound. You can keep it by closing the dialog box or click the Rack Setup button, select Distortion from the Current Effect Rack, click Remove, click OK, and then close the FX 8 dialog box.

▼

FIGURE 15.9
The Distortion
dialog box offers
presets plus
something a bit out
of the ordinary:
graphic controls.
Drag the handles
along the curved
line to further
adjust the sound.

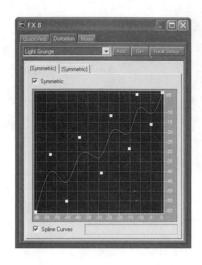

Did you
Know?

Drag and Drop Effects on to Tracks

The alternative means of adding an effect to a track is to simply drag it from the
Effects list on the left side of the Audition user interface, shown in Figure 15.10,
and drop it anywhere on a track.

FIGURE 15.10
Even if a track's FX
dialog box is
closed, you can
add an effect to a
track simply by
dragging it from
this collection to
anywhere on the
track.

▼

Track Effect Versus Clip Effect

When you're in multitrack view, all effects are applied to entire tracks, not to individual clips. Even if you drop an effect on a clip in a track, it still affects the entire track. To apply effects directly to clips, you need to open a clip in the Waveform window. I cover that starting in step 6.

By the Way ▼

6. Double-click the AA-VOICE1v clip to open that part of the narration in the waveform edit window (see Figure 15.11).

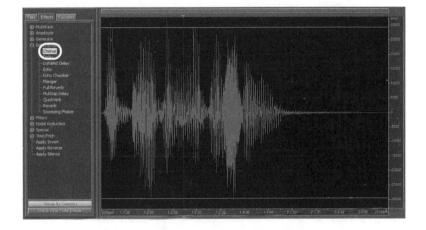

FIGURE 15.11
Double-clicking a clip segment opens It in the waveform edit window. You'll use the Chorus effect on this narration to give the clip some presence.

7. Add the Chorus effect to this clip by double-clicking it (it's in the Delay Effects group). That opens the Chorus settings dialog box shown in Figure 15.12. Note that it has a different look than the Track Effect settings dialog box.

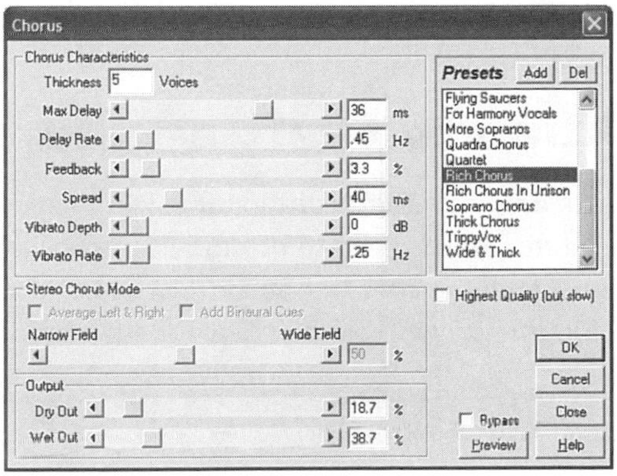

FIGURE 15.12
When adding effects to clips—in this case, the Chorus effect—the dialog boxes take on a different look but still offer virtually the same functionality.

▼

8. This dialog box also has a Preview button. Click it and try out the various presets. I like Rich Chorus. When you're done, click Cancel.

9. Open Time/Pitch and double-click Pitch Bender. This is a very cool effect (shown in Figure 15.13) that can give a narrator a whole new pitch. Select Down a Whole Step from the presets and click Preview. A deeper, more sonorous voice emits from your speakers. You can drag the pitch handles in the screen and make changes on the fly. Try the other presets as well. Cancel out of this effect.

FIGURE 15.13
Pitch Blender raises or lowers a clip's frequency, giving a narrator a high squeaky voice, for instance.

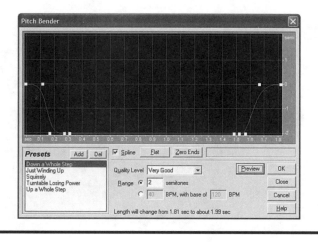

There is a passel of additional effects. Of particular interest is the Noise Reduction group. For instance, you can use its Click/Pop Eliminator to analyze recordings made from vinyl records and automatically remove scratches. Noise Reduction will analyze a quiet passage of a concert and remove the ever-present audience background noise from the music. Hiss Reduction will fix old audio tapes.

Using Audition to Craft a Tune

You've done multitrack and waveform editing; now you'll create a tune using Audition's loops. To do this, you'll need to download the Rockabilly loopology collection from the Adobe/Audition site: www.adobe.com/products/audition. If you feel like venturing off on your own, feel free to try a different set of loops.

 Composing Music Using Loops

Creating a tune using loops is great fun. The possibilities are endless. I give you a taste of that experience in this task. The basic process is to preview loops from an

Audition library. The loops are a variety of similar riffs (within the selected musical genre) using several different instruments. You'll want to select some that you think will play well together.

Feel free to experiment, head off on a different tack, or throw in some special effects. This is one of those activities where you might find yourself still at it in the wee hours of the morning, wondering where the night went. Here's how it works:

1. Close your Theme session by selecting File→Close All (Waves and Session).

2. If you're not in the multitrack view, click the multitrack button in the upper left to open a blank multitrack interface.

3. Start a new multitrack session by selecting File→New Session, choose 44100 from the New Multitrack Session dialog box, and click OK.

4. Click the File folder button in the upper left (below the File tab). That opens the Open a Waveform window shown in Figure 15.14. Things will get a bit tedious here, but one at a time, open each file folder, select all the loop files (they have the CEL suffix—a holdover to the pre-Audition, Cool Edit loop file naming convention), and click Open for each collection.

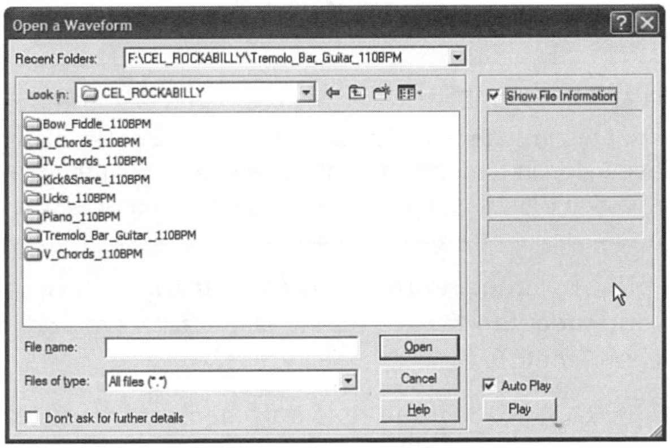

FIGURE 15.14
One at a time, open each of these folders, select all the CEL files, and click Open to add about 115 loops to your project.

5. When you're done, you'll have about 115 loops loaded into your workspace. As shown in Figure 15.15, select Sort By: Filename to get them into alphabetical order.

6. Now the fun begins. Click on the Auto-Play button (below the Sort By: drop-down list) to switch it on. Click on a loop to listen to it. Preview as many loops as suits you to get a feel for what's to come. You'll note that most play for four beats—in this case, one measure of music.

▼
FIGURE 15.15
How your work-
space should look
after adding the
rockabilly loops to
your project.
Select, Sort By:
Filename to alpha-
betized these
loops.

By the Way

Follow the Keys

Most of the clip names include their *key*, as in their musical key signature. It's a
good idea to place loops in the same key at the same time in the piece. If you're
not into music and don't get this, I think it will become clearer in a few steps.

7. Start your piece by dragging IntroPickup to Track 1. Once on the track,
   right-click and drag it to the beginning of the track (you use a left-click to
   change a clip's length).

8. Drag Kick&Snr07 to Track 1 and slide it up against IntroPickup. Extend it
   another three bars (four in all) by clicking on it to select it and then dragging its right edge to the right by left-clicking on the little diagonal hash
   marks in its lower-right corner. As shown in Figure 15.16, the cursor
   changes to something like the Premiere Pro Ripple Edit tool. As in Premiere
   Pro, Snap-to-Edges makes it easy to create four bars exactly (Audition displays those bar divisions with thin, vertical dashed lines). That five-bar
   track segment should look like Figure 15.16.

9. Play that segment and note how the IntroPickup loop moves seamlessly
   into Kick&Snr07.

▼

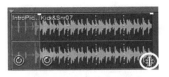

FIGURE 15.16 ▼
After adding a loop, you can grab its lower-right corner and drag it to build additional bars. In this case, four bars in all.

10. Add three more drum loops to Track 1: Kick&Snr10 (four bars), Kick&Snr05, and Kick&Snr04 (two bars each).

11. Here are the loops that I suggest you add to the rest of the tracks:

    ▶ **Track 2**: ChugginA starting at bar four (note the bar number ruler at the bottom of the multitrack screen) for two bars, Walkdown_A2 (two loops equaling one bar), WalkUpTo4 (two loops equaling one bar), ChugginA (two bars), Chuggin5 (two bars), ChugginA (two bars), WalkDownA_2 (two loops equaling one bar), and TremBarEndingChord02-E (one loop equaling two bars)

    ▶ **Track 3**: FunkierThanBilly-B starting at bar six for two bars, HappyGoLuckyB (two bars), and HappyGoLuckyA (two bars)

    ▶ **Track 4**: HonkyTnk04-A starting at bar eight for two bars, HonkyTnk05-B (two bars), HonkyTnk03-A (two bars), and PianoCmp03-A (one bar)

    ▶ **Track 5**: BowFidl07-A starting at bar four for four bars, BowFidl09-A (two bars), BowFidl12-B (two bars), and BowFidl10-A (two bars)

12. If you followed my song-building suggestion, your project should look like Figure 15.17. Play it. I think you'll enjoy it.

Key Consistency

To see what I meant in the "Follow the Keys" note, take a look at the clips in bar 8. All end with a large letter A. They are all in the key of A. At bar 10, they're all in the key of B (Chuggin5 is the exception, but it sounds like the key of B). At any rate, it's generally a good idea to match key signatures in the same bar.

By the Way

Coloring Clips

That the clips are uniformly green is Audition's default behavior. As in the Audition Theme session, if you want to give your clips different colors, simply right-click on a clip, select Block Color, move the slider to a color you like, and click OK.

Did you Know?

▼

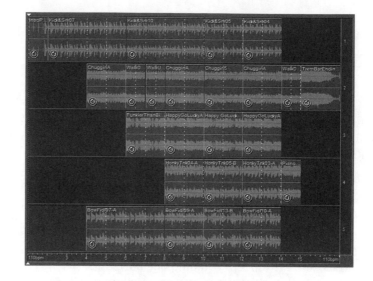

FIGURE 15.17
How your completed composition should look.

13. Make a waveform edit by double-clicking `TremBarEndingChord02-E` at the end of Track 2. Note that it has a little extra *scrunch* sound at the end of the waveform. Remove that by positioning the cursor between the stereo waveforms right before the extra noise starts, noting the cursor turns into an I-beam, and dragging it to the right to highlight the section to remove. Use Figure 15.18 as a reference. Press the Delete key. Audition automatically stretches the clip to fit its original two bars.

FIGURE 15.18
To remove an offending bit of noise, open the clip in the Waveform edit window, drag the cursor to highlight the offending segment, and press Delete.

14. Click the Multitrack button to return to that window. Feel free to add some effects to clips and/or tracks, change volume levels to highlight certain passages, and pan the instruments across the stereo field if that suits you.

▼

▲

Loopology Creation

Audition's 4,500 loops are essentially the product of one man: Jason Levine. As performer, engineer, and producer, he created, recorded, and mastered this entire library of original, royalty-free music. Levine has a lengthy history as an accomplished musician and recording studio engineer. He says that the "most exciting studio experiences of my life involved a two-year engagement working with one of the industry's most respected and honored engineers, Roger Nichols of Steely Dan fame."

Levine worked for Syntrillium as music director, with a heavy emphasis on Cool Edit Pro 2's concept and workflow. With Adobe's purchase of Syntrillium, he became Audition's main "evangelist," presenting the product at conventions and workshops across the globe.

During his Syntrillium tenure and before making the move to Audition evangelist, Levine created production-quality music loops. Using his home recording studio and Audition's multitrack recording capability, Levine (performing all keyboards and synthesizers, plus bass guitar and drums) worked with two other musicians: guitarist and Audition user interface designer Steve Fazio and drummer Fred Fung. Together they crafted the true, ensemble sound of the 4,500 loops that ship with Audition.

That is a big selling point for Audition. Because Levine recorded the loops as live performances by the three musicians working together in the studio, those loops have a real, ensemble feel and work well together. No other loop collection can tout that.

His recording setup probably has a few more bells and whistles than what you might have at hand or want to purchase. But if you want to create original audio content, I think you can learn from his methodology.

Audition—An Audio Recording Studio

Here's a basic rundown of the audio studio setup that Levine used to record the loops:

▶ Two M-Audio Delta 1010 audio cards—Street price: $599 each (http://www.m-audio.com/). These have eight analog input/outputs and one pair of digital I/Os (see Figure 15.19). Audition sees each of those discrete channels and can record them to individual tracks.

FIGURE 15.19
Jason Levine used two M-Audio Delta 1010 sound cards (20 input/output channels in all) to capture audio to his PC.

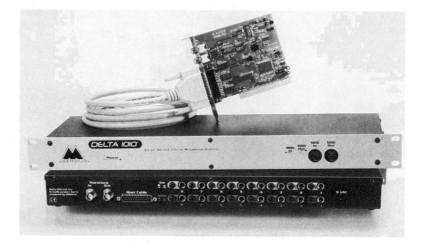

▶ Industry-standard Mackie mixers (http://www.mackie.com/) to ensure proper levels and mix. Basic Mackie mixers that will serve most purposes start at only about $200. The 1202-VLZ Pro has 12 channels and a street price of $400.

▶ Several different types of preamps captured and enhanced drum, bass, and guitar sounds. Preamps can be a bit expensive. When in doubt, you can always turn to the transparent, clean sounds inherent in Mackie mixer's built-in preamps.

▶ A varied collection of microphones rounded out the audio-capture process. Levine selected each mic to lend its distinctive quality to the many instruments recorded for the Audition content library. These included Shure's

SM57 ($147) and SM58 ($188) (http://www.shure.com) and the ubiquitous, high-end studio favorite C414 ($799 street price—see Figure 15.20) from AKG (http://www.akg.com).

FIGURE 15.20
You'll find the AKG C414 microphone in most professional audio production studios.

Even without all this gear, you can record audio using Audition. Simply plug a mic or musical instrument into the mic or line input, respectively, on your sound card. As shown in Figure 15.21, press the R record button on a track to switch to its record mode, open the Record Devices dialog box by clicking the Rec1 button, select the input channel (most standard sound cards offer only one stereo line input), and then click the Record button at the bottom of the multitrack window.

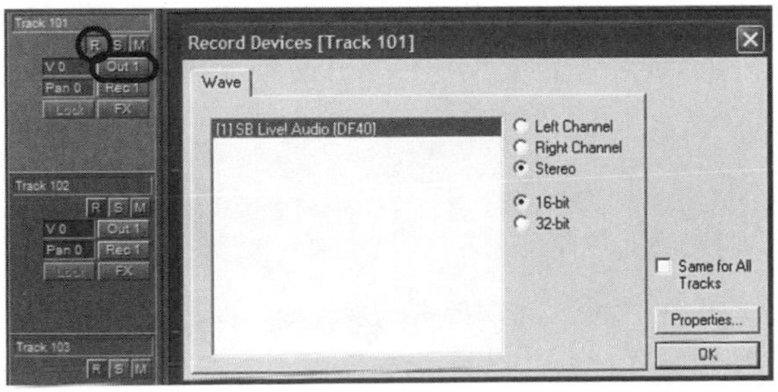

FIGURE 15.21
Access Audition's 32-track recording mode by clicking a track's Record button and assigning an input channel to that track.

Your sound card probably has only one stereo line input, but Audition enables you to split the channels onto two distinct tracks. This works well for radio announcers who record a narration on one of those mono channels while listening to the music accompaniment as it's being recorded to the other channel.

Summary

Music adds immeasurably to your video projects' overall quality. Finding just the right piece to fit or set a mood can be arduous. Two products that go a long way to simplifying that search are SmartSound Sonicfire Pro 3 and Adobe Audition.

Sonicfire helps you craft entire songs to fit a segment or project length and style. You select from a massive library of instrumentals, and then select and arrange song segments into a tune to fit your needs.

Audition is a much more powerful and higher-level product. It ships with 4,500 music loops that you can place on up to 128 tracks to create your own unique musical arrangements. In addition, you can add numerous audio effects, record your own audio (instruments and voice), and use Audition to remove tape hiss, vinyl record clicks, and ambient noise from live recordings.

Q&A

Q *I have the QuickTracks plug-in for Premiere 6.5. Is there any compelling reason for me to move to Sonicfire Pro?*

A It depends on your musical needs. QuickTracks is a fun product, but it has a limited library and you need to pay a licensing fee to SmartSound to use its tunes on commercial products. Sonicfire Pro's tunes are all royalty-free, meaning you can use them for virtually all productions: personal or professional. And Sonicfire Pro gives you absolute control over the editing of each tune or you can opt to automate that process.

Q *Why use Audition to add special effects to audio when Premiere Pro can do the same thing?*

A It's true that Premiere Pro has many of the same types of audio effects as Audition, but overall, Audition's collection has more control options, more presets, and better audio restoration capabilities than Premiere Pro. In addition, it ships with those 4,500 music loops and has a multitrack editor/mixer and a 32-track recording capability.

Workshop

Quiz

1. In Audition, how do you display both volume and panning characteristics for clips?

2. In Audition, you've already added QuickVerb to a track but want to swap that out for the more fully featured Reverb effect (you want to use its Shower setting—yep, as in singing in the shower). How do you make the exchange?

3. You want to speed up your announcer's delivery. How do you do that?

Quiz Answers

1. Make sure that the track on which your clips resides is unlocked. Then select the clip by clicking on it, and click the dB and the L/R buttons at the top of the screen to display the volume and panning handles. Note that moving the panning line to the top of the clip sets its value to –100 and places the audio completely in the left channel.

2. Click that track's FX button, click Rack Setup, select QuickVerb, click Remove, select Reverb from the Effects window, click Add, and click OK. That takes you back to the FX dialog box where you can change the preset for Reverb to Shower. Don't forget to sing a few bars: "Soap, soap, soap, soap."

3. The Tempo value at the lower-right corner of Audition's user interface works well for music with a beat, but it's not intended for voice. To change the speed of your announcer, try the Stretch effect in the Time/Pitch Effects group.

Exercises

1. Record some vinyl records to your hard drive. You'll probably need to use an amplifier connected to the line-in plug on your PC sound card. Use Audition's built-in Clip/Pop Eliminator to automatically remove most of those annoying clips. Then use the waveform editor to isolate single clicks (you'll see sudden, sharp jumps in the waveform) to remove the rest.

2. Jason Levine's (the Audition loopology creator) favorite loop content is Funk Rock. Those loop files (contained in two downloadable Zip files totaling 104MB) really lend themselves to the creation of some fun powerful music. If you have the Internet bandwidth, download them and take your loop music creation to new levels. After you've laid down a few tracks, give the clips and tracks some special effects—Reverb, Chorus, and Distortion, for example—as well as adjust their volume and pan characteristics. And try out some tempo changes.

PART IV

Higher-End Visual Effects and Editing Techniques

HOUR 16

Using Higher-Level Video Effects

What You'll Learn in This Hour:

▶ Making sense of the plethora of video effects
▶ Technical fix effects
▶ Blur/sharpen effects
▶ Distort effects
▶ Color and appearance effects
▶ Selected After Effects effects

I introduced you to several video effects in Hour 10, "Adding Video Effects." In this hour, I present most of the remaining effects. The major exception is the set of keying effects that I cover in Hour 17, "Compositing Part 1—Layering and Keying Clips." I also leave the Color Corrector effect and some effects that work best with clips on more than one video track for later hours.

Premiere Pro's 90+ video effects run the gamut from simple to complex. They have a wide range of uses. Some you might rely on regularly, whereas others fill such narrow niches they might never see the light of day.

With so many video effects staring up at you, it's darned hard to know when and why to use any one of them. In this hour, I'll single out my favorites and try to make sense of the rest.

Making Sense of the Plethora of Video Effects

It's not easy wading through Premiere Pro's 14 video effects categories, trying to unravel what their 90+ effects do and how they do it (see Figure 16.1). The category names do not necessarily match their functions. And some effects have multiple functions with numerous options.

By the Way

SteadyMove—In a Category By Itself

If you added SteadyMove when you installed Premiere Pro, that means you have 15 effect categories (it's in its own bin called *2d3*). SteadyMove is a third-party plug-in that smoothes out shaky camera work. I go over it and its professional version (available for an extra charge) in Hour 21, "Third-Party Products."

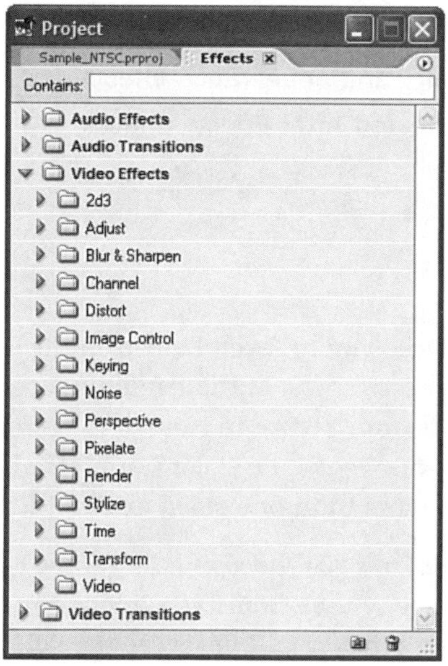

FIGURE 16.1
Premiere Pro's 15 category names for video effects do not necessarily describe their contents.

The categories themselves can be confounding. The Gamma Correction video effect is in the Image Control file folder, but is also a parameter of the Levels effect, which is in the Adjust file folder. Convolution Kernel is in the Adjust folder, but handles 10 different functions of several single-purpose effects in the Stylize and Blur & Sharpen folders. And the Transform effect is *not* in the Transform file folder, it's in the Distort folder.

Some effects resolve rarely encountered technical problems, such as missing fields or interlace flicker. Still others don't seem to achieve their stated purposes.

To minimize clutter, ease access, and keep things simple, I've organized this hour into my own set of categories. I suggest that you create several new video effects file folders to match those categories: Technical Fixes, Color and Appearance, and Selected After Effects. You'll continue to use the Blur & Sharpen and Distort groups.

To further eliminate clutter, I've placed the also-rans in one additional category: Other.

Did you Know?

Creating Custom Folders

To create these new categories, click the Video Effects tab in the Project window, click the fly-out menu triangle, and select New Custom Bin. It creates a folder named Favorites. Change that name by clicking on it to highlight it and then typing in a new name: Technical Fixes, Color and Appearance, and so on. To further clarify this new organization, you might add your initials to each bin name. Later, as I go over the various effects, you can drag and drop their icons to the new folders.

Even after you drag an effect to a custom bin, the effect remains in its default bin. You cannot delete effects or bins.

Technical Fix Effects

When you think of video effects, technical fixes do not come to mind. The primary reason you use video effects is to alter the appearance of your video clips—to blur, emboss, tint, or distort—or to add graphic elements, such as lightning and lens flare. So, I'll get this mundane but useful technical stuff out of the way first.

At first, you might use a variety of single-purpose effects from Premiere Pro's collection of technical fix effects. Eventually, you might settle on the one effect that can do just about anything those others can do: Levels.

I'll introduce Levels, list the technical fix effects with brief explanations, and then go over how to use the Levels effect.

My Favorite Technical Fix Effect: Levels

The Levels effect (shown in Figure 16.2 with all its parameters and its separate settings dialog box) is one of several jack-of-all-trades video effects. It manipulates the overall brightness and contrast of a clip and of its individual color channels, enabling you to adjust the following four image characteristics (each of which has its own separate video effect):

Brightness & Contrast—This is standard TV control stuff that can significantly enhance your video.

Color Balance RGB—You'll use this time and time again. No matter how carefully you use white balance when shooting your videos, some video clips will turn out too red, green, or blue. The Levels effect enables you to fix that by adjusting the individual RGB color brightness and contrast levels.

Gamma Correction—Anyone who's played a video game with a too-dark setting knows that bringing up the gamma levels brightens the scene without washing it out. This effect accomplishes that by bringing up the midtones while leaving dark and light areas unaffected.

Invert—This switches color information making your video look like a color negative.

FIGURE 16.2
The Levels Settings keyframable parameters and its dialog box and are not immediately intuitive.

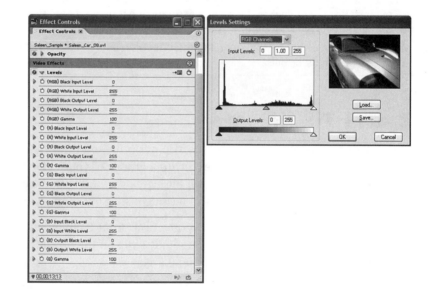

Using Levels to do these simple tasks might be overkill. Instead you might want to first use each of those four features' much more user-friendly, standalone video effects. In another Premiere Pro conundrum, you'll find them in two different video effects bins: Adjust and Image Control.

Using the Levels Effect

To see the Levels effect in action, drag it from the Adjust bin to a video clip (or select a clip and drag Levels to the ECW (Effect Controls Window). In the ECW, click on the Levels Settings dialog box icon (the little PC screen icon).

This is not your father's TV set brightness and contrast control. The interface takes some explanation. The chart is a histogram of your currently selected frame. Brightness values from dark to light run along the X-axis. The Y-axis represents the number of pixels at each brightness value.

Use the drop-down list at the top of the interface to choose whether you want the tonal adjustments to apply to one of the three color channels or to all three at once (RGB).

The sliders directly below the histogram control contrast and gamma. Drag the black triangle to the right to increase the shadows, the white triangle to the left to increase the highlights, and the gray triangle to control the gamma—the mid-tones.

The Output Levels slider reduces contrast. Dragging the black triangle to the right eliminates the darkest values in the clip, whereas sliding the white triangle to the left eliminates the brightest values.

Other Technical Fix Effects

In addition to Levels and its four siblings, here are the other technical fix effects that are available to you:

> **Broadcast Colors**—This effect ensures that color values will play back on PAL or NTSC TVs. It's a powerful tool with simple controls, but you might never need to use it.

> **Clip**—Trims away noise from the edges of your videos, replacing the removed pixels with a user-specified frame color. If you don't want a frame, use the Motion effect to zoom in on your video to push noisy frame edges offscreen. I demonstrate a practical use for Clip at the end of the "Bevel Alpha, Bevel Edges, and Edge Feather" section later this hour (I do it then because that's when I have you open a new project in which this effect works well).

> **Color Balance HSL**—This alters a clip's hue, luminance, and color saturation. It doesn't have the color accuracy of Color Balance RGB. Gamma Correction and Brightness & Contrast perform similar functions.

Field Interpolate—Rarely used. It's for instances when field loss (basically, half a video frame) occurs during capture.

Median—Median's strength is its oil painting effect (see the "Color and Appearance—Painting Effects" section later this hour). But its original purpose was to reduce video noise.

Reduce Interface Flicker—Very thin horizontal lines sometimes lead to disruptive flicker on some TVs. This seeks out those trouble spots and softens their edges to reduce flickering.

Blur & Sharpen Effects

As with the Levels effect and its narrower purpose siblings, at the core of most of the Blur & Sharpen effects is another jack-of-all-trades, the Convolution Kernel effect.

As shown in Figure 16.3, the Convolution Kernel effect also has a Settings dialog box and a lengthy list of keyframable parameters. It changes the brightness values of pixels using a three-by-three matrix and a mathematical formula. The formula divides the sum of those pixel values by another user-set variable and then adds yet another user-selected value to that quotient, thus creating the desired effect.

FIGURE 16.3
Convolution Kernel is fun to experiment with, but it's a heck of lot easier to use individual Blur & Sharpen effects than tweak its matrix values or presets.

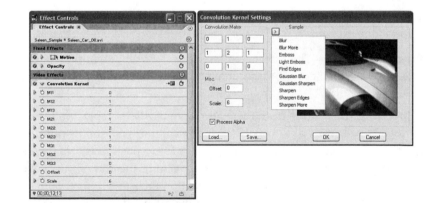

So, it's not surprising the Convolution Kernel effect can handle most of the effects in this category. But Adobe's Premiere Pro effects creators recognize that Convolution Kernel is not for the faint of heart. For all but two pre-set effects, it's easier to use individual, narrower purpose Premiere Pro effects rather than the Convolution Kernel's matrix calculations or even its presets.

Convolution Kernel Overview

Convolution Kernel is the workhorse of this category. But of its 10 presets shown in Figure 16.19 and in the following list, only Gaussian Sharpen and Sharpen Edges work as well or better than their single-purpose siblings. Stick to the other recommended Blur & Sharpen effects and experiment with Convolution Kernel to create your own effects.

▶ **Blur**—Very subtle. Use Directional Blur or Fast Blur instead.

▶ **Blur More**—Directional Blur and Fast Blur work better.

▶ **Emboss**—Use the Emboss effect instead. It gives you more control.

▶ **Light Emboss**—Use Emboss instead.

▶ **Find Edges**—This identifies and emphasizes areas of an image with obvious transitions/edges. The standalone Find Edges effect is a full-featured and powerful tool that I cover in the "Color and Appearance Effects" section later this hour.

▶ **Gaussian Blur**—This is nearly the same as Fast Blur.

▶ **Gaussian Sharpen**—This is on par with the separate Gaussian Sharpen effect.

▶ **Sharpen**—The After Effects Sharpen effect has a slider, so it works better.

▶ **Sharpen Edges**—This is the only Convolution Kernel preset that outshines the specialized effect.

▶ **Sharpen More**—Use Sharpen instead.

My Favorite Blur & Sharpen Effects

Each of the following video effects can either soften or sharpen entire clips or elements within clips:

Anti-alias—It softens edges between contrasting colors and light.

Channel Blur—This effect, illustrated in Figure 16.4, shifts RGB (red, green, and blue) colors individually, creating a blurring effect. It works well with alpha channels (transparent portions of some graphics), enabling you to shift the colors of graphics.

Directional Blur—By smearing pixels in a user-selected direction, this effect supposedly gives the illusion of motion. I don't think it's all that effective, but it is a good way to simply create a blurred image.

Fast Blur—This creates a much more blurred image than Directional Blur. Figure 16.5 shows how easy it is to use. Apply keyframes to create an ever-increasing blur over time. This works better than Gaussian Blur or Camera Blur.

FIGURE 16.5
Fast Blur creates
the blurriest
images.

Radial Blur—The "Psycho" look. It creates a whirlpool blur that simulates a swirling camera. Figure 16.6 shows that you can vary the location, type, and quality of the blur.

FIGURE 16.6
Radial Blur gives a
video clip a soft
swirling look.

> ### Radial Blur—A CPU Cycles Hog
> Radial Blur is a processor-intensive effect—thus the three Quality settings. At the highest quality, Premiere Pro's Real-time Preview might stutter through the clip. Rendering Radial Blur at its full quality takes extra time.

Sharpen—This effect sharpens a soft-focus image by increasing contrast where color changes occur. This effect uses only a single slider. It works better than Gaussian Sharpen or the Convolution Kernel's Sharpen and Sharpen More presets.

Duplicate Blur/Sharpen Effects

Feel free to place the following four video effects in your Other folder. Other effects handle their chores as well or better than they do:

Camera Blur—The Directional Blur effect handles this and adds a direction component.

Gaussian Blur—Same as the Fast Blur effect.

Gaussian Sharpen—The Convolution Kernel preset is as good as this standalone video effect.

Sharpen Edges—The Convolution Kernel preset is as good as this standalone video effect and has more options.

Distort Effects

With a few exceptions, these effects all do the same kind of thing. They twist and contort your clip into funhouse mirror shapes. To use them well takes some experimentation on your part. Rather than explain them in detail, I'll lump similar effects together and use figure captions to identify them.

I will give brief explanations of the *non*-funhouse distortion effects at the end of this section.

Pinch, Shear, Spherize, and ZigZag

You may have checked these effects out in Hour 11, "Putting Video and Still Clips in Motion." They all use a similar interface, as shown in Figures 16.7–16.10.

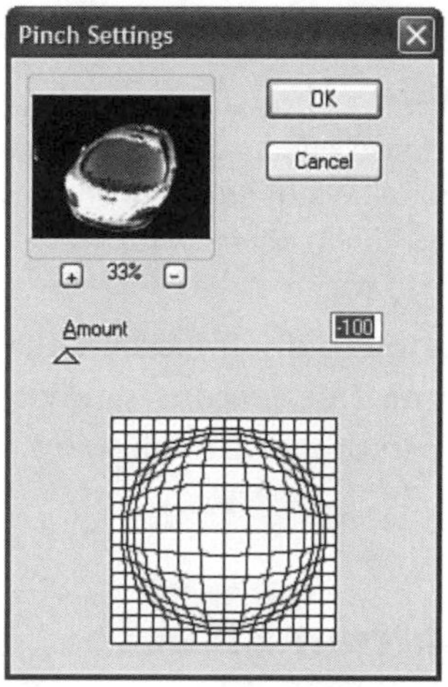

FIGURE 16.7
Pinch draws in or expands an image in the middle.

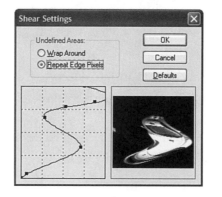

FIGURE 16.8
Shear creates a curve along a user-defined wavy line.

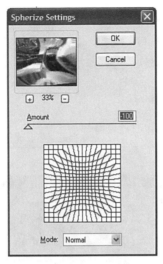

FIGURE 16.9
Spherize pushes out or pulls in the image using a ball shape.

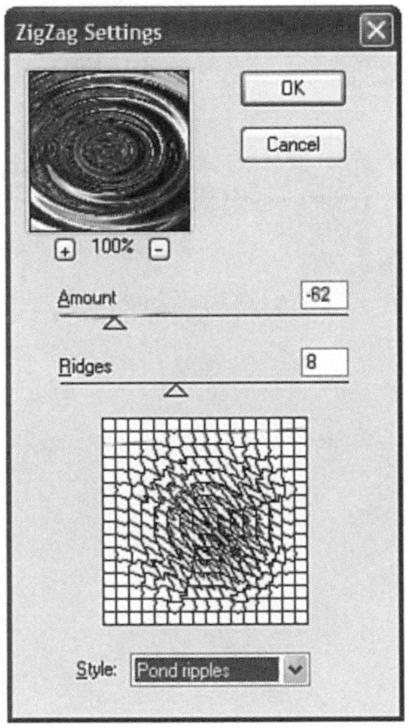

FIGURE 16.10
ZigZag creates several nice wave effects emanating from a user selected point.

Bend, Lens Distortion, Ripple, and Wave

The four effects shown in Figures 16.11–16.14 all create undulating, twisting effects.

FIGURE 16.11
Bend most closely re-creates a fun-house mirror effect. It fills the screen with the distorted image.

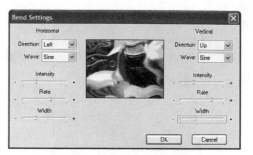

FIGURE 16.12
Lens Distortion's primary function is to reduce distortion effects; for example, when shooting at extreme angles or with special lenses. In addition, it has a feature that enables you to fill any gaps you create with a color selected from the clip (rolling the cursor over the small image automatically switches on the highlighted Eyedropper tool) or from the color picker window. Alternatively, you can turn that gap into a transparent alpha channel (discussed in Hour 18, "Compositing Part 2—Alpha Channels and Mattes") to allow clips below it on the sequence show through.

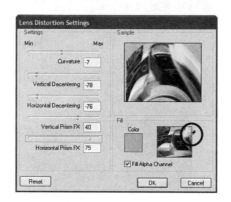

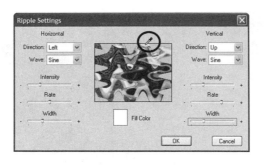

FIGURE 16.13
Ripple is like Bend but leaves gaps around the curves that you can fill with color, just as you can do with Lens Distortion. Except in this case you do not have an Alpha Channel option.

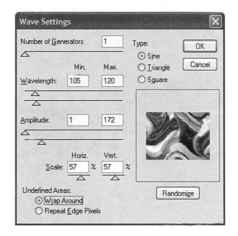

FIGURE 16.14
Wave looks a lot like the Bend effect.

Mirror, Polar Coordinates, and Twirl

These three effects, shown in Figures 16.15–16.17, are all After Effects effects. For one thing, that means they do not have separate Settings dialog boxes. Note that Mirror and Twirl are both motion-style effects (they have a bounding box cursor before their names in the ECW) and therefore have a crosshair you can drag around onscreen to set the focal point of the effect.

FIGURE 16.15
Mirror perfectly reflects the scene at the crosshair (switch it on by clicking on Mirror) using the angle selected, where 90 degrees creates a reflection along a horizontal line, and 0 degrees creates a reflection along a vertical line.

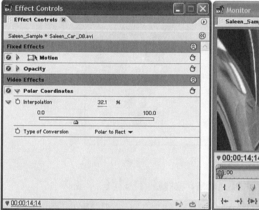

FIGURE 16.16
Polar Coordinates converts the clip's X/Y coordinates into polar coordinates (or vice versa) to create this odd little lens distortion. The slider intensifies the effect.

FIGURE 16.17
Twirl rotates a clip around the crosshair. The greater the radius and angle, the more intense the twirl. Animate this using keyframes to create a real cool effect.

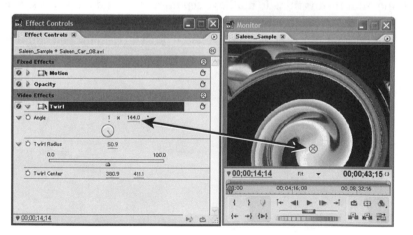

Horizontal Hold and Vertical Hold

The effects shown in Figures 16.18 and 16.19 give the impression that something is dreadfully wrong with the viewer's TV. You can use them both on the same clip to really make things go haywire.

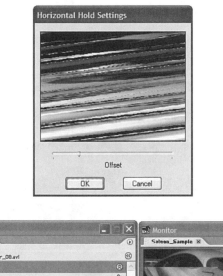

FIGURE 16.18
Horizontal Hold has a separate dialog box with slider control to set its severity.

FIGURE 16.19
Vertical Hold has no parameters. It's either on or off. When it's on, your image just rolls and rolls and rolls.

Noise—Give Your Clips That Old VHS Feel

You do what you can to create clean, sharp, noise-free video. So, what does Adobe do? It includes this Noise effect in Premiere Pro to give your videos that low-light, consumer, analog camcorder look.

The Amount of Noise slider sets the noise level by distorting or randomly displacing pixels. As illustrated in Figure 16.20, at a setting of 20% or so, the effect creates a very noisy image. Crank it up to 75% and your clip might become unrecognizable.

Checking the Use Color Noise box randomly changes the red, green, and blue values of the image's pixels. Unchecked means all color values change equally.

Checking the Clip Result Values box creates a more realistic Noise display by letting color values that reach their maximum value wrap around and start over at 0% noise. Leaving it unchecked means color values that max out stay at that maximum level, making some portions of your scene shimmer with noise.

Noise to the Max

To completely randomize Noise, turn on Use Color Noise and turn off Clip Result Values. To reproduce true noise, set the slider to about 20%, turn off Use Color Noise, and turn on Clip Result Values.

FIGURE 16.20
Noise can give your tape the look of a worn out VHS tape.

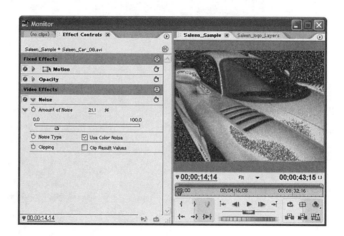

Camera View

This effect warrants special mention. As shown in Figure 16.21, Camera View gives the impression of a camera looking at your clip from different angles. It works a lot like the Basic 3D effect in that it rotates, flips, and zooms a clip. What makes it stand out from Basic 3D is that it gives immediate feedback in its Settings dialog box.

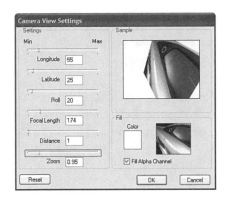

FIGURE 16.21
Camera View enables you to twist, flip, and zoom your clip, simulating a camera viewing the clip from varying angles.

Basic 3D—Create That Glint Shot

This effect is not all that different from the Camera View effect. In fact, Camera View has more options, the most important being Zoom-in and Roll. What makes Basic 3D worth your time is its Specular Highlight option. As shown in Figure 16.22, a simulated light source can create a little moving glint on the surface of your clip as it changes angles and moves around the screen.

A Glint Is Not a Lens Flare

Do not confuse this with Lens Flare (covered later this hour). In that case, the light is not reflecting off the surface of the clip, it's simulating a series of refractions that occurs when a camera lens is pointed at an oblique angle toward a light source.

FIGURE 16.22
Basic 3D's Specular Highlight gives a realistic touch when tilting a screen and moving it in 3D space.

The move takes place on only two axes:

Swivel—Controls horizontal rotation

Tilt—Controls vertical rotation

Go beyond 90 degrees in either direction and you see the back (mirror view) of your image. The Preview mode switches to a wireframe view. It notes the presence and location of the specular highlight using a green plus (+) sign (enlarged for emphasis in Figure 16.23). A red plus sign shows the highlight's location, but indicates that it won't be visible because the image is not tilted toward the simulated light source.

FIGURE 16.23
Switching to Preview mode turns on a wireframe view, making it easier to locate and follow the specular highlight.

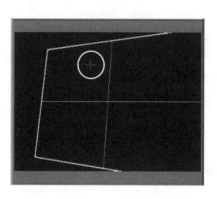

Specular Highlight Issues

Basic 3D's Specular Highlight (the main reason you'd want to use Basic 3D) is a surprisingly processor-intensive effect. Not even a single frame will display it if you have your Monitor window set to Draft Mode. To see it either switch to Highest Quality (click the wing menu to access that feature) or render the clip.

Also, it can be very bright if the reflection is straight at you—that is, if the highlight is at the center of the screen. To avoid that, try to make your moves so the highlight travels around the edges of the screen. Alternatively, use keyframes to turn on the highlight only when it reaches an edge.

Bevel Alpha, Bevel Edges, and Edge Feather

These effects create 3D beveled frame-like edges for your clips. Bevel Edges and Edge Feather are for regular video clips and Bevel Alpha works only with graphics or videos that have alpha channels. All three are great tools to use when you're using motion settings to fly clips over another image. Using them gives those flying clips extra depth.

Creating Beveled Images

Try it
Yourself
▼

In this case, rather than only showing you an effect, I want you to try both of these. The purpose is twofold: to show you how to combine effects and to introduce the concept of *alpha channels*.

1. When you installed Premiere Pro, you also might have copied the Sample Project NTSC or PAL to your hard drive. If not, you'll find those projects on the sample files CD that came with your boxed version of Premiere Pro. To do this task you need to copy that folder to your hard drive (wherever you store your media assets is a good location).

2. Open Premiere Pro, click on New Project, navigate to your Sample Project folder, select Sample Project (NTSC or PAL) and click Open.

The Saleen Assets

By the
Way

The Saleen S7 is a custom-built automobile (still a prototype as we went to press). Adobe worked out a deal with the manufacturer and the video production studio to include these assets with Premiere Pro and use them in numerous demos. Feel free to view this project. Some of the effects are from Premiere Pro and others were built in Adobe After Effects. I cover that latter product in Hour 22, "Using Photoshop and After Effects to Enhance Your DV Project."

---

3. Select the Saleen_Car_08 clip (you can choose any clip, but this one works well for the next few steps). Apply Edge Feather to it and, as shown in Figure 16.24, increase the edge thickness to make the soft frame obvious.

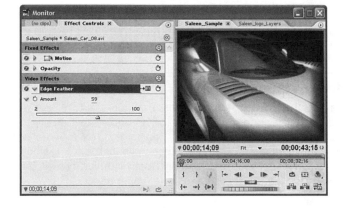

FIGURE 16.24
Edge Feather softens the look of a clip.

4. Delete Edge Feather and apply Bevel Edges to this clip. As shown in Figure 16.25, increase the edge thickness to make the bevel obvious.

▼

Give Frames to Clips in Motion

When you fly reduced-size clips onscreen using the Motion effect, giving them frames is a nice touch. Bevel Edges, Edge Feather, or Clip work well.

FIGURE 16.25
Bevel Edges gives video clips a nice 3D frame.

5. Apply Lens Distortion to this clip by dragging the effect to the ECW *below* Bevel Edges. Create a distortion and note that, as shown in Figure 16.26, the bevel matches that new shape.

Effect Order Counts

Premiere Pro applies effects starting at the bottom of the ECW and working its way up. So, in this case, it performs the Lens Distortion and then applies Bevel Edges to it. Premiere Pro's two fixed video effects—Opacity and Motion—are last in line. If you want to apply Motion earlier in the effect chain, use the Transform effect (it has the same parameters). If you want to apply Opacity earlier (I cover Opacity and other layering tools in the next hour) use the Alpha Adjust effect.

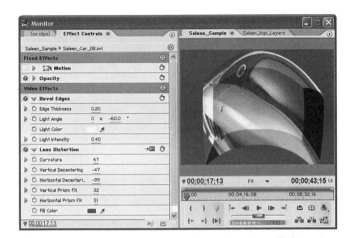

FIGURE 16.26 ▼
If you apply another effect—in this case, Lens Distortion—Bevel Edges adjusts its actions to match any changes to the clip's shape.

6. Remove all the effects (select them one at a time and press Delete) and add Bevel Alpha to the ECW. Increase the Edge Thickness setting and note that hardly anything happens. The reason: This effect works only with graphics that have an *alpha channel*. That is, a transparent layer. You'll see that in action in step 12.

7. The last clip in the sequence (highlighted in Figure 16.27) is not a standard video clip or graphic—it's a nested sequence (see the "What's a Nested Sequence?" Did You Know? for more information about that). Double-click that nested sequence to open it in the Timeline window.

What's a Nested Sequence?

Did you Know?

Saleen_logo_Layers is a nested sequence. That is, it's a separate sequence that is placed in another sequence as a clip. In this case, this nested sequence is simply two layered—or *composited*—graphics that have motion effects applied to them individually. Any work you do on this Saleen_logo_Layers sequence will show up in that nested sequence clip.

One advantage to working with nested sequences is that you can apply an effect to a nested sequence instead of having to do that with whatever number of clips made up that original sequence.

You can tell it's a nested sequence because its clip color on the sequence is a light blue/green, rather than the light blue for video clips, purple for graphics, and light green for audio (the color differences are subtle). And, as shown in Figure 16.27, if you select the clip with the Info palette open, it notes that it's a Sequence.

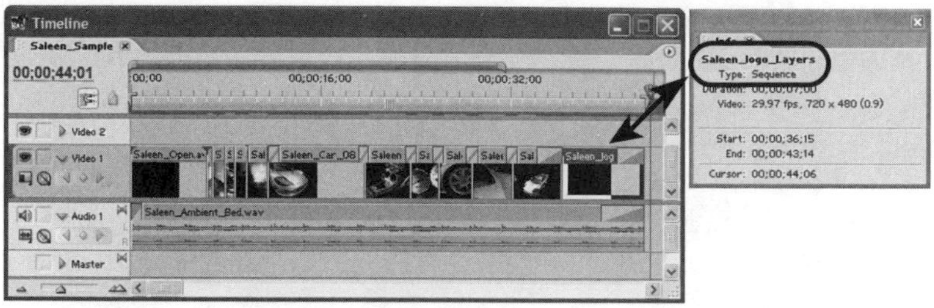

FIGURE 16.27
The last clip is a nested sequence— a separate sequence added to this sequence as a means to simplify the editing process.

8. Play the Saleen_logo_Layers sequence and note that it's simply two graphics that fly in from opposite sides of the screen.

By the Way

> ### Layered Graphics with Alpha Channels
>
> Two things to note: First, this sequence is an example of composited or layered clips. The clip on Video Track B (renamed by the Saleen video editor by right-clicking on the track header, selecting Rename, and typing in a new name) plays on top of the clip on the track below it.
>
> Second, the reason the clip on top (the word *Saleen*) does not cover the clip below is because the Saleen clip is a Photoshop graphic created with a transparent alpha channel. In other words, only the word *Saleen* is opaque. The rest of the graphic is clear, like putting a decal on a window.
>
> Because the default background color for a Premiere Pro sequence is black, that's the color that shows through the alpha channel transparency along with the red Saleen logo on the lower video track. It too is a Photoshop PSD graphic with a transparent alpha channel.

9. Turn off the Video track 2 (the upper track) display by clicking its eyeball to the left of the track name.

10. Select the red logo clip by clicking it (it's on the lower video track).

11. Switch on Motion by clicking on it in the ECW. Note that the motion line appears in the Monitor window Program screen. Expand the size of the logo by increasing the Scale to about 500%. Change its location to make it fit on screen. Use Figure 16.28 as a reference.

FIGURE 16.28 ▼
Adjust the logo
clip's Motion Scale
and Position
parameters to
expand the graphic
and center it
onscreen (I select-
ed a 25% screen
zoom level so that
you could see the
dotted line, diago-
nal motion path).

12. Apply Bevel Alpha to this graphic by dragging it to the ECW. Increase the Edge Thickness and Light Intensity settings and note how the graphic changes. As shown in Figure 16.29, because the areas between the parallel red bars are also transparent, Bevel Alpha gives each of those bars a beveled look.

13. To return this project to its original state, open the History palette (select Window→History), scroll to the top entry (it should be New/Open) and click on it.

▲

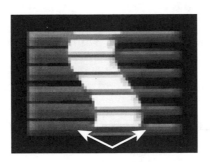

FIGURE 16.29
Bevel Alpha gives a
3D look to each
parallel bar in this
graphic.

Test Drive the Clip Effect

I mentioned in the "Technical Fix Effects" section that I'd show you one use for the Clip Effect. Select the `Saleen_Car_07` clip (second to last in the `Saleen_Sample` sequence) and apply Clip to it. As shown in the Figure 16.30 before-and-after images, that clip has a distracting element on the left side. Use the Clip effect to cover that with black (this works well because the original video has a black background).

Did you Know?

FIGURE 16.30
Use Clip to remove
unwanted junk from
the edges of your
video.

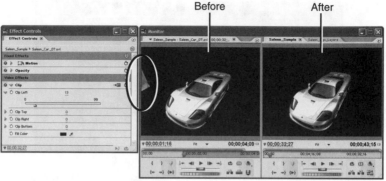

Duplicate Distort Effects

Feel free to place the following three effects in your "Other" folder: Horizontal
Flip, Vertical Flip (Camera View is better), and Roll. Note that Roll is not a duplicate. It's simply nearly useless. It rolls one edge of the screen around to the other
side. This would be very cool if you could set the amount of the roll or use
keyframes. Unfortunately, you can't.

Color and Appearance Effects

In Hour 10, I demonstrated several color appearance effects, including Black &
White, Crystallize, and Replicate. Some make your video look like a painting.
Others shift pixels or delay their display creating embossed or ghosting effects.

I've created subcategories to clarify differences within the Color and Appearance
category. I briefly explain most effects and go into detail on a handful.

Color and Appearance—Painting Effects

Eight video effects fit into this category: Crystallize, Facet, Median, Mosaic,
Pointillize, Posterize, Solarize, and Tint (I suggest including the Black & White
effect here as well for convenience). All are very easy to apply. You can use
keyframes for all but Facet. I covered three of them in Hour 10. I'll go over
Median, Mosaic, and Tint here.

Median

The Median effect replaces pixels with the median value of neighboring pixels. A radius of 1 or 2 pixels reduces noise (see the discussion of technical fixes), but at about 5 pixels, a video gets a nice soft-focus painting feel to it.

Try out Median by applying it to a clip. Note that the Radius slider, shown in Figure 16.31, goes only to 10 but you can type in higher values up to 255. The higher the number, the softer the focus (my example uses 15). Because you can use keyframes, you can change this effect over time.

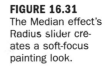

FIGURE 16.31
The Median effect's Radius slider creates a soft-focus painting look.

Mosaic

Mosaic is sort of like Pointillize with rectangles. As Figure 16.32 shows, you select the number of horizontal blocks and vertical blocks (rows and columns)—between 1 and 200—to create a collection of rectangles. The higher the number, the smaller the rectangles and the closer the image will match the original. At 200, it's simply jittery.

The Sharp Colors check box creates more distinct, clearly defined rectangles.

Mosaic—More Than Only an Effect

Use Mosaic as something like a transition. Using keyframes or simply the default start points and endpoints, start the "transition" near the end of the clip by setting both Horizontal and Vertical Blocks to 200. Then drop this setting to about 20 each at the end of the clip. Start the next clip at 20 and quickly build it to 200. Uncheck the Sharp Colors box; otherwise, the transition from 200×200 blocks to standard video will be somewhat abrupt.

Did you Know?

FIGURE 16.32
You can use Mosaic to create a faux transition.

Tint

Tint enables you to give a clip an overall color. Use it to set moods—a blue cast—or an era—a sepia tone. You select colors, either from within the original clip or using the Color Picker, and assign them to the image's black and white zones.

Color and Appearance—Color-Manipulation Effects

Channel Mixer—This effect, shown in Figure 16.33, enables you to modify each color channel. You can map one color onto another and increase or decrease a color's values to create high-quality tinted images.

The default value is 100% of each color. Dragging the sliders or inputting specific values will lead to sometimes dramatic results. Negative numbers invert the color.

Using keyframes with distinctly different values leads to some unique, gradual color changes as your clip plays.

Color Pass—You've seen those advertisements where one color stands out. Using Color Pass is one way to do it. Color Pass converts a clip to grayscale, with the exception of one user-selected color. As shown in Figure 16.34, select that color by moving the cursor into the image on the left and clicking on a color from that frame. Or select a color from the color picker. The Similarity slider expands or contracts that color on the spectrum. Use the right screen to find the sweet spot. Clicking Reverse grays out that selected color and retains all others.

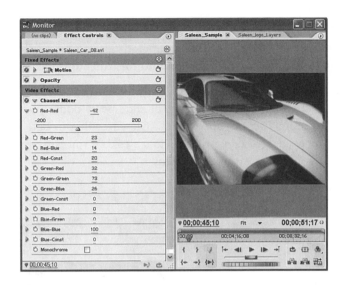

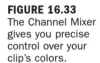

FIGURE 16.33
The Channel Mixer gives you precise control over your clip's colors.

Tricky Tasks

Color Pass is a super-slick effect that requires some careful pre-production preparation. To do it right, you need to create a setting where the object you want to highlight is a distinctly different color and evenly lit. Painting your object a color such as lime green will make it much easier to isolate with Color Pass later. Once it's converted, you can apply Color Replace to the same clip to alter that horrible lime green color into something more palatable.

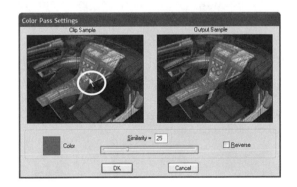

FIGURE 16.34
The Color Pass Settings dialog box's Eyedropper tool makes it possible for you to select a color to highlight.

Color Replace—This effect works more or less the same as Color Pass except that in this case it enables you to select a color and then *replace* it with another.

Extract—This effect converts a clip to grayscale and enables you to manipulate its appearance—from soft to harsh.

Color and Appearance—Color Shift Effects

Slightly altering or shifting some color characteristics can create dramatic visual effects. The following six video effects fall into this catchall subcategory:

Alpha Glow—This effect provides a very slick way to give a graphic (with an Alpha channel) a glowing fringe or shadow by adding color around its edges. To see it in action, apply Alpha Glow to either or both graphics in the Saleen_logo_Layers sequence (see Figure 16.35). You can apply keyframes to have the glow grow then fade away.

FIGURE 16.35
Alpha Glow adds a fringe around a graphic. Use keyframes to animate it.

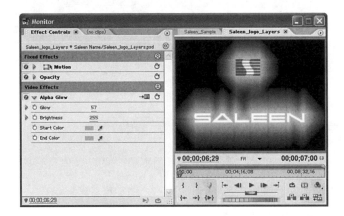

Color Emboss—This is the one Color and Appearance effect that does not appeal to me all that much. It's supposed to give elements within a clip a full-color embossed look, but it just seems to scramble colors haphazardly.

Emboss—This effect does in fact create embossed images. It offers more readily accessible controls than the Emboss element within the Convolution Kernel effect. As Figure 16.36 demonstrates, the "Blend With" slider makes it possible for you to add color to your image while making very distinct embossed edges. In that way you can use it to create both black-and-white and color embossed effects.

Find Edges

Find Edges—This effect locates elements in the image with obvious differences in contrast and color; then, as illustrated in Figure 16.37, it creates distinct dark edges on a white background. The slider enables you to combine a percentage of the original image with the converted image. Invert swaps black and white, creating white lines for edges.

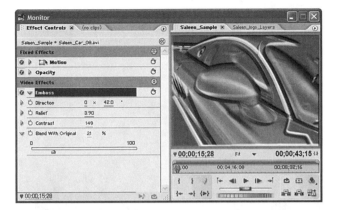

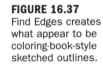

A Wild Combo: Find Edges and Color Replace

Here's one totally bizarre application of the Find Edges effect. Use it on any clip, add the Color Replace effect, and select any of the many black borders created by Find Edges. Replace that color with something distinct—bright red, for instance. Then click the Solid Colors check box to replace the black lines with the new color. Looks like you just strung everything with Christmas lights.

Did you Know?

Ghosting—This is a nifty effect where pre-production planning can be a big help. It creates ghost-like "comet trails" behind anything that moves. It works great if you hold the camera really steady while something moves through the scene.

Invert—This multifunction color shifter lets you substitute inverse RGB (red, green, blue) color information, HLS (hue, lightness, saturation), and YIQ

(NTSC luminance and chrominance values). It works much more easily than the Levels effect version. The Effect Controls window's options are deceptively simple. Use the drop-down menu, shown in Figure 16.38, to adjust those elements by their group type or individually.

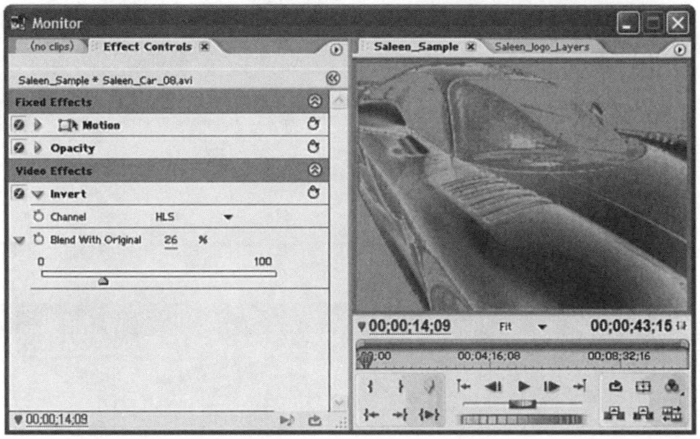

FIGURE 16.38
Invert packs a powerful color shifting punch in only a few controls.

My Favorite Color and Appearance Special Effects

My guess is that you will come to use each of the following three video effects, which create their own unique and nifty visual impression:

Lens Flare—Most of the time you shoot your scenes trying to *avoid* lens flare—that sudden appearance of glowing balls and halos, falling along a straight line. This effect, shown in Figure 16.39, enables you to *add* those glowing orbs to a scene. It works well for slow camera moves. If you use keyframes, you can add the effect gradually and adjust its location and brightness over time as your camera moves by the sun or other light source.

By the Way

Crosshair in Dialog Box, Not in ECW

Apply Lens Flare to a clip (I suggest Saleen_Car_08 in the Saleen_Sample sequence). Open its Settings dialog box and note it has crosshairs to place the flare. But if you want to add keyframes (true for all but static shots), you need to use the ECW. However, the crosshair feature is not available in the ECW; you'll need to use the Center X and Center Y parameters.

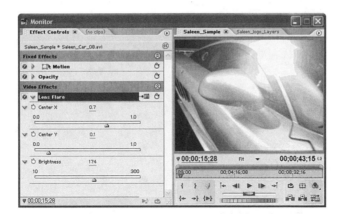

FIGURE 16.39
The Lens Flare effect coupled with keyframes enables you to insert a flare, change its brightness, and alter its location.

Replicate—You might have tried this effect in Hour 10. Use Replicate to display your clip in multiple, evenly distributed screens. The minimum setting is four rectangles—two by two. Maximum is 16 by 16. Each mini-screen displays the entire original clip.

Tiles—This effect slices your clip into jittering tiles, sort of like a mosaic in motion. As illustrated in Figure 16.40, the Tiles settings in the Effect Controls window enable you to select the number of tiles per column and how much space can be between them. You need to use the dialog box to set how you fill that space: with the background or foreground color (this varies depending on the original clip's colors), the inverse (like a film negative) of the original image, or the image itself.

Transparent Tile Gaps

The Tiles effect works well as a transparency, letting whatever is below it on the timeline show through the spaces between the moving tiles. I explain how to do this in Hour 18.

Did you
Know?

Introducing the Color Corrector

The addition of a Color Corrector video effect to Premiere Pro is a big deal. It is much more than a single, narrow-purpose technical fix effect. Rather, it is a full-featured suite of tools that go well beyond simply repairing color balance for example. I view it more as an artist's palette that you can use to create different moods. It's such a major improvement to Premiere that it has its own pre-set workspace.

FIGURE 16.40
The Tiles effect
slices your image
into shaking
squares.

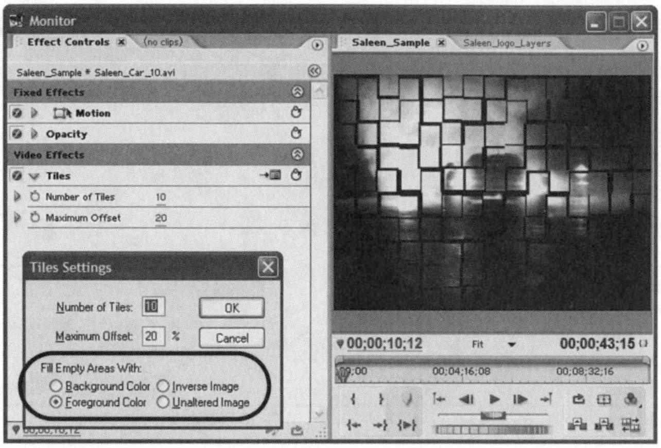

Instead of cramming more into this already fully loaded hour, I'm going to present the Color Corrector in Hour 20, "Tips, Tricks, and Techniques—Part 2."

Color and Appearance Effect—Limited Use

Color Offset fails to perform as designed. Its purpose is to create 3D images to use with red/blue 3D goggles, but I don't think it provides a practical means to accomplish that. Feel free to put it in your "Other" folder.

Adobe After Effects: Astounding Visual Effects

Some of Premiere Pro's best video effects come straight from another member of Adobe's Video Collection—the high-end, motion graphic tool: After Effects. (I give you an overview of that product's functionality in Hour 22.) You encountered some After Effects video effects earlier this hour, including Mosaic, Find Edges, Basic 3D, and Noise.

Three others—Blend, Drop Shadow, and Texturize—work only with clips on more than one track, so I cover them in Hour 18. And Transform is virtually identical to Premiere Pro's Motion video effect so I won't cover it at all. What's left then are three exciting After Effects effects: Echo, Strobe Light, and Lightning.

Adding Multiple Action Images Using Echo

Echo is an exciting effect with numerous possibilities. It layers multiple sequential frames of a clip to convert simple action into streaking, smearing, or a sequence. As Figure 16.41 demonstrates, you control Echo using five parameters:

Echo Time—The time, in seconds, between echoes. Negative values create echoes from later frames, causing ghosting or streaking to follow the action. Positive values use earlier frames, laying those echoed images ahead of the action.

Number of Echoes—The number of extra frames added to the original to make this effect. Two echoes create three images—the original plus two other (subsequent or preceding) frames. The slider values go from 1 to 10, but you can type in a number up to 3,000! From what I've seen, any value greater than 10 creates only 10 echoes.

Starting Intensity—The relative brightness of the first frame in the sequence. At the highest value (1), the first frame is at normal intensity. A setting of one half (0.5) displays the first frame at half its regular intensity.

Decay—Notes the decrease in intensity for each subsequent frame. A Decay setting of 0.5 means the first echo will be half as bright as the original frame, the second will be one quarter (0.25) as bright, and the third will be one eighth (0.125) as bright.

Smooth Out Jerky Streaks

To create smooth streaking and trail effects, use a large number of echoes (eight or more) and a short echo time (one tenth or so).

Echo Operator—Indicates how Echo combines frames. Here are the options:

▶ The Add option combines the echoes by adding their pixel values. If the Starting Intensity setting is too high, your action will turn into bright, white streaks.

Avoid Intense Echoes

To give the first frame and all echoes the same value while avoiding those bright white streaks, set Echo Operator to Add, set Starting Intensity to a value equal to 1 divided by the number of echoes, and set Decay to 1. For example, for four echoes, set Starting Intensity to .25 (1 / 4 = .25). A Decay setting of 1 means there will be no decay—all echoes will have the same value.

▶ Maximum uses the maximum pixel value from all the echoes, which emphasizes the brighter action elements.

▶ Minimum uses the minimum pixel value from all the echoes, displaying only the darker values.

▶ Screen is like Add but does not overload as easily.

▶ The two Composite options are for video clips with alpha channels (this will not work on graphics or most video clips). The Composite in Back option layers them back to front, whereas the Composite in Front option layers them front to back.

FIGURE 16.41
Echo converts motion into streaks, smears, and repeated actions.

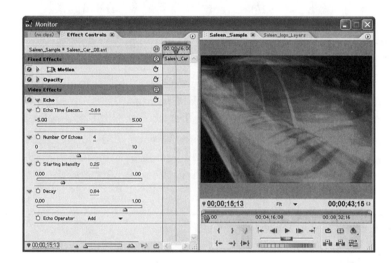

Echo Trumps Previously Applied Effects

Echo is a special video effect. By default, it switches off any other effects applied before it to the clip (those that appear above it in the ECW). Those that come below it on the Effect Controls window still work. However, there is a workaround: create a nested sequence. Apply all the effects you want to apply before Echo to a clip in a separate sequence, and then use that sequence as a clip in another sequence (making it a nested sequence) and apply Echo to that.

Giving Your Project Flash with the Strobe Light Effect

This effect opens the door to numerous creative possibilities. It works like a strobe light, flashing frames as your clip plays. Those frames can look like a super-bright strobe light or be black, transparent, or an inverse image.

The options, as illustrated in Figure 16.42, are listed here:

Strobe Color—This strobe effect can be any flashing color you want. Because color is keyframable, you can change that color over time.

Blend with Original—This option blends the Strobe Light effect with the original to adjust the intensity or brightness of the effect.

Strobe Duration—Sets the length, in seconds, for each strobe flash. Less than a half second is most like a real strobe, but you might want a strobe to stay on longer to show the inverse image or another image below this clip in the timeline.

Strobe Period—Sets the time, in seconds, between the start of subsequent strobes. Setting a strobe *period* of 2 seconds, for example, and a strobe *duration* of 0.5 seconds means that you would see the strobe effect for a half second. Then there would be a 1.5-second break until the next strobe effect. If the strobe period is less than or equal to the strobe duration, the strobe stays on all the time.

Random Strobe Probability—Set at a value other than zero means the effect will have a more realistic feel. It'll cause strobing even if the strobe period is less than or equal to the strobe duration.

Strobe drop-down menu—This menu has two options: Operates on Color Only and Makes Layer Transparent. A clearer way to state these options is Opaque and Transparent. If you choose Makes Layer Transparent, you can superimpose the strobe effect clip over another, revealing the lower clip during strobes. I'll cover transparency issues in Hour 18.

Strobe Operator—Gives you extra control if you choose Operates on Color Only (opaque). Copy is the default setting. Subtract displays a black strobe screen, and Difference pops on an inverse image. There are 10 other options.

FIGURE 16.42
The Strobe Light effect opens up numerous creative possibilities.

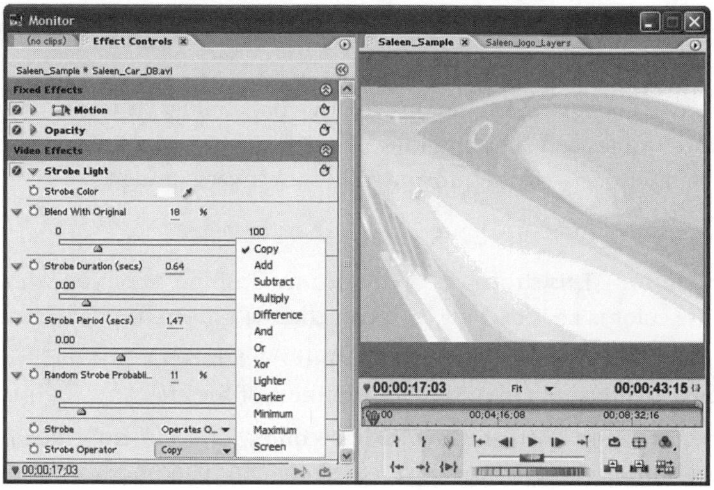

Did you Know?

Strobe Humor

For a little comic relief, use the Strobe Light effect with Strobe Operator set to Difference and Duration and Period set fairly low. The resulting strobe effect is reminiscent of a cartoon character sticking his finger in a light socket.

Adding Dazzle to Your Project with the Lightning Effect

Lightning is a wild and wacky effect. It produces a flashing electric arc like those used in old horror movies. As you'll see when you drag it to the Effect Controls window, its creators went overboard in the number of options—25 parameters! To avoid being equally guilty of overkill, I won't go over all of them.

As I've demonstrated in Figure 16.43, you use its two crosshairs to set start and end locations for the lightning. Setting keyframes enables you to alter those locations over the duration of your clip. In my case, I set two extra keyframes to have the lightning follow the car headlights.

The many options make it possible for you to set the size and intensity of the lightning. Increasing the number of segments, amount of branching, and level of detail make the flashes more jagged (kind of nastier looking). Choose any colors you like—both the core and outside colors. The default white/blue scheme works well but red/yellow provides an evil, organic touch.

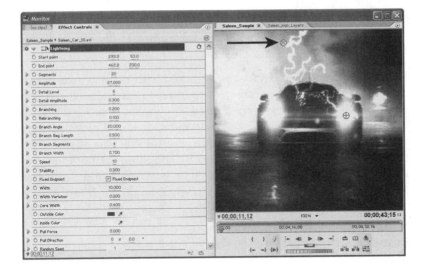

FIGURE 16.43
Experimenting with Lightning is great fun. Try a red/orange color scheme.

Summary

I introduced you to Premiere Pro's 90+ video effects in Hour 10. In this hour, I presented the full spectrum of effects from the mundane (but useful) technical fix variety to the exciting, high-end After Effects effects.

Premiere Pro's wide variety of video effects guarantee you'll have plenty of creative latitude as you build your video projects. You'll use them to change the appearance of your video clips or to repair poorly lit or color balanced footage.

Organizing the video effects into new, more descriptive file folders or bins goes a long way toward easing access. Removing redundant or underperforming effects further simplifies your video production process.

Q&A

Q *I added an effect to a clip and used keyframes to change its behavior during the clip, but I don't like the result. How can I change this?*

A Use the Keyframe Navigator—the diamond with the two triangles on the right side of each effect parameter—to move to the frame(s) you want to fix. Change the parameter setting. If you simply want to move a keyframe to a different time in the sequence, grab it and slide it to a new position. If you want to make the move frame-specific, put the edit line at your new location and create a new keyframe there by changing the parameter value in the ECW. Then delete the errant frame by selecting it and clicking the Keyframe Navigator diamond (or right-click on the keyframe and select Cut).

Q *I use Echo but the clip becomes so bright it washes everything out. What's up?*

A You've probably selected the Add or Screen option, which means that the brightness level of each echo adds itself to the original clip and its other echoes. If the Starting Intensity setting is high—near or at 1—then it takes only about two or three clips to obliterate your image. To keep the overall image intensity more or less equal to the original image, set the starting intensity to 1 divided by the number of echoes. For instance, if you use five echoes, set the starting intensity to 0.2 (1 / 5 = 0.2).

Q *I get that same kind of washed-out look when using Basic 3D to add a specular highlight to my clip. How do I avoid that?*

A Use the wireframe preview and the 3D move to keep the highlight (the green crosshair) near the edge of your clip. If it moves toward the center, the effect is like a mirror directly reflecting the sun.

Workshop

Quiz

1. You shot an interview indoors but near a window. The interviewee's face is blue! How do you fix this?

2. You "broke the plane" in a cutaway. How can you get your interviewer to face the right direction?

3. How do you create an "Electric Horseman"? If you missed this enjoyable Robert Redford/Jane Fonda flick, Redford rides out on a Las Vegas stage decked out with electric lights to promote breakfast cereal.

4. You can use the Mosaic effect to create a transition. How do you do that?

Quiz Answers

1. Use the Color Balance (RGB) effect, or if you're up to the extra level of detail involved, try adjusting individual Red, Green, and Blue channels in the Levels effect.

2. Use Camera View to flip the image on its vertical axis (Vertical Flip does this as well). That way, your interviewer faces the correct direction, and no longer breaks the plane (of course, her mother might notice that her face is a mirror image of the real thing).

3. Use Find Edges on a clip to create distinct outlines. Use Color Replace to swap a bright color for the black outline. Check the Solid Colors box to make the entire outline take on the new hue.

4. Use the Mosaic effect to give the illusion of a transition. This is not a true transition. It's simply a straight cut edit between two adjacent clips that appears to be a transition. Apply the Mosaic effect to both clips and use keyframes to have the effect start just a second or so before the end of the first clip and operate for a second or so at the beginning of the next clip. For the first clip, set the starting number of horizontal and vertical blocks to 200 and the end to something like 10; then reverse that process for the second clip.

Exercises

1. Use Lens Flare to create a moving glow that reacts to a light source. A panning shot, a tilt, or a light source moving through the image (a race car's headlights for example) all work well. Simply use keyframes in several locations to attempt to equal the light source's movement. It doesn't have to be exact because the lens flare does not have to rest directly on the light source.

2. Use keyframes to create a radial blur that gradually moves around an image.

3. Use Color Pass and Color Replace to isolate an object and give it a new color.

4. Experiment with the Lightning effect using the Saleen_Car_10 clip I used in Figure 16.43. The goal is to have two bolts of lightning emanating from the same source above the screen and splitting so that one each hits the car's headlights. To do that, you'll need to apply the effect twice (just drag it to the ECW two times), switch on keyframes for the start and end points, and set a few other keyframes for both moving end points. For extra credit, change the attributes of the lightning over the duration of the clip. Increase the intensity by changing values for segments, branching, and amplitude. Also, change the color of the lightning during the clip.

HOUR 17

Compositing Part 1—Layering and Keying Clips

What You'll Learn in This Hour:

- ▶ Making compositing part of your projects
- ▶ News-style cutaways and multitrack audio rules
- ▶ Your assignment: grab shots for compositing
- ▶ Working with the Opacity effect
- ▶ Keying clips

One great strength of Premiere Pro is its ability to layer (or **composite**) multiple clips over one another. Compositing can be as simple as placing a logo over a product shot or as complex as shooting actors in front of a green screen and then electronically placing them within a scene with both foreground and background elements.

Premiere Pro makes it possible for you to layer up to 99 video tracks. I can't imagine any project that would require so many layers, but I think you get the drift that permitting that level of complexity in Premiere Pro demonstrates that compositing can be a big part of any video production.

There are four basic compositing methods:

- ▶ Using the Opacity video effect to reduce the opacity of an entire clip so that a clip (or clips) below it on the timeline can show through

- ▶ Using keying effects to make portions of a clip transparent so that portions of clips below it on the sequence show through

- ▶ Blocking or **matting** parts of one clip to let parts of other clips show through

▶ Using a clip's alpha channel or using video effects with built-in alpha channels to create transparencies

This hour covers the first two topics. I save the latter two for the next hour, "Compositing Part 2—Alpha Channels and Mattes."

I start simple with some standard TV news–style cutaways—video clips placed on a track above an interview, for example—with the express purpose of covering whatever is below it. When you apply those you need to be aware of the rules Premiere Pro follows when handling the audio portions of those cutaways.

Some editors would argue that such cutaways aren't compositing because nothing on the first layer shows through. But because some cutaways use more than one video track, I consider it compositing and it's a good introduction to more complex layering to come.

That introduction begins when you take clips you've shot for this hour and make them partially transparent to let portions of the clips on lower tracks show through.

Making Compositing Part of Your Projects

If you've tried out Premiere Pro's Title Designer, used the Motion effect, or worked on video effects that use alpha channels, you've already moved toward compositing—that is, layering graphics or video clips over other clips.

For instance, anything you create in the Title Designer can display over another clip, layering text onto that clip while letting the rest of that clip show through. When you apply the Motion effect to a clip, you usually play it over another clip or a graphic background. And when you work with some video effects that have alpha channels, such as Lens Distortion, you can use them to combine two clips with portions of one clip showing around the edges of the distorted clip.

Compositing can add immeasurably to your video projects. Sometimes the effect is obvious—sliding videos in boxes onto the screen sends a clear message that you've done something out of the ordinary with your production. Other times the effect is more subtle. We don't think twice when we see a TV meteorologist gesturing at a map or graphics. As shown in Figure 17.1, in fact, that TV personality is standing in front of a green or blue wall. The program's technical director electronically makes that wall transparent and inserts videos, maps, and other graphics in its place. The meteorologist watches studio monitors to see what he is pointing at.

FIGURE 17.1
Matt Zaffino, chief meteorologist—KGW-TV, Portland, Oregon.

Most computer games with live actors and many movies use compositing. "Green screen" studios enable game developers and film directors to place actors in science fiction and other settings created with 3D computer graphics. Such sets make it possible for actors to work in relative safety while the finished product has them dangling from a skyscraper, hundreds of feet in the air.

For most budding professional video producers, such high-budget studio access might be out of the question. But you *can* add some nice composited special effects to your projects simply with a few tweaks of Premiere Pro's tools.

News-Style Cutaways and Multitrack Audio Rules

As an introduction to compositing or layering, you'll start by adding news-style cutaways over the edit point of two adjacent clips. This is a practical and often-used technique employed by TV news editors to cover an edit between sound bites and as a way to show viewers that the reporter actually did the interview.

In the coming Try It Yourself, some of the methods place the cutaway on a new track (compositing), whereas others cover a clip on the Video 1 track (not truly compositing). I've lumped both approaches together because they both fall into the cutaway category.

What works best for the upcoming task are two sound bites, from the same person, that you want to place back-to-back. If you don't have two such clips, you can use any two clips (plus a cutaway) just to get a feel for how this works. For instance, two soccer goals plus a crowd shot cutaway will work well. Make sure all three clips have video *and* audio.

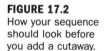

Creating TV News–Style Cutaways

There are several ways to add cutaways. I'll explain three. Here are the steps to follow:

1. Import the linked A/V sound bites (or whatever clips you're using) plus the cutaway to the Project window.

2. Delete all the clips in a sequence or open a new sequence (File→New→Sequence). Keep your sequence simple: one video track and one audio track.

3. Drag the two clips to the Video 1 track on the sequence, one right after the other. As shown in Figure 17.2, drag the Timeline window's top or bottom edge to expand it vertically a bit, creating some space above and below the video and audio tracks (you'll need that room later to automatically add video and audio tracks). Now play the clips. If this is an interview, there probably will be a slight image shift—a jump cut—between clip 1 and clip 2 because the interviewee moved a bit or you moved the camera.

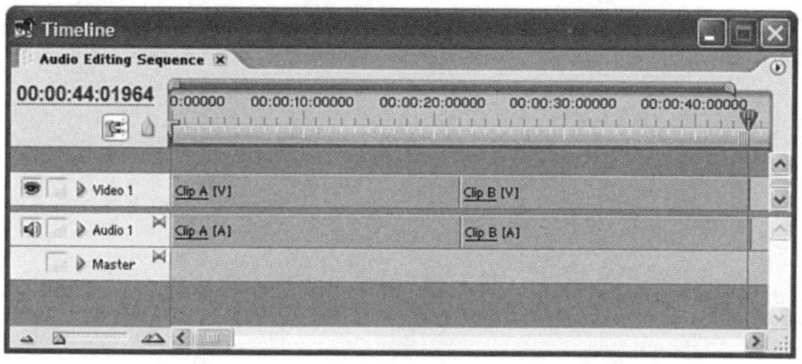

FIGURE 17.2
How your sequence should look before you add a cutaway.

4. Select a short clip from your Project window to use as a cutaway. Drag it to a point just above the Video 1 track (in the gray area where a new track will be automatically created). Line up its endpoint with the edit point between the two clips. As shown in Figure 17.3, Premiere Pro displays two icons: a black line with a triangle indicating you've aligned the end of the cutaway

with the cut edit between the two clips and an Insert edit marker indicating that if you release the mouse button, your clip will end up in the sequence at that point.

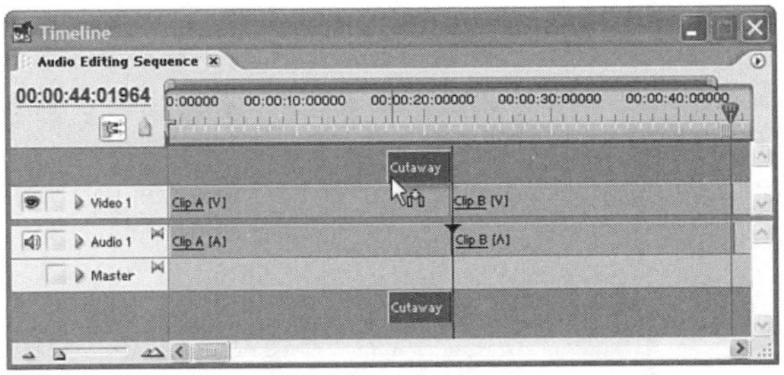

FIGURE 17.3
Add a cutaway by dragging it above the edit point you want to cover.

5. Release your mouse and take a look at what just happened. You automatically created two new tracks—video and audio—and your cutaway is positioned such that it covers the end of the first clip.

6. If you play this section, you'll hear audio from the cutaway "stepping" on the interview. To remove that audio, unlink the cutaway's audio and video (right-click on the clip, select Unlink Audio and Video, and click somewhere in the sequence to complete the unlink process). Right-click on the audio portion and select Cut. Now play this edit. You've just created a news-style cutaway.

Cutaway Locations

You might notice that using this technique means the cutaway ends exactly as the next sound bit begins. That's a method I like because the second sound bite is usually a new thought and it feels more natural to see the interviewee as he or she starts a new comment. That's not always the case, and you might want to slide the cutaway over clip B—covering the end of clip A and the beginning of clip B—or even start it right at the beginning of clip B.

Did you Know?

Keeping Cutaway Audio

You don't have to remove the cutaway's audio. If you're editing a sporting event and use a cutaway shot of a screaming fan, you'll want to leave in that sound and adjust its volume to fit the crowd noise in the two clips you just covered up.

Did you Know?

7. The problem with this method is that the cutaway might not be the exact shot or duration that suits your needs. To resolve that, use the Monitor

window Source screen to create a more accurate cutaway. First, delete the cutaway from the sequence, and then double-click on a longer clip to open it in the Source screen.

8. As shown in Figure 17.4, set an in-point and an out-point (use the curly brackets). I've set this cutaway to 3 seconds—a comfortable clip length.

9. Click the Toggle Take Audio and Video button until it becomes a video-only filmstrip icon, as shown in Figure 17.4. This means that when you add this trimmed clip to your production, only the video portion will end up in the sequence.

FIGURE 17.4
Use the Monitor window Source screen to trim your cutaway, and then set the Toggle Take Audio and Video to the video-only film-strip icon.

10. Click anywhere in the Source screen and drag that trimmed clip to the sequence. As before, you can drag it above the two clips to the newly created video track. Or, as shown in Figure 17.5, you can drag it right onto those two clips—positioning it where it suits you (you can always change this edit later on the sequence track). In either case, only the video portion will end up in your sequence.

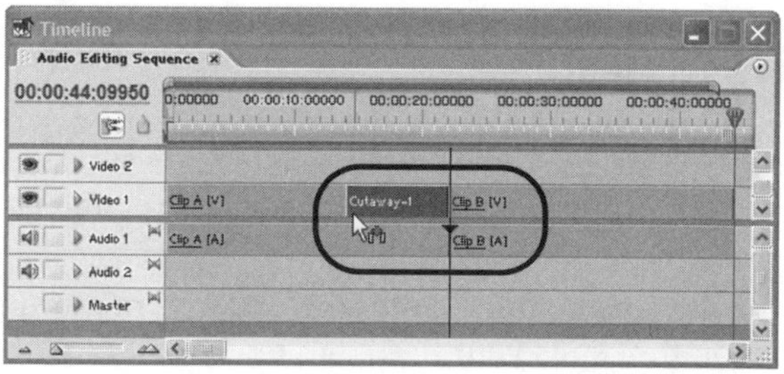

FIGURE 17.5
You can drag a trimmed clip from the Source screen directly to the sequence and easily line it up with the edit point.

Did you
Know?

Use the Source Screen Method to Add Audio

If you want to use this method to add a cutaway *with* its audio, you simply change the Toggle Take Audio and Video button to the combo filmstrip/speaker icon and then drag the clip to the sequence. If you drag it to a separate track, the audio will go to its own separate track. If you drag it on top of a clip, the cutaway audio will replace that clip's audio for the duration of the cutaway.

11. Finally, rather than dragging the clip to the sequence, use the Overlay button in the Source window instead. To do that, first set track targets. They are the track(s) on the sequence where you want the audio and/or video portions of the clip to go. The easiest way to target a track is to click its name (if you don't already have a Video 2 track, add one first by right-clicking on a track name and selecting Add Tracks). In Figure 17.6, I selected Video 2 and Audio 2 (changing the track headers to a darker beige).

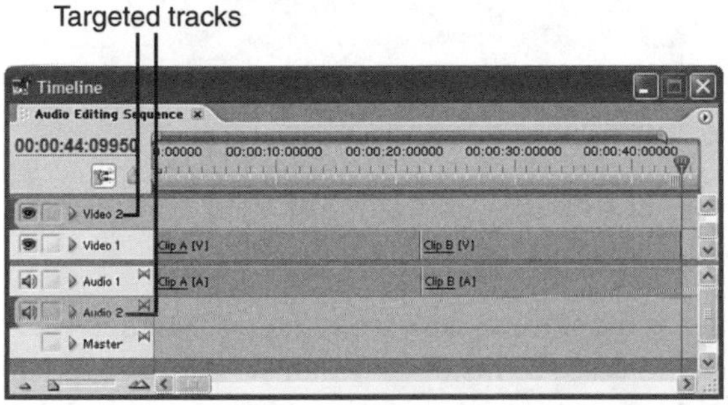

Targeted tracks

FIGURE 17.6
Clicking on a track name targets it so that when you click the Overlay button in the Source screen, the video or audio portions go to the tracks you've selected.

12. Move the CTI edit line to where you want to place the first frame of the cutaway and click the Overlay button (to the left of the Toggle Audio and Video button). Don't use Insert. It defeats the purpose of a cutaway because an Insert edit cuts (razors) the clip at that point, drops in the cutaway, and shoves everything to the right.

Did you
Know?

Edit Line Placement

Take a look at Figure 17.7. I purposely chose to have this cutaway cover the end of clip A and the beginning of clip B. I did that by moving the edit line a bit to the left of this edit point between the two clips (it automatically jumps to the end of the cutaway after it makes the overlay). If I don't like the exact placement, I can always slide the clip to the left or right and/or trim it. That's one advantage to putting it on a different track than the original clips.

FIGURE 17.7
Position the CTI edit line to your edit point and then click the Overlay button to drop your cutaway into your project (The CTI automatically jumps to the end of the cutaway once you have added it to the sequence.

Multitrack Audio Rules

You've already seen a bit of the Premiere Pro's rule set when it comes to adding clips to multitrack projects. For instance, when you dragged a clip above Video 1, Premiere Pro added new video and audio tracks and dropped the clip's video and audio segments there. The new, automatically created audio track also matched the source material: in your case, it was probably stereo.

But it can get much more complicated. There are two basic circumstances: when a user is dragging a clip *from* the Project window to a sequence and when the user is dragging clips *within* a sequence.

Dragging Clips from the Project Window

Premiere Pro's developers gave this a lot of thought. They concluded that when a typical user is dragging clips from the Project window, the user wants to **cascade** his layout (that is, match video track and audio track numbers). So, in this case only, Premiere Pro associates Video 1 with Audio 1, Video 2 with Audio 2, and so forth.

There are exceptions, of course. Premiere Pro matches audio clips to the next best track that fits the channel type (mono, stereo, 5.1). If you try to drop an A/V clip onto Video 1 and Audio 1, but the audio types don't match, Premiere Pro skips the audio tracks that are not compatible (as well as locked tracks) and finds the next best one or automatically creates a new track of the right channel type, if needed.

This also means that if you drag a clip to Video 1 and there is already audio in the same location on Audio 1, the new clip's audio goes to Audio 1 and covers up whatever was there.

Dragging Clips Within a Sequence

The rules change when working within a sequence. Again, Premiere Pro's developers gave this a lot of thought.

With the advent of track-based effects on the audio side, the developers wanted to give the user the opportunity to move around the video portion of an A/V clip that is already in the sequence, without changing its audio track assignment. In this way, you can bump the video portion up/down one track without messing up your audio mix. The same is true if you want to move the audio portion of the clip to a new track (with different track effects, for example) without moving the video around (because, for example, its relative layering is important).

Therefore, if you drag a clip to a new track and slide it off to one side or another, the audio remains on its original track. If you slide it to a portion of the track that already has audio, it replaces that audio.

Developer's Comment—Sequence Philosophy

Let me describe what has been our philosophy of the timeline:

In video, the relative vertical layering of each clip is important (but not the actual numeric track assignments).

In audio, the absolute track assignment of each clip is important because of track effects, submix track assignments, and so on, but the relative position of one clip track with respect to another is not important at all.

The most common reason to move clips to different video tracks is to alter the rendering order. However, audio tracks do not have a similar rendering order concept. Lower audio tracks do not block the audio on higher tracks.

Because of that, we're trying to slowly move away from the old paradigm that always matched V1 to A1, V2 to A2, and so forth. It now matters a lot what audio track you are on, so we don't want to make an automatic decision for you, which, in most cases, is going to mess something up. But we are still trying to be "nice" in some cases (for example, when dragging from the Project window to a sequence).

Did you Know?

Your Assignment: Grab Shots for Compositing

Most of the remaining tasks in this hour involve creating transparencies in clips by removing certain colors or luminance (brightness). To best see how that works in the real world, you need to grab your camcorder and tape a few quick shots.

> ### Locking Down Your Camcorder—Critical to Keying
>
> For images that you intend to key, you'd normally need to have your camera absolutely locked down. No camera movement at all. In this case, because it's just an experiment, don't worry too much about that. But after you've seen how much of a viewer disconnect there is when a keyed object bounces around over a keyed-in background, you'll understand why a rock-steady camera is critical. Use a tripod.

Here's your assignment:

1. Videotape an inanimate object—preferably a smooth object to minimize shadows within it—in front of a solid color. That color should be distinctly different from the color(s) of the object. Otherwise, when you later key out that background color, similar colors in the object will turn transparent, too, leading to some odd results.

2. Tape a person talking or moving in front of a solid color background. The best is light blue because that's complementary to skin tones. Seek out a smooth surface, not cloth or anything with obvious texture or shadows. Just make sure that your subject's clothes don't have colors that match or nearly match the background and avoid fly-away hair and fuzzy clothes (they create blurred edges in key shots). Most production studios use *chroma blue* (or *green*) screens. I'll highlight the advantages of each in a sidebar later in the hour.

3. Tape a dark object in front of a lightly colored surface (white is best) and a lightly colored object in front of a dark backdrop. Try this with a person as well. The greater the contrast between the subject and the background, the easier it'll be to make the background transparent.

4. Tape a distinct background with nothing moving in it—that is, no waving palm trees or soaring birds. Then, without turning off or moving the camera (this is the one exercise when you need a rock-steady shot), have someone walk into the left side of the scene, stand around for a while, and then walk back out the left side. Have that person do the same thing entering from the right side and then walking out to the right. For a bit of comic relief, have

your actor wave toward the center of the scene before walking off camera. You'll use this in the next hour to create split screen and difference mattes, but you might as well shoot it now while you're at it.

5. Finally, grab a few shots of background locations in which you'd like to place the objects/people you've videotaped. You'll later key your subjects onto those locations.

Working with the Opacity Effect

Before keying out colors or working with luminance, I want to cover opacity. Premiere Pro and other nonlinear editors like it have a general operating practice. Video tracks above Video 1 trump tracks below them on the timeline. In other words, whatever appears on the highest track covers up whatever is below it. However, the object *isn't* to use tracks above Video 1 to obliterate what's beneath them. It's to enhance what's down there. Premiere Pro offers up to 98 of those **superimposing** tracks (with Video 1, 99 tracks in all). Their purpose is for layering (compositing).

One easy way to see compositing at work is to place a video or graphic on a superimposing track and make it transparent—turn down its opacity to let video(s) on lower track(s) show through. A tool to accomplish this is the Opacity effect.

Use the Opacity Video Effect

Here's one way to see the Opacity effect in action. For this exercise, I'll have you place a super (text) in a superimposing track above a clip. Then you'll use the Opacity effect to fade that text in (its background is automatically transparent), display it over your clip for a while, and then fade the text out.

Here are the steps to follow for this task:

1. Place a video clip on Video 1. Any clip will do, but trim it to about 15 seconds to simplify things.

2. Open the Title Designer (File→New→Title) and create some simple text. Make it large and add color if you like. In my example (see Figure 17.8), I gave the text an outer stroke and a drop shadow to make it more visible over the background.

3. Save your text (File→Save). It'll show up automatically in the Project window.

4. As shown in Figure 17.8, drag the text to Video 2, drag its right edge to make it as long as the Video 1 clip, and expand the Video 2 track by clicking the triangle next to the words *Video 2*.

5. Click the Show Keyframes button (highlighted in Figure 17.8) and select Show Opacity Handles. That displays the Opacity line (I lightened it for emphasis in Figure 17.8), which for the moment is straight and at the top of the clip display (100% opacity).

FIGURE 17.8
Using text is a good introduction to the Opacity video effect. With Show Opacity Handles selected in the sequence, you'll be able to see any changes you make to opacity show up in the expanded track view.

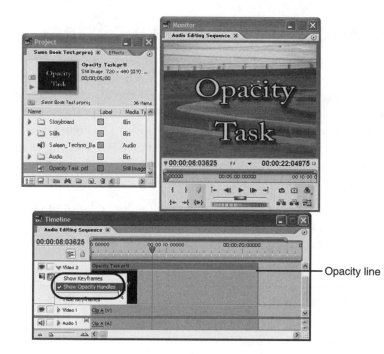

Opacity line

6. Select the text clip by clicking on it and open the Effect Controls window (ECW). Click the Opacity effect's two disclosure triangles to reveal the keyframable Opacity slider. Note that the keyframe stopwatch is turned on by default. Now set four keyframes:

▶ Press the Home key andSet the beginning of the clip Opacity slider to 0%

▶ Move the CTI to about 2 seconds into the clip and set Opacity to 100%

▶ Move to a couple seconds from the end and set Opacity to 100% (click the keyframe diamond to set that keyframe)

▶ Move to the end of the clip (press End and the left arrow key once) and set the opacity slider back to 0%

7. Your ECW should look like Figure 17.9. Note that Opacity handles have now shown up in the expanded view of the clip in the sequence (I've expanded them for emphasis in Figure 17.9).

8. Play your clip. The title should fade up, hold for a while, and then fade down. That's compositing in its simplest form.

FIGURE 17.9
Using the fixed Opacity video effect with keyframes enables you to fade in a super, hold it onscreen for a while, and then fade it out.

Superimpose Two Clips

Try a similar process with two video clips, but choose your clips with some care. If you select just any two clips, blending the two together can look way too busy.

The purpose is to let the clip on the lower track show through the higher clip in a pleasing fashion. Try to use a clip on the higher track with a distinct bright or well-lit area. The reason is that when you reduce its opacity, that bright area will let clips below it show through more clearly. For my example, shown in Figure 17.10, I used some flowers with the sky as a backdrop. Here's how this works:

1. Drag the clip you want to show through to Video 1 and the clip with the bright section to Video 2.

2. Follow the same four-step Opacity keyframe process you used in the previous task on the clip on Video 2.

3. Preview this effect. The lower clip should show through the upper clip, especially in the lighter areas of the upper clip.

FIGURE 17.10
Two superimposed clips. Reducing the opacity in the upper clip lets the lower clip show through, particularly through light areas such as the sky.

Keying Clips

The Opacity effect works great with text and some videos and images, but most of the time when you use it with two full-screen clips or graphics it can be an inexact science. You can get more precise compositing results using keying effects.

Take a look at Premiere Pro's keying effects by opening the Effects palette, selecting Video Effects, and then selecting Keying. As illustrated in Figure 17.11, that reveals 13 keying effects (14 if you include Alpha Adjust, which is simply the Opacity effect).

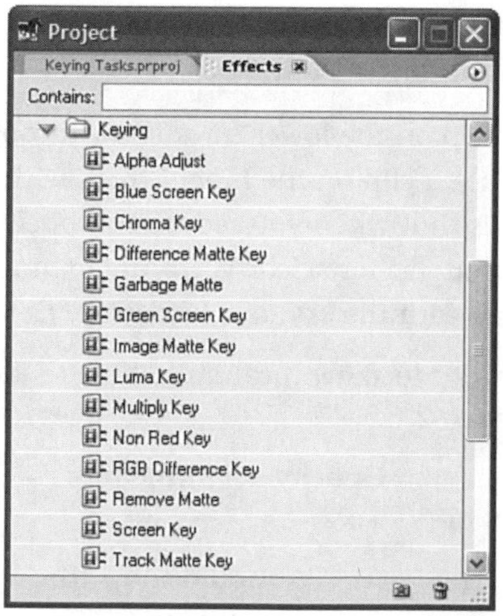

FIGURE 17.11
Premiere Pro's 14 keying effects give you a full range of possibilities.

I've grouped them into four categories:

- **Color**: RGB, Chroma, Blue Screen, Green Screen, Non-Red

- **Luminance**: Luma, Multiply, Screen

- **Matte**: Difference Matte, Garbage Matte, Image Matte, Remove Matte, Track Matte

- **Alpha**: Alpha Channel

In this hour, I'll go over the Color and Luminance keys. In Hour 18, I'll explain the Matte and Alpha Channel keys.

Using the RGB Difference Key

First up is the simplest key: the RGB Difference key. You use it to make a selected color transparent thereby making a background transparent.

This key works well when you have a brightly lit scene with no shadows, a solid-color background, and a subject with a color that's distinctly different from the background. Not many scenes will qualify. Almost all have some shadows, especially when the subject has texture. But it's a good way to see how keying works or—frequently—does *not* work.

Use the RGB Difference Key

Try it Yourself

▼

To use the RGB Difference key, follow these steps:

1. Place the clip from the first item in the assignment list—the inanimate object shot in front of a solid color—on Video 2.

2. Drag the location clip, the fifth item in the assignment list, to Video 1.

3. Select the clip on Video 2 and drag the RGB Difference Key to the ECW. In my example, shown in Figure 17.12, I will key out the sky in the right image (Video 2) to let the left image (Video 1) show through.

4. Click on the Eyedropper tool (I've highlighted it in Figure 17.13) and drag it to the clip image in the Monitor window Program screen. Use it to select the color you want to **key out**—that is, the color you want to make transparent.

5. Drag the Similarity slider to the right and watch the Program screen as your background disappears—becomes transparent—to reveal the clip on Video 1. Similarity expands or reduces the range of background color keyed out. However, the more you increase the Similarity value, the more likely you

▼

▼

are to key out colors and create transparencies in both the background and the subject itself. In my example in Figure 17.13, a similarity of 16 removed the blue sky without removing any colors of my wooden frog and his hovering lily pad.

FIGURE 17.12
Two clips that I'll combine using the RGB Difference Key.

▲

FIGURE 17.13
Use the RGB Difference key to remove a color from a clip.

Other RGB Difference Parameters

Smoothing enables you remove aliasing or jaggies, those stair-step edges common to diagonal lines in computer monitors and TV sets. Just as you did with transitions, you can turn on *antialiasing* to fix that. It blends the pixels around the edges of your object. Use the Smoothing drop-down menu, choose Low or High, and check your results in the Sample screen.

Mask Only turns your keyed clip into a black-and-white image to help you fine-tune the similarity setting.

Drop Shadow adds a thin drop shadow to give your clip a 3D feel. But there are no user adjustable parameters. It's either on or off. The shadow always falls down and to the right. Inconsistencies arise when your background scene has shadows going some other direction. If that's the case, you might consider using the Camera View video effect on the background to flip the image right-to-left to swap its shadow directions.

You might find that it's darned difficult to get the color and similarity just right. Welcome to keying. It can take some trial and error to find an approach that works.

Before using other keying types, try the RGB Difference key on the person you taped in front of a solid color. Doing so might be more challenging than using it on an inanimate object. Because the person you taped probably moves around a bit, it makes finding the right similarity around the edges of that person that much more difficult.

Using the Chroma Key

Because RGB Difference works only for very limited, well-planned shots, you'll likely rely on other color or transparency keying techniques. It's very easy to try them out. Chroma-keying is your best all-around method, but it's not as accurate as the more narrowly defined green/blue screens I'll cover later. It has more options than RGB Difference and therefore gives you a better chance to create a decent-looking key.

Delete the RGB Difference key from the ECW and replace it with the Chroma key. As I've highlighted in Figure 17.14, in addition to Similarity, you have sliders for Blend, Threshold, and Cutoff.

Blend—Softens the transition edges between the keyed subject and the clip below it. Gradually slide Blend to the right and watch as the image on Video 1 begins to replace the few remaining bits of your object's single-color background. Those snippets of background color typically fall right around the subject's outline.

Threshold—Controls the extent of shadowing thrown by the subject that will show up in the keyed clip. To see this in action, take a close look at any shadow on the solid background color and see how this looks in the composited image.

Cutoff—Darkens or lightens shadows. Its value must be less than the Threshold value; otherwise, it'll invert gray and transparent pixels and your screen will become black.

FIGURE 17.14
Chroma-keying
offers more options
that increase the
likelihood of a suc-
cessful key.

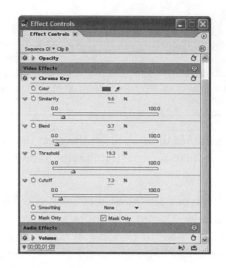

Using Threshold and Cutoff Effectively

A good way to use Threshold and Cutoff to your best advantage is to click the check box next to Mask Only, which displays only the silhouette of your subject and the keyed-out color/background. What you want is a black background and a white subject. What you'll probably start with is a dark gray background and a light gray subject. As you slide Threshold to the left, the background darkens. Try to turn it black. Then slide Cutoff to the right and try to get the subject as white as possible.

Despite your best efforts, even the Chroma key might not make the entire background color transparent without punching a few transparent holes in your subject.

Try the Chroma key on the person you taped. As with the RGB Difference key, you probably will find it difficult to make a clean key, especially in and around the subject's hair.

Using the Luma Key

To test this key, use the images from the third item in the assignment list—the dark object with a light background and vice versa. In my case, I'll combine the two images shown in Figure 17.15. I'll use the Luma key to remove the black background of the image on the right.

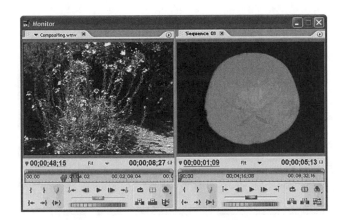

FIGURE 17.15
The Luma key works well if you have a highly contrasting subject and background and little texture to your subject.

Place your high contrast image on Video 2 and apply the Luma key to it. When you first open Luma, the Threshold setting is 100%, meaning the widest range of dark values will become transparent. As shown in Figure 17.16, reduce the Threshold value and you tighten that range. Cutoff sets just how transparent those dark areas will become. Higher values increase transparency.

As my subjects demonstrate in Figure 17.16 and 17.17, if you taped very contrasting scenes, the Luma key should work smoothly. It's similar to the Image Mask transition covered in the next hour. Whatever is dark gets keyed out (that is, it becomes transparent, letting images below it show through), and light areas remain opaque, displaying whatever is on the upper clip.

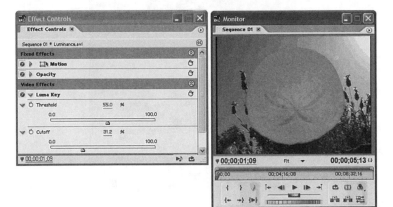

FIGURE 17.16
The Luma key works well if you have a highly contrasting subject and background and little texture to your subject.

FIGURE 17.17
Use the Luma key on a dark object like this clock shot against a light background to create this unique visual combination.

Blur the Background—Make It Realistic

Did you know?

To add a realistic feel to any keyed shot, make the background blurry. Typically, you want to make the subject, which you've shot with a key in mind, the focal point of your composited clip. By using a background that's a bit out of focus, the subject stands out even more. To create that illusion, simply use the Fast Blur video effect on the background clip. I used that effect with the sand dollar clip in Figure 17.18.

FIGURE 17.18
Using the Fast Blur video effect on the background clip makes the keyed image stand out.

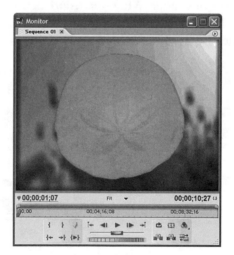

Again, this key takes some planning. When you're shooting, it's best to illuminate the light object or background and work to make the dark area as dark as possible. Objects with fine edge detail, such as hair, are very hard to key under any circumstances, including when you use Luma.

Put Keyed Clips in Motion

You can add motion to clips keyed with Luma and other keying effects. Simply click on the Motion effect to switch it on. Then, as shown in Figure 17.19, move the keyed clip around the screen just as you would any other clip or graphic (including rotating it).

Previous versions of Premiere displayed the entire clip as opposed to only the keyed subject. If you scaled it down a bit, you ended up with a rectangular box moving around the screen. You needed to take some extra steps to fix that. Now, thankfully, that's no longer necessary.

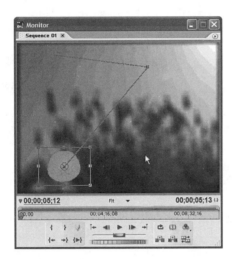

FIGURE 17.19
You easily can move, scale, and rotate a keyed clip using the Motion effect.

Using the Multiply and Screen Keys

The Multiply and Screen keys are like the Luma key, but they create more subtle superimpositions. They both examine the clip *below* the superimposed clip on the timeline to determine what areas of the keyed clip to make transparent. Multiply looks for bright areas and Screen looks for dark areas. Then they make portions of the superimposed clip transparent to match those areas.

Each effect has two sliders: Opacity and Cutoff. Higher values lead to less transparency.

Using the Blue Screen and Green Screen Keys

The Blue Screen and Green Screen keys are your best bets for accurate, relatively low-budget keying. To use them well, you'll not only need what are called *chroma blue* and *chroma green* backdrops, but you'll also need to follow a few procedures as well. Because this is sort of an involved process, I've included a sidebar on the subject.

The Blue Screen and Green Screen keys options work like other Premiere Pro keys, only they're simpler because Premiere Pro is looking for very specific chroma blue and green background colors.

There are only two principal slider controls: Threshold and Cutoff. Again, drag Threshold to the left to make the entire blue/green screen transparent. Drag Cutoff to the right to ensure that the opaque areas look satisfactory. I asked Matt Zaffino, my favorite weatherman, to demonstrate in Figure 17.20 how things look before and after applying keying effects.

FIGURE 17.20
KGW-TV's Matt Zaffino in front of a Chroma key green screen (left) and with the Green Screen key (right) turned on to display a weather graphic.

Did you Know?

Extra Keying Help Using a Nested Sequence

If at first your key does not succeed, try again. Sometimes, try as you might, you cannot remove all the jaggies from the edges of your green- or blue-screened actors. This is endemic to consumer/prosumer DV (technically, DV25) camcorders. To possibly remedy that, key them twice.

However, that won't work for the original clip on the timeline. Going back to Transparency Settings and tweaking the existing blue/green screen settings only changes them—it doesn't apply the settings twice.

To do that requires creating a nested sequence. I'll explain that concept in Hour 19, "Tips, Tricks, and Techniques—Part 1."

Making Blue and Green Screens Work

Setting up chroma green or blue backdrops can be a royal pain—especially on location. About 10 years ago, I hired one of Portland's top production companies to do a fairly involved blue screen shoot at a local college. They lit the heck out of that blue screen, got the dolly rails and the trucking move down perfectly, and rolled and recorded.

When we got back to the studio, try as we might, we could not completely key out the blue screen without creating some transparency in the actor. We ended up building an elaborate moving matte (it had to fit the actor's shifting silhouette). What a time-consuming hassle!

As someone once said, "It's not easy being green" (or blue). Here are some tips:

▶ Blue and green screens require flat lighting—no hot spots. If you can set up your screen outdoors, overcast or cloudy days work best. No need to overdo the lighting. Simply make it even.

▶ The actor's lighting does *not* have to be flat. Controlled spotlights or lights with "barn doors" work well. Using soft lighting with umbrellas and reflectors is less dramatic but also is effective. A key backlight aimed at the actor's head helps more clearly illuminate hair to eliminate or at least minimize blue or green screen halos.

▶ If you plan to key in an outdoor background, try to re-create outdoor lighting on your subject. If you're working with live actors, further enhance the illusion by using a fan to blow their hair around a bit.

▶ Avoid the dreaded blue or green spill. Actors' skin will pick up the reflected color of the backdrop if they're too close to it. Move them at least a few feet away. One other way to minimize this is to use a backlight.

▶ Tight shots work better than full-body shots. The closer you are to your subject, the more realistic the finished product will be.

▶ If there is fast-paced action in your shot, you might have trouble keying right to the edges of your subjects.

▶ Set your camcorder to Manual and open the iris (you'll probably need to increase shutter speed to avoid overexposure). A wide-open iris—1.8 or so— limits the focal plane to your subject and throws the green screen a bit out of focus, making it easier to key out.

▶ To build a backdrop on a budget, consider using unofficial chroma blue or green paint (the real stuff retails for about $40 a gallon). Grab a paint sample collection, videotape it, and then use Premiere Pro's blue screen or green screen transparency on it. Find a color that keys well and buy a gallon. Paint that on a large piece of plywood and you have a portable studio.

Alternatively, you can buy Chroma key fabric or wide rolls of Chroma key paper. Both run about $10 a square yard. One source is www.Filmtools.com.

> ▶ Which color to use? With chroma green, you have a reasonable assurance that no one will have clothing that matches and therefore will key out. Chroma blue works well because it's complementary to skin tones. The kind of scene you key in might be the determining factor. If you will have your actors keyed in to a scene with a blue sky, use a blue screen. In this case, the dreaded blue spill could be a nice feature.
>
> ▶ Consumer and prosumer camcorders do not key as well as professional camcorders. The 4:1:1 color sampling compression leads to some quality loss. Because the green portion of an RGB signal receives extra weight to correspond to the sensitivity of human eyes to different colors, green screens key more cleanly than blue. A mathematical analysis done a few years ago showed that using a green screen with a DV camcorder keys only 15% less cleanly than a broadcast-quality Betacam SP camcorder.

Using the Non-Red Key

The Non-Red key is your blue/green screen fall back. Both Blue and Green Screen keys look for very specific colors. They offer no similarity controls to select a color range. If you just can't quite dial in a Blue/Green Screen key because somehow the color is slightly off or there is too much fringing around the edges of non-transparent subjects, try the Non-Red key. It's a little more forgiving. As you move the Threshold slider, this key looks for non-red colors (blue/green) to key out.

As I've demonstrated in two before-and-after images with Matt Zaffino (Figures 17.20 and 17.21), the Non-Red key offers one other control: Blend. This ostensibly lets you smoothly blend two scenes together. I've found that it doesn't make much difference if you already have a reasonably good blue/green screen shot.

FIGURE 17.21
Sometimes, as in the left image, the Chroma or Green/Blue Screen keys fail to fulfill their promise. The Non-Red key (right) tends to clear up the jaggies along the edges of your opaque subjects.

Summary

Compositing tools enable you to greatly enhance your projects by adding multiple layers of video and images. First stabs at compositing typically involve adding cutaways to interviews and other video work.

Then you move on to creating transparencies. The principal transparency compositing tools are the Opacity and Keying video effects. The Opacity effect is always available in the ECW and has only one keyframable parameter: opacity percentage.

The Keying effects come in four flavors: Color, Luminance, Matte, and Alpha. I covered the first two in this hour, and will go over Mattes and Alpha channels in the next hour.

Making keys work well takes some extra effort. Proper backdrop colors, lighting, and keying techniques all come into play. Green/blue screens work best but invariably take some trial and error.

Q&A

Q *No matter how many different key types I try, I get a halo effect along the edges of my keyed objects, especially in their hair. What should I do?*

A This is endemic to this technology. Using consumer and prosumer DV camcorders and Premiere Pro's less-than-pixel-specific keying controls means you might never get rid of those halos. Some video capture cards, such as the Canopus DVStorm2, and software, such as Adobe After Effects Professional, have much higher quality Chroma key tools. You might notice that your local weather forecaster does not have such halos (unless you live in a tiny TV market that's behind the technology curve). Many of those stations use a keying technology from Ultimatte (www.ultimatte.com). It offers incredible flexibility and creates very clean keying in difficult situations, such as through smoke, hair, water, and glass. Ultimatte offers a $1,495 plug-in that works with three Adobe products: Premiere Pro, Photoshop, and After Effects. The hardware prices start in the neighborhood of $28,000.

Q *When I drag a linked audio/video clip to Video 2, the audio goes to Video 2 as I'd expect. But when I drag a linked A/V clip from Video 1 to Video 2, its audio stays on Audio 1 and covers up the audio that was there. What's going on?*

A Your clips are following Premiere Pro's new multitrack audio rules. When you add clips *from* the Project window, Premiere Pro tries to cascade the audio portions. That is, if at all possible, it tries to put them on track numbers that match where you placed the video. There are exceptions for locked tracks and mismatched track types (mono, stereo, and 5.1). When you move clips *within* a sequence, the audio stays on its track. The reasoning? With Premiere Pro's new track-based audio effects and controls, developers want to ensure any such clip moves don't lead to surprising results. If you want to move the audio to a new track, unlink audio and video and move both clips individually.

Workshop

Quiz

1. How do you blend two full-screen clips?

2. What's the difference between the two sets of Chroma key sliders—Similarity/Blend and Threshold/Cutoff? What's a more descriptive name for the Smoothing drop-down menu?

3. When do you use the Non-Red key?

Quiz Answers

1. Either of two ways: Use the fixed Opacity video effect (or its non-fixed twin: Alpha Adjust) to reduce the opacity of the superimposed clip, or use the Screen (or Multiply) transparency for a subtle blend that lets dark (or light) areas of the bottom track show through the superimposed clip. Screen more closely approximates the Opacity effect. Multiply acts more like a real key.

2. Similarity and Blend work together to set a width for the color range to key out of a superimposed clip and to blend the two clips smoothly together. Threshold and Cutoff deal with shadows. Threshold controls the amount of shadows from the superimposed clip that will display on the lower track's clip. Cutoff controls how dark or light those shadows are. Smoothing is the same as antialiasing. It gets rid of the jaggies along the edges of keyed objects.

3. Non-Red enables you to key out, well, non-red backgrounds (that is, green and blue). It's a helpful backup if the Green or Blue Screen keys don't work as well as you'd like, which might happen if the green or blue are not true Chroma key colors.

Exercises

1. Use the Luma key to isolate a ball by keying out a highly contrasting background. Then use motion settings to bounce it around a scene. Use keyframe interpolation with the bounces and apexes to more realistically mimic a bouncing ball.

2. Use the Title Designer to create several titles. Place them in various superimposing tracks and fade them in and out of your Video 1 clip at various

times, sometimes displaying more than one title at a time. Remember, you drag the edges of a title clip to make it any length you want. Finally, give a couple titles motion using the Motion effect.

3. Experiment with the Chroma and Green/Blue Screen keys. Find a backdrop color and a lighting setup that works well.

4. Ask to visit a local TV station or production studio to watch how the crew sets up green/blue screens. You'll see that they take great pains to light it evenly and to have the actor stand a good distance from the screen.

5. Start watching TV commercials more critically, looking for examples of compositing. It's a rare spot that doesn't use layering. This is a great source of ideas.

HOUR 18

Compositing Part 2—Alpha Channels and Mattes

What You'll Learn in This Hour:

- ▶ Working with alpha channel transparencies
- ▶ Using video effects with alpha channel transparencies
- ▶ Using the Motion effect to make pictures-in-a-picture
- ▶ Two multiple track video effects: Blend and Texturize
- ▶ Creating and working with matte keys
- ▶ Using mattes to build split screens

In the previous hour, I presented three ways to composite clips: the Opacity effect, and the Color and Luminance keying effects. Two other ways to make portions of a clip transparent—creating something like digital holes—are by using alpha channels and mattes. Alpha channels are common elements of graphics created in programs such as Adobe Photoshop and Illustrator. Premiere Pro makes them transparent.

In addition, several of Premiere Pro's video effects have built-in transparent alpha channels that enable portions of clips below them on a sequence to show through.

Mattes used for keying generally are simple black-and-white, opaque graphics, but Premiere Pro has several ways to use them to create transparencies. Both alpha channels and mattes are effective, useful means to composite clips in Premiere Pro.

Working with Alpha Channel Transparencies

Most video clips and many graphics have alpha channels. Coupled with a clip's visible red/green/blue (RGB) color channels, an alpha channel defines what parts of an image are transparent or semi-transparent. You don't see the alpha channel. Rather, Premiere Pro uses the grayscale information from that channel to set the level of opacity or transparency.

The alpha channel typically uses 8 bits of information to describe 256 shades of gray. In typical computer graphic applications, pure white regions of the alpha channel are opaque—that is, they cover any clips beneath them on the timeline. Pure black regions are transparent and let any lower clips show through. Finally, gray regions let some background come through, depending on the level of gray.

On the other hand, a typical video's alpha channel describes gray values on a pixel-by-pixel basis instead of by a larger region, making it impractical to use the Alpha Channel Transparency setting to carve out a transparent hole in a video clip. That's why the only work you'll do with alpha channels will be on graphics or as a parameter in a Premiere Pro video effect.

Alpha Channels—Straight or Premultiplied

An alpha channel is either straight or premultiplied. A **straight** alpha channel stores its transparency information only in the alpha channel. By default, Premiere Pro automatically makes any straight alpha channel transparent. You can make that alpha channel opaque if it suits you. I explain how in a moment.

Graphics with premultiplied alpha channels sometimes need some extra attention when working with them in Premiere Pro. The reason? Premultiplied alpha channels include transparency information in both the alpha channel and the edges of the graphic. When Premiere Pro makes those alpha channel areas transparent, the graphic elements frequently have halos—blurry edges or stray pixels of variable color around them. Premiere Pro's Remove Matte effect can fix that. I explain it later this hour in the "Fixing Premultiplied Alpha Channel Fringing" sidebar .

Make an Alpha Channel Visible

Try it
Yourself
▼

To see how an alpha channel transparency works, follow these steps:

1. Place any video clip on Video 1 in the timeline. I used Saleen_Car_01.avi from the sample project that shipped with Premiere Pro.

2. If you have a graphic with an alpha channel (most Photoshop graphics meet that criterion) import it to your Project window (File→Import). If you don't have such a file, use the Saleen_logo_layers.psd file from the sample project.

Import Layered Graphics as Sequences

By the
Way

If you use the Saleen Photoshop file or any other layered graphic file, when you attempt to import it, Premiere Pro will pop up a dialog box asking how you want Premiere Pro to deal with its layers. In this case, select Import as: Sequence and click OK. Doing so will create a new sequence in your Project window with the graphics layers listed as separate clips.

---

3. Drag that graphic to a superimposing track—Video 2 or higher—directly above the clip on Video 1. Your project should look like Figure 18.1 (I used the Motion effect's Scale parameter to blow up the logo for emphasis). By default, Premiere Pro makes the graphic's alpha channel transparent, allowing whatever is below it on the sequence to show through.

FIGURE 18.1
Premiere Pro automatically makes a graphic's alpha channel transparent, displaying whatever is below it on a sequence.

▼

▼

4. To see some alpha channel options, apply the Alpha Adjust video effect to this clip. This effect's primary function is to enable you to apply the Opacity effect at some point other than second to last in any collection of effects you set up (Motion is applied last). As shown in Figure 18.2, it does have some extra settings that give you a feel for alpha channels:

  ▶ Ignore Alpha—Switches off the alpha channel transparency and turns it into opaque white (its original color is black—the color seen as transparent by Premiere Pro).

  ▶ Invert Alpha—makes the alpha channel opaque and the graphic transparent. As highlighted in Figure 18.2, this is a very cool effect and it's keyframable (as are the other two check boxes). For example, if you use a graphic with a recognizable shape, you can easily insert other images and videos into that shape using the Invert Alpha parameter.

  ▶ Mask Only—Converts the opaque graphic into a solid white opaque object.

▲

  ▶ Opacity—This is the Alpha Adjust effect's primary function: duplicating Premiere Pro's fixed Opacity effect.

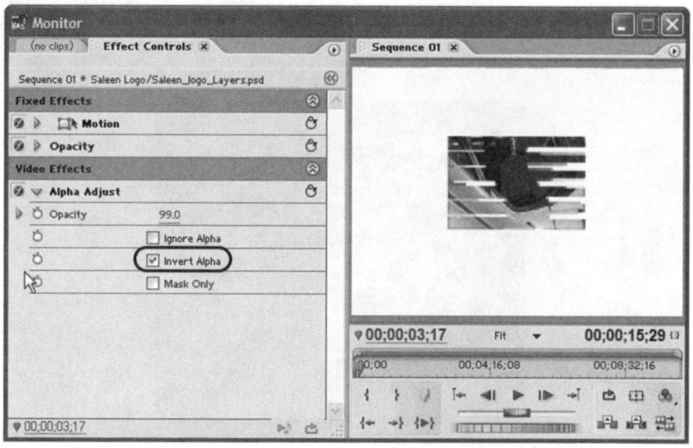

FIGURE 18.2
The Alpha Adjust effect enables you to manipulate the alpha channel and any associated graphics. Selecting the Invert Alpha parameter makes the graphic element transparent and the alpha channel opaque.

Put Alpha Channel Graphics in Motion

You can apply motion to a graphic using the Motion effect. To do that in this case, first delete Alpha Adjust from the Effect Controls window (ECW) and then click Motion to switch it on. Just as you did in Hour 11, "Putting Video and Still Clips in Motion," grab the crosshairs and move the graphic's bounding box around and change some other Motion parameters.

As shown in Figure 18.3, even though the bounding box defines the edges of the graphic's transparent alpha channel region, you won't see a rectangular, screen-sized object moving around the screen. You will see the clip's opaque graphic element.

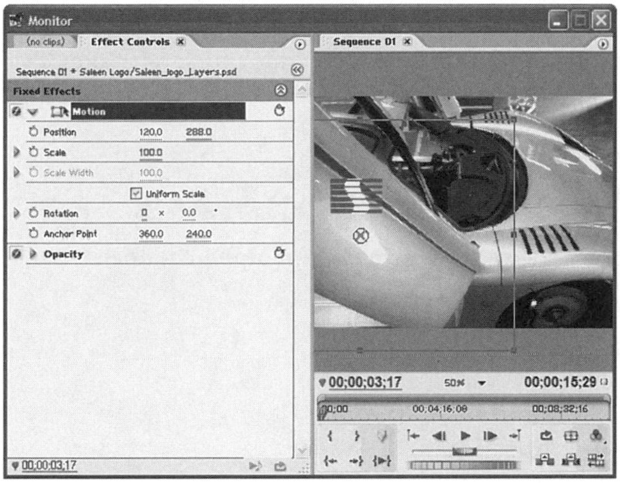

FIGURE 18.3
It's a simple matter to put alpha channel graphics in motion.

Fixing Premultiplied Alpha Channel Fringing

Think of straight alpha channels as cookie cutters. Graphic artists bleed some of their graphics slightly beyond the edges of the white portion of the alpha channel, knowing that when they apply an alpha channel transparency, it will act like a cookie cutter, slicing a sharply defined edge along the graphic and ensuring there will be no gaps along the border.

In a graphic with a premultiplied alpha channel, the white (opaque) portion of the alpha channel exactly matches the edge of the pixels in the RGB graphic. In most cases, premultiplied graphics have either black or white backgrounds. Because of anti-aliasing, the background color darkens or lightens these pixels along the edge of the graphics.

If you use graphics with premultiplied alpha channels in Premiere Pro, you might experience some unpredictable fringing around the edges. To fix that, use the Remove Matte key. Its only parameter is a drop-down list from which you select White or Black. Select whichever color matches your graphic's premultiplied background color. That will key out that background and create a sharper edge to your graphic.

Using Video Effects with Alpha Channel Transparencies

Of Premiere Pro's 90+ video effects, several have either an alpha channel or have special adjustments for clips with alpha channels. I'll go over 10 of them. In previous hours, I've touched on all of these effects and noted some of their alpha channel characteristics so I'll try to avoid too much repetition. I've placed them in two groups: video effects with alpha channels and effects that work well with graphics that have alpha channels.

Video Effects with Alpha Channels

Six Premiere Pro video effects have built-in alpha channels:

- ▶ Tiles
- ▶ Lens Distortion
- ▶ Strobe Light
- ▶ Motion and Transform
- ▶ Basic 3D
- ▶ Camera View

Transparent By Default

Typically, these effects move clips around the screen, revealing whatever is below them on a sequence. It used to be that you could block that see-through view by selecting one of the effect's parameters and opting for a background color or some other action. With Premiere Pro, transparency is the default setting and to block that, you need to apply the Alpha Adjust effect and select Ignore Alpha. I explain that further in a couple of the upcoming examples.

To see these effects in action, remove the alpha channel graphic from the Video 2 track and replace it with a video that's distinctly different than the one below it on Video 1. In my case, I used the Saleen_Car_01 and Saleen_Car_02 clips from the sample project. Then select the clip on Video 2 to open it in the ECW where you will apply video effects to it.

Breaking Up a Clip Using Tiles

This video effect can reveal the clip below it on the sequence. As I've demonstrated in Figure 18.4, to display more of the two lower clips, increase the Maximum Offset setting to something more than 50%. This widens the gaps between the jittering tiles.

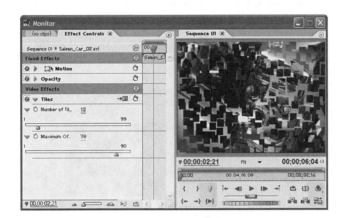

As I mentioned earlier, Premiere Pro sees any gaps between the tiles as alpha channel transparencies. That means that unless you take an extra step, none of the Tiles' four Fill Empty Areas With options will work properly. To use any of those parameters, as I've shown in Figure 18.5, apply Alpha Adjust to the clip and select its Ignore Alpha parameter. Now when you select Inverse Image (as I did in this example) it blocks the view through the tiles to the clip below it and displays an inverse image of the clip on Video 2.

FIGURE 18.5
To use the extra Tile Settings parameters, add the Alpha Adjust effect and click its Ignore Alpha check box.

Effect Testing Housekeeping

Before moving on from one alpha channel example to the next, make sure that you delete the previous video effect(s) from the Effect Controls window.

Twisting Away an Image with Lens Distortion

With this video effect, there is no need to use Alpha Adjust to switch transparency off. As shown in Figure 18.6, there is a check box to do that in the Lens Distortion settings dialog box.

FIGURE 18.6
Uncheck the Lens Distortion Fill Alpha Channel check box to reveal the clip below. Checking it displays a solid color background.

Check Box Bug

There was a bug in the shipping version of Premiere Pro that disabled the Fill Alpha Channel check box. Unchecking it made no difference. The gaps around the distorted image remained opaque and filled in with the user-selected color. Adobe does not announce bug fixes or patches, so there's no way to know whether Adobe will have fixed that bug and posted a patch by the time this book ships. Feel free to check for a download on www.adobe.com.

Flashing a Second Image with Strobe Light

To have each strobe flash reveal the clip on Video 1 instead of displaying a solid strobe color, use the drop-down menu highlighted in Figure 18.7 and select Makes Layer Transparent. You can use Blend With Original to reduce the opacity of the clip on Video 2, thereby making the strobe changes less abrupt.

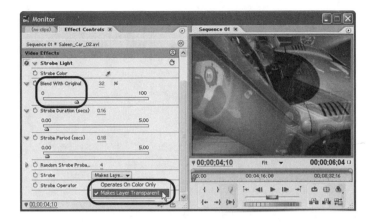

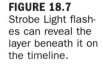

FIGURE 18.7
Strobe Light flashes can reveal the layer beneath it on the timeline.

Using Strobe on a Moving Object

Try it Yourself

You know how a strobe light can momentarily freeze a moving object. You can use Premiere Pro to do the same thing in what appears to be a 3D space. Here's how:

1. Add another video track to the timeline (unless you already have a Video 3 track) by right-clicking on a track header and selecting Add Tracks. Move the clip on Video 2 to Video 3.

2. Strobe Light should remain associated with that clip (if not, reapply it). Set a short duration (0.2 or so). Set a strobe period about twice as long (0.4 or so). Put some randomness in (5% works well). Also, set the Strobe parameter to Make Layer Transparent.

3. Add a graphic with an alpha channel to Video 2 (you can use the Saleen logo), and drag its ends to match the length of the other two clips.

4. As shown in Figure 18.8, give the graphic on Video 2 some motion, keeping it within the screen. The faster it moves the better, so feel free to give it a convoluted and long motion path, forcing it to zip around the screen.

5. Give that graphic a drop shadow to lend a bit of a 3D feel to this set of effects.

6. Now preview that section. The top clip should do the strobe thing, and if the graphic moves fast enough it'll be reminiscent of a disco dance nightclub.

7. To make upcoming tasks work smoothly, remove the video clip from Video 3, but leave the graphic on Video 2 and the video clip on Video 1.

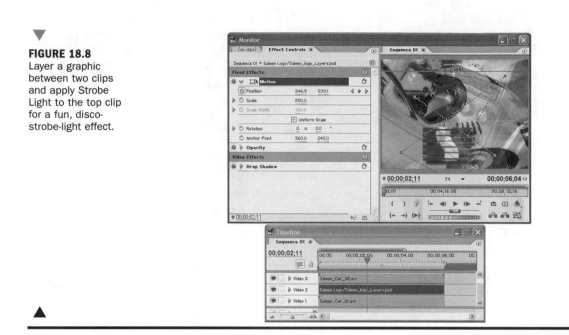

FIGURE 18.8
Layer a graphic between two clips and apply Strobe Light to the top clip for a fun, disco-strobe-light effect.

Working with Motion and Transform

Motion and its nonfixed video effect twin, Transform, move your clip in apparent 3D space. After it has been displaced from a normal full-screen aspect, both effects leave transparent gaps around the edges of the clip.

As shown in Figure 18.9, Transform has a few extra attributes not included in the Motion effect: Skew and Opacity. Once again, you can use Alpha Adjust if you want to turn off or invert the alpha channel transparency.

By the Way

Transform's Disabled After Effects Attributes

Transform is an After Effects effect and it has two parameters that work only in After Effects: Use Composition's Shutter Angle and Shutter Angle. Both are included as parameters in the ECW but are disabled.

Revealing a Clip with Basic 3D

As is the case with Transform and Motion, you can use Basic 3D to reveal a clip below it on a sequence. As shown in Figure 18.10, this is a good effect to use as something like a transition. You can spin and tilt the entire screen toward the front or back while changing the Distance to Image slider to move it away from the viewer. As I mentioned in Hour 16, "Using Higher-Level Video Effects," Basic 3D's primary appeal to me is its specular highlight.

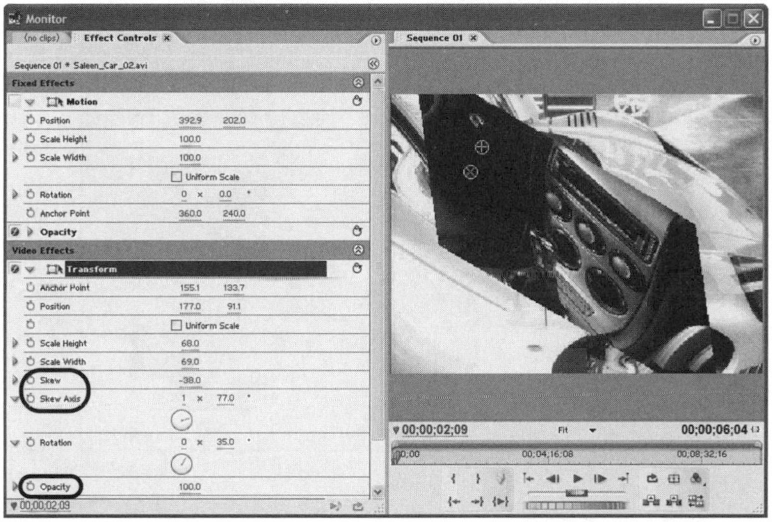

FIGURE 18.9
Transform can skew a clip to reveal the clip beneath it.

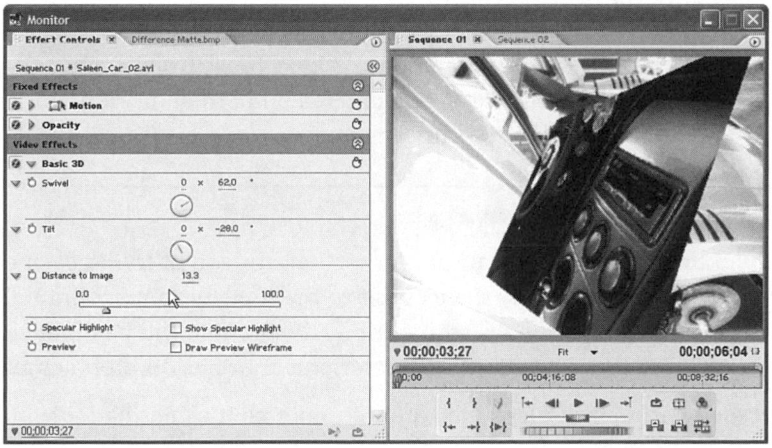

FIGURE 18.10
Basic 3D is another tool you can use to reveal a clip below it on the timeline.

Opting to Reveal a Clip Using Camera View

This effect works a lot like Basic 3D with a few additional controls thrown in. As shown in Figure 18.11, it has the same type of settings dialog box as Lens Distortion including a Fill Alpha Channel check box. Unchecking it reveals the clip below it on the sequence.

FIGURE 18.11
Uncheck the Camera View effect's Fill Alpha Channel box to display the clip below it on the timeline.

Effects That Work Well with Graphics That Have Alpha Channels

Four video effects work well with a graphic: Alpha Glow, Bevel Alpha, Channel Blur, and Drop Shadow. You briefly encountered all of them in Hour 16. I'll cover a few additional highlights in this upcoming task.

Try it Yourself   Using All Four Effects At Once

I'll ask you to take a different tack in this section. Instead of trying each effect separately, I'll have you apply these effects to the same graphic, eventually viewing all four at once. Admittedly, by that time, the graphic will be a hodgepodge. You can use the Saleen logo or any other graphic that has an alpha channel:

1. If you're using the Saleen logo graphic, enlarge it using the Scale parameter in the Motion effect—400% works well. Center it onscreen by dragging the crosshairs or adjusting the position parameters: 400 and 560 work well.

2. Apply Alpha Glow to the graphic on Video 2 and experiment with its settings (use Figure 18.12 as a reference):

▶ Glow—Sets the size of the glow.

▶ Brightness—Might be a little counter-intuitive. A high value (255 is the maximum) darkens the glow and a low value makes it lighter and more transparent.

▶ Start Color—The color closest to the graphic.

▶ End Color—The color at the outer edge of the glow.

3. Open Alpha Glow's Settings dialog box by clicking the little Setup button next to its reset button. Note that it has one extra option: Fade Out. By default, Fade Out is checked. Unchecking it gives your glow's perimeter a hard edge.

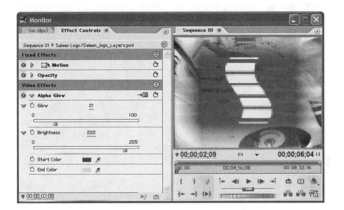

FIGURE 18.12
Alpha Glow creates a halo around a graphic that has an alpha channel.

4. Drag Bevel Alpha to the ECW. As you did in Hour 16, give this graphic a 3D beveled feel by adjusting this effect's parameters. Figure 18.13 shows one look you might come up with.

5. Add Channel Blur to the ECW. This shifts individual color values— red/green/blue—as well as blurs the graphic. Feel free to make adjustments using all the sliders. Figure 18.14 shows the results of my parameter adjustments.

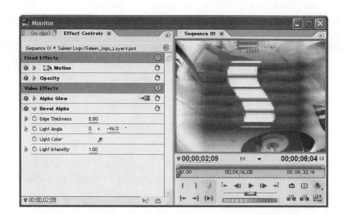

FIGURE 18.13
Bevel Alpha adds a
3D edge to the
graphic. Because
this clip also has
Alpha Glow applied
to it, the beveled
edges are not very
distinct.

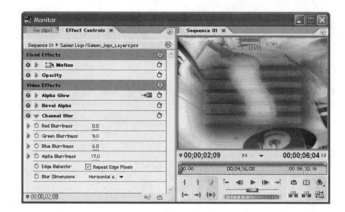

FIGURE 18.14
Because Channel
Blur is, for the
moment, the lowest
effect in the Effect
Controls palette, it
blurs all effects
above it.

Effect Order Makes a Difference

As illustrated in Figure 18.14, as you make changes using the Channel Blur effect sliders, the Bevel Alpha and Alpha Glow effects change. You might want to experiment as you add even more effects to the same clip.

Turn individual effects off and on by clicking the f in the check box. The order of the effects also alters the overall appearance of a clip. Premiere Pro renders effects from the top down (saving the fixed effects—Motion and Opacity—for last), reflecting the order in which you applied them to the clip.

You can change that order after the fact by dragging effects to new positions in the Effect Controls window. Try that for these three effects to see what happens.

For instance, as I've demonstrated in Figure 18.15, if you place Channel Blur at the top (below Motion and Opacity), any changes made when it's in that position will have a much more dramatic effect than if you place Channel Blur toward the bottom of the palette.

FIGURE 18.15 ▼
Placing Channel Blur at the top of the Effect Controls palette amplifies any adjustments you make to it.

6. Apply Drop Shadow to the ECW. Because the three other effects have softened the edges of the graphic, Drop Shadow won't have all that dramatic an effect. If you increase its opacity, as I did in Figure 18.16, you'll get a more distinct shadow.

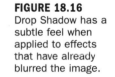

FIGURE 18.16
Drop Shadow has a subtle feel when applied to effects that have already blurred the image.

▲

Move Drop Shadow to the Top

Because Premiere Pro applies effects from the top of the ECW, down, if you drag this effect to the top of the effect chain in the Effect Controls palette, it will create a very distinct drop shadow. Toward the bottom of the palette, it acts much more in character with the other effects. In this case, because the graphic has soft edges applied to it, the drop shadow has a soft-edged look as well.

Did you
Know?

Applying Keyframes Within the Sequence

If you're in a particularly ambitious mood, feel free to apply keyframes to each individual video effect. You can access all the effects within the Effect Controls window or within the clip itself on the sequence.

To do that, expand the Video 2 track by clicking the Collapse/Expand Track triangle. Then click the Show Keyframes button and select Show Keyframes. That adds an effect drop-down list to the clip to the right of its name.

You can select any of the effects, and then select any of that effect's parameters. Once selected, you'll see that particular parameter's keyframe line. Use the Pen tool (keyboard shortcut P) to drag keyframes to new locations or create new ones by clicking it on the keyframe line.

Using the Motion Effect to Make Pictures-in-a-Picture

Pictures-in-a-picture is one of the top uses of the Motion effect. And it's one of the easiest ways to see how you can composite more than two clips.

Pictures-in-a-Picture Fundamentals

Because you worked with Motion in Hour 11, I won't repeat the basic instructions. Rather, I'll give you a few tips:

1. To do this, place several clips stacked one above the other on a sequence (for my example, I used six Saleen_Car AVI clips from the sample project).

Automatic Track Creation

There's no need to add video tracks to your sequence. Simply drag each new clip to somewhere above the current video tracks and drop it. Premiere Pro will create a new video track (and an audio track, if you're adding a linked A/V clip) to accommodate you.

2. To keep things easy, trim them so that they all are the same length and keep them short.

Top-Down Thinking

It's best to work from the top clip down because each clip covers the one below it. If instead you first apply Motion to a clip below the top track, you won't see it in the Monitor window Program screen.

If you must work from the bottom up, simply switch off the higher tracks' Toggle Track Output eyeballs. That way you can see what's on those lower tracks.

3. Click on the topmost clip to select it. You'll apply three effects to it then copy and paste those effects to the rest of the clips to create a uniform look.

4. Switch on Motion by clicking it in the ECW. Scale the clip down to about 25%. As you reduce its size, you reveal the clip in the video track below it in the sequence. Position it in a corner. Use Figure 18.17 as a reference.

Area Versus Perimeter

The 25% figure in step 4 refers not to a change in the clip's area, but rather to its perimeter. Each side becomes 1/4th its original length, which means the clip's area drops to 1/16th or .0625 its original size. That might be a bit counterintuitive to those who expect that scaling to 25% would create a clip that fills one quarter of a full screen.

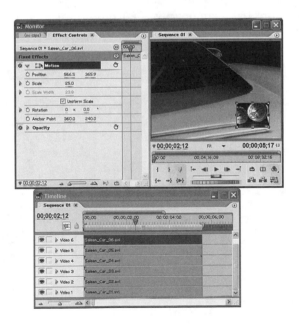

FIGURE 18.17
Create pictures-in-a-picture by stacking video clips in multiple tracks then applying motion settings to them.

5. To make your clips stand out from the background, use the Clip effect to give them frames. Drag that effect to the ECW, open its settings dialog box (shown in Figure 18.18), give your clips a frame size of five pixels or so and a color that complements the predominant colors of the clip on Video 1 that will serve as the background.

FIGURE 18.18
Add a frame to your clip using the Clip effect.

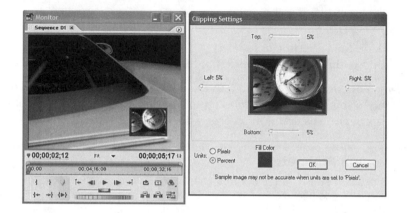

6. To further distance the moving clips from the background, drag the Drop Shadow effect to the ECW and create a fairly obvious drop shadow. As shown in Figure 18.19, an opacity of 80, a distance of 50, and a softness of 25 work well.

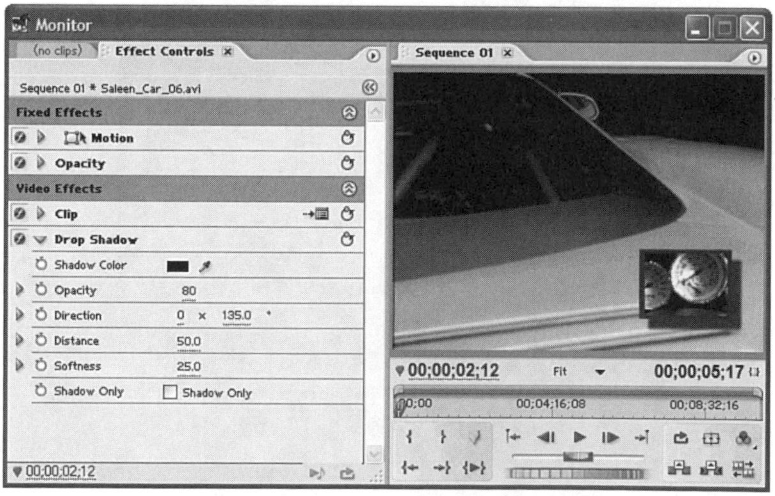

FIGURE 18.19
Using Drop Shadow gives a 3D feel to the moving clips. As you add more moving clips, those higher on the sequence will throw shadows on those below.

7. Right-click on this selected clip in the sequence and select Copy. Right-click on the clip below it and select Paste Attributes. That will change the scale of that clip, give it the same size and color frame, and add a drop shadow.

8. By right-clicking that clip, you also select it. Click on Motion in the ECW to display a bounding box around it (you'll see the bounding box but not the clip because the clip on the higher video track is covering it up). Grab the bounding box crosshairs and drag this clip to another corner (after you start moving it, you'll see the clip).

9. Working your way down the video tracks, follow the same procedure for each clip (right-click, select Paste Attributes, click Motion, move the clip), leaving the clip on Video 1 alone (it's the background video—the "picture"—of this pictures-in-a-picture). When you're done, your Program screen should look something like Figure 18.20.

FIGURE 18.20
Blend lets a clip that's on a lower video track show through a clip above it.

10. You can call it a day or you can take this further by putting each clip in motion. You can use keyframes to fly the clips onscreen at different times and then have them fly off. Or you can use the Opacity effect to have them fade in and then out. You can expand one of them to full screen as a way to transition to that clip. Using pictures-in-a-picture lends itself to many possibilities.

Two Multiple Track Video Effects: Blend and Texturize

Two video effects combine clips on two tracks. Blend works something like a cross-fade, but gives you extra options that can have some surprisingly colorful results. Texturize enables you to give a clip something akin to an embossed feel using a clip below it on the sequence.

Using Blend to Combine Two Clips

As illustrated in Figure 18.21, Blend has several parameters. The one you cannot keyframe is the track with which you're doing the blending. It can be any track, but if it's a track above the track you're working on, you need to switch off the upper track's eyeball to see the effect.

The Mode parameters drop-down list offers Crossfade, Color Only, Tint Only, Darken Only, and Lighten Only. Each lets different values of the lower clip show through. Blend With Original sets a relative percentage of opacity for the selected clip. A setting of 100% displays only the selected clip. 0% shows only the Blend With Layer clip, and 50% sets each at 50% opacity. You can use keyframes on the Blend With Original slider to gradually transition from one clip to another.

Did you Know?

> **Combine a Graphic and Video**
>
> For an unusual effect, use a graphic for one clip and a colorful video for the other. Selecting anything but Crossfade leads to some bizarre results. Try using the graphic as the selected clip, selecting Color Only, and moving the Blend With Original slider to 0%, which converts the graphic to grayscale and colors it using the Blend With Layer clip.

Using Texturize to Add an Embossed Look to Another Clip

Texturize has tons of possibilities. You apply Texturize to whichever clip you want to give some texture to, select the track that has the clip to use to create that texture, and then adjust the Light Direction and Texture Contrast settings to set the depth of the embossing (see Figure 18.22).

The Texture Placement parameter apparently is disabled; changing it had virtually no influence on the effect.

FIGURE 18.21
Blend lets a clip on a different video track show through the selected clip.

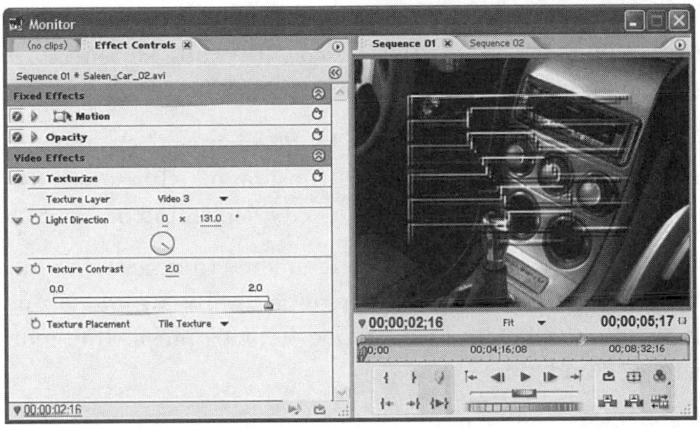

FIGURE 18.22
Texturize embosses one clip and imparts that 3D feel to a clip on a different track in the sequence.

Texturize Has Many Uses

The name *Texturize* is too narrow. Yes, you can use a clip with obvious texture—rug, sand, or rippling water—and impart that feel to another clip. But there are many other uses. You can bring up an embossed version of your logo beneath a product shot or place one distinctly different setting under another. How about embossed waving palm trees behind a frozen arctic tundra?

Did you Know?

> **Texturize Disables Motion Settings**
>
> Texturize will not work with motion settings. Therefore, if you want to move around your embossed logo under another clip, you'll have to create a nested sequence to do that. I cover this topic in Hour 19, "Tips, Tricks, and Techniques—Part 1." The basic approach is to create a new sequence, add only the logo to it, apply the Motion effect to it and adjust any motion parameters that suit you, drag that sequence to your other sequence as a separate clip, and then apply Texturize. That's a nested sequence—a sequence in a sequence.

Creating and Working with Mattes

On the surface, the matte is a straightforward concept. But confusing terms and applications can make using one counterintuitive. By definition, mattes are color or grayscale graphics or images. When used with Matte key effects, they create transparent and opaque areas in clips.

When you use mattes with Premiere Pro Matte keying effects, they follow standard transparency rules: Black areas are transparent, white areas are opaque, and gray areas create varying levels of opacity depending on the tone of the gray.

If the matte is a color image or graphic, Premiere Pro *removes* the same level of color from the clip you're keying, thus creating an inverse image. So, if you use a matte with green in it, the displayed image will look purple (the matte removes green, leaving red and blue).

You can create basic graphic mattes using Premiere Pro's Title Designer (except for image mattes), Photoshop, or any basic graphics program. Or you can use video clips or still images as mattes. You can use a Premiere Pro video effect to convert a color clip to a grayscale matte to avoid dealing with color inversions.

Most of the time, mattes are simply black-and-white graphics. In those cases, they work like scissors on white paper. Any (black) holes cut into the paper let those portions of the clip below it on the sequence show through and combine with the clip above it on the timeline.

Combine Clips with an Image Matte Key

Image Matte keys enable you to cut "holes" in one clip to allow portions of another clip to show through. For example, you can use an Image Matte key to highlight an element in a clip or insert a portrait in a frame. I offer up a practical example in the next hour. Here's how to use an Image Matte key:

1. The Image Matte key works only with graphic files supported by Premiere Pro. It does not work with files created in the Title Designer. So, open a graphics program such as Photoshop or Microsoft Paint. Set the image canvas to a resolution that matches your project: 720×540 for NTSC or 720×576 for PAL (see the following Did You Know for more on the canvas size).

Did you Know?

Image Matte Photoshop Setup

When using Photoshop to create a graphic to use as an Image Matte key, select File→New and choose one of the DV Preset Sizes: 720×540 Std. NTSC 601 or 720×576 Std. PAL. As I noted, the NTSC 720×540 does not properly fill the screen in Premiere Pro. But matching the project resolution means there will be no image quality loss. When opening a new canvas in Photoshop, set the mode to RGB color and if you want an opaque background, click the White radio button under Contents.

---

2. As I've demonstrated in Figure 18.23, start with a white background, create a simple shape, and fill it in with solid black. Create another shape and fill it with gray. Save your work and remember where you stored this file.

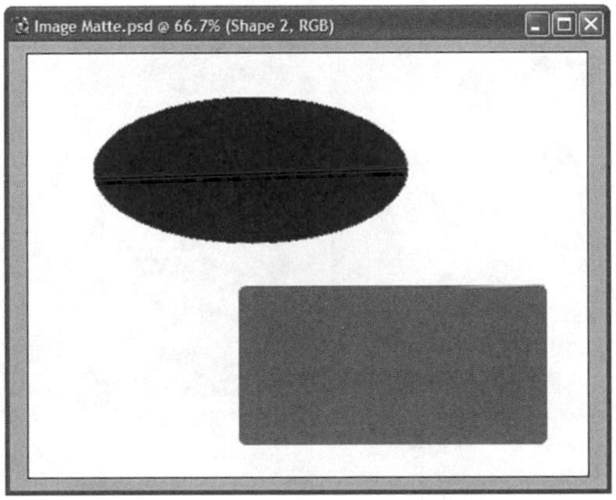

FIGURE 18.23
Use a graphic program such as Adobe Photoshop to create a basic image matte.

3. Return to the sequence and place two different video clips or still images on Video 1 and Video 2 (for my example, I used the Saleen_Car AVI clips).

4. Select the clip on Video 2 and apply the Image Matte key to it.

5. Twirl down the Image Matte disclosure triangle and change the Composite Using parameter to Matte Luma. (If you created a graphic with an alpha channel, you can leave the Composite Using setting to Matte Alpha.) As shown in Figure 18.24, your Program screen should now display the clip on

Video 2 with whatever holes you drew in the graphic showing portions of the clip on Video 1. Black holes are completely transparent; gray ones are partially transparent.

Image Matte Key Anomaly

The Image Matte key has an anomaly. No matter what size or aspect ratio graphic you use, Premiere Pro either expands its edges so that they fall off the right and left sides of the image, or shrinks its height, leaving gaps above and below it. This shows up most obviously when you use a matte that extends to the edges of the graphic. For example, at 720×540 (standard NTSC DV resolution) there are gaps at the top and bottom. At 720×480, the sides are pushed offscreen. I asked Premiere Pro's development team about this and they did not provide an answer. As I explain later, you need to use Motion's Scale parameter to expand the clip a bit to compensate for this.

6. If your clip now has gaps (refer to "Image Matte Key Anomaly" earlier) open the Motion effect and increase the Scale setting enough to have the clip on Video 2 fill the screen.

FIGURE 18.24
Using an Image Matte key enables you to cut holes in one clip, disclosing portions of the clip below it on a sequence. If you have gaps like those shown here, use Motion's Scale parameter to expand the clip.

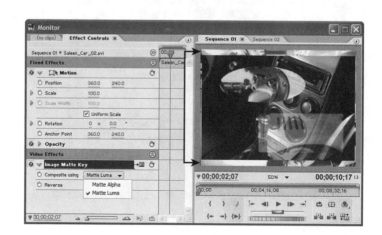

Reversing the Effect

You can electronically swap black with white by clicking the Image Matte Key's Reverse check box. That will swap transparent and opaque areas of the clip on Video 2, letting different portions of the clip on Video 1 show through.

Using a Track Matte Key

A Track Matte key works much like an Image Matte but has a few advantages and one obvious difference. What makes it different is that you place the matte on a video *track* rather than apply it directly to a clip.

As with an Image Matte, a Track Matte slices holes in a clip, revealing whatever is below it on a sequence. What makes it more convenient is that you can use Premiere Pro's Title Designer to create the graphic. What makes it more interesting is that you can use the Motion effect on that matte to turn it into a *traveling matte*.

Just about every older movie involving "impossible" motion—spaceships, Superman in flight, or giant spiders (such as the 1955 cult classic, *Tarantula*, with Clint Eastwood in a minor supporting role as a pilot)—uses traveling mattes.

Working with a Track Matte

Try it Yourself
▼

To give it motion requires using a *nested sequence*. In the next hour, I explain that concept plus demonstrate how to use a Track Matte to create a traveling matte that highlights action and conceals someone's identity. For now, follow these steps simply to see how to apply a static Track Matte key to a clip:

1. You can use the Image Matte graphic you created for the previous task or you can create a new one in Premiere Pro's Title Designer. To use the Image Matte, import it to your Project window (select File→Import). If you use the Title Designer, save your graphic, calling it something like Track Matte Key. It'll show up automatically in the Project window.

Creating Mattes in the Title Designer

Did you Know?

Both the Image Matte key and the Track Matte key can use graphics that have alpha channels. When you create a graphic, Premiere Pro's Title Designer, it'll have an alpha channel by default. At this point, things will make more sense if you don't use that alpha channel (I show you a cool way to use it in the next hour). So, if you use the Title Designer, first create a solid white rectangle that fills the screen, and then place whatever black/grayscale graphics you want to use to create transparencies on that. In that way, the white area will be opaque and the black/grayscale areas will be transparent as you'd expect.

2. Use the same two clips from the previous task. Drag whichever graphic you want to use as a Track Matte key from the Project window to Video 3 and drag its edges to fit the other two clips.

▼

▼

3. You need to disable the display of that matte (otherwise, it'll cover all clips below it on the sequence). As shown in Figure 18.25, do that by right-clicking on the clip and selecting Enable to uncheck that attribute. Alternatively, you can unclick the Video 3 eyeball, but that disables the entire video track, switching off the display for any other clip you might later put on Video 3.

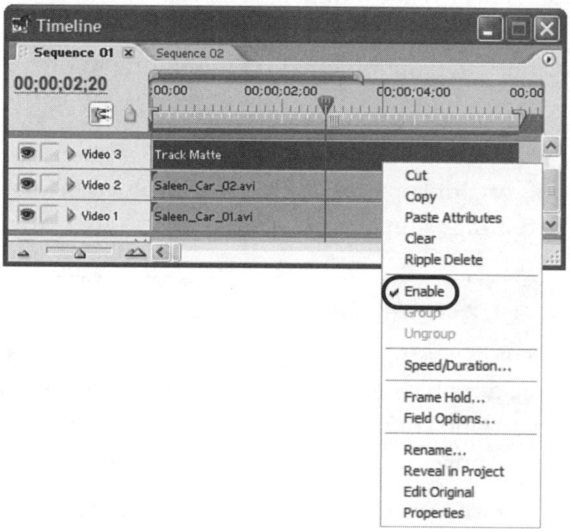

FIGURE 18.25
You need to uncheck Enable for this clip to keep it from covering up clips below it on the sequence.

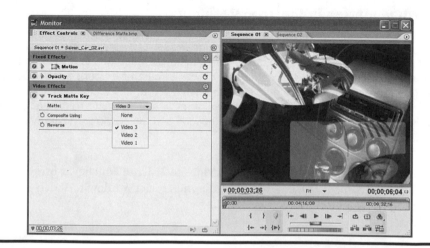

4. Select the clip on Video 2. Delete the Image Matte key from the ECW and apply the Track Matte key. Set Composite Using to Matte Luma. Your project should look something like Figure 18.26.

FIGURE 18.26
Track Matte uses a matte on a video track and applies it to the clip on a different track. The end result in this case is strikingly similar to the Image Matte key example, but there is no need to resize the clip to cover gaps.

▲

Using Mattes to Build Split Screens

There are several ways to create a split screen. For instance, you can use an Image Matte or a Track Matte with black on one side and white on the other, or a more complicated Difference Matte. But the Garbage Matte is the easiest method, so we'll start with that.

Working with the Garbage Matte Key

You've seen movies with the same actor playing multiple characters in the same scene. There are several ways to accomplish this. Using a split-screen matte is one. Using a Difference Matte key is another. I explain both in the next two tasks. So, what the heck is a Garbage Matte key doing in a nice place like Premiere Pro?

The Garbage Matte is so named because you use it to get rid of garbage in your image. Frequently, a boom microphone might be in a shot done in front of a chromakey screen. Or there might be some video noise around the edges of a keyed shot. The Garbage Matte key readily removes those things.

Take a look at Figure 18.27. I applied RGB Difference to this shot. That keys out the single-color background, but not the shadow on the right and that extraneous stuff in the lower-left corner.

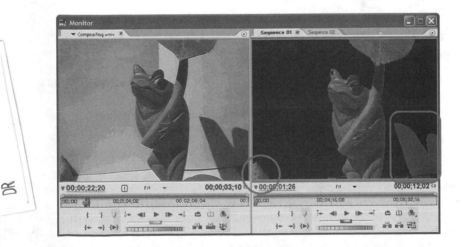

FIGURE 18.27
I can use RBG Difference to key out the background of this shot, but that doesn't remove the detritus—the shadow and that object in the lower-left corner.

I apply the Garbage Matte Key to remove those other items. As you can see in Figure 18.28, it's a bounding box with four handles in the corners. I can drag those handles into the clip and cover up those objects.

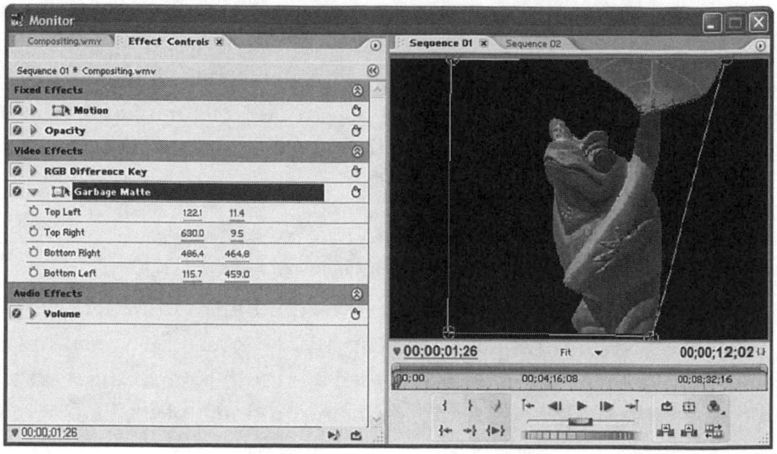

FIGURE 18.28
Use the Garbage
Matte key to slice
away those unwant-
ed items and
replace them with
transparent
regions.

Any gaps you create by dragging in the Garbage Matte's corners become transparent, letting whatever is below them on a sequence show through. You also can
use keyframes to adjust the size and shape of this box over time.

The Garbage Matte has its limitations. It's good at removing items along the
edges of a clip, but if you try to get at anything toward the middle you'll probably cut off the object you're keying.

Using the Garbage Matte Key to Make a Split Screen

This is where task number five from Hour 17, "Compositing Part 1—Layering and
Keying Clips," comes into play.

By the Way

Assignment Review

As a reminder, for the task in Hour 17, you were to tape a distinct background with
nothing moving in it—that is, no waving palm trees or soaring birds. Then, without
turning off or moving the camera (this is one exercise where you need a rock-steady
shot), have someone walk into the left side of the scene without crossing the center
line, stand around for a while, and then walk back out the left side. Have that person do the same thing entering from the right side and walking out to the right. For
a bit of comic relief, have your "actor" wave toward the center of the scene before
walking off camera.

Create a Split-Screen Effect

Try it Yourself

To create a split-screen effect using your video track assignment from Hour 17, follow these steps:

1. In the Project window, double-click the assignment clip to display it in the Monitor window Source screen.

2. Trim the left side of the clip to a point just before your actor enters the scene. Drag the trimmed clip to Video 1 at the start of the sequence.

3. In the Source screen, trim the clip to a point just before your actor enters the right side. Drag it to Video 2, right above the clip on Video 1. Move the CTI edit line far enough into the clips so that your actor has moved onscreen.

4. Apply the Garbage Matte key to the clip on Video 2. As shown in Figure 18.29, drag the corners to reveal the clip beneath it on the sequence.

5. Preview your split screen. Your actor should enter the scene from both sides, hang around, wave to his/her other self, and then walk off.

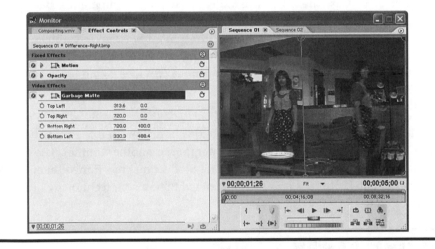

FIGURE 18.29
Using the Garbage Matte key enables you to place the same actor in two locations (or more) within the same setting.

Obviously, this takes some planning. The actor shouldn't cross the line that divides the set in two, for instance (you *can* keyframe the Garbage Matte box edges to accommodate some overlap). The lighting can't change from one shot to the next, and there can't be any movement in the vicinity of the scene's dividing line.

Using a Difference Matte

Split screens work fine if you can keep your actors from moving across the imaginary line dividing the image or don't have more than only a few actors (you can use the Garbage Matte key on more than two clips, but doing so takes some real planning).

You can resort to the Difference Matte when there is just too much action to neatly divide a scene into a few Garbage Matte–defined rectangles. The Difference Matte behaves more like a chromakey. As with the Garbage Matte key split-screen, the Difference Matte enables you to tape an actor working in one spot in the scene and then tape the same or another actor working in another section at a different time. It doesn't have to be distinctly left and right sides. And you can have multiple actors.

Here's how it works: Just as you did in your assignment, you use a locked-down camera to avoid any movement, tape a scene with a static background, and create a still image of that scene with no actors present. Then for each scene shot with an actor, you use the Difference Matte key to look for differences between the two scenes (in this case, the presence of an actor) and key out everything else. What you end up with is the actor over a transparent background. You can do that for any number of action elements, keying out the background and keeping the action. Then you place the static background on Video 1 and layer all the action scenes over it.

If you've seen the Eddie Murphy film *Dr. Doolittle 2* (hey, I'm the father of a 9-year-old child), you've seen technology like this in action. In one scene, they had a couple dozen animals all paying rapt attention to another animal. Those animals weren't all there at the same time. The production crew filmed them in several takes at different times and then combined them using technology like the difference matte.

Try it Yourself   **Working with a Difference Matte**

▼

Try it out by following these steps:

1. You could use the clips already on the timeline, but it's easier to start fresh. Therefore, clear the timeline and place the assignment clip on Video 2 (*not* Video 1).

2. Move the edit line to a section of the clip on Video 2 where there are no actors in the scene. You'll use that scene for your still image.

▼

3. To create a still image, go to the main menu and select File→Export→Frame. Navigate to the Scratch Disk file folder, name the image something such as Difference Matte, and click Save. The default image settings (BMP file) should work fine. This new still image automatically appears in your Project window. Leave it there for now.

4. Move the CTI Edit line to the point in the clip on Video 2 where the actor moves onscreen.

5. Apply the Difference Matte key to the clip on Video 2. Click the Settings button, find your newly created image, and click Open. You're going to use that still image to key out that static background, showing only the actor over a black (transparent) background.

6. Check the Reverse Key box and use the Similarity slider to fine-tune the removal of the background. In a perfect world, the background would disappear, leaving only the actor. If you're working with a standard prosumer DV25 camcorder, its less-than-razor-sharp images make it difficult to remove all but the actor. Glitches are common.

7. Trim your assignment clip in the Source screen to the point where your actor enters from the other side of the scene. Drag that to Video 3.

8. Apply the Difference Matte to it, and follow the same procedures used in step 7 to remove the background.

9. Drag the newly created Difference Matte still image you created in step 3 on Video 1 and drag its edges to make it long enough to match the action on the two clips above it.

Preview your project. You should see something akin to the split screen you worked on earlier. But you'll probably notice that this is far from a flawless process. As shown in Figure 18.30, sometimes no matter how you adjust the Similarity sliders, you'll still key out parts of your actors. You probably will have to experiment a lot to find two Similarity settings that allow the actors in both clips to look reasonably sharp.

Difference Matte Versus Chromakey

Did you Know?

You can use a Difference Matte to place an actor or object over a background other than the one you shot on the original set. But that's really the wrong technology for that effect. If you tape actors in front of a static setting, you probably want to use that setting in the final cut. If you want to place your actors into a *different* background, you might as well tape your actors in front of a blue or green screen.

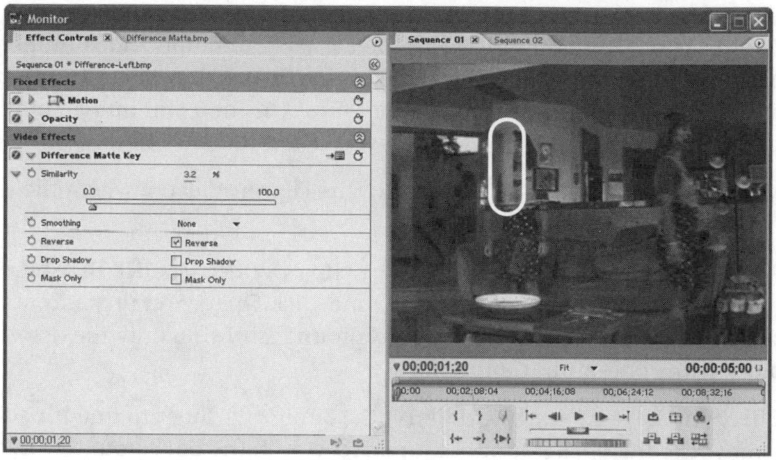

FIGURE 18.30
Using a Difference
Matte on two clips
frequently creates
jagged edges or
gaps in the actor(s)
like the one high-
lighted here.

Difference Mattes take a very controlled and simple background to pull off. In most cases, you might want to stick to split screens or blue/green screens.

Did you Know?

Improved Matte Key Previews

One way to see a more accurate preview of any matte or other key is to create a bright, solid-color matte (yes, the terms can be confusing) and place it on Video 1 to use as a temporary background. As a reminder, to create a solid-color matte, click the New Item button at the bottom of the Project window and select Color Matte. Select a color, name the matte, and save it. It'll appear in the Project window.

Summary

Alpha channels and mattes round out Premiere Pro's compositing tools. Graphics frequently have alpha channels built in. Premiere Pro "switches on" those alpha channels, creating distinct, easy-to-use transparencies. Premiere Pro has several video effects with alpha channel transparencies built in, as well as some effects that work only on clips on more than one track.

Matte keys are yet another way to combine or composite clips. They come in several styles. The most common is a simple black-and-white graphic. When applied to a clip, it makes portions transparent and other areas opaque.

Q&A

Q *I placed a graphic I wanted to use as a Track Matte on a sequence and I used the Motion effect on it to move it around the screen. But when I applied that graphic to another clip using the Track Matte Key, the graphic doesn't move. What's going on?*

A To get that Track Matte to move—to become a **traveling matte**—you need to put the graphic in a separate sequence that you will later nest inside the original sequence. I explain that process in the next hour.

Q *I tried using the Difference Matte, but when I move the Similarity slider, my actor disappears, not the background scene. Why?*

A The Difference Matte is an odd duck. It looks for *differences* between two images and removes them. But that's not what you want to do. You want to remove *similarities*. Therefore, check the Reverse Key box to do just that. Now when you move the slider, the background should disappear and your actor should remain.

Workshop

Quiz

1. You have a lovely logo created in Photoshop. How do you give it some sharp, beveled edges and fly it over a clip of your office exterior?

2. If black areas of an alpha channel are transparent, why is black text on a graphic with an alpha channel opaque?

3. What's the difference between an Image Matte and a Track Matte?

Quiz Answers

1. Place it in a video track above your office shot. Apply the Bevel Alpha effect to it. Adjust the Edge Thickness, Light Angle, Light Color, and Light Intensity settings to suit your needs. Then use Motion's parameters to fly it over your video clip.

2. The color of the graphic does not set opacity. The color of the alpha channel does. Typically, artists create graphics and build an alpha channel stencil to match the graphic's borders. In that alpha channel layer, areas beneath the graphic are white to ensure the graphic remains opaque no matter what color it is.

3. You apply an Image Matte directly to a clip by clicking that clip's Image Matte Settings box and selecting the Image Matte graphic file. Track Matte is not as direct. You place that matte clip on a separate video track. Then you apply the Track Matte key effect to a clip and select the video track with the matte graphic. You use track mattes to create traveling or moving mattes. I explain that in the next hour.

Exercises

1. Create a four-segment split screen. You can do this by applying the Garbage Matte key three times, adjusting its bounding box to display three different corners. Or you can make three mattes with black covering three-quarters of each one. Then place the same person/object in each quadrant of the same scene.

2. Use Camera View to have one clip move back to one side then spin away to reveal a second clip behind it. Then move that second clip back to the other side to reveal another clip behind it. You can apply the Motion effect to keep the "hinges" of each door attached to the side of the screen before twirling the clip off into the distance. On the other hand, you could use the Swing In or Swing Out transitions. But that would be too easy and your custom version will look much better.

3. Use the Strobe Light effect with keyframes on a clip on Video 2 (above another clip) to flash white frames, black frames, inverse frames (set the Strobe Operator to Difference), and transparent frames showing through to the clip below. For anything but transparent flashes, set Strobe to Operates on Color Only. For white, set Strobe Operator to Add or Copy; for Black, use Subtract; and for Inverse, use Difference. To see through to the lower video track, set Strobe to Makes Layer Transparent. All these parameters are keyframable.

HOUR 19

Tips, Tricks, and Techniques— Part 1

What You'll Learn in This Hour:

- ▶ Highlighting a portion of your clip
- ▶ Applying realistic drop shadows to rotating objects
- ▶ Working with nested sequences
- ▶ Enhancing two effects using nested sequences
- ▶ Giving motion to two immovable effects
- ▶ Obscuring someone's identity
- ▶ Fine-tuning keys using a nested sequence

In this hour and the next, I'm going to take things beyond the scope of most Premiere Pro how-to books by presenting tips, tricks, and techniques. These are the kinds of tools that experienced editors frequently use. But if you've never seen them in action, you probably wouldn't come up with them on your own. After you've tried them out, you'll find myriad ways to apply them to your projects.

In this hour, I focus on nested sequences—offering up six specific uses for them— plus I present two other practical Premiere Pro editing applications.

In the next hour, I take you through Premiere Pro's most important new video effect: the Color Corrector. Plus I offer up a couple fun tasks, several keyboard shortcuts, and a collection of expert tips from an Adobe corporate Premiere Pro evangelist.

Highlighting a Portion of Your Clip

Frequently, you'll want to draw attention to something within your clip without completely obscuring that portion of the clip. You might want to apply a graphic or a super there or highlight an object or person.

You do that by putting the same clip on Video 1 and Video 2, using an image or Track Matte key on the clip on Video 2 to highlight a portion of the clip, and applying a video effect to the clip on Video 1 to make the matted section of your clip stand out.

Try it Yourself — Highlight a Portion of Your Clip

How you choose to highlight your clip is up to you. You'll see what I mean as I take you through this task. The fundamental process works for a variety of situations. In this case, I go over how to change the color and sharpness of a portion of your clip so that when you add text it stands out from the image. Here are the steps:

1. Create a new sequence: select File→New→Sequence, name it Highlight a Clip, and click OK.

2. Using the sample project that shipped with Premiere Pro, drag Saleen_Car_10 to Video 1 and Video 2 (you *can* use your own clip: a brief scene—15 seconds or so—that does not have much action in it). For this effect to work properly, both clips must be lined up. Figure 19.1 demonstrates what I mean. Drag the CTI edit line into the clip a bit.

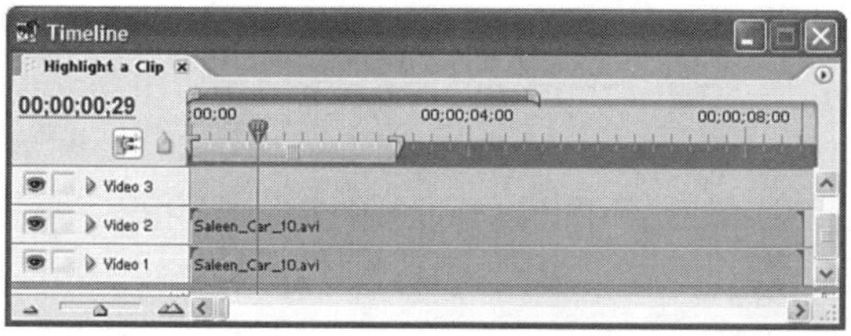

FIGURE 19.1
To highlight a location on a clip, start the process by placing that clip on both Video 1 and Video 2.

3. I prefer using the Track Matte key because it works with mattes created in the Title Designer. So, open the Title Designer (File→New→Title) to create the matte. Click Show Video to see your clip as you create the matte.

4. In this case, because you'll put text within the highlighted portion of your clip, create a black, rounded rectangle to define that area—something along

the lines of the one shown in Figure 19.2. Save your title by selecting
File→Save, give it a name like `Clip Highlight Matte`, and click Save (that
automatically puts it in the Project window).

Matte Creation Suggestions

In my example, I used the Rounded Corner Rectangle tool to create that vertical
oval. By default, the Fill color is black, which works fine. To give it that gray border, I
opened Strokes, clicked Add next to Outer Strokes, set the size to 10, clicked the
rectangle next to the word Color to access the Color Picker to pick gray, and set the
Opacity to 50% to let some of the clip show through when I apply the Track Matte
key in a moment.

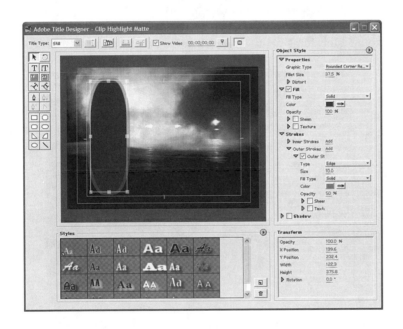

FIGURE 19.2
A rounded rectangle matte works well to frame text.

5. Drag your matte clip to Video 3 of your sequence and extend it to fit over
   the clips on Video 1 and 2. Switch off its display by right-clicking it and
   unchecking Enable.

What's Going on Here?

The object here is to change the appearance of the clip on Video 1 to have that slightly altered view show through the matte applied to the clip on Video 2. What you'll do is blur the clip on Video 1 and change its color. The tinted soft focus will let that clip's action show through but will serve as a relatively nondistracting backdrop for some text.

---

6. Switch off the eyeball on Video 2 so that you can see your work on Video 1.

7. Select the clip on Video 1 and apply Fast Blur and Tint to it in the Effect Controls window (ECW). As shown in Figure 19.3, a low blur setting works well. You have two tinting options: You can select a color to apply to light pixels in your clip and a color to apply to dark pixels. After these have been selected, adjust the Amount to Tint. The object is to make things look softer without losing some detail. You can make adjustments later if necessary.

FIGURE 19.3
Give the clip on Video 1 a slight blur and a different tint to make it stand out when placed inside the Track Matte key.

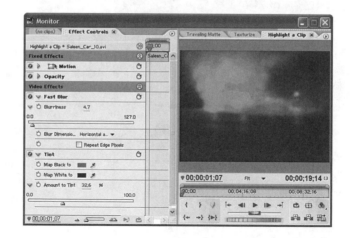

8. Turn on the eyeball for Video 2, select the clip on Video 2, and apply the Track Matte key. As shown in Figure 19.4, in the ECW, set Matte to Video 3, Composite Using Matte Alpha, and click Reverse. That latter parameter makes the alpha channel in this clip opaque (covering the clip on Video 1) and makes the oval and its border transparent, letting the altered clip show through. The end result should look something like Figure 19.4.

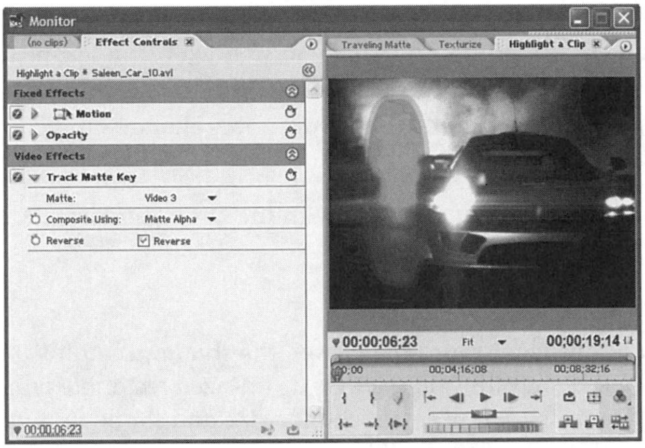

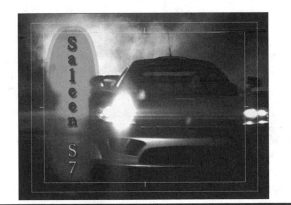

FIGURE 19.4
Applying the Track Matte key to the clip on Video 2 cuts a digital "hole" in that clip, letting the blurred clip on Video 1 show through.

9. Finally, you can add text to this clip by returning to the Title Designer. Using one of the vertical type tools would work well for this graphic. After creating the text, save it and add it to the sequence on a track above the two clips. Figure 19.5 shows one example. The blurred clip on Video 1 makes the text stand out.

FIGURE 19.5
Use a vertical type tool to create text for this Track Matte key.

Applying Realistic Drop Shadows to Rotating Objects

As I mentioned in Hour 11, "Putting Video and Still Clips in Motion," the Drop Shadow effect does not throw a realistic shadow when using the Rotation parameter. The shadow "sticks" to the clip, meaning it turns with it as if it were part of the clip, rather than a real shadow. It's as if Rotation also moves the position of the sun. You'll encounter this any time you create a picture-in-picture or layer a graphic over another clip. Drop shadows are just about standard for such effects, and if you spin those pics-in-pics, you want those shadows to behave realistically.

Two effects overcome that minor inconvenience: Transform and Camera View. A third, Basic 3D, works reasonably well with the Drop Shadow effect but it has two issues:

- ▶ It doesn't have rotation as a parameter.
- ▶ As you tilt the clip toward the viewer, the shadow remains the same size and shape as the clip. You see it as a clip-sized rectangle lying behind and parallel to the clip. It does not change size and shape to match the move.

Applying Drop Shadow to Transform

Rather than a fully fleshed-out task, I'll give you a basic run-through of how to use Drop Shadows with Transform. Using Figure 19.6 as a reference, I put a color matte on Video 1 and a clip on Video 2. I applied Transform to that clip, reduced its scale, and used keyframes to have it move across the screen, rotating twice along the way.

Then I applied the Drop Shadow effect. Now as the clip spins across the screen, the shadow always falls down and to the right. You need to apply Drop Shadow after you apply Transform (so it's below Transform in the ECW); otherwise, it will stick to the clip just as it does when used with Motion.

Using Camera View with Drop Shadow

You use Camera View when you want to simulate a changing clip viewing angle. As shown in Figure 19.7, updating some parameters distorts the clip shape, giving it perspective. Using the Roll parameter works much like Rotation in Transform, and the Drop Shadow effect works smoothly with that spinning clip.

The one caveat is that, just as with Basic 3D, as you tilt the clip toward the viewer, the drop shadow starts looking unrealistic, matching the shape and size of the clip and lying parallel to it.

One other point: For the Drop Shadow to work, you need to open Camera View's Setup dialog box and unclick the Fill Alpha Channel check box.

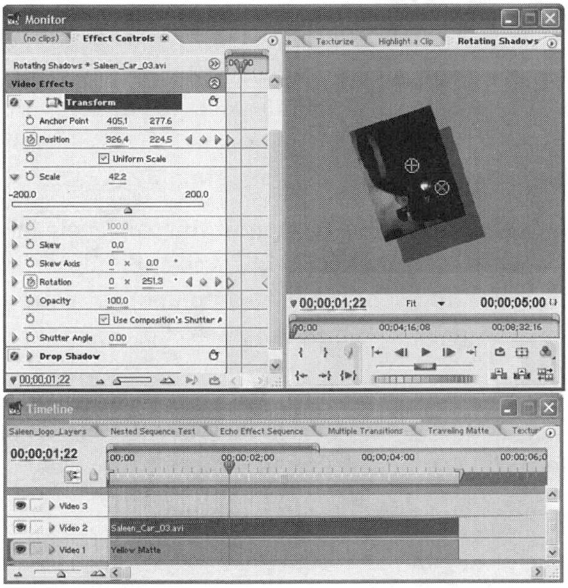

FIGURE 19.6
The Drop Shadow effect creates realistic shadows when used with the Transform effect.

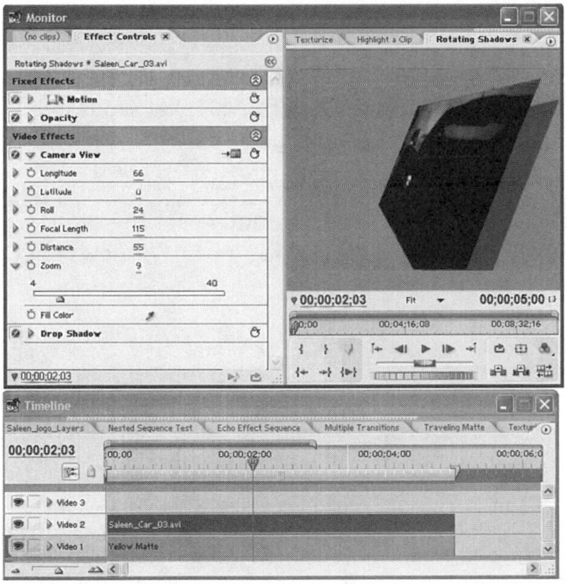

FIGURE 19.7
Camera View also works hand-in-hand with Drop Shadow to create realistic shadows to spinning clips.

Working with Nested Sequences

The **nested sequence** concept is new to Premiere Pro and replaces something called *virtual clips*. Nested sequences are a *huge* improvement. I won't explain virtual clips; I'll only say that all sorts of things could go wrong with them and they were very confusing. Nested sequences greatly simplify the virtual clip process.

A nested sequence is a sequence-in-a-sequence. You can create an entire project segment in one sequence and drop that sequence—with all its clips, graphics, layers, multiple audio/video tracks, and effects—into another sequence. There it will look and behave like a single, linked audio/video clip.

You use nested sequences for several reasons:

▶ Apply an effect or effects to a collection of layered clips. That saves having to do that to each layer or clip, one at a time.

▶ Apply more than one transition between clips.

▶ Build multiple picture-in-picture effects.

▶ Give motion or apply other effects to immovable effects.

▶ Reuse sequences, or use the same sequence but give it different looks each time.

▶ Simplify editing by creating complex sequences separately. This helps you avoid running into conflicts and inadvertently shifting clips on a track that is far from your current work area.

▶ They're also very helpful organizationally—for the same reason you might create subfolders in the project window or in Windows Explorer. They avoid confusion and shorten editing time.

By the Way

Developer Comment—Our Take on Nested Sequences

They have so many uses that aren't immediately apparent. Not only does this feature enable you to break up your project into more manageable chunks, it also allows you to treat longer segments as one piece.

A prime example is color correction or other effects. If you want a two-minute sequence of multiple cuts to have the same dreamy look or be in black-and-white, for example, rather than apply these effects to the individual cuts, you would apply the effects to the entire sequence that has been placed in another sequence.

Once nested, a sequence acts just like a clip, which means you can apply one effect to the entire time span. And if you want to change the settings, you can do it in one place rather than changing one and then setting the rest of the clips to the same setting.

I introduced nested sequences back in Hour 16, "Using Higher-Level Video Effects." As a reminder, open the sample project that shipped with Premiere Pro. In the Saleen_Sample sequence, double-click on the last clip: Saleen_logo_Layers. That clip is a nested sequence and double-clicking it adds that sequence to the Timeline window and switches the view to that sequence. As shown in Figure 19.8, this sequence is simply two graphic clips.

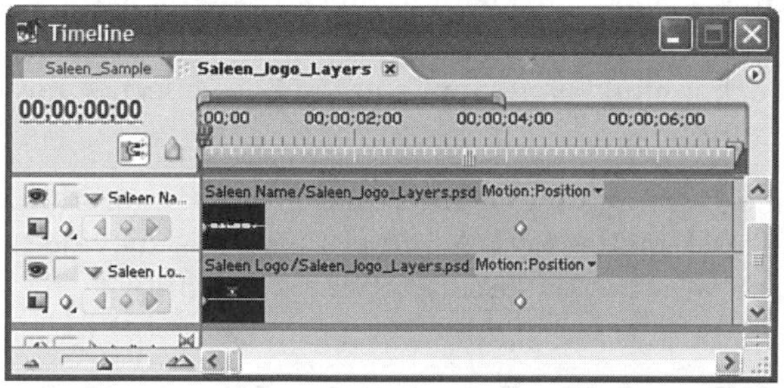

FIGURE 19.8
Double-clicking a nested sequence clip opens its sequence in the Timeline window.

The sample project's editor chose to create this two-layer sequence for a simple reason: to fade to black. To see that, return to the Saleen_Sample sequence by clicking its tab in the Timeline window. As shown in Figure 19.9, the last clip, the Saleen_logo_Layers sequence, has the Cross Dissolve transition applied to it. When used at the end of a piece, it fades the video to black.

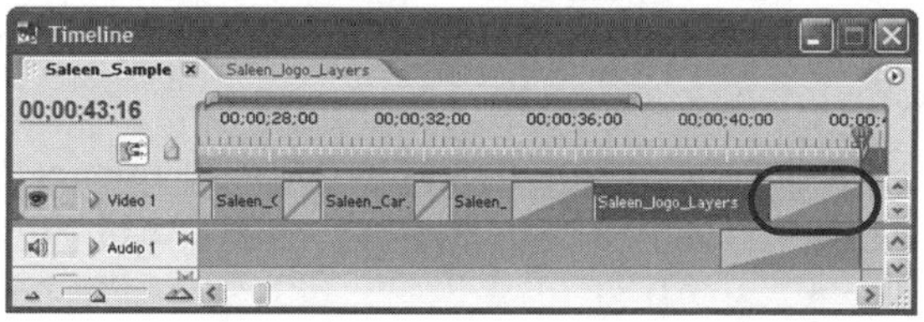

FIGURE 19.9
The highlighted clip, actually a nested sequence, has a Cross Dissolve applied to it—a minor time-saving step.

If this project's editor had not used this nested sequence, he would have had to apply the Cross Dissolve to both clips. In this case, the nested sequence avoided only a minor inconvenience. But I think you get the idea of how nested sequences can help.

Enhancing Two Effects Using Nested Sequences

In this section, I explain workarounds for two Premiere Pro video effects. Both have issues that only a nested sequence can address:

▶ The Echo video effect disables all effects applied above it (before it) in the Effect Controls window. Frequently, you want to apply some other effects before using Echo. For instance, you might want to use a key effect to remove a background before applying the Echo effect. A nested sequence lets you do that.

▶ You cannot apply motion to a Track Matte key. This is critical because you usually use track mattes to make *traveling mattes*—moving screens that, for example, follow action or obscure someone's identity.

Try it Yourself ▼   **Giving Echo More Attributes**

This can be fairly straightforward, but I've extended it a bit by adding a few housekeeping steps to help with upcoming tasks. In this task, you create a new sequence, add a clip, apply a key effect to it, open that nested sequence clip in another sequence, and apply Echo to it:

1. To keep things orderly, create a new bin in the Project window by clicking the Bin button at the bottom of that window. Name it Nested Sequences. It shows up in the Project window and is automatically selected. This is where you will store any new sequences.

2. Create a new sequence by selecting File→New—Sequence. Type in a name— I suggest Nested Sequence Test—and click OK. As illustrated in Figure 19.10, because the newly created Nested Sequences bin was highlighted, this new sequence shows up in that bin.

3. Follow the same process used in step two and create another sequence. Name it Echo Effect Sequence.

4. Take a look at the Timeline window. As shown in Figure 19.11, your new sequence should be open and there should be a tab at the top of the window denoting the presence of the other new sequence. The default new sequence layout is three video and audio tracks plus a master audio track.

▼

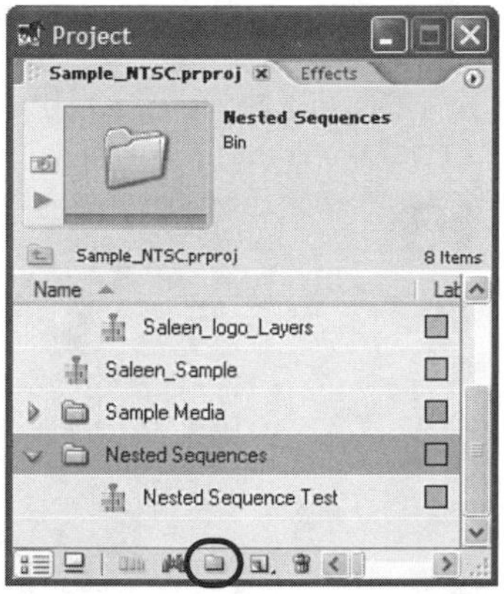

FIGURE 19.10 ▼
Click the highlighted Bin button to create a new bin to store the sequences you'll create in the upcoming tasks.

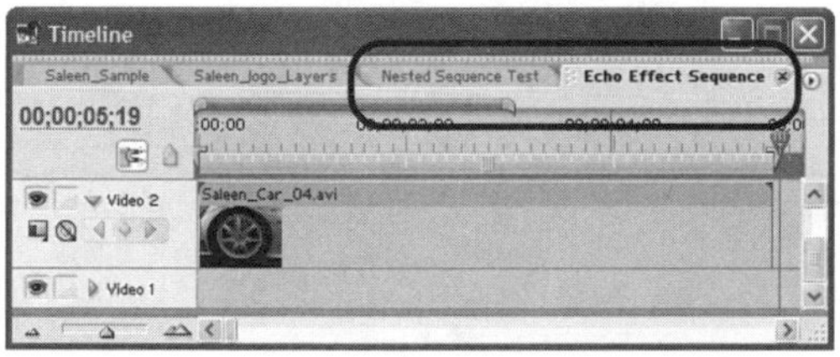

FIGURE 19.11
As you create new sequences, they show up as tabs in the Timeline window.

5. From the Project window, Sample Media bin, drag Saleen_Car_04 to Video 2 of Echo Effect Sequence (you'll add a color matte to Video 1 in a moment). You can drag both ends to lengthen it a bit.

Expanding Clip Display—Keyboard Shortcut

You might notice in Figure 19.11 that the Saleen_Car_04 clip fills the length of the Timeline window even though it's only five seconds long. That's because I used the keyboard shortcut \ (backslash). That automatically zooms the timescale in the Timeline window to fit the full length of the current sequence's clips—which might shrink or enlarge the current display. In this case, that amounts to one very brief clip taking up the entire sequence display.

Did you Know?

6. Create a color matte by clicking the New Item button at the bottom of the Project Window, selecting Color Matte, selecting a color (bright yellow works well), clicking OK, giving that matte a name, and clicking OK. Drag that matte from the Project window to Video 1 and extend it to match the length of the Saleen_Car_04 clip.

▼

7. Apply the Luma Key effect to the `Saleen_Car_04` clip. Adjust the Threshold and Cutoff sliders to remove the black background. As you can see in Figure 19.12, I chose values of 18% and 7% respectively.

FIGURE 19.12
Apply the Luma Key effect to key out the black areas of this clip.

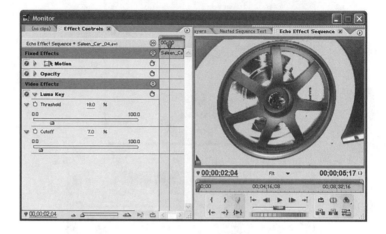

8. Remove the color matte from the sequence by selecting it and pressing Delete. You used it only as a reference and you don't want it showing up in the final project.

9. Switch to the `Nested Sequence Test` sequence by clicking its tab in the Timeline window.

10. Drag `Echo Effect Sequence` from the Project window to Video 2. It will be a different color than other clips (unless you've changed the default color for sequence clips) and it will display as a linked A/V clip despite the fact that the AVI clip has no audio.

By the Way

Unlink and Remove Audio

You don't have to remove the audio portion of the clip, but it's helpful to remove useless items. As a reminder, to delete the audio portion of a linked A/V clip, right-click on the clip, select Unlink Audio and Video, click in the sequence (but not on the clips) to complete the unlink process, click on the audio portion, and press the Delete key.

11. Drag `Saleen_Car_01` to Video 1. This will be the background for the keyed out areas of the `Echo Effect Sequence` clip.

12. Apply Echo to the Echo Effect Sequence nested sequence clip. Finding settings that reveal the clip while still creating an Echo takes some doing. Use Figure 19.13 as a guide. Preview your work.

Try Some Other Effects

Apply just about any video effect to the original clip in Echo Effect Sequence. I like Invert. It reverses color or luminance information, creating a color negative (inverse) effect. Try the HLS (Hue, Lightness, and Saturation) setting. Make adjustments to the Blend With Original slider. Less than 50% or so creates a dramatic color shift. Greater than 50% tends to be a more subtle change.

Any changes you make will show up immediately in the clip in the Nested Sequence Test sequence.

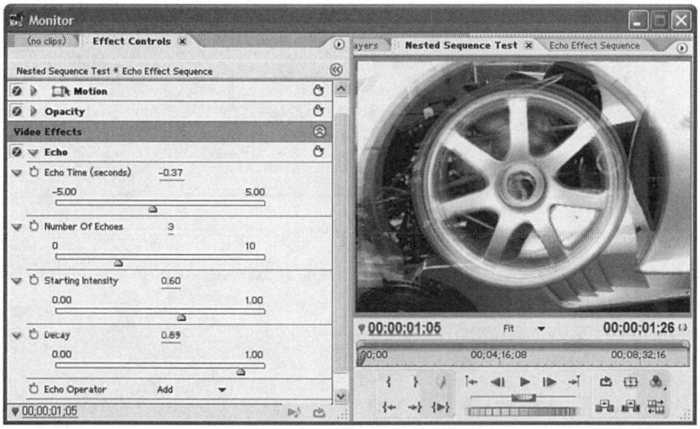

By the Way

FIGURE 19.13
Using a nested sequence means that you can use a key effect before applying the Echo effect.

Using More Than One Transition at a Time

Try it Yourself

Premiere Pro does not permit more than one transition at an edit point. But you can use a nested sequence if you want more. Here's how to do that:

1. Create a new sequence by selecting the Nested Sequence bin in the Project window, selecting File→New→Sequence, naming that sequence Multiple Transitions, and clicking OK.

2. Add two clips to that sequence in the Timeline window. Any two will work, but as long as you have the sample project open, add Saleen_Car_09 and Saleen_Car_10 to Video 1.

▼

3. Apply an obvious transition to them. I suggest Center Split. For my example, I added a white border.

4. Click on the Nested Sequence Test tab in the Timeline window and remove the two clips from the previous task.

5. Drag the `Multiple Transitions` sequence clip from the Project window to Video 1.

6. Move the CTI edit line to the center of the transition.

7. As shown in Figure 19.14 select the Razor tool (keyboard shortcut C) and cut the clip at that point.

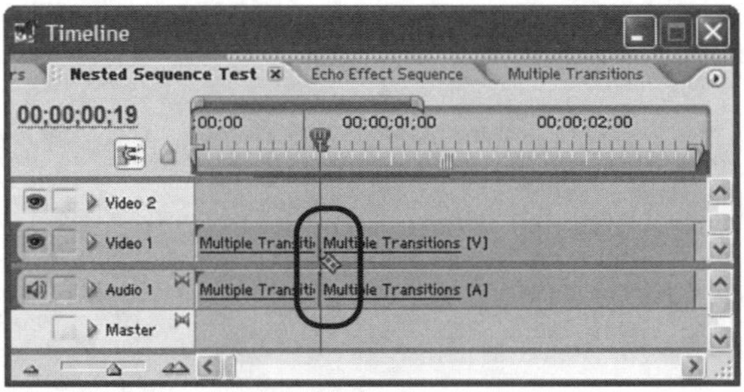

FIGURE 19.14
Create a double transition by razoring a nested sequence clip at the center of an existing transition, and then dropping another transition there.

8. Add an obvious transition here. As shown in Figure 19.15, I went with Center Split again and gave it a blue border. That gave me a very cool looking, split-in-a-split transition.

FIGURE 19.15
Adding the same Center Split transition to an existing Center Split transition leads to this wild effect.

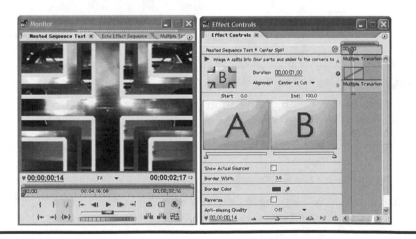

▲

Giving Motion to Two Immovable Effects

Premiere Pro will not allow you to apply any effects, including motion, to either the Texturize or the Track Matte key effects. They effectively switch off all other effects. Nested sequences resolve that.

Applying Motion (and Other Effects) to Texturize

Texturize has many possibilities, but the only way you can take advantage of them is by putting the clip you'll use to create the texture in a nested sequence. After it's there, you can apply any effect to it, including Motion. Here's how to do that:

1. Just as you did in the two previous tasks, make a new sequence. Name it `Texturize`.

2. Drag the `Saleen_logo_Layers` graphic to Video 1 in the `Texturize` sequence.

3. Apply Motion to it. As shown Figure 19.16, I scaled it up to 300% and used keyframes to have it move from the upper left to the lower right.

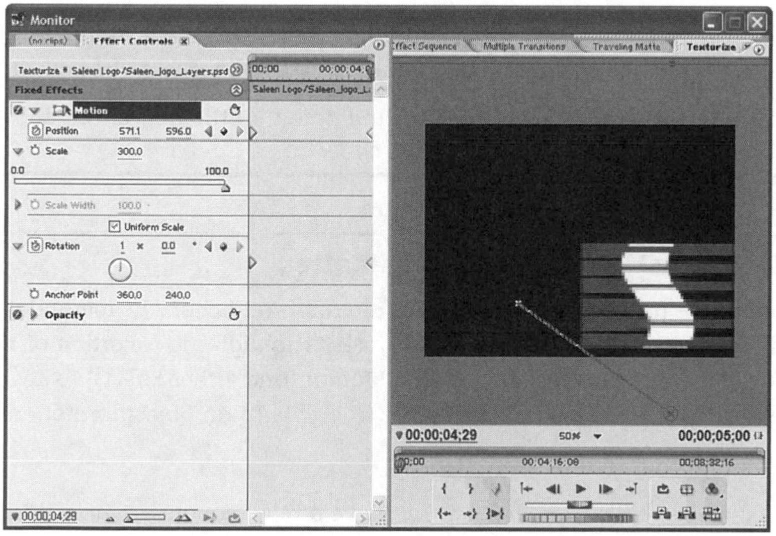

FIGURE 19.16
Apply motion settings to a graphic to prepare to demonstrate another use for a nested sequence.

4. Click the `Nested Sequence Test` tab to open it in the Timeline window. Remove all clips, add `Saleen_Car_08` to Video 1, and the `Texturize` sequence to Video 2.

▼

5. Apply Texturize to the clip in Video 1. As shown in Figure 19.17, set the Texture Layer to Video 2 (the track with the nested sequence), adjust the light direction for maximum texture, and raise the contrast.

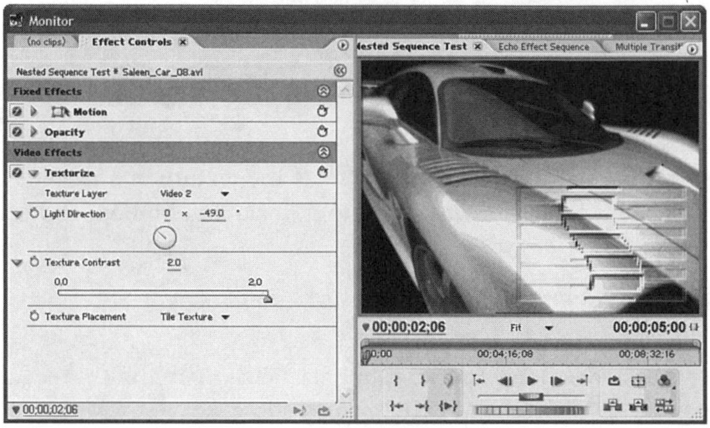

FIGURE 19.17
Give Texturize higher contrast to further emphasize a graphic.

6. Play the clip and note that the logo gives the Saleen car clip a moving, embossed look.

7. Return to the Texturize sequence and apply some other motion or effects to the graphic. Bevel Edges, for instance, will amplify the embossed effect.

8. Return to Nested Sequence Test, and note that the new effects show up immediately in the Saleen_Car_08 clip.

Try it Yourself   Following Action with Traveling Mattes

This method is an exciting way to focus attention on action. Its methodology is sort of a combination of this hour's first task, "Highlighting a Portion of Your Clip," and the previous task, "Applying Motion (and Other Effects) to Texturize." In this case, you'll use a Track Matte key to highlight an object in motion.

To accomplish this, follow these steps:

1. As you've done in previous tasks, make a new sequence. Name this one Traveling Matte.

2. Drag the Saleen_Car_10 clip to Video 1 and extend it to its full length by dragging both edges. The clip is just shy of nine seconds long. Move the CTI edit line to a few seconds into the clip so that you can see the car's headlights emerging from the fog.

3. Open the Adobe Title Designer by selecting File→New→Title.

4. As shown in Figure 19.18, switch on Show Video, create a solid color oval such that it covers the car's headlights. Choose a color other than black so that you can see it on a black background. As long as it's opaque, the color doesn't matter. Save this title: File→Save. Name it Traveling Matte. Saving it automatically places it in your Project window.

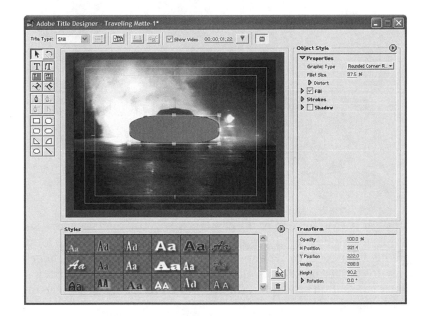

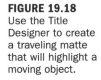

FIGURE 19.18
Use the Title Designer to create a traveling matte that will highlight a moving object.

5. Drag the Traveling Matte clip from the Project window to Video 2 of your Traveling Matte sequence. Extend it to fit completely above the Saleen_Car_10 clip.

6. Now you'll apply some motion characteristics to the Traveling Matte sequence to have it follow the car's headlights. As shown in Figure 19.19, do that by pressing the Home key to place the CTI on the first frame, reducing opacity (so that you can see the headlights), selecting Motion, turning on keyframes for position and scale, and then adjusting the location and the size of the matte to fit the headlights.

7. Move the CTI into the clip about five seconds (just before the car turns to its left) and adjust the Motion Position and Scale parameters again to match the growing headlights. Doing so will automatically add new keyframes for those parameters.

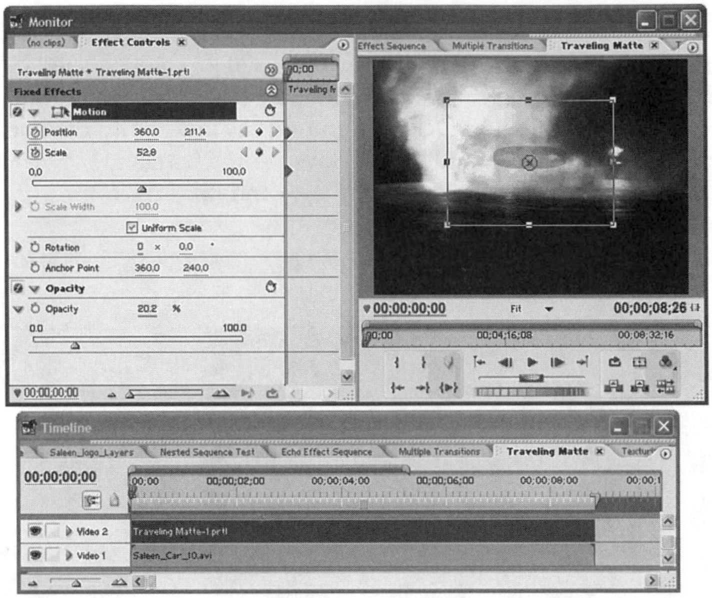

▼

FIGURE 19.19
Apply motion settings to have the oval move and expand as the headlights move through the scene.

8. Move the CTI to the end of the clip (press End and the Left Arrow key). Adjust the Motion settings again. Remember, you can set Scale to something greater than 100% by typing in a value higher than 100 (the slider goes only to 100%). You can fine-tune this parameter setting process by adding other points in the clip, but I think setting three points gives you an idea about how this works.

9. If you want, you can go back to the beginning of the clip and set keyframes for opacity to have the matte gradually reveal itself over the lights (start at 0% opacity and climb to 100% as lights appear through the fog). If not, click the Opacity reset button to put it back to 100% (the oval will switch back to black).

10. Remove the Saleen_Car_10 clip from Video 1 by selecting it and pressing the Delete key (you had it there only as a guide for your motion settings).

11. Open the Nested Sequence Test sequence, remove all clips, add Saleen_Car_10 to Video 1, extend it to its full length, do that again for Video 2 (you can Copy/Paste as well), and drag the Traveling Matte sequence from the Project window to Video 3. Your sequence should look like the one in the Timeline window in Figure 19.20.

▼

12. Right-click the Traveling Matte sequence and uncheck Enable.

13. Select the clip on Video 1, apply the Brightness & Contrast video effect to it and reduce its brightness to about −65%. This darkens the clip while the Track Matte key displays the headlight portions of the clip on Video 2 at full brightness.

14. Select the clip on Video 2 and apply the Track Matte key to it. Set the matte to Video 3 and Composite Using to Matte Alpha. Preview your sequence. It should look something like the video image in Figure 19.20.

FIGURE 19.20
How your Track Matte key sequence should look.

A Slicker Means to the Same End

As is the case with all things Premiere Pro, there is a slightly different, faster (when you get used to it) way to impart motion to a track matte. If your PC is reasonably fast, this approach should work smoothly. Slower PCs might require a little extra effort, but I recommend you try this, fast PC or not.

The principal difference is that you have both the nested sequence and the final project open in the two Monitor window screens and do your work there. It saves you a step and demonstrates yet another cool feature of Premiere Pro: ganging your Source and Program Monitor window screens. It also takes some reverse thinking because you will put your project sequence in the *Source* screen and your original track matte graphic clip in the *Program* screen.

Try it Yourself ▼ — Creating a Traveling Matte Using Both Monitor Screens

In any event, this is a very slick way to apply effects to a nested sequence and see immediate feedback in the final project. The process and setup for this method are very similar to the task you just completed. Here's how you do it:

1. Use the same two sequences: Traveling Matte and Nested Sequence Test.

2. Place only your Traveling Matte graphic clip in the Traveling Matte sequence on Video 1 (there's no need, in this example, to temporarily use a video clip as a reference for motion settings).

3. As before, put the clip you want to apply the Track Matte key to on Video 1 and Video 2 of the Nested Sequence Test sequence. And drag the Traveling Matte sequence clip from the Project window to Video 3 of the Nested Sequence Test sequence.

4. Drag the Nested Sequence Test sequence from the Project window to the Source screen.

5. Open the Traveling Matte sequence and put the CTI edit line on that Traveling Matte clip to display it in the Program screen.

6. As shown in Figure 19.21, gang the Program and Source screens by clicking either the Source or Program wing menu and selecting Gang Source and Program. With that feature enabled, when you move the CTI for one window, the CTI in the other window moves in sync.

FIGURE 19.21
Gang the Monitor Source and Program screens to help simplify the traveling matte creation process.

▼

7. Select the Traveling Matte clip. In the ECW, select Motion and move, scale, or rotate the clip, and add keyframes as needed. On faster machines, you should see all your motion attributes display in the Source window. On slower machines, you might need to drag the CTI a bit to force a screen update.

▲

Obscuring Someone's Identity

This is another use for a traveling matte. You've seen those TV programs that hide the identity of a witness or a suspect by making their faces look like animated mosaics (using black rectangles to cover eyes—or other body parts—is so old school). They typically use a traveling matte combined with an effect such as Crystallize to accomplish that feat.

Take a look at Figure 19.22. Here's how I obscured that person's identity (don't worry; she's neither a witness nor a suspect).

1. I used the Title Designer to create a black oval.

2. Just as you did in the previous task, I put it in motion and adjusted its size to match the motion of the subject.

3. In addition, I applied Fast Blur to it to soften its edges.

4. In a different sequence, I put the video clip on the first two tracks and the traveling matte sequence (making it a nested sequence) on the third.

5. I applied two video effects to the clip on Video 1: Mosaic and then Crystallize.

6. I applied the Track Matte key to the clip on Video 2, set the Matte to Video 3 and set Composite Using to Matte Alpha.

7. Finally, and this is the significant difference between this use of the Track Matte key and the use in the task you just completed, I clicked the Reverse check box. That reverses the alpha channels. What that does is use the clip on Video 2 to obscure the clip on Video 1 with the exception of letting the portion of Video 1 within the track matte oval show through. That means the Mosaic/Crystallize effect shows only within the oval.

A Faster and Easier Alternative

Using Premiere Pro to create a traveling matte and applying motion settings to it can be relatively simple if the motion is easy to follow and generally falls on a straight line. Curved or convoluted paths are a trickier proposition. That's where Adobe After Effects shines. The Professional version of that powerful video production tool has a Motion Tracker that automatically builds a traveling matte path in a matter of moments. I demonstrate that in Hour 22, "Using Photoshop and After Effects to Enhance Your DV Project."

FIGURE 19.22
Obscure someone's identity by using a Track Matte key and a combination of Mosaic and Crystallize.

Fine-tuning Keys Using a Nested Sequence

Keying can be hit or miss. Frequently, you'll be hard-pressed to remove pixels near the edges of the subject you want to key over a background. At other times, **hotspots**—unevenly lit areas of your green/blue screen—will not key out. Creating a nested sequence as a means to apply a key twice can help. It's not a guarantee, but it sometimes can be the difference between unusable and acceptable.

Fine-tune Keys with a Nested Sequence

Try it Yourself

To fine-tune keys with a nested sequence, follow these steps:

1. Open the Nested Sequence Test sequence you worked on in the "Creating a Traveling Matte Using Both Monitor Screens" task earlier this hour and remove all clips.

2. Use a clip from assignment number one back in Hour 17, "Compositing Part 1—Layering and Keying Clips." That called for you to tape a subject in front of a solid—and differently colored—backdrop. Drag that clip to Video 2.

3. Drag any clip that can serve as a background to Video 1.

A Color Matte Can Make Keying Easier

Did you Know?

Instead of a video clip background, consider using a color matte. This gives you a more accurate representation of how well your key is working. As a reminder, to make a color matte, click the New Item button in the Project window, select Color Matte, choose a color, give your matte a descriptive name, and click OK. The matte will appear in your Project window.

---

4. Apply a color-based key to the clip on Video 2. Your pick: Chroma, RGB Difference, Blue/Green Screen, or Non-Red.

5. Use the Eyedropper tool to select the color to key out then adjust the slider(s) as well as you can without impacting the subject. My example in Figure 19.23 has a hotspot that does not key out without creating a transparency in the subject. Click OK.

Try Different Keys or a Matte

Did you Know?

You might try different keys. RGB Difference might work better than Green Screen, depending on how closely your green screen matches true chroma green.

Or create a matte to block out the areas that did not key correctly. For example, you could use the Title Designer, switch on Show Video so that you can see where to place the mask on the screen, and use the Shape tools to build an object or objects to cover up the problem area(s).

---

6. Remove the background clip.

7. In a different sequence, drag the nested sequence you just created to Video 2, drag the background color matte to Video 1, and apply a color-based key to the Nested Sequence clip.

8. Once again, adjust the sliders to suit your needs. As shown in Figure 19.24, I managed to fine-tune the key effect enough to clean up those stray pixels.

Did you Know?

Leave Room for the Eyedropper Tool to Grab a Color

If you carefully adjust the Similarity or other values in the original clip so that almost no unkeyed areas are left, you might not be able to use the Eyedropper tool in the nested sequence clip to select a color to key out. Therefore, go easy on the first attempt.

FIGURE 19.24
Applying the RGB key a second time to a nested sequence cleans up most of the poorly keyed portion of the original key.

Summary

Experienced Premiere Pro users typically have a few editing tricks up their sleeves. Unless you see them at work, you might not come up with them yourself. In this hour, I've explained two of them: highlighting an area of your clip using a matte and a couple video effects, and adding realistic drop shadows to rotating clips.

In addition, I explained several uses for nested sequences, taking you through specific tasks that showed you how to enhance the Echo effect, use multiple transitions at one location, apply motion to the Texturize effect, follow action and obscure someone's identity with a Track Matte key, and fine-tune chroma keys.

Q&A

Q *I used the Track Matte key with a graphic I made using the Title Designer. My purpose was to highlight a portion of a clip by putting that area into a soft focus. But it's in sharp focus and the rest of the clip is blurred. Why?*

A You need to click the Reverse option check box in the Track Matte key's display in the ECW. Normally, when using a graphic with transparent alpha channel regions (almost always the case for graphics created with the Title Designer), the graphic elements of your matte are opaque and everything else is transparent. So, when you chose Matte Alpha for the Matte type, that let the clip on Video 1 show through those alpha channel regions. Selecting Reverse makes the alpha channel regions opaque and the graphic elements transparent, thereby creating the desired effect.

Q *I put a clip in a sequence, nested that sequence into another, and applied some effects. Later, I wanted to nest that sequence in another part of the project but I wanted it to look a bit different. So, I changed the clip's appearance before dragging that sequence to the new location. But now the first nested sequence clip has changed appearance too. What's up?*

A Basically, you defeated the purpose of nested sequences. When you want to use a nested sequence more than once, you have to make any changes to it after you apply it to a new sequence. Any changes you make to the original clip in its sequence ripple through the project to all instances where you added that sequence to a project.

Workshop

Quiz

1. When rotating a clip over another clip, what two effects ensure that Drop Shadow performs realistically? When do you apply Drop Shadow? Above or below those effects in the ECW?

2. For the Track Matte key tasks in this hour, you used graphics with alpha channels. How would using simple graphics that don't have alpha channels be different?

3. In the traveling matte task, you reduced the brightness on the clip in Track 1 to make the highlighted area stand out. How can you do that with the track matte graphic itself?

Quiz Answers

1. Use Drop Shadow with Transform and Camera View to give rotating clips shadows that fall in a same relative direction. Apply Drop Shadow after either of these effects (below them in the ECW).

2. You'd need to keep in mind that white portions of your graphic will be opaque and black will be transparent. Gray areas will have some transparency. And in the ECW, you'd set the Track Matte key's Composite Using parameter to Matte Luma. You can reverse that black/white transparency behavior by clicking the Reverse check box.

3. When you create a graphic in either the Title Designer or a graphics editing program, color the entire graphic gray. (In the Title Designer, you can reduce its opacity and use the Matte Alpha setting or keep the opacity at 100% and use the Matte Luma setting.) Then create a black shape you will use for the highlight. The only caveat here is that if you use Motion or some other effect to reduce the size of the graphic, you'll see that gray area as a rectangle in your clip. The way around that is to make a very large graphic or a smaller highlighted area that you expand to fit the area of the clip you want to highlight. As I've mentioned several times, Premiere Pro has so many options, you can almost always find other ways to accomplish the same tasks.

Exercises

1. Get used to working with nested sequences by creating a quad transition. Apply one transition to a clip. Drop it in a new sequence, add another transition to it, drop that into another sequence, and so on. With each additional transition, lengthen the duration by a second or so. As a means to get a clearer picture of what's going on, choose Transitions that have borders and make the borders thick to further emphasize each transition. When you're done, go back and change the attributes of a couple transitions and see how that affects the final quad transition.

2. Highlight an area of a clip using a track matte. Then try out a number of different video effects' combinations on the clip on Video 1 as a means to alter it and make it stand out. Conversely, try to make it less prominent to allow something else—a graphic, logo, or text—to stand out on it. Switch back and forth between using the Reverse option and not using it.

3. Creating traveling mattes that actually follow action should become part of your standard editing arsenal. They add some real visual interest to your projects. To gain facility with their creation, make a couple. Experiment a

bit. Change the shape of the matte by giving it a soft focus using the Fast Blur effect and add a border. Alter the appearance of the highlighted area using keyframes to fade in that change and fade it out. Try both traveling matte production methods: working on the matte in the sequence and ganging the Monitor window screens.

HOUR 20

Tips, Tricks, and Techniques— Part 2

What You'll Learn in This Hour:

▶ Adjusting color—three color-correcting effects
▶ Working in the Trim window
▶ Four fun editing techniques
▶ Five fast editing tips
▶ Using Timeline window keyboard shortcuts
▶ Checking out several workspace shortcuts and tools
▶ Tips from an Adobe corporate Premiere Pro evangelist

Premiere Pro's depth lends itself to discovery. Experienced editors frequently stumble across undocumented editing tricks that fall outside those described in the printed manual and the online help file that accompany your copy of Premiere Pro.

For this hour's lesson, I've assembled several such tips, tricks, and techniques, including a half-dozen favorites from Adobe's principal corporate Premiere Pro evangelist. They should help you become a faster, more efficient and creative editor.

I also take you on a tour of Premiere Pro's most important new video effect—the Color Corrector—and its two narrower purpose siblings—Broadcast Colors and Color Match. And I show you how to tap the power of another new and very helpful feature: the Trim window.

Adjusting Color—Three Color-Correcting Effects

The addition of the Color Corrector effect to Premiere Pro, along with its more specialized partners, Color Match and Broadcast Colors, is a big deal. They are much more than single, narrow purpose video effects. Rather, taken together, they are a full-featured suite of tools. The Color Corrector even has its own pre-set workspace.

Open a project then open that workspace by selecting Window→Workspace→Color Correction. Your interface should look like Figure 20.1. Those three graphical displays in the Monitor window are called (in clockwise order starting at the upper left) Waveform, Vectorscope, and RGB Parade. The one other available option not displayed in this default view is the YCbCr Parade.

Developer Comment—Two Sequence Views

This tip is from Adobe's Premiere Pro corporate evangelist, Daniel Brown. He provides five more tips in this hour's concluding section.

Using the Reference Monitor (screen) can give you two different views of the same timeline. This was created primarily to let you see a vector scope in one window while you see straight video footage in the other window, but you can have two video sources as well. As described later in the Color Match effect section, if you want to match colors across different parts of the timeline, this is tremendously helpful.

Color Correction Alphabet Soup

Venturing into the color correction arena opens up a whole new can of alphabet soup. In the case of the Reference Monitor display options, *RGB Parade* refers to the red, green, and blue elements used in PC monitor displays. *Y, Cb*, and *Cr* refer to the color mode used by the television industry for digital video. Y is luma and Cb and Cr are the chroma (color) components.

The power and scope of Premiere Pro's Color Corrector, Broadcast Colors, and Color Match effects go way beyond what I can cover in this small section. Entire books are written on color correction. I recommend *Color Correction for Digital Video* by Steve Hullfish and Jaime Fowler. If you become adept at the various color correction features, you can turn those skills into a marketable commodity. Good colorists command substantial salaries.

FIGURE 20.1
Premiere Pro's
Color Correction
workspace puts
several new tools
and displays at
your fingertips.

I don't think of these effects solely as means to *correct* something. They are also color *adjusters*. You can use the Color Corrector to set a mood and Color Match to ensure that a project has a consistent look as you go from one scene to the next. What follows is a basic overview of how they work.

Using the Broadcast Colors Effect

Consumer TV sets cannot handle the same luminance (brightness) as PC monitors. To compensate for that, some video editors apply the Broadcast Colors effect to selected clips or their entire project.

Applying an Effect to More Than One Clip

To apply the Broadcast Colors effect (or any other video effect) to more than one clip or even an entire project, use a nested sequence. Assemble your clips in one sequence and nest it into another sequence where it'll appear as a single clip. Then apply the effect to it.

You might not need to ever do this. Most TV stations have built-in limiters and other electronic gear designed to compensate for luminance problems. But in case you do need to keep your videos within broadcast specifications, give Broadcast Colors a try.

Try Out Broadcast Colors

I applied Broadcast Colors to the clip in Figure 20.2. Here's how to duplicate that process:

1. Opening the Color Correction workspace puts a Reference screen in the Monitor window on the left side (where you're used to seeing the Source screen). Switch to its Waveform view by clicking that screen's wing menu and selecting Waveform.

2. Gang the Reference Screen to the Program screen by clicking the Monitor screen's wing menu and selecting Gang to Program Monitor. That way, when you move the CTI in your clip, the Reference screen will display the selected frame's waveform.

3. Move the CTI somewhere inside your clip and note how the waveform changes. In my case, the vertical shafts of sunlight on the left show up on the left side of the waveform. Even the white blaze on the horse's nose creates a luminance peak.

Luminance Values

Typically, NTSC luminance values should run from 7.5 (dark areas) to 100 (bright areas) IRE (Institute of Radio Engineers—yes, *Radio*) units. Japan's implementation of NTSC allows for darker blacks and it starts at zero IRE units. Most DV typically peaks closer to 120—the maximum possible transmission amplitude. 110 is the default value in the Broadcast Colors effect.

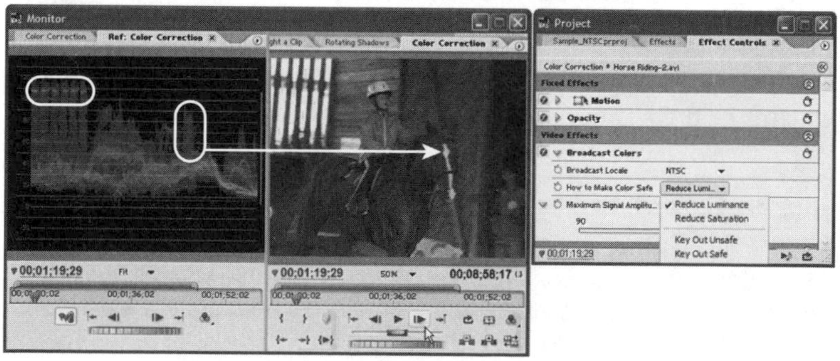

FIGURE 20.2
The Waveform display gives a graphical representation of the luminance values of your video. The Broadcast Colors effect enables you to reduce the maximum luminance as well as to desaturate colors.

4. Apply the Broadcast Colors effect to this clip. As shown in Figure 20.2, you select either PAL or NTSC as well as a few other features. Rather then enumerate them, I suggest you read about them in Premiere Pro's online help file. Select Help→Contents, navigate to Applying Effects and Video Effects, and then select Broadcast Colors.

5. Change the Maximum Signal slider and note that as you drop that amount, the clip takes on a duller cast. Selecting the Reduce Saturation option makes the clip even less colorful.

Creating a Consistent Look with Color Match

This is a great means to avoid the horrible color shifts common to video projects. Even the best lighting technicians cannot ensure that all scenes will have the same color temperature.

Fluorescent lights are notorious for giving off varying hues of green. Incandescent bulbs look orange. Sunlight is blue, and mercury vapor lamps are yellow. Use the Color Match effect to make all these scenes look as if they had the same lighting (that is, if that's the desired outcome).

Testing Color Match

Try it Yourself

Figure 20.3 is the typical setup for the Color Match effect. After it has been arranged, the color match process can become a bit tricky and takes some trial and error. My goal here simply is to get you started:

1. Place the clip you want fix and the one you want to match it to on your sequence.

2. Un-gang the Reference screen so that you can cue up the Master clip independently of the clip needing repair. Do that by opening the Reference screen wing menu and unchecking Gang to Program Monitor.

3. Using that same menu, set the screen display to Composite so that you can see the clip instead of the waveform.

4. Drag the CTI edit line in the Source screen to the frame you want to use as a reference.

5. Select the clip you want to fix, apply Color Match to that clip, and move the CTI in the Program screen or the sequence to the frame with subjects that have colors you can match with the reference clip.

6. Expand the ECW Color Match view. This is where the experimentation begins. Basically, you can match using HSL (Hue, Saturation, and Luminance), RGB (Red, Green, and Blue) or Curves (in this case, simplified versions of complex multi-point defined curves found in the Color Corrector). You use the Eyedropper tools to select reference colors from the Sample frame (the Source screen) and use the Target eyedropper tools to select colors to match for each instance in the clip you want to fix (in the Program screen).

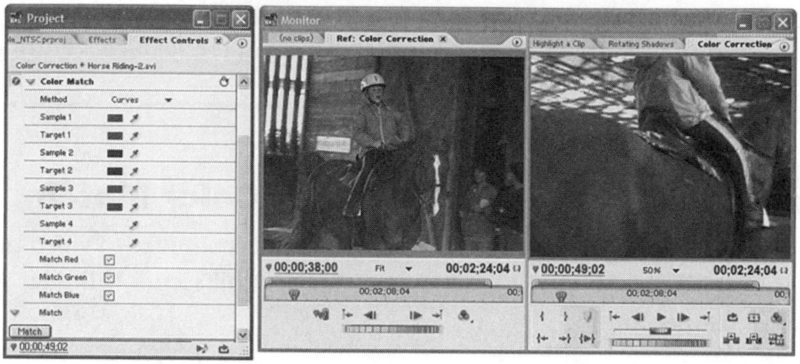

FIGURE 20.3
The Color Match effect enables you to give scenes shot in different lighting conditions a consistent color cast.

A Counterintuitive Color Match?

Sometimes I found that the standard approach to doing Color Match—using the Sample eyedropper to select a color from the master clip and using the Target eyedropper to select a color I want to fix in the off-color clip—didn't work. It might be a bug. But for an unexplained reason, sometimes when using the RGB setting, selecting a *sample* color with the Target eyedropper and choosing the *target* color with the Sample eyedropper yielded excellent results.

Venturing into Color Correction

This is the real workhorse of this trio. It has more than 40 parameters and sub-parameters. I can't begin to cover them all. It introduces concepts such as Pedestal (akin to Brightness), HSL Hue Offsets (Circular tools to adjust colors in shadows, midtones, and highlights), and Curves (graphical displays of red, green, and blue curves with user-added points for more precise control).

For brief explanations of most of the parameters, read Premiere Pro's online help section: Help→Contents, select Applying Effects, Video Effects Included with Premiere Pro, and then select Color Corrector. You apply Color Corrector to a single clip or a nested sequence. Figure 20.4 gives you a taste of its features.

I'll give you a brief rundown of some of the elements displayed in Figure 20.4:

▶ I use a Reference screen to clarify any changes I make. I set it to show the Vectorgraph, Waveform, and RGB Parade displays. As I make changes in the Color Corrector, those displays update in real-time.

▶ Split Screen Preview—This is darned near essential. As you make changes, you can see the before and after in the Program screen.

▶ Black/White Balance—In a normal workflow, these will likely be your first, and perhaps, only adjustments. They work extremely well. Drag each eyedropper in turn to locations in your clip that you determine best represent black, gray, and white. When you're done, even scenes shot under fluorescent lights can match sunlit locales.

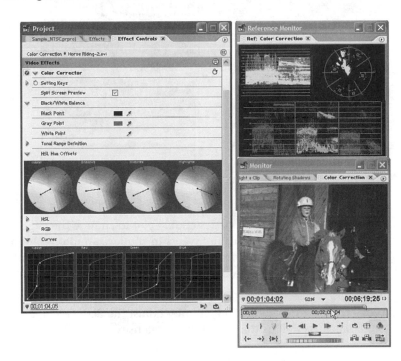

FIGURE 20.4
The Color Corrector is a powerful new tool in Premiere Pro that opens up a wide range of possibilities but takes a real commitment from the user.

To Avoid Instant Color Updating

As you drag the eyedroppers around, the colors in your clip update instantly. In the split screen, that can be good visual feedback, letting you know how things will look depending on your selections. But sometimes that can be distracting. If you want to turn off that constant color shifting, hold down the Shift key while dragging the Eyedropper tool around.

▶ Brightness, Contrast, and Gamma—These might be the other most used controls. You can find them under the HSL and RGB sections.

▶ Tonal Range Definition—This group of parameters makes it possible for you to define shadow and highlight zones using sliders and a visual representation of those regions. As shown in Figure 20.5, switch on the Tonal Range Definition Preview. The Program screen displays black for shadows, white for highlights, and gray for midtones. As you move the sliders, those zones expand or contract accordingly. This comes in handy when working the HSL Hue Offsets (next point).

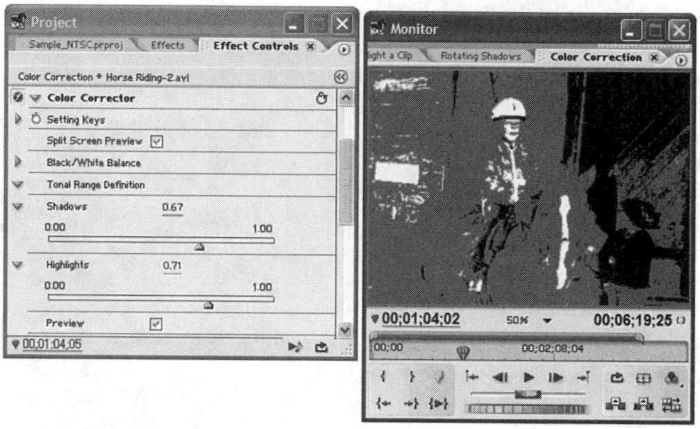

FIGURE 20.5
With the Tonal Range Definition Preview on, it's a simple matter to define the highlight and shadow regions of your clip.

- ▶ HSL Hue Offsets—These color circles enable you to change the clip's overall color value in addition to adjusting colors in shadows, midtones, and highlights. To make the adjustments, click on a color wheel's center point and drag in the direction of the desired color. The longer the line, the greater the color intensity.

- ▶ Curves—These enable you to individually adjust the Red, Green, and Blue color channels as well as the overall color intensity.

I'm barely tapping the Color Corrector's potential. To go beyond this introduction, I suggest that you work with it. Start simple by using Black/White Balance to fix improperly lighted or color balanced scenes. Then create a visual mood for a project. Give your clips a warmer, richer look by increasing the red values and contrast. Or attempt to duplicate the Saleen clips' green/blue cast.

Working in the Trim Window

The Trim window is yet another very helpful addition to Premiere Pro. It enables you to fine-tune edits in a sequence, performing either rolling or ripple edits with great precision and immediate visual feedback.

Rolling and Rippling Reminder

As a reminder, rolling edits do not change the length of your project. They take place at an edit point between two clips: shortening one and lengthening the other. Ripple edits do change the length of your project. You apply them to only one clip. Then the rest of the project slides over to accommodate the change.

By the Way

Open the Trim window by clicking the Trim button in the lower-right corner of the Monitor window Program screen (keyboard shortcut—Ctrl+T). I've circled it in Figure 20.6.

Select a Target Track

When you attempt to open the Trim window, you might receive this error message: `Target track must not be empty.` To open the Trim window, you need to select a track by clicking on its name. And that track has to have at least a clip in it.

Watch Out!

FIGURE 20.6
Open the Trim window by clicking the highlighted Trim button in the Monitor window.

Take a look at the Trim window in Figures 20.7 and 20.8. I'll give you two views as a means to explain what it can do. The first will go over some basic clip navigation and rolling edits. The second will display ripple edits.

FIGURE 20.7
The Trim window's
clip navigation and
rolling edit tools.

When you open the Trim window, the CTI edit line jumps to the nearest edit point. The two Trim window screens display the last frame of the clip to the left of the edit point and the first frame of the clip to the right.

To move to other edit points, use the clip navigation buttons (annotated in Figure 20.7) or the keyboard shortcuts: Page Down for the next edit, Page Up for the previous edit.

Trim Window Rolling Edits

As shown in Figure 20.7 earlier, there are five ways to perform a rolling edit:

1. Move your cursor between the two clip windows. It turns into a Rolling Edit tool. Simply drag it left or right and note the real-time changes in the two screens.

2. Change the center time code by dragging it or typing in a new value.

3. Shift the edit point one or five frames left or right by clicking on the associated number.

4. Type in the number of frames you want to shift the edit point in the center boxed number. Use a negative number to shift left.

5. Drag the center jog disk left or right.

Trim Window Ripple Edits

Take a look at Figure 20.8. There are also five ways to make ripple edits:

1. Move your cursor next to or on either clip. It turns into a Ripple Edit tool. Drag it to the left or right accordingly and note the changing out- or in-point for that clip.

2. Change the left or right clip's time code by dragging it or typing in a new value.

3. Drag the in- or outpoint bracket on either clip's mini-timeline.

4. Change the left or right time code shift by dragging it or typing in a new value.

5. Use the left or right jog disk to make the edit.

After you've made your edit, you can preview it in the Trim window. Simply use the Play button. Clicking the Loop button and then the Play button will loop the edit.

Ripple Edit Tools

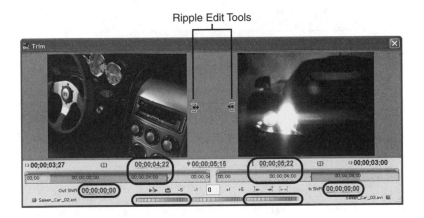

FIGURE 20.8
The Trim window also offers five means to make ripple edits.

Four Fun Editing Techniques

There's no real way to categorize these techniques. They are just some of the little editing tidbits one picks up over the years. I'll show you how to fix a slanted scene, produce true mirrored effects, use the Razor tool with effects, and create animated text.

Fixing a Slanted Scene

Even the best-planned productions can go awry. One common mistake is a tripod that wasn't quite level or the perspective in a scene looks cockeyed. Fortunately, a simple fix is available. Use the Motion effect to set things right. As shown in Figure 20.9, switch on the Motion effect for that clip, use rotation to align it properly, and then scale it up just enough to fill the gaps in the corners created by the rotation.

FIGURE 20.9
Use the Motion effect's Rotation and Scale parameters to fix an askew scene (I added the line for emphasis).

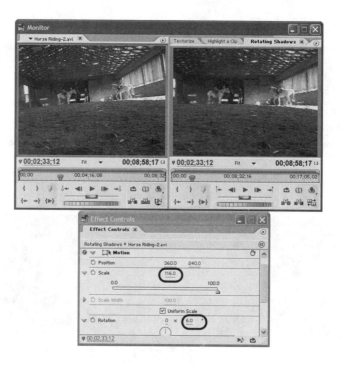

Creating Real Animated Mirrored Effects

Premiere Pro has a Mirror video effect. So, why bother trying some other way to create a mirrored effect? Because the methods I'm about to describe use an entire clip, whereas the Mirror effect divides a clip along a user-defined line and creates a reflection of that *portion* of the clip. In addition, using the upcoming mirror methods enable you to add mirrored animation to a graphic.

First, try a simple approach. Take a look at Figure 20.10. Here's how to create that:

1. Place the same clip on Video 1 and Video 2.

2. Apply Basic 3D to one of the clips (I chose the one on Video 2) and set its Swivel parameter to 180 degrees (minus or plus—it doesn't matter). That creates a reverse—mirrored—image.

3. Use Motion's Scale parameter on both clips to shrink them to 50%.

4. Use Motion's Position parameter to place the two clips side by side, creating a true mirrored effect using the entire (albeit smaller) clip.

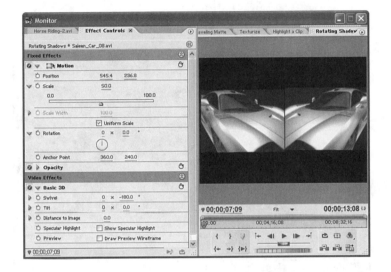

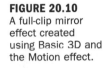

FIGURE 20.10
A full-clip mirror effect created using Basic 3D and the Motion effect.

Now for the trickier mirrored animation effect that displays two graphics spinning in opposite directions. Take a look at Figure 20.11. Here's how I set it up:

1. Place a clip to use as a background on Video 1.

2. Place the graphic you want to use above that clip on Video 2 and Video 3.

Centered Graphics Are Easier

By the Way

I pulled out a chestnut for this demo: the ubiquitous Veloman graphic from the Premiere 6 sample media assets. I chose this because the Veloman graphic is centered in its frame, thereby allowing me to rotate it without having to make some tricky adjustments.

If I had used the Saleen Logo (it's slightly above the frame's center point), for instance, I'd need to apply the Transform effect and carefully adjust that graphic's anchor point and position to get that logo to rotate on its center. If that anchor point were slightly off-center, the graphic would revolve around that anchor point like a ball on a string.

3. Use Motion's Position parameter to place the graphics in the upper- and lower-right corners.

4. As shown in Figure 20.11, I set Basic 3D's Tilt parameter to 180 degrees to flip the bottom graphic upside down, creating a mirror image of the graphic above it.

5. I applied keyframes and Rotation to both clips, giving one clip a positive spin and the other an equal but negative rotation value. Now they spin in opposite directions, further reinforcing their mirrored appearance.

6. You can take this approach one step further. Use keyframes and the Position parameter to roll the graphics across the screen.

FIGURE 20.11
Use Motion's Rotation parameter to rotate the graphics in opposite directions.

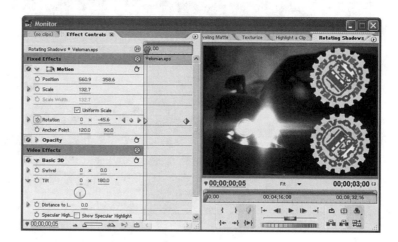

Using the Razor Tool with Effects

Keyframes allow smooth changes to an effect. To create sudden shifts or to start an effect mid-clip, use the Razor tool to slice a clip into smaller chunks and apply different effects or effect parameters to each segment. Here are some uses:

Apply the same effect to each clip chunk and give each instance drastically different characteristics. Use this method to make quick shifts in color or quick changes from inverted images back to positive. As I demonstrated in Hour 9, "Advanced Editing Techniques and Workspace Tools," the same razor-sliced clip approach works to make abrupt *or* smooth transitions from a full-motion clip to fast, slow, or reverse motion.

Slicing Leaves No Visible Wounds

Such slices do not leave any gaps in the clip, nor are they visible to viewers. With no effects applied, it appears the sliced clip is actually intact.

Abrupt changes work well when you want to draw attention to movement. Consider a gymnast's floor exercise. Just before a twisting flip, slice the clip and place slow motion on the flip. Or, you could gradually slow down a horse race photo finish. As the thoroughbreds pound down the straightaway, make two or three razor slices, gradually slowing the motion in each segment.

No Video Effect Bypass

Unlike audio effects, Premiere Pro video effects do not have a keyframable bypass option. That is, you cannot turn on or turn off an effect at selected points in a clip. In addition, most effects start at least partially on, so you can't apply them with a zero-parameter state and then use keyframes to switch on a parameter. Thus, the need to use the Razor tool.

Creating Animated Text

Another use for the Motion effect is to give text some zest. For this example, I used the Title Designer to create some large font text and placed that in a rounded rectangle backdrop.

Create Title Elements in Any Order

Whether you make the background graphic first or last is not critical. To place it behind the text, select Title, Arrange, Send to Back (from the main menu bar).

Place your text on Video 2 and place a background on Video 1. I chose a color matte. As shown in Figure 20.12, I applied the Motion effect's Rotation and Scale parameters to the title. In this case, I chose to duplicate that old newsreel effect of a spinning title appearing from a great distance, zooming to full screen (or beyond), and then zooming off the page. I also use the Camera View effect to spin the text like a top.

FIGURE 20.12
Apply motion set-
tings to your text
for a dramatic
effect.

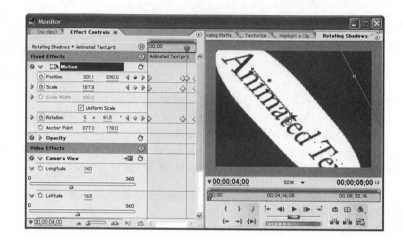

Five Fast Editing Tips

In this section, I give you a quick run-through of some easy and effective editing
ideas on setting keyframes, tinting clips, working with still images, fixing noisy
video, and using multiple transparencies.

Set Your Ending Keyframe First

When using keyframes with effects, your workflow will go more smoothly if you
think in terms of how you want the effect to end (it doesn't have to be the clip's
last frame). Move the CTI edit line to that point (either in the ECW mini-timeline
window or in your sequence) and switch on keyframes by clicking the little stopwatch icon in the Effect Controls window. Now set that effect's ending condition.
Move the CTI to where you want the effect to start and work your way toward
that concluding keyframe.

Using Title Designer for Tinting

Premiere Pro's Tint video effect does a fine job of creating a two-tone tint. But consider using Premiere Pro's Title Designer to take a different, single or massively
multihued, approach.

Create a Unique Tint with the Title Designer

Try it Yourself

The process is routine. Choosing which color scheme works for you is what will take some time. Follow these steps:

1. As I've illustrated in Figure 20.13, open the Title Designer and create a rectangle that goes well to the edges of the Title window to ensure that it entirely covers a clip.

2. Create a color matte. Open Fill and select a fill type. Solid gives you a single color tint, whereas 4 Color Gradient creates a rainbow effect. Couple the latter with a twisting, contorted video effect (I used the Twirl Video Effect) and it's the 1960s all over again. Click the Show Video check box to see how your clip works with this gradient.

3. Adjust the Opacity settings for each color stop to customize your matte further. Or, you can save this color rectangle at full 100% opacity and use the Opacity effect to change its overall transparency later.

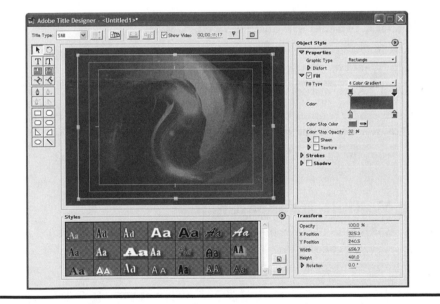

FIGURE 20.13
Use Premiere Pro's Title Designer to create color mattes to tint your clips.

Working with Still Images

As I mentioned in Hour 11, "Putting Video and Still Clips in Motion," Premiere Pro's Motion effect is a really effective way to make a static shot more interesting. Here are a few tips to consider when working with still images:

▶ If you plan to zoom or pan, set your scanner resolution at something greater than the standard 72 dpi (dots per inch) TV screen display. That way, when you zoom in, the image will remain crisp.

▶ Scan some images twice. Use one for your wide shot and the other for a tight shot. You can place them side-by-side on the timeline and do a cross-dissolve between them. Use motion settings to zoom in on each, but add a pause at the beginning on the tight shot to let the dissolve finish before starting the zoom.

▶ Consider putting a frame around your image. The easy way is to use the Clip video effect, drag in the edges a bit, and give the border a color. If you don't want to cut off the edges, place a color matte on the track below the clip and use the Motion effect Scale parameter to shrink the clip slightly. You can create a series of clips like this on a sequence, nest that sequence in another sequence, cut it up into each individual image, stack them on video tracks, and create a pictures-in-a picture effect.

Reducing Noise in Low-Light Clips

Video shot in low-light conditions typically looks noisy. There are a few tricks you can use to try and fix that problem:

▶ Adjust the contrast and brightness.

▶ Use the slider controls below the histogram in the Levels video effect to increase shadows and highlights.

▶ Try using the Color Balance video effect to boost red values a bit.

Using Multiple Transparencies

In previous versions of Premiere, you could apply only one type of transparency to a clip. Now you can stack multiple transparency effects. This is a slick way to create a transparent alpha channel in an otherwise opaque video clip.

Using a video clip from your Keying Effects exercises, apply a color key effect to it to make part of the clip transparent, apply the Alpha Adjust video effect to it, and then invert the alpha channel. That will make the otherwise opaque portion of your clip become transparent.

Timeline Window Keyboard Shortcuts

Premiere Pro has more keyboard shortcuts than you can use, much less memorize. And you can create dozens more while customizing existing ones. To get an idea of just how vast the shortcut opportunities are, select Edit→Keyboard Customization. That will open the dialog box shown in Figure 20.14.

FIGURE 20.14
The Keyboard Customization dialog box enables you to create shortcuts for just about any function in Premiere Pro.

Note that the default view listing reflects the main menu options. That is, File, Edit, Project, and so on. You can open each of those lists and find commands that match virtually everything available in the main menu.

Many mimic standard Windows shortcuts: Save = Ctrl+S, Copy = Ctrl+C, and Undo = Ctrl+Z. Some take far too much effort. For instance, when in the Monitor window Source screen, you frequently want to target a track for an overlay or insert edit. The keyboard "shortcut" to target the track *above* the current targeted track is Ctrl+Shift+=. It's a heck of lot easier simply to click on the targeted track's name.

That said, there are about a dozen shortcuts I use all the time. To see a bunch of them, as shown in Figure 20.15, click the Keyboard Customization drop-down list and select Tools.

Note that all the Tools shortcuts are single letters. The reason is obvious. You'll use most of them frequently. At the very least, Selection (V), Ripple Edit (B), Rolling Edit (N), and Razor (C) should be ingrained in your brain. In case you need reinforcement, roll your cursor over each icon in the Tools palette and Premiere Pro's tooltips will pop up, noting each tool's keyboard shortcut.

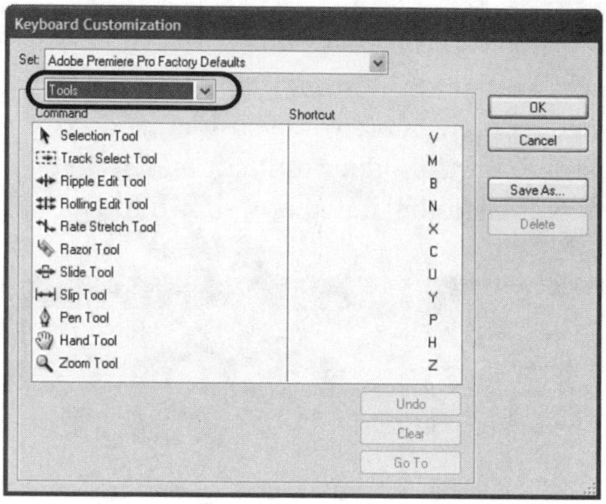

FIGURE 20.15
The Tools keyboard shortcuts are all single letters.

Editing Keyboard Shortcuts

Feel free to change these shortcuts. Simply click on the existing shortcut letter or keystroke-combination (or the blank space next to a command that doesn't have an assigned shortcut) to highlight it, click again, and then type in your customized shortcut. But be aware that other Premiere Pro functions have shortcuts and your new one might match an existing one. As shown in Figure 20.16, if that's the case, Premiere Pro lets you know and gives you a chance to opt out.

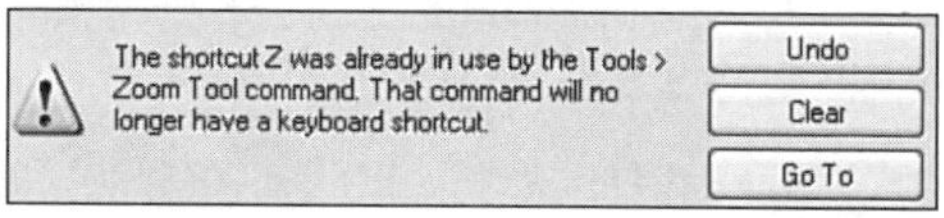

Watch Out!

FIGURE 20.16
Changing a short-cut frequently means stealing an existing shortcut. Premiere Pro warns you and lets you click Undo if you want to rethink that change.

Timeline Window Shortcuts

Most of your work takes place in the Timeline window. In no time at all, the following shortcuts will become second nature to you:

The backslash (\) key—This is my most frequently used keyboard shortcut. Pressing the backslash key resizes the timeline to display your entire project. It's a great way to get a handle on where you are in the workflow.

Did you
Know?

Slash Confusion

By the way, don't confuse the backslash (\) with the forward slash (/). Previous versions of Premiere used the forward slash to delete some clips. In Premiere Pro's default collection of keyboard shortcuts, the forward slash key is unassigned. You might want to use it as one of your customized shortcuts.

Playback Controls—The J, K, and L keys are great shortcuts. Normally, when working in the timeline, you play your project by pressing the spacebar. That's fine, but J, K, and L give you much more control.

The J key plays your project in reverse, the K key stops playback (as does pressing the spacebar), and the L key plays your project forward. What makes these shortcuts truly great is that pressing J or L two or three times incrementally speeds up playback.

The Home and End keys—When you're in the timeline window and don't have a clip selected, pressing the Home key places the edit line at the first frame of your project. Pressing End instantly moves the cursor to the last frame. Alternately, if you have a clip selected, Home and End move to the beginning and end of that clip, respectively.

Add Marker—While you're playing the timeline, pressing the **asterisk (*)** key on the numeric keypad (*not* Shift+8) adds a marker to the timeline. If you created a music video in Hour 13, "Editing Audio," you used the asterisk key. It marks in-points on the timeline for each clip from a storyboard. I'll cover markers in more detail when we discuss exporting your project to a DVD or for use on the Internet.

Snap-to-Edges—If Snap-to-Edges is not on (if the little two-pronged icon in the upper-left corner of the timeline window is not highlighted), pressing the **S key**, even while dragging a clip, switches it on.

CTI Does Not Snap

The CTI does not snap to items. Items snap to it. The reason: If the CTI did snap to edit points, scrubbing the sequence would become a jumpy mess.

By the
Way

Work Area Bar End Points—AltT+[and Alt+] set the work area bar ends. I've highlighted the work area bar in Figure 20.17. If you want to render a part of your project (you might do that to smooth playback of a complex section), you need to set the beginning and end of that section. Pressing Alt+[sets the beginning to wherever the CTI edit line is. Alt+] sets the end.

Note: Double-clicking the work area bar sets the bar ends to the visible area of the sequence. You can simply drag the ends of the bar to those points as well.

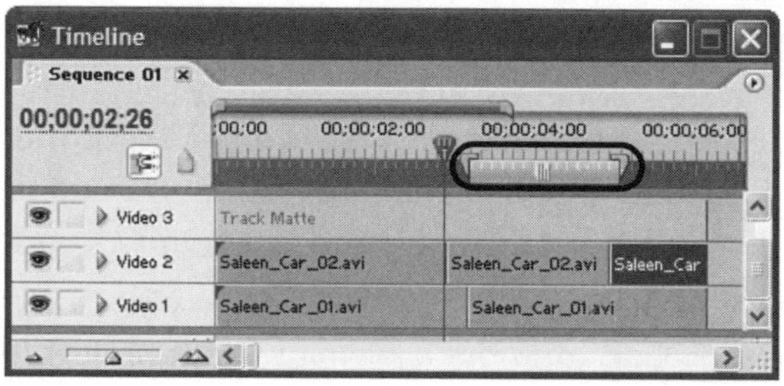

FIGURE 20.17
Use Alt+[and Alt+]
to set the begin-
ning and end
points of the work
area bar.

Temporarily Unlink Audio and Video—Press the Alt key as you click on the end of the audio or video portion of a linked clip and you can drag that end to make a J or an L edit. This saves the right-click/unlinking process and, if you drag the ends and not the entire segment, you won't make the audio and video get out of sync.

Move to the in or out of a selected clip—Use the Page Up key to jump to the previous edit or the Page Down key to jump to the next edit (the beginning of the next clip or the end of the current clip). This applies to all clips on all tracks. So, if you have many clips with outpoints that don't line up, this will move through them one at a time.

Jump to a specific time code—Use the numeric keypad (number lock needs to be switched on) to enter a time code and press Enter. If you use a whole number, Premiere Pro divides that by your project's frames per second, and then by 60, and so on down the line to make minutes, seconds, and so forth. If you type in numbers separated by periods (using the keypad's decimal key), Premiere Pro will consider them as hours:minutes:seconds:frames.

Entering a + (plus sign) and then numbers from the numeric keypad jumps forward the entered amount. Entering a – (minus sign) and then numbers from the numeric keypad jumps backward the entered amount.

Developer Comment—Unassignable Keys

The +/− keys in the keypad area are unassignable as shortcut keys by design. These keys and all numeric keypad keys (0–9) need to be unassignable to guarantee that you can reliably enter time code values (or time code deltas using the +/− prior to the time code value) when the sequence has focus (when it's active). As you enter new time code values via the keypad while the timeline window has focus, you'll see your numeric values display in the CTI Position time code control in the top-left corner of the timeline window.

By the Way

Checking Out Several Workspace Shortcuts and Tools

Although much of your work takes place in the timeline window, you'll venture to other user interface locations. Here are a few more shortcuts and nifty tools that I think will make your work go faster and more smoothly.

Hide/Show palettes—A great way to quickly free up desktop space or access a palette is the Tab key. Use it to display or conceal floating windows—the Tools, Info, and History palettes. For this to work, you need to have had the palettes open at some time and used the Tab key to hide them. Closing a palette by clicking the little X in the upper-right corner disables the Tab shortcut for that palette.

Horizontal Tools palette—As long as you're cleaning up the user interface, flip the Tools palette to a horizontal view by right-clicking an empty space around the tools and selecting Arrange Horizontal.

Snap to keyframes in the ECW—This is a very slick tool. Hold down the Shift key as you move the CTI in the Effect Controls window and it'll snap to any keyframes you've applied.

Open sequences in the Source screen—This is a very nifty way to trim a nested sequence. Hold down the Ctrl key as you double-click a sequence or collection of sequences and it (or they) will open in the Monitor window Source screen. This is a great way to trim a sequence before nesting it in another sequence.

Marquee selection—In previous versions of Premiere, a separate tool—Range Select—was required to select more than one clip in a sequence—

what was known as a *marquee selection*. One of the design goals of the Premiere Pro team was to reduce the number of tools so that editors could perform the most common editing tasks with the Selection tool (shortcut V). To select more than one contiguous clip on single or multiple tracks, use the Selection tool to click and drag from an empty area in the sequence and create a bounding box around the clips. If there is no empty space visible, use the vertical scrollbars on the right side of the timeline window.

Import folders—Instead of importing a file or collection of files, Premiere Pro now enables you to import an entire folder. If you've used folders to organize your media assets, this is a nice little time saver. When you launch the Import dialog box (File→Import), you'll see an Import Folder button in the lower-right corner. Selecting a folder and then clicking that button creates a bin in the Project window with the exact folder name and imports the associated files.

Program screen draft mode—If you open the wing menu in the upper-right corner of the Monitor window, you'll note three related options: Highest Quality, Draft Quality, and Automatic Quality. These refer to the playback display quality in the Program screen. Draft mode displays to the desktop at 1/4 resolution, whether or not you have rendered. If you use Automatic resolution, rendered material is displayed at full resolution and unrendered material is displayed at 1/4 resolution. In High resolution, everything is rendered at full resolution, rendered or not.

Staying centered while zooming—Note that when zooming in on a sequence, Premiere Pro always attempts to center the CTI edit line. This is a welcome addition to Premiere Pro. In previous versions, Premiere ignored the position of the playhead and attempted to zoom into different areas forcing you to find the playhead.

Tips from an Adobe Corporate Premiere Pro Evangelist

From database integration for AT&T to digital image retouching and graphic design for advertisements in *Newsweek* and *Time*, Daniel Brown has balanced a passion for right- and left-brain abilities. Daniel formed the Web development team at Metagraphics in Palo Alto, California, (now Artmachine.com) with clients such as Apple, Netscape, Sun, Silicon Graphics, and Hewlett-Packard.

Daniel Brown, Sr. Evangelist, DV/Motion Graphics, Adobe Systems, Inc.

In 1998, Daniel joined Adobe systems in the role of "evangelist," lending a hand in product development, marketing, interface design, and customer education. He is a frequent speaker at industry events worldwide and has taught classes at Santa Fe Digital Workshops, Anderson Ranch in Aspen, Colorado, and the Pacific Imaging Center in Makawao, Hawaii. Daniel currently handles Adobe After Effects, Adobe Premiere, and Adobe LiveMotion.

Here are five of Brown's favorite Premiere tips:

Title Designer External Monitor Preview—Take a look at Figure 20.18. Clicking the circled button will display the Title Designer window in any video device attached to your PC. Many times text looks different on a TV as compared to your PC's monitor, so this can be very helpful.

This is a vast improvement over previous versions of Premiere. Before, you had to click after every editing change. In Premiere 6.5, the Preview option was simply a "send frame to firewire" command. Hence you couldn't design in real-time on an external monitor. Now, when the check box is on, you see the results of your edits all the time.

Using the Project-Archive folder—If you accidentally erase or completely mess up a project file, don't panic. Every time you save a project, Premiere Pro saves over the file you're currently working on, but it will also save a copy of the previous version in its Auto-Save folder. Depending on the installation, it might be in your Documents folder or the folder that holds the actual application.

FIGURE 20.18
Use the Send
Frame to External
Monitor button to
view your work in
real-time on any TV
or monitor connect-
ed to your PC.

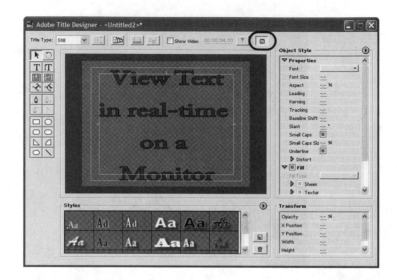

Project files are tiny compared to video files, and they're worth any extra disk
space they occupy. To specify how many versions of a single project Premiere Pro
will archive, select Edit→Preferences—Auto Save to open the dialog box shown in
Figure 20.19.

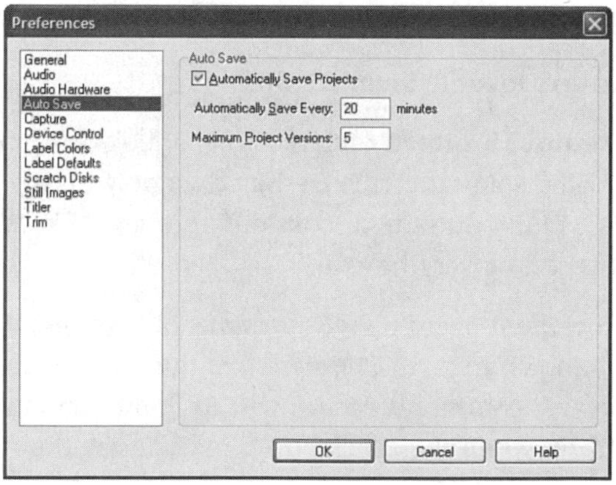

FIGURE 20.19
Use this dialog box
to set how many
versions of your
project Premiere
Pro will archive.

To restore an archived project, select File→Open and then navigate to the Project-
Archive folder and select a project.

Adding multiple clips to the Source screen—You can select multiple clips in the Project window, drag them to the Source window, and, as illustrated in Figure 20.20, choose from among them in the drop-down menu. To clear the active clip from the Source window drop-down menu, press Crtl+Backspace. This will delete the currently visible clip and move the others up the list.

FIGURE 20.20
Drag several clips to the Monitor window Source screen and then access them using this drop-down list.

Reuse clips from another project—In previous versions of Premiere, if you wanted to use the same collection of clips in another project, you could export a Project window's bin data to a text file. That's no longer the case.

Now, rather than exporting what you want, you simply import the other Premiere Pro project. This brings in all clips, online or offline, and imports the timeline as a sequence within the new project.

This is a great way to merge Premiere 6.5 projects with Premiere Pro projects. But I recommend converting the older projects to Premiere Pro first, and then importing them into one another.

Using a master clip—Double-clicking a trimmed clip in the timeline will open the original, full-length clip in the Monitor window Source screen with the current clip's in- and outpoints displayed. Using the Source screen, you can shift those edit markers to create new in- and outpoints and drag that trimmed segment from the Source screen to a different spot in the timeline.

This is a very easy way to pull more than one segment from a master clip. One other tip within a tip: If the in- and outpoints fall off the edges of the Source screen's mini-timeline, drag the end of the work area bar (highlighted in Figure 20.21) to zoom out and get the full clip-width view.

Summary

There's a lot more to Premiere Pro than you might expect. Software this deep is bound to foster plenty of undocumented or thinly referenced functionality. In this hour, I presented some editing tips and techniques running the gamut from fixing slanted scenes to using the Razor tool to make sudden effect changes.

Premiere Pro features dozens of customizable keyboard shortcuts. I listed my favorites. They likely will become second nature to you. You might also come to rely on the Trim window. It's a great way to fine-tune edits.

New to Premiere Pro is the Color Corrector. It and its two narrower purpose partner effects—Broadcast Colors and Color Match—bring a whole new level of quality and professionalism to this nonlinear editor.

Q&A

Q *When using Color Match, I selected the Reference Monitor but only those scopes showed up in the Source screen. How do I see my clip?*

A First, double-click on your clip to put it in the Source screen, and then open the Source screen's wing menu and select Composite. Doing so will display your clip. That wing menu is also where you can gang the Source screen to the Program screen when using the Waveform display with the Broadcast Colors effect.

Q *I tried using the Color Corrector's Black/White Balance features. When I dragged the Eyedropper tool into the Program screen, the colors in that clip shifted around wildly. What was going on?*

A The Color Corrector effect, by default, is always on. So, when you move the Black Point eyedropper around a scene, for instance, the effect thinks you're selecting that particular color as representative of black in the clip. It then immediately changes your clip colors to show that. Turn the effect off by holding down the Shift key as you move the eyedropper around. Or, select Split Screen Preview and opt to use Shift or not, depending on your needs.

Workshop

Quiz

1. You want to trim several edits in your project without changing its length. What is the best way to go about that?

2. What keyboard shortcuts enable you to rewind, stop, and play your project?

3. Why don't you want to use the Mirror video effect to create a split screen with mirrored animated action?

Quiz Answers

1. Use the Trim window and its various Rolling Edit tools. It's a simple matter to jump from edit to edit in the Trim window, so there's no need to move back and forth between it and the timeline window.

2. J, K, and L. Pressing J or L more than once speeds up the reverse and forward speeds. K stops playback.

3. Mirror is a wonderful video effect. It's easy to use and creates a perfect reflection, but it slices your clip and reflects only a portion of it. When using a graphic, unless it's entirely on one side of the screen, Mirror will chop it along a straight line. Using the Motion effect to make a mirror effect means that you can put an *entire* clip on *both* sides of the screen to create a true full-clip reflection.

Exercises

1. Create some tints using the Title Designer. There are so many possibilities, especially when using the various gradients. You can create partial screen tints and layer them to create even wilder effects.

2. Really try out the Color Match and Color Corrector effects. They are so powerful and fully featured that the only way you'll begin to discover all that they can do is to experiment with them.

3. Create a mirrored animation using a diagonal dividing line. Use a graphic with an alpha channel and use the Motion effect's Position parameter to move the graphic following the diagonal line from the upper-left corner to the lower-right corner. You'll need to think through the start- and endpoints a bit more than when the graphic moved horizontally, but otherwise this should be fairly routine.

HOUR 21

Third-Party Products

What You'll Learn in This Hour:

▶ Exciting effect and transition plug-ins
▶ Innovative graphics—Editor's Toolkit from Digital Juice
▶ High-definition video—Cineform's Aspect HD
▶ Multiple-camera editing with Multicam
▶ Creating multimedia movies with CyberCam
▶ Speeding up editing with Contour Design's Shuttle Pro

Premiere Pro is not an entity unto itself. Adobe gives third-party developers access to its internal code—its API or application programmer interface—through a freely available Software Development Kit (SDK). Using it, independent programmers can create effects, transitions, and other tools that work hand-in-hand with Premiere Pro.

In this hour, I give you an overview of the wide variety of exciting and powerful third-party products that complement Premiere Pro. I present collections of plug-ins—cool video effects and transitions—as well as standalone software and one hardware device that work in concert with Premiere Pro.

Exciting Effect and Transition Plug-ins

Topping the list of third-party products are several collections of effect and transition plug-ins. Premiere Pro already has dozens of effects and transitions, but I think you'll be pleasantly surprised at how many great-looking products are available from other developers.

Red Giant—Movie Looks

Your first encounter with Premiere Pro third-party plug-in video effects will likely be when you register Premiere Pro. Adobe sometimes offers registration incentives for its products. In the case of Premiere Pro, registering gives you the opportunity to download a plug-in video effect (with 10 presets) from Red Giant called *Movie Looks*.

Installation is easy. Simply unzip the downloaded file (`movielooks1_0.zip`) and double-click its EXE file. That install adds a subfolder to Premiere Pro's plug-ins folder and adds a new bin called Magic Bullet to the Video Effects palette in the Project window.

Open the Magic Bullet bin and drag its one effect—Movie Looks—to a clip or the ECW. Figure 21.1 shows you its setup.

By the Way

Why Magic Bullet?

Red Giant's principal product is Magic Bullet—a $1,000–$2,000 suite of tools intended to give video a film-like look. The 50 Movie Looks are a small subset of the features included in that powerful tool.

FIGURE 21.1
Movie Looks is a free plug-in that offers 10 film-like color scheme presets.

Movie Looks is an easy way to give your video a film-like style, be it a warm orange cast or a cool blue feel. The effects are very processor intensive (they're more than a simple tint) because they do a lot of floating-point calculations. So, to see how a preset really looks, you might want to render a brief clip before applying that preset to a longer clip or your entire project.

Because you're getting a free effect with 10 presets, there is a small catch: If you click the More Info. disclosure triangle, you're greeted by an advertisement to buy a $49 upgrade with 40 additional looks. I recommend checking out those additional offerings by visiting `http://www.redgiantsoftware.com/movielooks.html`.

> **VST Audio Plug-ins**
>
> In Hour 14, "Sweetening Your Sound," I suggested you check out `http://www.kvr-vst.com/` to check into VST plug-ins. These are audio effects, most of which will work in Premiere Pro. (Take a pass on its Quick Instrument Links—Premiere Pro does not support instruments.) If you exhaust that supply, simply use a search engine such as Google and search on `"VST plug-ins"` and `"VST plugins"`. You'll find more than you can ever use.

2d3—SteadyMove and SteadyMove Pro

The full retail version of Premiere Pro comes with a special plug-in called *SteadyMove*. It effectively smoothes shaky camera movement. To add it to your Video Effects palette, you need to install it directly from the main Premiere Pro installation CD. After it has been installed, you'll find it in its own folder, named "2d3" after the company that developed it (`http://www.2d3.com/`).

Figure 21.2 shows its interface. As with Red Giant's Movie Looks, SteadyMove too presents a marketing pitch for its Pro version ($99). This one is not as subtle. It greets you each time you use the effect.

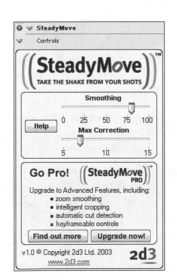

FIGURE 21.2
SteadyMove smoothes out shaky camera work.

The bundled version offers only two controls—Smoothing and Max Correction—but they are more than enough to fix most problem areas. In general, you can accept the default settings. SteadyMove works by slightly expanding your clips and applying motion to counter unsteady camera work. However, because SteadyMove expands your clips, it adds some graininess.

Making the Most of SteadyMove

SteadyMove needs to analyze a few frames before it kicks in. So, if you apply it to a trimmed clip in a sequence, the first few frames will still bounce around.

A nested sequence will fix that. Put the original—unsteady—clip in a separate sequence. Instead of trimming its beginning, leave that headroom in place. Apply SteadyMove. That will steady the entire clip with the exception of the first few frames. Then nest the sequence in another sequence and cut the unneeded (and unsteady) headroom.

To see the full SteadyMove effect, you need to have the monitor set to Highest Quality or Render the clip. If the monitor is set to Draft or Automatic, only one SteadyMove parameter is applied.

The SteadyMove Pro upgrade has additional features that smooth shaky zooms, minimize clip scaling to preserve quality, and detect and prevent smoothing across edits.

Plugin Galaxy from The Plugin Site

Plugin Galaxy for AE (available at The Plugin Site— `http://www.` `thepluginsite.com/`—for $99) is an inexpensive and wonderfully varied collection of 21 After Effects (AE) video effects with 150+ presets. I tried all the effects and they all seemed to work fine. That's not always the case for plug-ins created specifically for After Effects (see following By the Way).

Developer Comment: After Effects Plug-ins—Caveat Emptor

Many plug-ins created for After Effects work smoothly in Premiere Pro. And many don't. No guarantees.

We began adding AE plug-ins to Premiere in version 6; however, that was a fixed list of effects that we ported over to Premiere.

For Premiere Pro, we adopted the AE effects engine. So, many AE effects will work directly within Premiere Pro. However, some AE effects are not self-contained plug-ins and require AE core components. Those plug-ins will not work in Premiere because those core pieces are missing.

Typically, simple effects such as blurs and ripples will work fine. Those that have extra interface elements, such as paint or motion tracking, will not.

As shown in Figure 21.3, after installation, you'll find those 21 effects in Premiere Pro's Video Effects Plugin Galaxy bin.

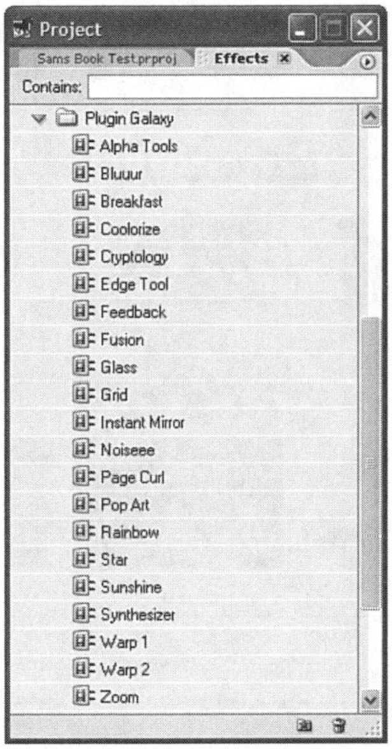

FIGURE 21.3
Plugin Galaxy's 21 effects.

Each Plugin Galaxy effect has a distinctive look and collection of parameters. The plug-in package comes with a help file that displays each preset's principal looks. Figure 21.4 shows a sampling of presets from the Glass, Edge Tool, and Fusion effects.

The man who designed Plugin Galaxy for AE, Harald Heim, is the driving force behind The Plugin Site. His site contains a massive collection of plug-ins for Photoshop, After Effects, Premiere, and several other products.

Heim, of Nuremberg, Germany, is one of the leading developers of plug-ins. His work began in 1997 when he was editing his own wedding video with Premiere. He now focuses his attention on Photoshop plug-ins. Photoshop users will find that Heim's Plugin Galaxy for Photoshop is well worth its $50 price tag.

FIGURE 21.4
Samples of Plugin
Galaxy's effects.

Feast or Famine

There is a plethora of Photoshop and After Effects plug-ins and a paucity of Premiere Pro plug-ins. Why? Four reasons: market share, cross-product compatibility, complexity, and a new API.

Photoshop dominates its market. It makes financial sense to create plug-ins for Photoshop users. It's a huge market, and Photoshop plug-ins are relatively easy to make and work on about 50 other image applications.

After Effects is a premium-priced product that dominates its smaller market. It's very complex (I demonstrate it in the next hour, "Using Photoshop and After Effects to Enhance Your DV Project") and just about anything that can automate its workflow is gratefully purchased. Third-party developers can command a premium price for several reasons: Their plug-ins are generally powerful, After Effects users tend to work in professional production houses with budgets for goodies like this, and AE plug-ins work on more than a dozen other applications.

Premiere Pro is the leader of a fairly populous market with virtually no cross-product compatibility. That fragmentation means third-party developers have fewer financial incentives to make plug-ins geared specifically for Premiere Pro. And older and current Premiere plug-ins work on only one or two other products.

In addition, Premiere Pro has a brand-new API and its developers rewrote the effects engine from scratch. Plug-ins that worked on previous versions simply will not work on Premiere Pro. It's taking a while for plug-in developers to get up to speed.

By the time this book ships, there might be other plug-ins available. To see what's out there, I suggest you simply do a Google search on "Premiere Pro plug-ins" and "Premiere Pro plugins".

ViviClip Video Filters 3

This is a massive product. Its Pro version lists for $329 and its slimmed down Basic version goes for $169. Both are available for download at http:// www.viviclip.com/index.htm. I tried the Pro version (see Figure 21.5).

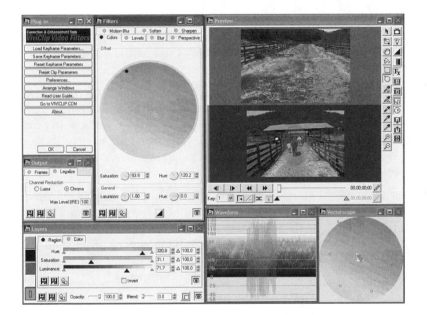

FIGURE 21.5
ViviClip Video Filters 3 Pro puts dozens of image controls, color corrections, and parameters in one interface.

ViviClip Video Filters 3 is unlike any plug-in I've seen for any product. When you drag it to a clip or the ECW, its interface fills your screen. Each of its windows is loaded with features and options. It has several basic effects that match those in Premiere Pro, such as Levels, Blur, and Sharpen, but each of those effects has its own collection of templates.

Those templates instantly transform clips into stylized looks that would normally have taken a lot of parameter tweaking for you to come up with on your own.

ViviClip Video Filters 3 has some excellent color correction features: instant color match, color balance, and tinting. What makes the Pro version stand out is that it offers five layers. You can apply effects to each layer as you see fit. You can highlight areas of the screen and apply effects only to them, obviating the need for a track matte, for instance, to obscure someone's identity.

Those two elements—layers and custom masks—along with a unique keyframe system, put this product into a high-end professional realm.

Other Third-Party Plug-in Providers

I scoured the Internet looking for other Premiere Pro plug-in creators. I found only a handful:

▶ **Boris FX** (http://www.borisfx.com/) is a major name in standalone special effects software and plug-ins, but it has only one set of plug-ins that work within Premiere Pro: *Continuum Basics* ($249). I received a copy just as I was wrapping up this book, so I can give you only a brief glimpse at it.

Figure 21.6 shows 4 of the 31 Continuum Basics effects. Each effect has a plethora of keyframable options as well as a help file with many examples, including ideas about some very cool ways to combine effects. In particular, Continuum Basics has Fire and Cloud effects. Previous versions of Premiere offered effects like those as part of the QuickTime effects package, but Adobe dropped those from Premiere Pro.

Boris FX also offers several massive collections of standalone special effects and text creation tools. Those compatible with Premiere Pro are Red 3GL, FX 7, and Graffiti 3. These are for serious video producers, have steep and lengthy learning curves, and commensurate price tags (from $600 to $1,000). You can download demo versions, but fair warning—they are huge files.

▶ **Burger Transitions** (http://www.burgers-transition-site.de/index2.html) offers a set of free plug-ins for Premiere and other products. Its creator is Stefan Burger, who, like the man behind the Plugin Galaxy, is from Nuremberg, Germany. (In a cool twist, neither knew they were neighbors until I swapped emails with them.) Burger acknowledges his transitions are a hobby and some are better than others. In any event, his easy-to-use plug-ins are worth downloading.

▶ **FlashAnts** (http://www.flashants.com/root/index.shtml) offers one plug-in—SWFVideo—that enables you to import Macromedia Flash SWF files. I tested it and discovered it's not quite fully functional. SWFVideo requires a restart of your project to complete the import and has no documentation. It does show promise and if its developer can make it more user-friendly, it can be a cool way to add some fun animations to your Premiere Pro projects.

▶ **Panopticum** (http://www.panopticum.com/), a Russia-based plug-in house, has many plug-ins for earlier versions of Premiere but none for Premiere Pro. Panopticum developed the Plugin Galaxy for After Effects for Harald Heim.

▶ **RE:Vision Effects** (http://www.revisionfx.com/) has several plug-ins, but they work only with progressive scan video clips, and even then it takes a few extra steps to get the plug-ins to work. Progressive videos typically are high-definition or transfers from film.

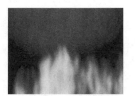

Fire

Rain

Particles

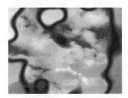

Burnt Film

FIGURE 21.6
Boris FX's Continuum Basics offers some excellent visual effects, some of which fill the gap left by Adobe dropping the QuickTime effects used in previous versions of Premiere.

Innovative Graphics—Editor's Toolkit from Digital Juice

Animated graphic backgrounds, or **beds**, can greatly enhance a video production. Digital Juice (http://www.digitaljuice.com/index.asp) is the de facto industry leader in this niche market. Its Editor's Toolkit (ETK) collection is loaded with visually innovative graphics as well as transitions that match their graphic look.

Just about any Digital Juice purchase is a significant investment. Each of the two Editor's Toolkits lists for $599, but you do get major bang for your buck.

Figure 21.7 gives you a little taste. Using the company's file management software—The Juicer—you can scan through the library of clips and images for each 10-DVD ETK.

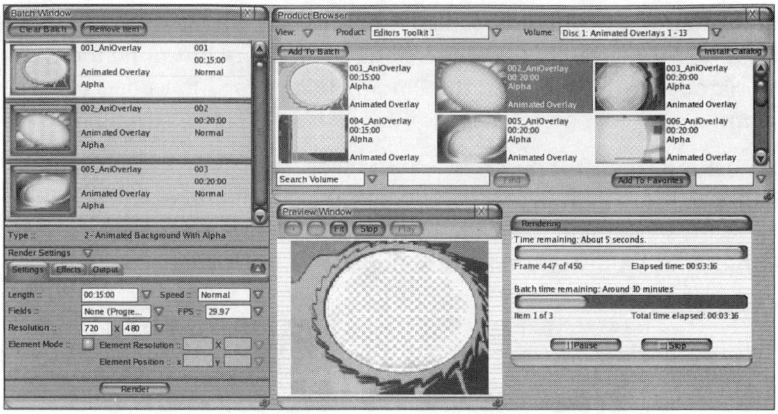

FIGURE 21.7
Each 10-DVD Editor's Toolkit comes packed with dozens of animated graphics, hundreds of still graphics, and thousands of images.

ETK 1 & 2 are 10 DVDs each totaling more than 110GB of content. As shown in Figure 21.8, their animated graphics have built-in alpha channels to allow footage on lower tracks to show through. You use the Juicer to build them to any length that suits you. Each is **loopable**—that is, you can place the same clip back-to-back on a track and they'll look like one uninterrupted animation.

FIGURE 21.8
The animated graphic beds have built-in alpha channel transparencies.

Each kit has animated lower-third graphics that you can use as backgrounds for supers. You can move them around the screen, placing them vertically along the sides or across the top. You can change the colors and select an output format (NTSC, PAL, DV, AVI, QuickTime) to match your project settings.

Editor's Toolkit 2 adds some uniquely fashioned transitions. None are true Premiere Pro video transitions, which means they will work on many nonlinear editors. Some, like the one shown in Figure 21.9, you place on a track above the edit point between two clips. They're animated graphics with transparent alpha channels. As the transitions play out, they eventually create full-screen effects, momentarily blocking anything below them on the sequence. It's at that point when the actual edit between the two clips takes place, looking for all the world as if there were some spectacular and gradual transition.

FIGURE 21.9
Full-screen, full-color transitions are actually animated graphics with alpha channels and brief moments of full-screen, non-transparent graphics, when the actual edit takes place.

Finally, in a feature that opened up a new editing approach that I'd never considered, Digital Juice includes a collection of animated, black-and-white mattes. You use them as track mattes as yet another means to create transitions.

Figure 21.9 shows one in action. Basically, you place the clip you're transitioning from on one track, and the clip you're transitioning to below it. Place the track matte transition above them and give the clips an overlap that matches the length of the track matte. Apply the track matte to the top clip and the animated black-and-white graphic will gradually reveal the clip below it. It's a very slick effect.

Applying a Track Matte Turns Off Clips

While testing the Editor's Toolkit's track matte transitions, I discovered what is probably a bug in Premiere Pro. If you apply a Track Matte key to a portion of a clip (the matte length does not equal the entire clip length), the uncovered part of the clip will not display.

In that setup, a track matte does not work as a transition because the video won't start playing until the CTI gets to the Track Matte graphic on the sequence.

The workaround is to make a razor cut on the video clip right before the first frame of the track matte (take a close look at Figure 21.10 and you'll note that I cut the clip on Video 2). Then apply the Track Matte to the portion under that matte and leave the rest of the clip untouched.

FIGURE 21.10
Using an animated black-and-white graphic as a track matte enables you to create transitions like this.

High-Definition Video—Cineform's Aspect HD

The video production industry is shifting to high-definition video. Premiere Pro can *output* HD video using Windows Media's HD file formats in the Adobe Media Encoder (for more on this, see Hour 23, "Exporting Premiere Pro Frames, Clips, and Sequences"). But you need some way to *import* HD footage. There are a couple hardware solutions in the $30,000 price range, but Cineform's Aspect HD (http://www.cineform.com/index.htm) is the first affordable solution.

At $1,200 for the software and $3,500 for the camcorder, it's still a significant chunk of change.

It works only with camcorders and tape decks that comply with a new format called HDV (see following By the Way). So far, that amounts to only two JVC camcorders and one JVC tape deck.

HDV—HD for the Masses?

HDV is a format created by four major camcorder makers: Canon, Sharp, Sony, and JVC (for more info, go to http://www.hdv-info.org). HDV allows for the recording and playback of HD on DV cassette tapes. It uses a recording format called *MPEG2 MP@HL Transport Stream*. Although it is not true full-resolution HD, it still records and plays back in a full 720p, 30 fps, 16:9 widescreen aspect ratio.

Normally, true transferring (capturing) HD video to a PC requires some expensive specialized hardware and different higher-speed cables and connections. But with HDV, all you need is a standard FireWire connection.

The JVC JY-HD10U camcorder (see Figure 21.11)—the first to market that uses this new format—has met with mixed reviews. But this commitment from such major players does point to a shift to HD-style video products.

Aspect HD, shown in Figure 21.12, operates seamlessly within Premiere Pro. When you start a new project, you'll see a new project setting option for HD. Upon opening your Premiere Pro project with an HDV setting, you'll note that the Monitor window Source and Program screens display in a 16:9 aspect ratio.

FIGURE 21.11
The JVC JY-HD10U
is the first HDV
camcorder and is
the device
Cineform worked
with when creating
AspectHD.

FIGURE 21.11
The JVC JY-HD10U
is the first HDV
camcorder and is
the device
Cineform worked
with when creating
AspectHD.

FIGURE 21.12
Cineform's
AspectHD brings
HD import and real-
time editing to
Premiere Pro.

AspectHD captures the MPEG2-TS video and converts it to a proprietary format, editable in Premiere Pro. The software ships with its own set of effects, transitions, color adjustment tools, slow-motion, frame hold, and static and moving video overlays geared specifically for HD video. If your output will be standard definition TV (a very common workflow), AspectHD enables you to pan/scan/rotate/zoom without any loss of pixel resolution.

You'll need a PC with above-average horsepower to play these HD clips and effects in real-time. A fast Pentium 4 with a RAID hard drive setup will suffice. AspectHD ran without a hitch on my Alienware dual-Pentium powerhouse.

Multiple-Camera Editing with Multicam

Wedding and other event videographers know what a pain it can be to sync up video from more than one camera and make clean, non-jump cut edits. One solution is Multicam from United Media (http://www.unitedmediainc.com/home/).

Some event videographers have the luxury of working with a remote production switcher. They connect all cameras to that switcher, and then make live camera changes during the event.

As mentioned in Hour 3, "Story Creation, Writing, and Video Production Tips," a fully equipped, two-camera remote setup can cost about $75,000.

Multicam gives you the advantages of that live switching gear for a whole lot less: $299 retail for a two-camera package and $599 for a four-camera version.

The basic concept is that you record an event with multiple cameras and you keep them rolling the entire time. (If you turn them off here and there, it becomes a real headache to sync them up, even using Multicam.)

You import the video into Premiere Pro and place each camera's video on a separate track. Save that project and then open it in Multicam. Figure 21.13 gives you an idea how it looks.

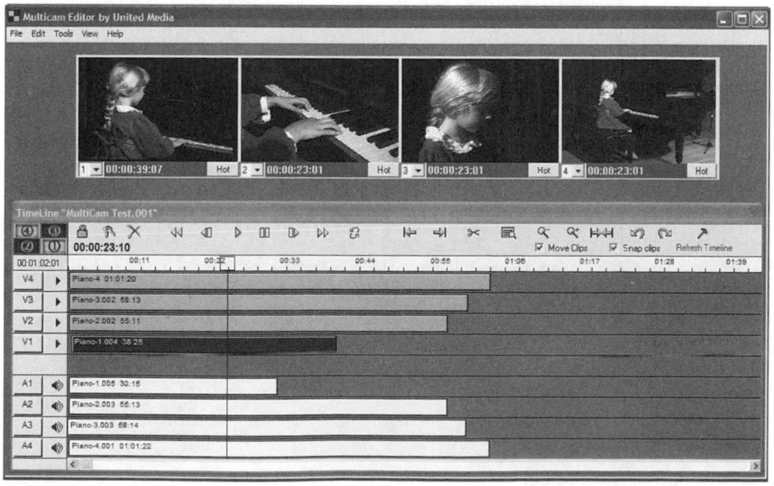

FIGURE 21.13
Multicam enables you to make what amounts to live cuts between cameras without all the remote location production hardware.

In the Multicam interface, you look for a spot in the clips to use to syncronize them. A movie-style clapper or a camera flash works well. You mark that spot in all the clips, and then use one menu command to slide all the clips to bring them into sync.

Now you do the live switching. It's as easy as hitting the 1-2-3-4 keys on the keyboard. As you watch the video, you press numbers representing the video tracks to cut from one to another. If you don't like a cut, undo it and try again. When done, you have Multicam automatically add some head and tail room to all the cuts so that you can add transitions later and then export it back to Premiere Pro.

It comes back to Premiere Pro as a collection of sub-clips on their original four video and audio tracks (you probably will settle on one master audio track, but you can mix them). It's a simple matter to add transitions (if desired).

Multicam is an intuitive tool that can save time and money.

Creating Multimedia Movies with CyberCam

CyberCam is a nifty little utility ($110 retail at `http://www.smartguyz.com/`) that captures whatever is playing on your PC screen. You end up with an AVI movie that is easily editable in Premiere Pro. Figure 21.14 shows you its simple interface.

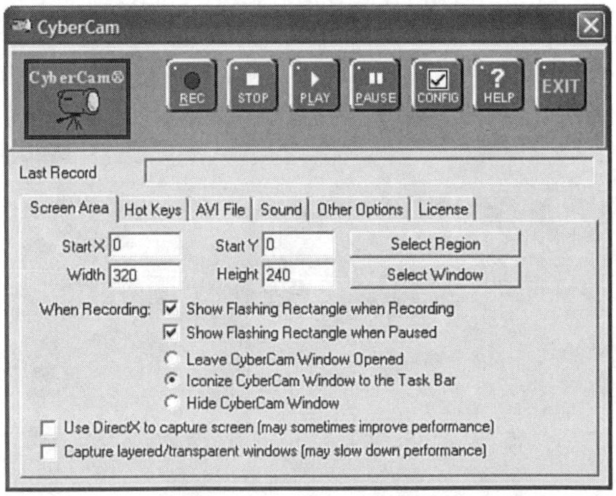

FIGURE 21.14
CyberCam captures whatever is displayed on your PC monitor in real-time.

You set the frame rate (low if you want to play these movies on the Internet, higher if you're putting them on a DVD or videotape), audio quality (if you choose to record audio), whether you want CyberCam to pan around the screen to follow your moving mouse, and the size of the screen area to capture.

This is a great way to present step-by-step instructions. I'm using CyberCam to create a series of videos to complement the tasks in this book. I plan to offer them for sale at my Web site: http://www.sengstack.com. My intention is to finish the videos and have the site up and running by the time this book ships. But please bear with me if things fall behind schedule.

Speeding Up Editing with Contour Design's ShuttlePRO V.2

Finally, I offer up one sharp piece of hardware, reminiscent of working with videotape machines. Contour Design's ShuttlePRO V.2 (see Figure 21.15) is a sleek, handheld controller with programmable keys and a smooth shuttle knob.

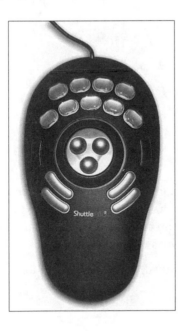

FIGURE 21.15
ShuttlePRO V.2 puts direct control of Premiere Pro's major Monitor window and some timeline functions into an ergonomic package.

Available for $130 at http://www.contourdesign.com/ and at many retailers, ShuttlePRO V.2 is preprogrammed to give you immediate access to more than a dozen Premiere Pro actions. As shown in Figure 21.16, with simple clicks, you can start, stop, fast-forward, and reverse, shuttle through the project, jump to edit points, and even insert or lift clips within a sequence.

FIGURE 21.16
ShuttlePRO V.2 software has a display option that shows default or user-programmed actions with labels.

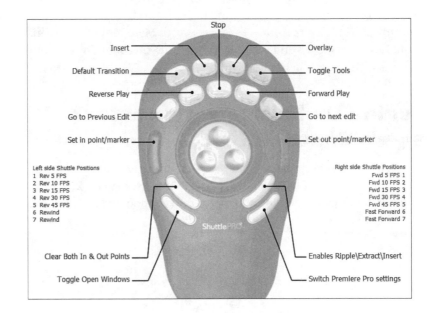

You can use ShuttlePRO V.2 for many other programs. Its cleverly programmed software recognizes whatever application you're using and changes its functions accordingly.

It's a simple matter to customize controls for Premiere Pro and other products. And you can create your own full set of personalized controls. After you've made changes, they show up in an easily accessible display and you can use the supplied button labels to serve as reminders.

This is a very slick, well-crafted, and labor-saving tool.

Summary

When you purchased Premiere Pro, you joined a community. The many third-party software and hardware developers who create products that work inside or with Premiere Pro are also part of that community. Those products enhance productivity, give you additional creative options, or streamline workflow.

In this hour, I covered effect and transition plug-ins. They represent a sparsely populated market, but I expect it will grow as developers explore Premiere Pro's Software Development Kit.

Other third-party products enable you to add some beautiful animated graphic beds and transitions to your Premiere Pro projects, sync-up and edit multiple camera views, import and edit high-definition video, create and edit mini-movies of your PC screen, and speed up editing with a handheld controller.

Exercises

This hour does not lend itself to a quiz, but I do have one suggested exercise: scour the Internet for other Premiere Pro third-party products. Start your search at `http://www.adobe.com`. Go to the Premiere Pro section and click on the Third-Party Plugins link.

When I last looked, there were no third-party products listed on that site for Premiere Pro. That might have changed by the time this book arrives on store shelves. After you've exhausted that resource, do a Google search on `"Premiere Pro"` with additional parameters such as `"plug-ins"`, `"plugins"`, `"third party"`, and `"compatible"`. To limit search results to those products most likely to fit the bill, use quotation marks and other parameters. A typical Google search might look like this: `+"Premiere Pro" "plug-ins" OR "plugins"`.

PART V

Working with Other Adobe Products and Exporting Your Videos

Using Photoshop and After Effects to Enhance Your DV Project

What You'll Learn in This Hour:

- ▶ Introducing Photoshop CS
- ▶ Using Photoshop CS in video production
- ▶ Introducing After Effects 6
- ▶ Animating text with After Effects 6
- ▶ Creating motion graphics with After Effects 6

Adobe's Video Collection Professional features five products: Premiere Pro, Audition, Photoshop CS, After Effects 6, and Encore DVD. Each stands alone at the top of its respective field. Taken together, they give video producers all the tools they need to do excellent work.

I took you through Audition's paces in Hour 15, "Professional Audio Tools: SmartSound Sonicfire and Adobe Audition." In this book's final hour, I will show you how to use Encore DVD to create Hollywood-style DVDs. In this hour, I introduce you to the two other products in the Adobe Video Collection Professional suite: Photoshop CS and After Effects 6.

Anyone who does anything with print graphics and photo retouching probably has Photoshop. It is the workhorse of the graphic design industry. But it is becoming an increasingly important part of the video world as well.

After Effects is the de facto video production industry-standard text animation and motion graphics tool. If it moves on your TV set or movie theater screen, someone probably used After Effects to create it.

Introducing Photoshop CS

Making the move to Photoshop CS (shown in Figure 22.1) means joining forces with just about every image-editing professional on the planet. It's that ubiquitous.

FIGURE 22.1
Adobe Photoshop CS is the undisputed photo- and image-editing tool of choice.

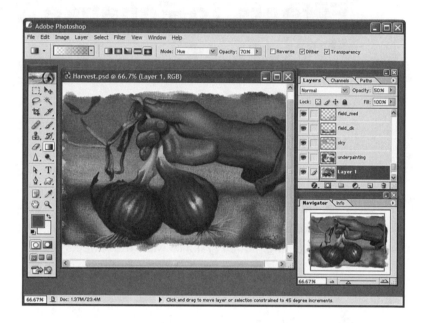

Photoshop CS (Creative Suite) offers deep customizability. The Layer Style dialog box in Figure 22.2—very reminiscent of Premiere Pro's Title Designer—is a case in point. Everything you need is at your fingertips.

FIGURE 22.2
Photoshop's Layer Style dialog box puts major functionality within one intuitive interface.

The drawing tools and Artwork palette in Photoshop CS enable you to create graphics, like the one in Figure 22.3, in only a few minutes.

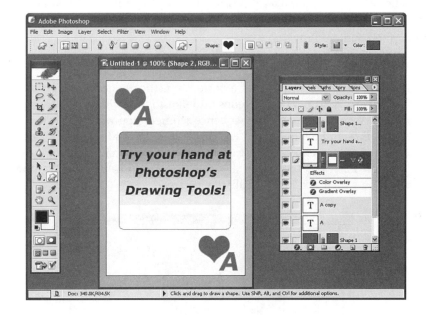

FIGURE 22.3
Photoshop's intuitive drawing tools speed up graphics creation.

Photoshop CS includes several creative paintbrush tools in that palette such as Charcoal, Pastel, and Oil Paint. Using them with a graphics tablet, such as the pressure-sensitive Wacom Intuos, means you can apply more or less texture as you draw.

Other Photoshop CS features include the following:

▶ A healing brush that does amazingly accurate and automatic dust, scratch, and blemish removal while compensating for differences in lighting, shading, and texture.

▶ Automatic color correction, which analyzes an image and balances color with a single click. This works well on photos shot under fluorescent lights.

▶ More powerful Web integration.

▶ A spell checker. This might not seem like a standard image-editing tool, but graphic artists have clamored for it.

Of primary importance to the scope of this book is just how strongly Photoshop CS is connected to Premiere Pro and to video production.

An obvious example is Premiere Pro's Edit Original command. Place any Photoshop graphic on the timeline, right-click it, and select Edit Original. This opens Photoshop CS and makes it possible for you to immediately edit the graphic. After it has been saved within Photoshop CS, the new version of the graphic shows up in Premiere Pro.

Here are three other Premiere Pro/Photoshop CS connections:

▶ Premiere Pro's filmstrip export feature is specifically designed to work with Photoshop CS. Convert video clips into *filmstrips*—collections of individual frames. To do that, mark the sequence segment you want to convert with the Work Area bar then select File→Export→Export Movie. Click Settings. For the file type, choose Filmstrip and then choose the frame rate. As shown in Figure 22.4, you then open the frames in Photoshop and paint directly on the clips, which is a process called *rotoscoping*.

FIGURE 22.4
Use Photoshop's Filmstrip file format and its paint tools to rotoscope Premiere Pro clips on a frame-by-frame basis.

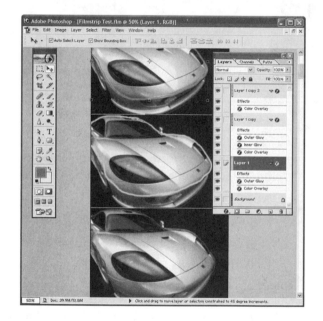

▶ Export a frame of a video to Photoshop CS to create a matte to mask or highlight certain areas of that clip. Here's how: Using that frame as a guide, create a shape using the Marquee or one of the Lasso tools. In the Tool Options bar, set Feather to about 15 px to give it a soft border. Fill the interior with black to make it transparent. Fill the rest with white to make that part opaque. Within Premiere Pro, you can use this mask as a track matte to adjust its location and size and to follow action. Plus, you can line up the original clip on both Video 1 and Video 2, apply some blur to Video 2, and use the soft-edged matte to highlight an element in your clip while throwing everything else out of focus.

▶ You can use Photoshop CS to cut objects out of a scene and fill in the gap using the Clone tool or the healing brush. Then place the removed object in a separate layer so that you can animate it using Premiere Pro's Motion video effect—Monty Python-esque comical situations come to mind. Consider a photo of a statue in a park. Move it off the pedestal and slide it next to an unsuspecting park patron seated on a bench.

Before you can start using these features, you'll need to learn the fundamentals. If you choose to add Photoshop CS to your digital video production repertoire, peruse the tips for first-time users provided by a Photoshop expert in the following section.

Using Photoshop CS in Video Production

If you aren't a Photoshop user, I strongly recommend downloading the Photoshop CS trial version. Go to http://www.adobe.com, locate the Photoshop CS page, and click the Tryout link.

One other alternative means to get up to speed on Photoshop CS is to start with its slimmed-down sibling: Photoshop Elements. It's a more user-friendly piece of software that features the same layered graphic approach used in Photoshop CS. It too has a downloadable trial version.

Expert Tips

Whichever approach you take, you'll want to follow a few standard procedures when creating graphics for use in video projects. I contacted a well-regarded professional in this use of Photoshop—Glen Stephens—to provide some tips.

Glen Stephens is an expert Photoshop user and designer for desktop and broadcast video. He has more than 10 years experience as a graphic designer, editor, and director in broadcast video.

Glen Stephens,
Pixel Post Studios.

Stephens is the developer of the Tools for Television Pro (`http://www.toolsfortelevision.com`)—a valuable productivity tool for people who want to integrate video production and Photoshop.

Stephens' company, Pixel Post Studios (`http://www.pixelpoststudios.com`), provides training and design services for the broadcast video industry.

Here are Stephens' tips for using Photoshop in your video productions. (Note that * indicates that actions (something like word processing macros that carry out a series of steps) are available on the Tools for Television–Photoshop Toolbox CD to automate the task.)

- ▶ **Place each element of your image onto a new and separate layer.** This enables you to keep your designs editable in case you decide to make changes later. It's tempting to flatten, or combine your image's layers when you're done to reduce their file size, but doing so prevents you from later making text or color changes.

- ▶ **Use the built-in features of Photoshop, such as layer styles, to create effects such as drop shadows, glows, and bevels.** Layer styles and adjustment layers are very valuable and allow you to create powerful image effects that are always adjustable later in the process, as long as you do not render or rasterize them. Experiment with these and get into the habit of using them.

▶ **Use safe areas.** * Overscan on television sets covers about 10% of each side of your image. Therefore, when creating graphics for video, use Photoshop CS's new Title Safe guides when you select a video preset when opening a new document. Make sure that you place all your content inside the delineated portion of your image (see Figure 22.5). It's okay to let background images and elements extend to the edges so that they appear to fill the screen, but overscan will cover any text that extends outside of the title-safe area.

Title Safe Zone

FIGURE 22.5
Keep your text within the title-safe area to avoid losing the edges in the overscan region.

▶ **Watch your font sizes.** Font sizes of 24 points or larger work best. Anything smaller might look like dust specks on a TV screen. For a header or primary text, 32 to 48 points work well, depending on how much text you use. (Note that typeface sizes vary. A 24-point font for one typeface might be smaller/larger than a 24-point font for a different typeface.)

Also, space your text evenly. Don't crowd the screen with too much large text, and avoid thin fonts that might become illegible in an interlaced video signal. Be very selective with text color (use NTSC safe color, for example) and use outlines or drop shadows to separate text from the video background.

▶ **Adjust image dimensions to compensate for non-square pixels.** *
Photoshop works only with square pixels. But some TV systems use *non-square* (slightly rectangular) pixels. To ensure that your Photoshop graphics translate well to the final video output format, use Photoshop CS' new Pixel Aspect Ratio Correction feature. It makes your images look square while you're working on them in Photoshop, but the pixels are actually non-square in their native form in Photoshop.

To ensure the proper pixel aspect ratio, use one of Photoshop's TV image presets. Select whatever output you'll use for your project when you open a new document in Photoshop. If you care to confirm that setting, choose the Advanced settings→Pixel Aspect Ratio drop-down menu in the new document setup dialog box.

After you've made that selection, don't change that from square to non-square or vice versa. Doing so could alter your image in an irreparable way.

Computer monitors, regular NTSC (non-D1 or DV), and HDTV (high-definition TV) use square pixels. NTSC D1, NTSC DV, and PAL use non-square pixels. If you do not use the Pixel Aspect Ratio Correction for non-square formats, your images will look like the graphics in Figure 22.6—stretched or squashed, depending on the video system.

FIGURE 22.6
Failing to use the correct resolution in a Photoshop graphic could lead to squashed or elongated images, depending on the output video format.

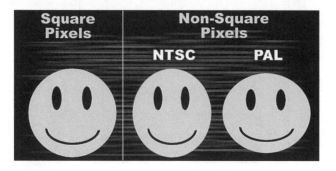

---

72 DPI Fits the Bill

Unless you plan to zoom in on a graphic within Premiere Pro, it's best to create all Photoshop images as RGB images at 72 DPI resolution (see the "Scanning Tips for Photographs" bullet later in this hour for more info).

▶ **Using bitmap versus vector graphics.** Computer graphics fall into two main categories: bitmap and vector. You can import both types into Premiere Pro, but Premiere Pro converts vector graphics to bitmap images before editing them. Here's a basic overview of both types:

 ▶ Bitmap images—technically called *raster images* —use a grid of colored dots known as *pixels*. Some pixels have been magnified in Figure 22.7 to illustrate this. Each pixel is assigned a specific location and color value. When working with bitmap images, you edit pixels rather than objects or shapes.

Bitmap images are the most common electronic medium for continuous-tone images, such as photographs, because they can represent subtle gradations of shades and color. Bitmap images are *resolution dependent*—that is, they contain a fixed number of pixels. As a result, they can lose detail and appear jagged if they're scaled larger.

All images created in Photoshop are bitmap.

FIGURE 22.7
Magnified bitmap pixels.

▶ Vector graphics are made up of lines and curves defined by mathematical objects called *vectors*. Figure 22.8 demonstrates how vectors describe an image according to its geometric characteristics. For example, a circle in a vector graphic is made up of a mathematical definition of a circle drawn with a certain radius, set at a specific location, and filled with a specific color. You can move, resize, and change the color of the circle without losing the quality of the graphic.

Vector graphics are *resolution independent*—that is, they can be scaled to any size and printed at any resolution without losing detail or clarity. As a result, vector graphics are the best choice for representing bold graphics that must retain crisp lines when scaled to various sizes (for example, logos).

All images created with Adobe Illustrator are vector based.

FIGURE 22.8
Vector graphics are made up of mathematical objects— lines and curves— to ensure sharp, crisp images, no matter how much they're scaled up.

▶ **Fixing interlacing and "shaky" graphics.** * If your Photoshop graphics vibrate when displayed on a TV set, this is likely due to interlacing.

This happens when thin horizontal lines, especially bright lines, in your graphic or image fall between the interlaced scan lines of your video signal. It's a common occurrence with scanned photographs. You want to avoid this.

You fix it by either making horizontal lines thicker or applying a motion blur. Figure 22.9 demonstrates the latter solution.

Select Filter→Blur→Motion Blur. This opens the Motion Blur dialog box. Apply one pixel at 90 degrees to the problem area in the image. This stretches the width of the horizontal lines into the next scan line in the video signal and corrects the problem. In some cases, one pixel will not be enough. Try two or three if the problem is really bad.

FIGURE 22.9
Use Photoshop's Motion Blur effect to resolve jitters on interlaced TV sets caused by thin lines in the graphic.

Limit Blurred Region

It generally works best if you apply the blur to only the problem areas in the image. If you apply the blur to the overall image, it might lose sharpness. There are exceptions: In the case of a scanned photo, you might need to apply the blur to the entire image.

You can use Premiere Pro's Edit Original command on the suspect graphic to automatically open Photoshop to do your graphic touch-up work. When you save the altered graphic, it will show up in its new form within Premiere Pro.

▶ **File-management tips.** When you're working in Photoshop, I suggest using a file folder system that keeps two sets of image files for a project: design and production.

Design files are the original Photoshop (PSD) images that contain text data, layers, adjustment layers, layer masks, and the safe grid and background.

Production files are the flattened files that you can export to other software applications. These files don't have any layered information and cannot be edited later. You can save these files in any format that your editing software will take. It's a good idea that these files be flattened because many applications cannot read layer styles or adjustment layers from Photoshop, and items such as drop shadows might be lost in the editing software. Simply select Save As in Photoshop and uncheck the Layers button in the Save dialog box to flatten the image.

▶ **Color-selection tips:** Certain colors work better than others when working with video. Any color that is highly saturated and too bright will cause problems when transferred to video. Muted, less bright colors will yield better results. Typically red is *not* a good color to use. However, if you keep the saturation and brightness down, you might be able to get away with it. Blues, yellows, and greens work well.

Photoshop has a filter that will help shift "illegal" colors into an NTSC safe-color space. Select Filter→Video→NTSC Colors to use it. However, just because a color is NTSC safe does not mean it will not bleed or look bad!

When working with text, make sure that there's a significant amount of contrast between the color of the text and the background. You want the text to jump off the screen at your viewers.

I rarely use color in text. If I do, it is just a faint shade. Your viewers' eyes will be drawn naturally to the brightest portion of your image. Try to guide your viewers to what you are trying to communicate with them.

By the Way

Color Theory

The book *Color Harmony* by Hideaki Chijiiwa is an excellent resource if you want to learn color theory and how to use colors to help communicate your message.

▶ **Scanning tips for photographs.** When scanning photographs for use in a video project, it isn't necessary to scan images at a high resolution. Because all video graphics end up at 72 DPI, anything more than that is overkill.

There are exceptions, though. If you plan to pan, move around, or zoom in on the image in Premiere Pro, you'll want to scan at a higher resolution than 72 DPI.

Because Photoshop works with pixels, if you scan a small image and try to scale it larger in Photoshop, you'll end up with a blurry version of your image. Scaling down does not make an image look obviously worse, but scaling up does.

In general, scan all images at a slightly larger size than the expected output video resolution so that you can scale the image down to the size you want it on your video screen.

Table 22.1 lists image sizes that will fill a screen at 72 DPI for each video format. If your original image is smaller than the sizes listed here, scan it at a higher resolution to ensure sharp details in the final edited video.

TABLE 22.1   Video Frame Size Versus Optimum Size of Original
Document to Ensure Sharp Onscreen Display at 72 DPI

Video Frame Size	Minimum Image Size to Ensure Sharp Onscreen Display
640×480	8 7/8 × 6 5/8 inches
720×480	10 × 6 5/8 inches
720×486	10 × 6 3/4 inches
720×576	10 × 8 inches
1280×720	17 2/3 × 10 inches
1920×1080	26 2/3 × 15 inches

Introducing After Effects

Recently, you might have noticed a change in video production techniques.
Suddenly, it seems, text is flying all over our screens. Advertisements, kids' programs, and entertainment shows feature jittery, shifting, ambling, and rambling
text. Why the sudden shift? Adobe After Effects 6.

FIGURE 22.10
After Effects 6 is
the industry-leading
motion graphics,
animated text, and
visual effects tool.

After Effects 6 features new, easy-to-use and wildly imaginative text animation tools. And video production houses around the world, most of which rely on After Effects for their day-to-day visual effects work, have enthusiastically exploited these new tools. In addition, they've started using AE 6's new Photoshop-style vector paint tools and its improved motion graphics features.

As you ramp up your Premiere Pro skill set, you might want to consider using After Effects in your productions. It is the industry-leading tool of choice for editors who want to produce exciting and innovative motion graphics, visual effects, and animated text for film, video, DVD, and the Web.

After Effects users tend to fall into two distinct camps: motion graphics artists and animated text artists. Some production houses specialize in one or the other. There is so much that After Effects can do, it's darned hard to wrap your brain around all of it. So, I'll focus on one main area at a time.

After Effects has a steep learning curve. So, rather than present a collection of tips or a series of tasks that would require a massive amount of explanation just to get you up to speed, I simply will demonstrate some of After Effects' features.

Tight Adobe Video Collection Integration

If you migrate to After Effects, you likely will use it to add special motion effects to Premiere Pro and Photoshop CS projects. Importing them into After Effects is easy.

Figure 22.11 shows the Saleen Premiere Pro project you worked on earlier in this book.

As with Premiere Pro, After Effects has a Project window but the icons and terminology are a bit different. For instance, Premiere Pro sequences are known as compositions in After Effects.

Double-clicking a sequence/composition opens it in the Timeline window. Each numbered line is an asset or effect from the original Premiere Pro project. Instead of tracks, you work with layers in After Effects.

Edits, effects, dissolves, motion keyframes, transparencies, nested sequences, crops, and clip speed changes built in the Premiere Pro project are all maintained when imported into After Effects.

As shown in Figure 22.12, those elements take on a different look in After Effects. Even with the highlighted basic cross dissolve, you have the option to control it to the minutest detail. In Premiere Pro, you can apply keyframe parameters that can smooth the dissolve, speeding it up or slowing it down as it approaches a keyframe. In After Effects, you build that effect curve exactly the way you want to for dissolves and just about any other effect.

FIGURE 22.11
Imported Premiere Pro projects retain their effects and transitions in After Effects.

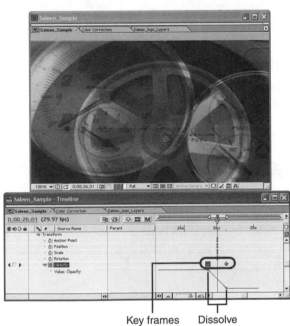

FIGURE 22.12
After Effects enables you to have absolute control of the minutest detail of virtually any effect.

Key frames   Dissolve

You can also import Photoshop layered files into After Effects. Figure 22.13 shows a DVD menu that you will work with in Hour 24, "Authoring DVDs with Encore DVD."

The Project window displays each Photoshop layer. You can apply effects to each layer, put each in motion on separate paths, and animate the text. Basically, you can start with a static layered image and turn it into an animated video menu that you can use in your DVDs.

For those of you who work with Adobe Illustrator, those files too can be imported into After Effects while retaining their layers.

Animating Text with After Effects

After Effects enables you to take text created in Photoshop and convert it to editable After Effects text, which means it will now behave as if you created it directly in After Effects (however, you might find that it's easier to create text directly in After Effects, as I explain later in this section). That opens the door to creative potential beyond anything you can imagine.

Figure 22.14 gives you an idea of what that entails. You can add text animation features to this composition layer, change attributes, and apply them over time using keyframes.

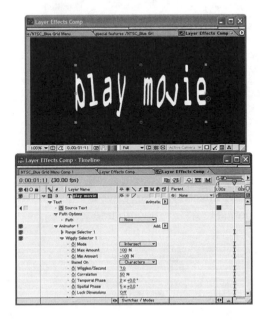

FIGURE 22.14
After Effects can convert text created in Photoshop to text you can animate down to a character-by-character basis.

Per-Character Animation

After Effects 6 has a new ground-breaking approach to text animation: per-character/word animation. Previously, you had to go through a laborious and tedious process to animate one letter or word at a time. Now you tell After Effects how many letters or whole words to animate at any one time.

To begin, you create text with a new set of text tools that work very much like those in Photoshop. As shown in Figure 22.15, it's a simple matter to choose the Text tool, add a bounding box to a video clip, set the font and its size, and then type in your text message. After the text has been written, you can select a portion of it and apply different font style attributes. I set the S7 to Book Heavy (the equivalent of bold for the Neuzeit S LT Std font) and gave it a **stroke** (an outer edge with a different color).

FIGURE 22.15
The new text cre-
ation tools in After
Effects work much
like those in
Photoshop.

Figure 22.16 demonstrates that you can place text on a path just as you can with Premiere Pro. But in After Effects, you can have the text move along that path and have the path change to fit the moving image.

FIGURE 22.16
Use After Effects to
animate text along
a moving path.

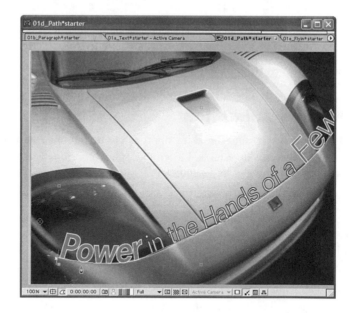

After Effects ships with a whole collection of text animation tools. In the case of Figure 22.17, I wrote a line of text, applied the per-character animation parameter, skewed the characters a bit (slanting them off to the right), set a bounding box within which I wanted the characters to animate, and then used the new Wiggly animation option. The characters jump all over the screen and settle down one at a time in a straight line.

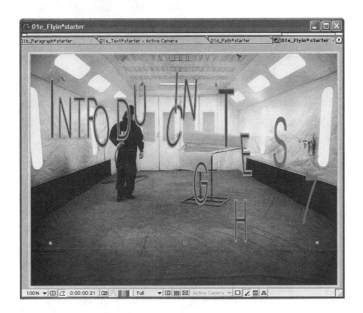

FIGURE 22.17
Using per-character animation enables you to create bouncing text like this.

There are many other animation characteristics. Letters can bounce, move through 3D space, twist, bend, curl, flip, invert, change colors and opacities, and even change to different characters.

One other item before moving on: You also can animate *within* text. Figure 22.18 shows an animated scribble effect that gradually fills the text. It's also a simple matter to draw outlines around text and have that animate as well. The possibilities are mind-boggling.

FIGURE 22.18
Not only can you animate individual letters, you can animate within letters.

Creating Motion Graphics with After Effects

The animated text examples give you an idea of how you can move objects through 2D or 3D space in After Effects 6. You can apply similar motion to any object and you can give that object keyframable parameters that change its characteristics over time.

What makes this different from similar keyframable motion effects in Premiere Pro is the minute level of control you have over the motion (including speed, curves, and the use of 3D space) and the number of special parameters.

In the following sections, I introduce that motion graphics concept with a simple example, show you a couple special effects, and then go over two higher-level motion tools.

Vector Paintbrush Tools

After Effects 6 includes a new set of Photoshop-style paint and touch-up tools. You can use them simply to create some wild, animated art and, as shown in Figure 22.19, to apply rotoscope-style animation to video. The huge advantage when using After Effects instead of Photoshop to do rotoscoping is the ability to animate it over time instead of tediously applying it on a frame-by-frame basis.

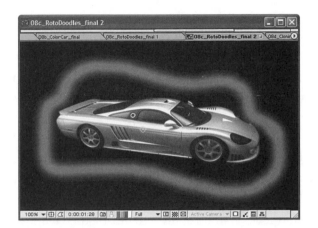

FIGURE 22.19
Use new Photoshop-style paint tools in After Effects to apply rotoscope-style animation to videos.

The paint tools, along with the additional Photoshop-style Clone tool, enable you to repair problem areas in a video. Figure 22.20 shows the paint tools and brushes. It's a simple matter to use the Eyedropper tool to select a color right next to that black smudge in the car door, and then select a soft-tipped brush to fix that smudge.

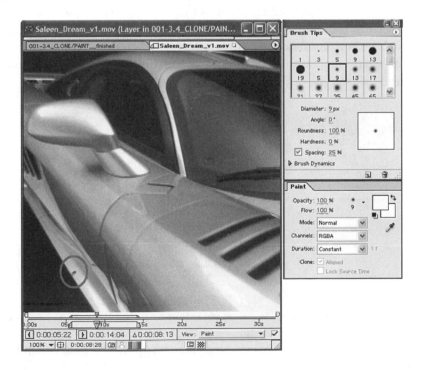

FIGURE 22.20
After Effects 6 uses Photoshop-style paint and touch-up tools that enable you to fix video miscues on a frame-by-frame basis if need be.

By using keyframes, you can apply touch-ups to multiple frames to track any movement in the video clip. That work can be mighty tedious—to fix this two-second clip required applying touch-up work to several dozen frames.

After Effects has a solution. Its new Motion Tracker can automate this touch-up process as well as perform some much more dramatic effects. I cover it later in this section.

Animated Effects

After Effects 6 has 17 new effects that enable you to correct and enhance your footage. For example:

- ▶ You can distort footage with Liquify's 10 brush-based tools.
- ▶ The Warp effect transforms layers into geometric shapes, arcs, waves, and fish-eye lens views.
- ▶ Turbulent Displace uses fractal noise to create distortions.
- ▶ Magnify simulates placing a magnifying glass over an area of the image.

Warp, illustrated in Figure 22.21, is one of the easiest effects to use. You select from a list of preset animations, and then adjust the degree and direction of the bend and the horizontal and vertical displacement. You can use multiple keyframes, but simply using a start and end keyframe will create a very cool flag wave feel, for example.

FIGURE 22.21
The Warp effect has a dozen preset animations and some simple, keyframable parameters that create some very cool effects.

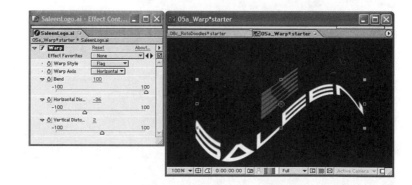

The Liquify effect (see Figure 22.22) enables you to manually distort portions of an image. To see how that distortion works, you can turn on the effect's Mesh view, which shifts and distorts as you drag one of Liquify's 10 tools around the screen.

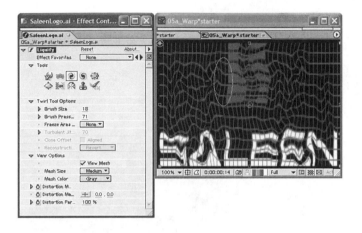

FIGURE 22.22
Liquify uses a mesh as a guide so that you can see the X/Y axis changes as you drag one of its distortion tools around the screen.

New Professional Edition Tools

New to the Professional Edition of After Effects 6 are two powerful and exciting tools: Keylight and Motion Tracker. Keylight offers better, more powerful chromakeying technology than you'll find in Premiere Pro. Motion Tracker makes it possible for you to accurately, quickly, and painlessly follow motion and then connect effects to those moving objects.

Keylight—Accurate and Clean-Keyed Effects

Keylight performs powerful chromakey analysis. It retains things such as reflections off the windows and does not leave jaggies around actors' hair.

Figure 22.23 shows the two shots that I'll key. It's difficult to see in print, but there are a few wisps of hair on the right and the windows have reflections.

FIGURE 22.23
Combining these two images and retaining elements such as reflections would be difficult if not impossible without a powerful chromakey analysis tool.

Applying Keylight to the scene and tweaking a few parameters led to the perfect key shown in Figure 22.24.

Follow Action with the Motion Tracker

After Effects 6 Professional's new Motion Tracker enables you to track any number of moving objects and then link effects directly to those objects. As I mentioned earlier in this section, you can do something as mundane as track something you want to touch up, and then apply that touch-up effect to the track (actually a collection of keyframes) to save a lot of time.

Its more exciting use is as a means to add cool effects to action items. You can highlight a skier by having a transparent, color matte match his every move. Follow a golf swing, leaving an arc that shows the swing's characteristics. Or, in the upcoming example, add headlights and lens flare to race cars.

As shown in Figure 22.25, the race car's headlights emit only a faint glow. After Effects can fix that and then some.

Using the Tracker controls, I place the highlighted square over a headlight and assign that target's motion to the Lens Flare Video Effect that I've already added to the composition. When completed the Lens Flare will simulate a bright headlight and will add a stream of halos running in a diagonal line away from the headlight.

Figure 22.26 shows how the Lens Flare layer looks after the Tracker controls add several dozen motion keyframes that track the headlights perfectly.

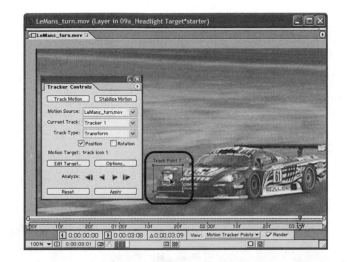

FIGURE 22.25
Use the Motion Tracker controls to target an object you want to track, and then assign an effect to that motion route.

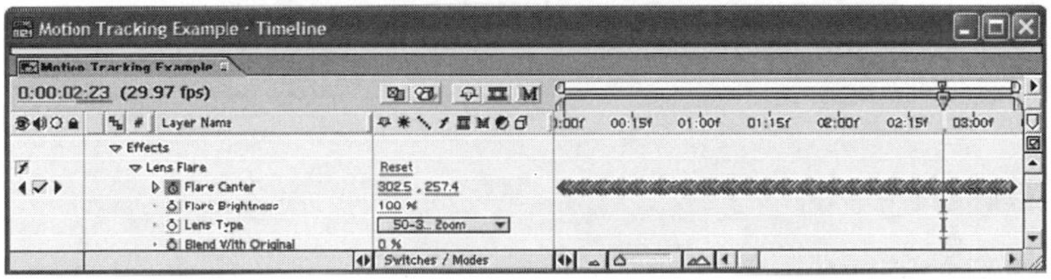

FIGURE 22.26
Opening the Motion Tracker's Motion Target layer shows the many automatically added motion keyframes that accurately follow the headlight.

After using the Tracker on both headlights, the video looks like Figure 22.27. For comparison purposes, take a look at Figure 22.25.

FIGURE 22.27
Adding Lens Flare to the motion tracking layers creates this very slick animated effect.

Summary

Adobe's Video Collection Professional contains everything you need to create high-end video projects. The two tools covered this hour—Photoshop CS and After Effects 6—are industry-leading powerhouses. Virtually everyone who works with digital images uses Photoshop, and the motion graphics and text animation tool of choice is After Effects.

Photoshop is geared to still image and photo work, but there are many ways to incorporate those layered graphics and stills into a video production. This hour I called on an expert in using Photoshop for DV work to offer some tips along those lines.

Those viewing After Effects for the first time might find its wealth of possibilities daunting. It's so big that many production houses literally specialize in either its text animation features or its motion graphics tools. In this hour, I gave you a taste of what After Effects can do on both fronts.

Q&A

Q *Your scanning tips in the Photoshop section say that there's no real need to scan at higher than 72 DPI. If I do use higher resolution settings, does that create a problem?*

A Probably not. At worst, you might experience minor inconveniences along the lines of disc space, CPU cycles, and scanning speed. Most people scan at 600 DPI or higher to ensure sharp printouts. That's serious overkill for TV sets that can't display at more than 72 DPI, and those files take up massive disc space versus images scanned at 72 DPI. High-res images also can take more processor horsepower to display quickly. On the other hand, if you plan to put your images in motion (pan or zoom) higher resolution is a must to avoid fuzzy photos.

Q *As long as I can put Photoshop graphics in motion in Premiere Pro plus apply keyframable animated effects to video, why use After Effects to do just about the same thing?*

A Premiere Pro is a professional-quality tool with a full feature set. But it has some limitations when compared to After Effects. All its motion paths are straight lines. You can animate text by crawling it or rolling it, but you can't begin to apply all the wild twists, turns, and character-based effects available in After Effects. Premiere Pro can handle the bulk of your day-to-day video editing needs, but if you want to match some of the really high-end video effects you see mainly in high-budget advertisements and Hollywood films, you'll need to move up to After Effects.

Workshop

Quiz

1. Photoshop primarily uses bitmapped graphics. Illustrator is geared to vector-based graphics. Describe the difference.

2. What's the principal difference between rotoscoping a two-second Premiere Pro clip in Photoshop versus After Effects?

3. In After Effects, what's the basic process used to apply an effect to an object moving through a video?

Quiz Answers

1. Bitmapped images are like photographs or paintings. After you've created them, you can't expand them without causing some damage. When you blow up bitmapped images, the graphics or video editing software fills in the expanding gaps between the existing color bits with a best guess color. The more you expand, the less distinct your image becomes. Vector-based graphics are defined by mathematical formulas and are geared primarily to higher-resolution print media. As you expand or shrink them, they always remain as sharply defined as the original image.

2. In Photoshop, you import that clip as a filmstrip of still frames and then apply your hand-drawn artwork one frame at a time. In After Effects, you work with the video clip itself. You can use the Paint tools to draw on its first frame, and then use some effect and motion controls to animate it for the length of the clip. After Effects can save you an enormous amount of time.

3. Add whatever effect or object (a graphic, text, touch-up artwork) you want to animate to the composition that also holds the original video. Use Motion Tracking on the video and assign its output to that effect or object.

Exercises

1. If you've never worked with Photoshop CS, download the trial version and check it out. The easiest place to start is scanning or importing some photos and painting on them, applying special effects, and doing touch-up work.

2. Download the trial version of After Effects 6 and take it for a test drive. It might seem overwhelming at first, but if you simply play around with it for a while—animating text is a good place to start—you'll begin to see its potential. As you add effects, open every newly added disclosure triangle in its timeline. That's a great way to see the plethora of options.

3. Start taking a closer look at TV advertisements with high production values. Knowing what After Effects can do, try to spot video edits that equal or go beyond what you can do with Premiere Pro. Try to figure out generally how they did them. Compile a list of the effects that you think are the most effective and see whether you can duplicate them in Premiere Pro or in your trial version of After Effects 6.

HOUR 23

Exporting Premiere Pro Frames, Clips, and Sequences

What You'll Learn in This Hour:

- ▶ Introducing exporting
- ▶ Recording your project to videotape
- ▶ Creating basic media files
- ▶ Using the Adobe Media Encoder
- ▶ Using Premiere Pro to burn a video to a DVD

Premiere Pro offers a dizzying array of export options—methods to record your project to videotape, convert them into files, or burn them to DVDs. Making sense of them is the goal of this hour.

The simplest task is to use Premiere Pro as a digital video recorder. In addition, you can export a still frame or frame sequence to your hard drive for use in other programs, record only the audio portion of your project, or convert a video segment or entire project into one of several standard (but somewhat dated) PC video formats.

Of greater relevance are the higher-level video encoding formats available in Premiere Pro: MPEG, Windows Media, QuickTime, and RealMedia. Premiere Pro's export workhorse—the Adobe Media Encoder—offers all four of those formats with many options for each. You'll use that powerful tool to create projects to post to a Web site, for multimedia CD-ROMs, and to create DVD movies.

Introducing Exporting

When you purchased Premiere Pro, you might have had only one basic concept in mind: to create video projects to put on a DVD or VHS tapes and play them on a TV. As it turns out, there are many other possibilities.

As technology has changed, Adobe has responded by adding new output features to Premiere Pro. A few years ago, the idea of creating a video for playback on the Internet was unheard of. And personal DVDs weren't even on the radar. Now they are both major elements of Premiere Pro.

So, before venturing off into recording to videotape (and later DVD), take a look at those possibilities.

Make sure that a sequence is active (otherwise Premiere Pro will not present Export as an option) by clicking somewhere in the Timeline window.

Select File→Export. As shown in Figure 23.1, Premiere Pro offers six export options:

- ▶ **Movie**—Create Windows AVI or Apple QuickTime desktop video files or collections of still images.

- ▶ **Frame**—Convert a selected frame into a still image using one of four formats: BMP, GIF, Targa, or TIFF.

- ▶ **Audio**—Record an audio-only file in one of four formats: WAV, AVI, DV AVI, or QuickTime.

- ▶ **Export to Tape**—Transfer your project to videotape.

- ▶ **Adobe Media Encoder**—Transcode your project or a segment into one of four high-end file formats: MPEG, Windows Media, RealMedia, or QuickTime. Use these for Web streaming video or, in the case of MPEG, to play on DVDs.

- ▶ **Export To DVD**—Burn your Premiere Pro project directly to a DVD.

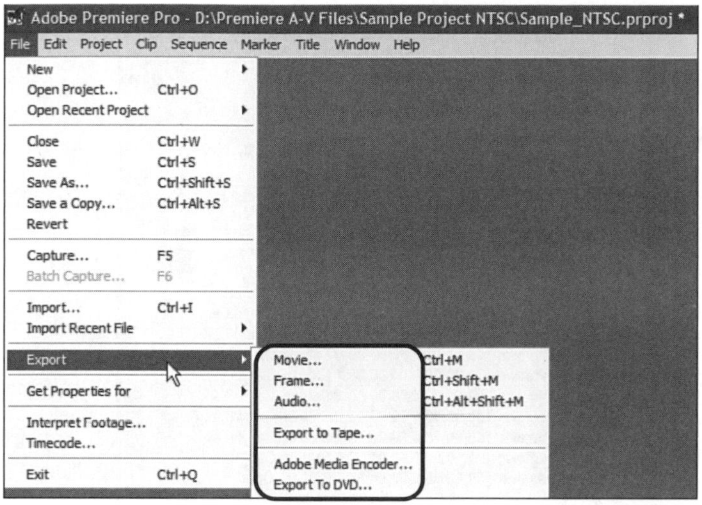

FIGURE 23.1
Premiere Pro's six
export options.

Two Other Export Options

Premiere Pro offers two other, infrequently used export options. To see them, make the Project window active by clicking somewhere inside it and then select Project from the main menu. Among other things, that drop-down menu displays the following two export options:

▶ **Export Batch List**—You might never use this option. As shown in Figure 23.2, an export batch list is a CSV (comma-separated value) file that lists only the video files used in your project. When imported, Premiere Pro considers batch list files as offline media; that is, you'll need to use their in- and out-point data to have Premiere Pro import them from a DV device. You use batch files to transfer projects between logging utility software and products such as Premiere Pro.

▶ **Export Project as AAF**—On the other hand, you might have an increasing need for this option. AAF (advanced authoring format) is replacing edit decision lists as the means to transfer media asset *and* editing information among various editing devices and software. It handles most common transitions, but does not support video effects or audio fade and pan information.

FIGURE 23.2
Exporting a project batch list creates a text file that you can read in a spreadsheet program such as Excel or in word processing software.

	Microsoft Excel - Sams Book Batch List.csv					

	A	B	C	D	E	
1	SAL-001	01;01;09;1	01;01;10;0	Horse Riding-2.avi		
2	Unknown	00;00;00;0	00;00;05;1	Saleen_Ambient_Bed.wav		
3	Unknown	00;00;00;0	00;00;06;0	Saleen_Car.avi		
4	Unknown	00;00;00;0	00;00;06;0	Saleen_Car_01.avi		
5	Unknown	00;00;00;0	00;00;06;1	Saleen_Car_02.avi		
6	Unknown	00;00;00;0	00;00;06;1	Saleen_Car_03.avi		
7	Unknown	00;00;00;0	00;00;07;0	Saleen_Car_04.avi		
8	Unknown	00;00;00;0	00;00;08;0	Saleen_Car_05.avi		
9	Unknown	00;00;00;0	00;00;08;1	Saleen_Car_06.avi		
10	Unknown	00;00;00;0	00;00;08;2	Saleen_Car_07.avi		
11	Unknown	00;00;00;0	00;00;11;0	Saleen_Car_08.avi		
12	Unknown	00;00;00;0	00;00;15;2	Saleen_Car_09.avi		
13	Unknown	00;00;00;0	00;01;27;0	Saleen_Car_10.avi		
14	Unknown	00;00;00;0	00;08;58;1	Saleen_Open.avi		

Sams Book Batch List

Recording Your Sequence to Videotape

Although a videotape is no longer the principal output medium for projects made using Premiere, it's still a very common choice. All you need is a DV recording device—most commonly, the same DV camcorder you used to *import* the original raw video. You can also use an analog videotape recorder, but doing so takes some extra effort (see "What About Analog Export?" later in this hour).

Export to Tape

Even with something as straightforward as dubbing your sequence to videotape, Premiere Pro gives you multiple options. Here's how to do it:

1. Connect your DV camcorder to your computer, just as you did when you captured video. Turn that device on and set it to VCR or VTR (not Camera as you might expect).

By the Way

What About Analog Export?

Premiere Pro offers only DV export. If you want to export (record) to an analog machine, you have three choices. You can record to DV and then record that to an analog device; record to a DV device and pass it through to an analog camcorder; or purchase a video card with Premiere Pro import/export plug-ins, such as the Canopus DVStorm2 discussed in Hour 4, "Premiere Pro Setup." After it has been installed, such a card adds its unique analog (and DV) export options to Premiere Pro. I explain how to export to what are known as *nondevice controlled recorders* in "Nondevice Control—Manual—Recording," later in this hour.

2. Select the sequence you want to record. The default process will export only an entire sequence, as opposed to a selected segment. To export only a segment, follow the nondevice control instructions listed in the Did You Know? presented later in this task.

Did you Know?

Leave a Little Room

To give your project a little breathing room on your DV tape, add black video to its beginning. You know the drill: Click on the New Item button at the bottom of the Project window (or right-click in the Project window and select New Item) and select Black Video. Drag that to the start of your project (hold down the Ctrl key to insert it and slide all other clips to the right).

If you're going to have a postproduction studio duplicate your tapes, add 30 seconds of bars and tone to the beginning so that the studio can set up its gear. Same drill as black video: Right-click the Project window, select New Item→Bars and Tone. Drag it to the beginning of your project and change its duration to 30 seconds (use the Trim window's Ripple edit option).

3. Select File→Export→Export to Tape. That pops up the dialog box shown in Figure 23.3. Here's a rundown of its options:

   ▶ **Activate Recording Device**—When checked, Premiere Pro will control your DV device. Uncheck it if you want to record to a device that you'll control manually.

Did you Know?

Nondevice Control—Manual—Recording

To record to a nondevice control machine, set up your camcorder for recording and then play the sequence to make sure that you see it display on your external recording device. Cue your tape to where you want recording to begin, position the CTI edit line to where you want recording to begin, press the Record button on your device, and press the Play button in the Monitor window Program screen (or press Enter).

When the sequence or segment finishes, press the Stop button in the Program screen and then stop the tape on the device.

It's best to render your sequence before doing manual, nondevice control recording. Otherwise, you'll have to wait with your finger on the device Record button and press it just as rendering ends.

▶ **Assemble at Timecode**—Use this to select an in-point on the tape where you want recording to begin. When unchecked, recording will begin at the current tape location.

▶ **Delay Movie Start**—This is for the few DV recording devices that need a brief period of time between receiving the video signal and recording it. Check your device's manual to see what the manufacturer recommends.

▶ **Preroll**—Most decks needs little or no time to get up to the proper tape recording speed. To be on the safe side, select 150 frames (five seconds) or add black video to the start of your project (see previous Did You Know?).

▶ **Options**—These are self-explanatory.

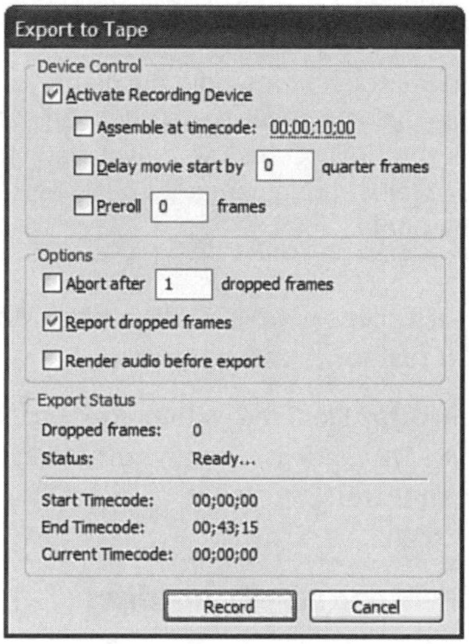

FIGURE 23.3
The Export to Tape dialog box enables you to fine-tune the export process before starting to record your project to your DV or analog device.

4. Click Record. If you haven't rendered your project (by pressing Enter for playback instead of the Spacebar), Premiere Pro will do that now. If you have a slower machine, this could take quite a while—several multiples of your project length. You can watch the progress in the Rendering Files display and by watching the red horizontal lines at the top of the sequence. After Premiere Pro has rendered their associated clips, those lines turn green.

5. When rendering is complete, Premiere Pro will start your camcorder and record your project to it. Because rendering might take several minutes, it's best to plug your camcorder into AC power, rather than use a battery. Not

only could your battery lose juice at a critical moment, your camcorder might go on auto-shutdown after a few minutes of inactivity.

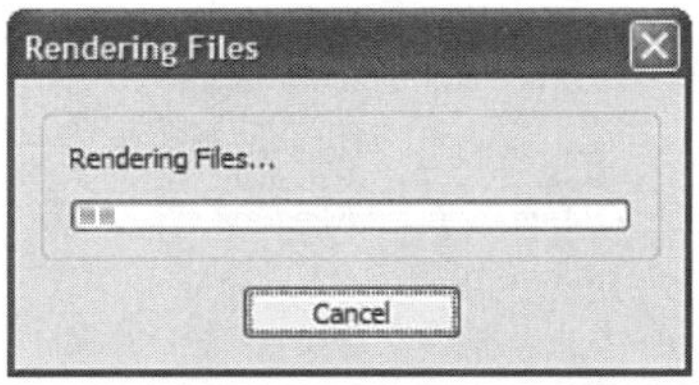

FIGURE 23.4
The Rendering Files display gives you one indication of rendering progress.

Creating Basic Media Files

Three of the export options are Movie, Frame, and Audio. All use older basic file formats such as AVI for the Movie and Audio option. My general view is that if you want to convert a sequence into an audio or audio/video file, use the Adobe Media Encoder. I cover it in the next section.

That said, you certainly will make still images (frames) from your video clips and WAV (Windows Audio Waveform) audio files are still heavily used in audio editing software such as Adobe Audition. So, there are still reasons to use these three export categories. I'll take you through each in turn.

Exporting Still Images

Try it Yourself

Grabbing still images of video frames is a common practice. You might want to use them for promotional literature, to post on the Web, as cover art for a video, and as a DVD menu background. This is a very simple process:

1. Move the CTI edit line to the video frame you want to save as a graphic file.

2. Select File→Export→Frame. As illustrated in Figure 23.5, that selection opens the Export Frame dialog box to your current project's file folder (you can opt to store this graphic in there or in any other folder).

3. The default file type is BMP (bitmap). You can accept that default, type in a filename, and click Save and that would be that. If you want to use one of the other three available file types—GIF, Targa, or TIFF—click the Settings button highlighted in Figure 23.5.

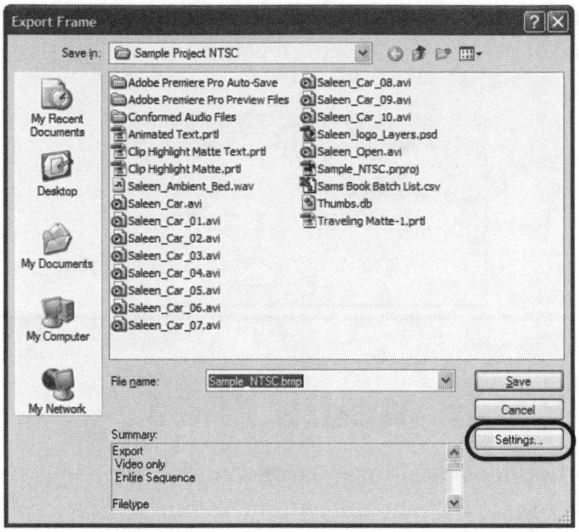

FIGURE 23.5
The Export Frame dialog box defaults to your project location.

4. In the newly opened Export Frame Settings dialog box shown in Figure 23.6, note the drop-down File Type list. Select one of the other three file types.

5. Note that you have one other option: Add to Project When Finished. If you don't want to add the file, uncheck the box.

6. Click OK to return to the Export Frame dialog box where you can give your image a filename using the newly selected file type. Then click Save.

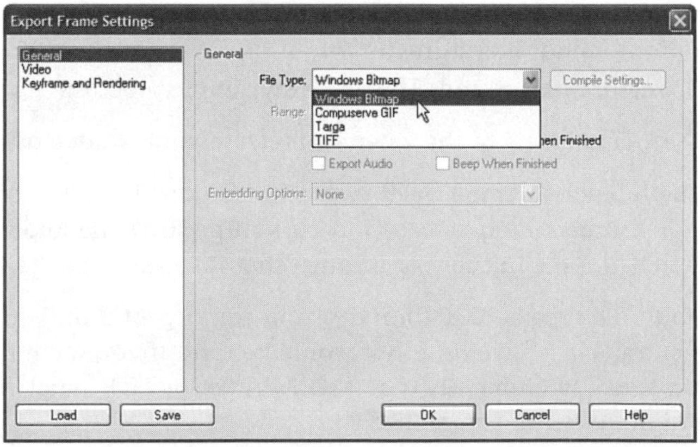

FIGURE 23.6
The Export Frame Settings dialog box offers only four file types.

Exporting Audio

Sometimes you might want to export only the audio portion of a sequence or clip—to do some higher-level editing in Adobe Audition, for example. Doing that follows the same steps as exporting a frame, but has a few more options. Again you choose from four file types, but you can tweak parameters such as the sample rate and the audio compression software used. And you can opt to export only a portion of your sequence. Here's how to do all that:

1. If you want to export a portion of your selected sequence, click and drag the work area bar's beginning and end points to define that segment.

2. Select File→Export→Audio to open the Export Audio dialog box.

Go Directly to Export Movie

After you've completed this task, there really is no need to use this Export Audio option again. Instead, select Export Movie, and deselect its Export Video option to leave the Export Audio option active.

---

3. As with the Export Frame dialog box, you can accept the default file type (WAV) or click Settings to open the Export Audio Settings dialog box shown in Figure 23.7.

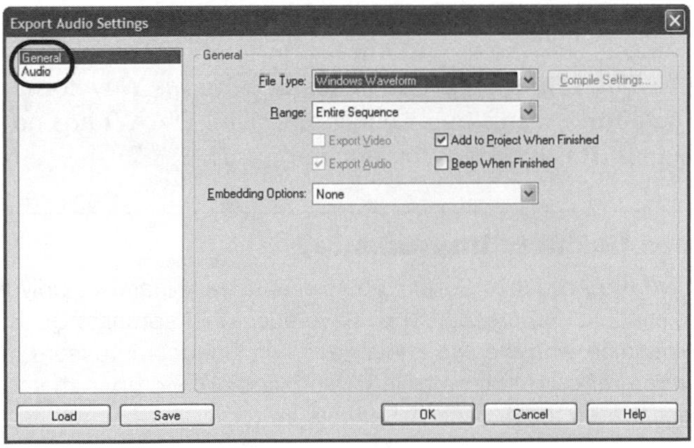

FIGURE 23.7
Like the Export Frame Settings dialog box, the Export Audio Settings dialog box offers only a few options.

4. Select whether you want the range to be the entire sequence or the work area bar.

5. Click the File Type drop-down menu. You have four choices, all of which are old Windows standbys. Windows Waveform is the only audio-specific format. Microsoft AVI, DV AVI, and QuickTime MOV are the same as those found in the upcoming Export Video Settings dialog box. In this case, so that you can see one extra feature, select QuickTime and then click the Audio option in the left column (highlighted in Figure 23.7).

6. The Audio section (shown in Figure 23.8) offers five options.

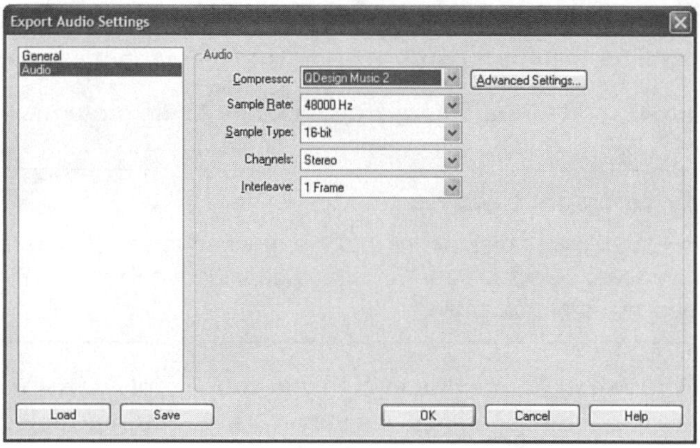

FIGURE 23.8
Switching to the Audio options window in the Export Audio Settings dialog box reveals five drop-down menus.

▶ **Compressor**—There is no way to briefly explain all the Compressor options. Click the drop-down list and note the 14 options associated with QuickTime. If you had chosen Windows Waveform or AVI, you would have seen similar but shorter lists. DV AVI has no compression options. It is by definition uncompressed.

Did you Know?

Is Advanced Settings Unavailable?

You'll likely note the Advanced Settings button is usually inactive. Only the following QuickTime-compatible compressor types have additional settings: QDesign Music 2, Qualcomm PureVoice, and the two Endian and two Float compressors (all use Endian technology, which refers to the order in which bytes are stored in memory). Selecting one of these activates the Advanced Settings button.

Just for grins, I assembled those three interfaces in Figure 23.9. Take a look at them. Because you should use the Adobe Media Encoder for virtually all audio compression, this might be the only time you see them.

▶ **Sample Rate**—Samples per second. 44,100 is CD-audio quality. A lower rate saves CPU cycles but audio quality suffers.

▶ **Sample Type**—Number of bits per sample. 16-bit is standard, but Premiere Pro supports up to 32-bit floating point.

▶ **Channels**—Stereo or mono. Dolby is not available for any of these audio files.

▶ **Interleave**—Usually refers to how audio information is inserted into video frames. This is kind of superfluous. Stick with the 1 Frame default setting.

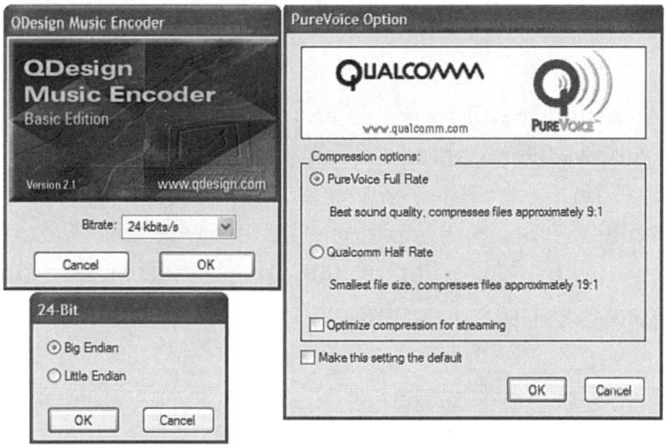

FIGURE 23.9
Only three compressor types have advanced options: QDesign Music 2, Qualcomm PureVoice, and the four Endian compressors.

7. After selecting your options, click OK to return to the Export Audio dialog box. Your new file type will show up as the default. Give your audio file a name and click Save.

Exporting a Movie

Because this process is so similar to exporting audio, I'll simply go over the various options rather than present a task.

When you open the Export Movie Settings dialog box (shown in Figure 23.10) and click the File Type drop-down list, you'll discover standard video file fare plus something that might be new to you: still frame sequences.

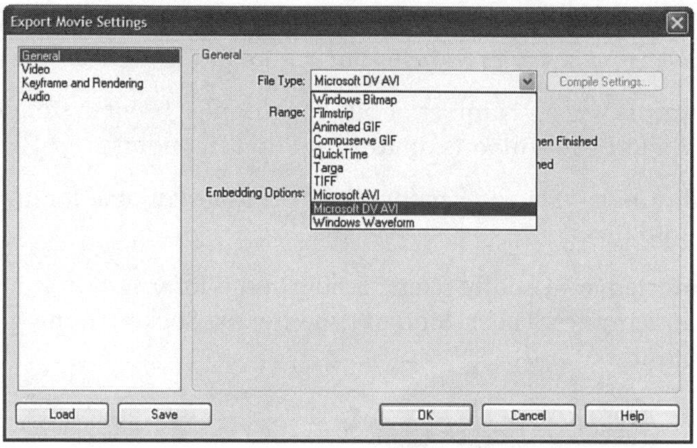

FIGURE 23.10
Export Movie
Settings offers
basic video files
plus still frame
sequences.

Frequently, editors transfer still frame sequences to programs such as Photoshop where they add graphic elements to them—a process referred to as **rotoscoping**—and then import them back into Premiere Pro for further editing. The Filmstrip option is specifically for use in Photoshop. On the other hand, animated GIF sequences work best with solid-color, motion graphics, typically for use on the Internet. They are a great way to animate a logo, for instance.

Did you Know?

> **After Effects: A Better Rotoscoper**
>
> Rotoscoping is even more effective in Adobe After Effects. In that powerful motion graphics product, you can apply animated artwork directly to video rather than use the frame-at-a-time method in Photoshop.

As I mentioned earlier this hour, Export Audio is a subset of Export Movie. Therefore, you can use Export Movie for all your A/V basic file creation needs. Export Movie has all the file types found in Export Audio (Windows Waveform is audio-only; AVI, DV AVI, and QuickTime are A/V). The same audio options you encountered in the Audio Export section are also available in the Export Movie Settings dialog box. You access them the same way: by clicking Audio on the left side of the dialog box. What's different about the Export Movie dialog box is the Video and Keyframe and Rendering sections.

Video Options

Click on Video to access those options (see Figure 23.11). If you start checking drop-down lists, you'll get the sense that things can become a bit complicated here. I'll try to simplify things by breaking the process down by file types available for export.

Some options make huge differences in the quality of your exported file, whereas others have minimal differences. Which options are available depends entirely on the file type you select in the General section of the Export Movie Settings dialog box.

The Video options include Frame Size, Frame Rate, Depth, and Quality. All are fairly self-explanatory. Some are dependent on the chosen **codec** (compression/decompression algorithm). The smaller the frame size and lower the frame rate, color depth, and quality, the smaller the exported file size. This used to be a critical issue. Many older computers could not handle higher data-rate A/V files. It's not that critical any more. Here are some of the other options (for additional information, check Premiere Pro's Help section under Video Export Settings):

▶ **Microsoft DV AVI**—It has virtually no options. It operates only at its default quality. You choose between NTSC and PAL. You also set the pixel aspect ratio—basically wide-screen or regular.

▶ **Microsoft AVI and QuickTime**—They present the most options. The most perplexing is the codec you'll use. AVI works with 9, QuickTime with 22. Which one you choose is largely up to your needs. Adobe does not offer documentation on any of the codecs used when creating AVI or QuickTime files. I wrote up a simplified rundown in the following sidebar.

Some of these codecs let you set a maximum data rate. Originally, this was done to ensure that the newly created video file did not exceed the speed ratings of lower-end CD-ROM drives. That, too, is ancient history. Checking Recompress gives you two options: Always recompresses every frame, even if it is below the stated maximum data rate, and Maintain Data Rate recompresses only those frames above the maximum rate.

▶ **Quality**—This setting can have a setting from 0 to 100%, and is another narrow-purpose option. If you captured video using a codec, you should use that same quality setting or less for export. Because you probably will work with DV source video most of the time—and therefore will not do any compression during capture—this issue rarely will be a factor.

Codec Characteristics

The number of codecs available in the Video section of the Export Movie Settings dialog box is overwhelming. You'll find no documentation on any of them in your Premiere Pro printed manual or online help file. The basic rule of thumb is to choose codecs that work on the PC that will be used to play the files. Here is a barebones rundown:

Standard video QuickTime/Windows AVI codecs—Cinepak and Indeo. Cinepak, developed in the late 1980s, is the old guard industry standard. Indeo is better than Cinepak but requires a fast computer.

Newer video codecs (QuickTime only)—Sorenson and Motion JPEG. Both are a step up from Cinepak and Indeo. In general, Sorenson is your best bet of all standard QuickTime codecs. Motion JPEG is used mainly for storage, not playback. (Note that Photo JPEG creates high-quality images but is slow.)

Graphic animation codecs (QuickTime only)—Animation and planar RGB.

Still image codecs (QuickTime only)—TIFF, BMP, TGA, and PNG.

Others (QuickTime only)—H.261 and H.263 are for video conferencing.

For more information on video codecs, see http://www.siggraph.org/education/materials/HyperGraph/video/codecs/Default.htm.

Keyframe and Rendering Options

With the exception of Fields, you may never use the settings in this dialog box, shown in Figure 23.12. Here's a rundown on what's available:

Fields—This is one of those easily overlooked "gotchas." The default setting for all DV output should be Lower Field First. For computer monitors, it's No Fields. Premiere Pro should automatically change this setting, depending on the file type, but it's a good idea to check this. Some video hardware needs to have an Upper Field setting. You'll have to check your documentation to find out.

Deinterlace Video Footage—Most video is interlaced. It consists of two fields: one containing the odd-numbered lines and the other the even-numbered lines. TV interlaces these fields to create the full-screen image. Select the Deinterlace option if you're exporting to a non-interlaced medium such as motion picture film or if you're going to apply high-quality effects in another program, such as Adobe After Effects.

Optimize Stills—With today's fast PCs, this will be a non-starter for most Premiere Pro users. Its primary goal is to save disk space, but that can have a drawback: playback problems. Optimize Stills converts still images within an exported video into single, longer-playing frames.

Keyframes—Offers a level of control few video producers will ever need or want to exploit. Some codecs—Cinepak, Intel Indeo, Sorenson, and others—offer this user-selected option. Basically, more keyframes means better-looking compressed video and more rendering time. But this is serious engineering overkill.

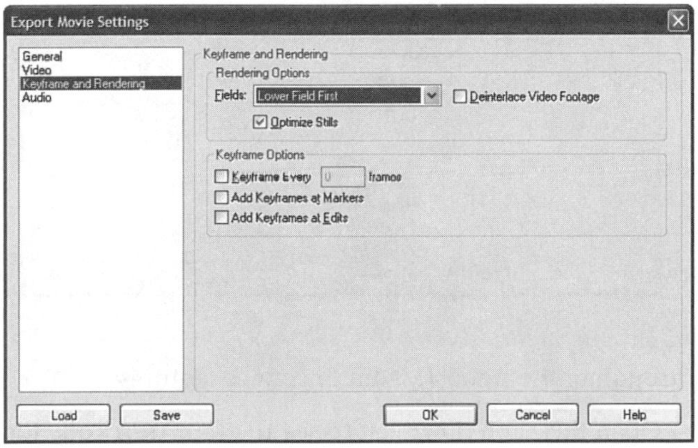

FIGURE 23.12
The Keyframe and Rendering dialog box within Export Movie Settings.

Using the Adobe Media Encoder

This is Premiere Pro's export powerhouse tool. It offers several flavors of MPEG encoding plus Windows Media, RealMedia, and QuickTime streaming media (as opposed to the QuickTime MOV files you encountered in Export Audio and Export Movie).

Each of the four basic encoding engines has so many presets that few editors will need to do any parameter tweaking. That said, there are customizable options aplenty but most are too arcane for me.

Rather than attempt to explain each encoding engine's unique characteristics, I'll show you how to access them and explain a couple general concepts. If you want to go beyond that and unravel, for example, the mysteries of QuickTime's Spatial Quality setting, you're on your own.

Open the Adobe Media Encoder by selecting File→Export→Adobe Media Encoder. As shown in Figure 23.13, that selection opens the Transcode Settings dialog box.

FIGURE 23.13
The Adobe Media Encoder has four transcode modules with uncountable options.

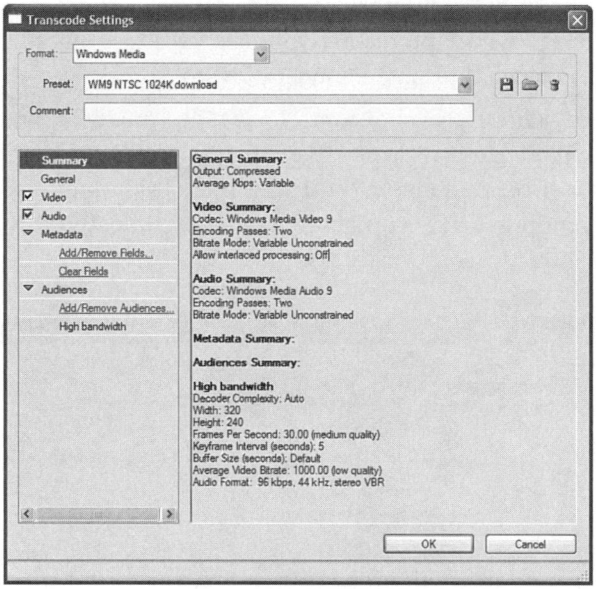

Here's a run-through of the Adobe Media Encoder's features:

▶ **Format**—Open this drop-down list to see the four transcode file types: MPEG (five varieties), QuickTime, RealMedia, and Windows Media.

▶ **Preset**—Depending on the format, opening this drop-down list could overwhelm you. Select Windows Media as a format and then check out the dozens of possibilities.

▶ **Comment**—You can create a custom preset. If so, you can add a comment here.

▶ **Summary**—Selecting Summary displays all the various attributes of the Format, Preset, and any other parameters selected from the Video and Audio options.

▶ **General**—Any additional options not available in the Video or Audio sections. Varies depending on the encoder format.

▶ **Video**—Selecting this enables you to choose a codec, frame size, and some other options. Again, each format has its own unique set of parameters.

▶ **Audio**—Same concept as the Video option.

▶ **Metadata**—Information about the video. Click on Add/Remove Fields to open the Select Metadata dialog box. Only Windows Media lets you add fields. But, in each case, you can select items such as Title, Author, and Parental Rating. Click OK and then input your metadata by selecting the word Metadata in the Transcode Settings dialog box. As shown in Figure 23.14, that selection displays whatever metadata tags you selected. As shown in Figure 23.15, you edit their contents by selecting Metadata in the Transcode Settings dialog box.

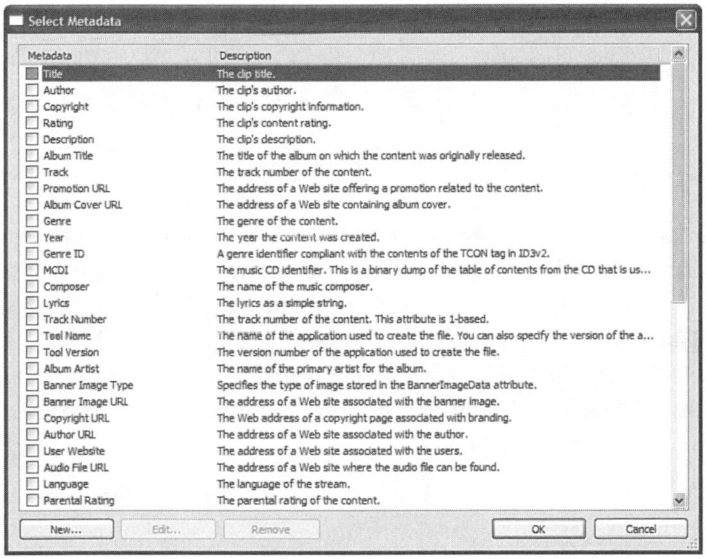

FIGURE 23.14
Use the Select Metadata dialog box to add some descriptive textual information to your encoded project.

▶ **Audiences**—This term is a bit misleading. *Bandwidth* would be more apropos. All three of the Adobe Media Encoder's non-MPEG formats are geared to Internet playback. As shown in Figure 23.16, the Audiences setting is where you can select bandwidths for your final file. In the case of Windows Media, you have 16 options ranging from 14.4 dial-up modems to T1 lines and faster.

FIGURE 23.15
After you've select
metadata tags, you
can edit their con-
tents by selecting
Metadata in the
Transcode Settings
dialog box.

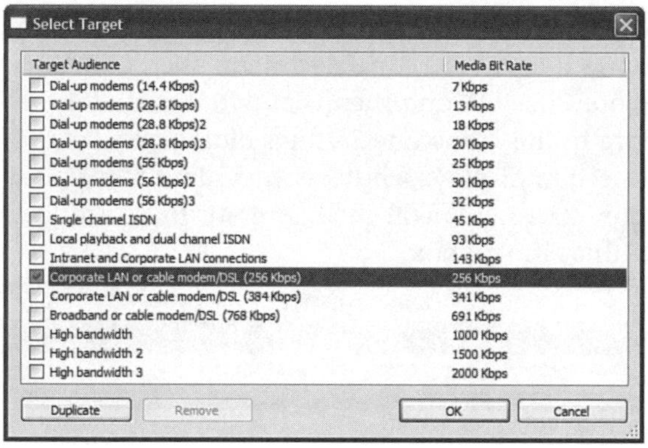

FIGURE 23.16
The Target
Audience dialog
box enables you to
select multiple
bandwidths (date
rates) you want to
include in your
transcoded file.

QuickTime

QuickTime offers the most options, but has a limited number of presets. To see what it has to offer, select QuickTime in the Format drop-down list. Take a look at the Preset drop-down list and select QT 256 streaming NTSC (or PAL). Now, as shown in Figure 23.17, select Video and note that as with QuickTime MOV files, you can select from a list of 20+ codecs, set frame size, frame rate, and a few other characteristics. Its General options also far outnumber any offered by RealMedia and Windows Media.

If you check out the Audio options, you'll note that it offers the same list of compression algorithms available for QuickTime MOV files. It has a fairly limited number of metadata fields and bandwidth options.

RealMedia

RealMedia takes a more consumer-friendly, hand-holding approach and offers the fewest user options and presets. Select the RealMedia format, keep the Summary window open, and click through a few presets. As illustrated in Figure 23.18, you might note that one option is two-pass encoding. Both RealMedia and Windows Media offer this option. If selected, the encoder analyzes the original video project before transcoding it. That means encoding will take almost twice as long, but the resulting video will look better than a single-pass version using all the same parameters.

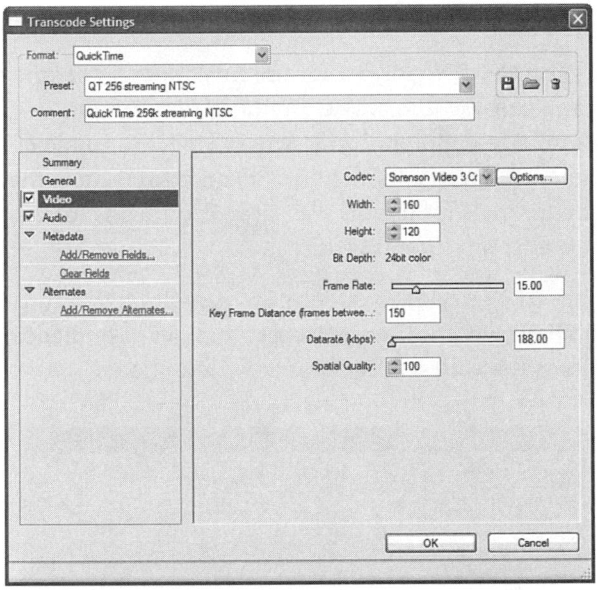

FIGURE 23.17
QuickTime's Video option offers more than 20 codecs and a number of other options.

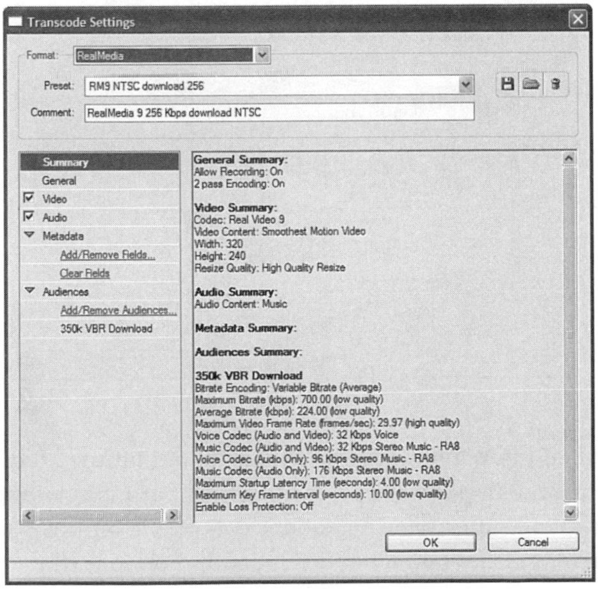

FIGURE 23.18
RealMedia offers fewer options, but unlike QuickTime, enables users to opt for two-pass encoding.

If you select the RM9 NTSC (or PAL) streaming modem preset, you'll note that RealMedia automatically selects six audiences (bandwidths). You can add or remove others, but that automatic setup approach is the hallmark of RealMedia.

Windows Media

This is the most versatile video format for use in Windows PCs and for playback on the Internet. You can use it to create anything from simple, low bitrate files for use on CD-ROMs to high-definition, wide-screen videos for playback in theaters or on high-def plasma TV screens. In addition, it can create single files with multiple bandwidth bit-stream rates for use on Web sites as a means to compensate for varying Internet user connection speeds.

As shown in Figure 23.19, its video options are very limited. But as I mentioned earlier, it has about 60 presets, has the largest number of audience (bandwidth) selections, and offers the widest range of metadata options.

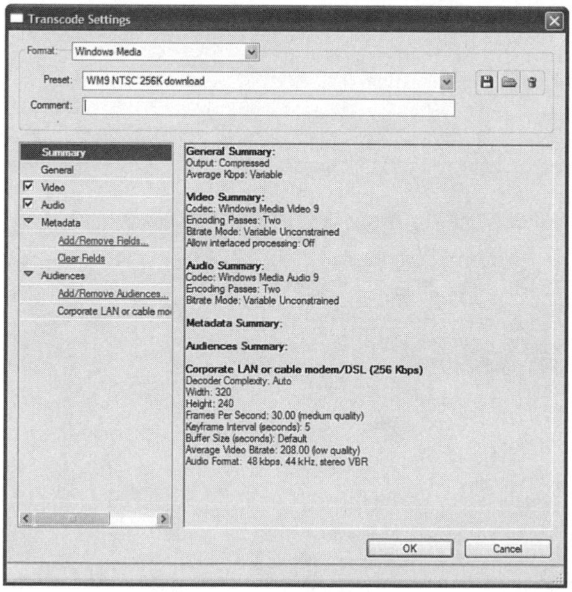

FIGURE 23.19
Windows Media has the fewest video and audio options, but by far the largest number of presets and bandwidth selections.

Note one feature of the Windows Media Video option: Bitrate Mode. Constant bitrate is best for smooth playback on the Internet, but high data rate scenes (typically fast action) will suffer some degradation. Variable bitrate is the better choice for consistent visual quality and is more appropriate when archiving video or creating projects for playback on a PC.

As illustrated in Figure 23.20, one other feature of the Adobe Media Encoder is the extra information it presents as it encodes your files.

FIGURE 23.20
The Adobe Media Encoder offers a more verbose render progress indicator than that used in the Export to Tape option.

MPEG

Why a special encoder for MPEG? MPEG-2 is the de facto standard codec for DVD movies and videos. It presents sharp video and CD-quality audio at about one thirtieth the data rate of regular analog video and one fourth the data rate of DV. You've seen movies on DVD and know how good they look. And you've seen those razor-sharp digital satellite TV images. Both systems use MPEG-2-encoded videos.

If you want to create DVDs to play on your home or business DVD video system, you must use MPEG-encoded video files. That's been the case ever since DVD movies arrived on the scene a few years ago.

You can use a DVD-authoring tool such as Adobe Encore DVD to convert video files to MPEG or you can convert in Premiere Pro—it's your choice. But if you do it in Premiere Pro, you need do it only once, you have a smaller file, and you know it will be compatible with all DVD-authoring applications (Encore DVD, for example, works only with MPEG or AVI files).

Prosumer DV Can't Match Film

By the Way

Because you probably shot your videos using prosumer DV (also known as **DV25**), they will not look as good as Hollywood DVD movies. Hollywood DVD movies start their lives as 35mm (or larger) film. DV25 can't touch that for quality. And those great video images you see on digital satellite systems—while running under MPEG-2 compression—probably started as broadcast-quality analog video signals—also a cut or two above prosumer DV.

Only now are professional video producers embracing this technology. It took the convergence of two technological advances to bring us to this point of putting a software-based MPEG encoder in Premiere Pro:

▶ First, MPEG is asymmetrical. It takes a lot of computer horsepower to *encode* a DV or analog TV signal into MPEG-2 or other MPEG formats On the other hand, *decoding* (playback on your DVD player) takes much less processor juice. Until relatively recently, encoding MPEG-2 required some expensive hardware that was priced beyond the reach of most video producers. Now increases in processor power and improved MPEG-encoding software have eliminated the need for hardware MPEG encoders.

▶ Second, DVD recorders have come way, way down in price. Pioneer Electronics is driving this continuing downward price spiral. By late 2003, Pioneer's standard DVD recorder retailed for less than $200. Along with this drop in hardware pricing, DVD recordable media prices have dropped dramatically, to as low as $3 per disc when purchased in bulk.

What this means is that now you have an opportunity to create media that will play on most DVD players and is interactive and high quality.

Using the Adobe Media Encoder to Export MPEG-1 and MPEG-2

Before we get into the exporting/encoding details, I want to give you a little background on exporting MPEG-1 and MPEG-2 from Premiere Pro. In Premiere 6.5, these capabilities were provided by the Adobe MPEG Encoder, a separate plug-in powered by MainConcept. Premiere Pro also uses the MainConcept MPEG-1 and MPEG-2 technology, but it's now included in the new Adobe Media Encoder interface. Figure 23.21 shows the Adobe Media Encoder set to export MPEG-2 for DVD.

MainConcept is a long-standing German firm (from the days of the Amiga) with a solid reputation as a creator of powerful multimedia tools and codecs. Premiere Pro also uses MainConcept's DV codec to maintain optimal quality and speed throughout the DV editing and exporting processes.

As I mentioned earlier, including a software MPEG encoder in Premiere Pro is a *big deal*. Before version 6.5, if Premiere users wanted to create MPEG-2 videos, they had to buy a third-party plug-in or use a hardware encoder. Now Premiere Pro users get a powerful encoder for free.

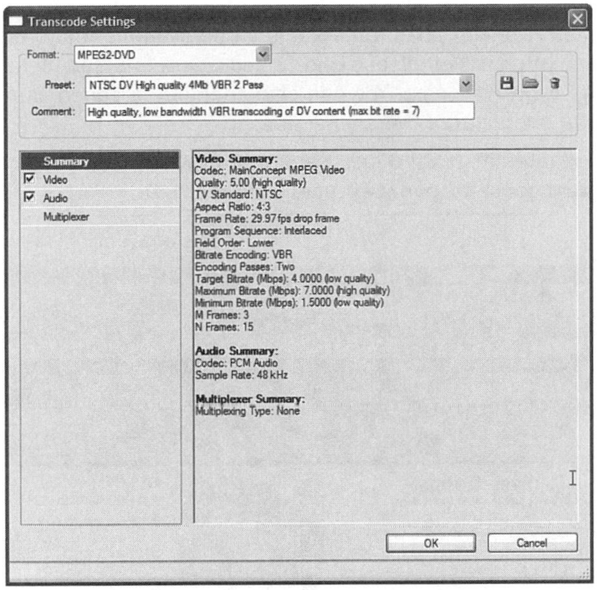

FIGURE 23.21
MainConcept's
MPEG encoding
technology is now
part of the Adobe
Media Encoder.

MainConcept's encoder is widely recognized as the leader in software MPEG encoding, and is used in a variety of video editing and DVD authoring software including Adobe Encore DVD. The MainConcept codecs offer exceptional quality, plus speed that can exceed that of hardware encoders in many situations.

Exporting MPEG for CD or DVD output using the Adobe Media Encoder is easy. Although the MPEG standards include many parameters, when you select a DVD, VCD, or SVCD preset, only the recommended parameters appear. Power users can expose other parameters by choosing a generic MPEG profile instead of one for a specific disc format such as DVD.

MainConcept has a support/resource site for the Adobe MPEG Encoder. It includes an FAQ about the encoder and MPEG in general, new settings files to download, test results, and a link to the relevant user-to-user forums on Adobe.com. The link to the support/resource site is http://www.mainconcept.com/adobemedia.html.

MainConcept.com—It's Worth the Visit

MainConcept's Web site is worth a visit at the very least because it offers free **texture loops**—four-second motion video clips that you can drop into Premiere Pro for some dazzling background animation. Figure 23.22 illustrates how they looks. One use for them is as text backdrops.

Did you Know?

It's a simple matter to copy/paste the same loop several times to create a smooth background animation. When placed end to end, there is a seamless transition from one copy of the clip to the next. You can also change the speed/duration of the clips to alter the character of the animations.

MainConcept updates its texture loop page with new offerings on a monthly basis: `http://www.mainconcept.com/texture_loops.shtml`.

FIGURE 23.22
Visit mainconcept.com to pick up a few texture loops for use within Premiere Pro.

Encoding an MPEG File

Here's a basic overview of the many options available in the MPEG encoder area of the Adobe Media Encoder.

There are five MPEG file formats, and most have multiple presets:

> **MPEG1**—This is a VHS-quality MPEG compression standard. If your goal is to create video to play on a VCD, use the MPEG1-VCD format instead. If you want to tweak the settings, this MPEG-1 format will suit your needs. As shown in Figure 23.23, access those settings by clicking on Video, Audio, and Multiplexer in turn.

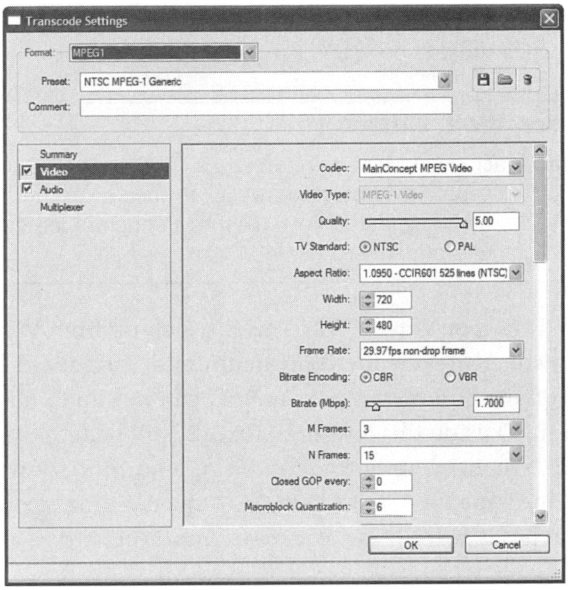

FIGURE 23.23
Selecting Video (or Audio or Multiplexer) in either the MPEG-1 or the MPEG-2 formats opens extensive lists of options.

MPEG1-VCD (Video CD)—If you select this option, the encoder will make a special kind of MPEG-1 file of your project. Later, using standalone CD-authoring and/or writing software that supports VCD, you can burn up to about an hour of MPEG-1 video onto a CD that will play on most consumer DVD video players and computer DVD and CD drives. A good online resource for VCD and SVCD issues is http://www.dvdrhelp.com/vcd.htm.

MPEG2—This is the high-end MPEG format geared to DVDs. As with MPEG-1, if your goal is to create DVD content, select MPEG2-DVD. If you want to tweak the MPEG-2 parameters, stick with the MPEG-2 format.

MPEG2-DVD—Selecting this option means the encoder will create MPEG-2 content for inclusion on a DVD. DVDs can hold up to 4.7GB of data, which can include as much as 133 minutes of MPEG-2 video depending on the bitrate. However, at the bitrates needed for very high-quality video, you should expect to fit much less data on a disc.

You also can place VHS-quality MPEG-1 video on them. Either flavor of MPEG plays in both standalone DVD players and in computers with DVD drives. Depending on the multiplexer settings, the encoder might create a **program stream** (a single file containing both video and audio) or **elementary streams** (separate video and audio files). Some DVD authoring programs require program streams, whereas some others prefer elementary.

Check your authoring software's documentation to find out the appropriate setting for you. Adobe Encore DVD works with both types.

By the Way

DVD Stands for, Well, Nothing

DVD is not an official acronym. Most companies say DVD stands for *digital versatile disc*, but that's not the case. DVDs started as *digital video discs*, but industry politics killed that idea. A journalist suggested *versatile* and through repeated usage that has become the de facto standardized name.

MPEG2-SVCD (Super Video CD)—This is a step up from VCD. In this case, the encoder will create a reduced bitstream rate, specialized MPEG-2 file. Depending on the parameters you set, you can put up to about 45 minutes of video on a CD using this low-end MPEG-2 (still better than MPEG-1) video. Again, you need authoring- and/or CD-burning software that supports SVCD to create an SVCD CD-ROM. A good online resource for VCD and SVCD issues is http://www.dvdrhelp.com/svcd.htm.

By the Way

SVCD Issues

SVCD creates videos in a 480×480 resolution (NTSC) or 480×576 resolution (PAL). If you play them back on standard video players such as the Windows Media Player or within Premiere Pro in the Source window, they'll look "tall" (that is, squashed in at the sides).

If you open these files in software that recognizes this standard MPEG format, such as DVD player software, they will play in the proper aspect ratio. If you place them on Premiere Pro's timeline and play them in the Monitor window, they will display in the proper aspect ratio, but as noted later in the sidebar, "Why Premiere Pro Does Not Edit Native MPEG Video," Premiere Pro is not intended to fully handle any MPEG format.

After you've made your format selection (MainConcept's MPEG encoder or any of the three other encoders), click OK. That selection takes you to a Save File dialog box. There you select whether you want to export the entire sequence or the segment under the work area bar.

Click Save and the rendering and transcoding begin. Depending on the quality level settings, this could take a long time. As I mentioned earlier this hour, rendering on its own can take several times the length of your sequence. Transcoding times might be about double the length of your piece.

By the Way

Is MPEG Encoding Taking Longer?

Users of the Adobe MPEG encoder in Premiere 6.5 might think that the MPEG encoder in Premiere Pro is slower. However, MainConcept testing shows it to actually be a bit faster at comparable settings.

The reason for the apparent disparity is that Premiere Pro's export settings default to the highest possible quality level, which can increase exporting time. The new support for two-pass encoding in Premiere Pro (the MPEG encoder analyzes the video twice to find the best means to compress while retaining quality) also roughly doubles the exporting time.

The PremierePro.README.pdf file (in Premiere Pro's main file folder) includes details on this issue. MainConcept's support/resource site also includes additional MPEG encoding presets for Premiere Pro, which are designed to speed encoding while still maintaining good quality.

Why Premiere Pro Does Not Edit Native MPEG Video

As I put together this hour on MPEG encoding, I swapped several emails with the MainConcept U.S. subsidiary's chief operating officer, Mark Bailey.

Bailey is the company's primary liaison with Adobe. His solid grasp of the MPEG compression universe completely impressed me. After reading emails from several beta testers on the Premiere Pro forum asking why Premiere Pro didn't offer native MPEG editing, I asked Bailey for his take on this topic. The remainder of this sidebar summarizes what he had to say.

Although MPEG is an excellent way to deliver material, it has some limitations as an editing format. Because of its high compression and the way that some frames are calculated, MPEG material can be subject to significant quality degradation when rendered multiple times. Because video editing and compositing projects often involve many generations of rendering, there is the potential for noticeable loss.

Although Premiere Pro does import MPEG material, it doesn't offer native MPEG editing. Imported MPEG files are transcoded to DV for editing, and then the DV data must be re-transcoded if a user wants to export the project as MPEG. This can result in two additional generations of compression.

Of course, it's best to start any editing or compositing project with the least-compressed source material available. Using highly compressed media from the start could present serious problems, except when special tools are used to work around these problems.

The workflow explained in this book—editing in DV and encoding the finished project to MPEG—works very well.

However, there are some cases in which people might need to edit MPEG and some companies offer plug-ins that enable it with varying results. As of earlier 2004, MainConcept is creating a plug-in that it believes will make MPEG editing a viable option and even make it advantageous in some circumstances. Planned features (which are subject to change) include

- ▶ Native MPEG editing in Premiere
- ▶ Real-time, high-quality capture to MPEG from a variety of source devices; for example, from a DV camcorder
- ▶ DV support, meaning that MPEG and DV material can be included in the same project with equal efficiency
- ▶ Smart rendering, meaning that only changed frames are re-encoded
- ▶ Smart requantizing—the ability to transcode from one MPEG format (such as Sony MICROMV) to another (such as DVD-compliant MPEG-2) without re-encoding
- ▶ High definition support
- ▶ Export to a variety of devices

This plug-in presents a very viable workflow. For example, you could capture directly to DVD-compliant MPEG-2, edit the captured material, and export the project with very minimal rendering.

Work on the plug-in is progressing very well. It might be available by the time you're reading this. For more details, visit MainConcept's Web site at www.mainconcept.com.

Using Premiere Pro to Burn a Video to a DVD

New to Premiere Pro is the capability to take a sequence or a video segment and burn it directly to a DVD. After the DVD has been completed, you can take the DVD and place it in a set-top player, which will automatically play your video. It won't have the menus, buttons, and other options associated with Hollywood DVDs. But it can have chapter points that you can jump to using your DVD player's remote control.

If you want to add DVD features such as menus, buttons, scene selection options, subtitles, and multiple languages, you'll need DVD authoring software, such as Encore DVD. I devote the final hour of this book to that excellent Adobe product.

Creating a DVD

Try it Yourself
▼

Here are the basic steps to take when exporting a video to a DVD:

1. You can give your video chapter points. That enables viewers to quickly navigate through your project using the chapter buttons on their DVD remote.

2. To add chapter points (called **sequence markers** in Premiere Pro), move your CTI to the beginning of a new scene (for example), right-click in the Time Ruler bar, select Set Sequence Marker→Unnumbered (keyboard short-cut—numeric keypad asterisk * key). Do that as many times as you like. The one caveat is that chapter points (sequence markers) must be at least 15 frames apart.

3. Select File→Export→Export to DVD. That opens the dialog box shown in Figure 23.24. Give your project a name by selecting Custom from the drop-down list. Check Timeframe Markers if you want to add chapter points, and check Loop Playback if you want your video to start over after it ends.

4. Select Encoding. As shown in Figure 23.25, this dialog box enables you to specify the encoding quality. The file format is MPEG-2 and you cannot change that. But you can tweak its settings using many of the features available in the Adobe Media Encoder. To access those features, click the Edit button.

▼

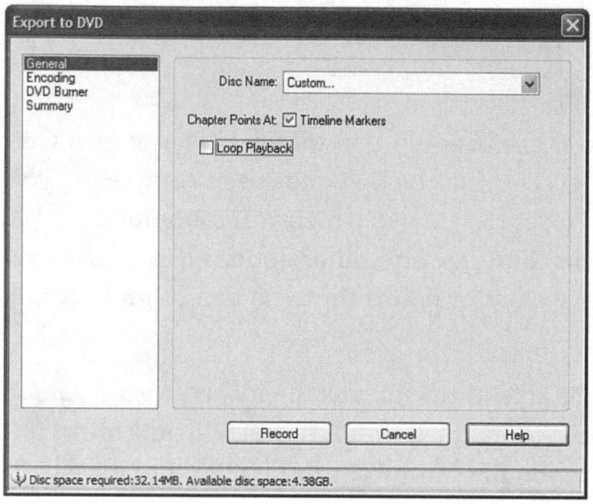

FIGURE 23.24
The first step in the DVD creation process: Give your disc a name and note whether you want the video to loop or have chapter points.

Did you Know?

Bitrate Settings

Select a bitrate that fits your needs and video length. If your project is less than approximately 90 minutes, you can use the highest target bitrate: 7Mbps. If your video is longer, it might not fit on a standard DVD-R/RW at that rate, so choose a 4Mbps preset. Selecting VBR (for *variable bitrate*) means the MainConcept encoder will find the best bitrate for each frame (maxing out at 9Mbps for the 7Mbps target and 7Mbps for the 4Mbps target setting).

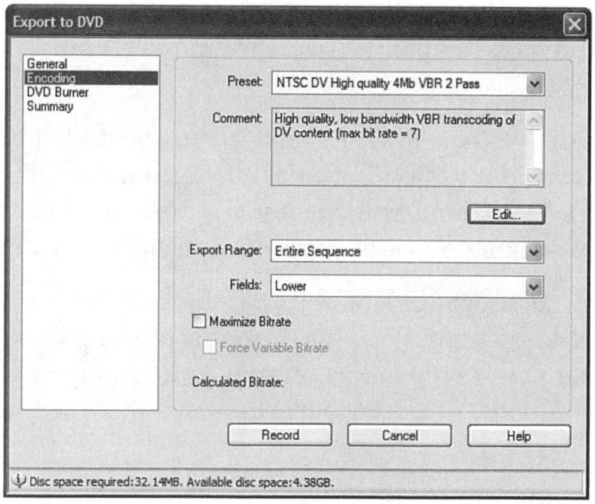

FIGURE 23.25
The Encoding section enables you to access the MPEG encoder parameters.

5. Select the Export Range: Entire Sequence or Work Area.

6. Check out the DVD Burner section. It identifies any burners on your PC and enables you to set the number of DVD copies and whether you want to record, test only, or test and record.

7. When done, click Record. You'll see a progress bar for transcoding and DVD burning.

Dolby AC-3 Licensing

If you select a preset that includes *SurCode for Dolby Digital*, a warning will pop up telling you that you can encode to AC-3 Dolby Digital Audio only three times. For encodings beyond that you'll need to purchase a license.

By the Way

Summary

Premiere Pro offers three basic means to export your project: recording to videotape, creating basic PC files, and transcoding your files using one of four high-end encoders. Recording to videotape is straightforward. Creating a file offers many more options. You can create video files, still frames, sequences of still frames, or animation files. In each instance, you can adjust various settings to reduce file size, generally as a means to streamline playback.

As more of your video projects move to DVD and the Internet, you'll rely heavily on the four high-end export modules available in the Adobe Media Encoder: MPEG, QuickTime, RealMedia, and Windows Media. Creating MPEG files opens the door to DVD authoring and placing MPEG files on CDs. The three other encoders all enable you to create single files that can play back your video at multiple bandwidths, which is a great feature for Internet playback. In addition, the Windows Media encoder offers high-end compression for wide-screen and high-definition videos.

Q&A

Q *When I use Export to Tape, and view a full-screen version of my project in the TV monitor attached to my PC, the playback on my computer is choppy. What's up?*

A Your computer might not have the power to process both video data streams. Select Project→Project Settings and in the General section, click Playback Settings. Because you probably want to view this on your computer monitor at the very least, uncheck Play Video on DV Hardware. Or, in the Real-Time Playback section, select Playback on Desktop Only. If you must view it on your DV/camcorder monitor, select Playback on DV Hardware Only.

Q *I encoded an MPEG-2 file, but it stutters on playback. Any idea why?*

A Did you select Upper Field First in the Fields drop-down menu in the MPEG encoder? If so, that might be the cause (a slow PC could be another reason). No Fields is the safest choice if you don't know which to choose, but its output quality is not as good as finding the correct setting—Upper or Lower.

Q *I encoded an MPEG-2 file and played it back in Windows Media Player, but there was no audio. What's up?*

A When you created that MPEG file using the Adobe Media Encoder, you probably built elementary stream (separate audio and video) files. To make a multiplexed (or *muxed*) file, click the Multiplexer option and select DVD (deselecting None in the process).

Workshop

Quiz

1. How do you create a sequence of still images, selecting one frame per second from your project?

2. How do you convert an AVI clip into a Windows Media file?

3. You have a two-hour video and you want to use Premiere Pro to burn it directly to a DVD. In general, what settings will work best?

Quiz Answers

1. Use the Export Movie process. Place the work area bar over the portion of your project from which you want to create still images, and select File→Export→Export Movie. Click Settings. Choose a sequence file type—TIFF, Targa, GIF, or Windows Bitmap—and move to Video. Select a frame size and change the Frame Rate setting to 1.

2. Add the clip to a sequence, place the work area bar over that clip, select File→Export→Windows Media Encoder, select Windows Media, and select from the various settings. To see if all went well, open Windows Media Player, select File—Open, locate your newly created file, and play it. You can view any metadata you added to it by selecting File→Properties and clicking the Content tab.

3. Two hours of the highest quality MPEG-2 video exceeds the capacity of a single-side, single-layer DVD. So, you need to crank down the encoding quality. Select a preset that has a 4Mbps bitrate. You can still use one that encodes using a variable bit rate (it tops out at 7Mbps at this level), and doing so will improve the overall quality. Use a constant bitrate only when you need a smooth flow of data, typically for Internet or network playback.

Exercises

1. Create both Windows Media and RealMedia files using similar settings and see how long the encoding processes take, how large the files are, and how the encoded clips look and sound.

2. Take a small step into the highly technical world of customized MPEG settings by selecting the MPEG-2 format and opening the three advanced settings sections: Video, Audio, and Multiplexer. Some are fairly self-explanatory: Bitrate Encoding (CBR or VBR), Encoding Passes (one or two), and Maximum Bitrate. But beyond that, you start entering the arcane world of I, B, and P frames and GOPs (groups of pictures). To learn more, start by visiting http://www.mpeg.org.

3. Do a personal test on video and audio codecs. Set the work area bar over a small section of your timeline and then export it using different codecs. Use the same Frame Size, Frame Rate, and Quality settings. When completed, note the file sizes and playback quality of the saved files.

HOUR 24

Authoring DVDs with Encore DVD

What You'll Learn in This Hour:

▶ Introducing the DVD authoring process
▶ Overview of Adobe Encore DVD
▶ Assembling assets and editing media
▶ Editing menus in Encore and Photoshop
▶ Linking menus, buttons, and media
▶ Burning the DVD

Authoring DVDs used to be solely for those with Hollywood budgets. As recently as the late 1990s, DVD recorders cost about $10,000 and the software used to put movies with menus and other interactive features on DVDs, cost more than $20,000.

Now DVD recorders sell for less than $200 and professional-quality authoring software, like Adobe Encore DVD, retails for about $500.

You're undoubtedly itching to create a multimedia DVD—one with menus, buttons, videos, music, and still images. In this hour, I introduce you to Encore DVD and give you some basics as a means to get you started along the path to DVD authoring.

I also give an overview of the authoring process, take you on a tour of Encore DVD, have you gather assets, and start building your project using menus, buttons, and media. Finally, you link those assets and see how to burn a DVD.

Introducing the Authoring Process

Authoring a DVD can be as simple as using Premiere Pro's Export to DVD function or as complex as creating a Hollywood-style DVD with multiple menus, dozens of buttons, several audio tracks, and subtitles.

The process varies from authoring project to authoring project, but the fundamentals remain the same.

Authoring Your DVD

Authoring typically begins in much the same way you start working with Premiere Pro. You assemble media assets into one readily accessible location. Then you venture off in a new direction as you build menus using static backgrounds (graphics, video still images, or photos) or you might opt to use a video or animation.

You also might want to add audio to your menus, such as music or a brief narration, and have them repeat (or *loop*) until the viewer takes some action. And you can add buttons or other graphics to those menus to serve as links to media assets or other menus.

Encore DVD offers a plethora of menu templates, buttons, and backgrounds. But its real strength is that it enables you to use menus you build from scratch in Photoshop.

In this hour, to keep things simple, you'll rely primarily on the library of assets that ships with both the retail and trial versions of Encore DVD.

Organizing Your DVD's Menu Structure

DVDs are interactive. That's one of their real fortes. You should therefore organize your DVDs to exploit that strength. To do that, use nested menus, intuitive navigation, and clearly labeled buttons.

Nested menus are menus within menus. You've encountered them time and again in Hollywood movie DVDs. Typically, those DVDs start with a main menu with buttons that take you to nested menus: special features, scene selection, or audio and subtitle setup menus.

Consider the family history DVD structure shown in Figure 24.1. Its main menu has button links to a video overview, immigration stories, photos, documents, and living history interviews. The stories nested menu offers links to other nested submenus, one for each family line.

To ensure a logical flow to your DVD, organize it using a flowchart similar to the one in Figure 24.1.

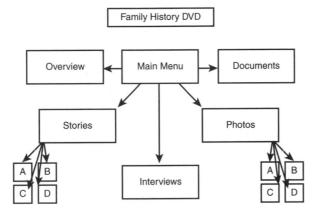

FIGURE 24.1
One possible DVD menu flowchart for a family history DVD.

Overview of Adobe Encore DVD

Adobe Encore DVD enables you to create full-featured, Hollywood-style DVDs complete with videos, motion menus with audio, animated buttons, scene selection, stills, Dolby digital audio, multiple language and audio tracks, and subtitles. Its tight integration with Photoshop (for menu and button creation), After Effects (for motion menus), and Premiere Pro (for videos and motion menus), plus its easy-to-use text and menu design tools, give you the freedom to present your media in its best light.

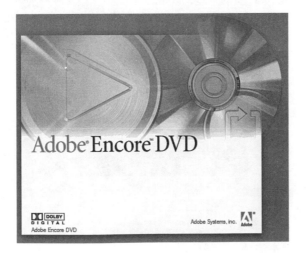

Its roots go back to Premiere 6.5. Adobe foresaw the explosive growth in the DVD authoring market and wanted to add a DVD authoring module to that immensely popular nonlinear editor (NLE). The company worked out a deal with Sonic Solutions, the DVD authoring market-leading firm, to bundle its popular DVDit! with Premiere 6.5.

That relationship led to another deal to license Sonic Solutions AuthorScript software (the engine that drives all its DVD authoring products) as well as provide a team of Sonic Solutions engineers to help Adobe develop the standalone DVD authoring product, Adobe Encore DVD.

At $549, it fits into a unique market niche: above Sonic Solutions consumer/prosumer DVDit! but below Sonic's high-end professional products such as DVD Producer and DVD Scenarist. Adobe geared Encore DVD specifically for those who are comfortable working with Premiere Pro and Photoshop.

Tour Encore DVD's User Interface

As shown in Figure 24.2, Encore DVD's user interface has the look and feel of other Adobe products. It uses timelines like those in Premiere Pro and After Effects for videos and slideshows. It incorporates graphics editing windows and text tools similar to those in Photoshop. Plus it features an Explorer-like window to tabulate menus, buttons, and their attributes, and Monitor windows with tabs to readily move from one function to another.

FIGURE 24.2
Adobe Encore DVD uses a familiar Adobe-style interface including file lists and window tabs to easily access and update menus and buttons.

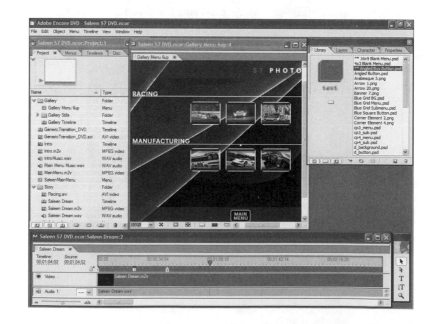

Encore DVD offers some neat twists on setting DVD menu and button navigation. Figures 24.3 and 24.4 show two such schemes: a collection of arrows that you can drag and drop to change button navigation routing (the order in which buttons highlight as viewers click up/down/left/right arrows on their remotes) within a menu and a means to create links using a cool drag-and-drop tool called the *Pick-whip*.

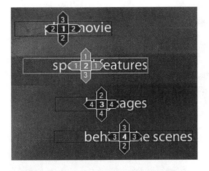

FIGURE 24.3
Use this four-point tool to drag and drop new button routing within a menu.

FIGURE 24.4
Use Encore DVD's Pick-whip to set button links by dragging and dropping them from a dialog box to a menu button.

Another strength is Encore's close ties to Photoshop. It has built-in means to recognize menus and other graphic elements created in Photoshop specifically for Encore, and uses Photoshop's layers approach to facilitate customizing button highlight colors and other characteristics (see Figure 24.5).

FIGURE 24.5
Encore emulates
Photoshop layers
to give users direct
control over setting
button highlight
attributes.

One other strength is Encore's menu design capabilities. It includes extensive menu layout options, full text editing functionality, and Photoshop design tools that enable you to make immediate, easily reversible changes.

Encore DVD also offers features you'd expect to see only in more expensive professional authoring apps such as precise control over chapters (for scene selection menus), 8 audio tracks (for multiple languages and director comments), 32 subtitle tracks, and the option to add DVD-ROM data files to your project. For those who have doubted the value of DVD authoring applications, Adobe's entry into this market should make believers out of them.

Assembling Assets and Editing Media

In most instances, the first stages of your Encore DVD workflow will run in parallel. You'll create media assets in video editing applications such as Premiere Pro, build static menus in Photoshop, and motion menus in After Effects. Then you assemble them all in Encore DVD.

Try it Yourself **Getting Started**

Much like Premiere Pro, Encore DVD's Project window serves as the asset repository. It gives you easy access to assets: menus, media, timelines, and project parameters.

After they've been assembled, you can add chapters, subtitles, and audio to those assets. Here how that works:

1. Start a new project by selecting File→New Project. Select NTSC or PAL and click OK.

2. As shown in Figure 24.6, that menu selection displays the Project window (with its four tabs) and the Library palette with its three tabs and Properties in a separate palette. But I dragged its tab into the top of the Library palette to simplify the workspace. Take a look at each Tab:

   ▶ **Project**—Displays all your imported assets—audio, video, and image files—as well as menus and timelines.

   ▶ **Menus**—When you import assets, you tell Encore which ones are menus. Those menus, plus any menus you build using Encore DVD, are stored here.

   ▶ **timeline**—You might want to add chapter points, subtitles, or extra audio tracks to your media assets. To do that, you place them on time-lines. You access all timelines you create within Encore DVD here.

   ▶ **Disc**—Take a look at the Disc tab shown in Figure 24.6. This is sort of the catchall Project window tab. You come here as you're wrapping up your authoring. The Check Links button displays any buttons, menus, or assets with missing links (if a viewer clicks an unlinked button, nothing will happen). It enables you to add region codes to your DVD as well as copy protection and a couple other odds and ends.

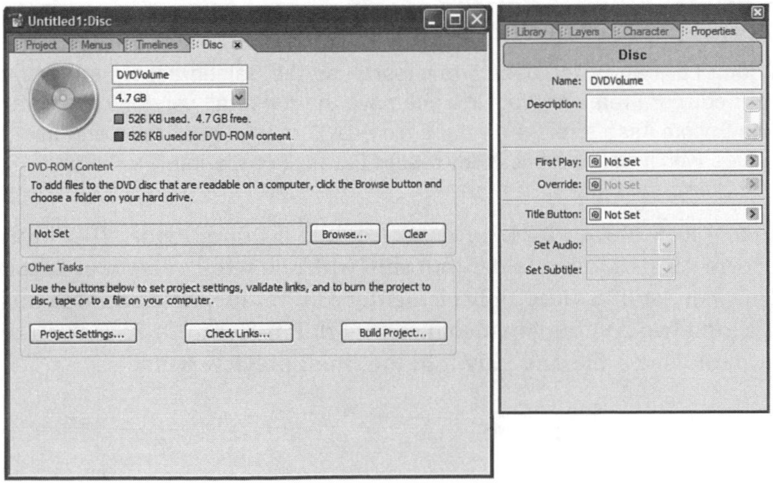

FIGURE 24.6
The Project window is your asset manager. The Library palette's four tabbed sections contain your menu-building and link-creating tools.

▶ **Library**—This holds your menu building assets: menus templates, buttons, and graphic elements (*images*, in Encore parlance). The trial version includes a couple dozen items. The retail version has about 200.

▶ **Layers**—This is something like a mini-Photoshop layers palette. It offers a subset of the standard Photoshop layers tools that enable you to make some simple fixes to menu items such as adjusting locations and sizes of banners and buttons.

▶ **Character**—Use this to add and edit text in menus and buttons.

▶ **Properties**—When you select an item, be it a button in a menu or an asset in the Project window, the Properties palette will display that item's characteristics such as duration, links, and name.

3. Click the Project tab and then import assets by double-clicking the blank space in the Project window to open the Import as Asset dialog box. Encore works with only two types of video files: MPEG and AVI. You can also import a variety of still image and audio file types.

Other Methods to Import

As with all things Adobe, there is more than one way to do a routine task such as importing assets. Here are three such options: right-click in the Project window and select Import as Asset or Import as Menu—or—select File→Import as Asset or Import as Menu—or—drag and drop from Explorer.

By the Way

Use Saleen Assets

If you don't have any video assets to import, use the Saleen assets that shipped with your copy of Premiere Pro. Or, if you have the full retail version of Encore DVD, copy the Encore-Assets folder off the Encore DVD to your hard drive and use its four media files (you'll use the DreamMovieSubtitles.txt file later).

4. Take a look at Figure 24.7. I imported the four audio/video files in the Encore-Assets/Movies folder that ship with the retail version of Encore DVD. They consist of a video-only elementary MPEG file, its associated audio WAV file, and two AVI audio/video files. As I did in Figure 24.7, click on an audio or audio/video file and play it in the small preview window.

No MPEG Transcoding Needed

The selected file's properties show up in the Properties palette. In particular, because this file is an MPEG-2 file, Encore will not do any additional transcoding of it before burning your DVD.

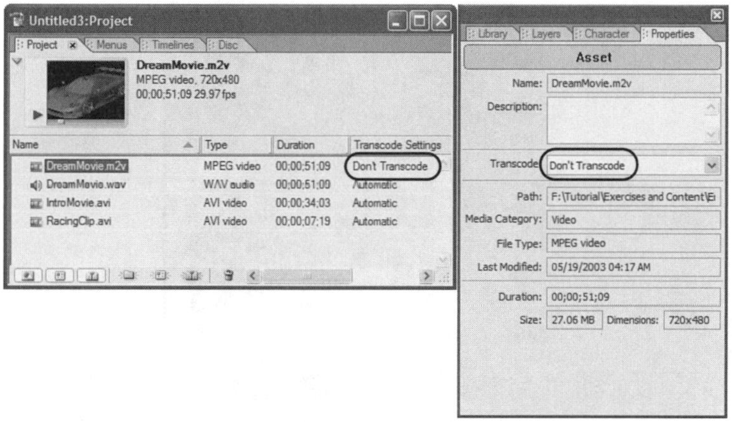

By the Way ▼

FIGURE 24.7
Organize assets in the Project window. Note that MPEG files need no additional transcoding before you make your DVD.

5. To have the audio and video play together on your DVD, you need to add them both to the same timeline. To do that, select Timeline→New Timeline (keyboard shortcut: Ctrl+T).

6. If you have the Encore-Assets, drag DreamMovie.m2v to the Video track and DreamMovie.wav to the Audio 1 track. Your timeline should look like the one in Figure 24.8. You can view your video in the Monitor window that opened when you created the timeline.

Missing Monitor?

There is a bug in version 1.0 of Encore DVD that can cause the Monitor window to not display. You might never encounter it because it tends to pop up only after multiple installs of Encore DVD (beta testers ran across it sometimes). Fix the problem by holding down Ctrl+Shift when you start Encore DVD. It won't start but that action will empty its preferences file. Now start it normally and the Monitor window should make its appearance when you open a timeline.

Watch Out! ▼

By the Way

Only One Video Track

Unlike Premiere Pro, Encore DVD has only one video track per timeline. The reason? You aren't using this for editing or compositing. Rather, this timeline is for adding chapters to the video plus audio tracks and subtitles.

FIGURE 24.8
Use the timeline to join an elementary video-only MPEG with its associated audio-only file.

7. Create another timeline by right-clicking `RacingClip.avi` in the Project window and selecting New timeline (you need to place this video on a timeline to enable you to link a menu button to it).

Did you Know?

Naming timelines

Encore DVD automatically names this new timeline RacingClip. You can name your other timeline by right-clicking it in the Project window, selecting Rename timeline, and giving it a new name.

8. You can add subtitles manually from the timeline's Monitor window or use a text file made in any word processor or Windows Notepad. First add a Subtitle track by right-clicking inside the timeline window and selecting Add Subtitle Track.

9. As shown in Figure 24.9, right-click on the newly added subtitle track and select Import Subtitles→Text Script. Using the Encore-Assets, navigate to Encore-Assets/Movies and select DreamMovieSubtitles.txt.

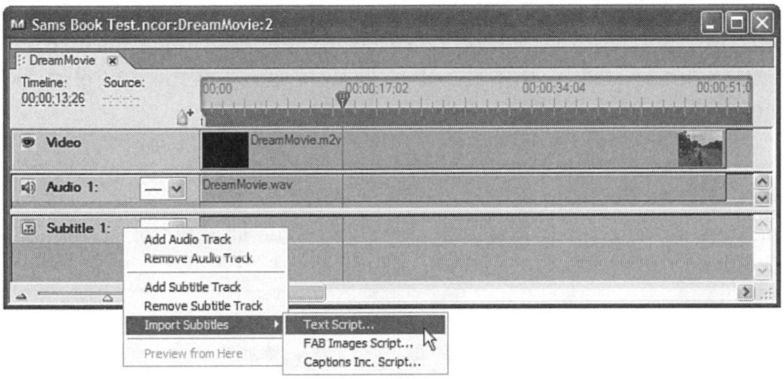

FIGURE 24.9
To add subtitles, add a subtitle track and then right-click on that new track to add a basic subtitle text file.

10. That opens the Import Subtitles (Text Script) dialog box shown in Figure 24.10. This is a very handy feature that no other DVD authoring product I'm aware of has (I tested more than a dozen for my book, *Sams Teach Yourself DVD Authoring in 24 Hours*). Here you can set several font attributes, such as size, placement on the screen, color, and justification. Click OK to accept the current settings.

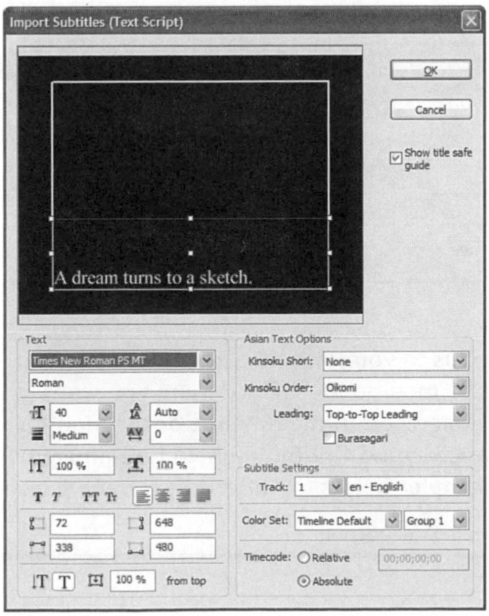

FIGURE 24.10
Before you finalize the import of subtitle text files, adjust their display attributes in this Import Subtitles (Text Script) dialog box.

▼

11. As shown in Figure 24.11, those subtitles now appear in the subtitle track as individual clips. You can edit them—move them and change their lengths— in the timeline window and edit their appearance in the Monitor window. Move the CTI edit line to one of them, click on the Character tab in the Library palette, select the Text tool from the Tools palette, highlight the text, and use the Character dialog box to make changes. I center justified the text and increased its size. It's also possible to move the text elsewhere on the screen.

Did you Know?

Switch Off Subtitles

You can turn off the display of subtitles by clicking the little button to the left of the word Subtitle 1 in the timeline window.

FIGURE 24.11
View and edit your subtitles in the Monitor window.

12. Add chapter points to your video for later inclusion in a scene selection submenu. Do that by moving the CTI to where you want to add a chapter and clicking the Chapter icon in the timeline or the Monitor window (keyboard shortcut: numeric keypad *). I highlighted both in Figure 24.12. Later, you will link these chapter points to buttons in a scene selection menu.

▲

13. Save your project: File→Save.

> ## Adding Chapters—An Inexact Science
>
> When you add chapters to an MPEG video, setting an exact location is a hit-or-miss affair. MPEG compression does not use each frame in a video. It selects scattered frames and then calculates the differences between those frames. In that way, an MPEG file has many fewer full frames than DV, for example. So, when you select a chapter point frame, Encore locates the nearest actual full frame and places the chapter point there.
>
> When you add chapter points to an AVI video in Encore DVD and later transcode it to MPEG, the transcoder ensures that the frame you selected remains associated with that chapter point.

By the Way

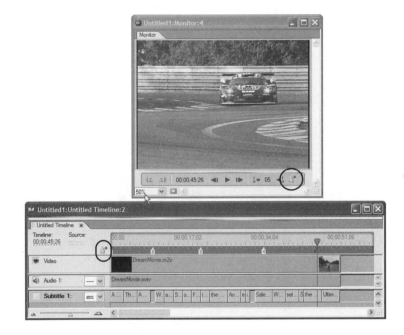

FIGURE 24.12
Add chapters to your video using the Chapter buttons in the Monitor or timeline window.

Editing Menus in Encore DVD and Photoshop

Menus are the focus of DVD authoring. They not only put a face on your production, but also provide all its interactivity. The full retail version of Encore DVD is loaded with menu templates, backgrounds, and buttons—certainly more than enough to create many DVDs. But as you become more facile with DVD authoring, you'll want to make custom menus. In those cases, Photoshop is the ideal candidate because it is fully integrated with Encore DVD.

Building Menus Within Encore DVD

For this task, I'll use both the Encore-Assets provided with the retail version of Encore and one of the three menu templates provided with all versions of Encore DVD. You can start with an empty background and add buttons, text, and graphics to suit your needs—or—edit an existing menu. We'll start with a blank slate:

1. In your project, open the Library palette (Window→Library) and select the Library tab. As shown in Figure 24.13, doing so displays the standard library of menu templates, images (graphic elements), and buttons that ship with all versions of Encore DVD.

Did you Know?

Highlighting Only Menus, Buttons, or Images (Graphics)

Take a look at Figure 24.13. The three buttons, starting in the bottom-left corner, control which menu-building assets display in the Library palette. From left to right, they are Menus, Buttons, and Images. When the button has a light background, its graphics will display. Click it to hide its items.

FIGURE 24.13
The Library palette contains all your menu building assets: buttons, menu templates, and graphics.

2. Right-click on Blue Grid Menu and select Create New Menu. Do the same with Blue Grid Submenu. They will appear in the Menu tab of the Project window.

Other Methods of Adding a Menu

There are two other ways to add a menu selected from the library to your project. Click on a menu name in the Library palette and click on the New Menu button (third from the right at the bottom of the Library palette). Or drag a menu from the Library palette to the Project window Menu tab. (If you drag it to the Project tab, Encore DVD will consider it only as a graphic, not a menu.)

If you have the Encore-Assets (or some other menus), you can add them to your project by double-clicking or right-clicking on an empty area in the Project window Menu tab to open the Import as Menu dialog box.

Did you Know?

3. Double-click on Blue Grid in the Project or Menu tab to open it in the Menu window.

4. As shown in Figure 24.14, add buttons to it by dragging them from the Library palette to that window.

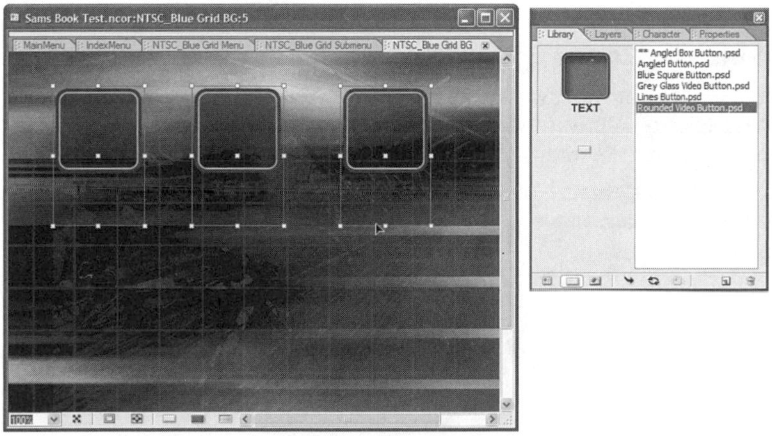

FIGURE 24.14
You can build a menu from scratch using a menu background and some buttons.

5. The text associated with these buttons is too dark. Fix that by selecting the Text tool (open the Tools palette by selecting Window→Tools), highlighting the text by dragging the tool on the text (or double-clicking on the text), clicking the Character tab and, as shown in Figure 24.15, changing the color to something lighter. You can also use the Text tool to add text directly to the menu—a title, for instance.

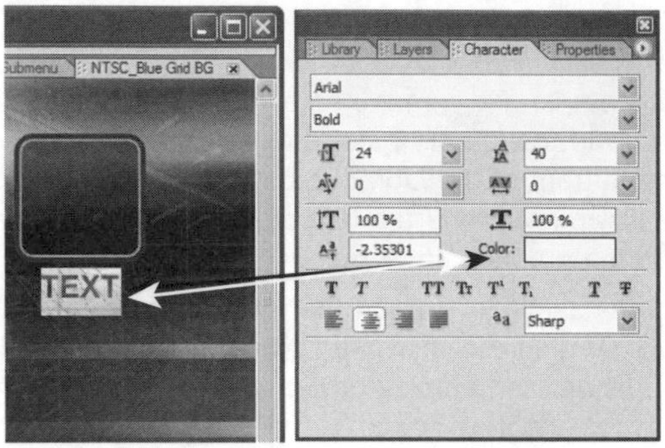

FIGURE 24.15

FIGURE 24.15
Edit text using the
Text tool and the
Character palette.

6. In the Menu window, select the Blue Grid Submenu. Click on the Layers tab
   in the Library palette. As shown in Figure 24.16, this shows the Photoshop-
   style layers for each element in the menu. Click the disclosure triangles to
   see the layers for each graphic element.

By the
Way

Symbols and Zones

Take a close look at the Layers palette. You'll see these items: (=1), (+), and (%).
Each tells Encore DVD what that graphic item does. I explain these further in the
upcoming section, "Encore DVD and Photoshop Integration."

Each of the Layers palette items defines a zone. You can't have overlapping button
zones or your viewers won't be able to use their remote to select a particular
button.

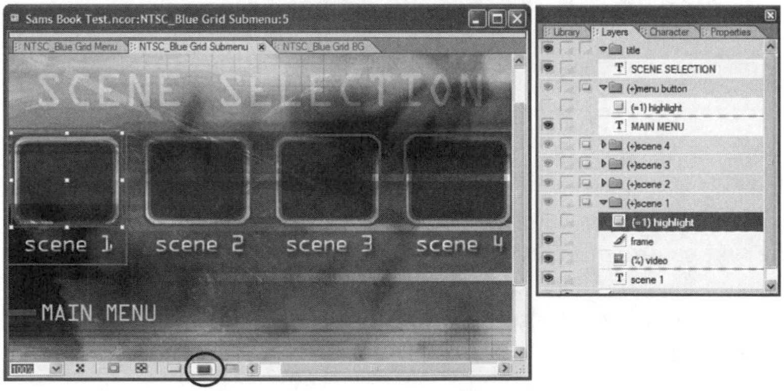

FIGURE 24.16
Displaying a
menu's layers
reveals each graph-
ic element. Clicking
the circled Selected
Subpicture
Highlights button
reveals how the
graphic will change
when the viewer
moves the remote
to a button.

7. Each of this menu's buttons has a *subpicture highlight*. This is a fairly obtuse and arcane part of the DVD specification. But its practical benefit is its capability to display button or text highlights as the viewer moves the remote to those menu elements (the selected highlight) and then clicks on one (activated). Click on the Show Selected Subpicture Highlights button, circled in Figure 24.16. It displays blue borders around the scenes and a blue rectangle to the left of the main menu (the activated state looks the same).

8. Change the selected subpicture color by clicking the Library palette Properties tab and selecting Menu Default from the Color Set drop-down list at the bottom of the palette. That is a different set of editable highlight colors. Depending on the default values in your version of Encore DVD, the blue highlight likely will change to orange.

9. Change the new color to one of your choosing by selecting Edit→Color Sets→Menu. Take a look at Figure 24.17. Select Menu Default from the Color Set drop-down list, and click the Preview button so that you can see changes in your menu as you make them in the Menu Color Set dialog box.

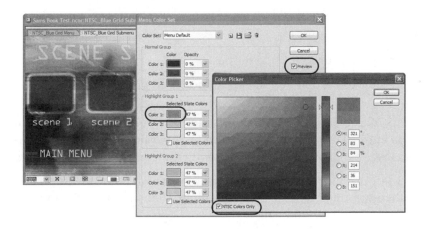

FIGURE 24.17
Use Menu Color Set dialog box to change the subpicture highlight colors for menu buttons.

10. Click on Selected State Color 1, click on NTSC Colors Only (to avoid smearing colors in NTSC TV sets), choose a new color, and click OK. Change the opacity to a higher number to make the color change more obvious and check out your work in the Menu window.

11. Change the Highlight Group 1 Activated State Color 1 to some other color and higher opacity. Now when you click on the Show Activated Subpicture Highlight button at the bottom of the Menu window, this new color will show up.

Encore DVD and Photoshop Integration

Because I covered basic Photoshop editing in Hour 22, "Using Photoshop and After Effects to Enhance Your DV Project," I won't offer up those kinds of editing tips. Rather I simply will point out how Adobe has integrated Encore DVD and Photoshop.

When editing menus in Encore DVD, you can do these things:

- ▶ Change or add text
- ▶ Alter the size of the scene button frames
- ▶ Copy and paste objects already in the menu
- ▶ Add graphic elements from the library
- ▶ Change the location of any element
- ▶ Turn graphic objects into buttons

In Photoshop, you can do all the items in the Encore DVD list plus these tasks:

- ▶ Create new graphics
- ▶ Apply filters and effects to the background
- ▶ Change colors and overall appearance of graphics

The crux of that integration is that you can edit Encore DVD menus in Photoshop or build Encore DVD menus from scratch in Photoshop. All it takes is some attention to layer naming conventions. Follow these steps to see how this works:

1. Select the Blue Grid Submenu by clicking its tab in the Menu window and then selecting Menu→Edit in Photoshop. Doing so opens Photoshop with that menu front and center.

2. Open the Layers palette by selecting Window→Layers.

3. Twirl down the disclosure triangles next to Title and Scene 1 and make sure that all eyeballs are on. Your layout should look like Figure 24.18.

Note the following layer and layer element naming conventions used in Encore DVD menus:

- ▶ (+) on a Layer set indicates this layer set is a button. You'll note the first layer—Title with the text *Scene Selection*—does not have a (+). That means that text string cannot be a button.

▶ (=1) or (=2) or (=3) selects the Highlight Menu Color Set Group. All such highlights in this menu are group 1. That's not required, but in this case, it ensures a consistent look to the menu in that all highlight colors will be the same throughout.

▶ (%) denotes that this graphic is a placeholder for a video placeholder image or video animation.

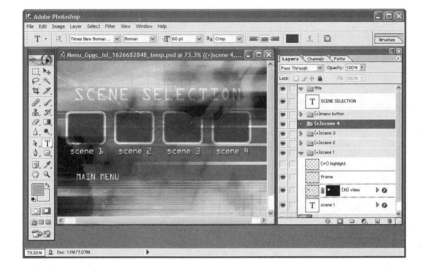

FIGURE 24.18
You can edit any Encore DVD menu in Photoshop.

To see how any changes made to an Encore DVD menu in Photoshop work, select the Background layer (click on the word *Background* in the Layers palette), select Image→Adjustment→Hue/Sat and move Hue slider to the right to about +72 (purple). Click OK. Then select File→Save.

Original Menu Remains Unchanged

These changes will not alter the original Encore DVD Library Blue Grid Submenu Photoshop file. Photoshop automatically creates a new file for this project.

Did you
Know?

Close Photoshop, return to Encore DVD and note that your menu has the new background color you gave it in Photoshop.

Linking Menus, Buttons, and Media

A strength of DVDs is their interactivity. Not unlike Web pages, you create menus with links to material behind those menus. In the case of DVD authoring, you decide what gets linked to what. Encore DVD offers several linking methods, most of which are simple drag-and-drop affairs or use drop-down menu lists.

On large projects with dozens of menus, buttons, and assets, tracking links can be a chore. Encore DVD takes care of that with another powerful feature. Encore DVD's link-checking tool lists all buttons, menus, and media that do not have links. Then you can drag and drop links to and from that list—a real nifty feature that no other DVD authoring product I know of has.

Try it Yourself　　**Linking Assets**

▼

To show you the breadth of Encore's linking capabilities, I'll present several scenarios. You could accomplish most of your linking tasks using only one of them, but there are unique benefits to each. Here's how they work:

1. Click on the Project window Project tab to open it.

2. Double-click on the Blue Grid Menu in the Menu (or Project) tab to open it in the Menu editor window.

3. From the Project window, click on the name of the first timeline you created (if you used the Encore-Assets in your timelines, select the one that has the DreamMovie video in it) and drag it to the Play Movie button in the Menu window. As shown in Figure 24.19, as you hover over Play Movie, its hot spot text box becomes highlighted. Creating this link means that when viewers play your DVD and click on Play Movie, it will do just that.

FIGURE 24.19
Drag a timeline from the Project window to the button/text you want viewers to click to access that timeline.

▼

4. Double-click on the Blue Grid Submenu tab in the Menu window to open it. Click on its Main Menu button (make sure that you use the Selection tool—V is the keyboard shortcut—as opposed to a Text tool).

5. Click on the Properties tab in the Library window. As shown in Figure 24.20, this context-sensitive palette should note that you've selected the menu button, the name given to the button's Photoshop layer (as opposed to its text string, "Main Menu"). To link it to this project's main menu, select Link→NTSC Blue Grid Menu→Default.

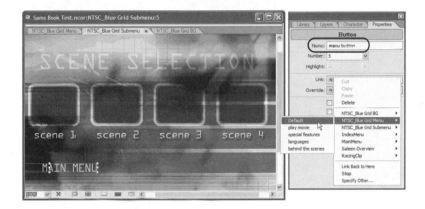

FIGURE 24.20
The Properties palette is context-sensitive. That is, it displays the properties of whatever you've selected in the Menu or Project windows. Set links using its Link drop-down list.

6. Now you'll use the Pick-whip tool. To prepare to do that, select the Menus tab in the Project window, click the Blue Grid Menu tab in the Menu window, and open the Properties palette in the Library window.

7. On the Blue Grid Menu, click the Special Features button to open its display in the Library window Properties palette.

8. As shown in Figure 24.21, drag the Pick-whip button (to the right of Link in the Properties palette) to the Menus palette of the NTSC_Blue Grid Submenu in the Project window. (Note how the line whips back to the Properties palette and the link name changes from "Not Set" to NTSC_Blue Grid Submenu.) The Blue Grid Submenu will serve as this project's scene selection menu.

9. Click the timelines tab in the Project window (it should have two timelines—in my case, Saleen Overview and RacingClip), click the Behind the Scenes button on the Blue Grid Menu, and drag its Pick-whip from the Properties palette to the RacingClip timeline listing.

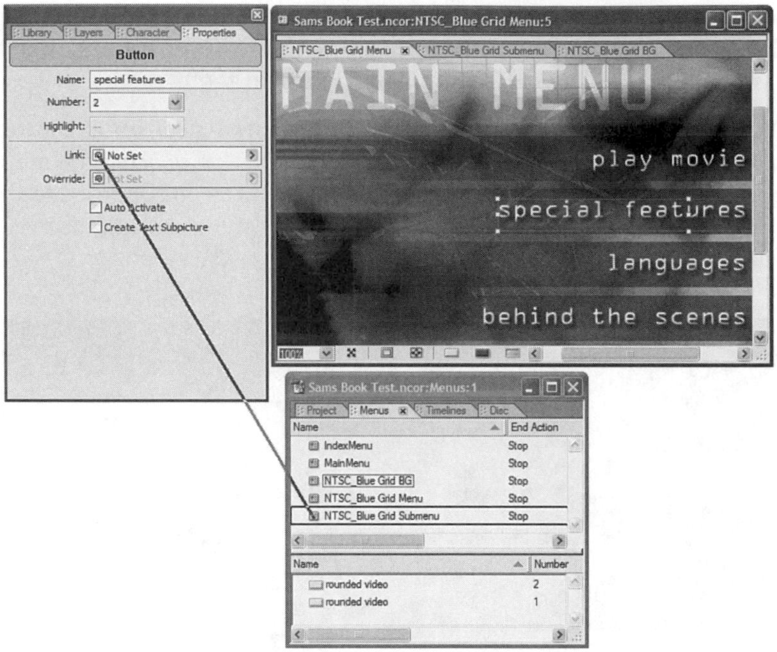

FIGURE 24.21
Use the Pick-whip
tool to link an
object in the
Properties palette
to a menu or media
asset in the Project
window.

10. Add poster frames (still images lifted from the video) and links to the video chapters in the scene selection menu by opening the main movie's timeline (double-click it in the Project window's timeline palette) and open the Blue Grid Submenu in the Menu window.

11. Click on individual chapter numbers (Chapter 1 is always the first frame and you can use it for a scene if that suits you), and then drag them in turn to their respective scene frames. Your scene selection menu has poster frame thumbnail images in each button and should look something like Figure 24.22.

Did you Know?

Changing Chapter Poster Frames or Locations

Using Figure 24.22 as a reference, drag a chapter point along the timeline to see how that updates the poster frame in the Monitor Window.

Change a chapter point poster frame (without changing the chapter marker location) by selecting a chapter point on the timeline, moving the CTI to a new location (view it in the Monitor window), right-clicking the chapter marker, and selecting Set Poster Frame (it shows up immediately in the menu window).

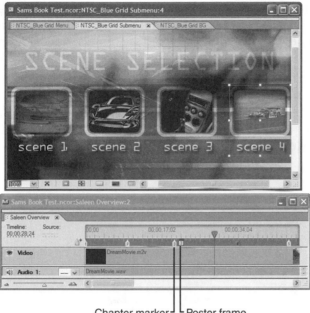

FIGURE 24.22 ▼
Drag chapter points to the scene frames to link those buttons to their respective scenes in the main video.

Chapter marker ─┘ └─ Poster frame

12. By default these scene selection buttons display only as static poster frames. To animate them—to have them play a few seconds of video—click on the Blue Grid Submenu tab to select it, click the Properties tab, and check the Animate Buttons check box. Put in a duration (Five seconds works well) and the number of loops until the buttons revert to still images (Forever is one choice).

13. Render these video buttons by selecting File→Render Motion Menu (this project might take 30 seconds to render—it's creating 120 full frames of that menu, not just the buttons, to play as a looping video).

▲

Setting First Play

You know that when you put a DVD in your set-top player, it doesn't just sit there waiting for you to tell it what to do. Depending on how its editor authored it, it might display a menu, play a brief video and then open a menu, or simply start playing the movie with no menu. In DVD specification parlance, those are all **first play** actions.

By default, Encore DVD sets the first menu or timeline you work on as the first play. Here's how to override that:

▶ If you have the Saleen-Assets material, you want to set `IntroMovie` as the First Play item. To do that, you need to put `IntroMovie` on a timeline. Do that by right-clicking `IntroMovie` and selecting New timeline. That opens the timeline window. Because you don't have to work in it, simply close it to free up screen real estate.

▶ In the Project window, look for the asset with the little triangle in its file type icon. As shown in Figure 24.23, in my case, it's the Saleen Overview timeline. That triangle indicates that it's the First Play item. Override that by right-clicking the newly added IntroMovie timeline and selecting Set as First Play.

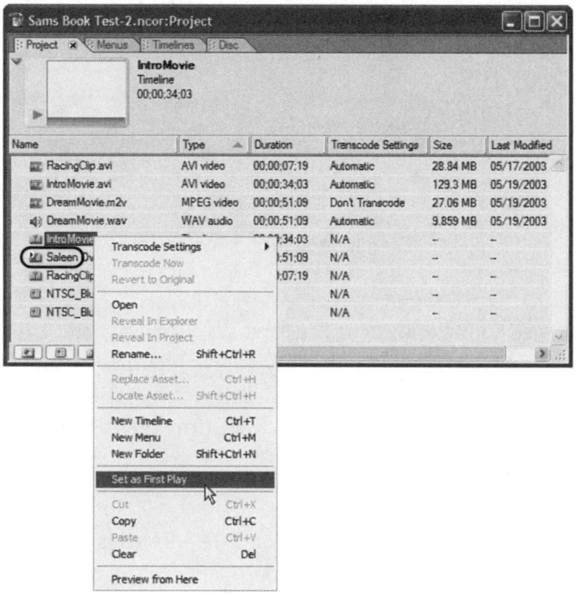

FIGURE 24.23
The asset with the little triangle in its icon is the project's first play item. Override that by right-clicking a different asset and selecting Set as First Play.

Setting End Actions

You need to tell `IntroMovie` what to do when it finishes playing or if the viewer presses the Stop button. That's called its **end action**. In this case, you want it to jump to the main menu.

▶ Select `IntroMovie` in the Project window and open the Properties tab.

▶ As shown in Figure 24.24, open the End Action drop-down list and select NTSC_Blue Grid Menu→Default.

▶ Set End Actions for the other two videos, having them both return viewers to the main menu.

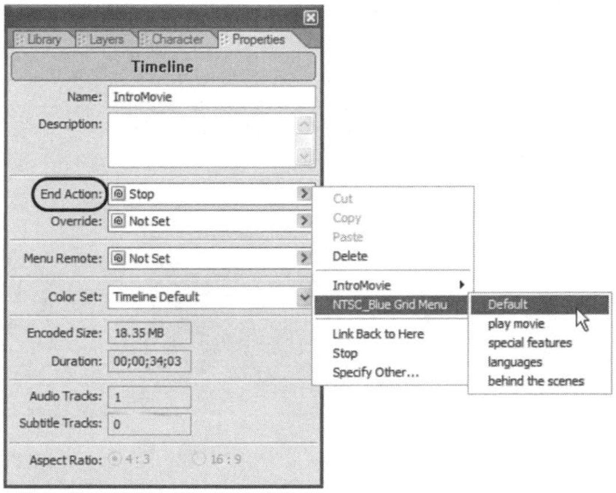

FIGURE 24.24
Set the end action in the asset's Properties palette.

Setting Overrides

You sometimes need to override default actions. For instance, the typical end action for most movies (or *timeline* in Encore DVD parlance) is to return to the DVD's main menu. But if your viewer accesses that movie via the scene selection menu, you want to return the viewer to the scene selection menu if he presses Stop. You set that using the Override drop-down list in the Properties palette.

Scene Selection Plays More Than One Scene

The scene selection concept might be confusing. At first glance, you might think that if you select a scene, the DVD would play only that scene. But that's not how it works. Selecting a scene simply starts playing the video at that point. If you don't take any further action, the video will play to its end.

But if viewers press the Stop button on their remotes, you might not want to throw them back to the main menu; you can return them to the scene selection menu. Thus, the need to use overrides when accessing the movie via a scene selection button.

Did you Know?

---

1. Using the Scene Selection menu you just created, click on the Scene 1 button.

2. As shown in Figure 24.25, in the Properties palette open the Override drop-down list and select Blue Grid Submenu→Scene 2. You choose Scene 2 because you want to have the button highlighted when the viewer returns to this menu; you assume that he won't want to view Scene 1 again.

3. Do this for the other three buttons, setting the Scene 4 button override to main menu to highlight that button because you assume that the viewer has exhausted the Scene Selection menu possibilities.

FIGURE 24.25
Set override
actions to ensure
viewers come back
to the correct
menu.

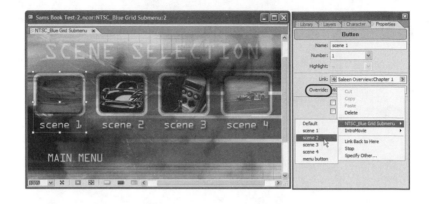

Changing Button Navigation

When you view Hollywood DVDs, you might notice that as you press the arrow
keys on your remote, you move through the menu button selections in what
seems like a logical order—typically top to bottom or left to right. By default,
Encore DVD determines what it calculates to be a logical order. It's best to check
that to see whether it matches your view of what constitutes a logical flow.

To see the order, click the Show Button Routing button circled in Figure 24.26.
That displays the four-arrow button routing symbols. The center number is the
button number set by Encore DVD, the left/right/up/down arrows indicate which
button will highlight when the viewer presses the associated button on the
remote.

FIGURE 24.26
Change the button
navigation to over-
ride the default val-
ues set by Encore
DVD.

In the case of the Blue Grid Menu, because the text buttons do not fall in a straight vertical column, the button navigation is illogical.

1. To adjust them, click the Blue Grid Menu tab to select it.

2. Open the Properties palette and uncheck the Automatically Route Buttons check box at the bottom of the palette.

3. Now, as shown earlier in Figure 24.26, drag and drop each arrow to set the navigation that suits you. Figure 24.27 shows you how I set the navigation for this project.

4. Change the navigation for any other menus you've created.

FIGURE 24.27
New button navigation settings have viewers move from top-to-bottom without skipping buttons as would have happened if I accepted the default navigation set by Encore DVD.

Previewing Your Work So Far

Encore DVD enables you to simulate how your project will function when played on a TV using a remote control. You can preview a specific menu by right-clicking on that menu and selecting Preview from Here. Or preview the entire project by selecting File→Preview. As shown in Figure 24.28, the latter action opens the Project Preview window, which then plays your first play video.

If you wait for the video to end, the Project Preview window will execute the end action and should display the main menu. To expedite that, click the Execute End Action button highlighted in Figure 24.28 (clicking the Stop button in this window has unpredictable results).

FIGURE 24.28
Open the Project
Preview window to
see how your proj-
ect will work when
it plays in a set-top
DVD player.

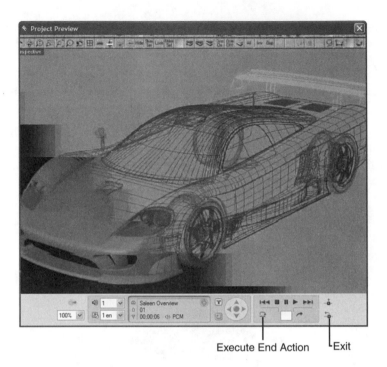

Execute End Action   Exit

1. Once in the main menu, move the cursor around to show the buttons'
   selected highlights and then click on Languages. Nothing will happen
   because the button does not have a link.

2. Click on Special Features to open the scene selection menu. Play the four
   scenes and click the Execute End Action button for each of them. That
   should take you back to the Scene Selection menu with the next scene's button highlighted.

3. Click its Main Menu button to return to the opening menu. Click Play
   Movie or Behind the Scenes and their respective movies will play. Use the
   Execute End Action feature on them and you should return to the main
   menu.

4. Click the Exit button, highlighted earlier in Figure 24.28, to return to the
   Encore DVD authoring interface.

Burning the DVD

Because this is just a demonstration project, there's no need to actually record this project to a DVD, but I'll show you how the process works.

Burning Your Project to a DVD

When doing these final steps, you get to take one last peek at your links and project settings. Here's how to make a DVD:

1. Click the Disc tab in the Project window to open it.

2. Click Check Links, select Links Not Set, and click Start. If, as is the case in Figure 24.29, there are assets with end actions that don't suit you, or links that are not set, you can change them in this dialog box. Simply click on one, open the Properties palette, and make the changes there. When you're finished, click Done.

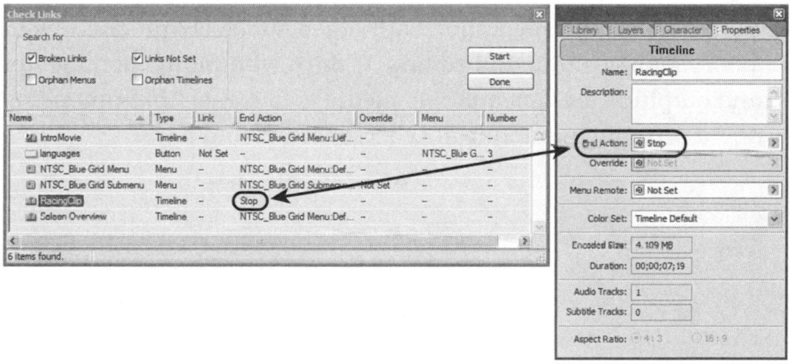

FIGURE 24.29
Use the Check Links dialog box (with the Properties palette) to repair any broken links or change end actions and overrides.

3. Click Project Settings and note that Encore DVD offers several copy protection options as well as region settings. These are for professionally mastered DVDs, and not for desktop burning to recordable media. Cancel out of that dialog box.

4. If you want to add DVD-ROM content—word processing files, spreadsheets, images, and other material users can work with on their PCs—use that feature in the Disc tab.

5. Click Build Project to open a dialog box that enables you to select a DVD burner.

▼

6. Insert a recordable DVD in your DVD burner and click Next. That displays a Make DVD Disc: Summary dialog box. If all seems to be in order, click Build. The progress indicator will display how things are going.

▲

7. When completed, you can take the DVD you just burned and play it in your set-top DVD player. Congratulations.

Summary

I saved Encore DVD for the final hour of this book because it's kind of the icing on a video project cake. You've worked hard to create a fine-looking video and Encore DVD gives you the opportunity to present that work in the best light.

No longer is DVD authoring for the few and the wealthy. With this $549 product, you can build Hollywood-style DVDs complete with menus, video buttons, scene selection options, multiple language audio tracks, and subtitles.

Encore DVD features tight integration with other Adobe DV products, notably Photoshop for menu creation and editing. It ships with many menu templates, buttons, and graphics. It offers multiple methods to create links among menus, buttons, and assets and automatically checks for missing links.

Q&A

Q *When I preview my DVD project, I play a video for a while and then click the Stop button, expecting the video to jump back to its menu. But all I get is a blank screen. What's going on?*

A When you clicked the Stop button, you expected the video to execute its end action. Were this a true DVD remote control, that would be the case. But in the Encore DVD Preview window, clicking Stop simply stops the video. To execute the end action, click that specialized button at the bottom of the screen.

Q *When I access a video chapter via my scene selection menu, it plays beyond the next chapter point. Why doesn't it stop automatically? And when I click the Stop button, it returns to the main menu. What's going on?*

A By default, clicking on a scene selection button simply starts the video at that point. It will continue to the end of the video if you don't click Stop. And the reason clicking Stop does not take you back to the scene selection menu is because you did not input an override value for that button, telling the video to return to the chapter menu.

Workshop

Quiz

1. You drag and drop chapters to buttons in a scene selection menu, but the poster frames thumbnail images don't represent the chapter's contents. How do you fix that?

2. You want your button navigation to go left-to-right, but when you click the right arrow in the Preview window, it skips a button. How do you fix that?

3. Instead of a selected highlight being a simple frame around a thumbnail image, you want little stars to appear with text, such as "Ouch!" How do you do that?

Quiz Answers

1. You can change the poster frame while keeping the chapter point at the same frame. Do that by moving the CTI to a frame that is more representative of the chapter's content, right-clicking on the chapter point number in the time ruler, and selecting Set Poster Frame.

2. Use the Show Button Routing feature in the Menu window. First you need to turn off the default Automatically Route Buttons feature by unchecking its check box in the menu's Properties palette. Then use the Show Button Routing four-pointer icons to drag and drop the proper navigation.

3. Edit the menu in Photoshop. Add a layer to the existing button and name it using the (=#) convention. Then simply use Photoshop's graphic building tools to create the stars and the text in a single layer. Back in Encore, you can give that new graphic its own unique color and opacity using the Color Sets dialog box.

Exercises

1. DVDs are great archive media. Use Encore DVD to create a basic menu, showing thumbnails of each of your video projects that take viewers to brief snippets, not the entire video clips. When you burn the project, use the Encore DVD's DVD-ROM feature to add the original DV AVI or MPEG (they take up less space) videos. That way you won't have to recapture them if you want to work on them in Premiere Pro again. And you can play them on your PC without having to hook up your camcorder and do a lot of fast forwarding or rewinding.

2. If you're in the video production business, use Encore DVD to author a demo reel. Have the main menu take viewers to screens that say more about who you are, what you do, and show some brief samples of your work.

3. One cool thing to do with a group photo—team, classroom, or old family portrait for example—is to create highlight graphics for each person. What you want the viewer to see, as he moves the remote from person to person, is a transparent oval on the person's head with that person's name below it. Then when the viewer clicks on that person, she goes to a submenu on that person—season statistics, school art project, family history narrative, and so on. Create such a highlight graphic and use it to create links to your DVD content.

Index

Symbols

A

C

How can we make this index more useful? Email us at indexes@samspublishing.com

How can we make this index more useful? Email us at indexes@samspublishing.com

G

H

J - K

How can we make this index more useful? Email us at indexes@samspublishing.com

O

P

How can we make this index more useful? Email us at indexes@samspublishing.com

How can we make this index more useful? Email us at indexes@samspublishing.com

How can we make this index more useful? Email us at indexes@samspublishing.com

How can we make this index more useful? Email us at indexes@samspublishing.com

Your Guide to Computer Technology

www.informit.com

Sams has partnered with **InformIT.com** to bring technical information to your desktop. Drawing on Sams authors and reviewers to provide additional information on topics you're interested in, **InformIT.com** has free, in-depth information you won't find anywhere else.

ARTICLES

Keep your edge with thousands of free articles, in-depth features, interviews, and information technology reference recommendations—all written by experts you know and trust.

POWERED BY

ONLINE BOOKS

Answers in an instant from **InformIT Online Books'** 600+ fully searchable online books. Sign up now and get your first 14 days **free**.

CATALOG

Review online sample chapters and author biographies to choose exactly the right book from a selection of more than 5,000 titles.

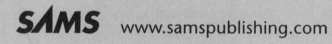

SAMS   www.samspublishing.com